I believe there are certain things that cannot be bought: loyalty, friendship, health, love and an American League pennant.

Edward Bennett Williams (1979)

THE

GREEN BAG

ALMANAC

&

READER

2010

John M. Ward.

ALLEN & GINTER'S

RICHMOND. Cigarettes. VIRGINIA.

JOHN MONTGOMERY WARD, 1860-1925

Lawyer, pitcher, shortstop, manager, labor leader, author.
See DAVID STEVENS, BASEBALL'S RADICAL FOR ALL SEASONS:
A BIOGRAPHY OF JOHN MONTGOMERY WARD (1998).

THE
GREEN BAG

ALMANAC

OF USEFUL AND ENTERTAINING TIDBITS FOR
LAWYERS FOR THE YEAR TO COME

2010

– AND –

READER

OF EXEMPLARY LEGAL WRITING FROM THE
YEAR JUST PASSED

2009

SELECTED BY THE
LUMINARIES AND SAGES ON OUR BOARD OF ADVISERS

EDITED BY ROSS E. DAVIES

GREEN BAG PRESS
WASHINGTON, DC
2009

Recommended citation form:

[author, title], *in* 2010 GREEN BAG ALM. [page number]

First Baseball Edition
limited to 2000 copies

Green Bag Press
6600 Barnaby Street NW
Washington, DC 20015

Green Bag Press is a division of
The Green Bag, Inc., publisher of the
Green Bag, Second Series, an Entertaining Journal of Law.

For more information, please email
editors@greenbag.org or visit
www.greenbag.org.

ISSN: 1931-9711
ISBN 13: 978-1-933658-10-0
ISBN 10: 1-933658-10-X
Library of Congress Control Number: 2009922229

TABLES OF CONTENTS

READER
OF EXEMPLARY LEGAL WRITING 2009

✴ OPINIONS FOR THE COURT ✴

✴ CONCURRENCES, DISSENTS, ETC. ✴

✴ BOOKS ✴

GREEN BAG ALMANAC & READER 2010

★ SHORT ARTICLES ★

★ LONG ARTICLES ★

★ NEWS & EDITORIAL ★

★ MISCELLANY ★

TABLES OF CONTENTS

ALMANAC
OF USEFUL & ENTERTAINING TIDBITS

LAST YEAR & THIS YEAR

BASEBALL CLASSICS

BASEBALL FEATURES

BASEBALL TIDBITS

OTHER TREASURES

PREFACE

This is the fifth *Green Bag Almanac & Reader*. For a reminder of the reasons why the world needs our almanac and our reader, read the "Preface" to the 2006 edition. It is available on our web site (www.greenbag.org), in the "Almanac & Reader" section.

OUR DILIGENT BOARD

Our selection process for "Exemplary Legal Writing of 2009" was, like past years', not your typical invitation to competitive self-promotion by authors and their publishers and friends. We did not solicit (or accept) entries from contestants, charge them entry fees, or hand out blue, red, and white ribbons. Rather, we merely sought to:

> (a) organize a moderately vigilant watch for good legal writing, conducted by people (our Board of Advisers) who would know it when they saw it and bring it to our attention;

> (b) coordinate the winnowing of advisers' favorites over the course of the selection season, with an eye to harvesting a crop of good legal writing consisting of those works for which there was the most substantial support (our "Recommended Reading" list);

> (c) ballot our advisers to identify the cream of that already creamy crop; and then

> (d) present the results to you in a useful and entertaining format — this book.

The nitty-gritty of our process for selecting exemplars is a simple but burdensome series of exercises:

Step 1: Our advisers read legal writing as they always have, keeping an eye out for short works and excerpts of longer works that belong in a collection of good legal writing. When they find worthy morsels, they send them to the *Green Bag*. "Good legal writing" is read broadly for our purposes. "Good" means whatever the advisers and the volume editor think it does. As one experienced scholar and public servant on our board put it, "there is good writing in the sense of what is being said and also in the sense of how it is being said." Our advisers are looking for works that have something of each. "Legal" means anything written about law — opinions, briefs, articles, orders, statutes, books, motions, letters, emails, contracts, regulations, reports, speeches, and so on. "Writing" means ink-on-paper or characters-on-screen.

Step 2: The *Green Bag* organizes the advisers' favorites into categories, and then sends a complete set to every adviser. Advisers' names are not attached to the works they nominate. In other words, everything is anonymized. Advisers vote without knowing who nominated a piece. Similarly, their rankings are secret. No one but the volume editor ever sees individual advisers' rankings or knows who voted in which categories. And the editor destroys all individualized records once the *Almanac* is in print.

Advisers are free to vote in as many categories — or as few — as they desire. That is, although there may be scores of nominated works in total, they are free to select the types of writing they want to evaluate. Almost all — but invariably not all — advisers vote in each category.

Step 3: The volume editor tallies the rankings and compiles the "Reader" portion of the *Almanac & Reader* based on the results, reserving, as editors tend to do, the right to add, subtract, and reorganize within reason. Nominated works not published in the book are listed in the "Recommended Reading" section.

Step 4: The advisers and the editor start all over again for next year's edition — a process which has been underway since last Halloween (recall that our annual cycle for selection of exemplary legal writing begins and ends on October 31), with dozens of nominees already in the queue for the 2011 *Almanac*.

Despite the substantial work involved in this business, most of our advisers seem to enjoy participating. Those who don't enjoy it appear to view it as some sort of professional duty. Either way, we're glad to have them. But these are people with day jobs, other commitments, and minimum sleep requirements. So not everyone can pitch in every year. Being listed as an adviser implies that a body has done some advising, however, and it doesn't seem right to burden someone with a slice of the collective responsibility (or credit, if there is any) for a project in which they did not participate, at least this time around. So the list of board members in this *Almanac & Reader* has changed since last year and will, we expect, continue to change from year to year. The fact that people come and go from the board does not necessarily indicate anything about their ongoing commitment to the *Almanac & Reader*, other than when they have had the time and inclination to participate. Of course, we hope they always will.

Where Are the Bloggers?
In the Almanac, and Above the Law

Two years ago I explained why we had not yet seen nominations from the blogosphere, and expressed hope that we would receive more over time. Last year one blog entry made it into the packet of nominees sent to our advisers, and they selected it for inclusion in the *2009 Almanac & Reader* (congratulations again Richard G. Kopf). This year, we had another, and it too merited republication here (congratulations to Eugene Fidell).

This year we have been blessed with another signal that the blogosphere is becoming part of the American establishment: a celebrity in that field has received the kind of treatment that some in our justice system provide to the local and international aristocracy. The associated judicial opinion (which does not endorse a one-law-for-the-few-and-another-law-for-the-many jurisprudence) was not nominated in time to be considered for this year's *Almanac & Reader*. And so it is reproduced here merely to illustrate the point: While it may be true that a "blogger can get away with less and afford fewer pretensions of authority" than the average writer,[*] it may also be true that a celebrity blogger can get away with just as much at the hands of the authorities as the average celebrity.

---

[*] Andrew Sullivan, *Why I Blog*, The Atlantic, Nov. 2008, at 106-13.

United States v. Andrew M. Sullivan

Case No. 2009-PO-0476-RBC
Memorandum and Order on Government's Request for Leave to File a
Dismissal of Violation Notice, September 10, 2009

Robert B. Collings[†]

I. Introduction

It sometimes happens that small cases raise issues of fundamental importance in our system of justice; this case happens to be an example.

II. Facts

The facts are straightforward. The defendant, Andrew M. Sullivan, who resides in Washington, D.C. but, according to his attorney, owns a home in Provincetown, Massachusetts, was in an area of the Cape Cod National Seashore on July 13, 2009 when he was charged by a National Park Service Ranger with a violation of 36 C.F.R. § 2.35(b)(2) which prohibits possession of a controlled substance on National Park Service lands. Specifically, Mr. Sullivan was charged with possession of marijuana. Title 36 C.F.R. § 2.35(b)(2) prohibits "the possession of a controlled substance . . . ."[1] The maximum penalty upon conviction of the offense is a fine of $5,000, six months imprisonment, a $25 processing fee and a $10 special assessment. As such, it is classified under the federal criminal code as a Class B misdemeanor;[2] it is also denoted a "petty offense."[3]

The charge was contained in a citation which the Ranger issued to Mr. Sullivan on July 13, 2009. The citation, which was on a form denoted "United States District Court Violation Notice," required Mr. Sullivan either to appear in the United States District Court when notified to do so or to forfeit collateral in the amount of $125.00.[4]

Mr. Sullivan was notified to appear before the Court on September 2, 2009 at Hyannis at a session at which the undersigned was to preside. On August 26,

---

[†] Magistrate Judge, United States District Court for the District of Massachusetts.
[1] Title 36 C.F.R. § 1.4(a) provides, in pertinent part, that "*[c]ontrolled substance* means a drug or other substance . . . included in schedules I, II, III, IV, or V of part B of the Controlled Substance Act (21 U.S.C. 812) . . . ." "Marihuana" is a Schedule I controlled substance. Title 21 U.S.C. § 812, Schedule I, (c)(10).
[2] *See* Title 18 U.S.C. § 3559(a)(7).
[3] *See* Title 18 U.S.C. § 19.
[4] *See* Rule 14(a), Rules for United States Magistrate Judges in the United States District Court for the District of Massachusetts ("A person who is charged with a petty offense may, in lieu of appearance, post collateral in the amount indicated for the offense, waive appearance before a magistrate judge, and consent to forfeiture of collateral . . .").

2009, the United States Attorney for the District of Massachusetts filed a "Dismissal of Complaint" [sic] seeking leave to file a dismissal of the Violation Notice issued to Mr. Sullivan because "further prosecution of the violation would not be in the interest of justice."

Because the reason given by the United States Attorney was so general ("interest of justice"), the Court scheduled a hearing on the request for leave to file the dismissal and directed that Mr. Sullivan appear. He did so on September 2, 2009 at Hyannis. He was represented by Robert Delahunt, Jr., Esquire, of Boston. The United States Attorney was represented by Assistant United States Attorney James F. Lang, Acting Deputy Chief of the Criminal Division.

When the case was called, the Court expressed its concern that a dismissal would result in persons in similar situations being treated unequally before the law. The Court noted that persons charged with the same offense on the Cape Cod National Seashore were routinely given violation notices, and if they did not agree to forfeit collateral, were prosecuted by the United States Attorney. In short, the Court explained that there was no apparent reason for treating Mr. Sullivan differently from other persons charged with the same offense. In fact, there were other persons who were required to appear on the September 2nd docket who were charged with the same offense and were being prosecuted.[5]

Both Assistant U.S. Attorney Lang and Attorney Delahunt explained that Mr. Sullivan is a British citizen who is applying for a certain immigration status in the United States. They stated that lawyers expert in the field of immigration law had advised them that if Mr. Sullivan were to forfeit the $125.00 in collateral, it would have an adverse effect on his application. The Court noted that Mr. Sullivan had been charged with the crime at the time the Violation Notice issued and that even if the Court did grant leave to dismiss the Violation Notice, Mr. Sullivan, if asked by immigration authorities, would have to answer truthfully that he had been charged with a crime involving controlled substances. In these circumstances, the Court asked the attorneys to explain why forfeiting collateral would have any additional adverse effect on his application. Neither attorney could answer the Court's query except to say that the lawyers they had consulted who practice immigration law said it would.

In these circumstances, the Court indicated that it would like Attorney Delahunt to file a brief answering the Court's query. Before Attorney Delahunt could reply, Assistant U.S. Attorney Lang stated that the Court was without power to ask for the brief, or, in fact, to inquire further into the decision of the United States Attorney to dismiss the charge.[6] He asserted, quite correctly, that the

---

[5] In point of fact, there were three other defendants on the list charged with the same offense.

[6] Research conducted by the Court after the hearing indicates that Assistant U.S. Attorney Lang is quite incorrect in his statement that the Court had no power to inquire. *See United States v. Ammidown*, 497 F.2d 615, 620 (D.C. Cir., 1973)(". . . [I]n the exercise of its responsibility [under Rule 48(a), Fed. R. Crim. P.], the court will not be content with a mere conclusory statement by the prosecutor that dismissal is in the public interest, but

United States Attorney has broad discretion as to when to dismiss a criminal charge and that the power of the Court in these circumstances is limited and able to be exercised only in special circumstances.[7]

The Court, still concerned about the apparent derogation of the principle that all persons stand equal before the law, decided to take the matter under advisement.

III. A Brief Detour

Before going any further, it is important to state with clarity those matters about which the Court is not concerned.

First, the Court is well aware of political discussion over whether the possession of a small amount of marijuana should be illegal. Whether or not the law should be changed to make such possession legal is a matter entrusted to state and federal lawmakers, and ultimately to the voters.[8] The Court's duty is to uphold the law as it is, and unless and until the law is changed, the Court must enforce it, regardless of whether or not the judge personally has any opinion as to how the law should be changed.

Second, the Court would not be concerned with any exercise of discretion by the United States Attorney not to prosecute the possession of small amounts of marijuana. The United States Attorney certainly has discretion to determine how best to allocate the resources of his office and could, if he deemed it appropriate, elect to focus those resources on more serious crimes while declining to prosecute the type of violation which Mr. Sullivan faces. However, from all that appears, the United States Attorney has not taken the position that persons who possess marijuana on federal property will not be prosecuted; rather, those persons are prosecuted routinely.

IV. The Issue Raised in the Instant Case

In the Court's view, in seeking leave to dismiss the charge against Mr. Sullivan, the United States Attorney is not being faithful to a cardinal principle of our legal system, i.e., that all persons stand equal before the law and are to be treated equally in a court of justice once judicial processes are invoked. It is quite apparent that Mr. Sullivan is being treated differently from others who have been charged with the same crime in similar circumstances.

---

will require a statement of reasons *and underlying factual basis*." (emphasis supplied; footnote omitted).

[7] See discussion of the Court's power in this regard at pp. [6-7], infra.

[8] The Court notes that voters in Massachusetts recently changed the penalty for possession of small amounts of marijuana from a criminal to a civil sanction. Possession of marijuana is still illegal in Massachusetts but the sanction for violation is a civil rather than a criminal penalty. Of course, on the Cape Cod National Seashore, a federal property, the federal regulation cited, *supra*, which provides for a criminal sanction for possession of marijuana is applicable and is unaffected by the change in Massachusetts state law.

If there were a legitimate reason for the disparate treatment, the Court would view the matter differently. But the United States Attorney refused to allow the Court to inquire into why, in the circumstances of this case where Mr. Sullivan had already been charged with the crime, either a forfeiture of collateral or an adjudication would make a difference in the immigration application.

But there is more. If, in fact, a determination that Mr. Sullivan had possessed marijuana is a factor which, under immigration law, the immigration authorities are legally charged with taking into account when deciding Mr. Sullivan's application, why should the United States Attorney make a judgment that, despite the immigration law, the charge should be dismissed because it would "adversely affect" his application?[9] If other applicants for a certain immigration status have had their applications "adversely affected" by a conviction or a forfeiture of collateral for possession of marijuana, then why should Mr. Sullivan, who is in the same position, not have to deal with the same consequences?

In short, the Court sees no legitimate reason why Mr. Sullivan should be treated differently, or why the Violation Notice issued to him should be dismissed. The only reasons given for the dismissal flout the bedrock principle of our legal system that all persons stand equal before the law.

V. THE BOTTOM LINE

In urging fidelity to these principles of our legal system, the Court must also be faithful to the constitutional principle of separation of powers — that the executive branch of the federal government (of which the United States Attorney is a part) and the judicial branch (of which the Court is a part) have both powers and limitations on their powers.

The law with respect to the limit of a Court's power to refuse to grant leave to the United States Attorney to dismiss a criminal matter is not entirely clear. The Supreme Court has written on the subject but declined to decide the issue. Over thirty years ago, the Court commented that:

> The words "leave of court" were inserted in Rule 48(a) without explanation. While they obviously vest some discretion in the court, the circumstances in which that discretion may properly be exercised have not been delineated by this Court. The principal object of the "leave of court" requirement is apparently to protect a defendant against prosecutorial harassment, *e.g.*, charging, dismissing, and recharging, when the Government moves to dismiss an indict-

---

[9] Again, the Court takes no position on what the law should be regarding the effect of a prior possession of marijuana on an application for immigration status. That is a matter which is in the province of the Congress. Similarly, the Court takes no position on how the immigration authorities should exercise their discretion when presented with applications by persons who have either been convicted or forfeited collateral for possession of marijuana. If the law gives the immigration authorities the discretion to determine the weight, if any, to be given this circumstance in making their decision on the applications, presumably authorities could determine that the application is not to be adversely affected.

ment over the defendant's objection. See, *e.g.*, *United States v. Cox*, 342 F.2d 167, 171 (CA5), cert. denied, sub nom. *Cox v. Hauberg*, 381 U.S. 935, 85 S.Ct. 1767, 14 L.Ed.2d 700 (1965); *Woodring v. United States*, 311 F.2d 417, 424 (CA8), cert. denied sub nom. *Felice v. United States*, 373 U.S. 913, 83 S.Ct. 1304, 10 L.Ed.2d 414 (1963). But the Rule has also been held to permit the court to deny a Government dismissal motion to which the defendant has consented if the motion is prompted by considerations clearly contrary to the public interest. See *United States v. Cowan*, 524 F.2d 504 (CA5 1975); *United States v. Ammidown*, 162 U.S.App.D.C. 28, 33, 497 F.2d 615, 620 (1973). It is unnecessary to decide whether the court has discretion under these circumstances, since, even assuming it does, the result in this case remains the same.

Rinaldi v. U.S., 434 U.S. 22, 30 n.15 (1977).

Obviously, the instant case does not involve the need to protect Mr. Sullivan from "prosecutorial harassment" since the United States Attorney, in seeking leave to dismiss the charge, is doing precisely what the defendant wants. Rather, the issue in this case is that which the Supreme Court declined to decide, i.e. whether the Court can refuse leave if, in the words of the Supreme Court, the request for leave ". . . is prompted by considerations clearly contrary to the public interest." *Id.*

While several Circuits have written on the subject since the *Rinaldi* decision, no consensus seems to have emerged, and the First Circuit has not had the opportunity to render its view. A good summary of the law in the various circuits is contained in the case of *United States v. Nixon*, 318 F. Supp. 2d 525, 527-30 (E.D. Mich., 2004). The Seventh Circuit Court of Appeals had the most recent opportunity to write on the issue in the case of *In Re United States of America*, 345 F.3d 450 (7 Cir., 2003). In that case, the Court held that a court would exceed the limits of judicial power under the Constitution if it refused to grant leave to dismiss a criminal charge on the grounds that the dismissal is "contrary to the public interest." *In Re United States*, 345 F.3d at 452-454.

The end result is that fidelity to the law requires that the Court grant leave to the United States Attorney to dismiss the Violation Notice against Mr. Sullivan, and the Court hereby grants such leave.[10] That the Court must so act does not require the Court to believe that the end result is a just one.

• • • •

---

[10] The Court also notes that the United States Attorney would have the last word in any event. If the Court were to refuse to dismiss the charge, the United States Attorney could merely decide not to present any evidence at the trial which would require the Court to enter a judgment of acquittal. *See United States v. Greater Blouse, Skirt & Neckwear Contractors Ass'n*, 228 F. Supp. 483, 489-90 (S.D.N.Y., 1964). Nevertheless, the Third Circuit has noted that "[e]ven though a judge's discretion under Rule 48(a) is severely cabined, the rule may serve an important interest as an information-and accountability-producing vehicle." *In Re Richards*, 213 F.3d 773, 788 (3 Cir., 2000). The Court is hopeful that its inquiry into the Government's reasons for seeking leave to dismiss the charge against Mr. Sullivan has served those purposes.

And now back to our regularly scheduled programming.

HOMER KEEPS NODDING . . .

We continue to struggle, and fail, to produce a flawless big fat book in a hurry. Here are the errors we are sure we made in the 2009 *Almanac & Reader*:

> Page 166: Rachel Davies of Willow Grove, PA, noted that "unconscsious" ought to be "unconscious." And while wringing our hands over that mistake we noticed that we'd spelled "pedagogical" "pedadogical" on the same page.

> Page 247: John Harrison of Charlottesville, VA, gently asked us two questions:

>> (1) "In discussing Measure for Measure, Bowdler says that the Duke acts 'curly.' Bowdler's error for 'cruelly'?"

>> and

>> (2) "What about 'untied' as opposed to 'united' in the second line of the third paragraph on that . . . page?"

> Professor Harrison is too kind. The answers are: (1) "curly" is the *Green Bag*'s error for Bowdler's "cruelly" and (2) "untied" is the *Green Bag*'s error for Bowdler's "united."

We will keep trying.

IN OTHER BUSINESS

Our goals remain the same: to present a useful and entertaining, perhaps even inspiring, monthly dose of our stock in trade — good legal reasoning and reporting, well-written — with moderate amounts of the traditional almanac potpourri of useful and distracting information thrown in. Like the law itself, the 2009 exemplars republished in this volume are wide-ranging in subject, form, and style. This year most of the potpourri has to do with baseball; next year is an open field. With any luck we'll deliver some reading pleasure, a few role models, and some reassurance that the nasty things some people say about legal writing are not entirely accurate.

• • • •

Finally, the *Green Bag* proffers the customary thanks to you, our readers. Your continuing kind remarks about the *Almanac* are inspiring. The *Green Bag* also thanks our Board of Advisers for nominating and selecting the works recognized here; the George Mason University School of Law and the George Mason Law & Economics Center for their continuing generous support of the *Green Bag*; Susan Davies, for her good reads; Susan Birchler, Nathan Chubb, Nicholas Frankovich, Paul Haas, and Tiger Jackson; and Green Bag Fellow Rob Willey.

Ross E. Davies
December 25, 2009

RECOMMENDED READING

We have tallied the ballots and printed the top vote-getters in this book. They are the ones listed in the Table of Contents above and marked on the list below by a little ✶. There were plenty of other good works on the ballot. We list them here. Congratulations to all.[1]

•   •   •   •

OPINIONS FOR THE COURT

William B. Chandler, III, *Rohm & Haas Co. v. Dow Chemical Co.*, 2009 WL 445609 (Del. Ch. 2009)

✶ Frank H. Easterbrook, *Buchmeier v. United States*, 581 F.3d 561 (7th Cir. 2009) (en banc)

Ferdinand F. Fernandez, *BNSF Railway Co. v. O'Dea*, 572 F.3d 785 (9th Cir. 2009)

Ralph D. Gants, *In re Birchall*, 913 N.E.2d 799 (Mass. 2009)

✶ Ruth Bader Ginsburg, *United States v. Hayes*, 129 S. Ct. 1079 (2009)

Per Curiam, *Spears v. United States*, 129 S. Ct. 840 (2009)

✶ Jed S. Rakoff, *Securities and Exchange Commission v. Bank of America*, 2009 WL 2916822 (S.D.N.Y. 2009)

James Robertson, *Hollister v. Soetoro*, 601 F.Supp.2d 179 (D.D.C. 2009)

Antonin Scalia, *United States v. Navajo Nation*, 129 S. Ct. 1547 (2009)

Paul A. Suttell, *Viveiros v. Town of Middletown*, 973 A.2d 607 (R.I. 2009)

CONCURRENCES, DISSENTS, ETC.

William A. Fletcher, *Cooper v. Brown*, 565 F.3d 581 (9th Cir. 2009)

✶ Alex Kozinski, *United States v. Cruz*, 554 F.3d 840 (9th Cir. 2009)

Carlos R. Moreno, *Strauss v. Horton*, 207 P.3d 408 (Cal. 2009)

✶ John T. Noonan, Jr., *Tucson Herpetological Society v. Salazar*, 566 F.3d 870 (9th Cir. 2009)

---

[1] Some publishers require consideration for republication that exceeds our modest resources. It was publishers' demands for money, not low supplies of votes, that precluded our presentation of Gene Weingarten's article and a slice of Melvin Urofsky's book.

Mark P. Painter, *Blust v. City of Blue Ash*, 894 N.E.2d 89 (Ohio Ct. App. 2008)*

Mark P. Painter, *State v. Roberts*, 904 N.E.2d 945 (Ohio Ct. App. 2008)*

John G. Roberts, Jr., *United States v. Hayes*, 129 S. Ct. 1079 (2009)

✷ John G. Roberts, Jr., *Virginia v. Harris*, 130 S. Ct. 10 (2009)

Conrad L. Rushing, *Miyamoto v. Department of Motor Vehicles*, 176 Cal.App.4th 1210 (Cal. Ct. App. 2009)

✷ David H. Souter, *United States v. Navajo Nation*, 129 S. Ct. 1547 (2009)

BOOKS

(including articles more than 25,000 words long)

✷ Amy Bach, *Ordinary Injustice: How America Holds Court* (Metropolitan Books 2009)

Lackland H. Bloom, Jr., *Methods of Interpretation: How the Supreme Court Reads the Constitution* (Oxford University Press 2009)

✷ Annette Gordon-Reed, *The Hemingses of Monticello: An American Family* (W.W. Norton & Co. 2008)

Philip Hamburger, *Law and Judicial Duty* (Harvard University Press 2008)

John Kroger, *Convictions: A Prosecutor's Battles Against Mafia Killers, Drug Kingpins, and Enron Thieves* (Farrar, Straus and Giroux 2008)

Goodwin Liu, Pamela S. Karlan, and Christopher H. Schroeder, *Keeping Faith with the Constitution* (American Constitution Society 2009)

Elizabeth Magill, *Standing for the Public: A Lost History*, 95 Va. L. Rev. 1131 (2009)

✷ David G. Post, *In Search of Jefferson's Moose: Notes on the State of Cyberspace* (Oxford University Press 2009)

Melvin I. Urofsky, *Louis D. Brandeis: A Life* (Random House 2009)

Carlos Manuel Vázquez, *Treaties as the Law of the Land: The Supremacy Clause and the Judicial Enforcement of Treaties*, 122 Harv. L. Rev. 599 (2008)

Steven T. Wax, *Kafka Comes to America: Fighting for Justice in the War on Terror* (Other Press 2008)

---

* Nominated by the author.

RECOMMENDED READING

SHORT ARTICLES

Michael Boudin, *A Response to Professor Ramseyer, Predicting Court Outcomes Through Political Preferences*, 58 Duke L.J. 1687 (2009)

✶ Pamela S. Karlan, *Voting Rights and the Third Reconstruction*, in *The Constitution in 2020* (Oxford University Press 2009) (Jack M. Balkin & Reva B. Siegel, eds.)

Leandra Lederman, *EBay's Second Life: When Should Virtual Earnings Bear Real Taxes?*, 118 Yale L.J. Pocket Part 136 (2009)

✶ David F. Levi, *Autocrat of the Armchair*, 58 Duke L.J. 1791 (2009)

✶ Michael J. Morrissey, *Dead Men Sometimes Do Tell Tales*, in *Your Witness: Lessons on Cross-Examination and Life from Great Chicago Trial Lawyers* (Law Bulletin 2008) (Steven F. Molo and James R. Figliulo, eds.)

Jeffrie G. Murphy, *Remorse, Apology & Mercy*, in *Criminal Law Conversations* (Oxford University Press 2009) (Paul H. Robinson, Stephen P. Garvey, and Kimberly Kessler Ferzan, eds.)

Henry E. Smith, *Does Equity Pass the Laugh Test?: A Response to Oliar and Sprigman*, 95 Va. L. Rev. in Brief 9 (2009)

LONG ARTICLES

Stephanos Bibas, Max M. Schanzenbach, and Emerson H. Tiller, *Policing Politics at Sentencing*, 103 Nw. U. L. Rev. 1371 (2009)

✶ Lani Guinier, *Courting the People: Demosprudence and the Law/Politics Divide*, 89 Boston U. L. Rev. 539 (2009)

Robert Henry, *Do Judges Think?*, 58 Duke L.J. 1703 (2009)

William Ranney Levi, *Interrogation's Law*, 118 Yale L. J. 1434 (2009)

✶ Frederick Schauer, *A Critical Guide to Vehicles in the Park*, 83 NYU L. Rev. 1109 (2008)

Steven D. Smith, *Discourse in the Dusk: The Twilight of Religious Freedom?*, 122 Harv. L. Rev. 1869 (2009)

Jeannie Suk, *Is Privacy a Woman?*, 97 Georgetown L.J. 485 (2009)

Jeffrey S. Sutton, *The Role of History in Judging Disputes About the Meaning of the Constitution*, 41 Tex. Tech L. Rev. 1173 (2009)

✶ G. Edward White, *Introduction to* Oliver Wendell Holmes, Jr., *The Common Law* (1881; Harvard University Press 2009 prtg.)

Verna L. Williams, *The First (Black) Lady*, 86 Denv. U. L. Rev 833 (2009)

NEWS & EDITORIAL

William W. Bedsworth, *The Moving Blues: A farewell serenade to an unconventional courthouse*, The Recorder, May 15, 2009

✴ Eugene R. Fidell, *Appellate Review of Military Commissions*, at Balkinization, Oct. 8, 2009

Rich Leonard, *Give Bankruptcy Judges the Power to Alter Mortgages*, Washington Post, Nov. 28, 2008

✴ Dahlia Lithwick, *Shit Doesn't Happen: The Supreme Court's 100 percent dirt-free exploration of potty words*, Slate, Nov. 4, 2008

✴ Kermit Roosevelt, *Justice Cincinnatus: David Souter—a dying breed, the Yankee Republican*, Slate, May 1, 2009

✴ Jeffrey Toobin, *Are Obama's judges really liberals?*, The New Yorker, Sept. 21, 2009

Bruce Weber, *Umpires v. Judges*, New York Times, July 12, 2009

Gene Weingarten, *Fatal Distraction*, Washington Post, March 5, 2009

MISCELLANY

Thomas E. Baker, *A Primer on the Jurisdiction of the U.S. Courts of Appeals*, §§ 1.01, 1-02, 3.01-05 (Federal Judicial Center 2d ed. 2009)

Mark E. Elias et al., *Memorandum of Law in Opposition to Contestants' Motion for Ruling Applying Feb. 13, 2009 Order to Previously Counted Absentee Ballots, Sheehan v. Franken*, No. 62-CV-09-56 (Minn. D. Ct. 2009)

✴ Elena Kagan et al., *Brief for the United States as Amicus Curiae Supporting Petitioners, Migliaccio v. Castaneda*, Nos. 08-1529 and 08-1547 (U.S. 2009)

✴ Martin S. Lederman, *Constitutionality of the Ronald Reagan Centennial Commission Act of 2009*, 33 Op. Office of Legal Counsel (2009)

Maureen Mahoney et al., *Brief of Petitioner, Union Pacific Railroad Co. v. Brotherhood of Locomotive Engineers*, No. 08-604 (U.S. 2009)

✴ Elizabeth B. Wydra, Douglas T. Kendall, and David H. Gans, *Brief of Constitutional Law Professors as Amici Curiae in Support of Reversal, McDonald v. City of Chicago*, Nos. 08-4241, 08-243, 08-4244 (7th Cir. 2009)

CHRONICLES OF

GRAMMAR, USAGE & WRITING

2009

Bryan A. Garner[†]

JANUARY

On New Year's Day, the peer-reviewed *Psychological Journal* published an article entitled "Fluency Training a Writing Skill," in which three Wisconsin professors argued that "the relation between good grammar skills and writing may be remote." They reinforced the point throughout the article, as they showed one but not the other, as illustrated in this snippet from their conclusion: "Our goal has been to enhance editing of one's own inconcise writing. Regarding this behavior, it is important to note that we have never preselected participants for high levels of inconcision. We have just assumed that most participants write inconcisely. Indeed, when we have asked participants, usually graduating seniors, to write concise essays after 1.5 hours of concision instruction, they have used, on average 1.8 words when 1 word would suffice. . . . The average confirms our assumption that participants typically write inconcisely." And who, exactly, was giving the "concision" instructions? • Eighty-eight-year-old James J. Kilpatrick retired from his last-remaining syndicated column, "The Writer's Art," after 70 years of bringing pleasure and knowledge to an appreciative readership. • The *Deseret News* (Salt Lake City) reported on a 29-minute speech by humorist Lynne Truss at Brigham Young University, during which the reporter counted 65 laughs over punctuational bungles (that's nearly a barrel). Truss concluded by saying that those who fight to improve punctuation will ultimately find the battle futile "because the enemy is so vast and hugely ascendant." • In support of that point, the *Sunday Telegraph* (London) reported that the Birmingham City Council has announced that it will no longer use apostrophes on street signs to make them "more consistent." Apparently, in the words of the newspaper, "if you have the misfortune to be a Mr. O'Dowd, needing a minicab from the King's Arms in D'Arcy Avenue, drivers can't find you." (For the civil unrest fomented by such decisions to scrap apostrophes, see August.)

[†] Bryan Garner is the author of more than a dozen books about words and their uses, including *Garner's Modern American Usage* (Oxford 3d ed. 2009). He is also the editor in chief of *Black's Law Dictionary* (West 9th ed. 2009) and president of Law-Prose, Inc. Copyright © 2009 Bryan A. Garner.

FEBRUARY

In the *Sunday Telegraph* (London), comedian Sandi Toksvig sardonically suggested a correlation between fraud and bad grammar: "If I told you that I believe I have won a million dollars on the Australian lottery without the annoyance of having to buy a ticket, you might think I needed a little time in a darkened room, but the truth will out. I have an e-mail that states: 'Congratulations your email address have won you US$1,000,000.00.' Clearly the organizers' desire to part with the money has left good grammar panting by the wayside, but nevertheless I believe the cash will be with me soon." (See more in this vein in July.) • The *Courier Journal* (Louisville, Ky.) announced: "Admirers of good grammar rejoice! Michael Lohan, feisty dad of Lindsay Lohan, has announced on his blog that he will stop blogging." A staff writer at the *Journal* claimed credit, noting that a week before he had pointed out Lohan's "horrible grammar" and "shamed him into stopping." Bravo! • The BBC's John Humphrys was quoted in the *Sunday Telegraph* (still London) as saying that text-messaging "is doing to our language what Genghis Khan did to his neighbors 800 years ago . . . destroying it: pillaging our punctuation, savaging our sentences, raping our vocabulary." (For Grammar Girl's differing view of text-messaging, see November.)

MARCH

National Grammar Day (March 4) passed almost without incident, as the entire country dutifully tried to abstain, for a day, from bad grammar. • Mike Clark, the monthly language columnist for the *Greensboro News & Record* (N.C.), commemorated the column's fourth year by noting the three most common peeves of his readership: (1) misused pronouns ("The prizes went to Bob and I"), (2) misused apostrophes ("white bean's and pinto's"), and (3) word-swapping ("No credit-card orders for under $10 excepted"). • Just down the road in Raleigh, *News & Observer* staff writer A.C. Snow announced that he would be accosting management at the building where his office is located: "I wish I had been present," he wrote, "when the lobby's restroom doors were recently repainted with 'Mens' and 'Womens.'" • *The Globe and Mail* (Toronto) noted that President Barack Obama has a tendency, "like a junior librarian," to engage in hypercorrection. He talks about "a very personal decision for Michelle and *I* [read *me*]," or "President Bush graciously invited Michelle and *I* [read *me*] to meet with him." (These pronoun problems, remember, are huge irritants in Greensboro.) Yet all reports suggest that, grammatical gaffes though there may be in the White House, they are fewer than in the preceding administration.

APRIL

The Sunday Times (Western Australia) mistakenly reported that in the second week of April 1828, "US lexicographer Noah Webster published his first dictionary." Not so: he published his first in 1806. He published his two-volume unabridged dictionary in 1828. • In Modesto, California, a quixotic sixth-grade teacher named Craig Mello decided to create a highly contagious "good-grammar virus," which works this way with his students: "As I e-mailed everyone back, I began correcting their mangled text-message language of abbreviated words and words with vowels intentionally left out, with proper grammar. . . . The plan was to infect every student who'd written me with correct language. Then, as they continue dialoguing with each other, they'll see their teacher's corrections on their MySpace sites and either start using correct langauge or be so annoyed that they stop writing me altogether. One way or another, they'll all be contaminated with my 'good-grammar virus' and be exposing all their friends." Good luck to him! • In Virginia, Hampton University officials announced $60,000 in scholarships at the journalism school's first-ever "grammar bee," in which competitors engaged in a game-show-style contest delving into grammatical terminology, differentiations between clauses and phrases, and (presumably) fused participles. As reported in the *Daily Press* (Newport News, Va.), Dean Tony Brown created the bee to combat "an education system that churns out college graduates who have poor vocabulary, grammar, and writing skills." • Almost prophetically (see August), James Yolles reported in the *Hamilton Spectator* (Ontario) on the annoyance that many people feel about misused and missing apostrophes in signs: "Take away the apostrophes, and we're left with anarchy. One can only imagine the horrific image: thousands of out-of-work copy editors and grammarians roaming the streets brandishing large red pens." (Again, see August!)

MAY

The Times (London) commemorated the death of Noah Webster on the 28th in 1843. In West Hartford, Connecticut, Fleming's Steakhouse sponsored a wine-tasting and silent auction at the Noah Webster House, which is West Hartford's only national landmark. The event raised $2,600. • *The Canberra Times* quoted Neil James, an Australian English professor, on the fallacy of believing that grammatical knowledge isn't important to becoming a competent writer: "We wouldn't send people out into the workforce to be practicing chemists without teaching them the difference between an element and a compound, so why are we sending kids out into the workforce to write where a large part of their output is written documents without teaching them the difference between a noun and a verb, or the active and passive voice?" James has identified what he calls the "Four Stages of Grammatical Grieving" that his students undergo: (1) indifference to or curiosity about the subject; (2) a pleasant sense of surprise at how easy syntax and punctuation are; (3) euphoria at mastering grammatical principles; and (4) anger at not having been taught this information earlier.

JUNE

In the *Leicester Mercury* (U.K.), a letter-writer named Mike Attenborrow complained that he'd had enough of being corrected by English professors (no details on the circumstances), saying: "I wonder if these academics who keep pulling us up for our spelling or pronunciation (did I spell that right?) could repair a car, or build a house, or install central heating." It must be the first such letter on record. • Scott Simon of NPR Weekend

Sunday Edition took to the airwaves to utter these words: "Not a week goes by in which our show, or me personally, doesn't receive notes from people who use good grammar . . . ." Oh dear. Couldn't he return the favor? • In London, the editor of the *Times Educational Supplement* editorialized about the importance of imagination, but he rightly warned: "There is no contradiction between rigor and imagination. Good grammar is as vital to an author as a grasp of tailoring is to a designer, or mathematical dexterity is to a computer whiz. Too many attacks on the standards agenda do not allow that it is a crucial ingredient of creativity." • Letter-writers in the *Milwaukee Journal-Sentinel* debated Ebonics. One Katie Herrmanns defended "the rich dialog that my family and friends create using the dialect I was taught and grew up listening to," adding that teachers of standard English are doing a "disservice to our children." One Bruce Tucker responded: "Bryant Gumbel became a well-known announcer partly by speaking flawless English. I'll bet Justice Sonia Sotomayor had teachers who demanded good grammar. Our new president speaks flawless grammar, too, which no doubt helps if you want to get accepted at Harvard." (On the supposed flawlessness of President Obama's grammar, see March — or call a friend in Greensboro.)

July

The February suspicion that good grammar is allied with conscientious scruples found support among realtors. *The Ledger* (Lakeland, Florida) reported that one way of spotting online rental-property scams is by their bad grammar, misspelled words, and punctuation errors. The illiterate scammers typically claim to be living overseas and ask victims to send a security deposit and the first month's rent via money transfer before turning over the keys. But beware the bad grammar. • The *Liverpool Daily Post* reported its decision not to send a photographer to a school whose headmaster had requested one with a message that began "To who it may be concerned." No dice, the paper said. • Steve Ballmer, a Microsoft chief executive, told Noam Cohen of *The New York Times* that the name of Microsoft's new search engine, Bing, has the potential to "verb up." In other words, he hopes that the proper noun will become a verb, and people will "bing" their queries. And Microsoft is happy about that. Traditionally, companies such as Xerox and Google have resisted "verbing up" because of the risk of losing trademark protection if their names become generic and lose their association with a particular business. But Rebecca Tushnet, a professor who teaches trademark law at Georgetown University, opined: "The risk of becoming generic is so low, and the benefits of being on the top of someone's mind are . . . high." Imagine the confusion, though, if Google became generic and Microsoft launched a campaign: "Use Bing for all of your most complicated googling!"

August

The *Hamilton Spectator* (Ontario) reported that "more and more students are stumped by . . . simple problems of English language usage," such as the difference between *it's* and *its*: "This past year, 30% of first-year stu-

dents failed [a basic English-proficiency exam], compared to 25% in 2004."
• The *Bournemouth Echo* (U.K.) reported that 62-year-old Stefan Gatward of Tunbridge Wells became exasperated by the missing apostrophe in a sign outside his home: "St Johns Close." He added the apostrophe and was accosted by a neighbor who accused him of vandalism. Citing frustrations with the Birmingham decision to scrap apostrophes (see January), Gatward defended himself by saying he was engaging in civil disobedience over the local council's decision to "scrap the punctuation from council signs for the sake of 'simplicity.'" Michael Diamond, street-naming and -numbering officer for the Bournemouth Borough Council was quoted as saying: "We endeavor to use apostrophes correctly but the use of an apostrophe in a street name has always been something of a grey area. . . . The monarch doesn't own Queens Park so it could be said it's no longer correct to include the possessive apostrophe." No word on when Mr. Gatward might become eligible for parole. • Seriously, though, two 28-year-old men who declared themselves members of the "Typo Eradication Advancement League" pleaded guilty to vandalizing a historic sign at Grand Canyon National Park. They had reportedly removed an unnecessary apostrophe and added a comma to the 60-year-old sign.

SEPTEMBER

William Safire, the longtime "On Language" columnist for *The New York Times Magazine*, was diagnosed with pancreatic cancer and died within the month. His loss was widely mourned. • On the 12th, the world celebrated the 300th birthday of Samuel Johnson, with mirth and wit and perspicacious remarks. The *Evening Standard* noted that "London's only full-length statue of the great lexicographer is at the end of St. Clement Danes, his local church in The Strand." True, but it's typically hard to get a glimpse of it because of the hordes of lexicologists who continually crowd around it. • In the *Phi Delta Kappan*, Kathleen Taylor noted that using *learn* as a synonym for *teach* (as Granny used it repeatedly on *The Beverly Hillbillies*), "occurred as long ago as the 13th century." She reported that "William Shakespeare used that sense, and so did Samuel Johnson. But American lexicographer Noah Webster noted the usage was falling out of favor in the 19th century. At the turn of the 20th century, the *Oxford English Dictionary* termed it 'vulgar,' and it's never regained its standing." • Emily Arsenault, an erstwhile lexicographer, published a novel, *The Broken Teaglass*, about how words find their way into published reference sources — amid a love story. • In the *Times Higher Education Supplement* (London), Matthew Reisz published his article "The Seven Deadly Sins of the Academy," in which he concluded: "The pedant is one who does care and thinks the difference really counts. And tells you. Pedantry has to be performed. You can have secret lusts; you can even be a snob in private, I suppose, imagining in solitude the invitations you would turn down if invited; but it is only when a pedant comes out that pedantry takes place. It needs an audience. . . . [W]e are all capable of falling dangerously in love with pedantry. Think of the lasting success of Fowler's *Modern English Usage*, a paean to pedantry where irony cannot conceal its true commitment." • The 24th was National Punctuation Day. In *USA Today*, columnist Craig Wilson explained that the day was officially "set aside to reflect on the fact that a semicolon is not a medical problem." • In the *Irish Daily Mail* comes an extended lament about the poor punctuation in Sandra Mara's new book *No Job for a Woman*. One perks up at reading that "this book is so badly and irritatingly punctuated that one has to wonder whether it was seriously edited at all." But then one begins to wonder about the reviewer, who writes (I kid you not): "Good punctuation is like good make-up you can hardly see it. . . . When you are reading a book littered with exclamation marks, its hard to concentrate. Especially if they come at totally inappropriate times! Like when the writer thinks theyve said something really funny! But actually they havent!" Nary an apostrophe appears in the piece. • *Sports Illustrated* reported on the stark differences between Lloyd Carr, the former coach of the Michigan Wolverines, and his replacement, Rich Rodriguez: "Carr kept an *Oxford English Dictionary* outside his office. Players who came to visit were expected to look up a word and jot its definition on one side of the index cards provided. He was known to quote Jefferson, Churchill, and Kipling. At his introductory press conference Rodriguez quoted Rafiki, the monkey in *The Lion King*. While Carr is a former English teacher and a stickler for grammar, Rodriguez is the bane of grammarians, some of whom have publicly complained about his use of 'ain't' in press conferences."

OCTOBER

The Canberra Times reported on a lexicographic development: "In the 20th century it took a long time for new words to find their way into dictionaries. Lexicographers had a rule of thumb for giving a guernsey to a new word: it should be widely used for at least five years, and used in at least five texts of different kinds. The internet has changed all this. New words spread around the world with remarkable speed, and the internet provides abundant information about how widespread use is." Quite right. • National Dictionary Day (Oct. 16) was joyfully celebrated as small children sang etymological carols and placed dictionary stands by the hearthstone, hoping that Noah Webster would come down the chimney with a shiny new dictionary. Not really. And so lexicographer Erin McKean mused in the *Pittsburgh Post-Gazette*: "If you think of Dictionary Day as being about a dusty book that's hardly ever opened, then sure, it's going to rank slightly further down the celebratory scale than National Corn Dog Day (which was March 21 this year, if you're curious). But if you think about dictionaries as being about the language, then isn't the English language well worth a holiday?" • Also on the 16th, the *Chicago Tribune* commemorated the birthdate in 1758 of Noah Webster. • *The Herald* (Glasgow) reported that the Chambers dictionary office in Edinburgh, created in 1819, is "under imminent threat of closure," reminding us all "how swiftly the publishing world has changed in the past few decades." According to Harrap, which acquired Chambers in 1992, "the onward march of the internet has spelt the end of reference publishing as it's been known for the past two centuries." • *The Times* (London) commemorated, on the 23rd, the birthdate in 1817 of the lexicographer Pierre Athanase Larousse. (He died in 1875.) • During the penultimate week of the month, according to *The Hindu* (India), "the Governor [H.R. Bhardwaj] felicitated the nonagenarian lexicographer G. Venkatasubbaiah and scholars N. Basavaradhya, T.V. Venkatachala Shastry, Kamala Hampana, and A.R. Mithra." That was the extent of the report on those festivities. ● Writing in *The Straits Times* (Singapore), Janadas Devan eloquently lamented: "I fear the distinction between 'enormity' and 'enormousness' will soon go the way of the once clear distinctions between 'momentary' and 'in a moment,' 'disinterested' and 'uninterested,' 'alternate' and 'alternative,' and so on. Try telling an airline pilot his plane can't possibly 'be landing momentarily,' for 'momentarily' means 'for a moment, briefly' — 'I wondered momentarily if he knew English' — not 'soon.' Try telling a teenager that Mother Teresa served the poor 'disinterestedly,' while he is just 'uninterested' in his work. What is the use of being careful about usage when it is changing so fast? In the long run, perhaps little, but in the meantime, such care does help foster a certain consciousness, a certain scrupulousness, a certain hesitation, even humility, in our choice of words. Apart from that, screaming at every erroneous 'enormity' is a waste of time.'"

NOVEMBER

The New York Times published a letter by Alma Graham of New York: "As the first lexicographer to put the courtesy title 'Ms.' into a dictionary (the *American Heritage School Dictionary*, 1972), I was gratified to read [a *Times* article] regarding its origins. I was also gratified when *The Times* finally, though belatedly, acceded to the use of the title in its pages. What annoys me, however, is the claim made by many that 'Ms.' is 'an abbreviation of nothing.' Just as 'Mr.' is the abbreviation of a form of 'master' so 'Ms.' is an abbreviation of 'mistress' in its original sense of 'a woman in a position of authority.' As the executive editor for dictionary publishing at American Heritage, I added the title and etymology to the 1975 edition of the *American Heritage Dictionary of the English Language*, but the etymology was subsequently removed." ● Yale University Press published Michael Slater's excellent biography of Charles Dickens. In it, Slater prominently notes that "nothing annoyed Dickens more than the idea that any kind of worthwhile writing could be done easily." ● Walker & Company published Jan Freeman's *Ambrose Bierce's Write It Right: The Celebrated Cynic's Language Peeves Deciphered, Appraised, and Annotated for 21st-Century Readers* — a fascinating updating of Bierce's linguistic bêtes noires. ● *The Hindu* (India) reported as follows on the 25th: "Lexicographer Prof. G. Venkatasubbaiah has been chosen for 'Bhageerati Sahitya Puraskar' [a major award for literature] instituted by the Bhageerathi Bai Narayana Rao Maanay Educational Institutions," which carries with it a cash prize of 25,000 rupees. Bravo! ● Former health minister Lord Warner criticized the Queen's speech at the opening of Parliament in which she mentioned at-home health care: "There's a big question mark as to whether there's even actually a Bill ready." A columnist at *The Times* (London) — called "The Pedant" — criticized Warner's phraseology: "The term 'question mark' should never be used as a synonym for 'question,' because it's a cliché. . . . If Warner had imagined the literal shape of a question mark hovering over Parliament, the absurdity of the phrase would have been clear to him. No one speaks of a big exclamation mark over Downing Street, a sizable semicolon over Strasbourg, or extensive ellipses alongside the Elyse. Punctuation marks belong in grammar; think hard before using them as metaphors, then choose something else." The editorialist then rightly objurgated Warner's *as to* and *actually*, together with this summation: "a collection of dead phrases . . . obscure rather than convey his point. It would have been more effective to say: 'Is a Bill even ready?'" • Lexicographers at Oxford University Press announced *unfriend* as their Word of the Year. Christine Lindberg, a senior lexicographer, was actually quoted as saying, "*Unfriend* has real lex-appeal." • Merriam-Webster, meanwhile, chose *admonish* because of the action taken against U.S. Representative Joe Wilson for shouting "You lie!" at President Barack Obama during a healthcare speech to Congress. • Interviewed by *The Columbus Dispatch*, Mignon Fogarty (a/k/a Grammar Girl) was asked whether text-messaging is ruining the English language. "I don't think it is," she replied. "It just tends to amplify whatever kind of writer you are." (For the militantly contrary view of John Humphrys of the BBC, see February.)

DECEMBER

On the 12th, *The Times* (London) remembered the death of writer and lexicographer Samuel Johnson on that date in 1784. • *The Irish Times* reported that the Global Language Monitor, based in Austin, Texas, announced that the most-used word in 2009 was "Twitter" and asked: will "the social networking site that condenses all human interaction into 140 characters or less [read *fewer*] . . . still rule in 2010, or will another online trend sweep the world and consign tweets to the recycle bin?" Stay tuned.

ANNIVERSARIES

300 years ago: Samuel Johnson was born in Lichfield, England. **100 years ago:** Ambrose Bierce's book appeared: *Write It Right: A Little Blacklist of Literary Faults*. **80 years ago:** Sterling Andrus Leonard's book appeared: *The Doctrine of Correctness in English Usage: 1700–1800*. **50 years ago:** *The Elements of Style*, by Strunk and White, was published. In the interim, it has sold 10 million copies. **35 years ago:** Edwin Newman's book appeared: *Strictly Speaking: Will America Be the Death of English?* **30 years ago:** William Safire started writing his "On Language" column for *The New York Times Magazine*. **25 years ago:** James J. Kilpatrick's book appeared: *The Writer's Art*.

✳ ✳ ✳

The interesting writer has an interesting mind and has led an interesting life (though perhaps uneventful to the outward eye), because he is interested in living.

Henry Seidel Canby (1926)

THE GRAMMATICAL HALL OF SHAME

THE TEN WORST LAW-REVIEW GAFFES OF 2009

Compiled by Bryan A. Garner

10. "Nor will it be sufficient for the commander to punish his troops for the atrocity itself if he does so only as a matter of *towing* [read *toeing*] the line." Amy J. Sepinwall, *Failures to Punish*, 30 Mich. J. Int'l L. 251, 294 n.225 (2009).

9. "Its approach *jives* [read *jibes*] with my scholarly interests and the parts of Federal Courts that my academic and practical experience enable me to teach about the big issues with passion and enthusiasm." Georgene Vairo, *Why I Don't Teach Federal Courts Anymore, but Maybe Am or Will Again*, 53 St. Louis U. L.J. 843, 854 (2009) (with extra points for the *Am* in the title and the ungrammatical *about*-phrase at the end of the sentence).

8. "Drawing a direct *corollary* [read *correlation*] between the 'deputizing' officer and acting officer, this framework would democratize collective knowledge . . . ." Sean D. Doherty, Note, *The End of an Era*, 37 Hofstra L. Rev. 839, 862-63 (2009) (with extra points for the dangling participle).

7. "The cause of action vests in the potential donee and could take a number of forms, including an action in negligence, *tortuous* [read *tortious*] interference, or invasion of privacy." Brian Morris, Note, *You've Got to Be Kidneying Me!*, 74 Brook. L. Rev. 543, 557 n.106 (2009).

6. "While temporal proximity is essential to the realm of law, its use must be *collaborated* [read *corroborated*] with other evidence." Liaquat Ali Khan, *Temporality of Law*, 40 McGeorge L. Rev. 55, 74 (2009) (with extra points for the *corroborated with* instead of *by*, and for corroborating not the evidence but the *use* of the evidence).

5. "A teacher motivated to 'prevail' in the classroom cannot *illicit* [read *elicit*] student understanding that genuine dialogue is a means of autonomous learning." Joseph A. Dickinson, *Understanding the Socratic Method in Law School Teaching After the Carnegie Foundation's Educating Lawyers*, 31 W. New Eng. L. Rev. 97, 113 (2009) (with extra points for the punning suggestion of illegalizing student understanding).

4. "[T]he canon generally *laid* [read *lay*] dormant in federal courts for more than fifty years after *White* . . . ." David R. Stras, *Pierce Butler: A Supreme Technician*, 62 Vand. L. Rev. 695, 755 n.426 (2009).

3. "Specifically, the Committee stated that the phrase 'dishonesty or false statement' was meant to cover 'crimes such as perjury, or *subordination* [read *subornation*] of perjury, false statement, criminal fraud, embezzlement, or false pretense . . . .'" Colin Miller, *Impeach-*

able Offenses?, 36 Pepp. L. Rev. 997, 1031 (2009) (with extra points for the punning suggestion that perjury might be subordinated to other crimes, and that doing so is itself a crime).

2. "Lincoln's position also became the main point of contention between *he* [read *him*] and Stephen Douglas in the well-known debates . . . ." Susan Schulten, *Barack Obama, Abraham Lincoln, and John Dewey*, 86 Denv. U. L. Rev. 807, 811 (2009) (with extra points for perpetrating such an error in a sentence about Lincoln).

1. "In addition to charging a base fee of $25.60 per ton, which applied *irregardless* [read *regardless*] of the wastes' origins, the statute added . . . ." William J. Cantrell, *Cleaning Up the Mess*, 34 Colum. Envtl. L. 149, 159 n.47 (2009).

✳ ✳ ✳

Take a conscious pride in our
language. Respect our English
tongue . . . . We, its students, are
also its servants; we have both
the privilege and the responsibility
of trying to write well, but we
shall bear neither if we go about
our work without joy in this
language [that] so many have
used so creatively.

Walter Nash (1992)

A TERM IN THE LIFE OF THE

SUPREME COURT

Tony Mauro[†]

Some developments involving the Supreme Court of the United States from November 1, 2008 to October 31, 2009 that are not likely to be memorialized in the United States Reports.

2008

Nov. 5: The Court heard oral argument in *FCC v. Fox Television Stations*, a test of the Federal Communications Commission's crackdown on broadcasters who allow "fleeting expletives" to reach the airwaves. Before the argument, Sidley Austin's Carter Phillips, who represented Fox, said he would use the unvarnished words, as he had before the U.S. Court of Appeals for the 2nd Circuit, "unless instructed otherwise." But Phillips did not use the controversial language, and declined to say why not. In a speech before the Second Circuit conference in June 2009, Justice Ruth Bader Ginsburg revealed that in fact "the lawyers were alerted that some of the justices might find that unseemly, so only the letters 'f' and 's' were used in our court." She did not specify which justices would have been offended, or who alerted the lawyers.

Nov. 10: Chief Justice John Roberts Jr. learned a new word during oral argument in *United States v. Hayes*, a case on the scope of a law that makes it a crime for those convicted of felonies to possess firearms. In discussing the statute at issue, 18 U.S.C. 922 (a)(33)(A)(i) and (ii), justices referred awkwardly to sections "little eye" and "little eye eye." But Assistant to the Solicitor General Nicole Saharsky called them "Romanette one and two," using an obscure but self-explaining term for a lower-case Roman numeral. "Romanette?" asked Roberts quizzically. "Oh, little Roman numeral," Saharsky replied. "I've never heard that before!" said Roberts.

Nov. 17: The first segment of the papers of the late chief justice William Rehnquist was made public at the Hoover Institution Archives at Stanford University. Released were case-related papers and some correspondence from Rehnquist's early terms on the Court, from 1972 to 1975. Rehnquist specified that case files could be released only after all the justices serving at the time had died.

Nov. 18: John Roberts Sr., the father of the chief justice, died after a long illness. In the manner of small-town newspapers everywhere, the headline

---

[†] Tony Mauro is Supreme Court correspondent for American Lawyer Media, the *National Law Journal*, the *Blog of Legal Times* and law.com.

on the Johnstown (Pa.) *Tribune-Democrat* story on his death focused on how he was known locally: "Former Bethlehem Steel Manager Dies." The story began, "Before John G. Roberts Sr. was known as the father of U.S. Supreme Court Chief Justice John Roberts, he was known in Johnstown as a steel man."

Dec. 1: During oral argument in the original jurisdiction case of *Kansas v. Colorado*, Justice David Souter asked a question of Colorado Attorney General John Suthers. Suthers paused and answered, "Justice Ginsburg . . ." Amid nervous laughter Souter said, "I'm greatly flattered," and as Suthers apologized, Souter added, "You're not the first to have done that." Indeed Suthers was not. In the April 24, 2007, argument in *Dayton v. Hanson*, a lawyer addressed Souter as Ginsburg, and then too, Souter said he was flattered by the mistake.

Dec. 31: In his annual year-end report on the state of the federal judiciary, Chief Justice Roberts praised the courts as frugal, dedicated, and crucial to the life and economic recovery of the nation. But to keep the courts strong, Roberts urged Congress to pass pay raises, or at least cost-of-living increases, for federal judges as soon as possible. "Given the judiciary's small cost, and its absolutely critical role in protecting the Constitution and rights we enjoy, I must renew the judiciary's modest petition: Simply provide cost-of-living increases that have been unfairly denied!" Roberts' plea fell on deaf ears; no pay raise was enacted, though the justices did receive a small cost-of-living adjustment.

2009

Jan. 14: President-elect Barack Obama and Vice President-elect Joseph Biden visited the Supreme Court late Wednesday afternoon for a private courtesy call that included chatting around a Court fireplace with eight of the nine justices — all but Samuel Alito Jr. Chief Justice Roberts had invited them to visit "so that colleagues in public service might become better acquainted," adding that the Court "would be pleased to see that sporadic practice become a congenial tradition." President-elect Ronald Reagan visited the Court in November 1980, and President-elect Bill Clinton visited in December 1992.

Jan. 20: John Roberts and Barack Obama, two verbally adept graduates of Harvard Law School, managed to muff the inaugural oath that launched Obama's presidency. Roberts, working without notes, started prompting Obama with the words. Obama jumped in a shade too early, which appeared to knock Roberts off stride. They started over, but then Roberts and Obama mixed up some of the words of the constitutionally mandated oath, locating the word "faithfully" in the wrong place. At least no one dropped the Bible, which occurred during one of Franklin D. Roosevelt's inaugurals.

Jan. 21: After a day of derision and debate over the flubbed presidential oath administered to President Obama, the two principals met again at the White House for a do-over. This time, according to a press pool report, Roberts and Obama said the right words in the right sequence. The constitutional cloud, if there was one, dissipated. When Roberts asked him if he was ready to take the oath, Obama said, "Yes, I am, and we're going to do it very slowly." After the oath was over, Roberts said to Obama, "Congratulations, again." White House Counsel Gregory Craig said the President had been "sworn in appropriately" the day before, but they decided to do it over "out of an abundance of caution."

Feb. 5: The Supreme Court announced that Justice Ginsburg had surgery in New York City for recently discovered pancreatic cancer. She had no symptoms prior to the "incidental discovery" of a lesion during a routine check-up, the Court announcement stated. It was the second bout with cancer for Ginsburg, 75. She had colorectal cancer in 1999, but recovered and has worked at full strength since. During her subsequent treatments, Ginsburg missed no Court sessions, though she did have brief hospital stays after adverse reactions to medication.

Mar. 19: The Senate confirmed the nomination of Elena Kagan to be the 45th solicitor general of the United States, by a vote of 61-31. Formerly the dean of Harvard Law School, Kagan is the first woman confirmed to the position. Some opponents to her nomination cited her lack of appellate experience as a reason for voting against her. Before her confirmation, Kagan had never argued before the Supreme Court, and she did not become a member of the Supreme Court bar until January 12, a week after President Obama nominated her as solicitor general.

Apr. 6: In a mock trial based on Shakespeare's *Twelfth Night*, Justices Ginsburg, Breyer, and Alito assessed the merits of Malvolio's suit against Olivia for false imprisonment, ultimately siding with Olivia. Explaining his vote, Breyer said simply, "I don't like Malvolio," which prompted Alito to comment, "I always wondered what 'Active Liberty' meant." Alito was referring to Breyer's 2005 book by that name.

Apr. 18: Speaking of Shakespeare, the *Wall Street Journal* reported that Justice John Paul Stevens, with the support of several other justices, subscribes to the view that the works ascribed to Shakespeare were actually written by the 17th earl of Oxford, Edward de Vere. For centuries, some scholars have doubted that Shakespeare, a commoner, could write plays with such intimate details of aristocratic life and faraway places. "A lot of people like to think it's Shakespeare because . . . they like to think that a commoner can be such a brilliant writer," Stevens told the *Journal*. "Even though there is no Santa Claus, it's still a wonderful myth."

Apr. 21: During argument in *Safford Unified School District v. Redding*, some comments by justices provoked Justice Ginsburg later on to make rare critical remarks about her colleagues to the press. The case involved a strip search of a middle school girl by school officials looking for prescribed medications. Justice Breyer wondered aloud, "How bad is this?" and later said "people did sometimes stick things in my underwear," when he was a schoolboy. In subsequent remarks to *USA Today*, Justice Ginsburg said of her male colleagues, "They have never been a 13-year-old girl" and did not seem to appreciate the embarrassment a strip search could cause. "It's a very sensitive age for a girl. I didn't think that my colleagues, some of them, quite understood," Ginsburg said. On June 25, the Court ruled 8-1 that the search violated the Constitution.

Apr. 30: Several news organizations, citing unnamed sources, reported that Justice David Souter told the White House of his plans to retire after 19 years on the Court. The following day, Souter formalized his plans with a letter to President Obama stating his intention to retire "when the Supreme Court rises for the summer recess this year." Chief Justice Roberts issued a statement lamenting Souter's departure: "His desire to return to his native New Hampshire is understandable, but he will be greatly missed in our deliberations."

May 4: In her first press interview as solicitor general, Elena Kagan told the *National Law Journal* that that in spite of the change in administrations, the Court did not want drastic changes in position from her office. But she did anticipate that, especially when the underlying law or regulation changed, the solicitor general would take positions different from the Bush Administration. She also said she did not mind being addressed as "General Kagan," telling the interviewer, "My thought basically was: the justices have been calling men SGs 'general' for years and years and years; the first woman SG should be called the same thing." But she declined to say whether she would wear the traditional swallow-tail morning coat to arguments. As it turned out, Kagan did not wear the morning coat to her first argument in the fall term.

May 20: Speaking in almost valedictory tones, retiring Justice Souter told a Georgetown University Law Center audience that the republic "can be lost, it is being lost, it is lost, if it is not understood." Recalling his own childhood in New Hampshire, Souter said that today's youth are not receiving an adequate education about government institutions. He said he had agreed to join a committee that was tasked with revamping civic education in New Hampshire schools.

May 26: Saying he wanted a candidate with a "common touch," President Obama announced he would nominate Judge Sonia Sotomayor of the U.S. Court of Appeals for the 2nd Circuit to succeed Justice Souter. In announcing his nomination, Obama reviewed her background as a district court and appellate court judge, and also her "extraordinary journey" as someone raised in a public housing project in the Bronx. In a September interview with C-SPAN, Sotomayor said she cried when President Obama told her by phone on May 25 that he would nominate her.

June 27: Asked what changes he would like to see at the Court, Chief Justice Roberts said he would prefer shorter briefs from parties and fewer questions from the justices. "There's no reason that a party's brief couldn't be even more effective at 35 pages, certainly at 40 pages." As for oral arguments, Roberts said, "I think we're getting carried away" with questioning. "It is a little too much domination by the bench." Roberts acknowledged that as a justice now and as a practitioner in the past, his remarks could be seen as hypocritical. He spoke at the judicial conference of the U.S. Court of Appeals for the 4th Circuit.

July 13: In opening remarks at her Senate Judiciary Committee confirmation hearing, Judge Sotomayor said her judicial philosophy is "simple: fidelity to the law. The task of a judge is not to make the law — it is to apply the law. And it is clear, I believe, that my record in two courts reflects my rigorous commitment to interpreting the Constitution according to its terms; interpreting statutes according to their terms and Congress's intent; and hewing faithfully to precedents established by the Supreme Court and my Circuit Court."

July 14: Under intense questioning, Judge Sotomayor disavowed her "wise Latina" remark as a "rhetorical flourish that fell flat." She also distanced herself from President Obama's statement that in tough cases, judges sometimes find the right answer in their hearts. "I don't approach the issue of judging in the same way the president does," she said matter-of-factly. "Judges cannot rely on what's in their heart."

July 28: Senate Judiciary Committee voted 13-6 in favor of Judge Sotomayor's nomination to the Supreme Court. Senator Lindsey Graham of South Carolina was the only Republican in the majority.

July 30: Retired Justice Sandra Day O'Connor was among 16 notables receiving the presidential Medal of Freedom from President Obama. In remarks at the White House ceremony, Obama said that each of the award winners "has been an agent of change. Each saw an imperfect world and set about improving it, often overcoming great obstacles along the way."

Aug. 8: A day after the Senate confirmed her nomination by a 68-31 vote, Sonia Sotomayor was sworn in by Chief Justice Roberts as the 111th justice of the Supreme Court. Significantly, the ceremony took place at the Court, unlike some in recent years that were held at the White House. Justice Stevens, among others, had urged that such ceremonies take place at the Court, to underscore the Court's independence and non-political character. In another break from tradition, the public segment of the ceremony was televised live on C-SPAN and other broadcast outlets.

Aug. 21: The next tranche of Rehnquist papers released at the Hoover Institution Archives included extensive personal and official correspondence of the late chief justice, including poignant notes that showed how deeply affected his colleagues were in 2005 when he was undergoing thyroid cancer treatments. "Top priority at Court," Justice Ginsburg wrote, is "to have our Chief back with us, steadily on course toward a cancer-free future." Justice O'Connor wrote, "You did not need another medical problem." Justice Clarence Thomas, referring to his wife Virginia, wrote, "Virginia & I want you to know that you are in our thoughts & prayers."

Sept. 2: The Associated Press reported that Justice Stevens had hired only one law clerk for the 2010-2011 term, a possible sign that he planned to retire at the end of the current term in June 2010, when he will be 90 years old. The fact that Stevens confirmed the report for AP gave the story more weight. Retired justices are permitted to hire only one law clerk, while sitting justices are allowed four.

Sept. 8: With President Obama and Vice-President Biden in attendance, Chief Justice Roberts swore in Justice Sotomayor again in a public ceremony at a formal sitting of the Court. Roberts wished her a "long and happy career in our common calling." After the ceremony, Roberts and Sotomayor came outside the Court for a "photo opportunity" with the press before returning to the mainly camera-shy institution.

Sept. 21: Justice Sotomayor confirmed she had joined the Court's "cert pool," the clerk-pooling arrangement whereby law clerks for the participating justices prepare memos about incoming certiorari petitions that are shared among the justices in the pool. During her confirmation hearing in July, Sotomayor said when asked about the pool that "my approach may be similar to Justice Alito's." Alito joined the pool when he became a justice in 2006, but jumped out in 2008.

Sept. 26: Justice Sotomayor threw out the first baseball at a New York Yankees game in her hometown, Bronx, N.Y. The diehard Yankees fan is already "the most important federal judge in the history of baseball besides Judge Kenesaw Mountain Landis," said University of Wisconsin law professor Brad Snyder, who has written about the Court and baseball. As a federal district court judge in 1995, Sotomayor issued a ruling in a labor dispute with major league baseball that purportedly "saved major league baseball."

Oct. 4: Timed to coincide with the opening of the Supreme Court term, C-SPAN aired an extraordinary series of programs on the Supreme Court, focusing on both the institution and the building that houses it. Included were interviews with all sitting and retired justices, including Justice Sotomayor. Justices discussed their rituals and traditions, including frequent lunches together. Justice Thomas said he joined the lunches after persuasion from Justice O'Connor, adding that "It was one of the best things I did. It's hard to be angry or bitter at someone and break bread and look them in the eye."

Oct. 5: In a rare move, the Court postponed its first oral argument of the term in *South Carolina v. North Carolina*, an original jurisdiction case. Court sources indicated the reason was the confluence of personal issues for two of the lawyers arguing: serious family illness for one, and the death of another lawyer's mother.

Oct. 15: Justice Ginsburg was hospitalized overnight after fainting as she prepared to fly from Washington to London for ceremonies marking the opening of the new Supreme Court of the United Kingdom. The episode was apparently a reaction to a combination of cold medication and a sleeping aid. Ginsburg missed the flight, but Chief Justice Roberts and Justices Breyer and Scalia represented the Court at the ceremonies.

Oct. 26: In a *New York Times* blog post, author Gay Talese reported he and his friends dined on October 24 at a New York City restaurant where they were seated next to Chief Justice Roberts and his wife Jane. As the Robertses were preparing to leave, the chief justice approached their table and said, "Excuse me, but we cannot possibly finish this wonderful bottle of wine, and I wonder if you'd like to try it." Talese accepted, but not without asking Roberts for his autograph — which Roberts supplied.

A YEAR OF

LOWERING THE BAR

2008-2009

Kevin Underhill[†]

2008

Oct. 31: After months of bickering over who will argue *Carcieri v. Kempthorne* to the U.S. Supreme Court, petitioners and their attorneys ask the Court to decide, but it refuses to intervene. Petitioners' two lead attorneys had discussed tossing a coin, but could not agree on the rules for the coin toss.

Nov. 1: Just days before the presidential election, Barack Obama finally takes a position on an issue that several state and local governments have debated during the year: whether excessively sagging pants should be outlawed. "Here's my attitude," he tells MTV News. "I think passing a law about people wearing sagging pants is a waste of time.... Having said that, brothers should pull up their pants."

Nov. 4: Barack Obama is elected the 44th President of the United States. Exit polls suggest that his last-minute pants-policy statement had absolutely nothing to do with the outcome.

Nov. 4: The same day, a debate takes place during argument in *FCC v. Fox Television Stations* as to why the "F-word" is "shocking." Chief Justice John Roberts: "[I]t is associated with sexual or excretory activity." Respondent's counsel: "There is no empirical support for that." Justice Antonin Scalia: "Of course there is." Scalia cites none, but advises listeners not to use "'gollywaddles' instead of the F-Word" if they hope to shock anyone.

Nov. 6: Law student Alex Botsios confronts a burglar who has broken into his apartment. Botsios hands over his wallet when threatened, but snaps when the burglar demands his laptop. "Dude, no — please, no!" Botsios tells the burglar. "I have all my case notes [in there]." When the burglar insists, Botsios punches him, knocks him down and sits on him until help arrives.

[†] Kevin Underhill is a partner at Shook, Hardy and Bacon LLP in San Francisco and is the author of the legal-humor blog *Lowering the Bar* (www.loweringthebar.net). More detailed reports on these items originally appeared there, and the blog includes links to sources confirming that these things actually happened. His two-part article "If Great Literary Works Had Been Written by Lawyers" appeared in the *Green Bag*'s Summer 1999 and Autumn 2000 issues.

Nov. 13: The town of Marshall, North Carolina, agrees to pay Rebecca Willis $275,000 to settle her claims that it unfairly barred her from the town dance hall for "overly provocative dancing." The case had been pending for seven years and had twice reached the U.S. Court of Appeals for the Fourth Circuit.

Nov. 28: French President Nicolas Sarkozy wins a lawsuit against a company selling a voodoo doll in his image. The court refuses to order a recall, but does require packages to bear stickers warning that poking the doll would constitute "an attack on the dignity of the person of Mr. Sarkozy." The court also awards Sarkozy one euro.

Nov. 28: A Texas driver who rammed another car at high speed tells police that Jesus told him to do so because the other motorist was not "driving like a Christian." Neither driver is seriously injured, leading one officer to say that "God must have been with them" because otherwise the crash would have been fatal.

Dec. 3: Prompted by a series of embarrassing incidents, some members of Australia's parliament call for periodic breath tests to ensure that legislators and government ministers are not drinking on the job. "I subsequently put it to former minister Brown last night," the country's premier is quoted as saying, "that there are 'too many reports of you in your underwear to ignore.'"

Dec. 5: Yoichi Shimamoto and his wife sue United Airlines over a 2006 incident in which Mrs. Shimamoto was punched by a drunken passenger whom the airline allegedly "overserved." The drunken passenger was Mr. Shimamoto. Plaintiffs seek, among other damages, the costs Mr. Shimamoto incurred in defending himself against criminal charges for punching his wife.

Dec. 9: The Minnesota Court of Appeals rejects Senator Larry Craig's argument that his airport-bathroom-stall conduct is protected by the First Amendment. The court holds that "even if Appellant's foot-tapping and the movement of his foot toward the undercover officer's stall are considered 'speech,' they would be intrusive speech directed at a captive audience, and the government may [therefore] prohibit them."

Dec. 10: "Dreier Troubles Show Danger of Single-Equity-Partner Structure," says a headline on the *ABA Journal*'s website, referring to Marc Dreier and the 250-attorney Dreier Law Firm. The article speculates that if the single equity partner is imprisoned for fraud, that might "spell trouble for other partners."

Dec. 18: The D.C. Court of Appeals affirms a lower court's decision against former administrative law judge Roy Pearson, who had sued his dry cleaners for allegedly losing a pair of his pants and then not resolving the dispute to his complete satisfaction. Pearson had demanded as much as $65 million in lost-pants damages.

Dec. 18: A bench-clearing brawl breaks out in the South Korean legislature over a proposed free-trade agreement. The controversial bill is referred to a committee, which promptly locks itself in a meeting room to avoid injury. Furious opposition members try to force their way in using sledgehammers and an electric saw before guards drive them away with fire extinguishers.

Dec. 23: Roy Pearson seeks *en banc* rehearing of the decision in his pants-deprivation case.

Dec. 29: In Florida, Tim Smith's bike is stolen while he tries to help the victims of a car accident. Fortunately, as a city commissioner Smith had sponsored an ordinance requiring bike owners to register their bikes to deter theft. Unfortunately, he did not register his own bike, and so in addition to losing the bike he is ticketed for violating his own law.

2009

Jan. 3: In an editorial, psychology professor Stephen Greenspan discusses the fact that he lost 30 percent of his life savings to Bernard Madoff. Greenspan had previously written a book entitled "Annals of Gullibility: Why We Get Duped and How to Avoid It."

Jan. 7: In divorce proceedings, Dr. Richard Batista demands that his wife turn over either $1.5 million or the kidney he donated to her in 2001. A medical ethicist suggests that Batista's chances of recovering the kidney are "somewhere between impossible and completely impossible." Batista's attorney concedes her client would rather have the money instead.

Jan. 9: The Ninth Circuit rejects a request by Ted Kaczynski, the convicted "Unabomber," that the personal property seized from his cabin be returned. The court is apparently persuaded by the government's unopposed evidence showing that many of the items could be used to make bombs.

Jan. 15: The American Life League objects to a Krispy Kreme promotion for Inauguration Day because it uses the phrase "freedom of choice." "The unfortunate reality of a post *Roe v. Wade* America," the League's president states, "is that . . . celebration of 'freedom of choice' is a tacit endorsement of abortion rights on demand." Krispy Kreme denies any connection between its donuts and any "social or political issue."

Jan. 16: After reluctantly approving a class-action settlement in which class members would receive a $10 gift card while their attorney collected $125,000 in fees, a California judge orders that the attorney also be paid in gift cards. His 12,500 gift cards are to be redeemable, like the class members' cards, only at Windsor Fashions for women.

Jan. 17: Walter Tessier returns a lobster to his local supermarket, saying the lobster is "bad" and asking to exchange it. Upon inspection, employees find that Tessier has eaten all the lobster meat and reassembled the empty shell. He is charged with larceny.

Jan. 21: Timothy Geithner's spokesperson says Geithner should not be treated harshly for a common mistake on an "arcane" personal tax matter. Some suggest that Geithner, who was an official at the International Monetary Fund at the time, moved on to be CEO of the Federal Reserve

Bank of New York, and has been nominated for Secretary of the Treasury, should be able to do his own taxes correctly.

Jan. 20: Chief Justice Roberts administers the oath of office to Barack Obama.

Jan. 21: Chief Justice Roberts administers the oath of office to Barack Obama again.

Jan. 29: Gov. Rod Blagojevich, who had declined to appear for his impeachment trial in the Illinois legislature, changes his mind and decides to show up. He makes a closing argument in his own defense in a dramatic bid to avoid being removed from office.

Jan. 29: Blagojevich is removed from office.

Feb. 9: Former Nebraska state senator Ernie Chambers files a brief arguing that his lawsuit against God was wrongly dismissed for failure to properly serve the Defendant. He says it is inconsistent for courts to "take judicial notice of God" when administering an oath, but ignore His omniscience when deciding whether He has notice of a lawsuit.

Feb. 10: The Brodsky Law Firm in New York runs ads offering to arrange a divorce in 60 minutes or less for $299. The firm uses the slogan, "Got an hour? Get a divorce!" As part of the package, couples receive one $10 gift card redeemable at a nearby McDonald's or Starbucks.

Feb. 11: Lucie Kim sues Miley Cyrus over an online image that appears to show Cyrus and some friends making "slant-eyed" faces. Kim, who claims to represent all people of Asian or Pacific Islander descent in Los Angeles County, demands four billion dollars in damages.

Feb. 11: Maryland state senator George Della, Jr., withdraws a bill that would have outlawed "beer pong," a popular game in which participants try to lob ping-pong balls into a cup. Della argues that the game tends to encourage drinking, but says he is withdrawing the bill due to overwhelming public opposition. "We're getting inundated with so many e-mails," he says, "that I don't have the time to fool with it."

Feb. 17: Harlyn Geronimo and other descendants of the famous Apache leader say they are pursuing a lawsuit demanding the return of their ancestor's skull, which they allege is being held in the crypt of the "Skull and Bones" society at Yale University. They claim that a group of Yale men including George W. Bush's grandfather, Prescott Bush, stole the skull from Geronimo's grave during World War I and carted it off to New Haven, where it allegedly remains to this day.

Feb. 26: Mark Rimkufski, late for a plane to Los Angeles, is allowed to board after he flashes a badge and identifies himself as an air marshal. Rimkufski is not actually an air marshal, however, and has failed to plan for the possibility that real air marshals might be on the plane who know what real air-marshal badges look like.

Feb. 28: Latreasa Goodman of Fort Pierce, Florida, is cited for misusing the 911 service after she uses it to report that her local McDonald's has run out of McNuggets. Told that 911 is reserved for emergencies, she insists that it is one, and demands that an officer be sent immediately. McDonald's later apologizes for the nugget shortage.

Mar. 2: The D.C. Court of Appeals denies Roy Pearson's petition for *en banc* rehearing.

Mar. 2: In Oakland, California, Rev. Dr. Cheryl Elliott sues Randy Keyes and the United Pentecostal Church of Modesto. Rev. Elliott alleges that Keyes knocked her down while "laying hands" on participants during a church service, and that he failed to apologize afterward.

Mar. 3: West Virginia lawmaker Jeff Eldridge (D-Lincoln) introduces a bill that would make it illegal to sell Barbie "and other similar dolls" in that state. Eldridge contends that the dolls "influence girls to place an undue importance on physical beauty to the detriment of their intellectual and emotional development." (Coincidentally, Eldridge grew up in Big Ugly, West Virginia.) GOP lawmakers opposing the bill proudly display Barbie dolls on their desks.

Mar. 4: A man charged with driving while intoxicated admits he consumed at least 15 beers before getting on the road. He had been involved in a minor accident while driving his motorized bar stool, which he says can reach speeds of almost 40 miles per hour.

Mar. 9: The California Court of Appeal rules that a contract for which there is no consideration is not enforceable even if it is written in blood.

Mar. 10: Scott Witmer tells a judge that he is immune from state DUI charges because he is an independent country. "I live inside myself, not in Pennsylvania," he declares. "Don't all our souls live within ourselves?" "Your metaphysical properties are not on trial here," the judge responds. Witmer ultimately pleads guilty.

Mar. 14: Reports say that the court in Morrow County, Ohio, has announced it will no longer accept new case filings because it only has enough paper for pending cases and cannot afford to buy more. Unless litigants want to provide their own paper, Judge Lee McClelland is quoted as saying, "we can't process anything."

Mar. 18: A Tennessee legislative subcommittee approves a bill making it illegal to "knowingly wear pants below the waistline, in a public place, in a manner that exposes the person's underwear or bare buttocks." The bill's sponsor insists on referring to it as "the crack bill." "I think any respectable citizen would be against crack," he says. A colleague argues in opposition that youth apparel should be regulated by parents, not the government, but denies being "pro-crack."

Mar. 25: A man who pleaded not guilty to indecent-exposure charges in Michigan is sentenced to 90 days in jail. He was arrested in 2008 after a caller alerted police to "suspicious activity" involving one of the vacuum cleaners at a local car wash.

Mar. 31: An attorney for a former San Francisco official who pleaded guilty to fraud, bribery, and extortion says his client has suffered head injuries that caused "social naiveté and exuberance." The positive aspects of these qualities helped him get elected, the attorney says, but "ultimately contributed to his downfall when more prudent judgment and impulse control were necessary," like when trying not to take bribes.

Mar. 31: Speaking to a group of students, Justice Clarence Thomas remarks that he still finds dishwashing machines somewhat miraculous: "I have to admit . . . that I'm one of those people that still thinks the dishwasher is a miracle. What a device! And I have to admit that because I think that way . . . . I like to load it. I like to look in and see how the dishes were magically cleaned."

Apr. 7: Robert Drawbaugh files for divorce, saying his marriage has "broken down irretrievably." The breakdown comes two months after police rescued Drawbaugh from his wife, who had handcuffed them together. She told police she had used the handcuffs "because it was the only way she could have a full conversation with her husband."

Apr. 17: Another lawsuit is filed, this one in Oregon, alleging a negligent "laying on of hands" during a church service. The plaintiff, who says she was injured when a congregant fell on her, claims that the church did not provide enough "catchers" for those taken by the spirit and did not instruct congregants on "correct falling procedures."

Apr. 21: During argument in *Safford Unified School District v. Redding*, involving a strip-search of a 13-year-old girl suspected of possessing ibuprofen, Justice Stephen Breyer suggests that it is not impossible for a third party to have hidden the contraband in the girl's pants. "In my experience," he recalls, "people did sometimes stick things in my underwear." Breyer quickly explains that he misspoke and had intended only to make the point that third-party involvement might not be "beyond human experience."

Apr. 22: A Louisiana woman sues Wal-Mart after suffering a broken foot in one of its stores during a run-in with a large wild rodent known as a "nutria." More specifically, she panicked after seeing the nutria and ran over her own foot with a shopping cart. She alleges that Wal-Mart knowingly harbored the rodent, claiming that an employee told her, "You had an encounter with Norman."

Apr. 27: Laurence Tureaud, better known as "Mr. T," reports for jury duty in Cook County, Illinois. T spends about five hours in court but is not chosen to serve. After being excused, he tells onlookers he would have been a fair but harsh juror. "If you're innocent, I'm your best man," he says. "But if you're guilty, I pity that fool!"

May 11: Former Minnesota Governor Jesse Ventura, who says he was waterboarded as part of his military training, tells Larry King that torture is not an effective interrogation technique. "I'll put it to you this way," he tells King. "You give me a waterboard, Dick Cheney and one hour, and I'll have him confess to the Sharon Tate murders."

May 20: Australian real-estate developer Harry Kakavas testifies that Melbourne's Crown Casino caused him to lose millions. He alleges that although the casino knew he was a compulsive gambler, it flew him to Melbourne 14 times and gave him $50,000 in "lucky money" each time to get him started. It did later ban him, allegedly just after he had lost $2 million at baccarat in 43 minutes.

May 20: Britain's Court of Appeals rules that Pringles do not qualify as "potato crisps" for taxation purposes. Proctor & Gamble UK had argued that Pringles should not be considered "made from the potato" because they are less than 50 percent potato and have "a shape not found in nature." The appellate court rules that the 50-percent criterion is not a requirement and that Pringles are, basically, close enough.

May 21: A federal judge in California dismisses a lawsuit against PepsiCo, the maker of "Cap'n Crunch with Crunch Berries." Janine Sugawara alleged that although the product is represented as a "combination of Crunch biscuits and colorful red, purple, teal and green [Crunch] berries," she has learned it actually contains "no berries of any kind." The court finds that "a reasonable consumer would not be deceived into believing that the Product in the instant case contained a fruit that does not exist. . . . So far as this Court has been made aware, there is no such fruit growing in the wild or occurring naturally in any part of the world."

May 21: The same judge dismisses a similar lawsuit against Kellogg USA, the maker of "Froot Loops," for reasons you can probably figure out.

June 8: The Washington Court of Appeals holds that honking is not protected speech. Irritated by a neighbor's complaint about her chickens, Helen Immelt honked repeatedly at the neighbor and a police officer, and was charged with violating a noise ordinance. She argues that the First Amendment protects her right to honk, but the court disagrees. It contemplates an exception for honking with "the intent to convey a particularized message in circumstances where it is likely the message would be understood," but says honking "done to annoy or harass others is not speech."

June 24: A committee of the Oregon Legislature passes a bill that critics say attempts to redefine "no" as "yes" for purposes of a controversial referendum vote. The bill provides that a measure "may not be adopted unless it receives an affirmative majority of the total votes cast on the measure rejecting the measure. For purposes of this subsection, a measure is considered adopted if it is rejected by the people."

June 27: *The Palm Beach Post* reports on a "Motion to Compel Opposing Counsel to Wear Appropriate Shoes." The motion argues it is "well known in the legal community that Michael Robb, Esq., wears shoes with holes in the soles when he is in trial . . . as a ruse to impress the jury and make them believe that Mr. Robb is humble and simple without sophistication." Allegedly, Robb "is known to stand at sidebar with one foot crossed casually beside the other so that the holes in his shoes are readily apparent to the jury . . . ." The motion is denied, but the case later ends in a mistrial after jurors admit they read the *Post*'s report about the motion.

June 29: A man caught speeding in Tennessee tells authorities that he does not have to obey national speed limits because he is a deputy director of the CIA. Scott Gibson is charged anyway after the CIA confirms that it does not have any deputy directors by that name.

June 30: A California court holds that a man who tripped and fell into the giant bonfire that ends the Burning Man festival in Nevada cannot sue the organizers for failing to keep him away from the fire. The man admitted he knew "fire was dangerous and caused burns" before he approached one, and the court holds that he therefore assumed the risk of injury.

July 1: Numerous sources report on a ruling by Judge Ronald McPhillips in a contract case pending in Toole County, Montana. This is news only because the case was filed in 1983 and so had been pending for over 26 years. Judge McPhillips, who retired in 1994, apparently found the file at home during a spring cleaning.

July 2: A D.C. federal judge dismisses yet another attempt to contend that President Obama is not a "natural-born citizen," this one initiated by a group calling itself a "Super American Grand Jury," which indicted Obama for treason. One problem with this plan, as the judge notes, is that a self-convened "grand jury" has no legal authority whatsoever.

July 10: H. Beatty Chadwick is released after serving 14 years on a contempt charge, said to be the longest term served for contempt in U.S. history. Chadwick was jailed in 1995 for refusing to pay his ex-wife $2.5 million. He has long claimed that he does not have the money to pay, but no judge has ever believed him. Nor did the one who let him go, but that judge said he had finally concluded that keeping Chadwick in jail would serve no further purpose.

July 23: Roy Pearson loses again, this time in a wrongful-termination suit he filed after he was not reappointed to another term as an ALJ. Officials claimed that Pearson's termination was not related to his $65-million-dollar lost-pants action.

July 27: The author of this piece encounters a law-review article entitled *YOU'VE GOT TO BE KIDNEYING ME!: The Fatal Problem of Severing Rights and Remedies From the Body of Organ Donation Law*, 74 Brook. L. Rev. 543 (2009). He says to himself that this is perhaps the worst title yet inflicted on the law-review-reading public.

July 31: In a story about judicial appointments in California, legal newspaper *The Recorder* quotes Court of Appeal Justice Anthony Kline as saying "That's bullcrap" in response to a comment.

Aug. 3: *The Recorder* publishes a correction to its July 31 story, saying that "[a]lthough another reporter and some audience members also thought they heard 'bullcrap,' a careful review of the videotape . . . indicates Kline actually said 'That's forthright.' We regret the error."

Aug. 5: Former U.S. representative William Jefferson is convicted of bribery. Jefferson's defense was not helped by the fact that FBI agents found $90,000 stashed in Jefferson's freezer at home.

Aug. 17: ABC announces that among the contestants on the next season of "Dancing With the Stars" will be former House majority leader Tom "The

Hammer" DeLay. DeLay has been indicted on money-laundering charges, but is allegedly a pretty good dancer. His critics are unimpressed. "It would be [more] interesting to see if Mr. DeLay can do the Perp Walk," says one. "Does he know that step?"

Aug. 28: Police in Massachusetts looking for a robbery suspect detain a man who has been cornered by their police dog. A search reveals that the man is not the armed robber the dog was supposed to track, but rather a shoplifter who chose an especially bad time to steal meat from a super-market by stuffing it down his pants. "The dog must have smelled a tasty dinner in his pants," a police spokesman suggests.

Sept. 2: Sallie Peake, the mayor of Wellford, South Carolina, orders police not to chase suspects after several officers are injured in pursuits, costing the town money. "As of this date," she writes in a memo, "there are to be no more foot chases when a suspect runs. I do not want anyone chasing after any suspects whatsoever."

Sept. 6: The final performance of *The Gonzales Cantata* takes place in Philadelphia. It is billed as the only concert opera based entirely on the transcript of former U.S. Attorney General Alberto Gonzales's 2007 testimony before the Senate Judiciary Committee.

Sept. 14: The U.S. Tax Court rules against tax attorney William Halby, who has claimed amounts he spent for what he calls "intimate therapy" services as deductions for "medical expenses." The court points out that paying for this kind of "therapy" is illegal in New York. It also criticizes Halby for failing to get itemized receipts.

Sept. 22: Undeterred by the dismissal in May of nearly identical cases, Roy Werbel sues PepsiCo and Kellogg's in San Francisco, also alleging that the terms "Crunch Berries" and "Froot Loops" misled him about the real fruit content of the fictitiously named cereals.

Sept. 24: Mayor Sallie Peake rescinds her no-chase policy after a prosecutor convinces her that not being able to chase felons would put officers in an "untenable position." She insists that she is not backing down, declaring "I meant what I said, and I say what I mean, and I stand by it!" although in fact she had just rescinded it.

Sept. 28: Reports say Parminder Singh Saini hopes to persuade examiners he should be allowed to practice law in Canada, notwithstanding the fact that he once hijacked a plane, shot someone, and entered Canada illegally after being exiled from Pakistan. Saini says he now realizes hijacking planes is "not legal," which is not quite a promise not to do it again.

Oct. 1: *The Wall Street Journal* reports that Justice Scalia has praised counsel appearing before the Court but expressed concern that so many good people are becoming lawyers: "[T]here'd be a . . . public defender from Podunk, you know, and this woman is really brilliant . . . . Why isn't she out inventing the automobile or, you know, doing something productive for this society? I mean, lawyers, after all, don't produce anything. They enable other people to produce and to go on with their lives efficiently and in an atmosphere of freedom. That's important, but it doesn't put food on the table .... And I worry that we are devoting too many of our very best minds to this enterprise."

Oct. 13: Justice John Paul Stevens is quoted as saying he could not recall anyone ever recognizing him outside of a courtroom, except once in a Florida video store. In a related story, reporter Linda Greenhouse remembers that she once saw a tourist hand a camera to a man he did not know was Justice Byron White and ask him to take his family's picture. Greenhouse says White "wordlessly complied."

Oct. 20: A Louisiana couple sues a judge who refused to marry them because they were not of the same race. Keith Bardwell denies he is a racist, claiming he is concerned for the children of mixed-race couples because their lives will be ruined by stigma. He appears to be unaware both that race-based restrictions on marriage were held unconstitutional forty years ago and that a son of a mixed-race couple has recently been elected President of the United States.

Oct. 26: Judge Michael Hecht denies wrongdoing during testimony in his trial on charges of felony harassment and patronizing a prostitute. Asked why he frequented a local adult theater, Hecht admits visiting hundreds of times but says it was only to buy chicken soup from a vending machine there. "It's very good soup," he testifies. He is convicted two days later.

Oct. 27: A French court finds the Church of Scientology and six Scientologists guilty of fraud for misleading plaintiffs through alleged "audits" conducted with "electropsychometers." Judges appear skeptical of Scientology's claims that humanity was brought to Earth 75 million years ago at the command of an alien space lord named Xenu who then released their souls with atomic bombs, but limit their holding to the fraud claims.

Nov. 1: The Washington Supreme Court grants review of Helen Immelt's case. The fact that a state supreme court will take up the question whether horn-honking can be protected speech suggests that next year will be at least as odd as this one was.

JANUARY

NAPOLEON LAJOIE

Defendant, *Philadelphia Baseball Club Co. v. Lajoie*, 13 Ohio Dec. 504 (1902).
See David Jones & Steve Constantelos, *Nap Lajoie, in*
THE BASEBALL BIOGRAPHY PROJECT, www.sabr.org (SABR 2009).

❧ JANUARY ❧

SUN	MON	TUES	WED	THUR	FRI	SAT
31					1	2
3	4	5	6	7	8	9
10	11	12	13	14	15	16
17	18	19	20	21	22	23
24	25	26	27	28	29	30

'INFORMATION PLEASE' — MOE BERG ON THE STAND

Sporting News, Nov. 16, 1939, at 4, 7

For some time, fans have been aware that Moe Berg, coach and catcher for the Boston Red Sox, is a highly educated ball player. However, not until Berg recently appeared on the "Information Please" program, over a national radio network, did they realize the full extent of his erudition — the broad scope of his learning in a wide variety of fields. It was our good fortune to meet Moe in New York recently, where in the course of an hour's talk, we discovered a lot of interesting points about "Professor" Berg's career, his world-wide travels and his educational attainments — including the fact that if he desires, he can address umpires in a choice of 11 languages, while the average player is limited to one.

We put the scholarly catcher on the stand with the following results: . . .

"I went through Columbia Law School and passed my bar examinations while I was with the White Sox.

"My presence in baseball today I owe to a grand man, Professor Noel Dowling of the Columbia Law School. In May, 1927, I was the property of the White Sox. I had had no spring training for two years, and I knew I had come to the cross roads. It apparently would have to be baseball or law. Which? I loved the game and hated to quit.

"One day I went into Prof. Dowling's office to discuss a lecture I had missed. The prof was reading a newspaper and much to my amazement, it was the sports page. He looked up and laughed, 'I see the Giants beat the Pirates yesterday. Great game, this baseball. You ought to get interested in it.'

"Very few folks around the law school, certainly none of the faculty, knew then of my connection with baseball.

"Prof. Dowling continued his effort to 'interest me in baseball.' He told me he had played first base for Vanderbilt University. I said, 'Professor, I played shortstop for Princeton.'

"He looked at me in amazement. 'Are you the Berg from Princeton?' I assured him I was and then came the whole story. I had found somebody to whom I could tell my difficulties. I told him that if I was to continue with the White Sox, I would have to report for spring training in 1928. He gave me a plan. He let me double up on courses the second semester of 1927.

"Thus Noel Dowling, who had played first base for Vanderbilt, saved my professional baseball career for me. I had about made up my mind to give up on the diamond. . . ."[1]

---

[1] To learn a great deal more about Berg, read Nicholas Dawidoff's *The Catcher Was a Spy: The Mysterious Life of Moe Berg* (1994).

"At the turn of the century we lived in this little town of Ouray in the southwestern part of Colorado, not far from places with names like Lizard Head Pass . . . . Dad was a lawyer there — his law partner was later the attorney general of Colorado — and he was involved in some big cases for the Western Federation of Miners. During several of these cases they had to send in the state militia to guard him. Feelings ran high about unions in Colorado back then. He was a great trial lawyer. Hardly ever lost a case in front of a jury." Joe Wood, in LAWRENCE RITTER, THE GLORY OF THÉIR TIMES 154-55 (1984 ed.).

SEC V. BANK OF AMERICA CORP.

Jed S. Rakoff[†]

In the Complaint in this case, filed August 3, 2009, the Securities and Exchange Commission ("S.E.C.") alleges, in stark terms, that defendant Bank of America Corporation materially lied to its shareholders in the proxy statement of November 3, 2008 that solicited the shareholders' approval of the $50 billion acquisition of Merrill Lynch & Co. ("Merrill"). The essence of the lie, according to the Complaint, was that Bank of America "represented that Merrill had agreed not to pay year-end performance bonuses or other discretionary incentive compensation to its executives prior to the closing of the merger without Bank of America's consent [when] [i]n fact, contrary to the representation . . ., Bank of America had agreed that Merrill could pay up to $5.8 billion — nearly 12% of the total consideration to be exchanged in the merger — in discretionary year-end and other bonuses to Merrill executives for 2008." Compl. ¶ 2. Along with the filing of these very serious allegations, however, the parties, on the very same day, jointly sought this Court's approval of a proposed final Consent Judgment by which Bank of America, without admitting or denying the accusations, would be enjoined from making future false statements in proxy solicitations and would pay to the S.E.C. a fine of $33 million.

In other words, the parties were proposing that the management of Bank of America — having allegedly hidden from the Bank's shareholders that as much as $5.8 billion of their money would be given as bonuses to the executives of Merrill who had run that company nearly into bankruptcy — would now settle the legal consequences of their lying by paying the S.E.C. $33 million more of their shareholders' money.

This proposal to have the victims of the violation pay an additional penalty for their own victimization was enough to give the Court pause. The Court therefore heard oral argument on August 10, 2009 and re-

---

[†] Judge of the United States District Court for the Southern District of New York. This opinion is reported at 2009 WL 2916822 (S.D.N.Y. 2009).

ceived extensive written submissions on August 24, 2009 and September 9, 2009. Having now carefully reviewed all these materials, the Court concludes that the proposed Consent Judgment must be denied.

In reaching this conclusion, the Court is very mindful of the considerable deference it must accord the parties' proposal, since it would seemingly result in the consensual resolution of the case. Society greatly benefits when lawsuits are amicably resolved, and, for that reason, an ordinary civil settlement that includes dismissal of the underlying action is close to unreviewable. *See Hester Industries, Inc. v. Tyson Foods, Inc.*, 160 F.3d 911, 916 (2d Cir. 1998)(citing cases). When, however, as in the case of a typical consent judgment, a federal agency such as the S.E.C. seeks to prospectively invoke the Court's own contempt power by having the Court impose injunctive prohibitions against the defendant, the resolution has aspects of a judicial decree and the Court is therefore obliged to review the proposal a little more closely, to ascertain whether it is within the bounds of fairness, reasonableness, and adequacy — and, in certain circumstances, whether it serves the public interest. *See S.E.C. v. Randolph*, 736 F.2d 525, 529 (9th Cir. 1984); *see also S.E.C. v. Wang*, 944 F.2d 80, 85 (2d Cir. 1991). *See generally, United States v. ITT Continental Baking Co.*, 420 U.S. 223 (1975); *United States v. North Carolina*, 180 F.3d 574 (4th Cir. 1999). But even then, the review is highly deferential. *S.E.C. v. Worldcom, Inc.*, 273 F.Supp.2d 431, 436 (S.D.N.Y. 2003).

Here, however, the Court, even upon applying the most deferential standard of review for which the parties argue, is forced to conclude that the proposed Consent Judgment is neither fair, nor reasonable, nor adequate.

It is not fair, first and foremost, because it does not comport with the most elementary notions of justice and morality, in that it proposes that the shareholders who were the victims of the Bank's alleged misconduct now pay the penalty for that misconduct. The S.E.C. admits that the corporate penalties it here proposes will be "indirectly borne by [the] shareholders." Reply Memorandum of Plaintiff Securities and Exchange Commission in Support of Entry of the Proposed Consent Judgment ("S.E.C. Reply Mem.") at 13. But the S.E.C. argues that this is justified because "[a] corporate penalty . . . sends a strong signal to shareholders that unsatisfactory corporate conduct has occurred and allows shareholders to better assess the quality and performance of management." *Id*. This hypothesis, however, makes no sense when applied to the facts here: for the notion that Bank of America shareholders, having been lied to blatantly in connection with the multi-billion-dollar purchase of a huge, nearly-bankrupt company, need to lose another $33 million of their money in order to "better assess the quality and performance of management" is absurd.

The S.E.C., while also conceding that its normal policy in such situations is to go after the company executives who were responsible for the lie, rather than innocent shareholders, says it cannot do so here because "[t]he uncontroverted evidence in the investigative record is that lawyers for Bank of America and Merrill drafted the documents at issue and made the relevant decisions concerning disclosure of the bonuses." Id. But if that is the case, why are the penalties not then sought from the lawyers? And why, in any event, does that justify imposing penalties on the victims of the lie, the shareholders?

Bank of America, for its part, having originally agreed to remain silent in the face of these charges, now, at the Court's request that it provide the Court with the underlying facts, vigorously asserts that the proxy statement, when read carefully, is neither false nor misleading, see Reply Memorandum of Law on Behalf of Bank of America Corporation ("BoA Reply Mem.") at 5, or that, even if it is false or misleading, the misstatements were immaterial because "[it] was widely acknowledged in the period leading up to the shareholder vote that Merrill Lynch intended to pay year-end incentive compensation," id. at 19. The S.E.C. responds, however, that these arguments are hollow. The Bank's argument that the proxy statement was not misleading rests in material part on reference to a schedule that was not even attached to the proxy statement, and "[s]hareholders are entitled to rely on the representations in the proxy itself, and are not required to puzzle out material information from a variety of external sources." S.E.C. Reply Mem. at 2. As for the Bank's argument that the investors were not materially misled because the press was already reporting the imminent payment of Merrill bonuses, "investors were not required to ignore Bank of America's express statements in the proxy materials and rely instead on media speculation that may have suggested that these statements were misleading." Id. at 9.

Moreover, it is noteworthy that, in all its voluminous papers protesting its innocence, Bank of America never actually provides the Court with the particularized facts that the Court requested, such as precisely how the proxy statement came to be prepared, exactly who made the relevant decisions as to what to include and not include so far as the Merrill bonuses were concerned, etc.

But all of this is beside the point because, if the Bank is innocent of lying to its shareholders, why is it prepared to pay $33 million of its shareholders' money as a penalty for lying to them? All the Bank offers in response to this obvious question is the statement in the last footnote of its Reply Memorandum that "Because of the SEC's decision to bring charges, Bank of America would have to spend corporate funds whether or not it settled," BofA Reply Mem. at 28, n. 20 — the implication being that the payment was simply an exercise of business judgment as to which alternative would cost more: litigating or settling. But, quite aside from the fact that it is difficult to believe that litigating this simple case would cost anything like $33 million, it does not appear, so far as one can tell from this single sentence in a footnote, that this decision was made by disinterested parties. It is one thing for management to exercise its business judgment to determine how much of its shareholders money should be used to settle a case brought by former shareholders or third parties. It is quite something else for the very management that is accused of having lied to its shareholders to determine how much of those victims' money should be used to make the case against the management go away.[1] And even if this decision is arguably within their purview, it calls for greater scrutiny by the Court than would otherwise be the case.

Overall, indeed, the parties' submissions, when carefully read, leave the distinct impression that the proposed Consent Judgment was a contrivance designed to provide the S.E.C. with the facade of enforcement and the management of the Bank with a quick resolution of an embarrassing inquiry — all at the expense of the sole alleged victims, the shareholders. Even under the most deferential review, this proposed Consent Judgment cannot remotely be called fair.

Nor is the proposed Consent Judgment reasonable. Obviously, a proposal that asks the victims to pay a fine for their having been victimized is, for all the reasons already given, as unreasonable as it is unfair. But the proposed Consent Judgment is unreasonable in numerous other respects as well.

For example, the Consent Judgment would effectively close the case

---

[1] Undoubtedly, the decision to spend this money was made even easier by the fact that the U.S. Government provided the Bank of America with a $40 billion or so "bail out," of which $20 billion came after the merger. Since $3.6 billion of that money had already been spent, indirectly, to compensate the Bank for the Merrill bonuses — not to mention the $20 billion in taxpayer funds that effectively compensated the Bank for the last-minute revelations that Merrill's loss for 2008 was $27 billion instead of $7 billion — what impediment could there be to paying a mere $33 million (or more than most people will see in their lifetimes) to get rid of a lawsuit saying that the bonuses had been concealed from the shareholders approving the merger? To say, as the Bank now does, that the $33 million does not come directly from U.S. funds is simply to ignore the overall economics of the Bank's situation.

without the S.E.C. adequately accounting for why, in contravention of its own policy, see Order, 8/25/08 (quoting the policy), it did not pursue charges against either Bank management or the lawyers who allegedly were responsible for the false and misleading proxy statements. The S.E.C. says this is because charges against individuals for making false proxy statements require, at a minimum, proof that they participated in the making of the false statements knowing the statements were false or recklessly disregarding the high probability the statements were false. But how can such knowledge be lacking when, as the Complaint in effect alleges, executives at the Bank expressly approved Merrill's making year-end bonuses before they issued the proxy statement denying such approval?[2] The S.E.C. states, as noted, that culpable intent was nonetheless lacking because the lawyers made all the relevant decisions. But, if so, then how can the lawyers be said to lack intent? Under these circumstances, how can a Court find reasonable a proposed Consent Judgment that otherwise violates S.E.C. policy?[3]

To give a different example, the proposed Consent Judgment seeks injunctive relief forbidding the Bank, on pain of contempt of court, from issuing false or misleading statements in the future. On its face, the proposed injunction appears too nebulous to comply with Rule 65(d) of the Federal Rules of Civil Procedure, which requires, among other things, that an injunction "describe in reasonable detail . . . the act or acts restrained . . . ." Moreover, since the Bank contends that it never made any

---

[2] Lurking in the background is the suggestion, affirmed by the Bank's counsel at the August 10 hearing, that the highest executives of Bank of America, upon learning that Merrill's loss was $20 billion more than had been represented at the time the merger was negotiated, were prepared to walk away from the merger until "coerced" by the Government into going through with it, following which the Government provided the Bank with an additional $20 billion in bail-out funds. But, quite aside from the fact that none of this appears to have been revealed to the shareholders prior to the merger, neither party suggests that any such coercion played any role in the alleged decision not to reveal the Merrill bonuses. The huge increase in Merrill's losses, however, did arguably render the providing of the bonuses more material, as well as more inexplicable.

[3] The S.E.C. also claims it was stymied in determining individual liability because the Bank's executives said the lawyers made all the decisions but the Bank refused to waive attorney-client privilege. But it appears that the S.E.C. never seriously pursued whether this constituted a waiver of the privilege, let alone whether it fit within the crime/fraud exception to the privilege. And even on its face, such testimony would seem to invite investigating the lawyers. The Bank, for its part, claims that it has not relied on a defense of advice of counsel and so no waiver has occurred. But, as noted earlier, the Bank has failed to provide its own particularized version of how the proxies came to be and how the key decisions as to what to include or exclude were made, so its claim of not relying on an advice of counsel is simply an evasion.

false or misleading statements in the past, the Court at this point lacks a factual predicate for imposing such relief.

To be sure, the Bank's initial position was that it neither admitted nor denied the allegations, and such a position, when coupled with proof by the S.E.C. that the alleged violations have occurred, may often be sufficient to support certain forms of injunctive relief. But here the further submissions of the Bank make clear its position that the proxy statement in issue was totally in accordance with the law: meaning that, notwithstanding the injunctive relief here sought by the S.E.C., the Bank would feel free to issue exactly the same kind of proxy statement in the future. Under these circumstances, the broad but vague injunctive relief here sought would be a pointless exercise, since the sanction of contempt may only be imposed for violation of a particularized provision known and reasonably understood by the contemnor, all of which would be lacking here. *See, e.g., Int'l Longshoreman's Ass'n, Local 1291 v. Philadelphia Marine Trade Ass'n*, 389 U.S. 64, 76 (1967); *Powell v. Ward*, 643 F.2d 924, 931 (2d Cir. 1981).

Without multiplying examples further, the point is that the Court finds the proposed Consent Judgment not only unfair but also unreasonable.

Finally, the proposed Consent Judgment is inadequate. The injunctive relief, as noted, is pointless. The fine, if looked at from the standpoint of the violation, is also inadequate, in that $33 million is a trivial penalty for a false statement that materially infected a multi-billion-dollar merger. But since the fine is imposed, not on the individuals putatively responsible, but on the shareholders, it is worse than pointless: it further victimizes the victims.

Oscar Wilde once famously said that a cynic is someone "who knows the price of everything and the value of nothing." Oscar Wilde, *Lady Windermere's Fan* (1892). The proposed Consent Judgment in this case suggests a rather cynical relationship between the parties: the S.E.C. gets to claim that it is exposing wrongdoing on the part of the Bank of America in a high-profile merger; the Bank's management gets to claim that they have been coerced into an onerous settlement by overzealous regulators. And all this is done at the expense, not only of the shareholders, but also of the truth.

Yet the truth may still emerge. The Bank of America states unequivocally that if the Court disapproves the Consent Judgment, it is prepared to litigate the charges. BofA Reply Mem. at 5. The S.E.C., having brought the charges, presumably is not about to drop them. Accordingly, the

Court, having hereby disapproved the Consent Judgment, directs the parties to file with the Court, no later than one week from today, a jointly proposed Case Management Plan that will have this case ready to be tried on February 1, 2010.[4]

So Ordered

✳ ✳ ✳

DAVID HERBERT DONALD

J. Gordon Hylton
Marquette University Law School Faculty Blog,
http://law.marquette.edu/facultyblog/2009/05/20/david-herbert-donald/ (vis. May 22, 2009)

The noted historian, Professor David Herbert Donald of Harvard University, passed away on Sunday, May 17, at the age 88. Professor Donald was a two-time winner of the Pulitzer Prize for Biography and was widely recognized as the preeminent Lincoln scholar of the twentieth century. Although not normally classified as a legal or constitutional historian, scholars who work in those fields are enormously indebted to Donald's work, particularly in regard to the era of the Civil War and Reconstruction. . . .

I also had the good fortune to later study under him at graduate school at Harvard in the late 1970's and early 1980's. He held the bar high, but he was also unfailingly gracious to his students and generous with his time. Although he is primarily associated with Lincoln and his era, his knowledge and interests were much broader than just that period and he supervised dissertations on a wide variety of topics.

He did, however, draw the line at the history of sports. After I passed my PhD general examinations, I met with him to discuss possible dissertation topics. He asked me what I thinking about, and I mentioned to him that I found it fascinating that in 1850 baseball was basically a folk game played informally with no set body of rules. However, by 1870, the rules had been standardized, there were professional leagues, and the sport was widely hailed as "America's national game." I told Donald that I thought it would be interesting to try to trace out the process by which this occurred, particularly since it happened against the backdrop of the Civil War and Reconstruction. Donald appeared to toss my idea around in his head for a minute or two, and then said, in his charming Southern voice, "You know, Gordon, I don't believe that I could come up with a less interesting historical question." On that note, I decided to write on the history of the legal profession in the South.

With his passing, the historical profession, and the United States, has lost one of its giants. . . .

---

[4] The trial would include both the application for permanent injunctive relief and the claim for monetary penalties. If the parties cannot jointly agree on a schedule, they should submit to the Court their competing proposals, and the Court will then resolve the differences.

49

Preston Woodlock's "Souvenir of First Yale-Waseda International Series 1935."

"How Can You Play the Game Like That?"

Douglas P. Woodlock[†]

My Dad played ball for Smoky Joe Wood.

For those of you who may need your recollections refreshed, Joe Wood was, according to Walter Johnson, the fastest pitcher ever to play major league baseball. He led the Boston Red Sox to the World Series championship in 1912, but he injured his shoulder the next year. Thereafter, he could throw only with great pain. As a consequence, he ended his major league career playing outfield. Shortly after beginning a several-decade second career as the Yale baseball coach, Joe Wood found himself accused with Ty Cobb and Tris Speaker of having bet on a game. It was a charge the Commissioner of Baseball, Judge Kenesaw Mountain Landis, never fully pursued and the Yale administration apparently never credited. But it is a charge that nevertheless continues to cast a shadow over his career.

In my Dad's case, playing for Joe Wood, ultimately as one of his captains, crystallized a sense of excellence in sportsmanship, of individual and collective responsibility, and of fair play. This was tempered by a sense for the vagary and frequent unfairness of fate and the ambiguity and terror of accusation.

He sought to pass those senses along to me.

My memories of springs and summers growing up are of watching ball games with my Dad at sand lots and town parks — with an occasional trip to New Haven to take in a college game, sometimes sitting with Mr. Wood — where my Dad would teach me the craft, explain the rules and warn of the dangers of becoming a bush leaguer, a status which roughly translated into someone who played ostentatiously for the grand stand or took his lumps with a whine.

It was amateur ball that delighted my father and among his favorite leagues to follow was a collection of pick up teams fielded by the tobacco farms in our Connecticut River Valley town where college kids and farm hands got together in the evenings for semi-organized play. Not infrequently, they would be short a position and my father would be drafted to play infield. I delighted in watching as the overcharged adolescent regulars looked on with growing appreciation that the game was better played, as my father did, with grace than, as they did, with muscle. My father is vividly etched in my mind as the fluid and ageless man who effortlessly covered most of the territory between second base and third base on a series of soft Southern New England summer evenings.

There came a time — I must have been all of six years old — when the umpire didn't show up for one of the Tobacco Farm League games. You should understand that being a Tobacco Farm League umpire was more like acting as a bouncer in a bar than presiding over an appellate argu-

---

[†] Judge of the United States District Court for the District of Massachusetts. This is a redacted version of the eulogy Judge Woodlock delivered at the memorial service for his father, Preston L. Woodlock, on August 27, 1998.

ment. When the teams turned to my Dad to ask him to umpire, he pointed to me and said, "Let the kid do it. He knows what he's doing." So the game proceeded with an umpire the size of a baseball bat peeking his head from behind the pitcher, calling the balls and strikes and periodically looking to his father sitting in the bleachers for confirmation.

And then it happened. A batter sent the ball well into the underbrush beyond the centerfielder. The batter, proud as a peacock, loped triumphantly around the bases. Except he didn't touch second base. I saw it; my father saw it; most importantly the second baseman saw it. The second baseman yelled to the centerfielder who finally recovered the ball and threw it to him. He touched second base and then for good measure ran to the opposing bench to tag the peacock who was accepting congratulations. I called the batter out.

There was a predictable uproar. I was surrounded by players each making a carefully reasoned, if somewhat forceful, argument. My father watched with bemused detachment from the bleachers but didn't move, except to restrain my mother who had some observations of her own to offer. When I had heard enough, I said, "Play ball" and all but the batter slowly went back to their positions. The batter had a few more thoughts he wished to share with me. I told him the game was going to go on but he persisted. Finally I looked him straight in the eye — from my vantage point considerably below his belt — and shouted as loudly as I could, "If you don't go back to the bench, I'm going to deballerize you." That threatened sanction, illustrating my early appreciation of the adaptability of remedies, was a sufficiently terrorizing deterrent to send the once proud peacock back to the bench and get the game going again.

As we drove home the only thing my father said was, "you made some good calls today, son, and you were decisive; but I don't think I've ever seen anyone deballerized. I'll have to check the rule books about that." He later told me he dined out the rest of his life on that story, which took on an extra dimension when I became a judge.

Needless to say, my Dad was drafted as a Little League coach and he had very firm rules and attitudes to communicate there as well. He was a great coach; he loved teaching every kid to reach his (only boys played Little League at that time) full potential and the rule during regular season was that every kid no matter how modest his skills would play in every game. That generally meant three 8 year olds would rotate two innings each in right field and two 9 year olds would rotate three innings each at second base. And everyone would pray we didn't face a strong left-handed batter or a right-handed hitter who knew how to push the ball.

This gave me an early insight into independent judgment and crank calls. Particularly as it came down to the wire, my parents would receive abusive anonymous calls demanding that my father play only the best players in order to win the league pennant. He didn't modify the rule; every kid played in every game during the regular season.

The rule, however, changed with the All-Stars. Despite the challenges of fielding the entire bench during the regular season, my Dad's teams regularly won the league and consequently he regularly became the league All-Star coach. For the All-Stars, only the players he thought best played in the game. The anonymous calls came again, this time demanding that every member of the All Star team — specifically including the caller's own youngster — be fielded in every game. But for my father the rules were clear: just as regular season was for everyone, All-Star season was for the best, as he saw them.

The principle cut close to home when we moved to Chicago just before I started eighth grade. I joined the Pony League in mid-season but I wasn't chosen for the All-Stars. When the first All-Star game took place, my father came home early to find me sulking about this failure of recognition and determined not to go to the game. "Put your hat on, we're going to the game," my father said. "Only bush leaguers pout about a bad call. You can't let anyone think that you only play the game when it's going your way."

I slipped out of the baseball orbit in high school and played football and ran track. My father was puzzled how anyone could forsake a nuanced, complex and civilized game for contests of brute force and singular skills. But he would arrange his travel to come to events anyway. He and my grandfather, another baseball player, however, found football in particular perplexing. Family friends who were in the stands with them at the Andover-Exeter game in 1964 report that, after I was knocked out in the closing minutes and carried off the field, my grandfather turned to my father and said to my father's nodding agreement, "Well maybe that will teach the silly fool to stop playing a stupid game like this."

Given his distaste for direct physical combat, it was not surprising that my father found war abhorrent. Yet, he served with distinction as a naval gunnery officer in the South Pacific during World War II. But he held no grudge against the Japanese. During the summer after his graduation from college in 1935 the Yale team he captained had toured Japan playing Japanese college teams. "They played serious baseball," he said "and there wasn't a bush leaguer among them."

He never, I think, was satisfied with his business career, except as it provided an occasion to help teach and develop colleagues, and he took the earliest possible opportunity to retire to the home he and my mother built on Cape Cod. There they pursued their respective interests together. When my mother took playwriting courses at Harvard, my father, who was born in the shadow of Harvard Stadium, enjoyed driving to Cambridge to visit old haunts. They made a deal; for every Cape Cod League game (he had played for Barnstable in the Cape Cod League while in school) she attended with him, he attended a little theater production (she had been an actress when they married) with her.

Throughout, he kept a light hand on my shoulder. His interest in the cases and controversies of the law was rarely substantive. What intrigued him was the thrust and parry of the game, just as my mother's interest was in the theater of the courtroom. Only once did he press me and I was startled. I was telling him about a bribery case I was about to try as a prosecutor in which the defendant had spoken in an expansive and incriminatory manner while an informant's tape recorder was on. "Are you going to use that kind of evidence," he asked regarding the consensual recordings. When I told him I would, he shook his head and said, "what a dirty business. How can you play the game like that?" We disagreed, as we sometimes did, over how the game should be played. His views were shaped, I'm sure, by the Irishman's distaste for the informant. But overarching was the image engendered by Joe Wood that the only game worth playing was one that was fair, that insured public and individual responsibility for the acts of all players yet recognized the permanence of human fallibility and the possibility of redemption. "How can you play the game like that?" It is the question my father's standards and example require me to answer every day, even though he is now no longer present periodically to pose it in person.

CODA

About a decade after this eulogy was delivered, my wife and I made our first trip to Japan, a journey my father had encouraged throughout his life and, by bequeathing me an elegantly crafted brass paperweight he had received on his own trip bearing the inscription "Souvenir of First Yale-Waseda International Series 1935," even after his death. In preparation, I read Robert Whiting's masterful history of Japanese baseball, "You Gotta Have Wa" (Vintage Departures ed. 1990). Surveying Whiting's sources, I was prompted to check in with the Japanese Baseball Hall of Fame and Museum to see if they had any materials regarding the 1935 visit of the Yale baseball team. To my surprise, they did. In addition to articles and box scores for the games the Yale team had played against Japanese college teams, they located a baseball the members of the Yale team had autographed and a transcript of a speech my father delivered at a banquet hosted by Waseda University. In that speech, my father identified "the outstanding difference" between Japanese and American teams as the

> attitude of the players towards the umpires. In Japan, the players are always respectful and polite and upon no occasion did any Japanese player question the judgement of the umpire regardless of how close the play was. In America, the majority of the players are ever ready to question the decision on any close play, the philosophy behind this habit being that the umpire might, in striving to be fair, lean towards the questioning team when judging the next close play. While this philosophy undoubtedly produces the desired result in many instances, it nevertheless detracts from the enjoyment of the game.

I wish I had known of the speech while my father was alive; I would have pressed him in debate. And I would have added some observations to my eulogy by way of dissent (from the proposition that the practice of questioning an umpire's — or judge's decision — on one close play might produce a more favorable call on the next) and concurrence (that the practice detracts from enjoyment of the game — or the trial — at least for the umpire and the judge) about playing the game like that.

THE CHILDREN OF NO ONE

from

THE HEMINGSES OF MONTICELLO: AN AMERICAN FAMILY

Annette Gordon-Reed[†]

Angling lawyers, indebted planters straining to meet their obligations to British merchants, enslaved Africans struggling to survive the cruel realities of their new home, and Anglo-Virginian colonists beginning to chafe at colonial authority were elements in the world outside as Elizabeth Hemings grew to adulthood in the home of John Wayles. Neither her first home at Bermuda Hundred nor the main house at the Forest still stands. We are left to imagine the kind of shelter Wayles chose to create, keeping in mind that he had every reason to build a home that reflected his much-strived-for station in life. Hemings worked in that house, doing household chores other than cooking, as she was too young for that task when she came to the Forest. By the time she had become an adult, another woman held the position of the Wayles family cook.[1]

Hemings's precise duties are unknown, although it has been suggested — given what happened later in her life — that she served as a nurse or "minder" of Wayles's daughter Martha. Martha was born two years after her parents' marriage, a year after her mother had given birth to twins who did not survive. As it has been for most of human history, childbirth was a dangerous event for women. In 1748, several weeks after bearing her daughter, Martha Eppes Wayles died.[2] A young enslaved girl who was used to working in the house would have been considered suitable for the task of looking after a young child, or at the very least for helping an older woman do it.

[†] Professor of Law, New York Law School. Excerpted from *The Hemingses of Monticello* by Annette Gordon-Reed. Copyright © 2008 by Annette Gordon-Reed. Used with permission of the publisher, W.W. Norton & Company, Inc. (And of the author.)

[1] John Wayle's will, April 15, 1760, *Tyler's Quarterly Historical and Genealogical Magazine* 6 (1924-25): 269.

[2] Jefferson Family Bible, LVa.

Whatever her early duties at the Forest, Hemings took on another role five years later, in 1753: motherhood. She gave birth to her first child, a daughter named Mary, when she was eighteen years old. After Mary came Martin in 1755, Betty in 1759, and Nancy in 1761. There is reason to believe that she had a daughter Dolly in 1757, who never resided at Monticello. The father of her first children, one described in later years as a "darker" mulatto was apparently a black man, though no record of his name or status has been found. Family tradition from one of Mary Hemings's descendants suggests that she may have been the daughter of a white man.[3] Hemings's pattern of childbearing resembled that of other slave women in Virginia. Eighteen was the average age at which enslaved women gave birth for the first time. Whether because of better diet or the lesser demands of cultivating tobacco compared with sugarcane or other crops, Hemings and other enslaved women in North America achieved fertility rates that allowed for the natural increase of the slave population — unlike their West Indian and South American counterparts. In the critical years that Hemings bore her first set of children, Virginia slave owners became able to keep up with the demand for slave labor without importing large numbers of slaves from Africa.[4]

With the decline in new imports from the continent, the multilingual, multicultural world of Elizabeth's African mother began to give way to the culture created by American-born children of slavery. This transformation

---

[3] *Farm Book*, 15, 18; Stanton, *Free Some Day*, 177 n. 178; Lucia Stanton, "Monticello to Main Street: The Hemings Family and Charlottesville," *Magazine of Albermarle County History* 55 (1997): 125. Mary Hemings's grandson described her as an octoroon, which is almost certainly incorrect. If Mary Hemings's father had been white, she would have been a quadroon like her siblings Robert, James, Thenia, Critta, Peter, and Sally Hemings. Hemings's situation is interesting. She is alternately described as Mary Hemings or Mary Bell by herself, Mary "Wells" by Thomas Bell, or Wales by a historian of Charlottesville. See Edgar Woods, *Albermarle County in Virginia, Giving Some Account of What It Was by Nature, What it Was Made by Man, and Some of the Men Who Made It* (1901; reprint, Berryville, Va., 1984). As was noted earlier, Mary was the name of John Wayles's sister. Madison Hemings, who knew Mary, does not mention her as a Wayles daughter. As of now, there appears to be no demonstrated oral history among the descendants of Mary Hemings that she was a Wayles daughter. It may well be that Mary Hemings's father was white and that the talk about Elizabeth Hemings and John Wayles led members of their community to assume that any of her older and lighter-skinned children belonged to him.

[4] Morgan, *Slave Counterpoint* (Chapel Hill, 1998), 81. "As early as the second decade of the eighteenth century, Virginia's slave population began to grow from natural increase, an unprecedented event for any New World slave population." Morgan also notes (p.87), "Whereas women in eighteenth-century England began childbearing in their midtwenties slave women in eighteenth-century North America tended to be in their late teens when they conceived their first child."

had lasting consequences for the development of the black community in what would become the United States. The memories of Africa faded more rapidly among blacks born in North America than among blacks carried to other parts of the New World, where the new cargoes of slaves that continued to arrive long after the legal slave trade in the United States ceased in 1808 constantly replenished connections to the African continent.

Hemings's children, who would eventually total fourteen, were one generation removed from their African ancestry. They were in a sense symbolic in that their individual family lines followed nearly all the various trajectories of black life during the eighteenth and nineteenth centuries. Some in those lines would become free well before the end of slavery in America (Hemings would live to see this), whereas others would not. Some, facing the enormity of white supremacy, would reject their African ancestry; others would continue to embrace it. These various pathways were forged out of the circumstances of Elizabeth Hemings's early life.

During the years between 1746 and 1760, Hemings's place at the Forest became firmly established. John Wayles himself gave a small indication that, at least in his eyes and those of his family, her status was in some way different. By the time he wrote his will in 1760, Wayles possessed many slaves, among them Elizabeth Hemings and a woman named Jenney, who came under his control in the marriage settlement between him and his wife. He singled these two women out for special mention in the document, calling Elizabeth Hemings "Betty" and identifying "Jenney" as the cook. Wayles directed that they, along with twenty-three others not named in the will itself, were to become the property of his new wife, Elizabeth Lomax, whom he married that same year, should he predecease her. Upon her death, they were to become the property of his oldest daughter, Martha, who was twelve at the time.[5] That Wayles gave his wife a life interest in Hemings reveals that, while he clearly thought Hemings should ultimately belong to Martha, he was thinking primarily about Hemings's — and the cook, Jenney's — usefulness to his wife, not her present value to his daughter. As far as anyone knew then, Elizabeth Lomax Wayles could have lived for several more decades. In that time Martha would surely have grown up, gotten married, and had her own household, and Hemings would still belong to her stepmother. This indicates that, as of 1760, Wayles did not think there was, or did not care if there was, a close association between his daughter and Hemings. He wanted to

---

[5] Wayles's will, cited above, n. 1.

provide his present wife with a good housekeeper and cook. His daughter, however, may have had different priorities.

Another item to note about Wayles's will is that he listed Elizabeth with her last name. One of the many ways that slave societies sought to drive home slaves' inferior status was to be careless about the use of slave surnames, signaling that bondpeople had no families that white society had to respect. Like the old practice among some southern whites of taking the liberty of calling every African American woman "Auntie" or every man "Uncle," the carelessness about names, both first and last, telegraphed white privilege. Throughout slavery, whatever whites may have thought, many, if not nearly all, slaves adopted last names that their owners either did not know about or acted as if they did not know or care about. To be sure, there were instances where masters and others did recognize slave surnames, which can be found on planters' slave rolls and in other documents. The origins of these names varied — some came from present or former owners, some were simply self-selected, and others grew out of family relationships.

In European culture surnames signal the paternity of those born in wedlock and those born out of wedlock whose fathers acknowledge them. Children of unmarried women typically carry their mother's name, which in most instances would have been the woman's father's last name. Enslaved women had no legal marriages, and fathers had no rights to their children, so it seems unlikely that Hemings's African mother had a last name that her white owner felt compelled to recognize and pass down to her daughter.

Given the family's explanation for why it was named Hemings, there is no reason to believe that Elizabeth herself simply plucked the name Hemings out of thin air and John Wayles abided by her decision so surely that he used it in a legal document. The only other slave mentioned in the will, the cook, Jenney, appears without a surname. This is additional evidence that a man named Hemings did acknowledge his daughter and communicated that fact to Elizabeth's original owner. Even though the law did not protect slave families, patriarchal views about family construction evidently influenced the way some masters saw them. If a man acknowledged a child, why not let the child carry his last name, even if it meant nothing legally? Law aside, having a recognized last name evidently meant a great deal to Elizabeth Hemings's family. Sixty-six years after her death, her grandson Madison Hemings would begin his family story by talking not about his African great-grandmother but about the uniqueness of the family's name, taking care to explain how they came to own it.

WITHIN THE DOZEN years following Martha Eppes's death, Elizabeth Hemings saw John Wayles marry and bury two more wives. His second marriage, to Tabitha Cocke, produced three daughters: Elizabeth, who would play a prominent and fateful role in the life of Hemings's daughter Sally; Tabitha; and Anne. After his second wife died, Wayles married Elizabeth Lomax, to whom he was married when he wrote his will, although she died the following year. It was sometime after her death that Wayles took Elizabeth as a "concubine." Over the course of roughly eleven years, they had six children together; Robert, born in 1762, James in 1765, Thenia in 1767, Critta in 1769, Peter in 1770, and Sally in 1773.[6] This set of children represented a further blurring of racial lines, moving branches of the Hemings family tree farther away from the African woman who was by law the reason for their enslavement, toward the Englishman who was the source of their last name. With three white grandparents and one black grandparent, these children were by the racial classification of the day "mulattoes," Virginia laws making no distinction between various gradations of racial mixture. But by a term that gained wider currency and greater meaning in the nineteenth century, these children would be called "quadroons." Their racial classification (legal or biological), however, made no difference to their legal status. Like their "darker mulatto" older siblings, these "bright mulatto" children were born of a slave woman. So they were slaves, too.

It would be very hard to find two people who occupied more vastly different positions than Wayles and Hemings — the prosperous white slave-trading lawyer and the Anglo-African female house slave. Given what we know about their world, the idea that these two would have children together seems utterly banal. Their society was set up for such things to happen, with a much touted, but essentially weak, barrier to prevent it. The pervasive doctrine of white supremacy supposedly inoculated whites against the will to interracial mixing, but that doctrine proved to be unreliable when matched against the force of human sexuality. People are prone to having sex, especially when they are in daily contact with potential objects of sexual attraction. That inclination has permeated every slave society, every frontier society, and every colonial society that has ever existed. Virginia was no exception.

Giving a group of males total dominion over the bodies of a group of females and relying on externally imposed notions of race ("I'm superior to her") and manners ("I'm a gentleman) to prevent them from having sex

---

[6] *Farm Book*, 24.

with those females was always a doomed proposition. That the mixing could be done entirely on the terms of the males, beyond the eyes and the scrutiny of the outside world, only increased the odds that it would happen — either through rape, using outright or implied force, or, in some cases, when the men and women were genuinely attracted to each other.

In all the ways that counted, the Virginia of the eighteenth century was designed to further the interests and positions of men like John Wayles. The opportunity to apply whatever talents he possessed allowed him to make a place for himself that he could never have made in his native England, where neither thousands of acres of land to be parceled out to men of lower or no rank nor a place to exploit the labor of an imported "alien" race existed. Abundant land and African chattel slavery, the engines of Wayles's success, gave him enormous power not only in economic terms but also culturally and socially. One cannot divorce the power to sell a shipload of slaves at Bermuda Hundred from the power to decide what to do with the slaves who are in one's home.

Elizabeth Hemings's place was exactly the opposite of Wayles's. Slavery, white supremacy, and male dominance — indeed, practically every feature of Virginian society — combined to keep her down. Law formed the foundation of this system, and its role in fashioning Hemings's oppression and Wayles's privilege can hardly be overstated. It determined their relative positions during their lives, and, as is often the point of legal rules, its influence has continued down the generations, helping to shape the way Hemings and Wayles are seen to this very day. Specifically, the laws of slavery, of what was called "bastardy," and of marriage set ironclad limits on Hemings's capacity to determine her fate and that of her children. These laws had everything to do with how Wayles and Hemings came to have children together, how the society of their time would protect Wayles in his activities as a slave owner, and how that protective instinct would thrive well beyond his life as a sort of patrimony bequeathed to his legal family and descendants, to be used as they saw fit.

Under cover of the laws of slavery, Wayles could sell slaves, punish them, and make them work for no pay without interference from outsiders. He could have sex with Hemings because she was his property. He could produce children with her who would never be recognized unless he chose to do so. She had no power to challenge this situation formally. Because of slavery and the dominant society's adherence to white supremacy, no one would have believed her had she named Wayles as the father of her children; or, one should say more properly, few if any white people would have admitted belief in her words, especially if Wayles had chosen to contradict them. Doing so would have run counter to one of the chief tenets of Virginia's culture — that the words of blacks could not legally be used against a white person.[7] Thus, blacks were never to be allowed to shape the "official" reality of a white person's life.

The laws and culture of slavery aside, that Hemings was not, and indeed could not, have been John Wayles's wife is also crucial to the way their relationship would be viewed by most people during their time and by many in our own. Under law any child born out of wedlock was considered *filius nullius*, "the child of no one." It was as if the child had dropped from the sky. At the same time, the children of a marriage were presumed to be the offspring of the husband. These were legal fictions and presumptions that deliberately ignored certain unassailable realities: everyone who has ever lived was the child of a mother and a father, a marriage license is no guarantee of biological paternity, and the fathers of children born out of wedlock can actually be known.

The fictions and presumptions about bastardy and marriage served definite purposes in a legal system seeking easy ways to determine who was eligible to inherit property, who had the right to a child's labor, and who could be held liable for support of a child. Efficient as they may have been, these fictions yielded answers that were not always truthful and certainly not always moral. Although they were tailor-made for the needs of the law, and not so perfect a fit for historical or biological conclusions, there is little doubt that they have come to represent what people take to be actual reality. They hover in the consciousness even when outside indicators suggest they should not be relied upon. If by law Hemings's children had no father, as even extralegal convention would have it, John Wayles could not be their father unless he was willing to say he was.

There is a twist. This way of thinking does not apply to the black men who fathered children with enslaved women to whom they could not have been legally married because the absurdity of the fiction as a statement of actual reality would then be too patently clear. Applying the precepts of *filius nullius* to enslaved families would require pretending that from the late 1600s to 1865 no American slave ever knew who his or her father was, an idea that is nonsense on stilts. Why would slaves have known who their fathers were when those men were black, but not know when the man was white? Indeed, if the black man who fathered Elizabeth Hemings's older children had been named, it is a safe bet that no question

---

[7] See Thomas D. Morris, *Southern Slavery and the Law, 1619-1860* (Chapel Hill, 1996), 230-37, on the subject of exclusion of testimony of blacks.

about his paternity would ever be raised. But when demonstrably mixed-race people speak of their white father or forefather, at most the white man is portrayed as the "alleged" father or the "said to be father," as if there had been some white "Mr. Nobody" ("Mr. *Nullius*"?) out there impregnating all the enslaved women in America. Presenting the life of mixed-race individuals in slavery poses a great challenge precisely because there is such hesitancy about accepting their competence when they explain how they came to be mixed race. The reluctance to accept the prevalence of interracial sex, other than as a generalization, avoids the perceived "cost" or "hazard" of naming a specific white man.

What accounts for this hesitancy? It cannot be the difference in the assessment of the ability to know black fathers versus white ones. That makes no sense. Race is certainly a factor. In a world where even today saying that a white man has black children is the ultimate put-down in some quarters, it is not surprising that some might pause over the claim that a white man in history had done so.[8] One is saying something negative about the man, and there is always a higher standard for saying something "bad" about a person than for saying something "good." Whole black family lines have been erased on that principle. Law, a powerful force, helps along the tendency to protect white slave owners against claims of paternity because it shapes our understanding of reality and what we are willing to accept as reality. People in history who, like John Wayles, were under the law's protection during life tend to remain under the law's protection — statutes, rules, presumptions, privileges, legal fictions, and all. People outside of the law's protection, like Elizabeth Hemings, generally remain outside, particularly when aspects of their lives do not comport with the law's strictures and fictions.

What we have in considerations of white male slave owner's paternity of slave children is a version of Anglo-American law without its usual complement of Anglo-American equity. The doctrines of equity exist alongside law to help mitigate the harsh and unjust results that come from too strict adherence to legal rules. For example, when no formal documents exist to prove that individuals entered into a contract, but the cir-

---

[8] Robert F. Bennett, then senator from Utah, commenting on the strength of candidate George W. Bush, listed the possible catastrophic things that could derail Bush's nomination. "Unless George W. steps in front of a bus, some woman comes forward, let's say some black woman, comes forward with an illegitimate child that he fathered within the last 18 months, or some other scenario that you could be equally creative in thinking of, George W. Bush will be the nominee." Bennett's remarks caused a furor, and he apologized for them. *New York Times*, Aug. 17, 1999, sec. A, p. 12, col. 1.

cumstances strongly indicate that an agreement was made and that one party will be severely damaged if the contract is not recognized, equity allows stepping outside formalities to consider other evidence and, when possible, to do justice.[9]

Law, not equity, lay at the heart of the American slave system. Under this regime of law with no equity, John Wayles's power as a slave owner remains as potent as the power he held as a legal husband and father. Slave owners like Wayles, who could force others to see the world through their eyes, virtually guaranteed that their lives and interests would be seen as of paramount importance in the writing of history. And because Wayles was a legally married man — three times — no one would ever think to suggest that the children born of his legal marriages could have been the children of someone else, though that was certainly possible. Even to open that inquiry, other than in the most extreme circumstances, would provoke outrage. Historians might pause at suggesting that a white man might have fathered a child of his own race outside of marriage, a so-called bastard, whom he did not acknowledge. That, too, would be considered a "bad" thing, although one wonders what stake a historian could have in protecting a subject's legal family against what could be legitimate, that is to say, historically and biologically accurate claims established through means other than a marriage license. One can understand a legal family's interest: they want to keep "Daddy" or "Grand Daddy" and his legacy all to themselves. Deeply felt as that desire may be, it simply cannot be taken seriously as a matter of history.

What do we make of this in the context of Hemings's life under eighteenth-century Virginia's system of slavery? We know she lived in a slave society with rules of law specifically fashioned to make possible, and then to obscure whenever necessary, the nature of one group's oppression of another. In ways that should be clear to modern observers, even if it was not to the people of the time, the law in that setting functioned essentially as a racket designed for the protection of whites. How does one begin to get at what was "real" or "true" in such a context? Playing along with the racket is an all too easy, wholly unworthy enterprise because it ratifies the view that "extralegal" blacks, like Elizabeth Hemings, deserve no protection and that "legal" whites, like John Wayles, are to be protected at all costs — even at the cost of all reason. This simply reenacts the world of master and slave in the pages of history. It is only through piercing the veil

---

[9] Stewart E. Stark, "Estoppel in Property Law," *Nebraska Law Review* 77 (1980): 756, 759-69.

of southern society's laws, including its fictions about family, that we can take the first step toward getting at the reality of black and white lives under slavery.

The law's protection of John Wayles in his absolute ownership of Elizabeth Hemings rendered his connection to the children she had with him invisible for all official purposes. Nevertheless, law, despite its power, is not the only word on the subject. The children of white men like Wayles who grew up in cohesive family units, often within the household of their fathers, knew who their fathers were in the same way that most people throughout the ages have known, even without the benefit of Anglo-American law. In addition, although white families could hide behind the protections that law and legal fictions afforded, there was still such a thing as the social knowledge of parenthood.

From time immemorial, people have "known" who others' parents were through a variety of extralegal ways, including reliance on a mother's word, observations of physical resemblances that indicate a family connection, interpreting a man's actions toward a set of children and their mother, overall reputation in the community for parenthood — in other words, through indicators that people pulled together to help them make sense of who was who in their world. The day-to-day experiences of life in a community, particularly small ones, give its members information about the nature of relationships among their neighbors. At times even the law (when seeking equity) has looked to these sources in the absence of a legal relationship between a man and a child to make judgments about the likelihood of a family connection.[10]

As Joshua Rothman, a scholar of the operation of social life in Virginia during the eighteenth century, has noted, "interracial sex was ubiquitous in urban, town, and plantation communities throughout the state. Moreover . . . knowledge of precisely who participated in it was widely shared."[11] While some may quarrel with the term "ubiquitous," there is no doubt that sex across the color line was a common part of life in Virginia. What is more, people were inclined to gossip about it. Why is easy to understand. People have always been interested in the lives of others, particularly in matters involving sex. And though some Virginians sought to replicate the lifestyles of the English gentry, they faced special circumstances in one area. Any illegitimate children fathered by an Englishman

---

[10] Laurel Thatcher Ulrich, *A Midwife's Tale: The Life of Martha Ballard, Based on Her Diary, 1785-1812* (New York, 1991).

[11] Joshua D. Rothman, *Notorious in the Neighborhood: Sex and Families across the Color Line in Virginia, 1787-1861* (Chapel Hill, 2003), 4.

with a servant girl or other lower-status woman in England would be white. Unless the child looked like the man, his or her existence signaled nothing beyond that fact that they were alive. The presence of a mixed-race child signaled something more; the child all but announced that some white person and some black person had broken the taboo against interracial sex.

Rothman goes on to note, "Virginians, like white southerners else-where, tolerated and accommodated a wide array of sexual activity across the color line, ranging from viable and supportive interracial families that bound extended networks of free and enslaved blacks and whites across space and time to family-shattering rapes that exposed the routine abuse, violence, and ruthless power of racial slavery. . . ."[12]

That is not the story most often told about interracial sex in the South. If views about slavery have been frozen in a particular image of immediate pre-Civil War southern society, beliefs about interracial sex during slavery have been heavily influenced by the sexual panic and hysteria of white southerners in the post-Civil War era and well into the twentieth century. That sex across the color line inspired legal and social opprobrium very early on in Virginia does not mean that there was one, continuing response to it among the citizenry over the course of slavery's existence.

It is often said that though the South lost the Civil War, it won the peace. As many scholars have noted, David Blight with particular force, as a gesture to promote national reconciliation southerners were given al-most unfettered power to define their prewar identities and, most devas-tatingly of all for black people, their prewar identities as well. White southerners declared war on the black people in their midst — ushering in the era of Jim Crow and the terrorism of lynching, as well as other meas-ures that grew out of a determination to reassert control through what-ever means available over the people they had once held as items of prop-erty. Rewriting the story of slavery in the South was a necessary part of the process.[13]

Southern racial laws and legal opinions, like those in Virginia which had determined whiteness by a formula of fractions — persons who were one-eighth black were legally white — and such evidentiary rules as "white by reputation in the community" fell by the wayside. The "one-drop rule" replaced them. The laws against interracial marriages became

---

[12] Ibid., 4-5.
[13] David W. Blight, *Race and Reunion: The Civil War in American Memory* (Cambridge, Mass., 2001).

more uniform, while interracial sex itself was not outlawed. The historian Charles Robinson cites two reasons for the attention to interracial marriages and cohabitation as opposed to interracial sex. "First, Southern white patriarchs had long enjoyed interracial liaisons. By the time of the Redemption period informal interracial sex constituted a white male privilege. . . . Second, Southern whites focused their attention on formal interracial relationships because of their growing concerns about the effects of black freedom on white supremacy." Sex itself was no threat. Legal marriages, and perhaps common law marriages, might give black partners property and some degree of power.[14] John Wayles's great-grandson Thomas Jefferson Randolph shed light on the differing sexual mores during slavery, insisting in his unpublished memoirs, written after the Civil War, that any married white man who took up with a black woman "lost caste" with his cohort. He made this claim despite the fact that married men in his own family (he purported to identify them) had children with black women and remained respected members of the community.[15]

Randolph's postwar statement dovetails with the prewar assessment of his grandfather Thomas Jefferson's close friend John Hartwell Cocke, who spoke frankly of the ways and preferences of white men in the Old South. Commenting upon Jefferson's relationship with Sally Hemings in a private diary, Cocke said that Jefferson's situation was common in Virginia: "bachelor and widowed slave owners" often took a slave woman as a "substitute for a wife."[16] There was no suggestion that *unmarried* men lost caste for doing this. His was simply a resigned statement about the way men lived in Virginia's slave society, as they have in every one that has ever existed. John Wayles had done exactly what Cocke described.

This is not to minimize white Virginians' announced hostility toward sex across the color line. It was there. The legal response to it shows that very clearly. But it would be unwise to read late post-Civil War and twentieth-century responses to interracial sex back into the days of John Wayles and Elizabeth Hemings. Theirs was a different time. The forces driving the post-slavery and pre-civil rights response to black people in the South simply did not exist in their age. And there are important reasons why. To expose Wayles, or a man like him, would have required blasting through deeply held beliefs and customs about the sanctity of the right to

---

[14] Charles F. Robinson II, *Dangerous Liaisons: Sex and Love in the Segregated South* (Fayetteville, Ark., 2003), 49-50.

[15] Thomas Jefferson Randolph's recollections, ViU:1874.

[16] Journal of John Hartwell Cocke, Jan. 26, 1853, in John Hartwell Cocke Papers, Box 188, Alderman Library, University of Virginia.

private property. Who could come to the Forest and inquire about the paternity of the obviously mixed-race children living there? On what basis would they complain? As long as Wayles did not try to elevate Elizabeth Hemings and their children to the status of white people — by going through a marriage ceremony, drawing attention to the children by publicly claiming them as his heirs, or making other public attempts to insinuate them into white society or bestow attributes of white privilege onto them — he would be left alone to do with his property as he pleased. With blacks firmly under the control of slavery, there was no need to interfere with the way planters conducted their lives with the slaves on the plantation. As the historian Philip Schwarz has shown, except in the most extreme circumstances, such as murder or a slave's intrusion upon the interests of a white person other than the master, slave owners in Virginia were the law in their realm.[17]

It is instructive that white Virginians' expressed disdain for interracial sex did not lead them to outlaw it more specifically in the context of the master-slave relationships that so obviously posed the greatest danger for the crossing of racial lines. Had the will of legislators been strong enough, they certainly could have taken such an action. They did not. The difficulty of enforcement does not explain their failure. Laws are sometimes put on the books not for purposes of strict enforcement but as statements about the community's values. Nor does the value Virginians placed on the sanctity of private property provide an adequate explanation. Throughout history even societies deeply committed to the right to property have enacted limitations on its uses when some other important competing interest was at stake. If its members really considered interracial sex so vile and destructive of public morals, the Virginia legislature could have passed laws specifically designed to outlaw interracial sex in the places it most easily thrived — the homes and plantations where Afro-Virginians lived in daily contact with whites.

It seems, then, that hostility toward racial mixing did not constitute an important enough interest to justify meddling with the notion that slave owners had absolute property rights to their slaves. As a result of this determination, the people who ran afoul of the state's laws regulating sexual activity — which pulled in whites who engaged in sex across the color line — were almost invariably members of the lower classes. Lower-class people's overrepresentation in prosecutions involving interracial fornication fueled the shibboleth that only "low status" people engaged in sex

---

[17] See, generally, Philip J. Schwarz, *Slave Laws in Virginia* (Athens, Ga., 1996).

across the color line. So might a not very insightful observer conclude. In much the same way, a historian from the twenty-second century who looked back at American society at the end of the twentieth and twenty-first centuries and concluded that middle- and upper-class whites did not take illegal drugs, because the overwhelming majority of people in prison for drug offenses were people of color and lower-class whites, would have missed a central reality of those times. Without understanding that deference to middle- and upper-class whites kept them out of the legal system, and without a commonsense understanding that poor people of color alone could not possibly have supported a multibillion-dollar drug industry in the United States, the truth would have been lost. The response to sex across the color line during John Wayles's time offered Virginia society an extremely useful narrative. Because there was no chance that a slave owner like Wayles could be penalized legally for producing children with his slave Elizabeth Hemings, his activities would never see the "official" light of day. Linking interracial sex with low-class criminality (through legislative choices and in the stories white slave owners told about their world) helped hide the behavior of the "best" of white society.

It is impossible to say exactly when the social knowledge of Wayles's relationship to Elizabeth Hemings and her children entered their community. By the time of the Chiswell affair, Wayles was fifty years old, and Hemings had given birth to his two oldest sons, Robert and James, who were both under five years old. Public references to Wayles as the father of Hemings's children appeared in a newspaper in 1805, long after his death, and in the reminiscences of Isaac Jefferson, in 1847, and in those of Madison Hemings, a Wayles grandchild, in 1873. In addition, historians have accepted the Hemings-Wayles connection for a variety of reasons that appeared after the time the two were together at the Forest. Specifically, observations of the way Hemings and her children were treated after they came under the ownership of Thomas Jefferson lent support to that conclusion.[18] From the very start, in ways that will become clear in large parts of the rest of this work, Jefferson viewed Elizabeth Hemings and all those connected to her in a light different from the one in which he viewed other enslaved people. Her children by Wayles did not drop from the sky; they were not the children of no one in Jefferson's eyes. His response to them, and the way it set the family's course in life, shows slavery as the immensely tragic and complicated institution that it was.

---

[18] *Boston Repertory*, May 31, 1805; Campbell, "Life of Isaac Jefferson," 566-82, 567-68; Gordon-Reed, *TJ and SH*, 245.

FEBRUARY

OCTAVIUS V. CATTO.—[PHOTOGRAPHED BY MESSRS. BROADBENT & PHILLIPS, PHILADELPHIA.]

OCTAVIUS V. CATTO

Officer, Pennsylvania National Guard (?–1871).
See LAWRENCE D. HOGAN, SHADES OF GLORY: THE NEGRO LEAGUES
AND THE STORY OF AFRICAN-AMERICAN BASEBALL (2006).

❧ FEBRUARY ❧

SUN	MON	TUES	WED	THUR	FRI	SAT
	1	2	3	4	5	6
7	8	9	10	11	12	13
14	15	16	17	18	19	20
21	22	23	24	25	26	27
28						

DEAD MEN SOMETIMES DO TELL TALES

Michael J. Morrissey[†]

Mike Morrissey probably knows more about medicine than most doctors — having represented so many members of the medical profession in malpractice cases over the past 30 years. He has had extensive successful trial experience in complex cases involving a variety of specialties, including neurosurgery, neuroradiology, orthopedics, general surgery, otolaryngology, psychiatry, obstetrics and gynecology, anesthesiology, infectious disease, and neuropsychology. He is well known in the medical community and frequently called on to defend the most serious of these matters. He is a founder and executive committee member of Cassiday, Schade LLP, one of Chicago's top defense firms, and a graduate of DePaul University College of Law.

Q. Have you ever been a resident of the Mt. Auburn Cemetery?

A. No.

Q. Have you ever given a contrary statement?

A. Yes.

OPPOSING COUNSEL: Your Honor, could we have a sidebar?

My friend and ex-partner Kevin Burke likes to tell people who ask him about his success as a plaintiff's attorney: "I'm not smarter than my opponents; I just work harder than they do." Although Kevin is being a bit disingenuous about his intellectual gifts, the statement about working harder than everyone else is what separates the successful trial lawyer from the also-rans. While I know and have had the good fortune to practice with and against some truly gifted lawyers, the ones who are the best cross-examiners are the ones who have worked the hardest in their preparation.

[†] *Of Cassiday, Schade LLP.* Copyright © 2008. Law Bulletin Publishing Company. All rights reserved. This work is one of 50 chapters in the book *Your Witness: Lessons on Cross-Examination and Life from Great Chicago Trial Lawyers,* available at yourwitnessbook.com. It is reprinted here with the permission of the author and the publisher.

The best example that I can think of to illustrate hard work and preparation is a case that I tried with my partner, Catherine Garvey, a few years ago, *Tornabene v. Paramedic Services of Illinois, Inc.* The case involved a middle-aged woman, Mrs. Tornabene, who had a history of chronic lung disease from smoking. Previously, a weakened area of her lung, called a bleb, had ruptured, causing a lung to collapse on one side. As a result, she had an open surgical procedure on that side of her chest to repair the collapsed lung. Despite her chronic obstructive pulmonary disease, she was able to hold down a job, work around the house, and apparently be the glue that held her large, loving extended family together.

On the night in question, she had difficulty breathing and her daughter — who, along with her husband, was living with her mother at the time — called 911 and the paramedics, our clients, were summoned. They arrived at the house to find a panicked family and an obviously distressed woman who could not breathe and, because she could not breathe, could not communicate very well. The family claims to have told the paramedics about the previous history of the ruptured bleb and surgical procedure. The paramedics gave the patient oxygen, put her in a special chair — they could not maneuver a stretcher up the stairs and around the corner in the small Northwest Side Chicago home — and took the patient out to the mobile ICU for transfer to the nearest hospital. Per procedure, the paramedics called their base hospital, Resurrection, and talked with a specially trained nurse who communicated directly with the emergency room physician on duty to direct the care rendered by the emergency medical technicians ("EMTs") and to learn what was happening with the patient, who presumably would arrive at the door of the emergency room shortly.

The patient was being given oxygen in the back of the ambulance with a bag and mask. Oxygen was being sent by a tube to a mask that covered the patient's nose and face and would be forced down into her lungs by one of the paramedics squeezing a bag attached to the mask. This is a life-saving procedure intended to keep the patient oxygenated en route to the hospital.

EMTs are a special breed of medical providers. They are not doctors or nurses, but in emergency situations they can provide life-saving care that ordinarily requires a medical license. Because it would be extremely expensive and virtually impossible to have all of the ambulances across the United States staffed by physicians, EMTs are given enough training to recognize and respond to medical emergencies. They are permitted under the law to render medical care under "standing orders." For example, if the paramedics arrive at a scene and find a patient without a heartbeat or whose heart is beating with an ineffectual rhythm, they are allowed to give specific drugs (depending on what the EKG shows) to start the heart or overcome an irregular rhythm.

"Standing orders" or standard operating procedures ("SOPs") are a kind of "cookbook." For example, if paramedics find a patient in ventricular fibrillation, the SOPs allow an EMT to give drugs and use an electric shock via a defibrillator, without contacting a doctor, to hopefully jumpstart the patient's heart.

In this particular case, Mrs. Tornabene had ruptured another bleb on the side opposite from where she had had the surgical repair several years before. Unfortunately for her, this hole in her lung allowed air to pass out of her lung and into the pleural cavity — the space around the lung inside the rib cage. The ruptured bleb acted as a one-way valve so that as the life-saving oxygen was forced into the patient's lungs with this bag and mask contraption, more and more air under pressure escaped out the hole into her chest cavity, collapsing the lung further.

The pressure began to build up until it actually caused compression on the heart and the vena cava, the main venous return to the heart. This condition is called a tension pneumothorax and it is life-threatening. If the air in the chest cavity is not allowed to escape, it will prevent the heart from filling properly and the patient will die.

The patient was taken to the hospital from her home after some delay — there was a dispute about how long this delay was. However, it is clear that the patient was at death's door when she finally arrived in the emergency room at Resurrection Hospital. She was blue and unconscious despite the oxygen. A quick portable chest film was taken, and a tension pneumothorax was diagnosed shortly after the patient arrived. A large bore needle was inserted on both sides to relieve the air pressure that had built up, but unfortunately, the patient died. Shortly after the incident, the family consulted with a lawyer and a lawsuit was filed.

The plaintiff claimed that the EMTs should have realized, from the history they were given by the family — of a previous ruptured bleb — along with the fact that there were no breath sounds noted on one side, that the patient had a tension pneumothorax and that the EMTs should have inserted a needle to relieve the air pressure.

The plaintiff claimed that the nurse should have talked with the ER physician on duty and made the diagnosis of a tension pneumothorax over the phone when the EMTs in the field did not do so.

On the eve of trial, the hospital had settled the case for a significant amount based on the alleged failure of the nurse on the radio and the ER physician to instruct the EMTs on what to do.

We argued that EMTs do not make diagnoses, and were exempt from liability for anything but willful and wanton conduct when they were operating within the framework of how they had been trained. They were not allowed to put a needle in the patient's chest because the procedure was not in their SOPs except for penetrating injuries to the chest.

The plaintiff's attorneys, two excellent trial lawyers, retained an EMT as an expert witness. This expert had been trained in the same system as the defendant EMTs and asserted that he had been trained — and therefore was allowed — to insert a needle into a patient's chest when a tension pneumothorax was suspected. He testified at his deposition that the procedure had been taught to everyone in the program and was supposed to be used when an EMT in the field suspected tension pneumothorax. This could have been devastating testimony, given that under Illinois law if the paramedics violated their training, this could be construed as willful and wanton conduct.

My partner, Cathy Garvey, went to work — the kind of hard work that makes for effective cross-examination. She left no stone unturned in looking into this expert EMT's background because we knew from the people in the paramedic program that the paramedics weren't trained to use a needle in a chest under these circumstances — we had talked with the people who taught the course and we had the medical director of the program indicating that he would not allow his EMTs in his system to use a needle unless there were a penetrating chest wound. These witnesses would help us to rebut plaintiff's expert's testimony, but it was still a toss-up on what the jury would believe.

We hit pay dirt when we heard that plaintiff's expert had gotten into some trouble with the law. It seems that a number of years before, he had been indicted in DuPage County for passing bad checks. Subsequently, he had taken a job at a hospital in Chicago, a large teaching institution where he had access to blank death certificates as part of his job. The very-much-alive paramedic expert filled one out for himself and in a creative burst noted that he had died of a drug overdose. He then took the death certificate and apparently sent it to the attorney defending him in the check-kiting proceeding. The unwitting attorney received a copy of the forged death certificate with a cover letter, also forged, purportedly from the expert's mother explaining the situation to the lawyer and asking him to get the charges against her now deceased son dismissed because her poor boy had died of a drug overdose.

In fact, the DuPage County State's Attorney then dismissed the indictment on the basis of the letter and death certificate from the attorney. At this point, the attorneys for the expert didn't know that they had been lied to, the expert's mother didn't know of her son's ruse, and the State's Attorney apparently took the word of both at face value. The expert resurrected himself by enrolling as an EMT candidate and completed the program that the defendant EMTs had completed. Unfortunately for him, the DuPage County State's Attorney's Office apparently did some follow-up investigation on his social security number and found that this "recently deceased" individual was working and that no death certificate had ever been filed in Cook County.

He was caught and ultimately pleaded guilty in the original check-kiting scheme and to additional charges associated with the forgeries, which created his fictitious demise. As part of his plea bargain, he was allowed to complete his EMT training, part of which included a six-month "ride-along" requirement in which a student EMT observes EMTs in the field, learns procedures, and assists more experienced EMTs within the system. This part of his training was done on a work release basis. The work release status and the special accommodations made for this individual had stuck in the mind of the administrator of the EMT program who put us on the right track.

The case itself was hotly contested. Our opponents were highly skilled and had an encyclopedic knowledge of the facts of the case and of the medicine involved in Mrs. Tornabene's demise. There was a continuing fight throughout the case regarding evidence of willful and wanton misconduct by the EMTs that would take away their statutory immunity. The plaintiff's attorneys hammered at our clients as having been trained to put a needle in a patient's chest, and we kept producing evidence that while they knew how to do the procedure, the SOPs did not allow them to perform it unless there was a penetrating chest injury. The plaintiff's attorneys called the EMT expert to provide them with the testimony they needed to convince the jury that not only were the paramedics trained to do the procedure; they were supposed to perform the procedure in circumstances like Mrs. Tornabene's — when a patient's life was on the line.

The expert testified on direct and did a credible job. The plaintiff's lawyer did a very good job with him on direct, but had no idea that the expert EMT she was dealing with was really Lazarus.

We had been afraid that plaintiff's attorneys might not call this EMT expert — after all, they had another one who had testified, but he was not trained in the same system. We made a half-hearted motion that the second EMT's testimony would be cumulative — this was denied by the trial judge in short order.

The night before the expert was due to testify, I considered different ways to go after him. The guilty plea to a felony was admissible as an attack on the witness's credibility. In cross-examining an expert, the Illinois courts have given lawyers wide latitude, but I knew that this trial judge would keep me on a tight leash, as she had done throughout the case. Still, I was looking forward to a once-in-a-lifetime opportunity for a trial lawyer.

I started off by asking the witness whether he took his obligation as an expert seriously and whether he would try to be fair to his colleagues, the EMTs who were the defendants in this case. Of course, he said yes, and I then asked whether he would ever invent a story about the training of the EMTs and the SOPs in the EMT program.

I then asked him where he lived, and then asked him about the name of the cemetery that he had filled in on the death certificate that he had forged.

Q. Have you ever been a resident of the Mt. Auburn Cemetery?

A. No.

Q. Have you ever given a contrary statement?

A. Yes.

The trial judge and the plaintiff's attorneys — who had no idea that this was coming — looked puzzled. The witness, however, looked at me with a realization that it was going to be a long afternoon for him. In fact, at least metaphorically, he ended up dying a second death in that courtroom that day.

Not many lawyers have the opportunity in their careers to examine an expert witness who has faked his death to avoid a criminal prosecution and then pleaded guilty to forgery when he was caught. I know I am lucky to have a good story that always gets a laugh from fellow trial lawyers — but I prefer to think of it as a good illustration of the principle that good cross-examination is not inspiration but is created from unrelenting hard work.

✳ ✳ ✳

This is the first day this week that I have not played baseball.

Woodrow Wilson (June 9, 1876)

THE COLOR LINE

from

SOL. WHITE'S OFFICIAL BASE BALL GUIDE

Sol. White[†]

In no other profession has the color line been drawn more rigidly than in base ball. As far back as 1872 the first colored ball player of note playing on a white team was Bud Fowler, the celebrated promoter of colored ball clubs, and the sage of base ball. Bud played on a New Castle, Pennsylvania, team that year. Later the Walker Brothers, Fleet and Weldy, played on prominent college teams of the West. Fleet Walker has the distinction of being the only known colored player that ever played in one of the big leagues. In 1884 Walker caught for Toledo in the old American Association. At this time the Walker brothers and Bud Fowler were the only negroes in the profession.

In 1886 Frank Grant joined Buffalo, of the International League.

In 1887 no less than twenty colored ball players scattered among the different smaller leagues of the country.

With Walker, Grant, Stovy, Fowler, Higgins and Renfro in the International League, White, W. Walker, N. Higgins and R. Johnson in the Ohio League, and others in the West, made 1887 a banner year for colored talent in the white leagues. But this year marked the beginning of the elimination of colored players from white clubs. All the leagues, during the Winter of 1887 and 1888, drew the color line, or had a clause inserted in their constitutions limiting the number of colored players to be employed by each club.

[†] Solomon White's "Base Ball Guide" was published in 1907 in Philadelphia. The author was, in his own words on pages 7-8 of his book,

[B]orn in Bellaire, O., June 12, 1868, and learned to play ball when quite a youngster. When but 16 years of age he attracted the attention of managers of independent teams throughout the Ohio Valley and his services were in great demand. His original position was short stop, but by playing on different teams, he developed into a great all-round player filling any position from catcher to right field.

His first professional engagement was with the Keystones, of Pittsburg, a member of the Colored League, in 1887. He was assigned to left field and later was placed at second base, where he played brilliantly. . . .

After the season of 1895 closed, Sol began a course at Wilberforce University. From 1896 to 1900 he played with the C.X. Giants in the Summer and attended school during the Winter. In 1900 he left school and joined the Columbia Giants of Chicago. In 1901 he played second base and captained the Cuban X-Giants. In 1902 he organized the Philadelphia Giants and has been captain ever since. Under his guidance the Philadelphia Giants have won the championship of the world every year since.

No colored ball player has had a wider experience in base ball than Sol, and no ball player has profited by experience greater than he has.

Colored base ball owes a great deal of its popularity of late to his hard, earnest, indefatigable work.

This color line has been agitated by A.C. Anson, Captain of the Chicago National League team for years. As far back as 1883, Anson, with his team, landed in Toledo, O., to play an exhibition game with the American Association team. Walker, the colored catcher, was a member of the Toledos at the time. Anson at first absolutely refused to play his nine against Walker, the colored man, until he was told he could either play with Walker on this team or take his nine off the field. Anson in 1887 again refused to play the Newark Eastern League with Stovey, the colored pitcher, in the box. Were it not for this same man Anson, there would have been a colored player in the National League in 1887. John W. Ward, of the New York club, was anxious to secure Geo. Stovey and arrangements were about completed for his transfer from the Newark club, when a brawl was heard from Chicago to New York. The same Anson, with all the venom of hate which would be worthy of a Tillman or a Vardaman of the present day, made strenuous and fruitful opposition to any proposition looking to the admittance of a colored man into the National League. Just why Adrian C. Anson, manager and captain of the Chicago National League Club, was so strongly opposed to colored players on white teams cannot be explained. His repugnant feeling, shown at every opportunity, toward colored ball players, was a source of comment through every league in the country, and his opposition, with his great popularity and power in base ball circles, hastened the exclusion of the black man from the white leagues.

The colored players are not only barred from playing on white clubs, but at times games are canceled for no other reason than objections being raised by a Southern ball player, who refuses to play against a colored ball club. These men from the South who object to playing are, as a rule, fine ball players, and rather than lose their services, the managers will not book a colored team.

The colored ball player suffers great inconvenience, at times, while traveling. All hotels are generally filled from the cellar to the garret when they strike a town. It is a common occurrence for them to arrive in a city late at night and walk around for several hours before getting a place to lodge.

The situation is far different to-day in this respect than it was years ago. At one time the colored teams were accommodated in some of the best hotels in the country, as the entertainment in 1887 of the Cuban Giants at the McClure House in Wheeling, W. Va., will show.

The cause of this change is no doubt due to the condition of things from a racial standpoint. With the color question upper-most in the minds of the people at the present time, such proceedings on the part of hotelkeepers may be expected and will be difficult to remedy.

It is said on good authority that one of the leading players and a manager of the National League is advocating the entrance of colored players in the National League with a view of signing "Mathews," the colored man, late of Harvard. It is not expected that he will succeed in this advocacy of such a move, but when such actions come to notice there are grounds for hoping that some day the bar will drop and some good man will be chosen from out of the colored profession that will be a credit to all, and pave the way for others to follow.

This article would not be complete did we not mention the effort of

John McGraw, manager of the New York National League, to sign a colored man for his Baltimore American League team.

While Manager McGraw was in Hot Springs, Ark., preparing to enter the season of 1901, he was attracted toward Chas. Grant, second baseman of the Columbia Giants of Chicago, who was also at Hot Springs, playing on a colored team. McGraw, whose knowledge of and capacity for base ball is surpassed by none, thought he saw in Grant a ball player and a card. With the color line so rigidly enforced in the American League, McGraw was at a loss as to how he could get Grant for his Baltimore bunch. The little Napoleon of base ball with a brain for solving intricate circumstances in base ball transactions, conceived the idea of introducing Grant in the league as an Indian. Had it not been for friends of Grant being so eager to show their esteem while the Baltimores were playing in Chicago, McGraw's little scheme would have worked nicely. As it was the bouquet tendered to Grant, which was meant as a gift for the colored man, was really his undoing. McGraw was immediately notified to release Grant at once, as colored players would not be tolerated in the league. This shows what a base ball man will do to get a winner and also shows why McGraw has been called by many, the greatest of all base ball managers.

The following open letter was sent to President McDermit, of the Tri-State (formerly Ohio) League, by Weldy Walker, a member of the Akron, O., team of 1887, which speaks for itself.

The letter was dated March 5th, 1888. The law prohibiting the employment of colored players in the league was rescinded a few weeks later.

> Steubenville, O., March 5 — Mr. McDermit, President Tri-State League — Sir: I take the liberty of addressing you because noticing in The Sporting Life that the "law," permitting colored men to sign was repealed, etc., at the special meeting held at Columbus, February 22, of the above-named League of which you are the president. I ascertaining the reason of such an action. I have grievances, it is a question with me whether individual loss subserves the public good in this case. This is the only question to be considered — both morally and financially — in this, as it is, or ought to be, in all cases that convinced beyond doubt that you all, as a body of men, have not been impartial and unprejudiced in your consideration of the great and important question — the success of the "National game."
>
> The reason I say this is because you have shown partiality by making an exception with a member of the Zanesville Club, and from this one would infer that he is the only one of the three colored players — Dick Johnson, alias Dick Neale, alias Dick Noyle, as the Sporting Life correspondent from Columbus has it; Sol White, of the Wheelings, whom I must compliment by saying was one, if not the surest hitter in the Ohio League last year, and your humble servant, who was unfortunate enough to join the Akron just ten days before they busted.
>
> It is not because I was reserved and have been denied making my bread and butter with some clubs that I speak; but it is in hopes that the action taken at your last meeting will be called up for reconsideration at your next.
>
> The law is a disgrace to the present age, and reflects very much upon the intelligence of your last meeting, and casts derision at the laws of Ohio — the voice of the people — that says all men are equal. I would suggest that your honorable body, in case that black law is not

repealed, pass one making it criminal for a colored man or woman to be found in a ball ground.

There is now the same accommodation made for the colored patron of the game as the white, and the same provision and dispensation is made for the money of them both that finds its way into the coffers of the various clubs.

There should be some broader cause — such as lack of ability, behavior and intelligence — for barring a player, rather than his color. It is for these reasons and because I think ability and intelligence should be recognized first and last — at all times and by everyone — I ask the question again why was the "law permitting colored men to sign repealed, etc.?"

Yours truly,
WELDY W. WALKER

* * *

JUSTICE HARLAN AND THE SEPARATION OF CHURCH, STATE, AND BASEBALL

from the Idaho Daily Statesman, May 21, 1905, at 1

WINONA LAKE, Ind., May 20.—In an endeavor to clear away the preliminary work of the convention, thereby expediting action on the important questions which will be disposed of within the next two weeks, the delegates to the general assembly of the Presbyterian church today disposed of nearly all the routine business . . . .

Following the adoption of the recommendation of the relief committee was the report on Christian work among seamen, which was taken up and discussed. Justice John A. Harlan of the supreme court of the United States spoke at length in support of a suggestion that President Roosevelt be petitioned for a larger representation of the Presbyterian church in the appointment of naval chaplains. Justice Harlan said in part:

"The United States has now become a world power, and a world power can only be such by a great navy. It is true that we have in the navy too few chaplains and too few Presbyterian chaplains in proportion to the other denominations. I believe that the same state of affairs exists in the army. We have only one Presbyterian chaplain in the American navy, while there are six Roman Catholics and six Episcopalians. I have seen a similar state of affairs in civil functions of state, when high dignitaries of the Roman Catholic or the Protestant Episcopal church were called upon to open the exercises with prayer or to close with the benediction. I do not remember a single occasion when a Presbyterian minister was called upon for this service, although we have a Presbyterian minister in Washington who is the peer of any; and no church has had a greater part in the founding of our nation and its subsequent history than ours has played." . . .

Justice Harlan this afternoon acted as umpire of a baseball game, which resulted in the defeat of a team composed of visiting ministers by the Winona agriculture team by a score of 11 to 5.

Home of the Pittsfield baseball ordinance. The Athenaeum, circa 1906.

BYLAW TO PREVENT DAMAGE TO NEW MEETING HOUSE WINDOWS:

NO BALL GAMES WITHIN EIGHTY YARDS OF THE BUILDING.

At a legal Meeting of the Inhabitants of the Town of Pittsfield qualified to vote in Town Meetings, holden on Monday the fifth day of Sept 1791 __

Voted, The following ByeLaw, for the Preservation of the Windows in the New Meeting House in said Town __ viz,

Be it ordained by the said Inhabitants that no person or Inhabitant of said Town, shall be permitted to play at any game called Wicket, Cricket, Baseball, Batball, Football, Cats, Fives or any other games played with Ball, within the Distance of eighty yards from said Meeting House – And every such Person who shall play at any of the said games or other games with Ball within the distance aforesaid, shall for every Instance thereof, forfeit the Sum of five shillings to be recovered by Action of Debt brought before any Justice of the Peace to the Person who shall and prosecute therefor –

And be it further ordained that in every Instance where any Minor shall be guilty of a Breach of this Law, his Parent, Master, Mistress or guardian shall forfeit the like Sum to be recovered in manner, and to the use aforesaid –[1]

---

[1] John Thorn, *Text of 1791 Pittsfield Ordinance*, SABR-L ARCHIVES, www.sabr.org (posted May 13, 2004); *see also* Frank Litsky, *Baseball: Now Pittsfield Stakes Claim to Baseball's Origins*, N.Y. TIMES, May 12, 2004; *cf.* Fred R. Shapiro, *Origin of Baseball*, N.Y. TIMES, May 23, 2004.

BRIEF OF CONSTITUTIONAL LAW PROFESSORS

AS AMICI CURIAE IN SUPPORT OF REVERSAL, NRA V. CITY OF CHICAGO, 567 F.3D 856 (7TH CIR. 2009)

Elizabeth B. Wydra, Douglas T. Kendall & David H. Gans[†]

INTEREST OF THE AMICI CURIAE

Each of the *amici curiae* is a law professor who has published a book or law review article on the Fourteenth Amendment and the Bill of Rights. Certain of *amici*'s relevant publications are cited in this brief. *Amici* are:

Prof. Richard L. Aynes	Prof. Michael K. Curtis
University of Akron Law School	Wake Forest University Law School
Prof. Jack M. Balkin	Prof. Michael A. Lawrence
Yale Law School	Michigan State University College of Law

Amici do not, in this brief, take a position on whether the particular regulation challenged in this case is constitutional in light of the individual privilege to bear arms, which, as the Court noted in *District of Columbia v. Heller*, 128 S.Ct. 2783, 2816 (2008), may be regulated to a certain extent.

All parties consent to the filing of this amicus brief.

SUMMARY OF ARGUMENT

The parties — and the district court below — all agree that the threshold question in this case is whether the individual right to bear arms recently recognized by the Supreme Court in *District of Columbia v. Heller*, and applied in the context of the federal government and the District of Columbia, must also be protected against state infringement. In modern Supreme Court jurisprudence, the most common means of "incorporating" rights enumerated in the Bill of Rights against the states has been under the Due

---

[†] Of the Constitutional Accountability Center, Washington, DC.

Process Clause of the Fourteenth Amendment. However, the textually and historically accurate approach to determining whether the Fourteenth Amendment protects an individual right to keep and bear arms is to look to the Privileges or Immunities Clause of the Fourteenth Amendment. Undertaking this inquiry, *amici* submit to the Court that it is clear that the framers of the Fourteenth Amendment sought to constitutionally protect an individual right to keep and bear arms against state infringement, in large part because they wanted the newly freed slaves to have the means to protect themselves, their families and their property against well-armed former rebels.

Precedent does not preclude the Court from following this constitutionally faithful method of incorporation. While the *Slaughter-House Cases* read the Privileges or Immunities Clause so narrowly as to render it practically meaningless — completely ignoring the contrary text, history and purpose of the Fourteenth Amendment — and its progeny stand for the proposition that the Fourteenth Amendment does not apply the Bill of Rights to the states, this line of precedent has been so completely undermined by subsequent Supreme Court incorporation decisions that there no longer remains any justification for its continued application.

ARGUMENT

I. THE PRIVILEGES OR IMMUNITIES CLAUSE OF THE FOURTEENTH AMENDMENT PROTECTS FUNDAMENTAL RIGHTS OF CITIZENSHIP AGAINST STATE INFRINGEMENT

Proposed in 1866 and ratified in 1868, the Fourteenth Amendment was designed to make former slaves into equal citizens in the new republic, securing for the nation the "new birth of freedom" President Lincoln promised at Gettysburg. In two short sentences, Section One of the Fourteenth Amendment wrote equal citizenship into our constitutional design, mandating that States abide by fundamental constitutional principles of liberty, equality, and fairness. Its words provide:

> All persons born or naturalized in the United States, and subject to the jurisdiction thereof, are citizens of the United States and of the State wherein they reside. No State shall make or enforce any law which shall abridge the privileges or immunities of citizens of the United States; nor shall any State deprive any person of life, liberty, or property, without due process of law; nor deny to any person within its jurisdiction the equal protection of the laws.

U.S. CONST. amend. XIV, section 1.

Leading proponents and opponents alike of the Fourteenth Amendment understood it to protect substantive, fundamental rights — including the rights enumerated in the Constitution and Bill of Rights. The framers of the Fourteenth Amendment acted against a historical backdrop that required them to protect at least the liberties of the Bill of Rights: they were keenly aware that southern states had been suppressing some of the most precious constitutional rights of both freed slaves and white Unionists. *See* AKHIL REED AMAR, THE BILL OF RIGHTS: CREATION AND RECONSTRUCTION 160 (1998) ("The structural imperatives of the peculiar institution led slave states to violate virtually every right and freedom declared in the Bill — not just the rights and freedoms of slaves, but of free men and women, too."). Starting around 1830, southern states enacted laws restricting freedom of speech and press to suppress anti-slavery speech, even criminalizing such expression; in at least one state, writing or publishing abolitionist literature was punishable by death. *Id.* at 161; MICHAEL KENT CURTIS, NO STATE SHALL ABRIDGE: THE FOURTEENTH AMENDMENT AND THE BILL OF RIGHTS 30, 40 (1986). Political speech was repressed as well, and Republicans could not campaign for their candidates in the South. *Id.* at 31. To prevent states from continuing to violate some of the core rights of our original Constitution, the Fourteenth Amendment framers added the Privileges or Immunities Clause to the Constitution.

A. The Plain Meaning Of The Privileges Or Immunities Clause Shows That The Provision Was Intended To Protect Fundamental, Substantive Rights

The opening words of the Fourteenth Amendment announce a new relationship between federal and state governments and between the people and their Constitution. By affirming U.S. citizenship as a birthright and declaring federal citizenship "paramount and dominant instead of being subordinate and derivative," *Arver v. United States*, 245 U.S. 366, 389 (1918), the Amendment marked a dramatic shift from pre-war conceptions of federalism and expressly overruled the Supreme Court's decision in *Dred Scott v. Sanford*, 60 U.S. (19 How.) 393 (1856), which held that a former slave was not a U.S. citizen under the Constitution because of his race. *See also* Robert J. Kaczorowski, *Revolutionary Constitutionalism in the Era of the Civil War and Reconstruction*, 61 N.Y.U. L. REV. 863, 884 (1986) (arguing that through the Reconstruction Amendments and civil rights statutes "Northern Unionists imposed upon the nation their view of national supremacy," including "the primacy of national authority to secure and enforce the civil rights of United States citizens").

The framers of the Fourteenth Amendment made sure that the full and equal citizenship they established in the first words of Section One was no empty promise. In the Privileges or Immunities Clause, they explicitly guaranteed that citizens would enjoy all fundamental rights and liberties: "the privileges or immunities of citizens of the United States."[1] From our very beginnings, Americans used the words "privileges" and "immunities" interchangeably with words like "rights" or "liberties." *See* AMAR, at 166-69; Michael Kent Curtis, *Historical Linguistics, Inkblots, and Life After Death: The Privileges or Immunities of Citizens of the United States*, 78 N.C. L. REV. 1071, 1094-1136 (2000). For example, when James Madison proposed the Bill of Rights in Congress, he spoke of the "freedom of the press" and "rights of conscience" as the "choicest privileges of the people," and included in his proposed Bill a provision restraining the States from violating freedom of expression and the right to jury trial because "State governments are as liable to attack these invaluable privileges as the General Government is . . . ." 1 Annals of Congress 453, 458 (1789); *see also id.* at 766 (discussing the proposed Bill of Rights as "securing the rights and privileges of the people of America"). This view of the privileges and immunities of citizenship was common ground in American constitutional thought from the founding up through the Civil War; those words had specific and powerful meaning to those who wrote them into the Constitution.

As crafted, the Privileges or Immunities Clause was meant to secure the substantive liberties protected by the Bill of Rights, as well as unwritten fundamental rights of citizenship. The Clause is also "the natural textual home for . . . unenumerated fundamental rights." *See* Michael J. Gerhardt, *The Ripple Effects of Slaughter-House: A Critique of the Negative Rights View of the Constitution*, 43 VAND. L. REV. 409, 449 (1990). It mimics the Ninth Amendment, which provides that there are rights protected

---

[1] This focus on full and equal citizenship did not mean that the Reconstruction framers were unconcerned with the rights of non-citizens. John Bingham, principal author of the Fourteenth Amendment, believed that no state could violate the Constitution's "wise and beneficent guarantees of political rights to the citizens of the United States, as such, and of natural rights to all persons, whether citizens or strangers." Cong. Globe, 35th Cong., 2d Sess. 983 (1859). As explained by Professor Akhil Amar, the "privileges-or-immunities clause would protect citizen rights, and the due-process and equal-protection principles (which Bingham saw as paired if not synonymous) would protect the wider category of persons." AMAR, at 182. *See also* Richard L. Aynes, *On Misreading John Bingham and the Fourteenth Amendment*, 103 YALE L.J. 57, 68 (1993) ("An examination of the language of the proposed Amendment shows that its 'privileges and immunities' clause would apply only to citizens, whereas its 'life, liberty, and property' clause would apply more expansively to 'all persons.'").

by the Constitution not spelled out in the text. *See* Randy Barnett, *The Ninth Amendment: It Means What It Says*, 85 TEX. L. REV. 1 (2006). As one member of the Reconstruction Congress observed during the debates on the Fourteenth Amendment:

> In the enumeration of natural and personal rights to be protected, the framers of the Constitution apparently specified everything they could think of — "life," "liberty," "property," "freedom of speech," "freedom of the press," "freedom in the exercise of religion," "security of person," &c; and then lest something essential in the specifications should have been overlooked, it was provided in the ninth amendment that "the enumeration in the Constitution of certain rights should not be construed to deny or disparage other rights not enumerated." This amendment completed the document. It left no personal or natural right to be invaded or impaired by construction. All these rights are established by the fundamental law.

Cong. Globe, 39th Cong., 1st Sess. 1072 (1866) (Sen. Nye). Indeed, one preeminent constitutional scholar has suggested that the individual right to bear arms for the protection of person and property at issue in *Heller* has more to do with the Ninth and Fourteenth Amendments than the words of the Second Amendment. Akhil Reed Amar, *Heller, HLR, and Holistic Legal Reasoning*, 122 HARV. L. REV. 145, 174-77 (2008). But whether the individual right to bear arms is protected by incorporating the Second Amendment or looking to an unenumerated right protected by the Ninth and Fourteenth Amendments, the textual home for the guaranteed protection of that substantive right is the Privileges or Immunities Clause.

B. The Legislative History Of The Fourteenth Amendment Shows That The Privileges Or Immunities Clause Was Intended To Encompass Fundamental Rights, Including The Bill Of Rights

The debates in Congress confirm what the plain text of the Fourteenth Amendment provides: the Privileges or Immunities Clause secures the fundamental, substantive constitutional rights of citizens.

Senator Jacob Howard, speaking on behalf of the Joint Committee on Reconstruction, offered the most comprehensive analysis of the Privileges or Immunities Clause in the Senate debates on the Amendment. Relying heavily on *Corfield v. Coryell*, 6 F. Cas. 546 (C.C.E.D. Pa. 1823), an influential 1823 decision interpreting the Privileges and Immunities Clause contained in Article IV, Section Two of the Constitution,[2] Sen. Howard

---

[2] Article IV, Section Two provides: "The citizens of each State shall be entitled to all Privi-

made clear that the Privileges or Immunities Clause of the Fourteenth Amendment would afford broad protections to substantive liberty, encompassing all "fundamental" rights enjoyed by "citizens of all free Governments": "protection by the government, the enjoyment of life and liberty, with the right to acquire and possess property of every kind, and to pursue and obtain happiness and safety, subject nevertheless to such restraints as the Government may justly prescribe for the general good of the whole." Cong. Globe, 39th Cong., 1st Sess. 2765 (1866) (quoting *Corfield*, 6 F. Cas. at 551).

Sen. Howard also made clear that these substantive "privileges or immunities" included those liberties protected by the Bill of Rights. *See* Bryan H. Wildenthal, *Nationalizing the Bill of Rights: Revisiting the Original Understanding of the Fourteenth Amendment in 1866-67*, 68 OHIO ST. L.J. 1509, 1562-63 (2007). He noted the "privileges and immunities" of citizens "are not and cannot be fully defined in their entire extent and precise nature," but to these unenumerated rights

> should be added the personal rights guarantied and secured by the first eight amendments of the Constitution; such as the freedom of speech and of the press; the right of the people peaceably to assemble and petition the Government for a redress of grievances, a right pertaining to each and all of the people; *the right to keep and bear arms*; the right to be exempted from the quartering of soldiers in a house without consent of the owner; the right to be exempt from unreasonable searches and seizures, and from any search or seizure except by virtue of a warrant issued upon a formal oath or affidavit; the right of an accused person to be informed of the nature of the accusation against him, and his right to be tried by an impartial jury of the vicinage; and also the right to be secure against excessive bail and against cruel and unusual punishments.
>
> . . . [T]hese guarantees . . . stand simply as a bill of rights in the Constitution . . . [and] States are not restrained from violating the principles embraced in them . . . .The great object of the first section of this amendment is, therefore, to restrain the power of the States and compel them at all times to respect these great fundamental guarantees.

Cong. Globe, 39th Cong., 1st Sess. 2765-66 (1866) (emphasis added).

Representative John Bingham, the principal author of Section One of the Fourteenth Amendment, also made it abundantly clear that the substantive privileges and immunities of citizens encompassed the liberties set forth in the Bill of Rights. In explaining why the Fourteenth Amendment

---

leges and Immunities of Citizens in the several States."

was necessary, Bingham cited the Supreme Court's opinions in *Barron v. Baltimore*, 32 U.S. (7 Pet.) 243 (1833), and *Livingston v. Moore*, 32 U.S. 469 (1833), both of which held that the Bill of Rights did not apply to the states. Cong. Globe, 39th Cong., 1st Sess. 1089-90 (1866). Bingham retained this understanding of what the Privileges or Immunities Clause protected. In 1871, after the ratification of the Fourteenth Amendment, he explained:

> [T]he privileges or immunities of citizens of the United States, as contradistinguished from citizens of a State, are chiefly defined in the first eight amendments to the Constitution of the United States. Those eight amendments are as follows. [Bingham read the first eight amendments word for word.] These eight articles I have shown never were limitations upon the power of the States, until made so by the fourteenth amendment.

Cong. Globe, 42d Cong., 1st Sess. 84 app. (1871). *See generally* Aynes, 103 YALE L.J. at 74.

Other prominent members of the Reconstruction Congress shared the same view of the privileges and immunities of national citizenship as Sen. Howard and Rep. Bingham. Prior to the drafting of the Fourteenth Amendment, Representative James Wilson, chairman of the House Judiciary Committee, stated that "[t]he people of the free States should insist on ample protection to their rights, privileges and immunities, which are none other than those which the Constitution was designed to secure to all citizens alike." Cong. Globe, 38th Cong., 1st Sess. 1202-03 (1864). *See* CURTIS, at 37-38. During debates in the House of Representatives on the Fourteenth Amendment, Thaddeus Stevens, a political leader in the House and head of the House delegation of the Joint Committee on Reconstruction, explained that "the Constitution limits only the action of Congress, and is not a limitation on the States. This amendment supplies that defect . . . ." Cong. Globe, 39th Cong., 1st Sess. 2459 (1866).

Accordingly, the most influential and knowledgeable members of the Reconstruction Congress went on record with their express belief that Section One of the Fourteenth Amendment — and in most instances, the Privileges or Immunities Clause specifically — protected against state infringement substantive, fundamental rights, including the liberties secured by the first eight articles of the Bill of Rights. Not a single Senator or Representative disputed this understanding of the privileges and immunities of citizenship or Section One. *See, e.g.*, AMAR, at 187; CURTIS, at 91; Kaczorowski, 61 N.Y.U. L. REV. at 932. To the contrary, whether in debates over the Fourteenth Amendment or its statutory analogue, the

Civil Rights Act of 1866, speaker after speaker affirmed two central points: the Privileges or Immunities Clause would safeguard the substantive liberties set out in the Bill of Rights, and that, in line with *Corfield*, the Clause would give broad protection to substantive liberty, safeguarding all the fundamental rights of citizenship. Time and again, members of the Reconstruction Congress explained that the Fourteenth Amendment would require state governments to adhere to the guarantees of the Bill of Rights,[3] as the original Constitution had not, and give Congress the power to enforce their guarantees.[4] As Sen. Howard had done, many invoked *Corfield*'s broad definition of privileges and immunities, promising that the newly freed slaves would have all the fundamental rights of citizenship.[5]

II. THE FRAMERS OF THE FOURTEENTH AMENDMENT INTENDED AN INDIVIDUAL RIGHT TO BEAR ARMS TO BE AMONG THE CONSTITUTIONALLY PROTECTED PRIVILEGES AND IMMUNITIES OF CITIZENSHIP

The text and history of the Privileges or Immunities Clause demonstrate that it was intended to protect substantive rights, including those enumerated in the Bill of Rights and other, unenumerated, fundamental rights of citizenship. The history of the Clause further shows that an individual right

---

[3] *See* Cong. Globe, 39th Cong., 1st Sess. 1072 (1866) (Sen. Nye) ("Will it be contended . . . that any State has the power to subvert or impair the natural and personal rights of the citizen?"); *id.* at 1153 (Sen. Thayer) ("if the freedmen are now citizens . . . they are clearly entitled to those guarantees of the Constitution of the United States, which are intended for the protection of all citizens."); *id.* at 2465 (Sen. Thayer) ("[I]t simply brings into the Constitution what is found in the Bill of Rights in every State of the Union.").

[4] *See* Cong. Globe, 39th Cong., 1st Sess. 586 (1866) (Rep. Donnelly) ("Are the promises of the Constitution mere verbiage? Are its sacred pledges of life, liberty, and property to fall to the ground for lack of power to enforce them? . . . Or shall that great Constitution be what its founders meant it to be, a shield and protection over the head of the lowliest and poorest citizen . . . ."); *id.* at 1088 (Rep. Woodbridge) ("It is intended to enable Congress to give to all citizens the inalienable rights of life and liberty . . . ."); *id.* at 1094 (Rep. Bingham) ("I urge the amendment for the enforcement of these essential provisions of the Constitution . . . , which declare that all men are equal in the rights of life and liberty before the majesty of American law.").

[5] See Cong. Globe, 39th Cong., 1st Sess. 474-75 (1866) (Sen. Trumbull) (invoking *Corfield*); *id.* at 1117-18 (Sen. Wilson) (same); *id.* at 1837 (Rep. Lawrence) (same); *see also id.* at 1266 (Rep. Raymond) ("[T]he right of citizenship involves everything else. Make the colored man a citizen and he has every right which you and I have as citizens of the United States under the laws and the Constitution of the United States."); *id.* at 1757 (Sen. Trumbull) ("To be a citizen of the United States carries with it some rights; and what are they? They are those inherent, fundamental rights, which belong to free citizens or free men in all countries . . . .").

to keep and bear arms for protection of person and property was among the privileges and immunities of citizens protected against state infringement under the Fourteenth Amendment.

The framers of the Fourteenth Amendment were particularly concerned with the right of freedmen to bear arms. *See* Robert J. Cottrol and Raymond T. Diamond, *The Second Amendment: Toward an Afro-Americanist Reconsideration*, 80 GEO. L.J. 309, 346 (1991). The efforts to disarm freed slaves "played an important part in convincing the 39th Congress that traditional notions concerning federalism and individual rights needed to change." *Id.* As constitutional historians have noted, "Reconstruction Republicans recast arms bearing as a core civil right . . . . Arms were needed not as part of political and politicized militia service but to protect one's individual homestead." AMAR, at 258-59. In fact, far from fulfilling the Founders' vision of state militias as bulwarks of liberty, various southern white militias perpetrated rights deprivations suffered by African Americans in the South: "Confederate veterans still wearing their gray uniforms . . . frequently terrorized the black population, ransacking their homes to seize shotguns and other property and abusing those who refused to sign plantation labor contracts." ERIC FONER, RECONSTRUCTION: AMERICA'S UNFINISHED REVOLUTION, 1863-1877 203 (1988). *See also* Cong. Globe, 39th Cong., 1st Sess. 40 (1866) (Sen. Wilson) ("In Mississippi rebel State forces, men who were in the rebel armies, are traversing the State, visiting the freedmen, disarming them, perpetrating murders and outrages upon them"); *id.* at 914, 941 (Letter from Colonel Samuel Thomas to Major General O.O. Howard, quoted by Sens. Wilson and Trumbull) ("Nearly all the dissatisfaction that now exists among the freedmen is caused by the abusive conduct of [the state] militia.").

Central in the minds of the framers were the Black Codes, the South's postwar attempt to re-institutionalize slavery in a different guise. The Black Codes systematically violated the constitutional rights of the newly freed slaves in myriad ways, including by prohibiting the former slaves from having their own firearms. *See* FONER, at 199-201; CURTIS, at 35.[6] *See also Heller*, 128 S.Ct. at 2841 (noting that "[b]lacks were routinely disarmed by Southern States after the Civil War" and that opponents of "these injustices frequently stated that they infringed blacks' constitutional right to keep and bear arms"). These abuses were investigated and re-

---

[6] For discussions of the Black Codes in Congress, see Cong. Globe, 39th Cong., 1st Sess. 93-94 (1865); *id.* at 340 (1866); *id.* at 474-75; *id.* at 516-17; *id.* at 588-89; *id.* at 632; *id.* at 651; *id.* at 783; *id.* at 1123-24; *id.* at 1160; *id.* at 1617; *id.* at 1621; *id.* at 1838.

ported to Congress by the Joint Committee on Reconstruction, composed of members of both the House and Senate (including Sen. Howard and Rep. Bingham). The Joint Committee drafted the Fourteenth Amendment in Congress, and thus their findings bear directly on the Amendment they constructed. Their findings, issued in a June 1866 report, were also distributed widely throughout the country — 150,000 copies were issued. *See* BENJAMIN B. KENDRICK, THE JOURNAL OF THE JOINT COMMITTEE ON RECONSTRUCTION 265 (1914). The Joint Committee's report confirmed through an exhaustive fact-finding effort the systematic violation of constitutional rights in the South and the need for guaranteeing basic human and civil rights.

On the issue of the right to bear arms the Joint Committee reported testimony that, in the South, "[a]ll of the people . . . are extremely reluctant to grant to the negro his civil rights — those privileges that pertain to freedom, the protection of life, liberty, and property," and noted that "[t]he planters are disposed . . . to insert into their contracts tyrannical provisions . . . to prevent the negroes from leaving the plantation . . . or to have fire-arms in their possession." REPORT OF THE JOINT COMMITTEE ON RECONSTRUCTION Pt. II, 4 and Pt. II, 240 (1866). *See generally* Stephen P. Halbrook, *Personal Security, Personal Liberty, and "The Constitutional Right to Bear Arms": Visions of the Framers of the Fourteenth Amendment*, 5 SETON HALL CONST. L. J. 341 (1995) (presenting chronologically key testimony heard by the Joint Committee on southern efforts to disarm freedmen and Unionists). Members of the Reconstruction Congress echoed these concerns. Senator Pomeroy explained that the newly freed slaves should guaranteed the "essential safeguards of the Constitution," including the right of bearing arms, and noted that southern states had denied blacks the right to keep and bear arms. 39th Cong. Globe, 1st Sess. at 1183, 1837-38. Representative Eliot decried a Louisiana ordinance that prevented freedmen not in the military from possessing firearms within town limits without special written permission from an employer. *Id.* at 517.

The Reconstruction Congress first acted to explicitly protect the right of the freedmen to keep and bear arms in the re-enacted Freedman's Bureau Bill.[7] Seeking to prevent the Black Codes from perpetuating the

---

[7] The Reconstruction Congress also passed the Civil Rights Act of 1866, which provided that "all persons born in the United States and not subject to any foreign power . . . are hereby declared to be citizens of the United States" and "shall have the same right . . . to the *full and equal benefit of all laws and proceedings for the security of person and property*, as is enjoyed by white citizens." 14 Stat. 27 (1866) (emphasis added). While the right to bear

wrongs of slavery, the bill provided that African Americans should have "the full and equal benefit of all laws and proceedings for the security of person and property, *including the constitutional right of bearing arms*." Cong. Globe, 39th Cong, 1st Sess. at 654, 743, 1292 (Rep. Bingham) (emphasis added). *See also id.* at 654 (Rep. Eliot) (proposing the addition of the words "including the constitutional right to bear arms"); *id.* at 585 (Rep. Banks) (stating his intent to modify the bill so that it explicitly protected "the constitutional right to bear arms"). Because there was some question over whether Congress had the power to enforce against the states the protections of the Bill of Rights and the fundamental rights articulated in Reconstruction civil rights legislation, the 39th Congress proposed the Fourteenth Amendment, which made explicit the constitutional guarantee of fundamental rights against state infringement.

As discussed *supra* Section I.B., the most prominent supporters of the Amendment expressly stated their understanding that the Privileges or Immunities Clause protected at least those rights set forth in the Bill of Rights. Sen. Pomeroy listed as one of the constitutional "safeguards of liberty" the "right to bear arms for the defense of himself and family and his homestead." Cong. Globe, 39th Cong., 1st Sess. 1182 (1866); *see also id.* ("And if the cabin door of the freedmen is broken open . . . then should a well-loaded musket be in the hands of the occupant to send the polluted wretch to another world . . . ."). Sen. Howard defined the privileges or immunities of citizenship protected by the Amendment to include "the personal rights guaranteed and secured by the first eight amendments of the constitution . . . such as . . . the right to keep and bear arms." *Id.* at 2765. Having expressly included "the right to keep and bear arms" as among the personal rights guaranteed by the Bill of Rights, Sen. Howard explained that "the great object of the first section of this amendment is, therefore, to restrain the power of the States and compel them at all times to respect these great fundamental guarantees." *Id.* at 2766. *See also id.* at 1073 (Sen. Nye) ("As citizens of the United States, they have equal right to protection, and to keep and bear arms for self defense.")

As noted *supra* in Section I.B., no member of Congress disputed the idea that the privileges or immunities of citizenship included at least those rights enumerated in the Bill of Rights. Indeed, in at least one instance opposition to the Privileges or Immunities Clause confirms that the Clause

---

arms was not expressly included in the Act, it was widely understood that "laws and proceedings for the security of person and property" included liberties set forth in the Bill of Rights, including the right to keep and bear arms. CURTIS, at 71-72.

would protect these rights, including the right to bear arms: Senator Reverdy Johnson of Maryland supported the Citizenship and Due Process Clauses of the Fourteenth Amendment but was opposed to the Privileges or Immunities Clause; having served as counsel for the slave owner in *Dred Scott*, Sen. Johnson was fully aware that protecting the privileges or immunities of citizenship for all "would give to persons of the negro race . . . the full liberty . . . to keep and carry arms wherever they went," *Dred Scott*, 60 U.S. at 416-17. *See also* Aynes, 103 YALE L.J. at 98 (noting that even "Fourteenth Amendment opponent Senator Reverdy Johnson" "agreed that the privileges and immunities protected by the Fourteenth Amendment included the right to keep and bear arms"). The Reconstruction Congress was fully aware — and the drafters of the Fourteenth Amendment fully intended — that the right to bear arms to protect self, family, and property was part of the full and equal citizenship guaranteed by the amended Constitution.

III. PRECEDENT DOES NOT PREVENT THE COURT FROM RECOGNIZING THAT THE PRIVILEGES OR IMMUNITIES CLAUSE PROTECTS AND INDIVIDUAL RIGHT TO BEAR ARMS AGAINST STATE INFRINGEMENT

This Court should follow the text and history described above to find that the Privileges or Immunities Clause of the Fourteenth Amendment protects an individual right to bear arms. While certain lines of precedent may be seen as impediments to this constitutionally-faithful method of incorporation, they do not in fact preclude such a decision here. *See* McDonald Br. at 33 (noting that the court "is not bound by precedent that does not speak to the claims before it").

A. Slaughter-House And Its Progeny Were Wrong As A Matter Of Text And History And Have Been Completely Undermined By The Supreme Court's Subsequent Application Of Most Of The Bill Of Rights To The States

Despite the clear understanding that the Privileges or Immunities Clause was included in the Fourteenth Amendment to protect substantive rights and liberties, the Clause has never fulfilled its promise. Within a few short years of ratification, the Supreme Court effectively wrote the Privileges or Immunities Clause out of the Fourteenth Amendment in its decision in the *Slaughter-House Cases*, 83 U.S. 36 (1873), and held that the protections of the Bill of Rights limited only the federal government in *United States v. Cruikshank*, 92 U.S. 542 (1876) (finding that the First and Second

Amendments secure rights only against federal infringement), reflecting a national mood that had grown weary of the project of Reconstruction. *See* Michael Anthony Lawrence, *Second Amendment Incorporation through the Fourteenth Amendment Privileges or Immunities and Due Process Clauses*, 72 MO. L. REV. 1, 38 (2007) (arguing that "there can be no doubt that Slaughter-House and Cruikshank reflected America's loss of will to memorialize the reforms begun in the late-1860s").

The actual decision in *Slaughter-House* is noncontroversial: the Court rejected petitioners' claim that the Louisiana legislature had violated their fundamental rights of citizenship by granting to a single slaughtering company a monopoly on the butchering of animals within the city of New Orleans. Indeed, kept to the four corners of the opinion, *Slaughter-House* is not necessarily dispositive on the question of whether the Privileges or Immunities Clause protects an individual right to bear arms against state infringement because such a right was not at issue nor is it anywhere referenced by the majority. While the Court provided some examples of privileges or immunities pertaining to national citizenship that could not be abridged by the states, it expressly "excused" itself from "defining the privileges and immunities of citizens of the United States which no State can abridge, until some case involving those privileges may make it necessary to do so." 83 U.S. at 78-79.[8] Unfortunately, in the process of rending a rather mundane decision, the *Slaughter-House* five-Justice majority did its best in *dicta* to eviscerate the full promise of the Privileges or Immunities Clause by interpreting the Clause to protect only rights related to the workings of the federal government, such as the right to access navigable waters, with virtually all fundamental rights remaining subject to the protection of the states. *Id.* at 74-75.

But even though *Slaughter-House* and *Cruikshank* together stand for the proposition that the Bill of Rights does not limit the states, this proposition has been completely undermined by the Supreme Court's subsequent incorporation of most of the Bill of Rights as a limit on the states. In over-

---

[8] None of the cases following *Slaughter-House* addressed whether the Privileges or Immunities Clause protected the right to bear arms. *See Maxwell v. Dow*, 176 U.S. 581 (1900) (holding that a state statute mandating a criminal trial with a jury of eight persons did not violate the Privileges or Immunities Clause, even though the Sixth Amendment requires a jury of twelve persons for federal criminal cases); *Twining v. New Jersey*, 211 U.S. 78 (1908) (holding that the Fifth Amendment's privilege against self-incrimination does not apply to the states under the Privileges or Immunities Clause). While *Cruikshank* held that the Second Amendment secured a right only against the federal government, it did not conduct an inquiry into whether the Fourteenth Amendment incorporated that right and did not consider the Privileges or Immunities Clause. *See Heller*, 128 S.Ct. at 2813 n.23.

ruling earlier cases such as *Maxwell*, *Twining*, and *Adamson v. California*, 332 U.S. 46 (1947),[9] the Court has rejected the foundation upon which *Slaughter-House* was built — the idea that the Fourteenth Amendment did not fundamentally change the balance of federal/state power and that Americans should look to state government for the protection of their rights, save only those few rights connected to the workings of the federal government.

The *Slaughter-House* majority opinion's analysis and reading of the Privileges or Immunities Clause has not only been undermined by subsequent precedent — it is fundamentally, unquestionably, troublingly wrong. It completely ignored the text and history described above in Sections I and II and refused to acknowledge that the Fourteenth Amendment did, in fact, nationalize fundamental rights of citizenship and intended to place important rights beyond the reach of the states. As one of the framers of the Fourteenth Amendment, Senator George Franklin Edmunds, said at the time of the decision, the *Slaughter-House* Court's view of the Privileges or Immunities Clause "radically differed" from the framers' intent. CURTIS, at 177. Other framers called *Slaughter-House* a "great mistake," Cong. Rec., 43rd Cong., 1st Sess. 4116 (1874) (Sen. Boutwell), which had perverted the Constitution by "assert[ing] a principle of constitutional law which I do not believe will ever be accepted by the profession or the people of the United States." *Id*. at 4148 (Sen. Howe). *See also* Lawrence, 72 MO. L. REV. at 29-35. Moreover, *Slaughter-House* and *Cruikshank* are inescapably tainted by political and social influence — a commentator as early as 1890 viewed *Slaughter-House* as "intensely reactionary" and predicted with confidence that the decision would be overruled. *Id*. at 33 (quoting an 1890 statement made by political scientist John W. Burgess). Finally, the reading given to the Privileges or Immunities Clause in *Slaughter-House* and its progeny is contrary to consensus among leading constitutional scholars today, who agree that the opinion is flat wrong.[10]

In short, the foundation for *Slaughter-House* has been utterly destroyed by modern Supreme Court jurisprudence and its fatal flaws revealed by

---

[9] *See, e.g.*, *Malloy v. Hogan*, 378 U.S. 1, 5-7 (1964) (overruling *Twining* and *Adamson*); *Duncan v. Louisiana*, 391 U.S. 145, 154-55 (1968) (rejecting dicta in *Maxwell*).

[10] *See, e.g.*, AMAR, at 163-230; JOHN HART ELY, DEMOCRACY AND DISTRUST: A THEORY OF JUDICIAL REVIEW 22-30 (1980); LAURENCE TRIBE: AMERICAN CONSTITUTIONAL LAW, § 7-6, at 1320-31 (2000). The arguments of these, and many other, scholars have demolished *Slaughter-House* everywhere but the Court. "Virtually no serious modern scholar — left, right, and center — thinks that [*Slaughter-House*] is a plausible reading of the Amendment." Akhil Reed Amar, *Substance and Method in the Year 2000*, 28 PEPP. L. REV. 601, 631 n.178 (2001).

the light of history and scholarship. The promise of substantive, fundamental rights protection the Reconstruction framers wrote into the Privileges or Immunities Clause should not remain buried by continuing reliance upon *Slaughter-House*.

B. *The Privileges Or Immunities Clause Is The Appropriate Vehicle For Incorporating The Substantive Rights Enumerated In The Bill Of Rights*

The Privileges or Immunities Clause is the appropriate vehicle for incorporating against the states the substantive fundamental rights secured to all Americans by the Bill of Rights, including the Second Amendment. As Section I, *supra*, demonstrates, the text of the Privileges or Immunities Clause is an explicit textual direction to protect the substantive fundamental rights of all Americans, and the natural starting point for finding these substantive fundamental rights is in the Bill of Rights itself. History overwhelmingly confirms that this was the original public meaning of the Clause. As Justice Harlan made the point in one of his prescient dissenting opinions: "[t]he privileges and immunities mentioned in the original Amendments, and universally regarded as our heritage of liberty . . . was thus secured to every citizen of the United States, and placed beyond assault by every government . . . ." *Twining*, 211 U.S. at 123 (Harlan, J., dissenting).

The Supreme Court's incorporation cases involving substantive fundamental rights have never considered these arguments. Instead, the Court has used the Due Process Clause of the Fourteenth Amendment as the vehicle to incorporate substantive fundamental rights. For example, in *Gitlow v. United States*, 268 U.S. 652, 666 (1925), the Court treated the First Amendment right to freedom of speech as properly incorporated because it is "among the fundamental personal rights and liberties protected by the due process clause of the Fourteenth Amendment from impairment by the States."

Gitlow is, of course, correct — states may not deprive individuals of their freedom of speech without observing the commands of due process, as they might by instituting a system of prior restraint. *See Near v. Minnesota*, 283 U.S. 697 (1931). But the Constitution demands that that States must respect the right of freedom of speech, and other expressive guarantees spelled out in the First Amendment, not only because it is part of the liberty protected by the Due Process Clause, but more fundamentally because freedom of expression is a substantive fundamental right secured and protected from abridgement by the Privileges or Immunities Clause.

The guiding principle of the Court's most recent incorporation cases is that it must "'look[] to the specific guarantees of the (Bill of Rights) to determine whether a state criminal trial was conducted with due process of law.'" *Benton v. Maryland*, 395 U.S. 784, 794 (1969) (quoting *Washington v. Texas*, 388 U.S. 14, 18 (1967)). As *Benton* observed, the Court has repeatedly held that the specific rights enumerated in the Bill of Rights are a measure of what due process requires, rejecting an earlier, nontextualist approach that simply asked whether a specific right listed in the Bill of the Rights was necessary for fundamental fairness. *See Benton*, 395 U.S. at 794-95. But the Due Process Clause is not, and was not written to be, the sole avenue for protecting all the rights enumerated in the Bill of Rights from state invasion. In this case, the Court should turn to the words of the Fourteenth Amendment that protect substantive rights of citizenship — the Privileges or Immunities Clause.

C. Previous Supreme Court Cases Addressing The Second Amendment Right To Bear Arms Are Not Dispositive Here

Supreme Court precedent addressing the Second Amendment right to bear arms does not preclude the Privileges or Immunities Clause analysis described above.

As argued by the appellants in their opening briefs, *see* McDonald Br. at 33-36; NRA Br. at 26-35, the Supreme Court's opinion in *Heller* explains in detail why precedent previously thought to preclude a constitutionally-protected individual right to bear arms does not, in fact, foreclose such an interpretation. *Cf. Quilici v. Village of Morton Grove*, 695 F.2d 261, 269-70 (7th Cir. 1982) (explaining that the Supreme Court's decisions in *Presser v. Illinois*, 116 U.S. 252 (1886), and *United States v. Miller*, 307 U.S. 174 (1939), foreclose the argument that there is an individual right to bear arms in self-defense that is protected under the Constitution against state action). Accordingly, with no general impediment in Supreme Court precedent to the recognition of an individual right to bear arms under the Constitution, the question is then whether such a right may be recognized to protect against *state* infringement.

The Court in *Heller*, while noting that the incorporation question was not before the Court, explained that its precedent applying the Second Amendment only to the federal government "did not engage in the sort of Fourteenth Amendment inquiry required by our later cases." 128 S.Ct. at 2813 n.23. A close reading of the cases bears this point out. *See* NRA Br. at 26-30. With the way cleared for an inquiry into whether the Fourteenth Amendment protects against state infringement an individual right to keep and bear arms, the Court should faithfully apply the text and history of the

Fourteenth Amendment, as recounted above, and find that the Privileges or Immunities Clause protects this individual right.

• • • •

The text and history of the Fourteenth Amendment establish that the Privileges or Immunities Clause was intended to protect substantive, fundamental rights — including at least those rights enumerated in the original Constitution and Bill of Rights — against state infringement. The legislative history from the Reconstruction Congress demonstrates that an individual right to keep and bear arms was among the rights protected as a privilege or immunity of U.S. citizenship. Accordingly, amici urge the Court to find that the Privileges or Immunities Clause protects an individual right to keep and bear arms against state infringement.

CONCLUSION

For the foregoing reasons, *amici* respectfully request the Court reverse the incorporation ruling and remand for further proceedings.

✳ ✳ ✳

THE GOOD OLD DAYS

In these days of large salaries baseball players are humored as though they were opera stars. They stay at the best hotels in the country. Their humors and their vanities are reported in detail, and recently, when it was reported that one of the stars was about to have an operation performed on his toe, the nation held its breath with anxiety. . . .

Moreover, if a national convention had to run in opposition to the final game between the champion teams of the two leagues, it is safe to say that the convention would have to take second place in the interest of the public.

The Washington Post (1912)

MARCH

JOHN KINLEY TENER

Member, U.S. House of Representatives (1909-1911).
See Daniel Ginsburg, *John Tener, in*
THE BASEBALL BIOGRAPHY PROJECT, www..sabr.org (SABR 2009).

✎ MARCH ✎

SUN	MON	TUES	WED	THUR	FRI	SAT
	1	2	3	4	5	6
7	8	9	10	11	12	13
14	15	16	17	18	19	20
21	22	23	24	25	26	27
28	29	30	31			

"BEAN HIM!"*

*Note for ignorami—Hit him in the head

MRS. WHITMAN TO TOSS BALL

New York Times, May 11, 1915, at 12

Governor and Mrs. Whitman have been invited to be the guests of honor of the suffragists at the baseball game on May 18 at the Polo Grounds, when the suffrage cause will share the gate receipts from the game between the Giants and the Cubs. Mrs. Norman de R. Whitehouse, Chairman of the Baseball Committee, asked Governor Whitman to toss the ball into the field and open the game, but the Governor, who is not certain of being present, has delegated this part of the program to Mrs. Whitman.

"The woman suffrage game at the Polo Grounds Tuesday, May 18. The Giants and the Cubs will play. Buy your tickets now at McBride's, Tyson's, Alexander's, or from the suffragists at 8 East Thirty-seventh Street." This is the wording of the sandwich boards which will be paraded at noon Tuesday by the Baseball Nine through Wall and Nassau Streets. Among the paraders are Miss Abastenia Eberle, Mrs. Lila Wheelock Howard, Miss Anges Morgenthau, Mrs. A.D. Martin, Miss Bessie Brainard, and Miss Emily Hooper.

The suffrage van will be stationed at Broad Street and Exchange Place on Wednesday to round up lukewarm fans. Mrs. A.D. Martin will speak at 1 o'clock.

On Thursday at 4:30 P.M. there will be a baseball rally at 8 East Thirty-seventh Street. Tea will be served, and the wives of baseball players will be guests of honor. Billy and "Ma" Sunday have also been invited to be special guests at this tea.

Editor's note: The Cubs won, 1-0. www.retrosheet.org/boxesetc/1915/05181915.htm.

TUCSON HERPETOLOGICAL SOCIETY V. SALAZAR

John T. Noonan, Jr.[†]

*Editor's note: As Judge A. Wallace Tashima explained in the opening
paragraphs of his opinion for the court,*

> Conservation organizations and individual biologists (collectively
> "Plaintiffs") contend that the Secretary of the Interior's (the "Secre-
> tary") decision to withdraw a rule proposing that the flat-tailed
> horned lizard (the "lizard") be listed as a threatened species is con-
> trary to the requirements of the Endangered Species Act ("ESA" or the
> "Act"), 16 U.S.C. § 1531 et seq., and the Administrative Procedure
> Act ("APA"), 5 U.S.C. § 706. They appeal from the district court's
> order granting summary judgment in favor of the Secretary.
>
> The district court had jurisdiction under 28 U.S.C. § 1331 and
> 16 U.S.C. § 1540(g)(1)(C) (authorizing "citizen suits" to compel the
> Secretary to perform non-discretionary duties required by the ESA).
> We have jurisdiction to review the district court's final judgment un-
> der 28 U.S.C. § 1291, and we reverse in part and remand.

This case began in 1993 when the Secretary of the Interior first proposed
listing the species. After careful and conscientious consideration by this
court, it is now in 2009 remanded to continue to be litigated for an indefi-
nite time. The pattern of the litigation is scarcely unfamiliar in environmental cases. Congress has enacted law designed to conserve species of
wildlife threatened with extinction. 16 U.S.C. § 1531 et seq. A federal
agency has been entrusted with enforcement. Using its expertise, the
agency has determined what protection should be afforded a particular
species. Its determination has been challenged by a private nonprofit organizations concerned with the existence of the species. The district court

---

[†] John T. Noonan, Jr. is a member of the United States Court of Appeals for the Ninth
Circuit.

has heard the resulting litigation more than once, and this court has heard it more than once. The various decisionmakers and participants — the agency, the nonprofits, the district court, and the court of appeals — are not motivated by private passion or grudge, but seek to see the fair application of broad legislation to highly particularized and often elusive data. The legal system does not confide the definitive judgment to the agency entrusted with enforcement of the law but subjects that judgment first to the challenges of the nongovernmental organizations and then to the supervision of judges who are not expert in the scientific matters at stake and not familiar with the species whose survival is at stake.

As if this interplay of governmental and private groups did not create room for tension, misunderstandings, and passionate disagreement, the problems in this case have been exacerbated by the simple absence of information. How many flat tailed horned lizards are there?

No one knows the answer to that question. Nor does anyone know how many lizards disappeared when portions of their range disappeared. It is supposed that a diminution in range correlates with a diminution in lizards. This hypothesis is plausible. It has not been shown to be probable. Yet the case turns on what measures are necessary to keep this unknown population in existence. The court concludes that the Secretary erred in finding that the lizard has not lost a significant portions of its range. The old method of counting lizards is out. A new method has not been tried very much. It's anybody's guess whether the lizards are multiplying or declining. In a guessing contest one might defer to the government umpire. The court, however, finds the Secretary's conclusion impacted by over-reliance on fragmenting evidence of the lizard's persistence; so the court decides to give the Secretary another crack at the problem.

If the Secretary does not know what the lizard population was to begin with, or what it was in 1993, or what it is now in May 2009, how will he know if it is increasing, staying the same, or declining?

A style of judging, familiar to readers of the old English reports, characterizes the judge as *dubitante*. That is probably the most accurate term for me, which leads me to concur in the majority opinion insofar as it rejects the contentions of the Tucson Herpetological Society and to dissent from the remand whose command to the Secretary of the Interior is, guess again.

JIM TUGERSON

Peter Morris[†]

Editor's note: Our readers might reasonably wonder why a base-ball-themed Almanac contains so few substantial profiles of law-yers who influenced the game or players who influenced the law. The short answer is that the job of producing and distributing such works is well underway and very well done by the Baseball Biography Project at the Society for American Baseball Research. See bioproj.sabr.org. And they do not need our help. Peter Mor-ris's biography of Jim Tugerson is (1) an especially fine example of the work being done by SABR, and (2) a story of baseball and the law that every lawyer and baseball fan should know.

While Jackie Robinson and some of the other pioneers who helped break the odious color barrier now receive credit for their accomplishments, others who showed just as much courage have been forgotten. Jim Tuger-son is one such player.

Tugerson was born in Florence Villa, Polk County, Florida on March 7, 1923, and christened James Clerence — at least that is how his middle name is spelled on his Florida death record, though it may be a mistake. He dropped out of school after grammar school and received training as a surveyor. On January 26, 1943, he enlisted in World War Two and served as a warrant officer.

In 1950, Jim's younger brother Leander, also a World War II veteran, signed to pitch for the Indianapolis Clowns of the Negro American League. The Clowns were the black touring team that was best known for mixing baseball with comedy, although they had scaled back the enter-tainment aspect in order to gain admittance to the Negro American League. Leander experienced a successful season as the Clowns captured the Negro American League's eastern title and he convinced Jim to join him in 1951.

With the help of the two brothers, the Clowns won both the first and second-half titles in 1951. Jim, a lanky 6'4", 194-pound right-hander, posted a 10-5 mark in his first year of professional ball. Leander was the big star, however, compiling a 15-4 record that included a no-hitter at Birmingham on August 22 in which he struck out sixteen.[1]

Following this standout performance, it was expected that Leander would be signed by a major league club, and he did indeed sign with the

---

[†] Researcher, Michigan Public Health Institute. With special thanks to Dick Clark. This article first appeared, and remains available, at The Baseball Biography Pro-ject, Society for American Baseball Research, bioproj.sabr.org/bioproj.cfm?a=v&v=l&bid=1643&pid=19546 (vis. Dec. 17, 2009). It is reprinted here with the permission of the author.
[1] *Sporting News*, September 5, 1951.

White Sox, who intended to have him play at Colorado Springs in 1952. But eventually he was returned to the Clowns, so the brothers spent their second straight season with the Clowns and (along with a new teammate named Henry Aaron) again won the first-half title.[2] After posting an 8-2 mark for the Clowns, Jim Tugerson ended the year with Oriente of the Dominican Summer League.

The Tugerson brothers finally joined organized baseball for the 1953 season, but the club they signed with was less than ideal. Slowly but surely, the minor leagues were being integrated, but there was still plenty of resistance, especially in the Deep South. This made the Tugersons' decision to sign with the Hot Springs Bathers of the Cotton States Leagues — a Class C league made up of four teams in Mississippi, three in Arkansas and one in Louisiana — a fateful one.

Their signing met with immediate resistance. On April 1, 1953, Mississippi Attorney General J. P. Coleman announced that integrated clubs did not have the right to appear on baseball diamonds in his state. Coleman acknowledged that there was no specific statute to that effect, but based his edict upon the emphasis placed on segregation in the Mississippi constitution.

Management of the Bathers apparently offered a compromise at this point, pledging to use the Tugersons primarily in home games, pitching them in road games only with the opponents' permission. Despite the offer, the league's other seven teams held a closed-door meeting on April 6, and then President Al Haraway announced that Hot Springs had been ousted from the Cotton States League. Haraway cited Article 5, Paragraph 13 and 14 of the league constitution, by which two-thirds of clubs can vote to dismiss a club that "prevents the league from functioning properly" and claimed: "Since the Hot Springs club has assumed a position from which it refused to recede, which would disrupt the Cotton States League and cause its dissolution, which position having been assumed without the courtesy of a league discussion, and since it is a matter of survival of the league, or transfer of the Hot Springs franchise, this action is taken."

The decision immediately came under fire, both for its rank bigotry and because the secret meeting had blatantly contravened the league's constitution. Leslie M. O'Connor, former assistant to Commissioner Kenesaw Mountain Landis and now a member of Major-Minor Executive Council, pointed out that the Cotton States League constitution provided any club facing dismissal with the opportunity to be notified in writing and reply to the charges before a vote was taken. Not only did this not happen, but there were also rumors that only five clubs had voted to expel Hot Springs, which was shy of the two-thirds requirement. Of course nobody knew for certain because of the secrecy surrounding the league's proceedings.[3]

So National Association President George M. Trautman stepped in and ordered that Hot Springs remain in the league until he had time to review the matter. With this hanging over their heads, the league owners held another secret meeting on April 14 and voted to readmit the Bathers.

---

[2] *Sporting News*, May 7, 1952.
[3] "Hot Springs Ouster for Using Negroes Halted by Trautman," *Sporting News*, April 15, 1953, 24.

There were rumors that some sort of compromise regarding the Tugersons had been agreed upon, but nobody was talking as there were threats of a $1,000 fine to anyone who disclosed what had transpired at the meeting.

The league's about-face gave Trautman the chance to avoid a controversial issue, but to his credit he did not do so. The next day he announced that the action taken on April 6 was illegal flouting of the league's constitution. But he did not stop there, stating that even if procedures had been followed correctly, that if the only reason for banishment was "the employment of two Negro players, this office would still be required to declare the forfeiture invalid. The employment of Negro players has never been, nor is now, prohibited by any provision of the Major-Minor League Agreement."[4]

While all this was happening, the Hot Springs' players were watching in enforced idleness. With the April 21 opener approaching, the team had played only a single exhibition game as their futures were being debated in the national press. It must have been especially frustrating for the Tugersons, but they kept their poise. Commenting on behalf of Leander and himself, Jim Tugerson said, "We hope this is not embarrassing to the city of Hot Springs, which has been so nice to us. We don't wish to keep the city from having baseball. But as long as the club wants us, we will stay here and fight."[5]

Then on the eve of the season, both brothers were suddenly optioned to Knoxville of the Class D Mountain States League. Hot Springs Secretary W.D. Rodenberry issued a puzzling statement indicating that the team didn't "want to embarrass the sport of baseball, the colored players or any other players or managers by giving the Tugerson brothers an opportunity to prove their ability in the Cotton States League." He added that on April 7 the brothers had asked to be transferred if their presence would mean the end of the league, as many feared.

Under the circumstances, the timing of the announcement seemed very suspicious. Rodenberry's comments left little doubt that the move was made under pressure, as he suggested that newspapers in league towns poll their readers to try to get the other owners to reconsider. The decision must have been especially disheartening to Jim Tugerson, who had recently turned thirty and must have seen the demotion as a crushing blow to any chance of reaching the white major leagues. But he again took the high road, thanking the Bathers, saying that he and his brother had no hard feelings toward anyone, and expressing hope that "some day we might be able to return."[6]

After being optioned to Knoxville, the two brothers combined to help the Smokies sweep a May 3 doubleheader. Jim pitched and won the opener, and then Leander took the mound for the nightcap. Clinging to a lead but clearly struggling, Leander was relieved by Jim, who even used

---

[4] "Cotton States and Trautman Revoke Hot Springs Ouster," *Sporting News*, April 22, 1953, 17.

[5] Harold Harris, "Cotton Loop Rocked Again; Jim Tugerson Sues for Fifty Grand," *Sporting News*, July 22, 1953, 13.

[6] "Hot Springs Options Negro Pair to End Cotton States Controversy," *Sporting News*, April 29, 1953, 28.

his younger brother's glove as he saved the game for him.[7]

Sadly, that was one of the last times that the two brothers would share a special moment on the baseball diamond. Leander Tugerson developed a sore arm and tried to pitch through it without success. In June, having won only three games for Knoxville, a physician advised him to go home and gave the arm a rest for the remainder of the season.[8] It was, as far as I can tell, the end of his once-promising pitching career.

Jim Tugerson, however, blossomed into the league's best pitcher. After recording six victories in the first four weeks of the season, he was recalled to Hot Springs to start a May 20 game against Jackson, Mississippi. While the move stirred the flames of racial intolerance, race was not the only factor involved. Injuries had reduced the Bathers' pitching staff to only four men, so team co-owner Lewis Goltz claimed that he was forced to recall Tugerson. In addition, suffering from low attendance, the team desperately needed the large crowd that could be expected to come out to watch the league's color barrier broken.

A large crowd did indeed turn out for the game. But as Tugerson threw his warm-up pitches, a telegram was received from league president Haraway stating that the use of Tugerson violated the agreement reached on April 14 and ordering home plate umpire Thomas McDermott to forfeit the game to Jackson. In vain, the crowd booed the announcement and loudly cheered Tugerson. Goltz must have been even more disappointed, as he was forced to refund the tickets of more than 1,500 fans and turn away many more who "were standing outside and crying to get in."

Goltz angrily telegraphed Haraway: "The Trautman ruling of April 15 decided it is club's decision to make on hiring of eligible negro players. Exception is taken to your illegal order. If game is forfeited as threatened the case will be appealed immediately and suit instigated." Haraway replied: "It is an intra-club matter. Take whatever action you see fit." Goltz did again appeal to Trautman, but he backed down and returned Tugerson to Knoxville. While his club still retained the right to recall the pitcher on twenty-four-hour notice, his comments suggested that he would not attempt to play Tugerson again.

Jim Tugerson must have been bitterly disappointed at this latest setback, but he once again showed great restraint in commenting, "I am the property of the Hot Springs baseball club. The club called me back. I didn't ask to come." He did, however, drop a hint that rocked the baseball world, telling a reporter, "It's just possible that I may sue [Haraway]. I'm not bitter, but I think he did the wrong thing in making Hot Springs forfeit that game. I hope I land in the majors some day. I want to be in a league where they will let me play ball." Tugerson's threat made news all across the country.[9]

George Trautman wasted little time reviewing the latest debacle and ruling that Haraway had again overstepped his authority. He ordered the forfeited game replayed and accused the Cotton States League of being "at war with the concept that the national pastime offers equal opportu-

---

[7] *Sporting News*, May 13, 1953.

[8] *Sporting News*, June 17, 1953, 36.

[9] *Valley Morning Star* (Harlingen, Texas), May 22, 1953; Emmett Maum, "Forfeit Over Use of Negro Revives Hot Springs Row," *Sporting News*, May 27, 1953, 13.

nity to all." The decision prompted Hot Springs club attorney Henry Britt to express pleasure and state that there was a "probability" that Tugerson would again be recalled to Hot Springs.[10]

So Jim Tugerson returned to Knoxville and continued to add to his league-leading win total and bide his time. There at least he received sympathy and support, with management staging a "Jim Tugerson Night" on June 5 at which African-American fans were admitted free of charge.

But as the weeks went by, it became increasingly clear that he was never going to have the chance to pitch in the Cotton States League. Haraway and the other league owners remained adamantly opposed to integration, with Haraway later claiming implausibly that he had received some 300 letters on the subject and only three of them favored the pitcher.[11] Even Britt finally admitted that he was hoping to end the controversy by selling Tugerson to a major league team, explaining, "The league does not want a Negro to play ball, so we are going to sell him in order to keep the league from breaking up." Yet being forced to pitch in a Class D loop made that solution far less likely. When former Pirates manager Bill Meyer scouted "Big Jim" he reported that he, "couldn't tell much ... he didn't have much opposition and he just loafed along. I want to catch him in a game where he has to bear down."

Finally, in mid-July, Jim Tugerson's seemingly endless patience ran out. After winning his twentieth game, on the advice of attorney James W. Chestnut, he left the Smokies long enough to travel to Hot Springs and file a lawsuit against the Cotton States League, Al Haraway, and several of the league officials who had prevented him from playing in the circuit. The lawsuit asked for $50,000 on the grounds that the defendants had breached his contract and violated his civil rights by preventing him from following "his lawful occupation of a baseball player" and enjoying the "equal protection of the law in his privileges as a citizen of the United States of America."[12]

As soon as he had filed the historic legal action, Tugerson returned to Knoxville and reaffirmed his status as the best pitcher in the Mountain States League with a three-hit shutout in his first game back. He finished the year with a league-leading 29 wins against only 11 defeats and also posted a circuit-best 286 strikeouts in 330 innings. Then he topped that off with four wins in the Shaughnessy playoffs to lead the Smokies to the championship.

After the season, Tugerson barnstormed with a Negro League all-star team and the tour finally gave him the long-awaited chance to pitch in Hot Springs on September 25. It proved a triumphant return, as he beat his onetime Indianapolis Clowns teammates 14-1 in front of 1,200 fans and even hit a home run.[13]

Two weeks earlier, he had received much less welcome news when circuit judge John Miller tossed out the civil rights part of Tugerson's law-

---

[10] *The New Mexican* (Santa Fe), June 7, 1953, UP; *Sporting News*, June 17, 1953, 36.
[11] *Sporting News*, October 28, 1953, 10.
[12] *Bradford* (Pennsylvania) *Era*, July 22, 1953, AP; Harold Harris, "Cotton Loop Rocked Again; Jim Tugerson Sues for Fifty Grand," *Sporting News*, July 22, 1953, 13.
[13] *Sporting News*, October 7, 1953, 30.

suit.[14] Miller reserved judgment on the breach of contract claim but before he could rule a compromise was reached. The right-hander's contract was sold to Dallas of the Texas League and, having received the opportunity he had sought, Tugerson dropped his lawsuit.[15]

Dallas represented an ideal situation for Jim Tugerson, as the league had integrated in 1952 and he would have an African-American teammate in Pat Scantlebury. But after winning his first game for Dallas, Tugerson struggled and he was sent down to Artesia, New Mexico, of the Class C Longhorn League.[16]

On top of the discouragement he must have felt, Tugerson was entering a league that was strongly skewed to hitters. Roswell slugger Joe Bauman would swat 72 home runs that season, a minor-league record that still stands, and none of the pitchers who spent enough time in the league to qualify for the title posted an earned run average below 3.60. Tugerson, however, was unhittable, tossing forty-four consecutive shutout innings and chalking up a 9-1 record before being recalled to Dallas.[17]

Tugerson was less dominant upon his return to Dallas, but by late July he boasted a 7-4 record. Then his luck took a turn for the worse, and he lost six straight games, during which his teammates provided him with only five runs. He ended the year with a 9-14 mark for Dallas, but his 3.98 ERA (in a league where the leader's ERA was 2.89) suggested that he pitched reasonably well.

The 1954 season also saw the Cotton States League finally integrate. When Hot Springs expressed interest in signing two African-Americans, new league president Emmet Harty polled all five other owners and heard no objections. On July 20, eighteen-year-old outfielder Uvoyd Reynolds from Langston High School in Hot Springs joined the Bathers and was followed the next day by first baseman Howard Scott of the Negro American League. The team, which had been averaging less than 350 fans per game, drew more than double that total for the first two games.[18]

Jim Tugerson returned to Dallas in 1955 and spent the whole season there. He posted a 9-12 record, but his 3.19 earned run average suggests that he again pitched better than his won-loss record indicates. Otherwise it was a successful campaign as Dallas captured the regular season title before bowing out in the first round of the Shaughnessy playoffs. Tugerson had two young teammates of color, Ozzie Virgil and Bill White, both of whom were destined for long major league careers.

He played professional ball in Panama that winter and started 1956 in Dallas, but did not stay there long. Shortly after a May 18 start in which he failed to retire a batter, Tugerson was optioned to Amarillo of Class A Western League, where he spent the rest of the season. Being in the Western League gave Jim Tugerson the chance to watch Dick Stuart take a run at Joe Bauman's home run record (he ended with 66) and to play on his second-straight pennant winner.

Otherwise, however, it was a disheartening season. Somehow he man-

---

[14] *Modesto Bee* and *News-Herald*, September 12, 1953.

[15] *Kingsport* (Tennessee) *Times*, December 8, 1953; *Sporting News*, December 23, 1953.

[16] *Sporting News*, April 14, 1954, 38.

[17] *Oklahoma City Daily Oklahoman*, May 25, 1954; *Sporting News*, June 2, 1954.

[18] *Sporting News*, July 28, 1954, 40.

aged an 11-6 record with Amarillo, but his 5.67 earned run average shows that, for a change, he was the beneficiary of good run support. His struggles in 1956 suggest that he may have been experiencing arm trouble, but whatever the reason, one thing was now crystal clear. Now 33 and having failed to pitch well even after a demotion, Tugerson's window of opportunity for reaching the major leagues was closing.

At season's end Dallas reacquired his contract, and he again pitched in Panama that winter.[19] Before the 1957 season could start, Jim Tugerson announced his retirement.

After staying out of baseball for the year, Tugerson made a spectacular comeback with Dallas in 1958. Now using a sidearm delivery, he led the Texas League with 199 strikeouts while posting a 14-13 record and a fine 3.33 earned run average.[20]

Dallas joined the American Association in 1959, and Tugerson went with them, meaning that at 36, he was suddenly one rung away from the major leagues. But he battled injuries, and when he was healthy his old trouble with run support recurred, as indicated by his ugly 5-12 won-lost record alongside his respectable 3.51 earned run average. After the year his contract was assigned to Sioux City and then reacquired by Dallas, but at that point Tugerson finally decided to retire for good.[21]

Both of the Tugerson brothers returned to Florida after their baseball careers. Little is known about the later life of Leander Tugerson, who was only thirty-seven when he died in Alachua County in January of 1965.

Jim Tugerson had joined the police force in Winter Haven, Florida, in 1957, becoming its second African-American officer (and receiving leaves of absence in 1958 and 1959 to resume his baseball career). He spent more than a quarter-century on the Winter Haven police force and earned promotion to the rank of lieutenant. He also coached local youth baseball and it was while coaching a youth team on April 7, 1983, that he suffered a fatal heart attack. In recognition of his long service to Winter Haven, the city council passed a resolution to rename the baseball field in his honor.

Was Jim Tugerson deprived of a major league career by bigotry? The evidence does not enable us to say with any degree of certainty. He undoubtedly had fewer opportunities than a white man would have had, and it is quite possible that an earlier start in baseball, better timing or avoiding arm trouble would have enabled him to reach the major leagues. Yet he did have opportunities to prove himself worthy of advancement and failed to do so, meaning that it is quite possible that he had the talent to excel in the minor leagues but not at the major league level.

We can be much more confident in asserting that both Tugersons showed great courage in pursuing their dreams of careers in baseball. Jackie Robinson is rightly remembered for his great talent and his great ability. But men like the Tugersons deserve to be remembered because they fought just as courageously to reach the white major leagues, even though they never achieved that goal.

Sources: Contemporary newspaper, sporting presses, censuses, military and vital records; Alan J. Pollock (edited by James A. Riley), *Barn-*

---

[19] *Sporting News,* October 10, 1956.
[20] *Sporting News,* April 9, 1958.
[21] *Sporting News,* December 23, 1959.

storming to Heaven: Syd Pollock and His Great Black Teams (Tuscaloosa: University of Alabama Press, 2006); Neil Lanctot, *Negro League Baseball: The Rise and Ruin of a Black Institution* (Philadelphia: University of Pennsylvania Press, 2004); Dick Clark and Larry Lester, editors, *The Negro Leagues Book* (Cleveland: SABR, 1994). Special thanks to John J. Watkins for information on Jim Tugerson's life after baseball.

❋ ❋ ❋

REDEFINING THE MD, JD, AND MBA

From Paul Dickson, The Dickson Baseball Dictionary 131, 242, 255, 390 (1989)

doctor 1. *v.* To gain an edge, by secretly tampering with the bat, ball or grounds. Most doctoring is both hard to detect and illegal. Real or imagined doctoring has lead to some of the most heated and prolonged debates in baseball. "I'm not accusing the Yankees of doctoring the infield but it's very thick-sodded and that's certainly a great help to their infield." (Tiger Manager Jack Tighe, quoted in an AP dispatch, May 1, 1958; PT)

2. *n.* Temporary nickname for someone caught or suspected of the act of doctoring. "Doctor Sutton not the only one." (reference to pitcher Don Sutton in a *San Francisco Examiner* headline, July 19, 1978; PT)

ETY The term was applied to baseball high jinks long after establishing itself elsewhere as a term for secret product adulteration. "There is very little beer that is not 'doctored' and made even worse than in its original state by deleterious drugs." (*Sunlight and Shadow, At Home and Abroad*, John B. Gough, 1881; PT)

lawyer 1. *n.* A player who talks a lot in the clubhouse.

2. *n.* A player, coach or manager who tends to contest umpires' decisions.

manager *n.* The person who has been given the job of running the team. Traditionally, the manager determines the lineup and batting order, makes substitutions and plans the game strategy. The professional manager is hired by the owner or owners of the club.

1ST 1880. (*New York Herald*, July 12; EJN)

teacher *n.* MANAGER.

1ST 1917. (*New York Times*, October 6; EJN)

George Wharton Pepper at a baseball game, circa 1921-22.

SENATOR PEPPER IN THE MAJOR LEAGUES

George Wharton Pepper received his law degree from the University of Pennsylvania in 1889, and taught at the Penn law school from 1894 to 1910. Later in life, he represented Pennsylvania in the United States Senate from January 9, 1922 to March 3, 1927.[1] At the same time, on April 19, 1922, he was engaged in representation of a different kind in the Supreme Court of the United States. His clients were the National League of Professional Baseball Clubs, the American League of Professional Baseball Clubs, John K. Tener (president of the National League), Bancroft A. Johnson (president of the American League), and August Herrmann (chairman of the National Commission, an unincorporated body composed of the presidents of the two leagues and a third person, selected by them) — that is, the defendants in error (whom we would today call the respondents) in *Federal Baseball Club of Baltimore, Inc. v. National League of Professional Baseball Clubs*.[2] He won the case. What follows is a report on that victory in the *Sporting News*.

---

[1] *Pepper, George Wharton, (1867-1961), in* BIOGRAPHICAL DIRECTORY OF THE UNITED STATES CONGRESS: 1774-PRESENT, http://bioguide.congress.gov/scripts/biodisplay.pl?index=P000219 (vis. Dec. 19, 2009).
[2] 259 U.S. 200 (1922).

KNOCKOUT OF BALTIMORE FEDS
RED LETTER DAY FOR BASEBALL

HAD THOSE DAMAGE SEEKERS WON IN SUPREME COURT THEN WHOLE SYSTEM
UNDER WHICH GAME IS ORGANIZED MIGHT HAVE BEEN ENDANGERED

Sporting News, June 8, 1922, at 3

Washington, D. C., June 5. — When the supreme court of the United States handed down its decision in the suit of the Baltimore Club of the now defunct Federal League against Organized Baseball on May 29, it marked a red letter day, for the decision was one of the biggest events in the history of the game. The judgment of the court was entirely favorable to Organized Baseball ["O.B."]. The opinion of the court was written and delivered by Justice Holmes and was una[nim]ously concurred in by the other members of the court.

The suit of the Baltofeds was a civil proceeding under the Sherman anti-trust law, to recover damages alleged to have been sustained by the dissolution of the Federal League. They claimed that Organized Baseball was a conspiracy in constraint of inter-state commerce, in violation of the Sherman law and that one of its effects was to make chattels of the players and reduce them to a condition of peonage.

The court held unanimously that professional baseball is not commerce at all, and that "the restrictions by contract that prevented the plaintiff (the Baltimore Club) from getting players to break their bargains" were not in restraint of trade or commerce.

This was not the only indication that the court had not a very high opinion of the methods of the Feds. One of their lawyers who was indulging in a spirited harangue in which he alleged that O.B's methods were those of highwaymen, was gently admonished by Justice McKenna, to the effect that his remarks were somewhat irrelevant.

COURT KNOWS ITS BASEBALL

The opinion of the court presents the matter in a very clear, common sense way. It indicates a much better knowledge of professional baseball than is usual among men not connected with the game. Perhaps the fact that Chief Justice Taft and Justice Day are veteran fans had something to do with this. Mr. Taft was already a regular when he was practicing law in Cincinnati and Ban Johnson was sporting editor of the Cincinnati Commercial, about 1883.

If baseball players are slaves, why do they compete so desperately to get into slavery and stay in? Every one with a good knowledge of baseball is aware that the players are and always have been the principal beneficiaries of the game. The club owners may make money or lose it, but the player always gets his.

The case was first argued in the supreme court of the District of Columbia, in September, 1920, before a jury and judge of the court. The jury awarded the Feds damages in the sum of $80,000, which under the terms of the Sherman law, would have been trebled. The judge held that major league baseball was inter-state commerce and that the reserve clause in contracts of players was violative of their rights.

Organized Baseball carried the case to the court of appeals of the District of Columbia, where the decision of the lower court was completely and unanimously reversed. The Baltofeds then appealed the case to the supreme court of the United States, with the result noted above.

The highest court held that games of teams operating under the National Agreement are purely state affairs, that the transportation of players and paraphernalia across state boundaries is merely incidental, and that the personal efforts put forth by the players are not related to production and therefore are not a subject of commerce.

It would be strange if this were otherwise as, in that case, it would be legal for a league whose clubs were all in one state to play out their schedule, while it would be illegal for a league whose clubs had to cross state lines to do the same thing. But would crossing a state line alter the right or wrong of the act done?

United States Senator George Wharton Pepper, the great Philadelphia lawyer, was O.B.'s leading counsel, and Benjamin S. Minor, former president of the Washington Club, who is one of the leaders of the District bar, was his principal assistant, and prepared the brief of the case.

The supreme court's opinion followed rather closely the opinion of the court of appeals and the brief of the defendants (Organized Ball). It was a great victory on all points presented. Senator Pepper had the principal part in formulating the players' contract now in use and the baseball law on which it is based with a view to avoiding conflict between the Unites States laws and those of the game, and so far his work has stood every test and placed the sport on a firm and safe legal basis. . . .

"Senator George W. Pepper of Pa. at the bat — enjoying a game [of baseball] with the Page boys at the Capitol, 25 March 1924."

SHIT DOESN'T HAPPEN
THE SUPREME COURT'S 100 PERCENT DIRT-FREE EXPLORATION OF POTTY WORDS

Dahlia Lithwick[†]

Well, shit. There was supposed to be swearing. They swore like sailors when this case was argued in the 2nd Circuit. (Watch here.[1]) Judges and lawyers both! Those same judges swore themselves silly in the appellate opinion.[2] Advocates swore (a lot[3]) in the merits briefs.[4] Promises were made.[5] But today, in a case about how and when the FCC can regulate so-called "fleeting utterances" of words like *fuck* and *shit*, the saltiest language comes when Solicitor General Gregory Garre, arguing for the FCC, warns that the agency had an obligation to guard against the possibility of "Big Bird dropping the F-bomb on *Sesame Street*."

The F-bomb? What, are we all of us in the *Dora the Explorer* demographic now?

There's a famous story about oral argument in *Cohen v. California*,[6] the landmark 1971 case about the right to wear a jacket bearing the words "Fuck the Draft" in a Los Angeles courthouse. Listen here.[7] Calling on Mel Nimmer, who represented Cohen, then-Chief Justice Warren Burger cautioned the lawyer: "Mr. Nimmer, you may proceed whenever you're ready. I might suggest to you that . . . the court is thoroughly familiar with the factual setting of this case, and it will not be necessary for you, I'm sure, to dwell on the facts." Nimmer waited a whole two minutes and 11 seconds before saying "fuck." But today? The F-bomb.

[†] Dahlia Lithwick is a *Slate* senior editor. This article originally appeared in *Slate* on November 4, 2008. It is reprinted here with permission from the author and the publisher.

[1] www.youtube.com/watch?v=QdCsup3zqyA.

[2] scrawford.net/courses/foxvfcc.pdf.

[3] www.firstamendmentcenter.org/analysis.aspx?id=20832.

[4] www.abanet.org/publiced/preview/briefs/pdfs/07-08/07-582_RespondentNBCTelemund-oCBSABC.pdf; scotusblog.com/wp/wp-content/uploads/2008/02/07-582_bio_fox.pdf.

[5] www.law.com/jsp/article.jsp?id=1202425027610.

[6] www.law.cornell.edu/supct/html/historics/USSC_CR_0403_0015_ZS.html.

[7] www.oyez.org/cases/1970-1979/1970/1970_299/argument/.

FCC v. Fox Television is not a First Amendment case. It's a First Amendment-minus case, in that while the various justices insist that it need not be decided on constitutional grounds, it nevertheless provokes one of the best First Amendment debates I have ever heard. Since the Supreme Court decided *FCC v. Pacifica*[8] in 1978, which found the midday radio broadcast of George Carlin's "Filty Words"[9] monologue to be indecent, the FCC rule has been this: The agency may regulate a daytime broadcast of the sort of "verbal shock treatment" of the Carlin monologue, but it will overlook the "isolated use" of one-off potty words. A 2001 clarification of the FCC policy provided that a finding of indecency requires that the naughty word "describe or depict sexual or excretory organs or activities" and be "patently offensive as measured by contemporary community standards."

Enter Bono, who accepted his 2003 Golden Globe with the heartfelt (live) declaration that the honor was "really, really fucking brilliant." Oh. And Cher, who received her 2002 *Billboard* music award with the gracious, "I've also had critics for the last 40 years saying that I was on my way out every year. So fuck 'em." And the ever delightful Nicole Richie, who wowed them at the *Billboard* awards the following year with the observation that "it's not so fucking simple" to remove "cow shit out of a Prada purse."

Kinda makes you long for George Carlin, doesn't it?

The FCC would have ordinarily ignored these fleeting expletives, but it announced in 2004 that "given the core meaning of the F-word, any use of that word or a variation, in any context, inherently has a sexual connotation" and thus constitutes indecency. Then the FCC went around tagging everyone and their uncle for various fleeting expletives, from *NYPD Blue* (for "bullshit" and "dickhead") to the CBS *Early Show* (for "bullshitter"). Fox and its friends appealed, arguing, among other things, that the FCC's sudden rule change violated the federal Administrative Procedure Act, which bars "arbitrary and capricious" agency policy changes or those made without a "reasonable basis." The federal appeals court didn't want to discuss the First Amendment issues when it squashed the FCC like a bug, but it did so anyhow. The Supreme Court does the same today, leading Justice Ruth Bader Ginsburg, at one point, to observe that the whole case has an "air of futility" because, if the court just decides the narrow administrative issue, the First Amendment problem is still "the elephant in the room."

---

[8] www.lectlaw.com/files/case22.htm.
[9] www.law.umkc.edu/faculty/projects/ftrials/conlaw/filthywords.html.

Garre, arguing for the FCC, defends the policy change because the FCC "concretely explained it" and it was "consistent with its mandate." Justice Ginsburg can't understand why an expletive-rich broadcast of *Saving Private Ryan* was spared the FCC's wrath while a program about the history of jazz was tagged for indecency. "There's very little rhyme or reason which one of these words is OK and which isn't," she tuts.

Garre points out that 28 percent of the viewing audience for the offending Nicole Richie broadcast were children under age 18. He says her swearing "was shockingly gratuitous and graphic." He adds that the "F-word is one of the most graphic, explicit, and vulgar words in the English language." Justice John Paul Stevens asks if that's still the case when the word is used "with no reference whatsoever to sexual function." Garre says yes because it "inevitably conjures up a coarse sexual image."

Ginsburg wonders how "contemporary community standards are determined." Garre says the FCC asks its "collective experts: lawmakers, broadcasters, courts, interest groups" and the Church Lady.[10] When Ginsburg points out that *Pacifica*, the Carlin case, was decided in 1978, before the Internet, Garre replies that the proliferation of smut on cable and the Internet are all the more reason to strictly regulate network TV: So people can turn on their sets and eat dinner, confident that they will "not be bombarded" with Big Bird. Dropping the F-bomb.

Justice Stephen Breyer wants to know how the five-second-delay-bleeping thingy works and why it only works sometimes. Garre explains that Richie's expletives weren't bleeped because "they only had one person working the bleeping machine" that night.

Stevens proves he is our kind of jurist when he asks whether the FCC ever "takes into consideration that the particular remark was really hilarious?"

Carter Phillips, representing Fox, says the FCC's change of policy about fleeting expletives was sneaky. From 1978 to 2004, words were only indecent if they described sexual or excretory organs or activities; that changed in 2004 for no discernible reason. Scalia retorts that the F-word *always* referred to sexual activities. Adds Chief Justice John Roberts, "The reason these words shock is because of the association." Scalia deadpans, "And that's why we don't use the word *jolly-woggle* instead of the F-word." Even Justice David Souter argues that if what changed between 1978 and 2004 was that the FCC determined that viewers were deeply offended by fleeting expletives, then the change of policy might not be

---

[10] sendables.jibjab.com/.

arbitrary and capricious. Phillips replies that this isn't the only question here. "This was not about regulating the price of oil going through a pipeline," he says. "This is about regulating speech." Neither Scalia nor Roberts will accept his argument that there is some higher standard to be met for administrative regulation just because speech is involved.

Phillips adds that this is a statute with criminal penalties—including potential fines of $325,000. The FCC policy represents an "extraordinary *in terrorem* regime," he argues, citing amicus briefs describing the writers block faced by TV writers and broadcasters who no longer know which circumstances will set off the FCC's moral whack-a-mole. (Disclosure: I am a trustee of the Jefferson Center for the Protection of Free Expression, which also filed an amicus brief in this case.) What, wonders Phillips, about small TV stations afraid to carry local sports for fear of a student letting loose?

Roberts says awards shows are different. Nicole Richie has many youthful fans because she is a "celebrity" and they "like her music" and "want to hear what she has to say." (Name one Nicole Richie fan, Mr. Chief Justice, I defy you.)

When Phillips says that allowing a handful of objectors to set broadcast policy is a "hecklers' veto," Scalia heckles him right back. "So those of us that don't like it are hecklers, and you can't take our position into account?"

Stevens asks whether Americans today are more tolerant of foul language than they were 30 years ago, and when Phillips agrees they probably are, Scalia says, "Do you think your clients had anything to do with that?" Phillips retorts, exasperated: "Go to a baseball game, Justice Scalia. You hear these words every time you go to a ballgame." Scalia snaps back that this is still "not normal in polite company" and a "coarsening of manners."

It's hard to say how this all shakes out. Three justices say very little. Two clearly favor granting the FCC even more standardless discretion. The rest keep offering peanuts to the elephant in the room. It's a safe bet that the court will try to stick to the narrow administrative question, despite the justices' itch to talk dirty. Mostly, though, it's a bitterly disappointing day for those of us who'd looked forward to hearing some filthy words at the high court. But, having run the whole case through the FCC's highly subjective, context-based smut filter, I did come up with the following list of dirty words from today's arguments: Briefs. Golden globes. First blow. Dung. Pipeline. Jolly-woggle. Perhaps it's true that the Supreme Court can take away our F-bomb. But they cannot touch our dirty, dirty minds.

APRIL

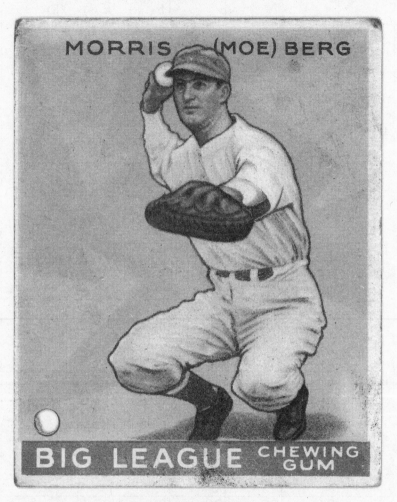

MORRIS (MOE) BERG

Associate, Satterlee and Canfield, www.ssbb.com (1930–?).
See Ralph Berger, *Moe Berg, in*
THE BASEBALL BIOGRAPHY PROJECT, www.sabr.org (SABR 2009).

❧ APRIL ❧

SUN	MON	TUES	WED	THUR	FRI	SAT
				1	2	3
4	5	6	7	8	9	10
11	12	13	14	15	16	17
18	19	20	21	22	23	24
25	26	27	28	29	30	

Democratic players (left) and Republican players (right), June 30, 1917.

'DONKEY' KICKS 22 TO 21

CONGRESS BASEBALL FOR RED CROSS SURELY WAS "SOME" GAME.

Washington Post, July 1, 1917, at 2

The Democratic donkey had a kick in all of its figurative four legs yesterday. He won the annual congressional baseball game from the Republicans by a ninth-inning rally — won it after the President of the United States had given up hopes for his party and returned with Mrs. Wilson to the White House.

The score was 22 to 21, but, despite the fact that 43 men crossed the counting board, it was the most exciting congressional game for years. The entire proceeds are to go to the Red Cross, and in addition to the sum realized from gate receipts, hundreds of dollars more were obtained from contributions and from the sale of score cards.

DODGES A FOUL BALL.

President Wilson with Mrs. Wilson sat through eight innings of the game. He was cheered when he caught a ball and then threw it out to Umpire Clark Griffith before the game started. In the seventh inning, Representative Sydney Mudd, pitcher for the Republicans, drove a foul ball into the presidential box, which Mr. Wilson barely managed to dodge.

Vice Pr[e]sident Marshall sat in a box behind the catcher and Speaker
Champ Clark was perched far back in the grand stand, and rooted for the
Democrats. Members of the diplomatic corps, cabinet members, army and
navy officials, members of Congress and officialdom in general attended
the game.

JONES AT IT AGAIN.

Marvin Jones, of Amarillo, Tex., doesn't like Republicans. He defeated his
Republican opponent in the 1916 election by [a] 30,000 majority and he
defeated the Republicans yesterday almost single handed. Seven times
Jones faced Pitcher Sydney Mudd and seven times he drove out ringing
base hits.

Four times the Texan led rallies which lifted the Democrats out of the
slough of despond. He stole five bases, and once he took a lead off base in
order to draw a throw and give a Democratic runner a chance to score.

HARRISON GATHERS BINGLES.

Aside from the hitting of Jones which was singularly like that of his fellow
Texan in the American League, Tristam Speaker, Pitcher Pat Harrision, of
the Democrats, gathered five bingles which aided materially in the victory.

The Democrats appeared to be favorites among the 4,000 or 5,000 persons who attended the game. They jumped right in and started scoring in
the first inning. Jones dropped a Texas leaguer back of third base, stole
second and third, and came in on Harrison's single to left. The Republicans tied it in their half.

In the second Jones singled, scoring Rouse and Webb. The Republicans
took the lead in the last of the second and maintained it until the sixth,
when the Democrats, in a wild batting orgy, sent ten runs over.

STRANGEST OF ALL INNINGS.

It was the strangest inning ever seen at American League park. Republicans stymied the ball all around the field with their hands, knees and
other portions of their anatomies.

But the G. O. P. batted out a lead again, and went into the ninth inning
with a four-run lead.

Jones started the ninth with a single and it became infectious. Before
the side could be retired six more runs had been chalked up and the Democrats were leading. The G. O. P. died hard. Prince Kalananiaole, Ha-
waiian delegate, walked and Representative Sydney Mudd, of Maryland,
Republican pitcher, stalked to the plate, stole second and third and scored
by a rolling slide on Morin's out.

BANKHEAD GETS BENCHED.

Most of the players who started went through the entire nine innings. The
Democrats made only one substitution. Bankhead was benched in the
sixth and Gard, of Ohio, went to right field. The Buckeye representative
hit safely three of the four times he faced the opposing hurler.

For the Republicans, Bacarach, of New Jersey, exhausted himself running bases and Elston went in to play third base. In the seventh Prince Kalananiaole supplanted Norton at second base.

Mudd led the Republicans at bat with four hits out of seven times, and in his galaxy of safeties was the only home run of the game. McClintic starred behind the bat for the Democrats.

Busy Day for Griffith.

Umpire Clark Griffith had a busy day. In the eighth inning McClintic tackled Farr in football style to prevent him from scoring and Jones tagged the Pittsburgh representative.

When the men arose Griffith waved Farr across the counting station and the Democrats gathered around Griffith and inserted some remarks into the record.

The sun was going down in the West when Harrison struck out Mudd, giving the Democrats victory after three hours of battling. The game netted the Red Cross about $1,000 an hour, or in all, $3,000. As the Democrats danced jubilantly to their bench the Marine Band struck up "Dixie."

Drill by Student Officers.

Preceding the game student officers from Fort Myer went through a snappy drill, which drew applause from the spectators. Lieut. Col. Charles W. Fenton, commandant at the training camp, watched his men drill from a box in the grand stand.

Little girls garbed to represent seven of the allied nations took up a collection at the gate. Mrs. S. P. Martin was in charge of the children. Elizabeth Martin represented America; Katherine Rickhardt, France; Helen Rickhardt, England; Julia Aukam, Russia, and Maude Winter, Japan.

The score of the game by innings was:

										R.	H.	E.
Democrats	1	2	0	0	3	10	0	0	6	22	30	16
Republicans	1	4	1	5	2	5	2	0	1	21	20	19

Line-Up of the Teams.

In the line-up were the following: Democrats: Jones, of Texas, third base; Bankhead, Alabama, left field; Harrison, captain, short stop and pitcher; Nicholls, South Carolina, center field; McClintic, Oklahoma, catcher; Rouse, Kentucky, first base; Webb, North Carolina, pitcher and shortstop; Whaley, South Carolina, second base; Sears, Florida, right field. Mr. Harrison concluded to be pitcher before the game was over, and, being the captain, Mr. Webb had to retire, much against his will.

Republican line-up: Miller, Minnesota, captain, shortstop; Morin, Pennsylvania, first base; Mudd, Maryland, pitcher; Johnson, South Dakota, catcher; Sanders, Indiana, center field; Ireland, Illinois, left field; Bacharach, New Jersey, and Elston, California, third base; Vestal, Indiana, right field; Norton, North Dakota, and Kalaniaole, second base.

RATIONING BASEBALL, JUNE 1943

"OPA (Office of Price Administration) lawyers hold nightly hearings for offenders in the pleasure driving regulations. Policemen, accompanied by OPA investigators, stop the drivers, question them. If there is any question about their reason for driving, they are asked to appear at a hearing that same night or any time in the next three days. This man is furious because his gas ration book was taken away when he was caught driving to a baseball game." *See* Farm Security Administration–Office of War Information Photograph Collection, Library of Congress Prints and Photographs Division, Reproduction No. LC-USW3-030777-D.

VOTING RIGHTS AND THE THIRD RECONSTRUCTION

Pamela S. Karlan[†]

At the signing ceremony for the Voting Rights Act of 1965, President Lyndon B. Johnson called the act "one of the most monumental laws in the entire history of American freedom."[1] The act is rightly celebrated as the cornerstone of the Second Reconstruction: Within two years of its passage, more African Americans had been added to voting rolls in the South than had managed to register in the entire preceding century. As a result of the original act and its amendments, politics in jurisdictions with significant numbers of black, Latino, and Native American voters has been significantly transformed, and the number of minority elected officials has skyrocketed. But that we *needed* a Second Reconstruction is a disquieting fact about U.S. history: The First Reconstruction, which at one point saw levels of voter turnout and black electoral success that would be the envy of any state today, ended with cynical political compromises, concerted vote suppression, and judicial indifference. It took the civil rights movement of the 1950s and 1960s to resuscitate the Fourteenth and Fifteenth amendments' promise of political integration.

In a number of unfortunate ways, the twenty-first century has seen a reprise of cynical political compromises, concerted vote suppression, and judicial indifference to voting rights that has undermined some of the promise of the Second Reconstruction. In Georgia, for example, Democratic incumbents of both races agreed to a redistricting plan that decreased the number of districts from which black voters could elect the represen-

---

[†] Kenneth and Harle Montgomery Professor of Public Interest Law at Stanford Law School. This article originally appeared as Chapter 14 of *The Constitution in 2020* (Oxford University Press 2009) (Jack M. Balkin & Reva B. Siegel, eds.), and is reprinted here with the permission of the author and the publisher.
[1] David J. Garrow, *Protest at Selma: Martin Luther King, Jr., and the Voting Rights Act of 1965*, 132 (1978).

tatives of their choice in an ultimately fruitless attempt to retain Democratic control of the state legislature. (Indeed, some of the white Democratic legislators whose reelection depended on black support actually switched parties after the election.) In many states, an ostensible concern with fraud has led to the imposition of draconian voter identification requirements that make it difficult for poor, elderly, disabled, and urban voters, who often do not have the requisite documents, to cast their ballots. Despite the conceded lack of any evidence of in-person vote fraud, in 2008 the Supreme Court upheld an Indiana law, finding that it protected public confidence in the election system and downplaying the burdens it imposed. The United States remains the only country in the Western world to disenfranchise millions of its citizens on the basis of criminal convictions, and the courts have repeatedly rejected challenges to this punitive practice, despite public opinion surveys finding that over 80 percent of Americans support allowing offenders to regain their right to vote and that more than 40 percent of the public would also allow offenders on probation or parole to vote.[2]

So, we need a Third Reconstruction. And this time around, two goals must be to transform the constitutional conception of the right to vote and to recognize that voting — while it expresses a critical recognition of individual dignity and full membership in the community — is also a fundamental structural element of our constitutional democracy. While a Third Reconstruction must achieve the full enfranchisement that has so far eluded us, it needs also to look beyond voting as an atomistic, individual act. It needs to consider political structure as well in order to provide fair, effective, and responsive representation after Election Day is over.

The Constitution is honeycombed with provisions regarding political participation; most of the amendments ratified since the original Bill of Rights deal with elections or voting in one way or another. But the most explicit protections of the franchise are phrased in the negative — that is, as prohibitions on particular forms of disenfranchisement. The Fifteenth Amendment, for example, forbids denial of the right to vote "on account of race"; the Nineteenth, "on account of sex"; and the Twenty-Fourth, "by reason of failure to pay any poll tax." Still other constitutional provisions

---

[2] See Pamela S. Karlan, *Convictions and Doubts: Retribution, Representation, and the Debate over Felon Disenfranchisement*, 56 Stan. L. Rev. 1147 (2004); Brian Pinaire, Milton Heumann, and Laura Bilotta, *Public Attitudes toward the Disenfranchisement of Felons*, 30 Fordham Urb. L.J. 1519, 1540 (2003); Jeff Manza, Clem Brooks, and Christopher Uggen, *"Civil Death" or Civil Rights? Public Attitudes towards Felon Disfranchisement in the United States* 21-23 (2003), available at http://www.socsci.umn.edu/~uggen/POQ8.pdf.

simply bootstrap off of states' decisions about the franchise; for example, the right to vote in congressional elections is protected for individuals who have "the qualifications requisite for electors of the most numerous branch of the State legislatures."[3] In light of this phraseology, the Supreme Court long ago expressed itself "unanimously of the opinion that the Constitution of the United States does not confer the right of suffrage upon any one."[4] And it reinforced this view in the notorious *Bush v. Gore* decision, with its almost offhanded declaration that "[t]he individual citizen has no federal constitutional right to vote for electors for the President of the United States unless and until the state legislature chooses a statewide election as the means to implement its power to appoint members of the Electoral College."[5]

That the right to vote is expressed in negative terms is not entirely surprising. The entire Constitution is characterized by negative rights. Even the Fourteenth Amendment, the centerpiece of the First Reconstruction, largely acts to restrict government action: "nor shall any State deprive any person of life, liberty, or property, without due process of law; nor deny to any person within its jurisdiction the equal protection of the laws." This conception can work well enough when the right at issue can fairly be framed as a right to be left alone: The right to privacy, for example, can be vindicated in large part simply by telling the government to stay out of our bedrooms, away from our e-mail, and off our property. But a negative conception doesn't work nearly so well when the ability to exercise a right depends on governmental action. A citizen who is handed an official ballot written in a language she does not understand is effectively denied the right to vote. A citizen who lives in a county that uses antiquated voting machines that frequently break down may effectively be prevented from voting by the press of other responsibilities that make it impossible for him to wait in line for hours to cast a ballot.

Moreover, the right to vote, while it is an important symbol of an individual's full membership in our political community, should not be seen as solely an individual right. Voting gets much of its meaning from the way individual votes are aggregated to determine election outcomes. If punitive offender disenfranchisement statutes bar over 1 million black men from voting, their disenfranchisement is not just their own business: It deprives the black community as a whole of political power and can skew

---

[3] U.S. Const. amend. XVII; see also U.S. Const. Art. I, § 2, cl. 1.
[4] *Minor v. Happersett*, 88 U.S. 162, 178 (1875).
[5] 531 U.S. 98, 104 (2000) (per curiam).

election results sharply to the right, creating legislative bodies hostile to civil rights and economic justice for the franchised and disenfranchised alike. If four-hour lines to vote in urban precincts in Ohio deter voters there from casting their ballots, their absence can swing a presidential election, thus impairing the political interests of voters across the country. Although we stand by ourselves in the voting booth casting a secret ballot, no one really votes alone.

What would it mean to develop an affirmative conception of the right to vote, one in which the government has an obligation to facilitate citizens' exercise of the franchise? One concrete context involves voter registration. It's a bedrock principle of the Fourteenth Amendment with respect to other government-recognized or -created entitlements that the kind of notice the government must give someone before it deprives her of life, liberty, or property should be the sort that "one desirous of actually informing" the individual "might reasonably adopt." A "mere gesture" is not enough.[6]

What would happen if we applied this view to voting and treated the right to vote as a kind of liberty or property that was inherent in the very notion of citizenship? When the government really cares about whether a citizen fulfills an obligation — ranging from registering for the draft to staying clean on parole to showing up for jury duty — it acts quite differently than it does with respect to political participation. It makes affirmative efforts to ensure that citizens are informed about their obligations. For example, the government mails jury summonses to individuals' homes with prepaid mailers for returning the forms, and it follows up with individuals who do not respond. It makes the forms for Selective Service registration available at every post office, and it conditions eligibility for government programs, such as student loans, on individuals' registration. By contrast, when it comes to voting, the government relies largely on individual initiative. And some states have created a series of hurdles that make registration difficult and time consuming. For example, one out of six individuals who tried to register to vote in Maricopa County, Arizona (the state's most populous county), had his registration papers rejected for failure to comply with the state's restrictive new voter identification bill.

If we treated voting as an affirmative right of citizenship, this could also help to reframe the way courts, legislatures, and the public think about the relationship between voter participation and vote fraud. Conservatives often claim that there is an inevitable tradeoff between making

---

[6] *Mullane v. Central Hanover Bank and Trust Co.*, 339 U.S. 306, 315 (1950).

it easier for citizens to vote and increasing the likelihood of fraud. And the Supreme Court in its opinions seems to see a related tradeoff between government-imposed barriers that preclude some citizens from casting ballots and a sort of disillusionment effect in which qualified voters stay away from the polls because they think their votes are being canceled out by ballots cast by unqualified individuals.[7] While, as a theoretical matter, these tradeoffs might exist, the available evidence suggests that the number of qualified citizens who are barred from the polls by so-called voter integrity measures exceeds many times over whatever fraud is actually prevented,[8] and there is no evidence whatsoever that voters stay away from the polls because they believe unqualified individuals are voting. (Indeed, there is a far more structural explanation for low turnout: Many voters believe, with a fair amount of justification, that the present system is rigged, through gerrymandering and other incumbent-protective devices, to produce foreordained outcomes. The available evidence shows that turnout is significantly higher in competitive races.)

Just as important as the evidence, though, is the way the potential tradeoff is discussed. In the criminal justice system, where individuals' freedom is at stake, the public understands that protections such as the requirement that a defendant be proven guilty beyond a reasonable doubt before he is convicted may occasionally result in acquitting guilty people. But our system is willing to bear that risk in order to protect the innocent — hence the phrase "better a hundred guilty men go free than that one innocent person be convicted." By recognizing that voting, like physical freedom, is a fundamental constitutional right, perhaps we can move toward a similar perspective with respect to the franchise.

Beyond easier registration, recognizing that voting is an affirmative right and that the government must therefore provide individuals with the means to exercise their right could also serve as a springboard for attacking, both politically and through litigation, states' failure to construct efficient, fair, and reliable voting systems. The "reforms" instituted in the wake of the 2000 election often fail to deliver on this promise. For example, the Help America Vote Act (almost as euphemistic a moniker as the USA PATRIOT Act) requires states to provide provisional ballots to individuals who appear at a polling place only to find that their names are somehow missing from the rolls, but it says nothing about whether states

---

[7] See *Purcell v. Gonzalez*, 549 U.S. 1 (2006); see also *Crawford v. Marion County*, 128 S.Ct. 1610 (2008).

[8] See, e.g., Spencer Overton, *Stealing Democracy: The New Politics of Voter Suppression* (2006).

must ultimately count those ballots, and many elections officials have refused to count such ballots even if the voter was entirely qualified to vote
but simply showed up at the wrong polling station. Similarly, the electronic voting machines that many jurisdictions adopted in the wake of the
butterfly ballot/hanging chad disasters can be difficult for elderly and disabled voters to use and may lack audit trails that allow the public to be
confident that votes are being accurately counted.

Finally, remaining mindful that the right to vote is not only an affirmative right but is also a collective right offers at least a starting point for
rethinking fundamental questions about who deserves representation and
how our representative institutions should be constructed. The Second
Reconstruction embraced a commitment to ensuring that members of
traditionally excluded racial and ethnic minority groups, such as African
Americans, Latinos, and Native Americans, achieve representation on
elective bodies. That representation has been accomplished largely
through the use of geographic districts, making lemonade out of the sorry
fact that the United States remains deeply residentially segregated. But the
use of geographic districts does nothing to enhance the electoral prospects
of female candidates or candidates representing numerical minorities who
do not live in discrete communities. Moreover, it can make it more difficult for liberal, progressive, and moderate white voters to elect candidates. One of the striking facts about the emergence of democracies in the
former Soviet bloc, in South Africa, and in the developing world is that,
while all these nations have adopted features of the U.S. Constitution such
as a bill of rights and judicial review, *none* has adopted our system of win-
ner-take-all single-member districts as the sole means of electing national
and provincial legislatures. Instead, they have all adopted systems that are
more explicitly proportional. By their nature, these systems are more democratic, since they leave to voters, rather than to those who draw the
districts, the decision about how to affiliate themselves. There's a traditional Korean saying that one should never let one's skill exceed one's
virtue. One of the lessons we have learned since the reapportionment
revolution that occurred during the Second Reconstruction is that the ger-
rymanderers' technical skill in manipulating district lines now exceeds the
power of our current legal doctrine to assure fair elections. Part of the
task of the Third Reconstruction must be to develop new principles that
can constrain the blatant manipulation of elections, which has replaced
elections where the people choose their rulers with redistricting processes
in which the rulers choose their constituents.

While some activists and legislators have suggested the need for a new constitutional amendment recognizing the affirmative right to vote, my own view is that the existing constitutional provisions are sufficient. A better tactic, it seems to me, lies in reviving — as conservatives have done for their own ends — Charles Black's approach to constitutional reasoning from the structure and relationship of constitutional provisions.[9] The federalism revolution of the later Rehnquist Court relied on this approach in using the language in the Tenth and Eleventh amendments to expand state sovereignty and to constrain congressional power to vindicate civil rights. It is time for liberals and progressives to make similar arguments with respect to the contours of the right to vote. The entire Constitution presupposes free and fair elections in which all qualified citizens can participate. The individual amendments that have expanded the electorate should be read to express a more general principle. The decision in the Seventeenth Amendment to take the selection of U.S. senators away from the state legislatures should be seen as fundamentally inconsistent with a decision to turn the selection of U.S. representatives into the province of the state legislatures, as the current hands-off approach to redistricting has done. The decision in the Twenty-Fourth Amendment to abolish poll taxes should be seen as reflecting a fundamental commitment to eliminating barriers to registration and to ensuring that wealth plays less of a role in our politics.

And even beyond our politics, arguing for an affirmative conception of the right to vote can perhaps serve as an opening wedge in arguing for affirmative conceptions of other rights. In part, if we can persuade the public that the government has a responsibility to enable all citizens, including poor people, people with disabilities, and members of minority groups, to participate fully in the electoral process, then perhaps we can also persuade them that the government has a responsibility to provide all individuals with the tools necessary to participate fully in other arenas of American life. But there is a more concrete way in which voting can contribute to a more affirmative politics. The politics we have is itself a function of who votes. That was the point of Dr. Martin Luther King's great Give Us the Ballot speech in 1957. Once the U.S. electorate is more representative of all its people, the people themselves will push for legislation that more fully serves their needs. One of the great victories of the Second Reconstruction was the way in which the Voting Rights Act of 1965 transformed black Americans' lives. The act's ambition separated it from preceding civil rights laws: It sought to transform black southerners into ac-

---

[9] See Charles L. Black, Jr., *Structure and Relationship in Constitutional Law* (1969).

131

tive participants in the governance process rather than simply recipients of congressionally or judicially conferred fair treatment in some discrete arena.[10] The aim of the Third Reconstruction must be both to preserve the gains the Second Reconstruction produced for racial minority groups and to expand those gains to reach other communities as well.

✣ ✣ ✣

HUGGINS TOOK LIKING FOR BASEBALL WHILE HE WAS LEARNING LAW

Washington Post, Dec. 24, 1917, at 8

Miller James Huggins, the new manager of the Yankees, is a midget with a big baseball intellect.

Urged by his father to become a grocer, Huggins studied law, but while in school became so engrossed in baseball that he adopted it as a profession.

Huggins inherited his love for athletics from his father, who played cricket in England. The senior Huggins gave Miller J. a good education. The new manager of the Yankees captained his primary school, high school and varsity baseball teams. So he is a college product, not a corner lot development.

He attended Cincinnati University for two years. Later he studied law for three years and graduated from Cincinnati Law School. He was admitted to the Ohio bar at Columbus. Former President William Howard Taft and Judson Harmon, Attorney General in Grover Cleveland's cabinet, taught Hug law.

He earned his own way through law school by playing professional ball during the summer months and working at various tasks between hours of study during the winter.

In his younger days Huggins was a right-handed hitter. Because it is closer to first base, he shifted and began to hit from the port side.

The smallest manager in big league baseball is a bachelor.[*]

---

[10] See Samuel Issacharoff and Pamela S. Karlan, *Groups, Politics, and the Equal Protection Clause*, 58 Miami L. Rev. 35 (2003); Karlan, *Loss and Redemption: Voting Rights at the Turn of a Century*, 50 Vand. L. Rev. 291, 316 (1997); Karlan, *The Rights to Vote: Some Realism about Formalism*, 71 Tex. L. Rev. 1705, 1719 (1993).

[*] Judson Harmon was no slouch as a baseball player himself:

> While at college and as a young man Judson Harmon was noted among other things for his proficiency in athletic sports. Traditions still linger about his native place concerning his skill and prowess in the game of baseball. An elderly member of the Cincinnati bar delights to relate how his first sight of the future jurist and statesman was when he was posing in the center of the diamond as pitcher for his village team . . . .

H.D. Peck, *Judson Harmon*, 20 GREEN BAG 239 (1908). Which leaves us wishing for some evidence that Harmon taught his student more than law.

INTRODUCTION

to

OLIVER WENDELL HOLMES, JR., THE COMMON LAW

G. Edward White[†]

The first question that needs to be asked about *The Common Law* is why, more than a century after its publication, it is still worth reading. A conventional response is that it continues to be regarded as a major work of American jurisprudence. But that answer does not tell us what makes *The Common Law* important; nor, for that matter, does it help the modern reader navigate through its dense and often obscure pages.

In the fall of 1880, Oliver Wendell Holmes, Jr., was invited to deliver the Lowell Institute Lectures in Boston. That lecture series was designed for professionals and lay people enthusiastic about the subjects covered by the talks.[1] The expected audience for Holmes's lectures, on the common law, would have been practicing lawyers and legal academics, some law students, and others with a particular interest in the scholarly treatment of legal topics, the sorts of people who would have been acquainted with Holmes's numerous articles in the 1870s in the *American Law Review*, a legal journal founded in the late 1860s.

[†] David and Mary Harrison Distinguished Professor of Law at the University of Virginia School of Law. "Introduction," by G. Edward White reprinted by permission of the publisher from THE COMMON LAW by Oliver Wendell Holmes, Jr., pp. vii-xxxiii, Cambridge, Mass.: The Belknap Press of Harvard University Press, Copyright © 2009 by the President and Fellows of Harvard College.

[1] Holmes delivered twelve lectures, but only eleven appeared in *The Common Law*: the twelfth was a summary. The "Closure of the Lowell Lectures," a précis of the twelfth lecture, was published in the Boston *Daily Advertiser* on January 1, 1881. The *Daily Advertiser* also noted that "[n]o other course in the [Lowell] institute has been attended by so large a proportion of young men," and that "having sketched his course," Holmes "gave a few minutes at the close of the [last] lecture to a picture of the scope, beauties, pleasures, and horrors of the law." A portion of the *Advertiser*'s précis appears in *The Collected Works of Justice Holmes: Complete Public Writings and Selected Judicial Opinions of Oliver Wendell Holmes*, ed. Sheldon Novick, 5 vols. (Chicago: University of Chicago Press, 1995), vol. 3, pp. 104-106.

Attorneys, legal scholars, law students, and occasional nonspecialists still make up the audience for *The Common Law* today. But though many readers recognize Holmes as one of the most famous judges in American history and *The Common Law* as his primary work of scholarship, few have more than a passing acquaintance with the book's contents. Most people, specialists and nonspecialists alike, find *The Common Law* a challenging book.

Consider this set of comments from a group of Holmes scholars. Holmes's first authorized biographer, Mark DeWolfe Howe, noted in 1963 that "though often started," *The Common Law* "is seldom finished by today's readers." In Howe's judgment, it was "a difficult book," being "made up for the most part of closely-reasoned analysis of certain aspects of English legal history and certain problems of jurisprudence" that Howe speculated were "less important" to his own, twentieth-century contemporaries than they were to Holmes's original audience. He noted that though many people still "found the mind and achievements of Holmes to be matters of absorbing interest," they "looked more to his judicial opinions, essays, speeches, and letters, than to *The Common Law.*"[2]

In 1977 Grant Gilmore, working to complete the biography that Howe had begun, went further.[3] The lectures in *The Common Law*, Gilmore wrote, "have long since become unreadable unless the reader is prepared to put forward an almost superhuman effort of will to keep his attention from flagging and his interest from wandering."[4] In 1993 Morton Horwitz, seeking to locate *The Common Law* in the late nineteenth- and twentieth-century history of American jurisprudence, largely agreed with Gilmore. Although he concluded that *The Common Law* was a "great work," Horwitz found it "obscure and inaccessible," and noted that it was "very rarely read."[5]

These comments suggest that difficulties with *The Common Law* are not simply a product of the arcane historical data Holmes surveys. Indeed, he

---

[2] Mark DeWolfe Howe, "Introduction," in Oliver Wendell Holmes, *The Common Law*, ed. Howe (Cambridge, Mass.: The Belknap Press of Harvard University Press, 1963), pp. xi-xii.

[3] Howe completed two volumes of his biography, *Justice Oliver Wendell Holmes: The Shaping Years* (Cambridge, Mass.: Belknap Press of Harvard University Press, 1957); and *Justice Oliver Wendell Holmes: The Proving Years* (Cambridge, Mass.: Belknap Press of Harvard University Press, 1963). He died in 1967. Subsequently the literary executors of Holmes's estate retained Gilmore to complete the biography. Both Howe and Gilmore were given exclusive access to Holmes's papers, which had been donated to Harvard Law School after Holmes's death in 1935. Gilmore died in 1983 without having published any further work on the authorized biography.

[4] Grant Gilmore, *The Ages of American Law* (New Haven: Yale University Press, 1977), p. 52.

[5] Morton J. Horwitz, *The Transformation of American Law, 1870-1960: The Crisis of Legal Orthodoxy* (New York: Oxford University Press, 1992), p. 110.

often does not make clear the relationship between that data and what he identifies as central themes in American jurisprudence. In some chapters, such as that on criminal law, historical evidence is largely absent. In others, Holmes's descriptions of the historical evolution of common law fields seem indistinguishable from his policy prescriptions about the scope of liability in those fields. Thus modern readers may fail not only to understand the details of Holmes's history but also to grasp the point of his historical exegesis.

These difficulties with *The Common Law* can be contrasted with another recurrent impression readers have had of the book. From its initial publication, many have recognized the suggestiveness and depth of the jurisprudential observations it contains. In 1889 the English legal historian Frederic Maitland predicted that "for a long time to come," *The Common Law* would "leave its mark wide and deep on all the best thoughts of Americans and Englishmen about the history of their common law."[6] It is a book of "wide and deep" statements about the nature of judge-fashioned law and the process of its development over time; those statements, often rendered in memorable language, have repeatedly given readers the impression that they are encountering a work of extraordinary quality.

But the difficulty of extracting Holmes's perspective from the obscure narrative in which he sought to present it remains. If *The Common Law*'s inaccessibility makes it difficult for most people to read, let alone understand, how can we appreciate its greatness? Prospective readers might be well advised, given the experience of the scholars quoted above, not to plunge directly into the text without first gaining a fuller view of its author.

• • • •

When he received the invitation to give the Lowell Lectures, Holmes was at a frustrating point in his professional life. He turned thirty-eight the year the invitation came, and he had been pursuing a variety of legal projects for the previous thirteen years. In addition to practicing law in Boston, he had published several scholarly articles and written a number of book notes, digests of reports of cases, and commentaries in the *American Law Review*. He had edited the twelfth edition of James Kent's famous legal treatise *Commentaries on American Law*, to which he also contributed a set of new annotations. He had served as an editor of *The American Law Review* and offered two lecture courses at Harvard College. In short, he had fol-

---

[6] Quoted in Howe, "Introduction," p. xi.

lowed the prescription he laid down for himself in a diary entry in 1866: "immerse myself in the law completely," which "a man must [do] . . . if he would be a first rate lawyer."[7]

Holmes's friends and colleagues were aware of the intensity and single-mindedness with which Holmes approached his professional pursuits. In 1869 John C. Ropes, a fellow Boston practitioner and one of the founders of the *American Law Review*, said that his contemporaries "had never known of anyone in the law who studied anything like as hard" as Holmes did, and the mother of William and Henry James, close friends of Holmes at the time, described him as having "a power of work."[8] Arthur Sedgwick, who would become co-editor of the *American Law Review* with Holmes in 1870, wrote to Henry James that year that Holmes "knows more law than anyone in Boston of our time, and works harder at it than anyone."[9] Three years later James's mother, noting that Holmes carried his manuscript on Kent to the dinner table on one occasion, observed: "His pallid face, and this fearful grip on his work, make him a melancholy sight."[10] By 1876 William James was describing Holmes as "a powerful battery, formed like a planing machine to gouge a deep self-beneficial groove through life."[11]

The intensity of Holmes's engagement with legal scholarship had deep roots. By the time he had enrolled in Harvard Law School at the age of twenty-three, a series of experiences had prompted him to search for an overriding philosophical perspective on his chosen profession, and on the universe in general. Those experiences had begun in the spring of his senior year at Harvard College, when he enlisted in a regiment of Massachusetts volunteer soldiers after the Civil War broke out. In the summer of 1861, having graduated from Harvard, he secured a commission in the Union Army and fought in active service, mainly as an infantry officer, until July 1864, when he declined to re-enlist for another three years and was honorably discharged. He was wounded three times in action, in the chest, neck, and foot, and spent about a third of his military service recu-

---

[7] Holmes, Jr., diary entry, November 24, 1866, Oliver Wendell Holmes Papers, Microfilm Edition, University Publications, 1985. Further references to the Holmes Papers are to the Microfilm edition. The originals are in the Harvard Law School Archives.

[8] William James to Henry Bowditch (quoting John C. Ropes), May 22, 1869, quoted in Ralph Barton Perry, *The Thought and Character of William James, as Revealed in Unpublished Correspondence and Notes, Together with His Published Writings*, 2 vols. (Boston: Little, Brown, 1935), vol. 1, p. 297; Mrs. Henry James, Sr., to Henry James, Jr., August 8, 1869, James Papers, Harvard University Archives.

[9] Arthur Sedgwick to Henry James, Jr., January 30, 1870, James Papers.

[10] Mary James (Mrs. Henry James, Sr.) to Henry James, Jr., February 28, 1873, quoted in Perry, *The Thought and Character of William James*, vol. 1, p. 58.

[11] William James to Henry James, Jr., July 5, 1876, quoted in ibid., p. 371.

perating from those injuries. By the time he left his regiment, nearly all his close friends had been killed, wounded, or transferred to other units.

Holmes had enlisted in the army under the influence of some close friends at Harvard who were abolitionists, and because he believed that fighting for a noble cause, such as antislavery, was a chivalric ideal. As late as April 1864, Holmes was referring to the war as "the Christian Crusade of the 19th century," fought on behalf of "the cause of the whole civilized world."[12] But a month later he told his parents that if he survived the remainder of his enlistment he would not return to service. He had come to believe that there was no clear connection between the ideals that might motivate soldiers and the arbitrary realities of wartime service. "I can do a disagreeable thing or face a great danger coolly enough when I *know* it is a duty," he wrote to his mother after resolving to leave the army, "but a doubt demoralizes me as it does any nervous man." "I am not the same man," he had written to his parents in May of that year. "[I] may not have the same ideas."[13]

The Civil War had been a deeply unsettling experience for Holmes and his generation. In the years between Holmes's birth in 1841 and the time he entered Harvard in 1857, the territory and population of the United States had grown significantly; the railroad and the telegraph had revolutionized long-distance transportation and communication; and American writers and artists had begun to attract international as well as national audiences. Holmes's father, who became editor of the *Atlantic Monthly* in 1857 and began to publish his highly popular "Autocrat of the Breakfast Table" stories in that journal, seemed to be at the very center of an American renaissance in which highbrow literature and the arts would become popularized on a large scale. The unique abundance of the American continent, and the geographic isolation of the United States from war-torn Europe, seemed to guarantee a promising future for Americans of Holmes's generation. The last major conflict involving the United States, the Mexican War, had ended in 1848, with the United States gaining more than a million square miles of territory, stretching from Texas to Oregon. American culture seemed to be opening up in all directions.

But as Holmes's undergraduate years came to a close, the continued existence of a union of American states suddenly seemed precarious. Instead of anticipating a leisurely, comfortable transition from college to a career in Boston, Holmes found himself, in his senior year at Harvard,

---

[12] Oliver Wendell Holmes, Jr., to Charles Eliot Norton, April 17, 1864, Holmes Papers.
[13] Oliver Wendell Holmes, Jr., to Amelia Jackson Holmes, June 7, 1864; and Oliver Wendell Holmes, Jr., to Dr. and Mrs. Oliver Wendell Holmes, Sr., May 30, 1864, Holmes Papers.

serving as a bodyguard for the abolitionist Wendell Phillips, whose anti-slavery speeches in Boston had been met with threats of violence. That commitment led Holmes to others, and instead of emerging from Harvard as a young Boston intellectual, pursuing literature, philosophy, and the choice of a profession, he had become a soldier and, eventually, a "demor-alized" and "nervous" one. Even the chivalric ideal of an antislavery crusade had not sustained him in the face of seemingly purposeless and random death. Lewis Einstein, a diplomat who had a long correspondence with Holmes in the first three decades of the twentieth century, recalled Holmes's once telling him that "after the Civil War the world never seemed quite right again."[14]

As the war ended, Holmes's generation struggled to reconcile Darwin-ist-inspired "scientific" explanations of change in the universe with belief in a basic moral order. They hoped that adherence to traditional moral and religious values would counter what now appeared to be the inevitable tendency of societies to be in a constant evolutionary state. Just as they began to internalize the Darwinist insight that the history of a civilization might be best described as a continuous progression of qualitative change, they were confronted with the first signs of modernity in American soci-ety. Against a cultural backdrop of advancing industrial capitalism, in-creased participatory democracy, and the weakening of a hierarchical class-based social order, they thus considered the potential displacement of religious-based theories of causation in the universe by theories based on the natural sciences. In this setting intellectuals of Holmes's generation struggled to fashion comprehensive secularized theories of knowledge that could help them make sense of a new and unsettling cultural experience.[15]

In an autobiographical sketch Holmes had written for his Harvard Col-lege album in July 1861, he stated, "If I survive the war, I expect to study law as my profession or at least as a starting point."[16] When he returned from the war in the summer of 1864, his commitment seems to have wa-vered, and he did not immediately take to the study of law. Harvard Law School at the time had no admissions standards and no examinations: its only requirement for a degree was periodic attendance at lectures. After three semesters Holmes stopped doing even that, attaching himself to the

---

[14] Lewis Einstein, "Introduction," in James B. Peabody, ed., *The Holmes-Einstein Letters: Correspon-dence of Mr. Justice Holmes and Lewis Einstein, 1903-1935* (New York: St. Martin's, 1964), p. xvi.

[15] For more detail on the "crisis of intellectual authority" in post-Civil War America, see Doro-thy Ross, *The Origins of American Social Science* (New York: Cambridge University Press, 1991), pp. 53-59.

[16] Harvard College, *Class of 1861 Album*, Harvard University Archives, quoted in Frederick C. Fiechter, Jr., "The Preparation of an American Aristocrat," 6 New Eng. Q. 5 (1933).

law office of a friend in January 1866 and "look[ing] up some cases."[17] Harvard still awarded him a degree in June 1866. In 1870 Holmes would describe the law school he had attended as "almost a disgrace to the Commonwealth of Massachusetts," an institution that had "[done] something every year to injure the profession . . . and to discourage real students."[18]

Between 1866 and 1868 Holmes remained interested in philosophical issues, maintaining a close friendship with William James and participating in "a philosophical society" that met regularly to discuss "the tallest and broadest questions" of metaphysics.[19] Holmes had earlier written to James that he had come to the "conviction" that "law . . . may be approached in the interests of science and may be studied . . . with the preservation of one's ideals."[20] Approaching law "in the interests of science" precipitated his ventures in legal editing, lecturing, and writing as well as in law practice in the 1870s. The idea of extracting the fundamental principles of the common law in America and placing them in some kind of "scientific" order remained at the back of his thoughts. It was as if Holmes viewed his efforts to order fields of legal knowledge as a chastened substitute for the chivalric ideals that had lost intelligibility for him in the carnage of the Civil War.

Holmes explained the intensity of his professional pursuits in an 1879 letter to James Bryce, an English legal scholar with whom he shared an interest in jurisprudential issues. "The men here who really care more for a fruitful thought than for a practical success are few everywhere," he wrote.

> I wish that the necessity of making a living didn't preclude any choice on my part — for I hate business and dislike practice apart from arguing cases . . . As it is I console myself by studying toward a vanishing point which is the center of perspective in my landscape — but that has to be done at night for the most part and is wearing, and my articles though fragmentary in form and accidental in order are part of what lies in a whole in my mind — my scheme to analyze what seem

---

[17] Holmes, diary entry, September 27, 1866, Holmes Papers.

[18] [Holmes], "Harvard Law School," 5 Am. L. Rev. 177 (1870). Holmes kept copies of bound volumes of the *American Law Review* beginning in 1868, and identified the unsigned notes or comments he had written. See Novick, *The Collected Works of Justice Holmes*, vol. 1, pp. 182-183.

[19] William James to Oliver Wendell Holmes, Jr., January 3, 1868, Holmes Papers. This discussion group should not be confused with the "Metaphysical Club," which was formed in January 1872 by the philosophers Chauncey Wright, Charles Pierce, William James, and Holmes. See Henry James, Jr., to Elizabeth Boott, January 24, 1872, in Leon Edel, ed., *The Letters of Henry James*, 4 vols. (Cambridge, Mass.: Belknap Press of Harvard University Press, 1974-1984), p. 269.

[20] Oliver Wendell Holmes, Jr., to William James, April 19, 1868, Holmes Papers.

to me the fundamental notions and principles of our substantive law, putting them in an order which is a part of or results from the fundamental conceptions.[21]

The Lowell Institute invitation would give Holmes a chance to pursue that scheme. The timing of the invitation, given Holmes's state of mind when he wrote to Bryce, might have been thought almost miraculous, but it was also awkward. The Lowell Institute course of lectures consisted of twelve sessions, given on Tuesday and Friday evenings in the months of November and December: Holmes's invitation was for the 1880 series, and since he wrote an entry in one of his notebooks for that year indicating that he had begun writing the lectures "about Jan. 1," one may surmise that the invitation did not come before the fall of 1879 at the earliest.[22] In June 1880, Holmes wrote to Pollock that his evenings had been "largely devoted to preparing a course of lectures for next winter."[23] Later, after the lectures were published as *The Common Law*, he sent Pollock a copy and noted that he had "failed in all correspondence and . . . abandoned pleasure as well as a good deal of sleep for a year" to produce the lectures.[24]

Despite the pressure that writing the lectures placed on Holmes, the invitation to synthesize the ideas he had been developing about law came at a felicitous time. He had been struggling since entering law school with a concern he was to describe much later in his life: how to reconcile the apparently prosaic and unorganized details of legal study with his interest in developing a scientific or philosophical — words he used as synonyms — approach to a field of knowledge. "When I began," Holmes wrote in 1913, "the law presented itself as a ragbag of details. . . . It was not without anguish that one asked oneself whether the subject was worthy of the interest of an intelligent man."[25] By the late 1870s he had concluded that law could open the way to philosophy, and he began the process of developing a wide-ranging jurisprudential perspective.

• • • •

---

[21] Holmes to James Bryce, August 17, 1879, Holmes Papers.

[22] That diary entry is quoted in Eleanor Little, "The Early Reading of Justice Oliver Wendell Holmes," 8 Harvard Library Bulletin 163, 202 (1954). Little's article was based on notebooks in the Holmes Papers in which Holmes listed the titles of books he had read in particular years.

[23] Oliver Wendell Holmes to Frederick Pollock, June 17, 1880, in Mark DeWolfe Howe, ed., *Holmes-Pollock Letters: The Correspondence of Mr. Justice Holmes and Sir Frederick Pollock, 1874-1932*, 2 vols. (Cambridge, Mass.: Harvard University Press, 1941), vol. 1, p. 14.

[24] Holmes to Pollock, March 5, 1881, ibid., p. 16.

[25] Oliver Wendell Holmes, "Introduction to the General Survey by European Authors in the Continental Legal Historical Series," in *Collected Legal Papers* (New York: Harcourt, Brace, 1921), pp. 298, 301-302.

Holmes's *Common Law* lectures, in the main, consisted of historical surveys of common law fields, in which Holmes charted the course of doctrine. Those surveys were designed to arrange common law subjects in a "philosophically continuous series."[26] Holmes wanted not only to trace the evolution of doctrine but also to "reconsider the popular reasons" on which doctrinal rules had been justified, and "to decide anew whether those reasons are satisfactory."[27] The result of his simultaneous attention to history and to the public policy implications of doctrine, he believed, would reveal the defining architecture of common law fields.

Holmes had some normative goals embedded in his approach, and he made no bones about them. His historical overviews were designed to reveal the unarticulated "views of public policy" undergirding established doctrinal rules, thereby freeing up those rules for re-examination.[28] He intended to "prove," he noted at the end of the first chapter of *The Common Law*, "that by the very necessity of its nature, [law] is continually transmuting [subjective] moral standards into external or objective ones, from which the actual guilt of the party concerned is wholly eliminated."[29]

The law was constantly evolving in the direction not only of establishing external and objective standards of liability, Holmes announced, but also of limiting the scope of liability as far as possible. Socially useful activities that injured others were to be subjected to liability only when they were, from the point of view of the community, intentionally or foreseeably dangerous.[30] The purpose of the criminal law was to deter antisocial conduct by identifying "blameworthy" behavior from an external point of view, rather than focusing on the motives of criminals.[31] Contract law reduced itself to a simple, universal proposition. Once a contract had been made, the promisor had the option of fulfilling the contract or "pay[ing] damages if the promised event does not come to pass." Whether a contract had been made, and whether it had been breached, were to be determined by objective and external standards. Damages for a breach of contract were limited to what reasonable persons would think its ordinary consequences.[32]

Holmes's methodology in *The Common Law* has alternately frustrated

---

[26] Holmes, *The Common Law*, p. 119. All page references are to the present edition.
[27] Ibid., p. 36.
[28] Ibid.
[29] Ibid.
[30] Ibid., p. 147.
[31] Ibid., pp. 46, 48.
[32] Ibid., p. 271.

modern readers or made them suspicious. In an age in which the view that historical scholarship primarily exists to "prove" the universality of prevailing contemporary values has largely been discarded, readers have become inclined to react skeptically toward the historical findings of work conducted in that vein. As a result, Holmes's historical exegesis in *The Common Law* has ceased to be regarded as presumptively persuasive and become, to many, simply bewildering. Some modern readers have been tempted to conclude that Holmes was reading his historical sources purposively, finding in them support for arranging legal subjects around theories of liability that he found congenial. Thus readers of *The Common Law* today, while noting some of its elegant language, have had difficulty empathizing with Holmes's methodological perspective. To surmount that difficulty, we must revisit Holmes's efforts, in his scholarship leading up to *The Common Law*, to derive an overarching jurisprudential point of view, and to connect those efforts to the intellectual and cultural predicament in which Holmes and his contemporaries found themselves in the decades after the Civil War.

By the time he wrote *The Common Law*, Holmes had identified three variables that, in his view, combined to shape the evolution of common law fields. "We must alternately consult history and existing theories of legislation," he announced, and "understand the combination of the two into new products at every stage." Determining the "combination" of the first two variables was the "most difficult labor" his approach required, and it was the most important.[33] It had taken him some time to recognize this.

None of the variables Holmes identified as central elements of his perspective in *The Common Law* had received emphasis in his first efforts at legal scholarship. In those works he had been preoccupied with constructing "arrangements of the law" that might be sufficiently comprehensive to organize, in some kind of philosophical order, the "ragbag of details" he had encountered in his early legal studies. Holmes's interest in organizing legal fields into philosophically integrated "arrangements" can be seen as part of a more general intellectual search for order that preoccupied American scholars after the Civil War.

As noted, Holmes had mustered out of the Civil War in an unsettled intellectual state, hoping to find some way of organizing knowledge and ordering experience in the methodologies of philosophy and natural science. But he had difficulty, in his early years as a scholar, finding the basis for an overarching philosophical organization of legal subjects. He found

---

[33] Ibid., p. 3.

no basis for constructing a scientific classification of legal subjects in the writ system,[34] in Austin's view that the law emanated from the command of a sovereign,[35] or in a conception of law that emphasized rights.[36] He also rejected the codification of common law fields, believing that codified principles could not fully resolve new cases, and "it is the merit of the common law that it decides the cases first and determines the principle afterwards."[37]

Between 1870 and 1873, he explored the idea that "a sound classification of the law" might be achieved by constructing arrangements of legal subjects "based on *duties* and not on *rights*."[38] In three articles written in that period he identified different types of duties and produced analytical tables outlining their nature and scope.[39] But he soon discovered areas of the law that did not seem consistent with a duty-based arrangement. After failing to explain them, he concluded, in 1878, that the term "duty" was "open to objection," and he abandoned the effort.[40]

By then Holmes had become interested in three other bases from which common law fields might be arranged in a "philosophically continuous series." One was the idea that law might best be described as a compilation of the recurrent sources on which judges grounded their decisions. As early as 1872 Holmes had remarked that "in a civilized state" it was "not

---

[34] "If the [common law writs] had been based upon a comprehensive survey of the field of rights and duties," Holmes wrote in 1871, "so that they embodied in a practical shape a classification of the law, with a form of action to correspond to every substantial duty," they might be the basis for a scientific arrangement of the law. "But they are in fact so arbitrary in character . . . that nothing keeps them but our respect for the sources of our jurisprudence." [Holmes], Notice of John Townshend, *The Code of Procedure of the State of New York, as Amended to 1870*, 5 Am. L. Rev. 359 (1871).

[35] In a notice of Frederick Pollock's article "Law and Command" in the April 1, 1872, issue of *The Law Magazine and Review*, Holmes said that "Austin's definition was not satisfactory from a philosophical point of view," because "there might be law without sovereignty, and . . . where there is a sovereign, properly so called, other bodies not sovereign might generate law in a philosophical sense against the will of the sovereign." [Holmes], 6 Am. L. Rev. 723-24 (1872).

[36] In 1872 Holmes wrote that in his "Codes, and Arrangements of the Law" article, written two years earlier, he had "expressed the opinion that a sound classification of the law was impossible" on the basis of "the derivative notion, *rights*." He reaffirmed that view. Holmes, "The Arrangement of the Law-Privity," 7 Am. L. Rev. 46 (1872).

[37] Holmes, "Codes, and Arrangements of the Law," 5 Am. L. Rev. 1 (1870).

[38] Ibid., 3. Italics in original.

[39] The articles were "Codes, and Arrangements of the Law," "The Arrangement of the Law-Privity," and "The Theory of Torts," 7 Am. L. Rev. 652 (1873).

[40] Holmes's first inclination was that duties to persons in particular situations could be determined by focusing on the identities of the persons. But then he realized that the same duties might extend to other persons, such as heirs or successors of the original persons. This led him to investigate the concept of privity. See "The Arrangement of the Law-Privity," 47-52. See also Holmes, "Possession," 12 Am. L. Rev. 688, 692 (1878).

the will of the sovereign that makes lawyers' law . . . but what . . . the judges, by whom it is enforced, *say* is his will." Thus "the only question for the lawyer is, how will the judges act?" Any source on which judges based their decisions, "be it constitution, statute, custom, or precedent, which can be relied upon as likely in the generality of cases to prevail, is worthy of consideration as one of the sources of law."[41] The critical portion of that sentence was "which can be relied upon as likely in the generality of cases to prevail." Holmes was suggesting that an examination of judicial decisions over time might unearth the general principles judges repeatedly identified as governing cases in a common law field.

At the time he made that comment, Holmes was in the process of reading and digesting numerous cases in his work on the twelfth edition of Kent's *Commentaries*. He had decided that his principal contribution to the edition would come through annotations of recent cases in common law fields that Kent had covered. He prepared extensive notes on those of Kent's topics that were "the present fighting grounds of the law," such as the history of property in land, vicarious liability, easements, covenants running with the land, and warranty in the law of sales.[42] Holmes engaged in extensive surveys of the relevant cases for the topics in question, compiling the various rationales on which judges grounded results in those cases. Here was evidence that the law itself might simply be a composite of the rationales that were most regularly advanced.

But Holmes had noticed something else during his research for Kent's work. He had observed that on many occasions an established legal doctrine was followed even though the original rationale on which it had been based was no longer regarded as sensible. In such instances the original rationale was not emphasized, and a "formal" reason for following the doctrine, such as fidelity to precedent, was advanced instead. But the formal reason was not the true basis for following the established doctrine: the true basis was that it was attractive from the standpoint of contemporary public policy. Eventually Holmes was to describe this phenomenon as "the paradox of form and substance in the development of law."[43] He would identify it as the second basis on which a comprehensive ordering of com-

---

[41] Holmes, Book Notice of *The Law Magazine and Review* (No. 3, April 1, 1872), 6 Am. L. Rev. 723, 724 (1872).

[42] Holmes to John Norton Pomeroy, May 22, 1872, Holmes Papers. For Holmes's notes on those topics, see James Kent, *Commentaries on American Law*, ed. Oliver Wendell Holmes, Jr., 12th ed., 4 vols. (Boston: Little, Brown, 1873): vol. 2, pp. 260, 479; vol. 3, p. 419; vol. 4, pp. 441, 480.

[43] Holmes first used the phrase in "Common Carriers and the Common Law," 13 Am. L. Rev. 609, 630 (1879).

mon law subjects might be erected. His elucidation of that paradox would stimulate him to articulate the core, defining elements of his jurispruden-tial perspective.

That articulation would not come until just before Holmes delivered the *Common Law* lectures. Between the completion of his work on Kent and his subsequent explorations of the paradox of form and substance in judicial decisions, Holmes would explore a third basis on which to con-struct a scientific classification of common law fields. That basis was his-tory. Between 1873, when he completed his edition of Kent and re-entered law practice on a full-time basis, and 1876, when he next pub-lished a scholarly article in the *American Law Review*, Holmes began to read widely in history sources. The titles he noted in his reading lists between 1873 and 1876 included works in ancient and medieval history and an-thropology, as well as more than fifty books on legal history. His lists re-vealed a particular interest in works on "primitive" societies, particularly their legal systems. Holmes was approaching history in the same fashion as many of his late-nineteenth-century contemporaries, attempting to show that the evolution of cultures over time confirmed the primacy of certain universal political principles, or demonstrated the inevitable progression from "primitive" to "civilized" stages of development. He was, at this stage, a Darwinist historian.[44]

Holmes initially anticipated using history "to prove," as he put it in an 1877 article titled "Primitive Notions in Modern Law," the soundness of general observations about law he had "arrived at analytically" in the arti-cles in which he had proposed "arrangements" of legal subjects.[45] But his forays in history did not necessarily reinforce those general observations. Historical surveys revealed the existence of common law doctrines that could not be accounted for in Holmes's duty-based classifications. One was a doctrine that allowed even a person who had wrongfully displaced a landowner holding an easement through the land of a neighbor to prevent anyone else, except the neighbor, from obstructing the easement. "How comes it," Holmes asked, "that one who neither has possession [of the right of way] nor title [to it] is so far favored?"[46]

---

[44] For a discussion of "evolutionary" methodologies in late nineteenth-century German scholar-ship, see Mathias Reimann, "Holmes' *Common Law* and German Legal Science," in Robert W. Gordon, ed., *The Legacy of Oliver Wendell Holmes, Jr.* (Stanford, Calif.: Stanford University Press, 1992). For comparable tendencies among American scholars, see Ross, *The Origins of American Social Science*, pp. 53-67.

[45] Holmes, "Primitive Notions in Modern Law, No. II," 11 Am. L. Rev. 641 (1877).

[46] Ibid., 654.

His answer to that question would eventually provide the critical element of his jurisprudential perspective, the recognition that history and unarticulated theories of public policy were constantly interacting in the doctrinal development of common law fields. An examination of historical sources led him to the conclusion that in ancient and medieval times inanimate objects, such as land, were personified in the language of legal decisions and commentary. Although the sources stopped short of treating estates as legal persons, land was nonetheless described in "personifying metaphors," such as the common statement that a "right of way" was "a quality of . . . a neighboring piece of land." Just as when "an axe was made the object of criminal process," the language of personifying land "survived . . . to create confusion in reasoning."[47]

That confusion resulted in easements in land being treated as if they were "owned" by the land itself, so that even people who wrongfully acquired titles to lands gained control of the easements that went with them.

But why, once the idea of inanimate objects possessing human qualities was abandoned, did this doctrine survive? Holmes concluded that "where a thing incapable of rights has been treated as if capable of them," it was "either by confusion of thought" or "on grounds of policy."[48] Even though the doctrine extending prescriptive easements to wrongful possessors had resulted from abandoned anthropomorphic conceptions of land, it had survived because it facilitated the quieting of land titles. Possessors of land were presumed to succeed to easements "running" with that land even when their possession might have been unauthorized. This prevented the question of who could enjoy, or not enjoy, rights of way across adjoining land from arising every time a parcel of land with an easement changed hands. A Darwinist approach, designed to reveal the survival of some legal doctrines and the extinction of others, had been modified to take into account the continued existence of doctrines whose "fitness" rested on unarticulated grounds of policy.

Holmes's identification of the paradox of form and substance in the development of the law was an example of the "difficult labor" involved in juxtaposing history with what he called "existing theories of legislation" at every stage of the evolution of common law fields. By the time he wrote *The Common Law*, Holmes was able to articulate that insight in general terms. "In order to know what [the law] is," he declared, "we must know what it has been, and what it tends to become," and to "understand the

---

[47] Ibid., 654-55.
[48] Ibid., 660.

combination of the two into new products at every stage." His methodology was designed to illustrate that "the substance of the law at any given time pretty nearly corresponds . . . with what is then understood to be convenient," but "its form and machinery, and the degree to which it is able to work out desired results, depends very much on its past."[49] Holmes had concluded, as he put it in the last scholarly work he published before the *Common Law* lectures, that "the law finds its philosophy in history and the nature of human needs."[50]

Holmes's methodology allowed one to consider simultaneously, in the course of engaging in historical surveys of legal doctrine, historical evidence and issues of contemporary policy. If one traced doctrine looking for logical consistency, "failure and confusion" would often result, because "precedents survive . . . long after the use they once served is at an end, and the reason for them has been forgotten."[51] If the "reason for them" was historically based it could be identified, as Holmes had done in his discussion of easements. If, however, doctrines survived as a result of unarticulated grounds of public policy, they could be "consider[ed] . . . with a freedom that was not possible before" their historical basis had been exposed.[52] The methodology thus enabled scholars to investigate the development of common law doctrine both as historians and as students of contemporary public policy. And that was just what Holmes did in *The Common Law*, merging his surveys of the historical development of common law doctrine with his goals of organizing common law subjects around external standards of liability and limiting the scope of that liability as far as possible.

We are now in a position to understand, from the point of view of its author, the celebrated passage with which Holmes began *The Common Law*. The passage reads:

> The object of this book is to present a general view of the Common Law. To accomplish this task, other tools are needed besides logic. It is something to show that the consistency of a system requires a particular result, but it is not all. The life of the law has not been logic: it has been experience. The felt necessities of the times, the prevalent moral and political theories, intuitions of public policy, avowed or

---

[49] *The Common Law*, p. 4.
[50] Holmes, Book Notice of C. C. Langdell, *A Selection of Cases on the Law of Contracts, with a Summary of the Topics covered by the Cases*, 2nd. ed., 2 vols. (1879); and William R. Anson, *Principles of the English Law of Contract* (1879), 14 Am. L. Rev. 233, 234 (1880).
[51] Holmes, "Common Carriers and the Common Law," 630.
[52] Ibid., 631.

unconscious, even the prejudices which judges share with their fellow-men, have had a good deal more to do than the syllogism in determining the rules by which men should be governed. The law embodies the story of a nation's development through many centuries, and it cannot be dealt with as if it contained only the axioms and corollaries of a book of mathematics. In order to know what it is, we must know what it has been, and what it tends to become. We must alternately consult history and existing theories of legislation. But the most difficult labor will be to understand the combination of the two into different products at every stage. The substance of the law at any given time pretty nearly corresponds, so far as it goes, with what is then understood to be convenient; but its form and machinery, and the degree to which it is able to work out desired results, depend very much upon its past.[53]

Because of Holmes's juxtaposition of the tool of "logic" with that of understanding "experience," and because of his apparently slighting references to "the syllogism" and "the axioms and corollaries" of mathematics, the passage has regularly been taken as an attack on jurists who sought, as Holmes put it in an earlier comment, to "reduce the concrete details of [the] existing [common law] system to the merely logical consequence of simple postulates." Holmes had suggested that such an approach was "always in danger of becoming unscientific, and of leading to a misapprehension of the nature of the problem and the data," and he had identified Christopher Columbus Langdell, the dean of Harvard Law School, as being "entirely . . . interested in the formal connections of things, or logic, as distinguished from the feelings which make the content of logic, and which have actually shaped the substance of the law."[54]

The Holmes-Langdell juxtaposition, pitting "logic" against "experience," has been a tempting story. But the above passage from *The Common Law* does not rule out "logic" as a useful tool for understanding the development of common law subjects. It only states that "other tools" are needed as well. "It is something to show that the consistency of a system requires a particular result," Holmes wrote in the passage. He had sought to do just that in his early "arrangements" of legal subjects. Nor was he uninterested in the syllogistic reasoning that common law judges regularly employed in applying established principles to new cases. He wanted to probe that reasoning, to identify the "feelings which make the content of logic."

---

[53] *The Common Law*, pp. 3-4.
[54] Holmes, Book Notice of Langdell and Anson, 234.

Next in the passage came alternative descriptions of what Holmes meant by "experience," which he had called "the life of the law." Experience included "[t]he felt necessities of the time," "prevalent moral and political theories," "intuitions of public policy, avowed or unconscious," and even "the prejudices which judges share with their fellowmen." Those sentences have caused twentieth- and twenty-first century devotees of Holmes to hail him for recognizing that common law judicial decisions can be seen as exercises in public policy undertaken by humans with their culturally driven prejudices. Holmes may have had more modest goals in writing the sentences. They reasserted his view that the common law could best be understood as a composite of the rationales judges used to ground the results they reached in cases, and pointed out several sources of those rationales that tended not to be explicitly articulated.

Holmes's point was that the form of legal reasoning adopted by judges often concealed its substance. This led him to suggest that to "know what [the law] is," one needed to get beyond the surface "logic" of decisions and consult history and theories of legislation. That suggestion brought him to the center of his methodology, the simultaneous consultation of those variables in order to understand the paradox of form and substance at the heart of the development of common law fields. It was that simultaneous consultation that ultimately freed the jurist from too single-minded a focus on the law's logical consistency, its history, or its underlying "theories of legislation," and made possible the integration of those variables into a comprehensive "general view" of the common law.

Historians have recognized that Holmes's generation of post-Civil War intellectuals had three abiding concerns, some of which have been mentioned. One was an interest in deriving organizing and stabilizing principles of secularized knowledge in response to the crushing influence of the war on early nineteenth-century religious-based versions of romanticism and idealism. A second was enthusiasm for the promise of science — notably the natural sciences — for developing theories and techniques for making sense of the universe. A third was a willingness to embrace the idea of history as qualitative change, so that the course of a culture's development could be seen, not as a cyclical process of birth, maturity, and decay, but as a constant progression in which the future was always an improvement on the past.[55] One can see all those aspirations in the per-

---

[55] In addition to Ross, *The Origins of American Social Science*, pp. 58-67, see George Frederickson, *The Inner Civil War: Northern Intellectuals and the Crisis of the Union* (New York: Harper and Row, 1965), pp. 79-112; and Edmund Wilson, *Patriotic Gore: Studies in the Literature of the American Civil War* (New York: Oxford University Press, 1962), pp. 743-796.

spective on American jurisprudence that Holmes offered in *The Common Law*. His methodology was secularized, "scientific" in the late nineteenth-century sense, historicist, and in search of a comprehensive general approach to the common law.

• • • •

The enduring feature of *The Common Law* is not the way Holmes presents his history, nor the policy conclusions he draws from it. Both those features demonstrate the time-boundedness of the work. But a third feature transcends time: Holmes's recognition that exploring the relationship between history, the formal "logic" of justifications for legal decisions, and the unarticulated cultural assumptions that help shape those decisions captures the essence of common law judging in America.

Common law judging is a product of both "external" and "internal" factors, and it cannot adequately be understood without attention to the way those factors interact in the formation of a judicial decision. The external factors lie in the culture in which judicial decisions are situated, emerging in the form of unarticulated "intuitions," "prejudices," and avowed and unconscious "motives of public policy" that emanate from that culture. The internal factors lie in the fact that judicial decisions require formal justifications which emphasize legal doctrine, and that those justifications seek to create a "logic" emphasizing governing doctrinal rules deemed to be apposite to the decision. In any judicial decision, at any point in time, the external and internal factors influencing it will be different, and in different combination. Holmes's point is that they will always be there and that history helps us understand their different combinations. To understand their interaction in a given case is to understand the decision in that case in a broad and deep fashion; and to understand their interaction in a number of cases, across time, is to understand, in a comparable fashion, how the common law develops.

We can think of all common law cases as simultaneously raising the imperatives of continuity with the past, of logical consistency with existing doctrine, and of a search for a "just result," that is, one in conformity with "prevailing moral theories" and current "intuitions of public policy." Thinking about common law judging in that fashion, we can see how Holmes's explanation of judicial decision-making highlights the incentives for common law judges to emphasize formal legal rationales for their decisions and to de-emphasize "what is then understood to be convenient," according to the unarticulated social and political assumptions of the age.

The paradox of form and substance exists in the common law because judges are not supposed to be deciding cases on the basis of their intuitions and "prejudices" about matters of public policy, even if those intuitions and prejudices are widely shared by other actors in the culture at the time. Judges, who are typically not as directly accountable to the public as elected officials, are supposed to be putting aside their idiosyncratic human reactions so as to decide cases impartially and neutrally. The fact that judges are not fully able to do that does not mean that they should not try. The ideal of a "rule of law," transcendent of human will and power, is bound up in that aspiration.

The perspective Holmes adopted in *The Common Law* captures the interplay between the aspirations for judicial behavior in a culture committed to the rule of law and the way the process of deciding cases actually plays out. The "form and machinery" of legal decisions and "the degree to which [established doctrine] is able to work out desired results" depend upon the past, because it is from the past that established precedents are drawn, and those precedents can be employed as "formal" signals that a judge's decision is based on the rule of law, not on that judge's prejudices or intuitions. And yet those prejudices and intuitions, understood as reflections of the "felt necessities of the times" and of "prevalent moral and political decisions," are helping drive the decision. *Helping* drive it, not fully driving it. The decision, Holmes suggests, will be a complex product of both form and substance.

Looking simultaneously at history, doctrine and its logical arrangements, and the messages of contemporary culture as they emerge in the form of prevalent moral and political theories takes us to the very center of judicial decision-making. No better description of judge-fashioned law, still the primary element of American jurisprudence, has been made. No more serviceable set of variables for studying the course of the development of that law in America has been put forth. Holmes managed to capture, in his elliptical, suggestive fashion, the trade-offs judges make in common law cases; why judicial opinions tend more in the direction of concealing rather than revealing those trade-offs; and why that understanding of common law judging can best be grasped by comparing judicial opinions across time.

Thus readers have good reasons to continue to tackle *The Common Law*, even if some of the detail on its pages is initially off-putting. Once they extrapolate the historical origins, and contemporary utility, of Holmes's perspective, that detail will prove less inaccessible.

"The Little Boy—They say that with a little practice at catching hot balls I'll be a wonder." The image of baseball and antitrust in 1901, courtesy of cartoonist Frederick Opper and publisher William Randolph Hearst. This was not Hearst's only contribution to baseball. When Ernest Lawrence Thayer wrote the poem "Casey at the Bat" in 1888, Hearst published it in his *San Francisco Examiner*. See Ernest L. Thayer, Casey at the Bat, S.F. Examiner, June 3, 1888, at 4.

MAY

OLD JUDGE CIGARETTES Goodwin & Co., New York.

WILLIAM BUCKINGHAM (BUCK) EWING

Defendant, *Metropolitan Exhibition Co. v. Ewing*, 42 F. 198 (C.C.N.Y. 1890).
See Death of "Buck" Ewing: At One Time the Greatest Catcher in the Country,
N.Y. TIMES, Oct. 21, 1906.

❧ MAY ❧

SUN	MON	TUES	WED	THUR	FRI	SAT
30	31					1
2	3	4	5	6	7	8
9	10	11	12	13	14	15
16	17	18	19	20	21	22
23	24	25	26	27	28	29

BUCHMEIER V. UNITED STATES

581 F.3d 561 (7th Cir. 2009) (en banc)

Frank H. Easterbrook[†]

Shane Buchmeier was sentenced as an armed career criminal following four firearms convictions: two for possessing firearms despite a prior felony conviction, 18 U.S.C. § 922(g)(1), and two for receiving stolen firearms, § 922(j). His sentence of 188 months' imprisonment is within the 480-month maximum for these crimes. (Each conviction carries a maximum sentence of 10 years, § 924(a)(2)). But the armed career criminal enhancement set a floor of 180 months, § 924(e), and without it Buchmeier might have received a sentence in the Guideline range of 121 to 151 months that would have applied, but for the enhancement.

We affirmed Buchmeier's conviction and sentence on direct appeal. 255 F.3d 415 (7th Cir. 2001). He then filed a collateral attack under 28 U.S.C. § 2255, contending that his lawyer had furnished ineffective assistance by failing to contest the recidivist enhancement. The prosecutor might have replied that solitary errors in the course of an otherwise vigorous and competent defense rarely violate the sixth amendment. See *Strickland v. Washington*, 466 U.S. 668, 695-96 (1984); *Williams v. Lemmon*, 557 F.3d 534 (7th Cir. 2009). Instead of making such a riposte, however, the prosecutor defended the § 924(e) enhancement on the merits. The United States thus has forfeited, if it has not waived, any contention that the overall performance of Buchmeier's lawyer was adequate; it has effectively consented to treating this collateral attack as a rerun of the direct appeal. Given the parties' litigating positions, we proceed to examine the propriety of the recidivist enhancement, without asking whether counsel furnished ineffective assistance. That issue has never been contested, and we

---

[†] Chief Judge, United States Court of Appeals for the Seventh Circuit, joined by Circuit Judges Richard Posner, Michael Kanne, Ilana Rovner, Diane Wood, and Ann Williams. Circuit Judge Diane Sykes dissented, joined by Circuit Judges Daniel Manion, Terence Evans, and John Tinder.

cannot tell how things would have come out on a complete analysis under *Strickland*.

Section 924(e) requires a lengthy sentence for anyone who violates § 922(g) after three convictions for violent felonies or serious drug crimes. Section 924(e)(2)(B) lists the offenses that count as violent felonies. Each must be "punishable by imprisonment for a term exceeding one year" and meet other conditions. One qualifying offense is burglary, and Buchmeier has eight of these on his rap sheet. He now maintains that they do not count because of 18 U.S.C. § 921(a)(20):

> The term "crime punishable by imprisonment for a term exceed-ing one year" does not include —
>
> (A) any Federal or State offenses pertaining to antitrust viola-tions, unfair trade practices, restraints of trade, or other simi-lar offenses relating to the regulation of business practices,
>
> or
>
> (B) any State offense classified by the laws of the State as a misdemeanor and punishable by a term of imprisonment of two years or less.
>
> What constitutes a conviction of such a crime shall be determined in accordance with the law of the jurisdiction in which the pro-ceedings were held. Any conviction which has been expunged, or set aside or for which a person has been pardoned or has had civil rights restored shall not be considered a conviction for purposes of this chapter, unless such pardon, expungement, or restoration of civil rights expressly provides that the person may not ship, transport, possess, or receive firearms.

The hanging paragraph's first sentence tells us that state law governs "[w]hat constitutes a conviction". This countermands *Dickerson v. New Ban-ner Institute, Inc.*, 460 U.S. 103 (1983), which had held that federal law defines "conviction" and that a diversionary disposition in state court is one. The first sentence also means that a pardon or automatic expunge-ment under state law is effective for federal purposes. The hanging para-graph's second sentence is a proviso to the first. It tells us that, no matter what state law provides, a person who has received a "pardon, expunge-ment, or restoration of civil rights" is not treated as convicted for federal purposes "unless such pardon, expungement, or restoration of civil rights expressly provides that the person may not ship, transport, possess, or receive firearms."

Buchmeier relies on the hanging paragraph's second sentence. When his state terms expired, and he was released from all supervision, he received from the Illinois Department of Corrections a notice (applicable to all eight burglaries) reading:

> We have been advised by the field services office of the Stateville Correctional Center that you have completed the maximum of your sentence as of 02/09/1994. On this date, your obligation to the department ceases.

> We are pleased to inform you of the restoration of your right to vote and to hold offices created under the constitution of the state of Illinois. You also have the right to restoration of licenses granted to you under the authority of the state of Illinois if such license was revoked solely as a result of your conviction, unless the licensing authority determines that such restoration would not be in the public interest.

Buchmeier contends that this notice is a "restoration of civil rights" and that, because it does not provide that he "may not ship, transport, possess, or receive firearms", none of the eight burglary convictions meets the definition of a "crime punishable by imprisonment for a term exceeding one year". With these eight convictions erased, Buchmeier no longer has three convictions for violent felonies and cannot properly be sentenced under § 924(e) as an armed career criminal.

Section 921(a)(20) does not say *which* civil rights, if restored, cause a state conviction not to count. We concluded in *United States v. Williams*, 128 F.3d 1128, 1134 (7th Cir. 1997), that three civil rights matter: the rights to vote, to hold office, and to serve on juries. If these are restored, then a conviction does not carry federal firearms disabilities or support a § 924(e) enhancement "unless such pardon, expungement, or restoration of civil rights expressly provides that the person may not ship, transport, possess, or receive firearms." The document that Buchmeier received mentions only two of the three civil rights; it is silent about jury service. As this civil right has not been restored (at least, Buchmeier was not told about its restoration), the district court held that the eight burglary convictions still count for federal purposes. In reaching this conclusion, it relied entirely on *United States v. Gillaum*, 372 F.3d 848, 859-61 (7th Cir. 2004), which holds that, when a pardon, expungement, or other restoration of rights omits one of the "big three" civil rights, there is no need for a firearms reservation. In *Gillaum* the notice said that "rights to vote and administer estates are regained." Nothing there about the right to hold public office or to serve on juries, so Gillaum's convictions still counted for federal recidivist enhancements.

It does not follow from *Gillaum*, however, that a notice counts as a "pardon, expungement, or restoration of civil rights" only if it mentions all three civil rights. Pardons often are unconditional ("full, free, and absolute"); they don't mention any particular rights but come within § 921(a)(20) because they restore *all* civil rights, unless they contain a reservation — and the second sentence of the hanging paragraph says that a firearms reservation must be mentioned expressly. More to the point, there is no need to notify a defendant that a given civil right has been restored, unless it was first taken away. A felony conviction in Illinois suspends a person's right to vote and hold many public offices until the sentence has expired; then these rights are restored automatically. 730 ILCS 5/5-5-5(b), (c). The right to serve on juries, by contrast, is not suspended — though as a practical matter it can't be exercised while a person is in prison. The notice Buchmeier received did not mention his right to serve on juries, because he had never lost it. This means, Buchmeier observes, that when his sentence ended he could again exercise all three of the civil rights commonly lost with a felony conviction. And, as the notice informing him of the rights' restoration did not mention a firearms disability, the eight burglary convictions are removed from the federal calculus.

Logan v. United States, 128 S. Ct. 475 (2007), holds that, if a person never loses *any* of the "big three" civil rights, then they cannot be "restored" for the purpose of the hanging paragraph's second sentence. To restore means to give back. Thus a person who never lost civil rights cannot insist that he be treated the same as a person who lost them, had them restored, and did not receive an "express" warning that the right to possess firearms had not been restored. But Buchmeier did lose civil rights; they could be, and were, "restored" to him; and the document announcing this restoration could have contained (but lacked) a warning that he must not possess firearms. Illinois law forbids felons to possess firearms, unless the Director of the State Police grants a dispensation. 720 ILCS 5/24-1.1(a). Buchmeier's convictions have not been set aside, so this rule applies, though it was not mentioned in the notice telling Buchmeier that his civil rights had been restored.

Questioning by the panel at oral argument implied to counsel that neither *Logan* nor *Gillaum* supports Buchmeier's § 924(e) enhancement. And because, under this circuit's decisions, the "express" notice must be in the document informing the convict of the pardon, expungement, or restoration of civil rights, rather than in the state's statutes at large, the enhancement appeared to be infirm. See, e.g., *United States v. Erwin*, 902 F.2d 510 (7th Cir. 1990); *United States v. Glaser*, 14 F.3d 1213, 1218 (7th Cir.

1994); *Dahler v. United States*, 143 F.3d 1084, 1086-87 (7th Cir. 1998); *United States v. Vitrano*, 405 F.3d 506, 509-10 (7th Cir. 2005). Four other circuits agree with *Erwin*, though a further four disagree and hold that an "express" firearms restriction anywhere in the state's statutes suffices for the hanging paragraph's second sentence. Compare *United States v. Chenowith*, 459 F.3d 635 (5th Cir. 2006); *United States v. Gallaher*, 275 F.3d 784 (9th Cir. 2001); *United States v. Fowler*, 198 F.3d 808 (11th Cir. 1999); and *United States v. Bost*, 87 F.3d 1333 (D.C. Cir. 1996) (all following *Erwin*), with *United States v. McLean*, 904 F.2d 216 (4th Cir. 1990); *United States v. Cassidy*, 899 F.2d 543 (6th Cir. 1990); *United States v. Collins*, 321 F.3d 691 (8th Cir. 2003); and *United States v. Burns*, 934 F.2d 1157 (10th Cir. 1991). See also *Logan*, 128 S.Ct. at 482-83 n. 4 (noting the conflict's existence).

We gave counsel an opportunity to file post-argument briefs to discuss whether this circuit should change sides in the conflict. The United States filed a brief asking us to overrule *Erwin* and its successors. The panel prepared an opinion that was circulated to the full court under Circuit Rule 40(e). A majority of the judges in active service voted to hear the appeal en banc in order to address the status of *Erwin*.

Overruling would not be consistent with a proper regard for the stability of our decisions. *Erwin* was issued 19 years ago and, though its discussion of § 921(a)(20) can be characterized as dictum, its approach became a holding at the first opportunity (*Glaser*) and has been followed ever since. Precedents are not sacrosanct; we have overruled many. But when the issue is closely balanced (the 5 to 4 division among the circuits reveals at least that much), there is less reason to think that a shift will undo rather than create an error. What is more, no circuit can resolve the question with finality. Only Congress or the Supreme Court can accomplish that. When one circuit's overruling would convert a 5-4 conflict into a 4-5 conflict, it is best to leave well enough alone. As so often, it is better that the question "be settled, than that it be settled right." *John R. Sand & Gravel Co. v. United States*, 552 U.S. 130 (2008), quoting from *Burnet v. Coronado Oil & Gas Co.*, 285 U.S. 393, 406 (1932) (Brandeis, J., dissenting). "To overturn a decision settling one such matter simply because we might believe that decision is no longer 'right' would inevitably reflect a willingness to reconsider others. And that willingness could itself threaten to substitute disruption, confusion, and uncertainty for necessary legal stability." 128 S. Ct. at 757.

Any one circuit's restless movement from one side of a conflict to another won't reduce the workload of the Supreme Court. Yet changing sides in one conflict will telegraph a propensity to change sides in others, and that message will induce conscientious lawyers to argue for overruling of circuit precedent whenever there is a conflict. Almost all such requests will prove to be unavailing — for, even apart from *stare decisis*, the fact that a court has reached a conclusion once implies that it will do so again. Litigants rarely would benefit by diverting lawyers' time away from arguments that make the best of circuit law and toward arguments for a change in circuit law. That's why it takes more than argument that a decision is mistaken to justify overruling. See *Tate v. Showboat Marina Casino Partnership*, 431 F.3d 580 (7th Cir. 2005).

Overruling circuit law can be beneficial when the circuit is an outlier and can save work for Congress and the Supreme Court by eliminating a conflict. Even when an overruling does not end the conflict, it might supply a new line of argument that would lead other circuits to change their positions in turn. Finally, overruling is more appropriate when prevailing doctrine works a substantial injury. None of these indicators is present, however. A 5-4 conflict will remain no matter what we do. The United States has not produced a new argument; it simply asks us to agree with a position that was first articulated by the sixth circuit in 1990, and that five circuits already have found wanting. And no one contends that *Erwin* causes a serious, ongoing harm; quite the contrary, its understanding of § 921(a)(20) protects people who might be snookered, by material omissions from governmental documents, into believing that they are *entitled* to possess firearms.

Erwin and its successors treat the second sentence of the hanging paragraph as an anti-mousetrapping provision. On this view the hanging paragraph's first sentence refers to state law for the basic definition of a "conviction," while the second sentence is a federal proviso: Even if a state deems a person "convicted" for purposes of its domestic law, if it sends a document that seems to restore all civil rights the conviction does not count for federal purposes unless the document warns the person about a lingering firearms disability. That is not the only possible reading; four circuits treat the second sentence as an extension of the first sentence's reference to state law, and they look for the "express" reservation not in a document sent to the convicted person but in the whole of the state's statutes. Having given the view of these four circuits a fresh look, we do not think that *Erwin* is so clearly wrong that it must be interred despite the prudential considerations we have mentioned.

If, as the prosecutor contends, a judge must look to the whole of state law, why does the statute tell us to inquire what "such pardon, expungement, or restoration of civil rights expressly provides"? A "pardon" or "restoration of civil rights" differs from "the entirety of state law." Many states remove some convictions from a person's record, or restore some civil rights, after the passage of time, without the need for a pardon or other special dispensation. If a state does this without sending the ex-prisoner a notice, then the final sentence of § 921(a)(20) does not require a firearms reservation; there is no document in which the reservation would be included, no risk that the ex-prisoner will be misled into thinking that he is entitled to possess firearms. But when the state does send a document saying that civil rights have been restored, there is a potential for misunderstanding unless the document "expressly provides that the person may not ship, transport, possess, or receive firearms." *Erwin* gives effect to the entirety of the statute's final sentence; the prosecutor's approach does not, treating the sentence as if it read: "Any conviction which has been expunged, or set aside or for which a person has been pardoned or has had civil rights restored shall not be considered a conviction for purposes of this chapter, unless [state law] expressly provides that the person may not ship, transport, possess, or receive firearms." Replacing "such pardon, expungement, or restoration of civil rights" with "state law" changes the meaning.

Illinois sent Buchmeier a poorly written document. It neglected to inform him that, though the expiration of his sentence restored his rights to vote and hold "constitutional" offices such as Governor, other rights, including entitlement to possess firearms, were not restored. The notice also did not mention that Illinois does not automatically restore a felon's right to hold statutory offices, such as mayor. But the United States has not argued that this omission is significant, so we need not decide whether a firearms reservation is essential in a notice announcing the restoration of the civil right to hold constitutional, but not statutory, public offices.

If someone asks Buchmeier "have you been convicted of a felony?" he must answer "yes"; restoration of civil rights differs from expungement as a matter of Illinois law. But because the state sent Buchmeier a document stating that his principal civil rights have been restored, while neglecting to mention the continuing firearms disability, the final sentence of § 921(a)(20) means that his burglary convictions do not count for federal purposes. He is entitled to be resentenced.

Ty Cobb (left) and Joe Jackson (right), circa 1913.

INTRODUCTION
TO ELIOT ASINOV'S *EIGHT MEN OUT*

Alan M. Dershowitz[†]

To Americans, baseball is more than a game. It is a pastime of memory and legend. At its apex stands the World Series. When I was growing up in Brooklyn, everything stopped during our secular "holy week." Our hometown favorites, the Dodgers, were always playing and almost always losing to the New York Yankees. Fifty years later, I remember every inning. I can only imagine how it felt to Chicago White Sox fans to learn, in 1919, that their hometown favorites, led by living legend Joe Jackson, had thrown the World Series.

Everybody remembers Shoeless Joe Jackson, the greatest natural hitter the game of baseball has ever seen. As legend has it, he was discovered playing mill-town ball in his stocking feet. In the second decade of this century, swinging Black Betsy, his famous homemade bat, he electrified the major leagues with his clutch slugging, bulletlike throws, and come-from-nowhere fielding.

But then, at the height of his career, he was disgraced and thrown out of organized baseball for his alleged role in fixing the 1919 World Series. The Black Sox Scandal, as it has come to be called, involved eight members of the Chicago White Sox who were indicted for throwing the Series to the Cincinnati Reds. The rise and fall of this great natural ballplayer, followed by his gutsy comeback as an aging start of semipro "outlaw" ball, has inspired numerous American writers, ranging from Nelson Algren to William Kinsella. His life and legend infuse Joe Hardy ("Shoeless Joe from Hannibal, Mo.") in *Damn Yankees* and Roy Hobbs, the hero of Bernard Malamud's *The Natural*, the character portrayed on the screen by Robert Redford. And he made another appearance in the movie *Field of Dreams*, based on Kinsella's novel *Shoeless Joe*. Whatever one thinks of his moral character, there is no doubt that he has become a unique figure in popular American mythology.

The most famous phrase to emerge from the Black Sox scandal, and perhaps from all of baseball, was the tearful question allegedly put to Shoeless Joe by a young fan: "Say it ain't so, Joe." But Joe did not say that it wasn't so. An illiterate country boy, he gave contradictory answers about his involvement in a gambling scheme. Although he denied that he threw any games, his major league career was over, and he entered history as a personification of corruption.

That was more than eighty years ago. Since then we have learned much about Jackson's real role in the Black Sox scandal, some of it uncovered by Eliot Asinov, some of it by subsequent writers such as Donald

---

[†] Felix Frankfurter Professor of Law, Harvard Law School. This essay first appeared as the *Introduction* to the Notable Trial Library Special Edition (copyright © 2003) of Eliot Asinov's *Eight Men Out: The Black Sox and the 1919 World Series*. It is reprinted here with the permission of the author and the publisher. *Eight Men Out* appears as a selection in the Notable Trials Library, a division of Gryphon Editions LLC.

Gropman. Recently discovered information strongly suggests that it wasn't so, or at the very least was not as bad as the powers of organized baseball have led us to believe.

These recent disclosures make the 1919-1920 White Sox seem like the 1972-1974 Nixon White House. The White Sox cover-up was intended to protect club owner and president Charles Comiskey, much like the White House cover-up was intended to protect President Nixon. The big difference is that the White Sox cover-up worked, as most probably do. Since we only learn of those that fail, we tend to believe that cover-ups never pay! And therein likes an interesting story about how much our legal system has changed for the better over the intervening half century.

The facts, as they have emerged, seem to be as follows: Jackson was approached by a teammate and offered $10,000 to throw the World Series. He declined. A short time later, the offer was renewed, this time for $20,000. Jackson refused again. This information, by the way, is from Jackson's own testimony before the Cook County Grand Jury, the very testimony that has, in garbled, twisted press accounts, been used as proof of Jackson's complicity. Furthermore, there is strong evidence that Jackson told one or more officials of the club before the Series began that a fix was in the making. He even asked to be benched for the Series to avoid any suspicion that he was involved, but his request was refused.

Several of Jackson's teammates did conspire to throw the Series, and the White Sox lost to the Reds, five games to three. Jackson, however, playing under the watchful eyes of club officials, was the star of the Series. He hit the only home run, fielded flawlessly, batted .375 to lead all players, and his twelve hits set a World Series record that stood for decades.

Like most of the known facts about the Jackson case, the event that is usually cited to prove his guilt has also been misrepresented. On the evening after the last game of the Series, one of Jackson's teammates came to his hotel room and offered him an envelope containing cash. Jackson refused to accept it, an argument ensued, and Jackson stormed out of his own room. His teammate, pitcher Lefty Williams, threw the envelope down and left. This version of the crucial event in Jackson's case was attested to, under oath, by the only two men who were there: Jackson and Williams. Their accounts agree. Jackson did not take the money, it was dumped on him.

Returning to his room, Jackson found the envelope and saw that it contained $5,000 in cash. He put it in his pocket. The next morning, he went to Comiskey's office at the ballpark but was told Comiskey would not see him. He waited an hour, then he left.

Comiskey, who at that very moment was in a secret meeting with two of the fixed players hearing the story of the scheme, chose a hypocritical course of action. While publicly proclaiming his commitment to "clean baseball," he privately spent the winter and almost all of the 1920 season denying the rumors that stubbornly clung to the full story that the White Sox honestly lost the 1919 Series and perpetrating a cover-up, in part to protect his valuable property, namely the guilty players. But in September

---

Some of the material in this Introduction comes form Donald Gropman's *Say it Ain't So, Joe! The True Story of Shoeless Joe Jackson* and from my Introduction to that book (New York, 1992).

of 1920, for reasons that had more to do with political in-fighting and greed than with "clean baseball," a grand jury was impaneled and the fix was exposed.

From that point on, Comiskey's priority was to protect his own reputation. His best option was to feed the suspected players to the grand jury, but only after they had been counseled by Comiskey's own lawyer, Alfred Austrian. They point of this exercise seems to have been damage control — Comiskey would have looked bad if the public learned what he knew and when he knew it. Of the players fed to the grand jury, Jackson was the most problematic. He had been the only one to warn Comiskey *before* the Series began. If he told everything, Comiskey's self-proclaimed integrity would be impugned and he would be revealed as a hypocrite and perhaps worse.

Jackson was working under two misconceptions when he met with Austrian. He believed that the truth would protect him, and he believed Austrian was his lawyer. Neither belief was true. Jackson began by protesting his innocence, but in a session that lasted for several hours, Austrian finally convinced Jackson that the truth would not be believed by the grand jury. We do not know exactly what Austrian suggested to Jackson (while Austrian admitted under oath that he had kept notes on his pretestimony meetings with the other players, he claimed he kept no notes during his session with Jackson), but we can make some logical deductions by analyzing the grand jury testimony Jackson subsequently gave. That testimony reveals that Jackson told two diametrically opposed stories, one confessing his guilt and the other protesting his innocence. Logic leads us to believe that the first story was probably Austrian's, the second Jackson's.

Jackson was eventually indicted, tried in criminal court, and found not guilty. Nevertheless, he was banished from organized baseball. That is when his love of the game led him to his second career in semipro "outlaw" ball.

In 1924, during a civil trial in which Jackson sued Comiskey for back wages on a three-year contract, the likely truth of how and why Jackson's name had been falsely implicated in the Black Sox scheme finally came to light. Sleepy Bill Burns, the fixer who put the players and the gamblers in touch with each other, testified under oath that he had *never talked to Jackson* about the fix. Instead, he took the word of Lefty Williams, who claimed he was empowered to speak for Jackson. And Williams himself, also under oath, swore he *never received Jackson's permission to use his name* with the fixers. This is perhaps the most compelling evidence we have, because it provides both motivation and means. The gamblers wanted a sure thing, and since Jackson was capable of going on a hitting streak that could carry the White Sox to victory despite the fix, they wanted Jackson in. So the fixed players, in the person of Williams, said he was. The means were equally simple: Williams and Burns both wanted the scheme to work, so one lied and the other took him at his word with no effort to substantiate his claim. In other words, Burns may have been telling the truth when he swore that Williams had assured him that Jackson was in on the fix, but Williams may have been lying to Burns. It is just this sort of situation that justifies both the general prohibition on the use of hearsay and the requirement that a defendant be permitted to confront his accuser.

The outcome of the civil suit was ambiguous. The jury found in Jackson's favor, but the judge overruled the verdict. Nevertheless, it was the second jury to hear Jackson's story and find him not guilty of culpable involvement in the Black Sox scandal. But the powers that be in organized baseball ignored the jury verdicts and refused to lift his lifetime banishment.

Jackson received shoddy treatment, but this probably would not happen today. A modern-day Jackson would have his own lawyer from the very beginning. The players' association would support him. Nor would the shenanigans employed by Comiskey's alleged lawyer be tolerated by the bar now. Most important, an honest prosecutor today generally seeks to follow the criminal trail to the top of the mountain. Convicting the Watergate burglars was not enough. The special prosecutor followed the trail to the attorney general and eventually to the president.

But in post-World War I Chicago, corruption tainted more than the White Sox. The entire city, judiciary and all, reeked with influence peddling and power brokering, and one of the most influential brokers was Charles Comiskey. No one should be surprised to learn that corruption was rampant in Chicago any more than *Casablanca*'s Captain Renault was shocked to discover that there was gambling in Rick's Place ("I'm shocked, shocked!").

It is a continuing scandal that Comiskey now holds an honored place in the Baseball Hall of fame while Shoeless Joe Jackson remains a scapegoat. Though both are long dead, the true story deserves to be known. In the last years of his life, former baseball commissioner A.B. "Happy" Chandler got behind efforts to clear Jackson's name. "I never in my life believed him to be guilty of a single thing," said the man who was privy to the secret files of the major leagues.

Because baseball is a game of legends, if it "ain't so" — or even if it wasn't as bad as legend had it — major league baseball should be big enough to admit it made a mistake about Shoeless Joe. Like any other institution, baseball can only be honest in the present if it is honest with its own past. And since baseball is still viewed by many as a metaphor for America itself, such an act of corrective justice would have meaning beyond baseball as a mere game.

I propose that major league baseball conduct a trial of Joe Jackson. I would be honored to defend him. I'm sure that a good prosecutor could be found to prosecute him. Let a retired judge preside, either with or without a jury. I am confident that Jackson would once again be acquitted. If he is, he belongs in the Hall of Fame, not in the annals of shame.

Cambridge, Massachusetts
August 8, 2003

George Mogridge (left), Roger Peckinpaugh (center), and Muddy Ruel (right) of the Washington Senators, circa 1924.

HEROLD (MUDDY) RUEL OF THE SUPREME COURT BAR

In January 1933, Muddy Ruel's 19-year career in the major leagues was approaching its end. As the *Sporting News* noted at the time, it was something of a surprise that Ruel had become a professional baseball player at all. When he was 17 years old, "He was too small for a catcher. Didn't have the right kind of frame. Small bones, skinny arms and legs. He wouldn't amount to anything in 'a hun'nerd years.'" Nevertheless, he managed to sign with the St. Louis Browns (Branch Rickey, manager) in 1915, and over the next two decades he would also play for the Yankees, Red Sox, Senators, and Tigers. But there's more:

> Ruel, in addition to making himself a useful ball player, and earning plenty of money, has shaped himself for something worth-while after his baseball days are ended. It took industry to do it, but Muddy is a full-fledged lawyer [educated at Washington University in St. Louis], qualified to practice in Missouri and before the United States Supreme Court.[1]

In fact, after he gave up playing for pay, Ruel continued to make himself useful to major league baseball, mostly as a coach and manager. His career was sufficiently long and interesting to justify a full-length biography, but that is unlikely to happen, as Bill James has observed, "because he wasn't a great player." At least not by conventional standards.[2]

---

[1] SPORTING NEWS, Jan. 12, 1933, at 4; SPORTING NEWS, Sept. 4, 1924, at 1.
[2] THE NEW BILL JAMES HISTORICAL ABSTRACT 404 (2001).

WHAT'S A DEFENSE?

from

ORDINARY INJUSTICE: HOW AMERICA HOLDS COURT

Amy Bach[†]

"I didn't know I was going to jail," I heard a defendant say as she stood before the judge in Greene County, Georgia. Of course she didn't. No one had told her the consequences of pleading guilty. Most people, educated or not, often have no idea what a guilty plea actually means: the conviction of a crime that subjects them to incarceration, fines, probation, a criminal record with unforeseen future consequences. Many do not even know that a guilty plea is not mandatory or that an appeal after conviction at trial is possible, even though a judge is required to correctly advise defendants before any plea.

I had first come to Greene County in 2001 after hearing about the chaos in its court system which seemed representative of a statewide problem; and I continued to visit for weeks at a time over the next five years. As required by the U.S. Supreme Court precedent, the county was fulfilling the obligation to provide attorneys to those who couldn't afford them. With little state oversight, court-appointed lawyers, for a variety of reasons, were sacrificing the interests of their most vulnerable and malleable constituency — the defendants they were supposed to be protecting. In this process, the defense lawyer, the judge, and prosecutor formed a kind of a tag team — charge the accused, assign a lawyer, prosecute, plead, sentence — with slight regard for the distinctions and complexities of each case.

Robert E. Surrency was under contract with Greene County to represent poor people accused of crime. He was not employed by the county

---

[†] From Chapter One from ORDINARY INJUSTICE: HOW AMERICA HOLDS COURT by Amy Bach (pp. 11-40). Copyright © 2009 by Amy Bach. Reprinted by permission of Henry Holt and Company, LLC. (And of the author.)

full-time; he continued to represent a number of paying clients as well. Even so, his private work was not lucrative enough, so he needed the indigent defense contract to support himself. On an annual basis, his caseload was double the national recommendation for a full-time attorney.[1]

Surrency was raised in Media, Pennsylvania, where his father, Erwin C. Surrency, had worked as the law librarian and assistant dean for Temple Law School. "I grew up in the stacks," he said of his upbringing. Surrency's father, whom he admired greatly, had been born and married in Georgia. In turn, Surrency attended Mercer University in Macon, where he had kin. Afterward, he headed back to Temple for law, passed the Pennsylvania Bar, and landed a clerkship with a state court judge for whom he helped write opinions. He then hung out a shingle as a solo practitioner and established a civil-law practice. In the mid-1980s his father decided to return to Georgia to become the director of the library at the University of Georgia Law School. Surrency, in his thirties, chose to move as well. He opened a law practice on Main Street in Watkinsville, Georgia, conveniently located near several other towns, Madison and Greensboro, and near his father in Athens. But he found it hard to make a living. Surrency seemed to lack the relationships those who had grown up there enjoyed. An old-time attorney explained that Georgians born and bred "kind of rule around here" and that Surrency constantly had to prove himself. "He was a stranger," the attorney said. Surrency's practice foundered.

One afternoon in 1987, he drove the thirty-five-minute trip to Greene County's courthouse and ran into Chip Atkins, a longtime local lawyer. Atkins had been the public defender but no longer wanted the job. He said that the contract to represent poor people was up for "bid," and urged him to apply. Surrency won the contract by offering to handle all the routine cases for fifteen thousand dollars, plus seventy-five dollars an hour for serious cases like murder; his bid, which came in at about twenty thousand dollars total, was slightly lower than anyone else's, he explained. In his first year, he represented forty defendants while maintaining a private

---

[1] Various national organizations, including the American Bar Association, have cited the 1973 National Advisory Commission on Criminal Justice Standards and Goals, which mandates the following limits on caseload: 150 felonies per attorney per year; or 400 misdemeanors (excluding traffic) per attorney per year; or 200 juvenile cases per attorney per year; or 200 mental commitment cases per attorney per year; or 25 appeals per attorney per year. National Advisory Commission on Criminal Justice Standards and Goals, *Report of the Task Force on Courts*, Chapter 13, "The Defense," (1973), 13.6. In 2001, Surrency was handling the maximum limit for both felonies and misdemeanors: 136 felonies (91 percent of the maximum); and 294 misdemeanors (98 percent of the maximum); plus 18 probation revocations, according to documents the clerk's office filed with the state.

practice. "It was a good side job," Surrency said.

In the fourteen years that followed, his public caseload multiplied ten-fold, while the amount of time he devoted to each case inevitably shrank. In 2001, the year I first met him, 1,359 people were arrested and held in the Greene County jail. Because the vast majority of criminal defendants nationwide are too poor to afford a lawyer, many of those arrested in Greene County would become his clients.[2] During the same fourteen years, Surrency's pay rose only to $42,150.

Nonetheless, Surrency claimed to have achieved good results. He settled a large number of cases through plea-bargaining, which he called "a uniquely productive way to do business." It got his clients in and out of the system quickly, which, he maintained, was what they wanted; and it saved him from having to defend clients whose cases he did not have time to try. Holding onto his contract depended on, among other things, expediting the process. If he got stuck on one client, he couldn't push the rest through. The judges expected him to perform — one had a motto, "Slow justice is no justice" — and could complain to the county commissioners, who had a lot of influence with the committee that awarded Surrency's contract.

Outsiders and a few insiders, such as the head clerk and Surrency's former paralegal, saw him as the quintessential "meet 'em, greet 'em, and plead 'em lawyer" who met his defendants minutes before they would face the judge and who, by then, had few options but to plead guilty. Even so, Surrency insisted he was helping people. He saw himself as a man of experience who was defending the poor. He helped extract the innocent from the system and shepherd the guilty through an imperfect and unjust world.

When I arrived at the Greene County courthouse just before nine in the morning to watch Surrency in action, he was trudging up the stairs to the courtroom. He had red tousled hair and wore a loose grey suit. The old courtroom, with its ceiling fans and creaky floors, was packed. Those

---

[2] The U.S. Department of Justice has published several reports showing the connection between criminal defendants and indigence. See, for example, *Indigent Defense Statistics*, "Summary Findings," U.S. Department of Justice, Office of Justice Programs, Bureau of Justice Statistics (Publicly financed counsel represented about 66 percent of Federal felony defendants in 1998 as well as 82 percent of felony defendants in the 75 most populous counties in 1996). These reports, as of January 2009, were available on the Bureau of Justice Statistics' Web site, http://www.ojp.usdoj.gov/bjs/id.htm. See also The Spangenberg Group, *Contracting for Indigent Defense Services: A Special Report*, U.S. Department of Justice, Bureau of Justice Assistance (2000): 3 ("It is widely estimated that 60 to 90 percent of all criminal cases involve indigent defendants"). Available at http://www.ncjrs.gov/pdffilesl/bja/181160.pdf.

who didn't have a seat overflowed into the hallways outside. Surrency looked distracted and then defeated as he saw the crowd that awaited him. Some, waving papers, laid into him with frustrated questions. Many had phoned him about their cases but had not heard back, or had spoken with him briefly and been told to meet with him before court. They were swarming around him like gnats. "Everybody back up. Back up," he said. "I'll try to get to talk to all of you before you go to the judge."

I had come on the first day of "trial week," the term of court when this rural court attempts to resolve cases that have built up over the previous quarter with jury trials. The label is a misnomer. In four years, Surrency had taken only fourteen cases to trial out of 1,493; he won five. The rest of the cases he managed during that period — more than 99 percent — he plea-bargained. In this particular session no cases went to trial. People either pleaded guilty or had their cases rescheduled, a drill that took only two days. There were 142 defendants on the court calendar and 89 were Surrency's. In a flash, it seemed, forty-eight of his clients rose from the rickety dark wooden benches, one after the other, to plead guilty. After the first day I spent in court observing him, he announced, "We have successfully done a ten-page calendar in one day!" For Surrency, speed meant success.

In court, he would yell out a client's name, like the hostess at a restaurant clearing the wait list. "Mr. Jones, are you here?" Then he would peruse the list of plea offers the prosecutor had given him and tell his defendant how much he or she would have to pay in fines or serve in jail time. If the defendant didn't want to plead, the matter was held over until the next trial week. Surrency theorized that the longer a case dragged on, the more likely it was that incriminating witnesses might forget what had happened. His job had devolved into this: Plead guilty or come back another day.

Can a defense lawyer plead virtually all his cases and still be doing a decent job? In assessing the quality of a lawyer's work, the number of cases he pleads out is less significant than the amount of attention he gives to each one. What is required of him is not necessarily research in law books, but investigation and client contact: initial interviews about what led to the arrest or the charge; discussions, for example, with the prosecutor's witnesses to assess their strength, or with the arresting police officer; perhaps a review of any forensic reports or psychiatric evaluations. What's needed is a range of basic inquiries involving phone calls or brief meetings that go toward deciding strategy for everything from bail setting to finding evidence.

Surrency had little time to talk in detail to his clients, and so he often had limited information to use in their favor. It was thus difficult for him to bargain with prosecutors to secure a more lenient sentence, nor could he produce the ultimate trump card: a willingness to go to trial when his clients claimed innocence. Many of them risked losing their homes, children, and livelihoods if they pleaded guilty, and yet his actions remained the same: His caseload often made it hard for him to clarify the facts — for example, whether his client had been the ringleader or had acted without intent or was guilty of a lesser crime — which is the kind of information that can mitigate the severity of a sentence or get charges dropped in negotiation.

Part of Surrency's problem was that his contract did not fund investigations or expert witnesses. For these, Surrency would have to ask the judge to provide funds or just lay out the money and then ask for reimbursement, which he didn't like to do. He didn't want to get people riled up about spending the county's money. Moreover, he claimed not to need these resources, anyway, because most of his cases were "pretty open and shut." Under the weight of too many clients to represent, he seemed to have lost the ability both to decide which cases required attention and to care one way or the other.

Defendants, of course, didn't like Surrency's way of doing things. The then-clerk of the court, Marie Boswell, had received many complaints, but none had been formally filed. Instead, those accused of crimes banded together as if they were on one team and their lawyer on another, at times passing around advice, and a few proclaiming that the best solution was to represent themselves. I spoke with one woman, in her mid-twenties, smoking with her friends outside court, who was there on charges of selling cocaine. She dug into her savings to hire her own lawyer. "He meets with me. He talks with me about the case," she said, as if this were exceptional.

H,[§] another defendant, twenty-eight years old, a heavily built black man with a shaved head, was sitting in the back row of the courtroom, charged with aggravated assault and battery of his boyfriend. He said he had never been in trouble with the law before. The crime, which he did not dispute, involved hitting his lover with his car after he learned that the victim had knowingly exposed him to HIV and now H had tested positive. "I guess I panicked," H says. "A lot of emotions were going through me."

H's explanation constituted a defense. But Surrency never returned

---

[§] "H" asked to be called by a single initial to maintain his privacy.

H's phone calls. "I bet if [his clients] all lined up in a lineup he couldn't pick a person out," H said.

Surrency, I found, was resolute in his defense of himself. He did not allow for the prospect of having ill-treated his clients. "Nobody was treated bad," he said. "Nobody could say that they didn't have their day in court." But in his mind, it hardly mattered since most defendants wanted to plead guilty from the outset, whether they had or had not committed the exact crime with which they were charged. And if he went to trial rather than taking the plea, he risked a judge giving the maximum sentence. Plus, pragmatically, he said, people wanted to move on. The employed wanted to avoid missing work (which could mean days if the case was postponed over and over), while the unemployed found coming to court burdensome. Many didn't have cars, and there was no public transportation in Greene County. "A car don't run by itself," said one woman I met, who had been charged with committing aggravated assault with a heavy meat grinder. She had paid a friend ten dollars for a ride.

More often than not, what a defendant really wants is what Harvard Law School professor Charles Fried calls "a special-purpose friend," an attorney who, perhaps with a hand on the client's shoulder, "acts in your interests, not his own; or rather he adopts your interests as his own," guiding a client through the process and defending him against injury.[3]

This was not Surrency. Witness a conversation between him and a client, a woman in an orange prison jumpsuit.

"I know I'm pleading guilty," she said. "But I don't know why."

"Well, we talked about that," he said.

She shook her head. No, they hadn't.

"Don't you remember when we talked?" said Surrency, as he flipped through a file.

"We *never* talked," she said, calm and resigned, mocking her lawyer as if she knew she would get nothing from him and just wanted him to admit as much.

Rejecting this complaint, Surrency told me that he talked to all his clients at some point, but that the average defendant would usually protest that he or she didn't get enough time. Clients seemed bottomless in their need for attention. "You have to draw the line somewhere," he said.

It seemed that after seventeen years, he was exhausted — by the job and the system. As Surrency put it, the local governing agency that hired

---

[3] Charles Fried, "The Lawyer as Friend: The Moral Foundations for the Lawyer Client Relation," *Yale Law Journal* 85 (1976): 1071.

him, the Greene County Board of Commissioners, "didn't want these people" — indigent defendants — "to get an even break just to start with. 'They are guilty anyway, what do they need a lawyer for?' — that is their attitude today. There is really a consensus among the local people paying their taxes that these people don't need any defense, much less a quality legal defense."

And so it went. Frequently, Surrency was not even in court when his defendants pled. He'd stand in the hallway talking to other clients. Another lawyer, Rick Weaver, who knew even less about the cases, would often take his place. Surrency regularly paid Weaver, a former prosecutor, six hundred dollars for one day of work, which allowed Surrecy the freedom to communicate plea deals to his clients while Weaver stood before the judge. Surrency would talk to the prosecutor to receive the plea offer, then he would pass it on to the client, often on the day of court. The next step was sending the client, with his file, to see Weaver, who would accompany the accused as the plea occurred before the judge.

An attorney who is present in court and armed with specific information about a case stands a good chance of influencing the outcome for his client. Nevertheless, Surrency, in a letter that recapped his work load to the local government budget committee, wrote that there were times "when an attorney needs to be in two places at one time and Mr. Weaver has solved that problem." He maintained that "the trial judge and the District Attorney were very pleased with the addition of Mr. Weaver to the business of the day."[4]

Weaver stood up awkwardly beside Terrical Lashay Porter, who was in court on drug charges. Porter, in her early twenties, came from a family in which two of her uncles, as well as her brother and her mother, had served time for drug crimes, including trafficking or selling. On a search warrant based on her brother's conduct, the police had found a bag of marijuana that Porter admitted was hers. "It was in my bedroom," she told me; a friend had given it to her after a party. She was charged with possessing more than an ounce of marijuana with intent to sell — a felony for which the law mandates a maximum of ten years in prison. Porter had never been arrested for a crime before.

After the charge, she had heard nothing about her case for two years until the day before her appearance in court, when a neighbor brought her a subpoena sent to an old address. Porter raced to court early, but Sur-

---

[4] Robert E. Surrency (Office of the Public Defender), memorandum to the Greene County Commissioners, January 11, 2000.

rency had too many people around him to talk to her. When their turn came to meet, she learned that the prosecution was offering her five years of probation on "conditional discharge" — a special, one-time deal for people charged with drug possession as a first offense that resembles the "first offender" law in which a felony record is dismissed and discharged — with no conviction, if the "terms or conditions" of probation, such as paying a fine and seeing a probation officer once a month, are met. If, however, Porter got convicted of another crime — *any* crime — during the probation period, a judge could nail her with the maximum sentence for her original offense. Given that her family was clearly on the police radar, Porter might well get arrested, even for something as minor as driving without a license and she could conceivably end up getting sentenced to a full ten years. The risk seemed not worth it to Porter. She said she told Surrency she would rather accept the five years of probation, but without the conditional discharge, even if it meant a permanent record instead.

Soon after the meeting with him, Porter stood before the judge. She looked nervous. Her foot was twitching. She was sweating. Rick Weaver, a lawyer she had never met, stood at her side. Surrency wasn't there.

The prosecutor described Porter to the judge. "We believe she is much less involved in all of that than her mother and her brother and her uncles," he said, though he described her home briefly as "a place to buy drugs" and her mother as "the main one operating out of there." He then explained the offer of conditional discharge he was making to Porter. After, Judge Hulane George began a "colloquy" to explain to Porter her rights. She asked if Porter understood that she had the right to plead not guilty and demand a jury trial.

"Yes, ma'am," Porter said.

Did she understand that she was waiving her rights, including the presumption of innocence, the right to subpoena any witnesses, the right to a lawyer at trial?

"Yes, ma'am."

Despite Porter having told Surrency that she didn't want to take the conditional discharge gamble, the judge informed her that she was pleading under the conditional-discharge provision. "Do you understand that under this particular provision of the law, in five years, you will have no felony record? Do you understand that?"

"Yes, ma'am," Porter said.

"But if you get into trouble I could come back and sentence you to what is left of your five years. Do you understand that?"

"Yes, ma'am."

"All right, do you want to plead under conditional discharge?"

"Yes, ma'am."

"Do you freely and voluntarily enter your plea of guilty to the charge against you?"

"Yes, ma'am."

"You are represented here by Mr. Weaver, who is with you. Have you been talking to Mr. Surrency or Mr. Weaver?

"Mr. Surrency."

She then asked Porter if she had any problems with Mr. Weaver and if there was anything else she wanted Surrency or Weaver to do.

"No, ma'am," Porter said.

"Anything you want to say to me before I rule?"

"No, ma'am."

"All right. Mr. Weaver, is the sentence recommendation the State made the same one to which you and your client agreed?"

"It is, Your Honor."

"Have you had enough time to discuss this case with her?" Judge George asked Weaver.

"I would like about thirty seconds, if I could, just to make sure," Weaver said.

He and Porter conferred. And then he stepped forward: "I do not believe she is interested in the conditional discharge," Weaver said. "I don't think she fully understood."

Porter looked panicked. "I told Mr. Surrency that I didn't want to be under that," she said. "The first offender."

"But this isn't first offender," the judge said.

"But it operates exactly the same way, Your Honor," Weaver said.

The judge turned to the prosecutor. "It's my understanding, I could only sentence her to what's left on five years rather than the first offender up to ten," she said.

The prosecutor had to correct her. "I think you could sentence her up to the total amount she could have received."

The judge said, "Well, she said she doesn't want it."

"Well, it'll take us a minute to redraw the sentence."

Porter, nervous and disoriented before the judge, said later that she didn't understand what she was agreeing to. "I had never been up there before and everything was kind of moving together," she said of the panic.

The judge seemed confused and began to go on in a way that had little to do with Porter's case: "But this is not the time to impress me! It's the time to be honest. You know, if you don't think you can be successful on it, you're the one who'll have to go to prison! Not me!"

Maybe the judge was trying to be tough or thought Porter was intentionally playing games. Later, she explained that she had been especially irritable because she had a horrible cold, and because she had been forced to backtrack when she had a large number of cases to get through.

In court, Weaver tried to take control. "Your Honor, what I advised her is that if she is in a position where she is around drugs, whether they're hers or not, she can face a very real possibility of taking a hit for that."

But the judge was not listening. "Do you have children?" she asked Porter.

"No, ma'am."

"Do you work?"

"Yes," she said.

"Well, you need to get out of the environment or you're going to end up in prison . . . What color are the women's prison uniforms anymore?"

Porter stood there while a lawyer shouted out the answer.

"Brown? Are they brown? Not a pretty color!" said Judge George. "I don't think you want to go. But that is your decision."

In the end, Porter got what she wanted: She pleaded guilty and received five years of probation — not under conditional discharge.

Outside the courthouse, she bawled. She had no idea that her lawyer could have made the experience easier for her. A lawyer in a different position might have presented arguments to ameliorate the punishment or advance Porter's cause. She would have gotten considerably more than a five-minute conversation before court and would not have been exposed to a nuts-and-bolts consultation in court. But Porter wasn't angry at her lawyer; she seemed hurt by Judge George. "The judge told me to get out of the environment but I have no place to go," she said. "I don't want to leave my sister. I am the only one taking care of her." Another lawyer might have conveyed these concerns to a judge, as well as the plea Porter had wanted, not let her panic and nearly plead to something different.

In her hand, Porter had a pink slip that listed the costs she had agreed to as part of the plea: a $500 fine; $50 for the police officers and prosecutors training fund; $50 to the jail fund; $25 to the victims assistance program; $250 to the drug fund; $50 crime lab fee; $23 per month for the probation supervision fee; and one hundred hours of community service. Somehow, it amounted to $75 a month for the next year, which she could pay off if her boss at Wendy's, where she worked as cook and cashier, gave her additional hours. "I got to find me another job," she said.

Back in the courtroom, another case was breaking down. This time a young woman in a leather blazer was talking in muffled sobs with the judge. While Weaver was looking for the file, Tasha McDonald stood before the judge alone. She was asking for her case to be continued.

"How many times has he talked to you?" Judge George asked about Surrency.

"Once," said the woman. The judge wearily announced that her case would be rescheduled to a different day.

In the hallway, McDonald was crying hard. When she calmed down she told her story. A single mother of three young girls, she freely admitted to having applied for a Sears credit card in the name of a colleague with whom she worked at a luxury vacation community. McDonald had the card sent to her own address, made herself a secondary user, and then bought $1,895.35 worth of merchandise: beds, sheets and pillowcases, a CD player, a microwave, a toaster oven — "everything for the house." She also bought a small trampoline for her eldest daughter, a ten-year old, who had just been diagnosed with scleroderma, a hardening of the skin that can weaken limbs. The trampoline, she said, was therapeutic, to help her daughter regain muscle control and mobility.

McDonald had been charged with financial identity fraud. She knew she had to be punished, but had only found out from Surrency in the hallway that the prosecutor wanted her to serve 90 to 120 days in a detention center or jail. If incarcerated, she feared she would lose her job, her mobile home and car, both of which she was still paying off, and become a burden to the state. "If I do four months in boot camp you know where my home is going," she said. She had already repaid Sears for the goods.

There were alternatives. Instead of jail, she could be sentenced to do community service or to attend one of various halfway houses or work release programs designed so people convicted of minor felonies can keep their jobs if they have them. She could also have been sent to a diversion center, which collaborates with minimum-wage employers like processing plants or fast-food restaurants. Inmates work during the day to pay for room and board, and then, if there is money left over, to pay fines, a mortgage, or to support family members.

Surrency contends that the results would have been the same, no matter how much investigation he did. However, if he had argued that McDonald shouldn't be taken away from her children, due to her circumstances, she might not have ended up facing any jail time at all. Certainly prosecutors and judges are likely to be more sympathetic to a defendant whose motive comes down to poverty or an ill child. Yet the odds that the judge or prosecutor knew about McDonald's particular situation were slim. You could hardly blame them.

On the other hand, maybe you could. Weren't there questions a decent prosecutor could ask if he suspected defense counsel was asleep on the job? Wasn't it apparent that Surrency was overloaded to the point of neglecting his clients? I started to get curious about the prosecutor and just how complicit he was when it came to pushing defendants through the system. It seemed like most everyone who appeared before the judge was confused and uninformed. What was the prosecutor's role in all this?

Wilson B. Mitcham Jr., had been the assistant district attorney in charge of Greene County since 1993 and had appeared in court with Surrency hundreds of times. They seemed on good terms with each other and with the judge. Often the courtroom felt like a private party, with the lawyers and judge huddled around the bench, preventing anyone else from hearing. It looked like they were teammates rather than opposing advocates duking it out before a neutral arbiter.

In an interview, Mitcham was surprised to learn of McDonald's situation. "I am shocked," he said, "because no one told me she has a disabled child." He was essentially admitting that he knew Surrency was doing a disservice to his clients by not discussing their cases with them. Still, he seemed defensive of their convivial rapport in court, noting that "even though we are cordial . . . we do have certain disagreements." But these were not enough to change the way Surrency conducted business. While Mitcham knew Surrency waited until the last minute to talk to his clients, he still maintained that cases were getting the attention they needed.

As for McDonald, Mitcham said he would look into it and possibly change his plea offer, which he eventually did. It turned out this was not her first crime of deception. A decade earlier she had received probation for using a bad check knowing it wouldn't be honored by the bank. For her identity theft she could have received a maximum of ten years in prison, but given his knowledge about her family, Mitcham asked the judge that she serve only the mandatory minimum of one year on probation and some time at a diversion center "until released by the center director." The center would allow her to leave on weekends to visit her daughters, who would be cared for by her mother.

For McDonald's subsequent court appearances, she fired Surrency and hired a private lawyer. Her case went before a new judge who seemed annoyed by how light Mitcham's negotiated plea was. Judge John Lee Parrott criticized McDonald for her premeditation — that she "went through too many steps" to commit the crime. "[I]'ve got some doubts about whether I ought to let her off even this light," said Parrott before agreeing to the plea. "To be honest with you, most of the time I put people straight in jail," he said. "I'm giving you a chance to get your ducks in a row with your kids." Since he understood McDonald's circumstances, he made an exception. McDonald apologized to the coworker whose identity she stole. "[I] was desperate. I knew that she had good credit," she said. "That's why I used her."

McDonald said she ended up serving only two months in the Macon Diversion Center. There, she worked in a factory pressing shirts, which helped her pay off her mortgage on her trailer. She left on weekends to see her family, and also took care of all the various penalties and of her one hundred hours of community service. Most important, she wasn't whisked away to jail. McDonald is still incredulous at the way Surrency told her that she was going to jail. She wanted to ask him, "How could you be for me when you have never talked to me?"

In the case of H, when Mitcham was informed about the boyfriend who might have intentionally given him HIV, he recognized that H's crime might have been done "in the heat of passion." "I wish I had known," he said; he would have thought about it differently. Still, H had gotten a good deal. When Surrency hadn't returned his calls, H pulled some strings: He called a prosecutor friend in a different county who vouched for H as a good citizen. As a result, Mitcham had changed his original offer from five years in prison to five months in a detention center plus ten years' probation.

It is not explicitly the prosecutor's job to ask for more information than the defense has provided, though nothing precludes him from doing so, either. The ethics are murky. Codes of professional responsibility require a prosecutor only to "do justice" but provide little guidance about what this means.[5] In theory, a prosecutor who realizes that a defense attorney isn't performing aggressively could ask him to improve his performance or else withdraw from the trial. If that doesn't work, he could tell the judge or make a motion to disqualify counsel, though this is un-

---

[5] For a discussion of the ethics' codes failure to define ethical obligations see Fred C. Zacharias, "Structuring the Ethics of Prosecutorial Trial Practice: Can Prosecutors Do Justice?" *Vanderbilt Law Review* 45 (1991); for an elaboration of the dilemma a prosecutor faces see Vanessa Merton, "What Do You Do When You Meet a 'Walking Violation of the Sixth Amendment' if You're Trying to put that Lawyer's Client in Jail?" *Fordham Law Review* 69 (2000).

likely as lawyers view "most reporting obligations with distaste."[6] In reality, many prosecutors consider defense attorneys a nuisance and don't think they need to know anything besides the crime and a defendant's prior record to assess sentencing recommendations.

But Mitcham was not a stereotypical, aggressive prosecutor who invoked protection of the community as his top priority. He sometimes helped defendants, as he saw it. Like Surrency, Mitcham had hundreds of cases piled up in his office; he seemed to think that by putting them off he was showing compassion to those charged and, in a complicated way, doing God's work. But he admitted that he couldn't keep up with his workload and had a problem with procrastination. "I am an administrative nightmare walking," he said. Mitcham had a rather unusual view of how and why he did things. "I was raised to be a good Christian," he said over lunch at Subway, as tears welled in his eyes and he stopped eating his turkey sandwich. He had begun his career as a defense lawyer then left to become a minister. But he found this path didn't suit him, either; the politics of the church bothered him. In the end, being a prosecutor was the best way he could find to show his forgiveness. "You can mete out a lot more mercy as a prosecutor than as a defense attorney," he said.

At the same time, he was cautious about appearing too compassionate on the job. "I have a bleeding heart, but I try to disguise it. I don't want anyone to think that I have a hair-trigger to dismiss a case." With good reason: If he showed his mercy openly, he could seem soft on crime and get fired. Prosecutors are supposed to be strict and aggressive. To solve his quandary, Mitcham found a silver lining in his procrastination problem. By delaying cases and letting things slide, he compensated for the defense attorney's failure to defend his clients — no one defends, no one prosecutes, and, as it turns out, no one benefits.[7]

Surrency and Mitcham had created a stable but dysfunctional relationship; and Judge George, who had presided over the two lawyers for years, seemed to compound it. A former schoolteacher, she wanted to keep things orderly. "I like to clean things up," she said. At the same time, under her authority, the lawyers had been permitted to treat the dizzying disarray of the courtroom as if it were the norm. She claimed that the day I visited had been one of the worst, insisting that in other trial weeks she took more care of the defendants. However, the other Greene County

---

[6] Zacharias, "Structuring the Ethics of Prosecutorial Trial Practice," 73.

[7] Ibid., 70 ("Prosecuting weakly, however, does not repair the defects in adversarial justice; it eliminates adversariness altogether").

judges I observed during trial week seemed to have similarly bad days. They all blamed the problems on sheer volume, a lack of funding for public defense, and on the community's reluctance to spend money on the town's poorest and least law abiding. They also seemed resigned to an unwritten obligation to put the court on auto pilot — to make justice quick and easy and to dispense with the complications that accompany a true exploration of the facts. Judge George conceded to acting out of pressure. The jails were overflowing, so she needed to move cases forward. "Part of it is that you're standing up above everyone, in front of hundreds of people, all of whom want their cases to be number one," she said.

Besides its ease, auto pilot has certain advantages for the judge. If, for instance, a defense lawyer actually put forth arguments, the judge might have to make difficult calls about issues like admitting questionable evidence. Some decisions might be unpopular. Defendants considered guilty in the public's eye might have to go free. Doing justice would become much harder — both in and outside the courtroom — and messier. It was easier to take pride in maintaining the routine and the schedule. "[Too] many judges, consciously or subliminally, prefer the less aggressive advocate who cooperates in disposing of cases and helping to clear the judge's docket," writes Vanessa Merton, a professor at Pace Law School.[8]

In Greene County, there were additional incentives for judges to preserve the status quo. There, the opinion of the Board of Commissioners (the five citizens who control the county budget) carries a lot of clout. While judges are elected and often run uncontested, they are mindful of the influence of the commission and the sheriff, and of the possibility that these powerful bodies might support an opponent in the next election. Judges throughout the state are sensitive to the costs of a trial. Judges do not want to seem wasteful. "I'm a politician," said Judge James Cline, who also sat in Greene County. "Every four years I want fifty-one percent of the people to vote for me."

Like Surrency and Mitcham, Judge George denied rushing cases forward against the defendants' interests. When asked if being elected to her position every four years had anything to do with her need to please, she said no. She emphasized that what I saw was unusual. "It was just a godawful day." She did, however, feel badly about the impression she had made. "The whole thing was hurry up and get it done. I fault myself for allowing myself to get pushed around and I am better about it."

With Surrency, Mitcham, and Judge George faulting the system, each

---

[8] Merton, "What Do You Do," 1023.

other, and occasionally themselves, the court began to seem like a runaway train. It was hard to tell who was at the controls and if anyone there was awake.

•   •   •   •

Of course, Greene County is not unique. The real issue here is the poor quality of defense representation throughout the nation. There are three basic systems for providing attorneys. It is difficult to rank them comparatively by quality since all three are flawed and tend to come apart when underfunded, poorly staffed, or subject to the whimsy of judges and prosecutors.[9] Still, one can quantify the differences among them. The arguably best system is called the "public defender" structure, in which full-time defense lawyers, employed by the state, are provided with central offices, secretaries, computers, investigators, and legal research tools.[*] A public defender system aims to put the defense on equal, or near-equal, footing with the prosecution. In the more bountiful programs, public defenders are overseen by a statewide agency that sets uniform standards and expectations for counties or circuits. A variation on this program contracts with a non-profit program funded by public money and other sources.[10]

The second system is a panel program, in which private attorneys on a pre-approved list are appointed and paid to represent indigent defendants as needed. The idea, in theory, is for an independent agency or clerk to select lawyers from a list who want and are qualified to do the work. In many jurisdictions, however, a judge makes the assignments, which may affect the independence of the attorney, who depends on future assignments from the judge for his or her income. Lawyers who line up for assignments are paid by the case or by the hour (for which there is usually a

---

[9] The last survey conducted by the U.S. Department of Justice Bureau of Justice Statistics on indigent defense systems was by Carol J. DeFrances, "Indigent Defense Services in Large Counties, 1999" *Bureau of Justice Statistics Bulletin*, (November 2000): 1. The report details the methods by which criminal indigent defense systems are delivered in the nation's one hundred most populous counties. It found that public defenders handled about 82 percent of the 4.2 million cases received by the providers, assigned counsel 15 percent, and contract attorneys about 3 percent.

[*] In this chapter, a public defender system refers to the ideal form where the public defender works full-time with equal or near-equal resources as the prosecutor. At other times in this book, people use the term "public defender" to refer to an attorney or an office that represents the poor part-time in addition to their private practices.

[10] The three types of systems are described in Robert L. Spangenberg and Marea L. Beeman, "Indigent Defense Systems in the United States," *Law and Contemporary Problems* 58 (1995): 32-41.

fee cap) and can become accustomed to the quick disposal of cases. And in some places an attorney who is totally unqualified to do criminal work — an expert in real estate or matrimonial law — will be appointed unpaid as part of community service to the local bar association.

Further, private lawyers with paying clients may not want to make time for poorly funded cases. For years Virginia had the lowest fee caps in the nation for indigent representation.[11] In March of 2007, the legislature, under threat of a class-action lawsuit led by the Virginia Fair Trial Project, increased the fee cap for appointed attorneys and authorized judges to waive the caps, subject to a higher court's approval. However, the amounts are still meager and judges are unlikely to intervene. In 2007, the caps were as follows: $2,085 for clients charged with felonies that carry a sentence of twenty years to life, $600 for lesser felonies, and $240 for misdemeanors and juvenile felonies.[12] A lawyer who wants to prove his client's innocence could easily spend those amounts on the investigation alone. Prior to the fee hike, one Richmond attorney admitted that the fees were so low he reserved nearly all his time and labor for paying clients: Looking for witnesses, considering discovery, or using outside experts were impossible with so little funding. He tells court-appointed clients, who accounted for about 20 percent of his income, "to investigate the case themselves, look for witnesses and if they find them bring them to the office or to court."[13]

The third option for indigent defense is the contract system, in which one attorney or several contract with a county or circuit (group of counties) to represent a fixed or maximum number of cases for a fee, as with Robert Surrency in Georgia. Many counties prefer this method because it allows them to budget public defense for the entire year. It's also easier to administer than a panel program, which requires keeping track of many different lawyers and a complicated payroll.

There is much debate about which system is preferable, especially among county officials, who want to save money. Houston County in Georgia, for example, has employed full-time public defenders for decades. Three superior court judges, in a letter to their county commissioners, explained why the county shouldn't change to a less expensive contract system.

---

[11] The Spangenberg Group on behalf of the American Bar Association Standing Committee on Legal Aid and Indigent Defendants, "Indigent Defense in Virginia, Assigned Counsel," *A Comprehensive Review of Indigent Defense in Virginia* (January 2004): 40.

[12] Editorial, "Overdue Relief on Attorney Fees," *Virginian-Pilot*, March 1, 2007.

[13] The Spangenberg Group, *A Comprehensive View of Indigent Defense in Virginia*, 50.

> Having a public defender system means having a group of lawyers
> who are obligated to handle the county's indigent defense work
> full time. . . . [P]rivate attorneys under a contract system . . .
> would simply be operating with a lot of competing interests
> which a public defender does not have. . . . It is naïve to think
> that any private attorney in this area would, or could, completely
> close their private practice and handle only the indigent contract
> cases. Expecting that attorney to neglect "paying" clients, or to
> make them a lower priority so that he or she may give first prior-
> ity to indigent cases is equally implausible. . . .[14]

Another problem with the contract system is the implicit power it
gives judges over lawyers. In a report by a commission convened by the
Georgia State Bar to assess the state's indigent defense practice, the findings were that "[s]everal court-appointed and contract attorneys expressed
concern that if they were viewed by some judges as zealous advocates —
e.g., if they filed several motions in one case or demanded trials — they
ran the risk of being removed from the *ad hoc* counsel appointment list or
denied a future contract."[15]

So for the panel and contract systems, the problem is one of incentives. If these defense attorneys are going to be paid poorly and if, for
what little effort they make, the consequence might be dismissal, they
have little reason to work hard on an indigent client's behalf.

The better contract systems insist on quality controls, like limited
caseloads and reviews of lawyers before awarding contracts. In San Mateo
County, California, a contract attorney's fee will go up in a particular case
that requires more work than is covered by a lump sum or flat fee. Also,
lawyers have caps on numbers of cases based on a "weighted" study of how
difficult they are; additional work is paid by the hour, with a higher rate
for jury trials. For example, in a misdemeanor, a lawyer is paid a case fee
of $190 plus $80 for a pretrial conference; if an attorney goes to trial he
receives $125 per hour plus a per diem of $260 for preparation work. "By
the time you add it up you're getting pretty much what retained lawyers
get," said John S. Digiacinto, the county's chief defender. "We are able to
keep our staff."

---

[14] The Spangenberg Group, *Status of Indigent Defense in Georgia: A Study for the Chief Justice's Commission on Indigent Defense–Part I* (2002), quoting Superior Court Judges George F. Nunn and Edward D. Lukemire, letter to the Houston County Board of Commissioners, January 29, 2002. This report is available at http://www.georgiacourts.org/aoc/press/idc/idc.html.

[15] Ibid.

The worst contract systems, like Greene County's, feature a part-time lawyer who is hired based solely on how cheaply he is prepared to do the work. By 1985, even before Surrency took over the job, such "low bid" or "fixed fee" contracts had been condemned by the American Bar Association (ABA) House of Delegates, the policy-making body of the organization, for compromising the integrity of the justice system.[16] Unfortunately, local governments are often unaware of what the ABA says or consider its rulings advisory. In 2000, a report on the status of the country's contract defense practice by the Department of Justice's Bureau of Justice Statistics "noted a decline in the number of cases taken to jury trial, an increase in guilty pleas at first-appearance hearings, a decline in the filing of motions to suppress evidence, a decline in requests for expert assistance, and an increase in complaints received by the court from defendants" — virtually all of which described what was happening in Greene County.[17] Further, the county spent only $75.38 per case, the fifth lowest cost-per-case in the state.

Beginning in 1969, when adopting a plan for Georgia, the state legislature left it up to each county to determine which of the three systems to use. A decade later the legislature created the Georgia Indigent Defense Counsel (GIDC), which was based in Atlanta to oversee the different systems. The GIDC issued 11 percent of the total monies used to run 152 of 159 counties statewide. Of the 152 counties, only 20 decided on full-time public defenders, seventy-three employed a panel system, and 59 used contracts as their primary method.[18]

In exchange for the money, the GIDC asked counties to adhere to a detailed set of guidelines. These guidelines fixed standards for how to determine indigence and mandated appointment of counsel within seventy-two hours of arrest or detention, among other things. The GIDC also required that a tripartite committee of three volunteers be responsible for enforcing the standards. The tripartite committee, however, lacked a staff and often included nonlawyers or local businesspeople who had no interest in meaningfully supervising the indigent defense program, other than approving vouchers. The GIDC might admonish a county based on an anecdotal complaint, but a county could ignore a reprimand at will. A report

---

[16] American Bar Association, Criminal Justice Section, Standing Committee on Legal Aid and Indigent Defendants, *Report to the House of Delegates* (February 1985). Available at http://www.abanet.org/legalservices/downloads/sclaid/110.pdf.

[17] The Spangenberg Group, *Contracting for Indigent Defense Services*, 10.

[18] *Report of Chief Justice's Commission on Indigent Defense–Part I*, Georgia Supreme Court (2002): 2, http://www.georgiacourts.org/aoc/press/idc/idc.html.

in 2002 by the Spangenberg Group, a research and consulting firm in West Newton, Massachusetts, which specializes in improving justice programs, found that in recent years, the GIDC had not refused to provide funding for any county "in part because it fears political fallout or possible complaints from judges and other local people" to the state legislature. The GIDC "has no teeth," the report stated.[19]

. . . .

Traditionally, the country's legal apparatus favors the office of the district attorney. The states instinctively supported the creation of prosecutors' offices because of a political will to solve crime and punish those who commit it. By contrast, the need to provide counsel for poor people accused of crimes is a burden that the U.S. Supreme Court thrust on the states in the sixties. Thus with a more popular mandate, prosecutors tend to receive more money and resources. For instance, Congress spent $26 million building the National Advocacy Center in Columbia, South Carolina, to train prosecutors. There is a similar school in Reno, Nevada, for training state and local judges. No federally funded counterpart exists for defense lawyers. Also, the Bureau of Justice Assistance gives federal aid to state and local law-enforcement agencies (e.g. $170,433,000 through the Edward Byrne Memorial Justice Assistance Grant Program in 2008) with no equivalent moneys for the defense.[20]

Nationwide, prosecutors also receive more funding because they have a higher caseload. District attorneys (sometimes called state's attorneys or county prosecutors or county attorneys) represent the state in virtually all prosecutions, so the state foots the entire bill. But when it comes to defendants, the state pays only when they are poor and only for minimum defense. In California, for example, reports show discrepant funding between prosecutors and public defenders — for every $100 the prosecution receives, indigent defense receives an average of $60.90, which is on the high end of what most states provide.[21] A report by the Spangenberg

---

[19] The Spangenberg Group, *Status of Indigent Defense in Georgia*, 20.

[20] American Bar Association, Standing Committee on Legal Aid and Indigent Defendants, *Gideon's Broken Promise: America's Continuing Quest for Equal Justice* (December 2004): 14. Available at http://www.abanet.org/legalservices/sclaid/defender/brokenpromise/full-report.pdf. The annual appropriations to state and local law enforcement, including the information cited here about the Edward Byrne Memorial Justice Assistant Grant Program in 2008, Public Law 110-161, can be found on the Library of Congress Thomas Web site: http://thomas.loc.gov.

[21] American Bar Association, *Gideon's Broken Promise*, 14 (citing testimony of Gary Windom,

Group in 2002 estimated that states and counties nationwide spent $3.3 billion on indigent defense;[22] whereas in 2001, the ABA reported that $5 billion was spent in prosecuting criminal cases in state and local jurisdictions — a $1.7 billion gap.[23] (Both of these statistics are dated and experts say the discrepancy is probably greater, but an absence of nationwide statistics exists.)

With such a difference in resources, even the "best" public defender offices, which have full-time professional lawyers, cannot protect attorneys from problems like high caseloads. Instead, the overload has prompted new oversight measures in several states. Broward County, Florida, for instance, with a $15 million budget, has a prestigious public defender's office, but in 2005 the head of the office announced, to the dismay of some judges, that attorneys could not plead defendants guilty at arraignment without first having some "meaningful contact" with them. "We will make every effort to meet with clients prior to any court hearings," a memo to judges stated from public defender Howard Finkelstein, according to the *Broward Daily Business Review*. "However, if such a meeting has not taken place, we are legally and ethically constrained from recommending any plea to a client."[24] What should be a baseline standard has become so hard to reach that special requirements are needed to enforce it.

If the GIDC was failing to notice the problems in Green County, others were not. Stephen B. Bright, the president and senior counsel of the Southern Center for Human Rights in Atlanta, had decided in the mid-1990s that Georgia's indigent defense system was so bad that his organization was going to keep challenging it until it was brought into line with the ideals of American justice. Bright, in his fifties, has made a career of championing unpopular causes. He became the director of the struggling Southern Center in 1982 and has often worked without pay in defense of people facing the death penalty and on litigation to improve prison and jail conditions throughout the South. The organization has eleven attorneys,

---

chief public defender, Riverside County Public Defender Office, Riverside County, California).

[22] The Spangenberg Group, *50 State and County Expenditures for Indigent Defense Services FY 2002* (September 2003). Available at http://www.abanet.org/legalservices/downloads/sclaid/indigentdefense/indigentdefexpend2003.pdf.

[23] American Bar Association, *Gideon's Broken Promise*, 13-14 ("The U.S. Department of Justice's *Sourcebook of Justice Statistics* reports that in 2001, nearly $5 billion was being spent in prosecuting criminal cases in state and local jurisdictions").

[24] Dan Christensen, "Broward PD Says No to Instant Plea Deals," *Broward Daily Business Review*, June 6, 2005.

an equal number of investigators, and a stream of student interns and volunteers.

The center is fueled by a profound sense of purpose and by Bright's inspiration. One staffer wondered when Bright ate, and then, one night at around three a.m., saw him downing an energy drink at his computer. For years, Bright had set his sights on creating a state-wide public defender system in Georgia with full-time lawyers. He toured clubs and community halls to arouse the public's interest, making speeches wherever possible. He told it like it is: People charged with crimes, no matter how small, whether they are guilty or not, are treated "like hamburgers in a fast-food restaurant." He discussed the defense attorney's need for independence from the prosecutor and judiciary "so that judges would not use lawyers for the poor as clerks to process their cases." He wanted to get rid of the hodgepodge system that contracted out defense for the poor and ended up with the likes of Surrency or worse. He sought more resources from the state and counties to train both new lawyers and existing public defenders.

Until the state made proper changes, Bright planned to expose and root out bad defense systems, one by one, by observing various courts in action and filing a series of lawsuits claiming violations of the state and federal Constitutions. I had learned about Greene County's problems from a series of phone calls with advocates in Atlanta, and when I told Bright it was one of the courts I was considering looking at, he said he had never been. I asked him to join me so I could get his perspective on how this court matched up to others he had seen. Even though he had appeared on *Nightline*, on the radio, and in various newspaper articles, legal professionals knew him by name but not always by face. In Greene County, Bright slipped into Judge Hulane George's courtroom unnoticed. He sat with a yellow legal pad in his lap, at the end of the first row, near a few other lawyers who had cases that day.

Bright believes that change begins on the ground, in the courtroom, and he doesn't hesitate to speak his mind, much to the annoyance of judges, who feel like he lectures them when it should be the other way around. As the day went on, the proceedings in Greene County became harder to hear. The less people could understand, the more frustrated, bored, and restless the audience became. Spectators shifted loudly in their seats. They whispered. I sat a few people away from Bright, attempting to take notes. The people couldn't hear a thing, and Bright sensed their frustration.

He leaned over and whispered, "Why don't you go and ask the judge to speak up?" I laughed. I considered myself an observer and wanted to be as inconspicuous as possible. I was also embarrassed to make a ruckus. This was court, after all.

I went back to straining to follow.

Suddenly Bright was on his feet. "Your Honor," he said in a deep, loud voice. "This is a public hearing and there are people here who want to listen to what is going on. So if you wouldn't mind speaking up that would be much appreciated."

Judge George looked like she had been slapped. Bright didn't seem like a commanding man, more like the lanky Kentucky farm boy he had been growing up. He had a wholesome face and full red hair parted to the side. His clothes didn't match his pedigree — he teaches at Harvard and Yale law schools in his free time but prides himself on buying eighty-dollar suits on the road. A deadening, somber silence followed his interruption.

"Excuse me, could you please come before me? I would like to talk to you," Judge George said.

"No, ma'am, that's fine. I don't need to appear before you. I will stay right here. I am just an observer. And I would just appreciate it if you would speak up. Thank you, ma'am."

Bright sat down, refusing to budge.

"Sir, I order you to come stand before me," Judge George said.

Bright climbed his way over the packed row. With gravitational force, whipping himself around to play to the audience, he took control of the courtroom.

"Your Honor, my name is Steve Bright and I am a lawyer visiting court today from Atlanta. I am here to listen to this public hearing. People have a right to hear what is going on. We're all here, missing work, having left our children in the care of others. And we want to hear what is going on in court today. You are denying us our right to listen to a public hearing. So if you wouldn't mind, please speak up."

The exhausted, twitchy crowd was now focused. Someone started to clap, and soon the entire courtroom was applauding with cries of "Amen" and "That's right," and "We can't hear anything," and "Thank you, sir."

"I have this viral junk in my throat," Judge George said. She did seem tired. Alarmed, too.

For the rest of the day the judge used a microphone and would tap it regularly asking, "Can everyone hear? I just want to make sure. There seems to be a lot of interest here today."

In a court where people had grown accustomed to being ignored, merely asking the judge to speak louder was blasphemously glorious. It shook things up so that someone in the audience shouted out, "We can't hear you," at Surrency, who was now also taking the heat. Surrency, tensely flipping through his notes, had to respond to the audience, most of whom were his clients. "Can you hear me now?" he said, facing the crowd.

"No!" people shouted.

Judge George clapped her hands together. She used to teach school, she told the crowd, and couldn't stand noise.

Bright had become a celebrity. In the breaks, people patted him on the shoulder and shook his hand in gratitude.

"I got something to tell you," said a man in denim overalls, and then he launched into the complexities of his case.

"Come talk to me next," said a woman hitting Bright on the arm.

• • • • •

Bright was not the only one trying to accomplish reform on the ground. There were courageous whistle-blowers in Greene County, but unlike Bright, they could not simply return to Atlanta unscathed; they had to stay put, where they didn't fare so well.

Cathy Crawford, who was in her forties, had started working for Surrency right after obtaining a degree in paralegal studies. She found his papers were "just thrown in a box. I remember looking at this system, or lack thereof, and wondering: Is this man a complete idiot or is he just so brilliant that he can get away with this and still do his job?"

Yet she liked Surrency. He had an easygoing manner. When they carpooled to court they sang, "We're off to see the wizard." She would laugh.

In court, when the line to see Surrency sometimes snaked down the hallway stairs, he would announce that clients could conference with either him or Crawford, as if they were both lawyers. Crawford began to listen to their stories. She advertised office hours when people could come talk about their cases. "I had a tremendous turnout three days a week," Crawford said. "I would pull reports and look at them. We had people sitting in the hallways to see me." When she tried to talk to Surrency about the cases, however, he often didn't return her calls. She didn't see him in person because she didn't work out of his office. "You could never find him," she said.

Crawford also noticed that Surrency rarely filed motions to ask the court for certain pre-trial hearings. These usually involve requesting that evidence, a statement, or identification be excluded. Judges don't grant them very often, but that's not the point. Motion practice is a way of discovering information about the prosecutor's case. For example, a police officer might testify at arraignment and then the defense is entitled to his reports and has the chance to cross-examine the officer about his practices. "Any investigative leads unearthed in this manner are most useful if they come sufficiently early so that the defense has ample time to follow them up thoroughly," reads a seminal treatise on how to defend a criminal case.[25]

Sometimes, when other lawyers' motions were being heard, Surrency would ask Crawford to come to court and sit in with him because the county commissioners might come by. "I said to him," Crawford recounted, "You're willing to sit there for a whole day just so someone will think you're working?" The answer was, apparently, yes. Crawford advised him to start filing some motions of his own and turned to the codebooks. She drafted up some documents based on sample forms she found and had Surrency sign them. Then she filed them with the court.

Crawford's next "assignment" was to begin visiting with the prosecutor alone. "Don't bother calling Surrency," she'd tell Mitcham, explaining, presumably on Surrency's behalf, that he would rather see ten than fifteen years on probation, or, for example, that he was considering a motion to suppress evidence.

Mitcham, who sat on the board of governors for the state bar, the governing body that recommends changes to ethical standards to the state supreme court, claimed that he "didn't feel comfortable negotiating with Cathy." The Georgia Code of Professional Responsibility prohibits a lawyer from assisting a non-lawyer in the unauthorized practice of law.[26] An advisory opinion by the state disciplinary board explains, "competent professional judgment is the product of a trained familiarity with law and legal processes, a disciplined, analytical approach to legal problems, and a firm ethical commitment." Among those duties that the board specified should not be delegated to paralegals are "negotiation with opposing parties or their counsel on substantive issues in expected or pending litigation."[27]

Yet Mitcham negotiated with Crawford anyway, risking sanction or disbarment. "She was very zealous on behalf of her clients," he said. Mitcham claims Crawford was simply a messenger in a negotiation with Sur-

---

[25] Anthony G. Amsterdam, *Trial Manual 5 for the Defense of Criminal Cases* (Philadelphia: American Law Institute, 1988), l:§ 184, at 320.

[26] Rule 5.5(a) of the *Georgia Rules of Professional Conduct* states: "A lawyer shall not practice law in a jurisdiction in violation of the regulation of the legal profession in that jurisdiction, or assist another in doing so." Available at http://www.gabar.org/handbook/rules_index/.

[27] State Disciplinary Board, "Guidelines for Attorneys Utilizing Paralegals," Advisory Opinion No. 21 (September 16, 1977). Available at the Georgia State Bar Web site: http://www.gabar.org/handbook/state_disciplinary_board_opinions/adv_op_21/.

rency, but it is unclear how often Surrency was involved. After some back-and-forth, a plea deal would emerge and Mitcham would write it down. Then, according to Crawford, she would put the terms in a folder, which Surrency would open in court. Surrency would stand in court with Crawford while she related the facts in a defendant's case.

"I was actually asking her to come close to the line in order to handle caseloads," Surrency said of an ethical boundary he knew existed. "There were only so many hours in a day. . . . I was working sixty hours a week. A lot of it was homework — I was talking to the families."

Surrency believed he was overworked. But it was hard to establish whether he actually had the time to spend on cases or not, whether he was overloaded, lazy, or something else. Mitcham felt that Surrency's competence was not an issue. "He is a bright young fellow and operates well on his feet, but his discipline and preparation may have been lacking." And in truth, Surrency's performance kept with the environment in which he worked, where just getting by, making do, pushing cases through was considered acceptable. Mitcham recalled that at one point Surrency didn't even bring files with him — relying on his memory for loads of cases, a hard if not impossible task for anyone, given the enormous number of dates and legal charges. Yet he was allowed to get away with it.

Cathy Crawford complained about Surrency's disservice to his clients to Marie Boswell, clerk of the court. Boswell had watched Surrency for hundreds of hours, and concluded that too many people were being railroaded into pleading guilty. "I can't get in touch with him! I can't get in touch with him!" she said, imitating the calls she received from his clients.

Boswell wrote to Michael Shapiro, then the executive director of the GIDC, and went to a county commission session as well as to the tripartite committee, which was supposed to ensure the competence of indigent defense attorneys. Boswell expressed her concern that Surrency was not meeting with his clients before court and rarely visited the jail. She said that judges expected little unless Cathy Crawford was in court.[28] According to a letter from Shapiro to Boswell, the tripartite committee agreed to "re-energize the current defender" or hire someone to replace him to improve services.[29] Despite this, no action was taken.

Walter "Bud" Sanders, vice-chair of the Greene County Board of

---

[28] Boswell's concerns were relayed in Michael B. Shapiro (executive director of the Georgia Indigent Defense Council), memorandum to Greene County File, September 16, 1999.
[29] Michael B. Shapiro (executive director of the Georgia Indigent Defense Council) letter to Marie Boswell, clerk of Greene County Superior Court re: meeting of May 10, 2000, undated.

Commissioners, also served on the tripartite committee. Sanders didn't recall a need to overhaul the office. "The only complaints I used to hear about were from the attorneys who said that the inmates were having trouble getting in touch with [Surrency]," he said, which he felt the committee had addressed by setting up a local phone at the jail. Sanders didn't hear of "real problems . . . Judges never complained. Many judges never complained," he said.

Crawford confirmed that no one complained. The only reason she was allowed to do the lawyer's work that she did is because "the system allowed it — the judge, the DA, the probation officer, nobody cared." So she took her complaints elsewhere, to the local indigent defense committee — "and they listened to me rant." Not that it made a difference, she noted. Crawford left her job soon after she complained; though the circumstances of her departure are unclear, there appear to have been financial issues. "It got to the point where I had to beg for my check," she said.

Boswell quit, too. She wanted no part of what was happening in Greene County's courts. "The commission thinks that if you don't talk about it, it is going to go away. But this is not going to go away. It's only going to get worse."

What was happening was routine injustice. Before she took a new job as a clerk for a judge, Boswell predicted that Greene County would "get hit with a lawsuit that is going to rock the world."

✳ ✳ ✳

I'd rather ride the buses managing in Triple A than be a lawyer.

Tony La Russa (1986)

JUNE

MYRTLE ROWE

Player under contract, Antler Athletic Club (1910).
See HARRY KATZ, FRANK CERESI, PHIL MICHEL,
WILSON MCBEE & SUSAN REYBURN, BASEBALL AMERICANA (2009).

❧ JUNE ❧

SUN	MON	TUES	WED	THUR	FRI	SAT
		1	2	3	4	5
6	7	8	9	10	11	12
13	14	15	16	17	18	19
20	21	22	23	24	25	26
27	28	29	30			

THE AUTOCRAT OF THE ARMCHAIR

David F. Levi[†]

Richard Posner is a marvel.[1] He carries a full caseload as a U.S. circuit judge on the Seventh Circuit, teaches at the University of Chicago Law School, blogs with a Nobel Prize-winning economist (Gary Becker), and writes at least a book a year as well as any number of articles. His opinions are nicely written and explained. His scholarly writing covers a wide range of academic and public policy topics, from sex to literature, from jurisprudence to aging. Any large issue or event, such as the impeachment of a president or the treatment of captured Al Qaida members, is likely to elicit an interesting and thorough treatment of the topic from Judge Posner. Somehow he manages to be in the thick of things without diminishing his judicial role, although it is not unlikely that his more provocative academic writing kept him from an appointment to the United States Supreme Court in the 1980s. By all accounts, he is also a generous judicial and academic colleague. How he does all of this is one of the mysteries. Perhaps the explanation is simple: he is brilliant, hard working, and intellectually fearless. He is all of these things and more.

But is he an empiricist?

[†] Dean and Professor of Law, Duke University School of Law. Previously, United States District Judge for the Eastern District of California (1990-2007), Chair and Member of the Civil Rules Advisory Committee (1994-2003), and Chair of the Standing Committee on the Rules of Practice and Procedure (2003-2007). I am grateful to Mitu Gulati, Ernest Young, Lauren Collins, and Jennifer Dominguez for their many helpful comments and suggestions. I also thank the *Duke Law Journal* for its part in organizing this Symposium and particularly for its understanding of why this subject matter is of such importance. Copyright © 2009 by David F. Levi. This article originally appeared at 58 DUKE L.J. 1791 (2009). It is reprinted here with the permission of the author and the publisher.
[1] Judge Posner is a great admirer of Oliver Wendell Holmes Jr. *See* THE ESSENTIAL HOLMES: SELECTIONS FROM THE LETTERS, SPEECHES, JUDICIAL OPINIONS, AND OTHER WRITINGS OF OLIVER WENDELL HOLMES, JR. (Richard A. Posner ed., 1992). The allusion in the title is to Oliver Wendell Holmes Sr.'s popular *Atlantic Monthly* column, *The Autocrat of the Breakfast-Table*.

To be more precise, as a researcher who purports to describe how most judges think at all levels of the legal system, does he identify a reliable, sufficiently large data set and then apply appropriate statistical tests to the data such that others can evaluate the strength of his generalizations and replicate his conclusions using the same or other reliable data sets? Put somewhat differently, if Judge Posner were to take the stand as an expert on how most judges think most of the time, would his testimony be based upon "sufficient facts or data" to qualify as "reliable" under the Federal Rules governing admissibility of expert testimony?[2] Furthermore, as a distinguished judge who advocates for a particular approach to judging, an approach he calls "pragmatism,"[3] does he give sufficient attention to the need for reliable "empirics": transparent factfinding that can be challenged and tested, at the very least, by the parties to the litigation?

These questions might seem impertinent, even churlish. After all, Judge Posner has written several articles and at least one book that draw heavily on databases to answer questions about the legal system.[4] He is one of the founders of law and economics, and has been a key part in the upsurge of law and economics scholarship and law and social science research more generally, much of which consists of empirical study.

Judge Posner is certainly capable of empirical work and understands how it is done and its importance. But in his latest work on judging, *How Judges Think*,[5] he is no empiricist unless we are satisfied with "armchair empiricism." His generalizations about the ways of the judge and the world are ex cathedra pronouncements that generally lack any identified objective support outside of his own experience and belief. For many of

---

[2] Federal Rule of Evidence 702, Testimony by Experts, provides:

> If scientific, technical, or other specialized knowledge will assist the trier of fact to understand the evidence or to determine a fact in issue, a witness qualified as an expert by knowledge, skill, experience, training, or education, may testify thereto in the form of an opinion or otherwise, if (1) the testimony is based upon sufficient facts or data, (2) the testimony is the product of reliable principles and methods, and (3) the witness has applied the principles and methods reliably to the facts of the case.

FED. R. EVID. 702. The notes to Rule 702 caution: "If the witness is relying solely or primarily on experience, then the witness must explain how that experience leads to the conclusion reached, why that experience is a sufficient basis for the opinion, and how that experience is reliably applied to the facts." *Id.* advisory committee's note; *see also* Daubert v. Merrell Dow Pharmaceuticals, Inc., 509 U.S. 579, 585-98 (1993).

[3] *See* text accompanying *infra* note 13.

[4] *E.g.*, RICHARD A. POSNER, THE FEDERAL COURTS: CHALLENGE AND REFORM (1996); Tomas Philipson & Richard A. Posner, *A Theoretical and Empirical Investigation of the Effects of Public Health Subsidies for STD Testing*, 110 Q.J. ECON. 2 (1995); Richard A. Posner, *The 2000 Presidential Election: A Statistical and Legal Analysis*, 12 SUPREME CT. ECON. REV. 1 (2004).

[5] RICHARD A. POSNER, HOW JUDGES THINK (2008).

his assertions, it would appear that his dataset of judges is a set of one — himself. Further, as an advocate for a particular kind of pragmatic judging — consciously and explicitly making law embodying sound social policy — Judge Posner gives little or no attention to the critical, what I would call "empirical," question: How does the judge, particularly the appellate judge, know what the consequences of a new rule of law will be and whether those consequences are likely to be good for society? These are contestable issues that can be the subject of testimony and challenge within the courtroom and the litigation process. When the record is not developed, how does the judge make sound decisions about the social policy consequences of different legal rules?[6]

I write from the perspective of one who served as a U.S. district judge for almost seventeen years and who was deeply involved in the federal rulemaking process. Much of what I have to say about the book stems from these two experiences. These experiences and that perspective lead me to question a description of judging that pays so little attention to the average case or to the processes of fair adjudication, including the roles of the advocate and of our procedural rules and practices. Indeed, one detects not just Judge Posner's well-known disdain for legal formalism,[7] but something else more troubling and fundamental: a resistance to the limitations on a judge that are basic to our system, particularly that judges sit to decide the issues actually presented within the confines of a particular case and record. One senses that for this judge — a brilliant man steeped in

---

[6] For example, a party might contend that affirmative action programs in professional schools are necessary to the development of leaders in the military and in business. *See* Grutter v. Bollinger, 539 U.S. 306, 330-31 (2003). This assertion can be established or contested by expert testimony, based upon data and statistical tests, or perhaps by other evidence, including personal experience, offered under oath and subject to cross-examination. Without such evidence and testing processes, however, a judge would have no reliable basis for believing or disbelieving the mere assertion of this causal relationship. Appellate judges who go beyond the record to rely on factual contentions in amicus briefs or academic literature that have never been tested in the courtroom, that have been "mailed in," and that would not be admissible, start down a perilous path inconsistent with the carefully constructed truth-seeking process that has served well for many years.

[7] *See, e.g.*, POSNER, *supra* note 5, at 371-72 ("Legalists invent canons of construction (principles of interpretation) and distinctions between dictum and holding; embrace statutory and constitutional literalism but carve narrow exceptions for literal readings that produce absurd results; exalt rules over standards; [and] wash their hands of messy factual issues by adopting principles of deferential appellate review . . . ."); Richard A. Posner, *What Has Pragmatism to Offer Law?*, 63 S. CAL. L. REV. 1653, 1663 (1990) ("Legal formalism is the idea that legal questions can be answered by inquiry into the relation between concepts and hence without need for more than a superficial examination of their relation to the world of fact. It is, therefore, anti-pragmatic as well as anti-empirical.").

economics and academic learning, eager to make his mark on the development of the law and to exercise his broad lawmaking powers in the tradition of the great appellate lawgivers — such matters as precedent, the procedural posture of a case, the strategic decisions of the lawyers to advance certain positions and forego others, and the actual facts in the record simply get in the way.[8]

Judge Posner's basic point is that judicial decisionmaking is not governed strictly by logic or the reasoned application of the law — text and prior decisions — to facts, a process he calls "legalism" and the adherents of which he calls "legalists." According to Posner, "there is a pronounced political element in the decisions of American judges, including federal trial and intermediate appellate judges and U.S. Supreme Court Justices."[9] There is also a personal element to judging, he avers, because a judge's personal characteristics "such as race and sex; personality traits, such as authoritarianism; and professional and life experiences, such as having been a prosecutor or having grown up in turbulent times influence judging."[10] Political and personal factors, according to Posner, generate preconceptions, often unconscious, that affect judicial decision making.[11]

Furthermore, Judge Posner contends that there is a significant legislative aspect to judging; judges inevitably must make the law in the open areas where the law is unclear and undeveloped. According to Posner, this lawmaking role is unavoidable: "A combination of structural and cultural factors imposes a legislative role on our judges that they cannot escape."[12] Having established to his satisfaction that legalism fails to explain judicial behavior and that the legalist approach cannot resolve cases in the open areas of the law, Posner offers his own template for judging, an approach he calls "pragmatism" and describes as "basing judgments . . . on consequences, rather than on deduction from premises in the manner of a syllogism."[13]

Curiously, Judge Posner considers that these are controversial claims, even ones as banal as the claim that judges make the law by applying it to new fact settings or that judges could be influenced by their own life expe-

---

[8] *See generally* Linda E. Fisher, *Pragmatism is as Pragmatism Does: Of Posner, Public Policy and Empirical Reality*, 31 N.M. L. REV. 455, 491-92 (2001) (documenting how Judge Posner's "pragmatist agenda" leads to his reliance on "extra-record facts").

[9] POSNER, *supra* note 5, at 369-70.

[10] *Id.* at 370.

[11] *Id.* at 11. Relying upon Bayesian decision theory, he calls such preconceptions "Bayesian priors." *Id.* at 67; *see also infra* note 30 and accompanying text.

[12] POSNER, *supra* note 5, at 372.

[13] *Id.* at 40.

riences. These claims may have been shocking in the late nineteenth century when Justice Holmes asserted that history has more to do with the development of the law than logic,[14] but in a post legal-realist world, these claims are the new orthodoxy. According to Posner, however, most judges would vociferously deny that their decisions are ever influenced in the slightest by "political"[15] or personal considerations, and most judges pretend that they are finding the law and not making it.[16] For what it's worth, from the ease of my own armchair, I would take just the opposite position: I would say that most judges are more than aware that they are "making law," in the sense of amplifying it, when they apply precedents or statutory language to particular factual settings. I would also contend that most judges, particularly the very best ones, are acutely aware of the potential of personal factors, including judicial philosophy, life experience, and personality, to affect how judges approach and then decide legal issues. I would further say that part of the art of judging rests in recognizing the existence of these potential influences and then dealing with them in

---

[14] "The felt necessities of the time, the prevalent moral and political theories, intuitions of public policy, avowed or unconscious, even the prejudices which judges share with their fellowmen, have had a good deal more to do than the syllogism in determining the rules by which men should be governed." OLIVER WENDELL HOLMES, THE COMMON LAW 1 (Mark DeWolfe Howe ed., Harvard Univ. Press 1963) (1881). The idea that legal materials sometimes leave an open area within which the judge is freer to develop the law goes back many years. See H.L.A. HART, THE CONCEPT OF LAW 121-50 (1961); HANS KELSEN, PURE THEORY OF LAW 348-56 (Max Knight trans., Univ. of Calif. Press 1967) (1934); EDWARD H. LEVI, AN INTRODUCTION TO LEGAL REASONING 2-3, 7 (1949).

[15] Judge Posner continues the unfortunate use of the term "political" — with its overtone of partisan bias — to describe a judge's reliance on judicial philosophy. Judge Michael Boudin, a participant in this Symposium, comments upon the misleading use of the term in one of his contributions to this Issue. See Michael Boudin, A Response to Professor Ramseyer, Predicting Court Outcomes Through Political Preferences, 58 DUKE L.J. 1687, 1688 (2009) (calling the "political" label of a judicial opinion "mere provocation"). For a compelling argument that much of what Posner and others think of as "political" is actually quite consistent with legal decisionmaking, see Ernest A. Young, Just Blowing Smoke? Politics, Doctrine, and the Federalist Revival After Gonzales v. Raich, 2005 SUP CT. REV. 1, 14-15, 18-21.

[16] Judge Posner pokes a good deal of fun at Chief Justice John G. Roberts Jr. He repeatedly points to and then mocks the Chief Justice's assertion at his confirmation hearing that judges are like baseball umpires who just apply the rules to the facts as they unfold on the ground. E.g., POSNER, supra note 5, at 78-81; see also Confirmation Hearing on the Nomination of John G. Roberts, Jr. to Be Chief Justice of the United States: Hearing Before the S. Comm. on the Judiciary, 109th Cong. 56 (2005). Yet even Judge Posner concedes that much of the time this is exactly what judges do, POSNER, supra note 5, at 8, although one doubts that it is what Supreme Court Justices do much of the time, see Neil S. Siegel, Umpires at Bat: On Integration and Legitimation, 24 CONST. COMMENT. 701, 708 (2007) ("Supreme Court Justices cannot even agree on the basic contours of the 'strike zone' . . . because the constitutional text itself is indeterminate and the potential source materials for gleaning its meaning in particular settings are both numerous and contested.").

some appropriate way, depending on the nature and strength of the influence.

There are a number of problems with Judge Posner's descriptions and prescriptions. Most fundamentally, much of what he asserts about how judges think is just assertion, lacking any factual support in empirical study or even anecdote. One suspects that most of Posner's claims are based on examination of his own decisional processes or, perhaps, on his personal observations of some of his colleagues. Yet unfortunately, the book is neither structured nor argued as an autobiography.[17] Here are some of the many generalizations one finds in the book drawn from one knows not where:

- "Most judges who oppose abortion rights do so because of religious belief rather than because of a pragmatic assessment of such rights."[18]

- "A judge in a nonjury proceeding who has to decide whether to believe a witness's testimony will often have formed before the witness begins to testify an estimate of the likelihood that the testimony will be truthful."[19]

- Judges are more inclined to convict than jurors because "judges learn that prosecutors rarely file cases unless the evidence against the defendant is overwhelming."[20]

- "[M]any, maybe most, judges would if asked deny that they bring preconceptions to their cases[.]"[21]

- "[J]udges whose background is law teaching rather than private practice tend to be harder on the lawyers who appear before them."[22]

- "Appellate judges promoted from the trial court may be more likely than other appellate judges to vote to affirm a trial judge."[23]

- "[A] former trial judge promoted to the court of appeals may be more likely to focus more on the 'equities' of the individual case . . . and less on its precedential significance than would his colleagues who had never been trial judges."[24]

- "Most judges blend the two inquiries, the legalist and the legislative, rather than addressing them in sequence."[25]

---

[17] An intellectual autobiography by Judge Posner would be a wonderful addition to the sparse literature of judicial autobiography.

[18] POSNER, *supra* note 5, at 13.

[19] *Id.* at 65.

[20] *Id.* at 68.

[21] *Id.* at 72.

[22] *Id.* at 74.

[23] *Id.*

[24] *Id.*

[25] *Id.* at 84.

- "Accustomed to making nonlegalist judgments in the [nonroutine cases], the judge is likely to allow nonlegalist considerations to seep into his consideration of the [routine case]."[26]
- "Intuition plays a major role in judicial as in most decision making."[27]
- "[T]here are a few professions . . . in which the negative correlation between age and performance is weak. Judging is one of them, though part of the reason is that judges in our system are appointed at relatively advanced ages; this means that early decliners tend to be screened out and judges tend not to get bored, or run dry, at the same age at which persons in other fields do who have been in the same line of work for many years."[28]
- "Rather than a shortage of applicants for federal judgeships, there is a surplus."[29]

There are many more similarly rank assertions in the book. No studies are cited because there is nothing to cite to. The problem with these assertions for the most part is not that they are clearly untrue — some of them are couched tentatively, perhaps in acknowledgement of the lack of data and supporting empirical research — but that, in the absence of data and empirical studies, it is impossible to know how true or untrue they are. Thus, if Judge Posner's assertion were based upon data, it would be possible to test and then calibrate the significance of some of these assertions, and then to ask important follow-up questions. For example, to say that intuition or preconception plays a role in judicial decisionmaking is not to say anything useful. Judge Posner takes great delight in relying on Bayesian decision theory to make the point that judges have preconceptions, "priors" in Bayesian jargon,[30] which can affect their decisions. The existence of

---

[26] *Id.* at 85.

[27] *Id.* at 107.

[28] *Id.* at 161.

[29] *Id.* at 164.

[30] Judge Posner is unapologetic in his use of such jargon. "Judicial preconceptions are best understood, we shall see, with the aid of Bayesian decision theory. Not that this is how judges themselves would describe their thought process. And 'Bayes's theorem' is not the only term I shall be using that is likely to alarm some readers of a book about judges." *Id.* at 11. Like Monsieur Jourdain, who was so delighted and surprised to learn that he had been speaking in prose all of his life, see MOLIÈRE, THE BOURGEOIS GENTLEMAN 30-31 (Bernard Sahlins trans., Ivan R. Dee, Inc. 2000) (1670), I believe that most judges would be startled to learn that their preconceptions are actually Bayesian priors. I question whether Posner's addition of this label advances the central preoccupation of all who are involved in the litigation process with finding ways of neutralizing preconception and bias — by jurors, judges, and witnesses, whether conscious or unconscious. Because there are no data, it is difficult to know whether unconscious priors have any significant effect on judges in some or most cases. As to conscious priors, I find it difficult to believe that a good trial judge would ever rely in significant part on a hunch or prior to find any

preconception in the legal system is well known. Many of the procedures in a trial or other proceedings attempt to neutralize the effects of bias or preconception.[31] In a jury trial, for example, lawyers and judges use voir dire to expose potential jurors' preconceptions. Once exposed, the judge can address and neutralize these preconceptions to the satisfaction of the participants or the lawyer will strike the juror. Judges and lawyers constantly remind jurors to keep an open mind as a trial proceeds to guard against premature conclusions based upon only some of the evidence. In court trials, I frequently reminded myself to simply listen and not attempt to reach tentative views of how the case ultimately would be decided. I did not like to discuss ongoing court trials with law clerks or colleagues precisely because I did not wish to start characterizing the evidence until I had heard all of it. For the same reasons, many judges continue to instruct jurors not to discuss the case until deliberations have begun and the jurors have heard all of the evidence, the arguments of counsel, and the judge's instructions. Good lawyers attempt to predict the sorts of preconceptions that a judge may have and then address them with either facts or arguments.[32] Good judges are constantly on the lookout for their own preconceptions. When preconception rises to the level of bias, good judges will recuse themselves on their own motion.

It is not nearly good enough to point out that judges and jurors, like others, have preconceptions. What would be useful and important to know is whether these preconceptions are fixed and strong, whether they

---

material fact by a preponderance of the evidence. Indeed, addressing such preconceptions is one of the critical goals of a fair trial proceeding and of the rules that govern such proceedings.

[31] There is a large body of literature on debiasing techniques. *See, e.g.*, Linda Babcock, George Loewenstein & Samuel Issacaroff, *Creating Convergence: Debiasing Biased Litigants*, 22 LAW & SOC. INQUIRY 913, 914-23 (1997) (proposing debiasing mechanisms for negotiations); Christine Jolls & Cass R. Sunstein, *Debiasing Through Law*, 35 J. LEGAL STUD. 199, 200-02 (2006) (considering how debiasing through law works to address a range of legal questions in areas "from consumer safety law to corporate law to property law"); Jerry Kang & Mahzarin R. Banaji, *Fair Measures: A Behavioral Realist Revision of "Affirmative Action,"* 94 CAL L. REV. 1060, 1108-15 (2006) (advocating for new debiasing techniques in the race context). One might expect an empirical account of preconceptions to include a thorough investigation of these debiasing techniques and an analysis of whether they actually work in practice.

[32] When I was the U.S. Attorney for the Eastern District of California from 1986-1990, my office lost a suppression motion involving the search of a home that contained a methamphetamine laboratory, because the judge found that the affiant had omitted from the affidavit that the surveillance officers had seen young children present at the scene. The judge assumed that young children would not typically be present at the site of a methamphetamine lab because of the danger of explosion and fire, and that therefore this was material information detracting from probable cause. It was a failure of advocacy not to demonstrate to the judge that this assumption was incorrect: Methamphetamine manufacturers often show little concern for the safety of their children or neighbors.

may become fluid as a trial develops, and whether there are fair procedures for addressing them. Judge Posner does not seem to appreciate the
dynamic nature of litigation and how many times in a case or trial a judge
will rule one way and then reverse course later. What does this say about
the strength of initial preconceptions? It would be important to know
whether the ability to overcome preconception and keep an open mind is a
part of the judicial craft that can be studied, learned, and improved upon.
If scholars and judges could study preconceptions in some systematic way,
they could ask many interesting empirical questions about them. And they
might develop new methods for neutralizing, cabining, or, at least, revealing their role. Without data, however, Posner is at a loss to move forward
our understanding and procedures. His bare assertion that judges are prisoners of their conscious and unconscious preconceptions diminishes the
judicial role and the striving by conscientious judges for objectivity and
fairness. His assertion will become fodder for ideologues who believe that
everything is "political" and that all relationships are defined by power.[33]

Another empirical problem with the book as a description of how
judges think is that Judge Posner is simply uninterested in the vast majority of cases that come before the courts. At least at the appellate level, he
concedes that judges will decide the quotidian case in precisely the same
way. The law will be clear, or clear enough, and the facts will be
uncontested, assumed, as on an appeal from a summary judgment ruling,
or found by the court below by trial or hearing. Applying the law to the
facts in these cases may require a degree of discernment and elbow grease,
but most appellate judges will come to the same conclusions on the arguments presented. In Posner's lexicon, these cases can be decided by the
application of "legalist" techniques, which treat the law as a system of rules
that produces predictable outcomes based on logic, reason, precedent, and
common sense. These cases do not interest Posner even though, he concedes, they account for most of the cases that appellate judges are thinking
about.[34] It is these cases that end up in "unpublished" dispositions from the

---

[33] In my brief experience as a law teacher, I find that law students are particularly susceptible to
the belief that judges are political actors who routinely decide cases according to their own self-
interest, partisan beliefs, previous experience, and such personal characteristics as gender, religion, and race.

[34] POSNER, *supra* note 5, at 8 ("Legalism drives most judicial decisions, though generally they are
the less important ones for the development of legal doctrine or the impact on society."). Judge
Posner now concedes that although his book purports to describe how all judges think, it is
concerned mainly with the appellate courts, *see* Interview, *A Conversation with Judge Richard A.
Posner*, 58 DUKE L.J. 1807, 1816 (2009), and only a subset of their cases — those in the "open
area." Considering that unpublished opinions account for more than 80 percent of the appellate

courts of appeals.[35] The overall dominance of such cases within the system is probably even greater than the appellate statistics suggest if one considers that in many cases the parties do not elect to appeal from the judgment of the district court.[36]

Judge Posner is interested in the comparatively few cases that produce disagreement among judges and that tend to end up in the Supreme Court or in the casebooks. Though a fraction of the caseload, these are the cases that command his attention. These are the cases, he contends, that cannot be decided only by reference to prior case law, the language of statute, and the like, but seem to call forth some application of the judge's personal policy beliefs or judicial philosophy. These are the cases that generate disagreement and appeals, that drive the development of the law, and that create reputations for our great appellate judges.

But the typical case must have its due in any description of how judges think most of the time.[37] For an empiricist, the observation that in the vast majority of cases judges of different political stripes, genders, religions, races, ages, and experience all reach the same conclusion might be seen as the important point if one were to describe how judges think most of the time, instead of how appellate judges think a little bit of the time in uncertain cases.[38] The very fact that judges are usually "legalists" might cause one to ask if the legalist approach is the starting point in every case, including those that eventually require the judge to draw upon policy preferences. Judge Posner contends otherwise. He asserts that "[a]ccustomed to making nonlegalist judgments in the [nonroutine cases], the judge is

---

courts' dockets, *see infra* note 35, Judge Posner is actually focused on a relatively small number of cases within the remaining percentage.

[35] *See* JAMES C. DUFF, ADMIN. OFFICE OF THE U.S. COURTS, 2007 ANNUAL REPORT OF THE DIRECTOR: JUDICIAL BUSINESS OF THE UNITED STATES COURTS 48 tbl.S-3 (2007), *available at* http://www.uscourts.gov/judbus2007/JudicialBusinespdfversion.pdf (noting that 83.5 percent of opinions of cases in the U.S. courts of appeals are unpublished).

[36] Many cases are not appealed at all. District judges decide them in whole or in part and the parties accept the rulings or come to some settlement based on their understanding of the value of the case according to their own "legalist" analysis. *See generally* U.S. Courts, Federal Courts Management Statistics, http://www.uscourts.gov/fcmstat/index.html (last visited Mar. 23, 2009) (showing that 349,969 cases were filed in federal district courts in 2008, whereas only 61,104 appeals were filed in the courts of appeals during that same time period).

[37] *Cf.* Frederick Schauer, *Easy Cases*, 58 S. CAL. L. REV. 399, 401-08 (1985) (emphasizing the need to consider less-litigated constitutional provisions when creating constitutional theories).

[38] *See* Thomas J. Mills & Cass R. Sunstein, *The New Legal Realism*, 75 U. CHI. L. REV. 831, 841 (2008) (noting that a "great deal might be learned by incorporating unpublished opinions" into New Legal Realism analysis because most studies are now limited to published opinions that, because of their atypical nature, overstate the actual effects of judicial ideology and other characteristics).

likely to allow nonlegalist considerations to seep into his consideration of the [routine case]."[39] Why the reverse is not just as or more plausible, Posner does not say. And if the experience of our legal system by the people who use it matters, and I suggest that it should, the handling and disposition of the typical case would be of very great importance.

Judge Posner is not interested in the typical case. Like some other appellate judges, he seems to have a deep-seated enmity toward the everyday case. The dislike of the average case by certain federal appellate judges, including Posner, became clear during the 2004 debate over a proposed change to Appellate Rule 32.1 that made citable so-called "unpublished" opinions.[40] The unpublished opinion, a misnomer given that all opinions are now published and available electronically, is a phenomenon of the federal circuit courts and some state appellate courts. Before electronic publishing, an unpublished opinion was truly unpublished; the court did not send the opinion to West or other publishers and it was usually available only to the parties in the litigation in slip form or in the file maintained at the courthouse. These opinions were not citable because they were not generally available, and to permit citation would give unfair advantage to institutional, repeat litigants who would have their own collections of these cases. But with the advent of electronic research and with the requirement that court filings be available on public court websites, it makes no sense to consider these opinions unavailable or unpublished. They are easily obtainable and they appear in any electronic search. Nonetheless, many of the circuits continued to treat such opinions as second-class citizens.[41] Some courts denied them precedential effect, but permitted citation for whatever guidance the opinion might offer, but other courts went a step further, barring the parties from even citing the opinion on pain of sanctions. Given that more than 80 percent of the output of the

---

[39] POSNER, *supra* note 5, at 85.

[40] The new rule invalidated local appellate rules that forbade the citation of "unpublished" opinions:

Rule 32.1. Citing Judicial Dispositions
(a) Citation Permitted. A court may not prohibit or restrict the citation of federal judicial opinions, orders, judgments, or other written dispositions that have been:
(i) designated as "unpublished," "not for publication," "non-precedential," "not precedent," or the like; and
(ii) issued on or after January 1, 2007.

FED. R. APP. P. 32.1.

[41] Patrick J. Schiltz, *Much Ado About Little: Explaining the* Sturm Und Drang *over the Citation of Unpublished Opinions*, 62 WASH. & LEE L. REV. 1429, 1430-31 (2005) (summarizing the ways circuit courts treat unpublished opinions).

courts of appeals consists of unpublished opinions,[42] this prohibition was no small matter. This is not the place to rehash the arguments over the rule amendment.[43] The rule changed, and all unpublished opinions from all federal appellate courts at least may now be cited, even if they lack precedential force in some circuits.[44]

Judge Posner lined up with the opponents to the rule change in his circuit.[45] Like most of his colleagues,[46] he considered that citation of unpublished opinions would cause the judges a great deal of needless effort to distinguish cases that were best left undisturbed and unread.[47] He did not think then and he does not think now that these cases contribute anything to our understanding of how the legal system works or how judges think. Yet this point of view is questionable given the very large number of these cases. Indeed, one might have expected Posner, a sometime empiricist and an observer of the judicial system, at least to have appreciated the use that

---

[42] *See supra* note 35 and accompanying text.

[43] Letter from Samuel A. Alito, Jr., Chair, Advisory Comm. on Appellate Rules, to David F. Levi, Chair, Standing Comm. on Rules of Practice and Procedure 2-13 (May 6, 2005), *available at* http://www.uscourts.gov/rules/Reports/AP5-2005.pdf (summarizing the debates, arguments, and public comments over the proposed new rule 32.1); Letter from Samuel A. Alito, Jr., Chair, Advisory Comm. on Appellate Rules, to David F. Levi, Chair, Standing Comm. on Rules of Practice and Procedure 53-93 (May 14, 2004), *available at* http://www.uscourts.gov/rules/Reports/AP5-2004.pdf (chronicling the arguments on each side of the debate); *see also* Schiltz, *supra* note 41, at 1458-90.

[44] *See supra* note 40.

[45] Letter from Richard A. Posner et al., to Samuel A. Alito, Jr., Chair, Advisory Comm. on Appellate Rules 1 (Feb. 11, 2004), *available at* http://www.uscourts.gov/rules/ Appellate_Comments_2003/03-AP-396.pdf.

[46] Judge Easterbrook was a notable exception. *See* Letter from Frank H. Easterbrook, Circuit Judge, to Peter G. McCabe, Sec'y, Standing Comm. on Rules of Practice and Procedure 1 (Feb. 13, 2004), *available at* http://www.uscourts.gov/rules/Appellate_ Comments_2003/03-AP-367.pdf; *see also* Tony Mauro, *Difference of Opinion; Should Judges Make More Rulings Available as Precedent? How an Obscure Proposal Is Dividing the Federal Bench*, LEGAL TIMES, Apr. 12, 2004, at 1 (quoting Judge Easterbrook's remark that barring citations to unpublished opinions "implies that judges have something to hide").

[47] A letter to the Appellate Rules Committee Chair read, in part:

> Because the order is not citable, the judges do not have to spend a lot of time worrying about nuances of language. . . . [We] do not need to worry about nuances of language because the order will not be thrown back in our faces someday as a precedent. And thrown back they will be, no matter how often we state that unpublished orders though citable (if the proposed rule is adopted) are not precedents. For if a lawyer states in its brief that in our unpublished opinion in *A v. B* we said X and in *C v. D* we said Y and in this case the other side wants us to say Z, we can hardly reply that when we don't publish we say what we please and take no responsibility. We will have a moral duty to explain, distinguish, reaffirm, overrule, etc. any unpublished order brought to our attention by counsel.

Letter from Richard A. Posner et al., *supra* note 45, at 1.

a lawyer could make of unpublished opinions to mount an empirical argument. One reason a lawyer might wish to cite to unpublished opinions is to show an appellate court how a rule is actually working in practice, where it is being applied, whether it is being applied consistently, and the like. There are many contexts in which knowing how a rule of law is actually coming to the courts will be important to advocacy, to the court, and indeed to the very pragmatism that Posner advocates. For example, when a defendant asserts qualified immunity, a party might wish to show how earlier rulings demonstrate that a rule of law either is or is not "clearly established." Or if one wishes to argue about the consequences of a particular rule of law for other cases and factual circumstances — and consequences are the lodestar of Posner's pragmatism — one would want to look at the vast majority of cases in which the consequences are most likely to occur. In this sense, the unpublished opinion contains important data, not because the reasoning in the opinion may or may not be persuasive, but because of the very existence of the opinion, the outcome, and the controversy. Yet Posner is not interested in such data, and one may wonder why.[48]

This tendency to undervalue the data and the processes of the legal system is observable in *How Judges Think* in additional ways. Judge Posner purports to describe how all judges think, but he seems to have very little feel for the trial court and for the role of the bar and the parties. There is hardly any discussion of the influence on judicial thinking of the briefs, the arguments, and the lawyers' strategic decisions to press certain contentions and let others slide. The failure to discuss the effect of lawyering on how judges think leaves the impression that the briefs and other work product, including argument and direct- and cross-examination, are not of much significance. I disagree with this, and I think other trial judges would

---

[48] If the reason were simply the time it would take to distinguish the reasoning or holding in such cases, and a view that the cases are so inadequately prepared that they do not deserve this expenditure of time and attention, then it should satisfy that the cases have no precedential value and the court is free to ignore their reasoning and wording. But in an interview posted on the *How Appealing* website, Judge Posner indicates that he neither understands nor could accept such an approach:

> I don't like the idea of allowing unpublished opinions to be cited, which is another way of saying that I think courts should be permitted to designate some of their decisions as nonprecedential and therefore not worth citing. (Apparently under the new rule, we won't be allowed to forbid citation of unpublished opinions, but will be allowed to deny precedential force to them, a combination that seems to me to make no sense.)

20 Questions for Circuit Judge Richard A. Posner of the U.S. Court of Appeals for the Seventh Circuit, HOWAPPEALING.COM, Dec. 1, 2003, http://howappealing.law.com/20q/2003_12_01_20qappellateblog_archive.html.

as well. In a courtroom, with the parties often present and intensely interested in the fairness of the proceedings, a judge feels quite constrained to
address the questions and issues presented by the lawyers. A judge who
declines to address those issues will appear unfair or biased. Similarly, a
judge who generates arguments that the lawyers did not raise will appear
to assist one side or the other. Lawyers and parties who face a judge acting
as a roving commissioner will view the judge as yet another adversary in
the courtroom, and as biased or even co-opted in some way. Perhaps I
overstate these constraints or perhaps I was too sensitive to them as a
judge. The point is that in a description of how all judges think, it leaves a
huge hole to ignore the effect of lawyers and their clients, and the need to
run a fair courtroom, on judicial thinking.

Nor does Judge Posner consider the way in which the record is developed in a case and the constraints that the record might impose on a fair-
minded trial or appellate judge. Trial judges spend a good deal of their
time deciding what evidence is sufficiently reliable to be admitted. Lawyers devote their attention to challenging and countering testimony that
they view as misleading or inaccurate. The system imposes certain requirements, most notably, in the common law tradition, that witnesses
cannot "mail" it in. They have to submit themselves to rigorous questioning under oath.

And this process for reliable, fair, and transparent factfinding points to
another problem in Judge Posner's theory and discussion: He never addresses how a carefully constructed factual record relates to his theory of
pragmatic judging. Yet without such a record, pragmatic judges are at sea
and at large, making it up according to their own lights. For Posner, a
good judge is one who develops the law in directions that are sensible and
that produce beneficial consequences for society.[49] This is unobjectionable
if the judge includes the lawyers in this quest such that there is a sound
factual basis in the record — data — upon which the judge reliably can
project those consequences. But judges who think that they know what is
sensible or beneficial merely by dint of education or intellect are just as
formalist as the "legalists" to the degree that they rely upon a fixed set of
theories of human nature, economics, history, or political economy out in
the ether to deduce rules of law, rather than building such rules from the
ground up by responding to the particular facts of a particular situation
and dispute. The trial judge who, after hearing argument, honestly identi-

---

[49] See POSNER, supra 5, at 13 ("A pragmatic judge assesses the consequences of judicial decisions
for their bearing on sound public policy as he conceives it.").

fies what the grounds of decision will be and permits the parties to address those grounds and develop in the record a factual basis in support or derogation of those grounds — including consequences to the greater society, if those consequences will be a basis for the decision — is to my mind the best trial judge. Similarly, the appellate judge who plays by the rules, abiding by the record presented and remanding to the district court for additional factfinding when necessary, is the best kind of appellate judge. And these judges are neither legalists nor pragmatists. These judges are empiricists.

* * *

EARLY COVERAGE OF BASEBALL
IN THE GREEN BAG

We note a decision which holds the debatable doctrine that it is a crime for one base-ball captain to kill another. This is the doctrine of Byrd *v.* Commonwealth (Supreme Court of Appeals of Virginia), 16 S.E. Rep. 727.

Killing a Base-ball Player,
5 Green Bag 247 (1893)

In Mace *v.* State, Supreme Court of Arkansas, in July, 1893, it was held (two judges dissenting) that baseball is a game of skill, within a statute making it a criminal offence to bet on a game of hazard or skill. That seems unanswerable. "A game of baseball" is a very common phrase, and it requires skill to play it, especially to "throw" it. One might well argue too that it is a game of hazard, — at all events, it is a hazardous game.

Betting on Baseball,
5 Green Bag 530 (1893)

Above: Chief Justice Fred M. Vinson (front row, white hat) sits between President Harry Truman (standing, autographing baseball) and Judge William P. Cole, Jr., of the Court of Customs and Patent Appeals at a Washington Senators game in 1952. **Below:** Truman throws out the first ball.

FRED VINSON AND THE NATIONAL PASTIME

Adam Aft[†]

Frederick M. Vinson enjoyed an extraordinary career in public service, from City Attorney for Louisa, Kentucky (1914-15), to Chief Justice of the United States (1946-53), with several important stops in the federal executive and judicial branches in between. Even as he rose in office, with the associated elevations in personal and professional prestige and power, he continued to find time to watch, and occasionally play, baseball. An accomplished player in his youth, Vinson retained a love for baseball and a deep appreciation for the game throughout his adult life.

Vinson played baseball as a schoolboy, and went on to become a star at Centre College in Danville, Kentucky, where he played shortstop and helped the team win three state championships. Vinson then moved on to play for various semi-professional baseball teams in and around Kentucky. Finally, turning down a tryout for the St. Louis Browns, Vinson stopped played semi-pro baseball and spent more time pursuing careers in law and politics.

In his mature years Vinson did from time to time take the field for fun or bragging rights. He played, for example, on the Democratic side in the annual inter-party Congressional baseball game while he was serving in the House of Representatives (1924-29, 1931-38).[1] Vinson remained a fan of the annual game even after he left Congress. His social calendar kept by his assistant at the Supreme Court noted the game each May. In 1951, the calendar even notes that he brought Justice Sherman Minton along with him. When he was serving as a judge, Vinson could be relied upon to tell each crop of law clerks about the news coverage of the 1928 Congressional game, which included a report of Vinson's running from the shortstop position all the way back into left field to catch a ball.[2] On one occasion, Vinson also took his brother to the exact spot where he had made a great catch during one of the games.[3] As he grayed, though, Vinson was more often to be found in the stands, where he was a relatively frequent and prominent celebrity spectator.

What follows is a short photographic review of the love affair between Vinson and America's national pastime.

[†] Much of the material in this article is drawn from two fine biographies: Francis A. Allen & Neil Walsh Allen, *A Sketch of Chief Justice Fred M. Vinson* (2005), and James E. St. Clair & Linda C. Gugin, *Chief Justice Fred M. Vinson of Kentucky* (2002). The photos are reproduced with the permission of the University of Kentucky Libraries, Special Collections and Archives, and, for the two on the next page, with the permission of Centre College as well. Thanks to Jeffrey Suchanek, Head of the Public Policy Archives at the University of Kentucky, for his kind advice and assistance.
[1] *See, e.g.*, *Democrats Defeat Republicans' Team in Ball Game*, WASH. POST, May 2, 1926.
[2] University of Kentucky, *Vinson Oral History Transcripts* ("Oral History") (interview of Howard J. Trienens & Newton N. Minow) (February 27, 1975).
[3] Oral History (interview of James R. Vinson) (November 12, 1975).

Above: The 1909 Centre College team on the steps of Old Main Street in Danville, Kentucky. Front: Diederich, Devant, Hawkins. Back: Johnson (coach), Cave, Prichard, Duffy, Seelbach, Vinson, Arnold, Harper, Webber, Hager (mgr.). The team went 13-4 and was state champion. Vinson played shortstop, as he did all three years he was on the team. He once quit to devote more time to his studies, but his friend Hager convinced him to return. **Below:** Vinson and three of his Centre College teammates in 1909 (left to right): Hawkins, Vinson, Diederich, Prichard. Vinson and Prichard were good friends and remained close after college, through family (there were numerous friendly connections between the Prichards and the Vinsons) and the Kentucky Democratic Party. Oral History (interview of Edward F. Prichard Jr.) (October 11, 1974).

Vinson (fourth from the left in the front row) captained the Centre College team to a third state championship in 1911, the year he graduated from the college's law school. As a formal matter, he attended law school while party to a baseball contract with his mother. Before starting law school Vinson had signed a contract to play for the Lexington, Kentucky professional team. His mother objected, preferring that her son go to law school. Virginia Vinson took the train to Lexington and bought the baseball rights on her son for 25¢. Oral History (interview of James R. Vinson) (Nov. 12, 1975). After graduating from law school Vinson continued to play baseball on various semi-pro teams. By 1915, he was on the Paintsville semi-pro team. Before that he had played for the Lexington, Kentucky team in the Blue Grass League and in various other towns including Louisa, where he was a city attorney. Vinson did not have a long semi-pro career, and he was not an overpowering player. But he was a crowd favorite in Louisa, where he was known for his good glove and what would now be called "small ball" play — short base hits and bunting to reach, good base running, and so on. Oral History (interview of W.E. Crutcher) (Jan. 8, 1975). Vinson played semi-pro baseball until 1916, when he turned down a chance to try out for the St. Louis Browns and instead campaigned for the office of Commonwealth Attorney for Kentucky's 32nd judicial district. He won the election and embarked on a long and successful career in law and politics. He did, however, carry for the rest of his life one regret about his playing days. While playing for Centre College, Vinson put on an especially impressive performance in a road game against what was then known as Trinity College and is now Duke University. He went 5-for-5, with two doubles and six stolen bases, and made some sensational plays in the field. Unfortunately, the next day's newspaper account of the game mistakenly credited Vinson's prowess to one of his teammates. Oral History (interview of James R. Vinson) (Nov. 12, 1975).

Above: Vinson served under President Truman as Director of War Mobilization and Reconversion (1945) and Secretary of the Treasury (1945-46), before taking office as Chief Justice on June 24, 1946. Here, Vinson sits in the President's entourage (in the background, in line with Truman's left shoulder) on April 16, 1946, as the Truman throws out the first ball for the Washington Senators' opening day game at Griffith Stadium against the Boston Red Sox. **Below:** In the late summer of 1949 the St. Louis Cardinals were locked in a tight pennant race with the Brooklyn Dodgers. Vinson (right) attended a Cardinals-Cubs game in St. Louis on September 7. The Cardinals won the game 3-2, but eventually lost the league championship to the Dodgers.

Above: Vinson (left), Truman (center), and Senators owner Clark Griffith (right), at September 1, 1951, loss to the Yankees. The big leagues were in need of a new commissioner in 1951. Griffith lobbied for Vinson to take the job, but he declined to be a candidate — not an easy decision. Oral History (interview of Trienens & Minow) (Feb. 27, 1975). **Below:** Vinson participates in a traditional adjudication, probably at a Congressional game in 1952. His college teammates would have seen the irony of Vinson in an umpire-like role. In his playing days he had earned a reputation for frequent and vigorous disputation with umpires. Oral History (interview of Kit Carson Elswick) (Nov. 12, 1974).

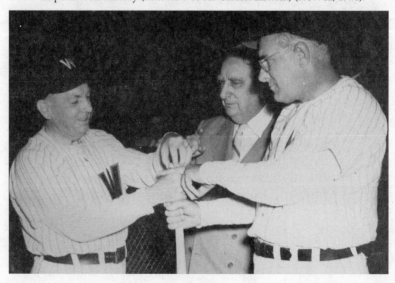

217

The 1953 season was Vinson's last. He would die on September 11 of that year. Here he attends the Senators' home opener with President Dwight D. Eisenhower on April 16, 1953. It would be another loss to the Yankees. While discussions in Vinson's chambers at the Supreme Court were usually about work, after hours Vinson frequently talked baseball with his clerks. Former clerk Howard Trienens recalled fielding questions ranging from what Joe DiMaggio's batting average was to who won the third World Series game of 1936. Oral History (interview of Trienens & Minow) (Feb. 27, 1975). (The New York Yankees beat the New York Giants 2-1, and went on to take the Series four games to two.) "Until his death," wrote Francis and Neil Allen, Vinson

> enjoyed astonishing friends and acquaintances with his ability to recite from memory the batting averages of major league ball players and even more esoteric baseball statistics. It was an ill-advised young person, wishing to serve as a Vinson law clerk, who failed at least to note the current standings of the major league teams before being interviewed by the Chief.

✳ ✳ ✳

I have no expectation of making a hit every time I come to bat. What I seek is the highest possible batting average, not only for myself, but for my team.

Franklin D. Roosevelt (1933)

Nos. 08-1529 and 08-1547

In the Supreme Court of the United States

EUGENE MIGLIACCIO, ET AL., PETITIONERS

v.

YANIRA CASTANEDA, ET AL.

CHRIS HENNEFORD, PETITIONER

v.

YANIRA CASTANEDA, AS PERSONAL REPRESENTATIVE
OF THE ESTATE OF FRANCISCO CASTANEDA, ET AL.

*ON PETITIONS FOR A WRIT OF CERTIORARI
TO THE UNITED STATES COURT OF APPEALS
FOR THE NINTH CIRCUIT*

**BRIEF FOR THE UNITED STATES
AS AMICUS CURIAE SUPPORTING PETITIONERS**

ELENA KAGAN
  *Solicitor General
    Counsel of Record*
TONY WEST
  Assistant Attorney General
EDWIN S. KNEEDLER
  Deputy Solicitor General
PRATIK A. SHAH
  *Assistant to the Solicitor
    General*
BARBARA L. HERWIG
HOWARD S. SCHER
  Attorneys

DAVID S. CADE
  *Acting General Counsel
  Department of Health and
    Human Services
  Washington, D.C.*

  *Department of Justice
  Washington, D.C. 20530-0001
  (202) 514-2217*

QUESTION PRESENTED

Whether 42 U.S.C. 233(a), which provides that a suit against the United States under the Federal Tort Claims Act is exclusive of any other action against a commissioned officer or employee of the Public Health Service for injury resulting from the performance of medical functions, bars a suit against such an officer or employee based on *Bivens* v. *Six Unknown Named Agents of Federal Bureau of Narcotics*, 403 U.S. 388 (1971).

(I)

In the Supreme Court of the United States

No. 08-1529

EUGENE MIGLIACCIO, ET AL., PETITIONERS

v.

YANIRA CASTANEDA, ET AL.

No. 08-1547

CHRIS HENNEFORD, PETITIONER

v.

YANIRA CASTANEDA, AS PERSONAL REPRESENTATIVE OF
THE ESTATE OF FRANCISCO CASTANEDA, ET AL.

---

*ON PETITIONS FOR A WRIT OF CERTIORARI
TO THE UNITED STATES COURT OF APPEALS
FOR THE NINTH CIRCUIT*

**BRIEF FOR THE UNITED STATES
AS AMICUS CURIAE SUPPORTING PETITIONERS**

INTEREST OF THE UNITED STATES

The court of appeals held that 42 U.S.C. 233(a)—which makes an action against the United States under the Federal Tort Claims Act (FTCA) the exclusive remedy for all damage claims arising out of medical care provided by commissioned officers or employees of the federal Public Health Service (PHS) while acting within the scope of their employment—does not bar tort claims premised on *Bivens*

(1)

2

v. *Six Unknown Named Agents of Federal Bureau of Narcotics*, 403 U.S. 388 (1971). The government has a significant interest in proper resolution of that issue. The government raises Section 233(a) as a bar to suit against individual PHS personnel when they are sued for conduct arising out of medical treatment. Further, the court of appeals' decision will likely have an adverse impact on the government's ability to recruit, hire, and retain medical personnel for the PHS, and may affect other federal entities that have medical missions covered by similar immunity statutes.

STATEMENT

1. The PHS, which is part of the Department of Health and Human Services (HHS), see 42 U.S.C. 201 *et seq.*, employs, among others, over 6,000 commissioned officers as physicians, dentists, nurses, pharmacists, and other medical personnel, and nearly 14,000 civilian employees whose duties involve patient care. PHS personnel are detailed to a number of agencies, including the Department of Homeland Security, Bureau of Prisons, Indian Health Service, and United States Marshals Service. They provide medical care in every State and in numerous foreign countries—often in communities most in need of medical care providers. PHS personnel also staff quarantine stations to limit the introduction of communicable diseases into the United States and to prevent their spread. See 42 U.S.C. 264; 42 C.F.R. 71.32, 71.33.

PHS's Commissioned Corps is one of the seven uniformed services of the United States. 42 U.S.C. 201(p), 204, 207. The Commissioned Corps, which includes the Surgeon General, may be called into military service in times of war or national emergency, at which point its personnel become subject to the Uniform Code of Military Justice. 42 U.S.C. 217.[1]

2. a. Following a December 2005 conviction, Francisco Castaneda, an alien, was imprisoned by the California Department of Corrections (DOC). During that incarceration, Castaneda met several times with DOC medical personnel regarding a lesion on his penis. Although those personnel recommended a biopsy, Castaneda did not receive one. Pet. App. 2a-3a.[2]

On March 27, 2006, Castaneda was transferred from DOC to Immigration and Customs Enforcement (ICE) custody in San Diego in connection with removal proceedings that had been commenced against him. According to the complaint filed in district court, Castaneda immediately complained to medical staff—consisting of PHS personnel—that a lesion on his penis was growing, becoming painful, and producing a discharge. He was examined by a physician's assistant, who noted both Castaneda's personal history of genital warts and his family history of cancer, and recommended a urology consultation and a biopsy. Although that recommendation was approved, Castaneda did not receive a biopsy. Over the ensuing months, he repeatedly complained that his condition was worsening. He was seen by several different doctors (including urologists) and physician's assistants, some of whom were concerned about the possibility of cancer and recommended a biopsy.

---

[1] The Secretary of HHS may also activate the National Disaster Medical System (NDMS) to provide health services to victims of a public-health emergency. 42 U.S.C. 300hh-11(a). The Secretary may appoint individuals to serve as intermittent NDMS personnel; such individuals are considered PHS employees for purposes of 42 U.S.C. 233(a). 42 U.S.C. 300hh-11(c).

[2] All citations to "Pet. App." are to the appendix to the petition for a writ of certiorari filed in No. 08-1529.

4

Others considered the problem to be genital warts. Pet. App. 3a-7a, 42a-48a.

In January 2007, Castaneda saw another urologist, who concluded that the lesion was "most likely penile cancer" and ordered a biopsy. On February 5, 2007, before the scheduled biopsy, Castaneda was released from ICE custody. Three days later, he went to a hospital and was diagnosed with penile cancer. A week after that, his penis was amputated, and he began undergoing chemotherapy for the metastasized cancer. He died in February 2008. Pet. App. 7a-8a.

b. Castaneda commenced this action months before his death.[3] He asserted claims against the United States under the FTCA, against state officers and employees under 42 U.S.C. 1983, and against various federal officers and employees of the PHS under *Bivens*. Castaneda alleged that the individual federal defendants violated the Fifth and Eighth Amendments of the Constitution by failing to treat his known serious medical condition, purposefully denying treatment, and acting with deliberate indifference to his serious health needs. Pet. App. 8a.

At all relevant times, the individual federal defendants (petitioners in this Court) were either commissioned officers or civilian employees of the PHS. After certifying that petitioners had acted within the scope of their employment, the government, which then represented petitioners, moved to dismiss the claims against petitioners on the basis of 42 U.S.C. 233(a). Pet. App. 8a-9a. Section 233(a) provides:

> The remedy against the United States provided by sections 1346(b) and 2672 of title 28 [the Federal Tort Claims Act] * * * for damage for personal injury, in-

---

[3] The representative and heirs of Castaneda's estate have been substituted as plaintiffs. Pet. App. 8a.

cluding death, resulting from the performance of medical, surgical, dental, or related functions * * * by any commissioned officer or employee of the Public Health Service while acting within the scope of his office or employment, shall be exclusive of any other civil action or proceeding by reason of the same subject-matter against the officer or employee (or his estate) whose act or omission gave rise to the claim.

42 U.S.C. 233(a).

The district court denied petitioners' motion to dismiss. Pet. App. 41a-80a. The court concluded, *inter alia,* that Section 233(a), via its reference to 28 U.S.C. 1346(b) and an ensuing "statutory trail" that the court believed led to Section 2679(b)(2)(A), "incorporates the provision of the FTCA which *explicitly* preserves a plaintiff's right to bring a *Bivens* action." *Id.* at 59a, 61a.

c. The government, on behalf of petitioners, filed an interlocutory appeal. The government also admitted liability on plaintiff's FTCA claim against the United States for medical negligence. Gov't Notice of Admission, CV 07-7241 Docket entry No. 110 (C.D. Cal. Apr. 24, 2008). Shortly thereafter, and before appellate briefing, the government authorized each petitioner to retain private counsel for representation throughout the remainder of the litigation to ensure that each received independent legal advice and that their personal interests were separately considered and represented in the case. Private counsel took over briefing in the court of appeals, and the United States (which remained a party in the underlying district court case) filed an amicus curiae brief in support of petitioners.

The court of appeals affirmed. Pet. App. 1a-40a. The court focused its analysis on *Carlson* v. *Green*, 446 U.S. 14 (1980), in which the Court had held that the availability of an FTCA remedy did not preclude a *Bivens* action against

6

federal officials. According to the court of appeals, a *Bivens* action is available under *Carlson* unless (1) an alternative remedy is both (a) "explicitly declared to be a substitute" for a *Bivens* remedy and (b) "viewed as equally effective," or (2) there are "special factors" that militate against a *Bivens* remedy. Pet. App. 10a. Applying that test, the court of appeals held that Section 233(a) did not preclude a *Bivens* claim—a result that it acknowledged "conflicts with" the Second Circuit's decision in *Cuoco* v. *Moritsugu*, 222 F.3d 99 (2000). Pet. App. 35a; see *id.* at 10a-40a.

The court of appeals determined that the FTCA remedy offered by Section 233(a) was not "equally effective" as a *Bivens* remedy for the same reasons an FTCA remedy was not deemed equally effective in *Carlson*: (1) FTCA damages, unlike *Bivens* damages, are not awarded against individual defendants; (2) punitive damages are unavailable under the FTCA; (3) FTCA cases, unlike *Bivens* claims, are not tried before a jury; and (4) FTCA remedies are not governed by uniform nationwide rules. Pet. App. 13a-18a.

The court of appeals also determined that Congress did not "explicitly declare" in Section 233(a) that the FTCA was a substitute for a *Bivens* action. The court pointed out that Section 233(a) does not mention constitutional claims and that it was enacted before *Bivens* was decided. According to the court, Section 233(a) was intended only to preempt a particular set of common-law tort claims related to medical malpractice. The court also noted that other federal medical personnel are not afforded comparable immunity from constitutional claims. Pet. App. 18a-35a.

The court of appeals expressly disagreed with the Second Circuit's conflicting decision in *Cuoco*. The court stated that the Second Circuit misread language in *Carlson* that appeared to confirm that Section 233(a) made the FTCA an exclusive remedy. Further, the court argued that the Second Circuit failed to address the prong of *Carlson*'s analysis stating that an alternative statutory remedy must be "equally effective" to a *Bivens* action. Pet. App. 35a-37a.

Finally, the court of appeals held that there were no "special factors" warranting hesitation in creating a cause of action under *Bivens* in this setting. In the court's view, Section 233(a) does not provide a comprehensive remedial scheme precluding *Bivens* relief. Pet. App. 37a-39a.

DISCUSSION

The Court should grant review of the court of appeals' decision holding that 42 U.S.C. 233(a) does not provide PHS personnel with immunity from *Bivens* claims arising out of the provision of medical care. First, that decision directly conflicts with the Second Circuit's decision in *Cuoco* v. *Moritsugu*, 222 F.3d 99 (2000). Second, the scope of Section 233(a)'s grant of immunity presents an important federal question because the court of appeals' ruling may undermine the ability of PHS to fulfill its statutory mandate and may affect the interpretation of immunity provisions governing other federal medical personnel. Third, the court of appeals' decision is contrary to the plain language of Section 233(a) and the Court's interpretation of that language in *Carlson* v. *Green*, 446 U.S. 14 (1980).

A. The Courts Of Appeals Disagree On Whether Section 233(a)'s Grant Of Immunity Covers *Bivens* Claims

As the court of appeals acknowledged (Pet. App. 35a-37a), its decision directly conflicts with the Second Circuit's decision in *Cuoco*. In *Cuoco*, the Second Circuit held that Section 233(a) barred a *Bivens* action brought against individual PHS physicians and other employees working at a federal prison facility for inadequate medical care that allegedly rose to the level of an Eighth Amendment violation. The Second Circuit specifically rejected the plaintiff's argu-

8

ment "that § 233(a) provides immunity only from medical malpractice claims," because "there is nothing in the language of § 233(a) to support that conclusion." *Cuoco*, 222 F.3d at 108. The Second Circuit thus held that PHS employees are absolutely immune from suits arising out of medical treatment, including suits claiming that such treatment violated federal constitutional norms. *Id.* at 107-109.

A number of other courts of appeals have reached the same conclusion as *Cuoco* in unpublished decisions. See *Anderson* v. *BOP*, 176 Fed. Appx. 242, 243 (3d Cir.) (per curiam), cert. denied, 547 U.S. 1212 (2006); *Butler* v. *Shearin*, 279 Fed. Appx. 274, 275 (4th Cir. 2008) (per curiam), aff'g No. 04-2496, 2006 WL 6083567, at *7 (D. Md. Aug. 29, 2006); *Cook* v. *Blair*, 82 Fed. Appx. 790, 791 (4th Cir. 2003), aff'g No. 02-609, 2003 WL 23857310, at *2 (E.D.N.C. Mar. 21, 2003); *Montoya-Ortiz* v. *Brown*, 154 Fed. Appx. 437, 439 (5th Cir. 2005) (per curiam); *Schrader* v. *Sandoval*, No. 98-51036, 1999 WL 1235234, at *2 (5th Cir. Nov. 23, 1999); *Walls* v. *Holland*, No. 98-6506, 1999 WL 993765, at *2 (6th Cir. Oct. 18, 1999); *Beverly* v. *Gluch*, No. 89-1915, 1990 WL 67888, at *1 (6th Cir. May 23, 1990). Indeed, even the Ninth Circuit had previously so held in unpublished decisions. See *Miles* v. *Daniels*, 231 Fed. Appx. 591, 591-592 (2007); *Zanzucchi* v. *Wynberg*, No. 90-15381, 1991 WL 83937, at *2 (May 21, 1991).[4]

---

[4] In addition, all but two of the district court decisions of which the government is aware agree with the Second Circuit's conclusion. See, *e.g.*, *Brown* v. *McElroy*, 160 F. Supp. 2d 699, 703 (S.D.N.Y. 2001); *Teresa T.* v. *Ragaglia*, 154 F. Supp. 2d 290, 299 (D. Conn. 2001); *Seminario Navarrete* v. *Vanyur*, 110 F. Supp. 2d 605 (N.D. Ohio 2000); *Lewis* v. *Sauvey*, 708 F. Supp. 167, 168-169 (E.D. Mich. 1989); see also 08-1529 Pet. 6-7 n.4 (collecting unpublished district court decisions); but see *Vinzant* v. *United States*, No. CV 07-00024, 2008 WL 4414630, at *4 n.3 (C.D. Cal. Sept. 24, 2008) (unpublished); *McMullen* v. *Herschberger*,

The Court should grant the certiorari petitions to resolve the conflict between the Ninth Circuit's decision in this case and the decisions of the Second Circuit and other courts of appeals.

B. The Scope Of Section 233(a)'s Immunity Presents An Important Federal Question

The Court's review is further warranted because PHS conducts nationwide operations that should be subject to uniform immunity rules. The immunity conferred by Section 233(a) is of material importance to PHS's personnel and operations. As a result of the decision below, PHS medical personnel serving in or deployed to the Ninth Circuit will be denied protection from suit that their colleagues in other parts of the country are afforded. That disparity will cause significant administrative problems, hindering the efforts of the government to recruit physicians and other medical providers to work in a large geographic region that relies heavily on PHS personnel to deliver health care services. The court of appeals' decision, if left standing, could force HHS to indemnify PHS personnel for the costs of defending or resolving *Bivens* claims arising out of performance of their medical duties—a potentially significant drain on limited agency resources. In addition, that court's decision would affect the immunity provided to medical personnel beyond the PHS, because 42 U.S.C. 233(g)-(n) confers on employees, officers, and certain individual contractors of federally funded community health centers the same immunity afforded PHS commissioned officers and employees. The court of appeals' interpretation of the scope of Section 233(a) therefore will create similar problems for the government in supporting these health centers.

No. 91-CIV-3235, 1993 WL 6219 (S.D.N.Y. Jan. 7, 1993) (unpublished; superseded by *Cuoco*).

10

The Ninth Circuit's interpretation of Section 233(a) also may have implications for medical personnel in other agencies who operate under immunity provisions using similar language. See 38 U.S.C. 7316(a) (making the FTCA the exclusive remedy "for damages * * * allegedly arising from malpractice or negligence of a health care employee" of the Department of Veterans Affairs); 10 U.S.C. 1089(a) (making the FTCA the exclusive remedy "for damages * * * caused by the negligent or wrongful act or omission of any [medical personnel]" in the armed services). Indeed, in *Carlson*, this Court discussed the immunity provisions in 38 U.S.C. 7316(a) (formerly codified as 38 U.S. 4116(a) (1988)), 10 U.S.C. 1089(a), and Section 233(a) in a single breath—all as statutes "explicitly stating when [Congress] means to make FTCA an exclusive remedy." 446 U.S. at 20; see p. 18, *infra*.

C. **The Ninth Circuit Erred In Holding That Section 233(a) Does Not Bar *Bivens* Claims Against PHS Personnel Based On Medical Treatment**

1. a. The court of appeal's holding is contrary to the plain language of Section 233(a). Section 233(a) states:

> The remedy against the United States provided by sections 1346(b) and 2672 of title 28 [the FTCA] * * * for damage for personal injury, including death, resulting from the performance of medical, surgical, dental, or related functions * * * by any commissioned officer or employee of the Public Health Service while acting within the scope of his office or employment, shall be exclusive of any other civil action or proceeding by reason of the same subject-matter against the officer or employee (or his estate) whose act or omission gave rise to the claim.

42 U.S.C. 233(a).

11

The text unequivocally provides that the "remedy against the United States" under the FTCA for "damage for personal injury, including death, resulting from the performance of medical, surgical, dental, or related functions" "by any commissioned officer or employee of the Public Health Service while acting within the scope of his office or employment" "*shall be exclusive of any other civil action or proceeding*" arising out of the same subject matter. 42 U.S.C. 233(a) (emphasis added). The statute draws no distinction between "other civil action[s]" predicated on common-law tort theories and those based on the Constitution. It instead makes plain that the "exclusive" remedy for injuries resulting from medical treatment provided by PHS personnel is an action against the United States under the FTCA. The statute's text could not be clearer: it reflects Congress's intent to afford PHS officers and employees absolute immunity from "any" damages actions arising out of medical care provided in the course of their employment.

The limited legislative history concerning Section 233(a) confirms that statutory purpose. The overarching objective of the Emergency Health Personnel Act of 1970, Pub. L. No. 91-623, 84 Stat. 1868 (of which Section 233(a) was a part) was to facilitate PHS's provision of medical care in underserved areas. See § 2, 84 Stat. 1868; H.R. Rep. No. 1662, 91st Cong., 2d Sess. 1 (1970). Because PHS personnel were not paid enough to afford malpractice insurance, the Surgeon General requested an amendment—Section 233(a)—to protect employees from damage suits arising out of the medical care they provided. See, *e.g.*, 116 Cong. Rec. 42,543 (1970) (Rep. Staggers, the sponsor in the House of Representatives) (PHS physicians "cannot afford to take out the customary liability insurance as most doctors do," "because of the low pay that so many of those who work in the [PHS] receive."); *id.* at 42,977 (Sen. Javits) (PHS per-

12

sonnel "just could not afford to take out the customary liability insurance."); see also *Cuoco*, 222 F.3d at 108 ("[Section 233(a)] may well enable the Public Health Service to attract better qualified persons to perform medical, surgical and dental functions in order to better serve, among others, federal prisoners."). Allowing a *Bivens* claim would thus undermine Section 233(a)'s grant of immunity to protect PHS personnel from personal financial liability arising out of their medical duties. And in doing so, it would undermine as well PHS's ability to recruit qualified medical personnel to furnish critically needed services.

b. Notwithstanding Section 233(a)'s plain language, the court of appeals held that the provision does not foreclose a *Bivens* actions. The court reached that conclusion based in part on the 1988 amendments to the FTCA. Pet. App. 24a-25a. Those amendments extended the personal immunity provided by 28 U.S.C. 2679(b) (originally enacted in 1961, see Act of Sept. 21, 1961, Pub. L. No. 87-258, 75 Stat. 539) to a broader class of injuries while carving out *Bivens* claims from that enhanced scope. See Federal Employees Liability Reform and Tort Compensation Act of 1988 (Westfall Act), Pub. L. No. 100-694, § 5, 102 Stat. 4564. Prior to the 1988 amendments, Section 2679(b) made the FTCA the exclusive remedy only for injury resulting from a federal employee's operation of a motor vehicle.[5] The

---

[5] The pre-Westfall Act provision read as follows:

The remedy against the United States provided by sections 1346(b) and 2672 of this title for injury or loss of property or personal injury or death, resulting from the operation by any employee of the Government of any motor vehicle while acting within the scope of his office or employment, shall hereafter be exclusive of any other civil action or proceeding by reason of the same subject matter against the employee or his estate whose act or omission gave rise to the claim.

28 U.S.C. 2679(b) (1982).

Westfall Act, via new Section 2679(b)(1), extended the exclusivity of the FTCA remedy to *any* injury "resulting from the negligent or wrongful act or omission" of any federal employee. 28 U.S.C. 2679(b)(1). At the same time, however, the Westfall Act added Section 2679(b)(2)(A), which states that Section 2679(b)(1)'s provision of an exclusive FTCA remedy "does not extend or apply to a civil action against an employee of the Government * * * brought for a violation of the Constitution." 28 U.S.C. 2679(b)(2)(A).

Based on Section 2679(b)(2)(A), the court of appeals read the Westfall Act to reinforce its view that Section 233(a)—though enacted long before the Westfall Act and in legislation separate from the FTCA more generally (see pp. 11-12, *supra*)—does not bar a claim based on the Constitution. Pet. App. 25a-26a. The district court went even further. That court stated that Section 233(a)'s reference to "the remedy against the United States" provided by 28 U.S.C. 1346(b) of the FTCA incorporates Section 1346(b)(1)'s statement that the FTCA remedy is "[s]ubject to the provisions of chapter 171 of this title," and that, therefore, Section 2679(b)(2)(A)—a provision found in chapter 171—directly limits Section 233(a)'s exclusivity. Pet. App. 59a-62a.[6]

---

[6] Section 1346(b), part of the FTCA, provides in relevant part:

Subject to the provisions of chapter 171 of this title, the district courts * * * shall have exclusive jurisdiction of civil actions on claims against the United States, for money damages * * * for injury or loss of property, or personal injury or death caused by the negligent or wrongful act or omission of any employee of the Government while acting within the scope of his office or employment, under circumstances where the United States, if a private person, would be liable to the claimant in accordance with the law of the place where the act or omission occurred.

28 U.S.C. 1346(b)(1).

14

Both courts erred in attaching such significance to 28 U.S.C. 2679(b)(2)(A). Section 2679(b)(2)(A) was added in 1988, eighteen years after Section 233(a)'s passage. It excluded constitutional torts only from the personal immunity that those same 1988 amendments to the FTCA newly conferred. See 28 U.S.C. 2679(b)(1) (as amended by Westfall Act, Pub. L. No. 100-694, § 5, 102 Stat. 4564). Nothing in the 1988 amendments to the FTCA or their legislative history purported to limit or otherwise have a bearing on the distinct (and more expansive) personal immunity conferred in separate statutes like Section 233(a). To the contrary, as the House Judiciary Committee Report noted, the 1988 amendments did "not change the law, as interpreted by the courts, with respect to the availability of other recognized causes of action, nor does it either expand or diminish rights established under other Federal statutes." H.R. Rep. No. 700, 100th Cong., 2d Sess. 7 (1988). Indeed, the absence in Section 233(a) of an exception for *Bivens* actions similar to that in Section 2679(b)(2)(A) seriously undermines the interpretation of the courts below.

To give operative legal effect here to Section 2679(b)(2)(A), a statute of general applicability, despite Section 233(a)'s unqualified mandate of exclusivity, would amount to an implied repeal of Section 233(a), a more specific statute. See *Long Island Care at Home, Ltd.* v. *Coke*, 551 U.S. 158, 170 (2007) ("normally the specific governs the general"). As this Court has noted, "repeals by implication are not favored." *Randall* v. *Loftsgaarden*, 478 U.S. 647, 661 (1986) (citation omitted).

The court of appeals also concluded that its decision was supported by Section 233's title in the public law ("Defense of certain malpractice and negligence suits"),[7] on the ground that this title excludes constitutional torts. Pet. App. 22a-23a & n.11. The title of a statutory provision, however, cannot trump the unambiguous language of the statute's operative terms. See *Pennsylvania Dep't of Corr.* v. *Yeskey*, 524 U.S. 206, 212 (1998) ("[T]he title of a statute * * * [is] of use only when [it] shed[s] light on some ambiguous word or phrase.") (internal quotation marks and citation omitted; brackets in original). As discussed above, there is nothing ambiguous about Section 233(a). In any event, Section 233(a)'s title does not refer solely to actions sounding in common law or negligence. The term "malpractice," in particular, does not refer to a specific type of legal proceeding or claim but rather to the underlying conduct—*i.e.*, the professional misfeasance that may give rise to a cause of action. See, *e.g.*, *Webster's Third New International Dictionary* 1368 (1993) ("malpractice" is "a dereliction from professional duty whether intentional, criminal, or merely negligent by one rendering professional services that results in injury"). In addition, the title's reference to both "malpractice" and "negligence" suits strongly suggests that "malpractice" refers to a species of tort beyond "negligence" and covers as well reckless or intentional conduct—including deliberate indifference, the constitutional standard for deficient medical care (*Estelle* v. *Gamble*, 429 U.S. 97, 106 (1976)).

---

[7] Section 233's title was changed to "Civil actions or proceedings against commissioned officers or employees" and the subtitle "Exclusiveness of remedy" was added to subsection (a) when the provision was codified in title 42. Compare Emergency Health Personnel Act of 1970, Pub. L. No. 91-623, § 4, 84 Stat. 1870 (Dec. 31, 1970), with 42 U.S.C. 233 (1970). Title 42 has not, however, been enacted into positive law. See 1 U.S.C. 204(a) & note; *United States Nat'l Bank* v. *Independent Ins. Agents of Am., Inc.*, 508 U.S. 439, 448 & n.3 (1993).

16

The court of appeals also reasoned that, because Section 233 was enacted in 1970, one year before the Court's decision in *Bivens*, Congress could not have had constitutional claims in mind. Pet. App. 21a. But that fact is irrelevant in light of Section 233(a)'s unqualified text stating that the FTCA remedy against the United States shall be the "exclusive" remedy for injuries arising out of medical care provided by PHS personnel. Under the court of appeals' reasoning, no pre-*Bivens* statute—no matter how absolute its text or how categorical its intent—could create an exclusive remedy. Moreover, five years after *Bivens*, Congress passed the Gonzalez Act, Pub. L. No. 94-464, § 1(a), 90 Stat. 1985, which affords immunity to medical personnel in the armed forces and which, like Section 233(a), makes the FTCA remedy "exclusive of any other civil action or proceeding by reason of the same subject matter." 10 U.S.C. 1089(a). Congress relied on Section 233(a) as a model for that provision. See S. Rep. No. 1264, 94th Cong., 2d Sess. 8 (1976) ("legislation having a comparable effect presently exists for * * * medical personnel of the * * * Public Health Service"). As the accompanying Senate Report indicated, "[t]his protection is designed to cover *all* potential financial liability." *Id.* at 2 (emphasis added). Thus, after *Bivens*, Congress reaffirmed the completeness of Section 233(a)'s immunity.[8]

---

[8] In any event, Congress would have been well aware of the concept of a constitutional tort when it enacted Section 233(a) in December 1970. See *Bivens*, 403 U.S. at 389 (noting that the Court's decision in *Bell* v. *Hood*, 327 U.S. 678 (1946), had held that a damage action against federal agents for constitutional violations stated a claim arising under the Constitution for purpose of federal question jurisdiction, but that *Bell* v. *Hood* had reserved judgment on whether the plaintiff had successfully stated a cause of action). Indeed, the Court had granted certiorari in *Bivens* itself six months before Congress enacted Section 233(a). 399 U.S. 905 (1970).

2. The court of appeals' decision is also inconsistent with this Court's precedents. In *Carlson*, the Court held that the FTCA standing alone did not bar a *Bivens* claim against federal officials. 446 U.S. at 18-23. *Carlson* involved the situation in which the relevant statute (the FTCA, as then written) was *silent* on the question whether remedies beyond an action against the United States were excluded.[9] The Court stated that a *Bivens* claim is generally available unless (1) "special factors counsel[] hesitation in the absence of affirmative action by Congress;" or (2) "Congress has provided an alternative remedy which it explicitly declared to be a *substitute* for recovery directly under the Constitution and viewed as equally effective."[10] *Id.* at 18-19. The Court in *Carlson* found neither condition satisfied there. In particular, the Court found nothing in the FTCA itself indicating that Congress meant to preclude *Bivens* actions; to the contrary, it stated that a post-*Bivens* amendment to the FTCA made it "crystal clear" that Congress viewed the FTCA and *Bivens* as complementary. *Id.* at 19-20.

But *Carlson* did not involve Section 233(a)—an immunity statute separate and apart from the FTCA that expressly made the FTCA remedy against the United States the "exclusive" remedy available for the type of injury asserted (personal injury arising from the provision of medical care by PHS personnel). As the Court in *Carlson* itself

---

[9] As noted previously, Congress amended the FTCA in 1988 to exempt *Bivens* actions from the newly conferred exclusive FTCA remedy against the United States for suits arising out of the conduct of federal employees in certain contexts. See 28 U.S.C. 2679(b)(2)(A); see also pp. 12-13, *supra* (discussing the Westfall Act).

[10] The Court clarified that Congress did not have to recite any specific "magic words" to satisfy the alternative-remedy requirement. See *Carlson*, 446 U.S. at 19 n.5.

recognized, that distinction is dispositive. In rejecting the argument that the FTCA was the exclusive remedy for the constitutional tort alleged there, the Court in *Carlson* explained:

> This conclusion is buttressed by the significant fact that Congress follows the practice of explicitly stating when it means to make FTCA an exclusive remedy. See 38 U.S.C. § 4116(a), *42 U.S.C. § 233(a)*, 42 U.S.C. § 2458a, 10 U.S.C. § 1089(a), and 22 U.S.C. § 817(a) (malpractice by certain Government health personnel).

446 U.S. at 20 (emphasis added). By identifying Section 233(a) as a quintessential example of when Congress has made the FTCA an exclusive remedy, which precludes a *Bivens* action against individual federal officers and employees, *Carlson* strongly supports the government's interpretation.[11]

Since *Carlson*, the Court has consistently expressed a strong reluctance to expand the availability of a *Bivens* cause of action. See, *e.g.*, *Ashcroft* v. *Iqbal*, 129 S. Ct. 1937, 1948 (2009) ("Because implied causes of action are disfavored, the Court has been reluctant to extend *Bivens* liability 'to any new context or new category of defendants.'") (quoting *Correctional Servs. Corp.* v. *Malesko*, 534 U.S. 61, 68 (2001)); *Wilkie* v. *Robbins*, 127 S. Ct. 2588, 2597 (2007) (*Bivens* remedy "is not an automatic entitlement no matter what other means there may be to vindicate a protected

---

[11] Although Congress's affirmative statement in Section 233(a) of the exclusivity of the FTCA remedy should resolve the matter, PHS's status as a uniformed service (pp. 2-3, *supra*) and the important purpose of protecting PHS personnel in lieu of liability insurance (pp. 11-12, *supra*), combined with the FTCA's reticulated remedial scheme, constitute "special factors counseling hesitation" against judicial creation of a cause of action under *Bivens* in this context.

interest, and in most instances we have found a *Bivens* remedy unjustified."); *Malesko*, 534 U.S. at 68-69 ("Since *Carlson*, we have consistently refused to extend *Bivens* liability to any new context or new category of defendants. * * * So long as the plaintiff had an avenue for some redress, bedrock principles of separation of powers foreclosed judicial imposition of a new substantive liability."); *Schweiker* v. *Chilicky*, 487 U.S. 412, 421-423 (1988) ("Our more recent decisions have responded cautiously to suggestions that *Bivens* remedies be extended into new contexts. The absence of statutory relief for a constitutional violation, for example, does not by any means necessarily imply that courts should award money damages against the officers responsible for the violation."); *Bush* v. *Lucas*, 462 U.S. 367, 374-390 (1983) (refusing to provide *Bivens*-type remedy given alternative remedial scheme created by Congress).

Thus, as the D.C. Circuit has noted, "subsequent to *Carlson*, the Court clarified that there does not need to be an equally effective alternate remedy" in order to bar the fashioning of a cause of action under *Bivens*. *Wilson* v. *Libby*, 535 F.3d 697, 708 (2008), cert. denied, No. 08-1043 (June 22, 2009); see *Spagnola* v. *Mathis*, 859 F.2d 223, 228 (D.C. Cir. 1988) (en banc) ("As we read *Chilicky* and *Bush* together, then, courts must withhold their power to fashion damages remedies when Congress has put in place a comprehensive system to administer public rights, has 'not inadvertently' omitted damages remedies for certain claimants, and has not plainly expressed an intention that the courts preserve *Bivens* remedies."). Accordingly, the Court's precedents support the government's plain-text interpretation of Section 233(a) as precluding a *Bivens* remedy against individual PHS personnel, above and beyond the FTCA remedy against the United States that Congress expressly declared to be "exclusive."

20

CONCLUSION

The petitions for a writ of certiorari should be granted.

Respectfully submitted.

ELENA KAGAN
Solicitor General

TONY WEST
Assistant Attorney General

EDWIN S. KNEEDLER
Deputy Solicitor General

PRATIK A. SHAH
Assistant to the Solicitor General

DAVID S. CADE
Acting General Counsel
Department of Health and
Human Services

BARBARA L. HERWIG
HOWARD S. SCHER
Attorneys

JULY 2009

✳ ✳ ✳

There is a cliché that major league baseball players are fond of repeating, which is that hitting a round ball with a round bat is the hardest undertaking in sports. This is why no one in baseball succeeds as much as 40 percent of the time and even Hall of Famers typically have success rates below one in three. . . . [G]etting certiorari granted by the United States Supreme Court makes hitting a baseball look more like throwing a ball and hitting the broad side of a barn.

Carter G. Phillips (2004)

JULY

WESLEY BRANCH RICKEY

Graduate, University of Michigan Law School (1911).
See LEE LOWENFISH, BRANCH RICKEY:
BASEBALL'S FEROCIOUS GENTLEMAN (2007).

❧ JULY ❧

SUN	MON	TUES	WED	THUR	FRI	SAT
				1	2	3
4	5	6	7	8	9	10
11	12	13	14	15	16	17
18	19	20	21	22	23	24
25	26	27	28	29	30	31

VIRGINIA V. HARRIS

130 S. Ct. 10 (2009)

John G. Roberts, Jr.[†]

Every year, close to 13,000 people die in alcohol-related car crashes — roughly one death every 40 minutes. See Dept. of Transp., Nat. Hwy. Traffic Safety Admin., Traffic Safety Facts, 2007 Traffic Safety Annual Assessment – Alcohol-Impaired Driving Fatalities 1 (No. 81106, Aug. 2008). Ordinary citizens are well aware of the dangers posed by drunk driving, and they frequently report such conduct to the police. A number of States have adopted programs specifically designed to encourage such tips — programs such as the "Drunkbusters Hotline" in New Mexico and the REDDI program (Report Every Drunk Driver Immediately) in force in several States. See Dept. of Transp., Nat. Hwy. Traffic Safety Admin., Programs Across the United States That Aid Motorists in the Reporting of Impaired Drivers to Law Enforcement (2007).

By a 4-to-3 vote, the Virginia Supreme Court below adopted a rule that will undermine such efforts to get drunk drivers off the road. The decision below commands that police officers following a driver reported to be drunk *do nothing* until they see the driver actually do something unsafe on the road — by which time it may be too late.

Here, a Richmond police officer pulled Joseph Harris over after receiving an anonymous tip that Harris was driving while intoxicated. The tip described Harris, his car, and the direction he was traveling in considerable detail. The officer did not personally witness Harris violate any traffic laws. When Harris was pulled over, however, he reeked of alcohol, his speech was slurred, he almost fell over in attempting to exit his car, and he failed the sobriety tests the officer administered on the scene. Harris was convicted of driving while intoxicated, but the Virginia Supreme Court overturned the conviction. It concluded that because the officer had failed to independently verify that Harris was driving dangerously, the

---

[†] Chief Justice of the United States, joined by Justice Antonin Scalia, dissenting from the denial of a petition for a writ of certiorari.

stop violated the Fourth Amendment's prohibition on unreasonable searches and seizures. 276 Va. 689, 696-698, 668 S.E.2d 141, 146-147 (2008); see Pet. for Cert. 4 (citing record).

I am not sure that the Fourth Amendment requires such independent corroboration before the police can act, at least in the special context of anonymous tips reporting drunk driving. This is an important question that is not answered by our past decisions, and that has deeply divided federal and state courts. The Court should grant the petition for certiorari to answer the question and resolve the conflict.

On the one hand, our cases allow police to conduct investigative stops based on reasonable suspicion, viewed under the totality of the circumstances. *Terry v. Ohio*, 392 U.S. 1, 22 (1968); *Alabama v. White*, 496 U.S. 325, 328-331 (1990). In *Florida v. J.L.*, 529 U.S. 266, 270 (2000), however, we explained that anonymous tips, in the absence of additional corroboration, typically lack the "indicia of reliability" needed to justify a stop under the reasonable suspicion standard. In *J.L.*, the Court suppressed evidence seized by police after receiving an anonymous tip alleging that a young man, wearing a plaid shirt and waiting at a particular bus stop, was carrying a gun. The majority below relied extensively on *J.L.* in reversing Harris's conviction.

But it is not clear that *J.L.* applies to anonymous tips reporting drunk or erratic driving. *J.L.* itself suggested that the Fourth Amendment analysis might be different in other situations. The Court declined "to speculate about the circumstances under which the danger alleged in an anonymous tip might be so great as to justify a search even without a showing of reliability." *Id.*, at 273. It also hinted that "in quarters where the reasonable expectation of Fourth Amendment privacy is diminished," it might be constitutionally permissible to "conduct protective searches on the basis of information insufficient to justify searches elsewhere." *Id.*, at 274.

There is no question that drunk driving is a serious and potentially deadly crime, as our cases have repeatedly emphasized. See, *e.g.*, *Michigan Dept. of State Police v. Sitz*, 496 U.S. 444, 451 (1990) ("No one can seriously dispute the magnitude of the drunken driving problem or the States' interest in eradicating it. Media reports of alcohol-related death and mutilation on the Nation's roads are legion"). The imminence of the danger posed by drunk drivers exceeds that at issue in other types of cases. In a case like *J.L.*, the police can often observe the subject of a tip and step in before actual harm occurs; with drunk driving, such a wait-and-see approach may prove fatal. Drunk driving is always dangerous, as it is occurring. This Court has in fact recognized that the dangers posed by drunk drivers are unique, frequently upholding anti-drunk-driving policies that might be constitutionally problematic in other, less exigent circumstances.[1]

In the absence of controlling precedent on point, a sharp disagreement has emerged among federal and state courts over how to apply the Fourth Amendment in this context. The majority of courts examining the question have upheld investigative stops of allegedly drunk or erratic drivers, even when the police did not personally witness any traffic violations before conducting the stops.[2] These courts have typically distinguished *J.L.*'s general rule based on some combination of (1) the especially grave and imminent dangers posed by drunk driving; (2) the enhanced reliability of tips alleging illegal activity in public, to which the tipster was presumably an eyewitness; (3) the fact that traffic stops are typically less invasive than searches or seizures of individuals on foot; and (4) the diminished expectation of privacy enjoyed by individuals driving their cars on public roads. A minority of jurisdictions, meanwhile, take the same position as the Virginia Supreme Court, requiring that officers first confirm an anonymous tip of drunk or erratic driving through their own independent observation.[3] This conflict has been expressly noted by the lower courts.[4]

---

[1] See, *e.g.*, *Michigan Dept. of State Police v. Sitz*, 496 U.S. 444, 455 (1990) (approving use of field-sobriety checkpoints of all approaching drivers, despite fact that over 98 percent of such drivers were innocent); *South Dakota v. Neville*, 459 U.S. 553, 554, 560 (1983) (upholding state law allowing a defendant's refusal to take a blood-alcohol test to be introduced as evidence against him at trial); *Mackey v. Montrym*, 443 U.S. 1, 17-19 (1979) (upholding state law requiring mandatory suspension of a driver's license upon a drunk-driving suspect's refusal to submit to a breath-analysis test); see also *Indianapolis v. Edmond*, 531 U.S. 32, 37-38 (2000) (noting that in the Fourth Amendment context the Court has upheld government measures "aimed at removing drunk drivers from the road," distinguishing such measures from those with the primary purpose of "detect[ing] evidence of ordinary criminal wrongdoing").

[2] See, *e.g.*, *United States v. Wheat*, 278 F.3d 722 (CA8 2001); *People v. Wells*, 38 Cal.4th 1078, 136 P.3d 810 (2006); *State v. Prendergast*, 103 Haw. 451, 83 P.3d 714 (2004); *State v. Walshire*, 634 N.W.2d 625 (Iowa 2001); *State v. Crawford*, 275 Kan. 492, 67 P.3d 115 (2003); *Bloomingdale v. State*, 842 A.2d 1212 (Del.2004); *State v. Golotta*, 178 N.J. 205, 837 A.2d 359 (2003); *State v. Scholl*, 2004 SD 85, 684 N.W.2d 83; *State v. Boyea*, 171 Vt. 401, 765 A.2d 862 (2000); *State v. Rutzinski*, 2001 WI 22, 241 Wis.2d 729, 623 N.W.2d 516.

[3] See, *e.g.*, *McChesney v. State*, 988 P.2d 1071 (Wyo.1999); *Commonwealth v. Lubiejewski*, 49 Mass. App. 212, 729 N.E.2d 288 (2000); *State v. Sparen*, No. CR00258199S, 2001 WL 206078 (Conn. Super. Ct., Feb. 9, 2001) (unpublished).

[4] See, *e.g.*, *Wheat*, *supra*, at 729-730 (reviewing cases upholding stops, then noting that some courts "have reached a different conclusion"); *Wells*, *supra*, at 1084, 136 P.3d, at 814 ("split of authority").

The conflict is clear and the stakes are high. The effect of the rule below will be to grant drunk drivers "one free swerve" before they can legally be pulled over by police. It will be difficult for an officer to explain to the family of a motorist killed by that swerve that the police had a tip that the driver of the other car was drunk, but that they were powerless to pull him over, even for a quick check.

Maybe the decision of the Virginia Supreme Court below was correct, and the Fourth Amendment bars police from acting on anonymous tips of drunk driving unless they can verify each tip. If so, then the dangerous consequences of this rule are unavoidable. But the police should have every legitimate tool at their disposal for getting drunk drivers off the road. I would grant certiorari to determine if this is one of them.

LAWRENCE ON THE LAW

The Legal World, 25 Green Bag 491 (1913)

President A. Lawrence Lowell of Harvard University, in an address delivered to the entering class of Harvard Law School at the beginning of the academic year, said, according to a newspaper report which appears to be authentic: "Criminal law, as administered in our courts today, is a disgrace to the country. The great criminal trials are conducted like pitched battles — like tournaments or baseball games — to be displayed for the enjoyment of the public in the front pages of the newspapers in a way that is shocking to civilized men. The reform in criminal law of the future is in the hands of the lawyers of the future, and this is the duty for which law students should prepare themselves."

THE *INFIELD FLY* ASIDE

AND THE

LEGAL ENTERTAINMENT

Robert A. James[†]

Graham Greene divided his writings into two categories. The first he unsurprisingly dubbed his "novels," creations like *The Power and the Glory* and *The End of the Affair* intended to be read as serious literary works. But he also tossed off what he called "entertainments," tales and scripts like *The Third Man* and *Our Man in Havana* that donned the form of the escapist pulp fiction crime or spy story, but that nonetheless explored profound truths. Over time, some of Greene's entertainments have been valued more highly than some of the novels he thought were more legitimate.[1]

A similar division exists in the law reviews, and that division can be dated to 1975 and the publication of the famous Aside reprinted here.[2] There have been attempts at legal humor since time immemorial, probably starting shortly after the appearance of the first lawyer. But a then anonymous University of Pennsylvania law student — later revealed to be Will Stevens, who died in 2008[3] — employed the gentle tools of satire and parody while advancing legal thought in innovative ways. The present series of the *Green Bag* is the modern embodiment of Stevens's great gift, the useful legal entertainment.[4]

This foreword will not pile onto the Infield Fly Rule itself or the baseball lore cited in the Aside, or the broader relation between law and baseball.[5] Instead, let us celebrate the elements of style and substance that are

---

[†] Rob James is a partner in the San Francisco and Houston offices of Pillsbury Winthrop Shaw Pittman LLP and a lecturer at the University of California, Berkeley, School of Law. His own student legal entertainments include the *Journal of Attenuated Subtleties* trilogy from 1982, updated and reprinted at 1 GREEN BAG 2D 377 (1998), 2 GREEN BAG 2D 267 (1999), and (with Ben Zuraw) 11 GREEN BAG 2D 341 (2008).

[1] See PETER WOLFE, GRAHAM GREENE THE ENTERTAINER (1972); MICHAEL SHELDEN, GRAHAM GREENE: THE MAN WITHIN (1994).

[2] Aside, The Common Law Origins of the Infield Fly Rule, 123 U. PA. L. REV. 1474 (1975).

[3] Obituaries of Stevens can be found in the *New York Times* (Dec. 12, 2008) and the *Philadelphia Inquirer* (Dec. 15, 2008).

[4] The editors of the first series of the *Green Bag* self-deprecatingly labeled it "a useless and entertaining journal of law," but the editors of the second series appropriately omitted "useless" from the slogan. See David P. Currie, Green Bags, 1 GREEN BAG 2D 1 (1997).

[5] These topics have been handled at great length elsewhere, in addition to this Almanac. See John J. Flynn, Further Aside, A Comment on "The Common Law Origins of the Infield Fly Rule," 4 J. CONTEMP. L. 241 (1978); Robert A. Jarvis & Phyllis Coleman, The Uncommon Origins of "The Common Law Origins of the Infield Fly Rule," 19 ENT. & SPORTS LAW. 17 (2002); Neil B. Cohen & Spencer Weber Waller,

both common and distinctive in the works of Stevens and those who followed his path.

The legal entertainment usually cannot resist the temptation to satirize
the pedantry of scholarship. The pedant has been a stock figure in comedy
since Aristophanes and Terence, and worthies including Karl Llewellyn
and A.P. Herbert took scholastic excess to task in their own excursions
into legal humor.[6] A novice like the Stevens of 1975 was no exception in
his footnotes, documenting his very first word with a reference to the *Oxford English Dictionary*, digressing into the Book of *Genesis*, and musing
about a wonder chicken.[7] Some humorists seize the pedantic element and
never lose hold of it, even to the present day. But once Stevens got the
nyuk-nyuks out of his system, the text of the Aside assumed a higher style
and conveyed a deeper substance.

The legal entertainment regularly presents the law as a game. Sort of.
As Art Leff observed in his anthropologist's-eye view of American justice,
"[if] the Usa Trial is not a game, it is not not a game either."[8] Law can be
literally a matter of life or death, and the fates of millions can turn on the
choices made, but the entertainment frequently portrays an all-too-human
contest of wills conducted under arbitrary or perverse rules. Stevens
launched a genre of law review scholarship on gamelike aspects of our
society.

The legal entertainment aims to startle and provoke the reader. Grant
Gilmore, contemporaneous with the Aside but late in his career, declared
in memorable prose that Contract is Dead, the consideration theory having been murdered by rival tort doctrines.[9] For his pains, Gilmore was
visited with a surfeit of critical book reviews poking holes in his thesis
and his facts, sometimes ignoring or missing the remarkable truths in the
general picture he painted. As Richard Danzig concluded, the reviewers
had mistaken a "plum" — an entertainment — for "meat," and thereby
missed out on the fun.[10]

The *Infield Fly* Aside drew an audacious analogy between the centu-
ries-old evolution of the common law and a rough-hewn rule of play
quickly improvised on dusty urban ballfields. What is more, Stevens carried it off with élan. His conclusion, crediting both baseball and the com-

---

Taking Pop-Ups Seriously: The Jurisprudence of the Infield Fly Rule, 82 WASH. U.
L.Q. 453 (2004); Anthony D'Amato, The Contribution of the Infield Fly Rule to
Western Civilization (and Vice Versa), 100 NW. U. L. REV. 189 (2006); see generally
Charles Yablon, On the Contributions of Baseball to American Legal Theory, 104
YALE L.J. 227 (1994).

[6] See Diogenes Jonathan Swift Teufelsdröckh, Jurisprudence: The Crown of Civilization, 5 U. CHI. L. REV. 171 (1938) (Llewellyn writing under pseudonym, affecting
style of Thomas Carlyle in *Sartor Resartus*); A.P. HERBERT, UNCOMMON LAW (1935).

[7] Even Stevens's celebrated footnoting of his opening "The" has proven prescient,
as there are now scholars who agonize over that particle of speech. See Glenda
Browne, The definite article: acknowledging 'The' in index entries, 22 THE INDEXER
119 (2001) (asking whether one should index "The Who" under "T" or "W").
Browne cautiously and ominously notes that treatment of "A" and "An" is "beyond
the scope of this article" (*id.* at 121).

[8] Arthur Allen Leff, Law and, 87 YALE L.J. 989, 1011 (1978).

[9] GRANT GILMORE, THE DEATH OF CONTRACT (1974).

[10] Richard Danzig, The Death of Contract and the Life of the Profession, 29 STAN. L.
REV. 1125 (1977).

mon law with "changing . . . only to the extent necessary to remove the need for further change,"[11] could with profit be carved in marble above the entrance to every administrative agency building in America.

Stevens wrote practical articles for continuing legal education programs, but not again in the academic law reviews. He wistfully remarked, "My ego is simultaneously flattered and bruised by the notion that something I cranked out more than 25 years ago would prove to be the highlight of my professional and academic careers."[12] The *Green Bag* publications carry his entertainer's torch. Reader, if you seek his monument, flip the pages around you.

❋ ❋ ❋

In those days Daddy just could not understand me at all. I loved Henry "Heinie" Manush, the left fielder of the 1933 Washington Senators, and so I saved by carrying the Washington *News* to get a Senator cap with Heinie's number "3" on it. When Daddy saw it he said, "Lord, wouldn't you know my boy would want to be like Heinie Manush instead of Thomas Jefferson."

Hugo Black, Jr. (1975)

In 1986, as my first term [as Chairman of the EEOC] was winding up, I was sounded out by several headhunters, one of whom wanted to know whether I'd consider becoming president of one of baseball's major leagues. "Would I have to go to the games?" I asked. He said it was part of the deal, to which I replied that no amount of money could possibly make me sit through that many baseball games.

Clarence Thomas (2007)

---

[11] Aside, supra note 2, at 1481.
[12] N.Y. TIMES (Dec. 12, 2008).

THE COMMON LAW ORIGINS OF THE INFIELD FLY RULE

Anonymous[†]

The[1] Infield Fly Rule[2] is neither a rule of law nor one of equity; it is a rule of baseball.[3] Since the[4] 1890's it has been a part of the body of the official rules of baseball.[5] In its inquiry into the common law origins[6] of the rule,

---

[†] Copyright 1975 by the University of Pennsylvania. Reprinted by permission of the publisher and William S. Hein Company. Original at 123 U. Penn. L. Rev 1474 (1975).

[1] 11 OXFORD ENGLISH DICTIONARY 257-60 (1961).

[2] OFF. R. BASEBALL 2.00 & 6.05(e). Rule 2.00 is definitional in nature and provides that:

> An INFIELD FLY is a fair fly ball (not including a line drive nor an attempted bunt) which can be caught by an infielder with ordinary effort, when first and second, or first, second and third bases are occupied, before two are out. The pitcher, catcher, and any outfielder who stations himself in the infield on the play shall be considered infielders for the purpose of this rule.
>
> When it seems apparent that a batted ball will be an Infield Fly, the umpire shall immediately declare "Infield Fly" for the benefit of the runners. If the ball is near the baselines, the umpire shall declare "Infield Fly, if Fair."
>
> The ball is alive and runners may advance at the risk of the ball being caught, or retouch and advance after the ball is touched, the same as on any fly ball. If the hit becomes a foul ball, it is treated the same as any foul.
>
> NOTE: If a declared Infield Fly is allowed to fall untouched to the ground, and bounces foul before passing first or third base, it is a foul ball. If a declared Infield Fly falls untouched to the ground outside the baseline, and bounces fair before passing first or third base, it is an Infield Fly.

Rule 6.05(e) gives operational effect to the definition, by providing that the batter is out when an Infield Fly is declared.

Depending upon the circumstances, other rules which may or may not apply to a particular situation include, *inter alia*, FED. R. CIV. P., Rule Against Perpetuities, and Rule of *Matthew* 7:12 & *Luke* 6:31 (Golden).

[3] Although referred to as "Rules" both officially and in common parlance, if the analogy between the conduct-governing strictures of baseball and a jurisprudential entity on the order of a nation-state is to be maintained, the "rules" of baseball should be considered to have the force, effect, and legitimacy of the statutes of a nation-state. The analogy would continue to this end by giving the "ground rules" of a particular baseball park the same status as the judge-made rules of procedure of a particular court.

[4] Note 1 *supra*.

[5] It is only with the greatest hesitation that one hazards a guess as to *the* year of origin of the Infield Fly Rule. Seymour considers it to have been 1893. 1 H. SEYMOUR, BASEBALL 275 (1960). Richter, on the other hand, in an opinion which *The Baseball Encyclopedia* joins, considers the rule to have entered the game in 1895. F. RICHTER, RICHTER'S HISTORY AND RECORDS OF BASEBALL 256 (1914); THE BASEBALL ENCYCLOPEDIA 1526-27 (1974). Finally, Voigt considers 1894 the correct year. 1 D.

this Aside does not seek to find a predecessor to the rule in seventeenth-century England. The purpose of the Aside is rather to examine whether the same types of forces that shaped the development of the common law[7] also generated the Infield Fly Rule.

As a preliminary matter, it is necessary to emphasize that baseball is a game of English origin, rooted in the same soil from which grew Anglo-American law and justice.[8] In this respect it is like American football and unlike basketball, a game that sprang fully developed from the mind of James Naismith.[9] The story of Abner Doubleday, Cooperstown, and 1839, a pleasant tribute to American ingenuity enshrined in baseball's Hall of Fame, is not true.[10] The myth reflects a combination of economic opportunism,[11] old friendship,[12] and not a small element of anti-British feeling.[13] The true birthplace of the game is England; thence it was carried to the western hemisphere, to develop as an American form.[14]

VOIGT, AMERICAN BASEBALL 288 (1966).

Although independent investigation of primary sources has led to the belief that the rule first developed in 1894 and 1895, notes 25-35 *infra* & accompanying text, a certain sense of justice would be satisfied if the rule developed as a result of play during the 1894 season. For that season was the first of the championship seasons of the Baltimore Orioles, the team that developed what is now known as "inside baseball," including such plays as the Baltimore chop and the hit-and-run. The Orioles not only played smart baseball; they played dirty baseball. "Although they may not have originated dirty baseball they perfected it to a high degree. In a National League filled with dirty players they were undoubtedly the dirtiest of their time and may have been the dirtiest the game has ever known." D. WALLOP, BASEBALL: AN INFORMAL HISTORY 88 (1969); *accord,* L. ALLEN, THE NATIONAL LEAGUE STORY 68 (1961); *see* R. SMITH, BASEBALL 136-46 (1947). Even if the Infield Fly Rule was not developed as a result of the event of the 1894 season, perhaps it should have been.

[6] For a discussion of origins, *see generally* Scopes v. State, 154 Tenn. 105, 289 S.W. 363 (1927); *Genesis* 1:1-2:9. *But see even more generally* Epperson v. Arkansas, 393 U.S. 97 (1968); R. ARDREY, AFRICAN GENESIS (1961); C. DARWIN, THE DESCENT OF MAN (1871); C. DARWIN, THE ORIGIN OF SPECIES (1859).

[7] For a discussion of common law in a non-baseball context, see W. HOLDSWORTH, A HISTORY OF ENGLISH LAW (1903-1938); O.W. HOLMES, THE COMMON LAW (1881).

[8] *Cf.* Palko v. Connecticut, 302 U.S. 319, 325 (1937).

[9] R. BRASCH, HOW DID SPORTS BEGIN? 41 (1970).

[10] R. HENDERSON, BAT, BALL AND BISHOP 170-94 (1947). The Doubleday theory of origin is outlined in 84 CONG. REC. 1087-89 (1939) (remarks of Congressman Shanley) (*semble*). Congressional approval of the theory, however, was never forthcoming. H.R.J. RES. 148, 76th Cong., 1st Sess. (1939), seeking to designate June 12, 1939, National Baseball Day, was referred to the Committee on the Judiciary, never again to be heard from. 84 CONG. REC. 1096 (1939). Nor did the Supreme Court formally adopt the Doubleday theory. Flood v. Kuhn, 407 U.S. 258, 260-61 (1972) (opinion of Blackmun, J.) (not explicitly rejecting the theory either). An interesting, if unlikely, explanation, offerable as an alternative to both the Doubleday and English theories of origin, is found in J. HART, HEY! B.C. 26 from the back (unpaginated, abridged & undated ed.).

[11] R. BRASCH, *supra* note 9, at 31-32.

[12] R. HENDERSON, *supra* note 10, at 179. The chairman of the commission suggested by A.G. Spalding to investigate the origins of the game was A.G. Mills, who had belonged to the same military post as Abner Doubleday.

[13] R. SMITH, *supra* note 5, at 31.

[14] *See generally* H. SEYMOUR, *supra* note 5; D. VOIGT, *supra* note 5. The American qualities of the game are also revealed in other than historical or legal contexts. *Cf.*

The original attitude toward baseball developed from distinctly English origins as well. The first "organized" games were played in 1845 by the Knickerbocker Base Ball Club of New York City,[15] and the rules which governed their contests clearly indicate that the game was to be played by gentlemen. Winning was not the objective; exercise was.[16] "The New York club players were 'gentlemen in the highest social sense' — that is, they were rich. . . . The earliest clubs were really trying to transfer to our unwilling soil a few of the seeds of the British cricket spirit."[17] This spirit, which has been variously described as the attitude of the amateur, of the gentleman, and of the sportsman,[18] would have kept the rules simple and allowed moral force to govern the game.[19] Such an attitude, however, was unable to prevail.

As baseball grew, so did the influence of values that saw winning, rather than exercise, as the purpose of the game.[20] Victory was to be pursued by any means possible within the language of the rules, regardless of whether the tactic violated the spirit of the rules.[21] The written rules had to be made more and more specific, in order to preserve the spirit of the game.[22]

The Infield Fly Rule is obviously not a core principle of baseball. Unlike the diamond itself or the concepts of "out" and "safe," the Infield Fly Rule is not necessary to the game. Without the Infield Fly Rule, baseball does not degenerate into bladderball[23] the way the collective bargaining process degenerates into economic warfare when good faith is absent.[24] It is a technical rule, a legislative response to actions that were previously permissible, though contrary to the spirit of the sport.

Whether because the men who oversaw the rules of baseball during the 1890's were unwilling to make a more radical change than was necessary to remedy a perceived problem in the game, or because they were unable to perceive the need for a broader change than was actually made, three changes in the substantive rules, stretching over a seven-year period, were required to put the Infield Fly Rule in its present form. In each legislative response to playing field conduct, however, the fundamental motive for action remained the same: "To prevent the defense from making a double play by subterfuge, at a time when the offense is helpless to pre-

---

M. GARDNER, THE ANNOTATED CASEY AT THE BAT (1967); B. MALAMUD, THE NATURAL (1952).

[15] R. SMITH, *supra* note 5, at 32-35.

[16] KNICKERBOCKER BASE BALL CLUB R. 1 (1845), *reprinted in* R. HENDERSON, *supra* note 10, at 163-64, *and in* F. RICHTER, *supra* note 5, at 227.

[17] R. SMITH, *supra* note 5, at 37.

[18] Keating, *Sportsmanship as a Moral Category*, 75 ETHICS 25, 33 (1964).

[19] R. SMITH, *supra* note 5, at 68-69.

[20] 1 D. VOIGHT, *supra* note 5, at xvii; *cf. Hearings on S. 3445, Federal Sports Act of 1972, Before the Senate Committee on Commerce*, 92d Cong., 2d Sess. 94-95 (1973) (statement of H. Cosell). *See generally* Keating, *supra* note 18, at 31-34.

[21] Perhaps the most glaring example of this attitude is contained in the career of Mike "King" Kelly. When the rules permitted substitutions on mere notice to the umpire, Kelly inserted himself into the game after the ball was hit in order to catch a ball out of reach of any of his teammates. R. SMITH, *supra* note 5, at 89-90.

[22] *Cf. id.* 68-69; 1 D. VOIGT, *supra* note 5, at 204-05.

[23] *See* Yale Daily News, Oct. 29, 1966, at 1, col. 1.

[24] NLRB v. Insurance Agents Int'l Union, 361 U.S. 477, 488-90 (1960).

vent it, rather than by skill and speed."[25]

The need to enforce this policy with legislation first became apparent in the summer of 1893. In a game between New York and Baltimore, with a fast runner on first, a batter with the "speed of an ice wagon"[26] hit a pop fly. The runner stayed on first, expecting the ball to be caught. The fielder, however, let the ball drop to the ground, and made the force out at second.[27] The particular occurrence did not result in a double play, but that possibility was apparent; it would require only that the ball not be hit as high. Although even the Baltimore Sun credited the New York Giant with "excellent judgment,"[28] the incident suggested that something should be done, because by the play the defense obtained an advantage that it did not deserve and that the offense could not have prevented. Umpires could handle the situation by calling the batter out,[29] but this was not a satisfactory solution; it could create as many problems as it solved.[30] The 1894 winter meeting responded with adoption of the "trap ball" rule, putting the batter out if he hit a ball that could be handled by an infielder while first base was occupied with one out.[31]

The trap ball rules of 1894, however, did not solve all problems. First, although the rule declared the batter out, there was no way to know that the rule was in effect for a particular play. The umpire was not required to make his decision until after the play, and, consequently, unnecessary disputes ensued.[32] Second, it became apparent that the feared unjust double play was not one involving the batter and one runner, but one that, when two men were on base, would see two baserunners declared out.[33] The 1895 league meeting ironed out these difficulties through changes in the rules.[34] The third problem with the trap ball rule of 1894, one not perceived until later, was that it applied only when one man was out. The

---

[25] 1 H. SEYMOUR, supra note 5, at 276.

[26] Baltimore Sun, May 24, 1893, at 6, col. 2. Raised by this statement is the issue of the speed of an ice wagon in both relative and absolute terms. Such inquiry is beyond the scope of this Aside.

[27] Id. The fielder who made the play was Giant shortstop and captain John Montgomery Ward, who became a successful attorney after his playing days ended. 1 D. VOIGT, supra note 5, at 285.

[28] Baltimore Sun, May 24, 1893, at 6, col. 2.

[29] E.g., the Chicago-Baltimore game of June 8, 1893. "In the second inning . . . Kelley hit a pop fly to short-stop. Dahlen caught the ball, then dropped it and threw to second base, a runner being on first. The muff was so plain that Umpire McLaughlin refused to allow the play and simply called the batsman out." Baltimore Sun, June 9, 1893, at 6, col. 2.

[30] Text accompanying notes 45-46 infra.

[31] Baltimore Sun, Feb. 27, 1894, at 6, col. 3. The rule stated that "the batsman is out if he hits a fly ball that can be handled by an infielder while first base is occupied and with only one out." Id. Apr. 26, 1894, at 6, col. 2.

[32] Baltimore Sun, Apr. 26, 1894, at 6n col. 2.

[33] 1 H. SEYMOUR, supra note 5, at 275-76. Seymour developed yet another reason for the change in the rule: that "teams got around it by having outfielders come in fast and handle the pop fly." Id. 276. This does not appear to be a valid thesis because, from the beginning, the rule referred not to whether an infielder, as opposed to an outfielder, did handle the chance, but to whether an infielder could handle it. Note 31 supra.

[34] Baltimore Sun, Feb. 18, 1895, at 6, col. 4. Id. Feb. 28, 1895, at 6, col. 5.

danger of an unfair double play, however, also exists when there are no men out. This situation was corrected in 1901, and the rule has remained relatively unchanged since that time.[35]

The Infield Fly Rule, then, emerged from the interplay of four factors, each of which closely resembles a major force in the development of the common law. First is the sporting approach to baseball. A gentleman, when playing a game, does not act in a manner so unexpected as to constitute trickery;[36] in particular he does not attempt to profit by his own unethical conduct.[37] The gentleman's code provides the moral basis for the rule; it is the focal point of the rule, just as the more general precept of fair play provides a unifying force to the conduct of the game. The principle of Anglo-American law analogous to this gentleman's concept of fair play is the equally amorphous concept of due process, or justice[38] itself.

Baseball's society, like general human society, includes more than gentlemen, and the forces of competitiveness and professionalism required that the moral principle of fair play be codified so that those who did not subscribe to the principle would nonetheless be required to abide by it.[39] Thus the second factor in the development of the Infield Fly Rule — a formal and legalistic code of rules ensuring proper conduct — was created.[40] In the common law, this development manifested itself in the for-

---

[35] THE BASEBALL ENCYCLOPEDIA 1527 (1974). The current rule is set forth in note 2 *supra*.

[36] *See, e.g.*, Pluck (the wonder chicken).

[37] In the law, this belief is reflected in the clean hands doctrine, which "is rooted in the historical concept of [the] court of equity as a vehicle for affirmatively enforcing the requirements of conscience and good faith." Precision Instrument Mfg. Co. v. Automotive Maintenance Mach. Co., 324 U.S. 806, 814 (1945). For a statutory codification of the clean hands rule, see CAL. HEALTH & SAFETY CODE, § 28548, ¶ 2 (West 1967) (requiring food service employees to "clean hands" before leaving restroom). *See generally* Z. CHAFEE, SOME PROBLEMS OF EQUITY, chs. 1-3 (1950).

To be contrasted with the doctrine of "clean hands" is the "sticky fingers" doctrine. The latter embodies the reaction of the baseball world to the excitement caused by the emergence of the home run as a major aspect of the game. Applying to the ball a foreign substance, such as saliva, made the big hit a difficult feat to achieve. As a result, in 1920, the spitball was outlawed. L. ALLEN, *supra* note 5, at 167. The banning of the spitball was not, however, absolute. Seventeen pitchers were given lifetime waivers of the ban, *id.*, possibly because the spitball had become an essential element of their stock-in-trade, and depriving them of the pitch would in effect deny them the right to earn a living. *See* Adams v. Tanner, 244 U.S. 590 (1917); McDermott v. City of Seattle, 4 F. Supp. 855, 857 (W.D. Wash. 1933); Winther v. Village of Weippe, 91 Idaho 798, 803-04, 430 P.2d 689, 694-95 (1967); *cf.* RESTATEMENT (SECOND) OF CONTRACTS § 90 (Tent. Drafts Nos. 1-7, 1973). *But see* Ferguson v. Skrupa, 372 U.S. 726, 730-31 (1963).

[38] *See generally, e.g.*, U.S. CONST. amends. V & XIV and cases citing thereto; Poe v. Ullman, 367 U.S. 497, 539-55 (1961) (Harlan, J., dissenting); J. RAWLS, A THEORY OF JUSTICE (1971); Bentley, *John Rawls: A Theory of Justice*, 121 U. PA. L. REV. 1070 (1973); Michelman, *In Pursuit of Constitutional Welfare Rights: One View of Rawls' Theory of Justice*, 121 U. PA. L. REV. 962 (1973); Scanlon, *Rawls' Theory of Justice*, 121 U. PA. L. REV. 1020 (1973); *cf., e.g.*, Byron R. "Whizzer" White (1962-), Hugo L. Black (1937-71), & Horace Gray (1881-1902) (Justices). *But cf., e.g.*, Roger B. Taney (1836-64) (Chief Justice).

[39] Keating, *supra* note 18, at 30. *See also* R. SMITH, *supra* note 5, at 68-69.

[40] Text accompanying notes 25-35 *supra*.

malism of the writ system.[41] Conduct was governed by general principles; but to enforce a rule of conduct, it was necessary to find a remedy in a specific writ.[42] The common law plaintiff had no remedy if the existing writs did not encompass the wrong complained of; and the baseball player who had been the victim of a "cute" play could not prevail until the umpire could be shown a rule of baseball squarely on point.

To the generalization set forth in the preceding sentence there is an exception, both at common law and at baseball. At common law, the exception was equity, which was able to aid the plaintiff who could not find a form of action at law.[43] At baseball, the exception was the power of the umpire to make a call that did not fit within a particular rule.[44] The powers of equity and of the umpire, however, were not unlimited. The law courts circumscribed the power of the chancellor to the greatest extent possible, and this process of limitation has been defended.[45] Likewise, the discretionary power of the umpire has been limited: Additions to the written rules have reduced the area within which the umpire has discretion to act. Strong policy reasons favor this limitation upon the umpire's discretionary power. Because finality of decision is as important as correctness of decision, an action that invites appeal, as broad discretion in the umpire does, is not valued. The umpire must have the status of an unchallengeable finder of fact.[46] Allowing challenges to his authority on matters of rules admits the possibility that he may be wrong, and encourages a new generation of challenges to findings of fact.

The fourth element in the development of the Infield Fly Rule is demonstrated by the piecemeal approach that rules committees took to the problem. They responded to problems as they arose; the process of creating the Infield Fly Rule was incremental, with each step in the development of the rule merely a refinement of the previous step. Formalism was altered to the extent necessary to achieve justice in the particular case; it was not abandoned and replaced with a new formalism. Anglo-American law has two analogies to this process. The first is the way in which common law precedents are employed to mold existing remedies to new situations. Although the rigid structure of the common law was slow to change, it did change. The substantive change took place not only as a result of judicial decision; it was also caused by legislation, which is the second analogy. The legislation, however, was to a great extent directed at specific defects perceived to exist in the system.[47] Adjustment of the law, not its reform, was the goal of the legislative process. The rules of baseball and of Anglo-American jurisprudence are thus to be contrasted with the continental system of complete codes designed to remedy society's ills with a single stroke of the legislative brush.[48]

The dynamics of the common law and the development of one of the

---

[41] 2 F. MAITLAND, COLLECTED PAPERS 477-83 (1911).

[42] F. POLLOCK, THE GENIUS OF THE COMMON LAW 13 (1912); 2 F. POLLOCK, & F. MAITLAND, HISTORY OF ENGLISH LAW 558-65 (2d ed. 1952).

[43] F. MAITLAND, EQUITY 4-5 (1909).

[44] Note 29 *supra*.

[45] 2 F. MAITLAND, *supra* note 41, at 491-94.

[46] OFF. R. BASEBALL 4.19.

[47] F. POLLOCK, *supra* note 42, at 72.

[48] *Cf.* H. GUTTERIDGE, COMPARATIVE LAW 77-78 (2d ed. 1949).

most important technical rules of baseball, although on the surface completely different in outlook and philosophy, share significant elements. Both have been essentially conservative, changing only as often as a need for change is perceived, and then only to the extent necessary to remove the need for further change. Although problems are solved very slowly when this attitude prevails, the solutions that are adopted do not create many new difficulties. If the process reaps few rewards, it also runs few risks.

"Funny thing, I never expected to be a ballplayer in the first place. I wanted to be a lawyer. Well, as a matter of fact I *became* a lawyer. I went to law school at Dixon College in Illinois and graduated in 1901, but I got to playing ball and never did go back to the law." Davy Jones, *in* LAWRENCE RITTER, THE GLORY OF THEIR TIMES 38 (1984 ed.).

APPELLATE REVIEW OF MILITARY COMMISSIONS

Eugene R. Fidell[†]

In the coming weeks there will be no shortage of analysis of the military commission provisions that have emerged from the conference committee on the National Defense Authorization Act. As good a place as any to kick off the discussion here on Balkinization is the bill's provisions for appellate review of military commission trials. The appellate process will include automatic, but waivable, review by a "United States Court of Military Commission Review" followed by appeal as of right to the United States Court of Appeals for the District of Columbia Circuit, with the usual opportunity for Supreme Court review on writ of certiorari. If you think this is just fine, here are three points to ponder.

First, why create an intermediate appellate court for so few cases? After all, no one seems to think there will be more than a couple of dozen military commission trials, especially after the Administration completes its screening to decide which of the potential military commission cases can wisely be shunted into the district courts. In a time of austerity, one would hope that budget-conscious legislators would have thought twice about the cost of this court. This is particularly so because the military services already have intermediate appellate courts. These are the four service "courts of criminal appeals," created by the Uniform Code of Military Justice (UCMJ). The slight case load associated with review of a handful of military commission cases could easily have been accommodated by these courts, which have existed under one name or another since 1951, when the UCMJ took effect. The judges of these courts are either active duty senior judge advocates or, in a few cases, retired judge advocates

---

[†] Senior Research Scholar in Law and Florence Rogatz Lecturer in Law, Yale Law School. This essay originally appeared at *Balkinization*, http://balkin.blogspot.com/2009/10/in-coming-weeks-there-will-be-no.html, on October 8, 2009. It is reproduced here with the permission of the author and the publisher.

now employed by the government as civil servants. There is plenty of military law expertise on these courts. Admittedly, these courts are separate from one another, and it may be awkward to refer all military commission cases to, for example, the Army Court of Criminal Appeals, but there's really no reason these cases could not be centralized in one of the service courts, as the accuseds are obviously not members of our armed forces. Of note, the judges of the Court of Military Commission Review do not enjoy the benefit of fixed terms of office, which is a key hallmark of independence. Although the Supreme Court decided in *Weiss v. United States*, 510 U.S. 163 (1994), that due process does not require military judges to have fixed terms, the Army and the Coast Guard (my old outfit), to their credit, have introduced three-year terms for their trial and appellate military judges. Military Commission accuseds' first tier of appellate review will be heard by at-will judges.

Did I mention that our military personnel do not even get access to the courts of criminal appeals unless their sentence extends to death, a punitive discharge, or a year or more of confinement, 10 U.S.C. § 866(b)(1), whereas anyone convicted by military commission is entitled to review by the Court of Military Commission Review, regardless of the sentence?

Second, why involve the District of Columbia Circuit? We have had a specialized civilian appellate military court since 1951 — originally known as the Court of Military Appeals and later renamed the United States Court of Appeals for the Armed Forces (CAAF). Although the judges must be drawn from civilian life and may not have been retired after 20 years' service, 10 U.S.C. §§ 942(b)(1), -(b)(4), the court has overwhelmingly been populated by jurists who have served in the armed forces. This is true of each of the five currently sitting judges and all but one of the senior judges. It remains a mystery why Congress has not seen fit to confer on these judges appellate jurisdiction over military commission cases, unless it was felt that the District of Columbia Circuit could be counted on in ways that CAAF could not be. I am not expecting any member of the House or Senate to explain the reasoning in the choice between these two courts. It certainly cannot have been CAAF's workload; although the court screens many petitions for review, it decided only 46 cases in its last Term of Court by full opinion.

Adding to the mystery surrounding this avoidance of our country's specialized court is the fact that military commission accuseds will, at this second stage of the appellate process, receive review by life-tenured Article III judges, whereas members of our own forces — most of whom by far are United States citizens — who fall afoul of the UCMJ can expect to appear before the Article I CAAF judges who serve for 15-year terms. This is not to impugn the CAAF judges' independence and impartiality, but there is a difference between Article I and Article III status, and Congress has repeatedly declined to confer Article III status on the CAAF judges. Result: military commission accuseds will receive the benefit of the Article III gold standard of judicial independence, while our own personnel who are convicted by courts-martial get second-best. Someone will have to explain this anomaly to me.

Finally, it is entirely appropriate that Congress has provided for Supreme Court review of military commission cases. The difficulty here lies in the fact that our own personnel who are convicted by courts-martial cannot even seek certiorari unless CAAF, in its discretion, grants review or an extraordinary writ. 10 U.S.C. § 867a(a); *see also* 28 U.S.C. § 1259. (This limitation does not apply to capital cases and the occasional cases that are referred to CAAF by the Judge Advocates General.) Indeed, the Solicitor General has taken the position — wrong in my view — that it is not enough that CAAF have granted review of the case, as the statute indicates, but that it have granted review of the particular issue sought to be presented to the Supreme Court. Once again, the result is that military commission accuseds enjoy greater rights than do our own personnel. How can this be defended?

Legislation is pending to remove CAAF's gatekeeper function (S. 357, The Equal Justice for United States Military Personnel Act of 2009; H.R. 569, The Equal Justice for Our Military Act of 2009), so that any court-martial accused whose case has reached CAAF would be able to seek certiorari, whether or not CAAF granted discretionary review or extraordinary relief. It is a scandal that Congress did not rectify this defect if it was committed to granting military commission accuseds untrammeled access to the Supreme Court.

I recognize that some of what I have suggested here smacks of saying of the provisions for appellate review of military commission cases that (to use a colorful phrase I once heard Attorney General Mukasey use to good effect in a related context) "the bride is too beautiful." I'm not interested in making this bride less beautiful by reducing anyone's rights, but Congress owes it to the country to produce legislation that makes sense against the larger canvas of our legal system.

FEDERAL JURISDICTION

Professor FREUND

3 hours

1. The State of California, claiming ownership of submerged coastal lands within the three-mile limit, has leased certain of those lands to the Sunmist Oil Co., a California corporation, which is producing oil from them. The United States also asserts ownership, and has issued a license to the Cosmic Oil Co., a California corporation, to drill wells and produce oil on the same lands, but the licensee has not gone into possession. The claim of the United States rests on the treaty of Guadelupe Hidalgo, by which Mexico ceded the lands; the claim of California rests on the subsequent act of Congress admitting her to statehood on an equal footing with the original states. As an expert in Federal jurisdiction, you are consulted by counsel for the United States and for Cosmic, requesting an opinion on how to proceed in order to obtain an authoritative decision in the dispute. What do you advise?

2. P, a baseball club incorporated in North Carolina, brings suit in a state court in South Carolina against D, the leading batter of the Piedmont League, who is a citizen of South Carolina, and E, a rival club incorporated in North Carolina, alleging that D has broken his contract with P by failing to report for duty and that E has induced the breach by making a contract with D with knowledge of P's prior contract. The complaint prays for specific performance against D and damages of $5000 against E. D answers, admitting P's allegations, asserting readiness to play for P, defending on the ground that E has secured an injunction against him in a North Carolina court, and interposing a complaint against E praying cancellation of its contract for fraudulent misrepresentations and an order directing E to dismiss its injunction suit. E answers, denying inducement of breach of contract or misrepresentation, asserting the invalidity of P's contract, and praying for dismissal of the complaints of P and D. (a) May D remove the case to a federal court? (b) May E remove it?

(3) An Act of Congress imposes a tax on electric utility companies but exempts companies operating in a state which provides for rate regulation on the prudent investment rate base. State X enacts a statute directing its public service commission to fix electric rates on that basis; jurisdiction to review rate orders is given to the state supreme court, with power to affirm, reverse, or modify the orders. The state statute contains the following proviso: "This Act

PAUL FREUND'S
FEDERAL-BASEBALL JURISDICTION

In the November 1992 issue of the *Harvard Law Review*, Professor James Vorenberg recalled his recently deceased colleague Paul Freund. In addition to commenting on Freund's qualities as a scholar and a citizen, Vorenberg summarized and quoted from a newspaper article published many years earlier in Freund's hometown:

> Among the papers Paul left was a clipping from a 1918 issue of the *St. Louis Post Dispatch* with a picture of a smiling but determined youngster, and the headline: "11-Year-Old Boy Graduated From the Wyman School" — and the sub-headline: "Paul Freund who reads poetry and speaks from the platform would like to be a lawyer." The story explained that Paul entered high school at 11, spoke in public without embarrassment, wanted to be a lawyer — or maybe "a plain business man" or a "moving picture actor" — but that deep down in his heart he knew that "supreme happiness could come if he could only grow up to be a big-league baseball player."[1]

Freund missed out on supreme happiness, but he was a success as a lawyer. And he did manage to weave a little bit of baseball into his work in the law. See Question #2 on the facing page. Now comes the *Green Bag*, inviting readers to send us their answers to Question #2 (written on the lines below and on the next page, then mailed by October 31, 2010 to The Green Bag, 6600 Barnaby St. NW, Washington, DC 20015). The author of the best answer will receive a prize, and that answer will be published in the next *Green Bag Almanac & Reader*.

_____

_____

_____

_____

_____

_____

_____

_____

---

[1] James Vorenberg, *In Memoriam: Paul Freund*, 106 HARV. L. REV. 13 & nn. 1, 2 (1992) (quoting *"11-Year Old Boy Graduated from the Wyman School*, ST. LOUIS POST-DISPATCH (undated copy on file at the Harvard Law School Library)") (footnote omitted).

AUGUST

JENNINGS, DETROIT

HUGH AMBROSE (HUGHIE) JENNINGS

Member, Maryland Bar (1905).
See C. Paul Rogers III, *Hughie Jennings, in*
THE BASEBALL BIOGRAPHY PROJECT, www.sabr.org (SABR 2009).

❧ AUGUST ❧

SUN	MON	TUES	WED	THUR	FRI	SAT
1	2	3	4	5	6	7
8	9	10	11	12	13	14
15	16	17	18	19	20	21
22	23	24	25	26	27	28
29	30	31				

COURTING THE PEOPLE

DEMOSPRUDENCE AND THE LAW/POLITICS DIVIDE

Lani Guinier[†]

America's first black President signed his first major piece of legislation on January 29, 2009: the Lilly Ledbetter Fair Pay Act.[1] Since the Act carried Lilly Ledbetter's name, she fittingly stood beaming by President Obama's side during the signing ceremony.[2] For nineteen years, however, this seventy-year-old grandmother had less reason to be joyful, working in supervisory blue-collar jobs in a Goodyear Tire and Rubber Plant in Gadsden, Alabama earning fifteen to forty percent less than her male counterparts. This pay gap, which resulted from receiving smaller raises than the men, "added up and multiplied" over the years.[3] But Ledbetter did not discover the disparity until she was nearing retirement and "only started to get hard evidence of discrimination when someone anonymously left a piece of paper" in her mailbox listing the salaries of the men who held the same job.[4] Ledbetter sued and a federal jury awarded her $223,776 in back pay and more than $3 million in punitive damages, finding that it was "more likely than not that [Goodyear] paid [Ledbetter] a[n] unequal salary because of her sex."[5] The Supreme Court nullified that verdict. The five-

---

[†] Bennett Boskey Professor of Law, Harvard Law School. I thank Niko Bowie, Tomiko Brown-Nagin, Richard Chen, Andrew Crespo, Jean-Claude Croizet, Christian Davenport, Pam Karlan, Jennifer Lane, Jane Mansbridge, Martha Minow, Janet Moran, Robert Post and Gerald Torres for their invaluable contributions to this Essay. This article originally appeared at 89 B.U. L. Rev. 539 (2009), and is reprinted here with the permission of the author and the publisher.

[1] Lilly Ledbetter Fair Pay Act of 2009, Pub. L. No. 111-2, 123 Stat. 5.

[2] *See* Richard Leiby, *A Signature with the First Lady's Hand in It*, WASH. POST, Jan. 29, 2009, at C1 ("It seemed to be all about Lilly Ledbetter at the White House yesterday — her name was enshrined in history, affixed to the first piece of legislation signed by President Obama.").

[3] *Justice Denied? The Implications of the Supreme Court's* Ledbetter v. Goodyear *Employment Discrimination Decision: Hearing Before the H. Comm. on Educ. & Labor*, 110th Cong. 10 (2007) [hereinafter *Hearing*] (statement of Lilly Ledbetter); *see also* Lilly Ledbetter, Address to the Democratic National Convention (Aug. 26, 2008) [hereinafter Ledbetter, Address], http://www.demconvention.com/lily-ledbetter/.

[4] *Hearing*, *supra* note 3, at 10. Ledbetter's salary was $3,727 a month. The salary of the lowest paid man, with far less seniority, was $4,286. *Id.* at 12.

[5] Ledbetter v. Goodyear Tire & Rubber Co., 127 S. Ct. 2162, 2178 (2007) (Ginsburg, J., dis-

Justice majority held that Ledbetter waived her right to sue by failing to file her complaint within 180 days of the first act of discrimination.[6] In Ledbetter's words, the Court "sided with big business. They said I should have filed my complaint within six months of Goodyear's first decision to pay me less, even though I didn't know that's what they were doing."[7] By contrast, the Lilly Ledbetter Fair Pay Act sided with ordinary, working women across the nation.

Justice Ruth Bader Ginsburg, on behalf of herself and three colleagues, dissented from the Court's May 2007 decision.[8] A leading litigator and advocate for women's equality before taking her seat on the Court,[9] Justice Ginsburg read her dissent aloud from the bench — an act that, in her own words, reflects "more than ordinary disagreement."[10] Her oral dissent, which made the front page of the *Washington Post*,[11] signaled that something had gone "egregiously wrong."[12] In a stinging rebuke to the Court majority, she used the personal pronoun, speaking not to her colleagues but directly to the other "you's" in her audience — women who, despite suspecting something askew in their own jobs, were reluctant to rock the boat as the only women in all-male positions:

> Indeed initially you may not know the men are receiving more for substantially similar work. . . . If you sue only when the pay disparity

---

senting) (quoting record from below), *superseded by statute*, Lilly Ledbetter Fair Pay Act of 2009, Pub L. No. 111-2, 123 Stat. 5.

[6] *Id.* at 2165 (majority opinion).

[7] Ledbetter, Address, *supra* note 3; *see also Hearing*, *supra* note 3, at 10.

[8] *Ledbetter*, 127 S. Ct. at 2178 (Ginsburg, J., dissenting).

[9] In an interview with the ACLU, Ginsburg's co-counsel described the first case Ginsburg argued before the Court: "I've never heard an oral argument as unbelievably cogent as hers. . . . Not a single Justice asked a single question; I think they were mesmerized by her." *Tribute: The Legacy of Ruth Bader Ginsburg & WRP Staff*, AM. CIVIL LIBERTIES UNION, Mar. 7, 2006, http://www.aclu.org/womensrights/gen/24412pub20060307. html.

[10] Justice Ruth Bader Ginsburg, The 20th Annual Leo and Berry Eizenstat Memorial Lecture: The Role of Dissenting Opinions (Oct. 21, 2007) [hereinafter Ginsburg, Eizenstat Lecture], http://www.supremecourtus.gov/publicinfo/speeches/sp_10-21-07.html.

[11] Robert Barnes, *Over Ginsburg's Dissent, Court Limits Bias Suits*, WASH. POST, May 30, 2007, at A1 ("Speaking for the three other dissenting justices, Ginsburg's voice was as precise and emotionless as if she were reading a banking decision, but the words were stinging."). Barnes noted that Justice Ginsburg's oral dissent was a "usually rare practice that she has now employed twice in the past six weeks to criticize the majority for opinions that she said undermine women's rights." *Id.*

[12] Ruth Bader Ginsburg, Celebration Fifty-Five: A Public Conversation Between Dean Elena Kagan '86 and Justice Ruth Bader Ginsburg '56-'58 at the Harvard Law School Women's Leadership Summit (Sept. 20, 2008) (from notes taken by and on file with author) [hereinafter Ginsburg, Leadership Summit]; *see also* Ginsburg, Eizenstat Lecture, *supra* note 10 ("A dissent presented orally . . . garners immediate attention. It signals that, in the dissenters' view, the Court's opinion is not just wrong, but importantly and grievously misguided.").

becomes steady and large enough to enable you to mount a winnable case, you will be cut off at the Court's threshold for suing too late.[13]

Justice Ginsburg's dissent reflected an acute sense, missing from the majority's opinion, of the circumstances surrounding women in male-dominated workplaces. In a job previously filled only by men, women "understandably may be anxious to avoid making waves."[14]

Justice Ginsburg was *courting* the people.[15] Her oral dissent and subsequent remarks hinted at a democratizing form of judicial speech that, were it heard, could be easily understood by those outside the courtroom.[16] By speaking colloquially — using the personal pronoun "you" to address her audience — Justice Ginsburg signaled to ordinary women that the majority should not have the last word on the meaning of pay discrimination. Her goal was to engage an external audience in a conversation about our country's commitment to equal pay for equal work.[17]

While Justice Ginsburg spoke frankly to and about the Lilly Ledbetters of the world, her real target was the legislature. Appalled by the Court's "cramped interpretation" of a congressional statute to justify its decision nullifying the favorable jury verdict, Justice Ginsburg explicitly stated that the "ball again lies in Congress's court."[18] During a public conversation in September 2008, then-Harvard Law School Dean Elena Kagan asked Justice Ginsburg to describe her intended audience in *Ledbetter*. Ginsburg replied: "[I]t was Congress. Speaking to Congress, I said, 'you did not mean what the Court said. So fix it.'"[19]

Democrats in Congress responded quickly. Initially called the Fair Pay

---

[13] Oral Dissent of Justice Ginsburg at 4:25, *Ledbetter*, 127 S. Ct. 2162 (No. 05-1074), *available at* http://www.oyez.org/cases/2000-2009/2006/2006_05_1074/opinion; *see also* Lani Guinier, *The Supreme Court, 2007 Term—Foreword: Demosprudence Through Dissent*, 122 HARV. L. REV. 4, 40-41 (2008).

[14] Oral Dissent of Justice Ginsburg, *supra* note 13, at 8:30-8:37; *see also* Guinier, *supra* note 13, at 41.

[15] By "courting" I mean enlisting or inspiring rather than wooing or currying favor with.

[16] Guinier, *supra* note 13, at 40.

[17] *Cf.* Timothy R. Johnson, Ryan C. Black & Eve M. Ringsmuth, *Hear Me Roar: What Provokes Supreme Court Justices to Dissent from the Bench?*, 92 MINN. L. REV. (forthcoming 2009) (manuscript at 14, *available at* http://black.wustl.edu/webfiles/announcements/johnson-black-ringsmuth-2009.pdf) (finding that Supreme Court Justices use their oral dissents strategically to signal strong disagreement as well as the need for action by third parties to change the majority decision). As was her practice, Justice Ginsburg handed out her bench announcement right after the delivery of her oral dissent. Her press-release-style opening paragraphs in her opinions are intended to help reporters under tight deadlines get it right.

[18] Oral Dissent of Justice Ginsburg, *supra* note 13, at 10:17-10:58; *see also* Guinier, *supra* note 13, at 41 n.179.

[19] Ginsburg, Leadership Summit, *supra* note 12.

Restoration Act, the House-passed bill would have eliminated the Court-sanctioned time limit.[20] That bill, however, died in the Senate, where Republicans — including John McCain — publicly denounced it as anti-business.[21]

As the initial Fair Pay Restoration Act languished in Congress, Lilly Ledbetter emerged as a real presence in the 2008 election campaign.[22] Despite her initial misgivings about partisan campaigning, she was infuriated by John McCain's refusal to support a congressional fix. She cut an ad[23] for Barack Obama that had a "stratospheric effect" when poll-tested by Fox News's political consultant Frank Luntz.[24] In August 2008, Ledbetter was a featured speaker at the Democratic National Convention in Denver.[25] There, as well as in her testimony before Congress, she acknowledged the significance of Justice Ginsburg's dissent both in affirming her concerns and directing attention to a legislative remedy.[26]

In her testimony before Congress, for example, Ledbetter echoed Justice Ginsburg's emphasis on the isolation many women feel when they first integrate the workplace.[27] Both Ledbetter and Justice Ginsburg used the pronoun "you" to speak directly to other women. At the same time that Ledbetter's story animated Justice Ginsburg's dissent, Justice Ginsburg's dissent amplified Ledbetter's own voice. Suitably emboldened, this Alabama grandmother went before Congress to speak directly to women about their shared fears of making waves in a male dominated environment:

> Justice Ginsburg hit the nail on the head when she said that the majority's rule just doesn't make sense in the real world. You can't expect people to go around asking their coworkers how much they are mak-

---

[20] H.R. 2831, 110th Cong. (2007).

[21] The initial bill passed the House in July 2007, but never came up for a vote in the Senate. GovTrack, H.R. 2831: Lilly Ledbetter Fair Pay Act of 2007, http://www.govtrack.us/congress/bill.xpd?bill=h110-2831 (last visited Mar. 17, 2009); *see also* Carl Hulse, *Republican Senators Block Pay Discrimination Measure*, N.Y. TIMES, Apr. 24, 2008, at A22.

[22] *Morning Edition: Fair Pay Law Strikes a Blow for Equal Pay* at 4:12 (National Public Radio broadcast Jan. 29, 2009), http://www.npr.org/templates/player/mediaPlayer.html?action=1&t=1&islist=false&id=99995431&m=99995549 (describing Ledbetter's prominent role and reporting that Ledbetter's husband, a retired National Guard Sergeant Major, voted for a Democratic President for the first time in fifty years when he cast his ballot for Barack Obama).

[23] In the ad, Ledbetter says, "John McCain opposed a law to give women equal pay for equal work. And he dismissed the wage gap, saying women just need education and training. I had the same skills as the men at my plant. My family needed that money." *Id.* at 2:35-2:58.

[24] *Id.* at 3:07-3:18.

[25] Ledbetter, Address, *supra* note 3.

[26] *Hearing*, *supra* note 3, at 10.

[27] *Id.* at 11.

ing. Plus, even if you know some people are getting paid a little more than you, that is no reason to suspect discrimination right away. Especially when you work at a place like I did, where you are the only woman in a male-dominated factory, you don't want to make waves unnecessarily. You want to try to fit in and get along.[28]

Justice Ginsburg also continued to engage in a more public discourse about the *Ledbetter* case and her role as an oral dissenter. In an October 2007 speech posted on the Supreme Court website, she parodied the majority's reasoning: "'Sue early on,' the majority counseled, when it is uncertain whether discrimination accounts for the pay disparity you are beginning to experience, and when you may not know that men are receiving more for the same work. (Of course, you will likely lose such a less-than-fully baked case.)"[29] As reframed by Justice Ginsburg, Ledbetter's story was not about a negligent plaintiff who waited an unconscionably long time to sue; it was about an ordinary woman struggling to comprehend and eventually document the pay disparities in her all-male work environment. Justice Ginsburg frankly acknowledged the zigzag trajectory of change, especially given the real world employment challenges such a woman faces. In "propel[ling] change," her oral dissent had to "sound an alarm" that would be heard by members of Congress, Lilly Ledbetter and women's rights advocates more generally.[30] Her dissent had "to attract immediate public attention."[31]

Eventually social activists, legal advocacy groups, media translators, legislators and "role-literate participants" (in Reva Siegel's terminology)[32] not only heard but acted upon the alarm bells Ginsburg sounded. Marcia Greenberger of the National Women's Law Center was one of those "role-literate participants" who helped carry Justice Ginsburg's message forward. Greenberger characterized Ginsburg's oral dissent as a "clarion call" to the American people "that the Court is headed in the wrong direction."[33] Lilly Ledbetter became another such participant as her story, with

---

[28] *Id.* at 10; *see also* YouTube, Ledbetter v. Goodyear Equal Pay Hearing: Lilly Ledbetter, http://www.youtube.com/watch?v=jRpYoUu5XH0 (last visited Mar. 10, 2009).

[29] Ginsburg, Eizenstat Lecture, *supra* note 10.

[30] *See id.* Justice Ginsburg's willingness to participate in a more expansive conversation is not entirely unexpected, given her view that conversation should run both ways. "If we don't listen we won't be listened to." Ginsburg, Leadership Summit, *supra* note 12.

[31] Ginsburg, Eizenstat Lecture, *supra* note 10; *see also* Johnson, Black & Ringsmuth, *supra* note 17 (manuscript at 7-8).

[32] Guinier, *supra* note 13, at 51; *see also* Reva B. Siegel, *Constitutional Culture, Social Movement Conflict and Constitutional Change: The Case of the de Facto ERA*, 94 CAL. L. REV. 1323, 1339-48 (2006) [hereinafter Siegel, *Constitutional Culture*].

[33] Mother Jones, Ginsburg's Famous White Gloves Finally Come Off, http://www.mother-

Justice Ginsburg's assistance, helped ground and frame the discourse.[34] And for the first time in more than a decade, Congress pushed back against the Supreme Court. In January 2009, Lilly Ledbetter's name was enshrined in history when Congress passed and President Barack Obama signed the Lilly Ledbetter Fair Pay Act.[35]

In her *Ledbetter* dissent and subsequent remarks, Justice Ginsburg was courting the people to reverse the decision of a Supreme Court majority and thereby limit its effect. In Robert Cover's "jurisgenerative" sense,[36] she claimed a space for citizens to advance alternative interpretations of the law. Her oral dissent and public remarks represented a set of *demosprudential* practices for instantiating and reinforcing the relationship between public engagement and institutional legitimacy.

In Justice Ginsburg's oral dissent we see the possibilities of a more democratically-oriented jurisprudence, or what Gerald Torres and I term demosprudence.[37] Demosprudence builds on the idea that lawmaking is a collaborative enterprise between formal elites — whether judges, legislators or lawyers — and ordinary people. The foundational hypothesis of

---

jones.com/mojoblog/archives/2007/05/4556_ginsburgs_famou.html (May 31, 2007, 22:19 PST) (quoting Marcia Greenberger).

[34] Justice Ginsburg's dissent and Lilly Ledbetter's public statements converge on a common explanation for Ledbetter's delay in filing her lawsuit, an explanation that influenced both the media coverage and the Obama campaign's framing of the case. *See* Adam Liptak, *Justices Hear Bias Case on Maternity, Pensions, and Timing*, N.Y. TIMES, Dec. 11, 2008, at B7; Sheryl Gay Stolberg, *Obama Signs Equal-Pay Legislation*, N.Y. TIMES, Jan. 29, 2009, http://www.nytimes. com/2009/01/30/us/politics/30ledbetterweb.html?hp. Their mutually reinforcing explanation for Ledbetter's delay in filing her lawsuit, their joint outreach to Congress and their success in sparking favorable media coverage of the new legislation became key talking points on conservative blogs. *See, e.g.*, Posting of Hans Bader to OpenMarket.org, http://www.openmarket. org/2009/03/04/ distorting-the-news-to-obamas-advantage/ (Mar. 4, 2009, 15:29); Posting of Orin Kerr to Volokh Conspiracy, http://volokh.com/posts/1236629897.shtml (Mar. 9, 2009, 16:18); Posting of Ed Whelan to Bench Memos, National Review Online, http://bench.nationalreview.com/post/?q=YzA0Zjk1MzViMWUwMWNlYWEwZTkyYTIzY mY3MzAxYWE (Mar. 9, 2009, 13:51). Indeed, Lilly Ledbetter soon came to symbolize a populist message. Ledbetter not only was present at the signing ceremony for the bill named in her honor, but sat with First Lady Michelle Obama during President Obama's first address to a joint session of Congress. Michael Falcone, *Guests of the First Lady, Reflecting Main Themes of the Speech*, N.Y. TIMES, Feb. 25, 2009, at A16.

[35] Lilly Ledbetter Fair Pay Act of 2009, Pub. L. No. 111-3, 123 Stat. 5. The Act passed the Senate with "Yea" votes from every present Democrat and all four female Republicans. U.S. Senate Roll Call Votes 111th Congress–1st Session, http://www.senate.gov/legislative/ LIS/roll_call_lists/roll_call_vote_cfm.cfm?congress=111&session=1&vote=00014 (last visited Mar. 17, 2009).

[36] *See generally* Robert M. Cover, *The Supreme Court, 1981 Term–Foreword: Nomos and Narrative*, 97 HARV. L. REV. 4 (1983) (conceptualizing the law as normative in nature).

[37] *See* Lani Guinier & Gerald Torres, Linked Fate: Toward a Jurisprudence of Social Movements 1 (Sept. 17, 2006) (unpublished manuscript, on file with author).

demosprudence is that the wisdom of the people should inform the law-making enterprise in a democracy. From a demosprudential perspective, the Court gains a new source of democratic authority when its members engage ordinary people in a productive dialogue about the potential role of "We the People" in lawmaking.[38]

Demosprudence is a term Professor Torres and I initially coined to describe the process of making and interpreting law from an external — not just internal — perspective. That perspective emphasizes the role of informal democratic mobilizations and wide-ranging social movements that serve to make formal institutions, including those that regulate legal culture, more democratic.[39] Demosprudence focuses on the ways that "the demos" (especially through social movements) can contribute to the meaning of law.

Justice Ginsburg acted demosprudentially when she invited a wider audience into the conversation about one of the core conflicts at the heart of our democracy.[40] She grounded her oral dissent and her public remarks in a set of demosprudential practices that linked public engagement with institutional legitimacy. Those practices are part of a larger demosprudential claim: that the Constitution belongs to the people, not just to the Supreme Court.

The dissenting opinions, especially the oral dissents, of Justice Ginsburg and other members of the Court are the subject of my 2008 Supreme Court foreword, *Demosprudence Through Dissent*.[41] The foreword was addressed to judges, especially those speaking out in dissent, urging them to

---

[38] Guinier, *supra* note 13, at 48 ("The demosprudential *intuition* is that democracies, at their best, make and interpret law by expanding, informing, inspiring, and interacting with the community of consent, a community in constitutional terms better known as 'we the people.'").

[39] *See, e.g.*, LANI GUINIER & GERALD TORRES, CHANGING THE WIND: THE DEMOSPRUDENCE OF LAW AND SOCIAL MOVEMENTS (forthcoming 2010) (draft manuscript at 1, on file with author).

> We coin the term demosprudence . . . as a critique of lawmaking that is historically preoccupied with moments of social change as if they occur primarily within an elite enterprise. Demosprudence is a philosophy, a methodology and a practice that views lawmaking from the perspective of informal democratic mobilizations and disruptive social movements that serve to make formal institutions, including those that regulate legal culture, more democratic. Although democratic accountability as a normative matter includes citizen mobilizations organized to influence a single election, a discrete piece of legislation, or a judicial victory, we focus here on democratic responsiveness to popular, purposive mobilizations that seek significant, sustainable social, economic and/or political change. In this lecture, therefore, we discuss demosprudence primarily as the jurisprudence of social movements.

Id.

[40] *See id.* (manuscript at 14).

[41] Guinier, *supra* note 13.

"engage dialogically with nonjudicial actors and to encourage them to act democratically."[42] The foreword focuses on oral dissents because of the special power of the spoken word, but Justices can issue demosprudential concurrences and even majority opinions, written as well as spoken.[43] Moreover, true to its origins, demosprudence is not limited to reconceptualizing the judicial role. Lawyers and nonlawyers alike can be demosprudential, a claim that I foreshadow in the foreword and which Torres and I are developing in other work on law and social movements.[44]

Supreme Court Justices can play a democracy-enhancing role by expanding the audience for their opinions to include those unlearned in the law. Of the current Justices, Justice Antonin Scalia has a particular knack for attracting and holding the attention of a nonlegal audience. His dissents are "deliberate exercises in advocacy" that "chart new paths for changing the law."[45] Just as Justice Ginsburg welcomed women's rights activists into the public sphere in response to the Court majority's decision in *Ledbetter*, Justice Scalia's dissents are often in conversation with a conservative constituency of accountability.[46] By writing dissents like these, both Justices have acknowledged that their audience is not just their colleagues or the litigants in the cases before them. Both exemplify the potential power of demosprudential dissents when the dissenter is aligned with a social movement or constituency that "mobilizes to change the meaning of the Constitution over time."[47] Thus, Justice Ginsburg speaks in her "clearest voice" when she addresses issues of gender equality.[48] Similarly, Justice Scalia effectively uses his originalist jurisprudence as "a language that a political movement can both understand and rally around."[49] Both Justices Ginsburg and Scalia are at their best as demosprudential dissenters when they encourage a "social movement to fight on."[50]

---

[42] *Id.* at 50; *see also id.* at 10 (describing Justice Breyer's passionate oral dissent in *Parents Involved in Community Schools v. Seattle School District No. 1*, 127 S. Ct. 2738 (2007), where he "hinted at a new genre of judicial speech" that could resonate with a less educated audience were his oral dissent more widely distributed). Demosprudential dissents are those that 1) probe or question a particular understanding of democracy, 2) using an accessible narrative style to 3) reach out to an external audience — beyond the other Justices or litigants in the case. *Id.* at 51, 90-92, 95-96.

[43] *Id.* at 52-56.

[44] *Id.* at 102-07, 113 & nn.517-18.

[45] *Id.* at 110.

[46] *See, e.g.*, Lawrence v. Texas, 539 U.S. 558, 586 (2003) (Scalia, J., dissenting).

[47] Guinier, *supra* note 13, at 114.

[48] *Id.*

[49] *Id.*; *see also* Reva Siegel, *Dead or Alive: Originalism as Popular Constitutionalism in Heller*, 122 HARV. L. REV. 191, 192 (2008) [hereinafter Siegel, *Dead or Alive*].

[50] Guinier, *supra* note 13, at 112; *see also* Ginsburg, Eizenstat Lecture, *supra* note 10; *cf.* Siegel,

Robert Post, writing in this symposium, reads my argument exactly right: "[C]ourts do not end democratic debate about the meaning of rights and the law; they are participants within that debate."[51] As Post explains, I argue that the "meaning of constitutional principles are forged within the cauldron of political debate," a debate in which judges are often important, though not necessarily central, actors.[52] Law and politics are in continuous dialogue, and the goal of a demosprudential dissenter is to ensure that the views of a judicial majority do not preempt political dialogue. When Justice Ginsburg spoke in a voice more conversational than technical, she did more than declare her disagreement with the majority's holding. By vigorously speaking out during the opinion announcement, she also appealed to citizens in terms that laypersons could understand and to Congress directly.[53] This is demosprudence.

Robert Post eloquently summarizes and contextualizes the argument I make about demosprudence. He also corrects the misunderstanding of the law/politics divide that beats at the heart of Gerald Rosenberg's criticisms of that argument.[54] Post neatly restates my premise: "Law inspires and provokes the claims of politically engaged agents, as it simultaneously emerges from these claims."[55]

In his companion essay, Professor Rosenberg polices the law/politics distinction to create a false binary. Rosenberg dismisses the possibility of an ongoing and recursive conversation between law and politics that *may* produce changes in the law and eventually in our "constitutional culture," meaning changes in the popular as well as elite understanding of what the law means. Constitutional culture is the fish tank in which the beliefs and actions of judicial as well as nonjudicial participants swim. It is the "dynamic sociopolitical environment" in which ideas about legal meanings circulate, ferment, compete and ultimately surface in formal venues such as legal advocacy or legislative actions.[56] As political scientist Daniel Ho-Sang explains, the goal of demosprudence is "to open up analytic and po-

---

Dead or Alive, supra note 49, at 196, 237-38.

[51] *See* Robert Post, *Law Professors and Political Scientists: Observations on the Law/Politics Distinction in the Guinier/Rosenberg Debate*, 89 B.U. L. REV. 581, 582 (2009).

[52] *Id.*

[53] My claim in the foreword that Justices, not just Justice Ginsburg, use their oral dissents strategically to appeal to third parties is consistent with the findings of a recent study by several political scientists. *See* Johnson, Black & Ringsmuth, *supra* note 17 (manuscript at 30-31).

[54] *See* Gerald N. Rosenberg, *Romancing the Court*, 89 B.U. L. REV. 563, 564 (2009).

[55] *See* Post, *supra* note 51, at 581.

[56] *See* Guinier, *supra* note 13, at 59 ("That there is a healthy dialectic between an oppositional constitutional culture and the 'legal constitution' is the organizing idea behind demosprudence through dissent.").

litical possibility to build and sustain more dynamic and politically potent relationships between [legal elites] and aggrieved communities."[57]

Professor Rosenberg's critique of demosprudence rests on several misunderstandings of my work and that of other legal scholars.[58] First, Professor Rosenberg wrongly assumes that my claims are descriptive rather than aspirational.[59] Second, Professor Rosenberg's concern about my "Courtcentric" analysis overlooks the occasion for my argument;[60] that is, the traditions associated with the Supreme Court foreword published every year in the November issue of the *Harvard Law Review*. Third, he orients his entire critique around polling data and other social science research to trivialize the relationship of narrative to culture, to exaggerate the predictive capacity of a data-driven approach to quantify causation and to preempt other useful analytic approaches.[61]

First, my foreword posits that judges *can* play a demosprudential role and that oral dissents are one *potential* vehicle for allowing them to do so.[62] While it is true that oral dissents *currently* face obstacles to their demosprudential efficacy, those obstacles need not be insurmountable. Moreover, Rosenberg's critique arguably makes my point. He is saying "people don't pay attention,"[63] while I am saying "yes, they can!" Indeed, they might pay more attention if Justices took the time to talk to them.[64] He characterizes the past; I aim to sketch out the contours of a different future. Rosenberg is absolutely right that one next step might be to deploy the tools of social science to explore the extent to which this claim has been realized.[65] But the foreword is suggestive, not predictive. Justices of the Supreme Court can be demosprudential when they use their opinions to engage nonlegal actors in the process of making and interpreting law over time. They have democratically-based reasons to seek to inspire a mobilized constituency; it is not that they invariably *will* cause a social

---

[57] Daniel HoSang, Assistant Professor of Ethnic Studies and Political Science, University of Oregon, Remarks on Lani Guinier and Gerald Torres's "Demosprudence" Paper, University of Oregon School of Law (Oct. 24, 2008).

[58] *See generally* Post, *supra* note 51.

[59] *See* Rosenberg, *supra* note 54, at 565.

[60] *See id.* at 573-77.

[61] *Id.* at 577-79.

[62] *See* Guinier, *supra* note 13, at 4.

[63] *See* Rosenberg, *supra* note 54, at 566 (stating that "most Americans do not have a clue as to what the Court is doing or has done").

[64] I thank my faculty assistant, Janet Moran, for highlighting this formulation of my argument. *See* Guinier, *supra* note 13, at 24-25 & 29 n.126 (discussing debate over cameras in the courtroom); *infra* notes 110-111 and accompanying text.

[65] *See* Rosenberg, *supra* note 54, at 564, 577-79.

movement to emerge.

Similarly, the idea that Court opinions do not invariably inspire social movements does not mean they cannot have this effect. Nor do I argue that oral dissents are the only, or even the single most important, communication tool at the Court's disposal. When the Supreme Court announced *Brown v. Board of Education*[66] in 1954, there were no dissents. Moreover, the orality of the opinion announcement was not a central feature of the event. No one heard the voice of Earl Warren reading his decision on the radio. Nevertheless, the decision had a powerful effect, in part because it was purposely drafted to speak to "the people."[67] Justice Warren consciously intended that the *Brown* opinion should be short and readable by the lay public.[68] In his work, Professor Rosenberg focuses on the white backlash the *Brown* decision inspired.[69] But a demosprudential analysis also focuses on the frontlash, the way that *Brown* helped inspire the civil rights movement. *Brown*'s accessibility and forcefulness helped inspire a social movement that in turn gave the opinion its legs.[70]

In 1955, Rosa Parks refused to give up her seat on a bus in Montgomery. She was arrested. Four days later, when she was formally arraigned and convicted, a one-day bus boycott by the black citizens of Montgomery was unexpectedly, amazingly, successful.[71] Dr. Martin Luther King, Jr. delivered a sermon that evening before a mass meeting of 5000 people gathered at and around Holt Street Baptist Church.[72] He prepared his audience to take the bold step of continuing the boycott indefinitely. He did so by brilliantly fusing two great texts: the Supreme Court's pronouncement a year earlier in *Brown* and the Bible.[73] Dr. King roused the crowd at that first mass meeting in Montgomery with a spirited refrain: "If we are wrong — the Supreme Court of this nation is wrong. If we are

---

[66] 347 U.S. 483 (1954).

[67] *See* Guinier, *supra* note 13, at 52.

[68] *Id.* at 52 & n.233.

[69] *See* GERALD N. ROSENBERG, THE HOLLOW HOPE: CAN COURTS BRING ABOUT SOCIAL CHANGE? 74 (2d ed. 2008).

[70] *See* Guinier, *supra* note 13, at 134-35 & n.613 ("Its message was heard in the hamlets of Georgia and in the churches of Alabama.").

[71] TAYLOR BRANCH, PARTING THE WATERS: AMERICA IN THE KING YEARS 1954-63, at 131-32 (1988). The Women's Political Council, led by women like Jo Ann Robinson, undertook the "mammoth task" of printing letters "asking every Negro to stay off the buses on Monday in protest of [Rosa Parks's] . . . arrest and trial." *Id.* The effort required "stealth, because . . . [i]f white people ever learned that state-employed teachers had used taxpayer-owned facilities to plot a revolt against segregation laws, heads would roll." *Id.*

[72] *See* Guinier, *supra* note 13, at 116 (citing BRANCH, *supra* note 71, at 138-42).

[73] *Id.* at 116 n.531.

wrong God Almighty was wrong."[74]

In the foreword, I argue that Dr. King was a classic example of a "role-literate participant."[75] His theological and strategic acumen enabled him to invoke *Brown* as "authorization" and "legitimation" to sustain the actions that 50,000 blacks in Montgomery, Alabama would take for over thirteen months when they refused to ride the city's buses.[76] But as Robert Post rightly points out, the word "authorize" meant something more like embolden or encourage.[77]

My point is that *Brown* shows judicial actors can inspire or provoke "mass conversation." It is when the legal constitution is narrated through the experience of ordinary people in conversation with each other that legal interpretation becomes sustainable as a culture shift.[78] And if a majority opinion can rouse, so too can a dissenting one. Thus, demosprudence through dissent emphasizes the use of narrative techniques and a clear appeal to shared values that make the legal claims transparent and accessible.

Although demosprudence through dissent is prescriptive rather than descriptive, it was never my intent to suggest that the Court *should be* central to any social movement. Like Justice Ginsburg, I am not a proponent of juridification (the substitution of law for politics).[79] In Justice Ginsburg's words, "[t]he Constitution does not belong to the Supreme Court."[80] At the same time, I recognize that the Court has been deeply influential, albeit unintentionally at times, in some very important social movements. Studying the 1960s student movement in Atlanta, Tomiko Brown-Nagin argues that the lunch counter sit-ins were, in fact, a reaction to the Supreme Court's decision — not because of what the Supreme Court said, but because of what it did not say.[81] The Court initially raised,

---

[74] *Id.* (quoting Dr. King).

[75] *Id.* at 116; *see also supra* note 32 and accompanying text.

[76] Dr. King specifically referred to *Brown* as *authorizing* what the black residents of Montgomery were contemplating doing, meaning that they were fighting for a right the Supreme Court of the United States had determined to exist. Guinier, *supra* note 13, at 116 n.531, 135 n.613.

[77] *See* Post, *supra* note 51, at 585-86.

[78] *See* Thomas B. Stoddard, Essay, *Bleeding Heart: Reflections on Using the Law to Make Social Change*, 72 N.Y.U. L. REV. 967, 972-73 (1997) (describing the difference between the law's "rule-shifting" and "culture-shifting" capacities).

[79] *See* Ruth Bader Ginsburg, Madison Lecture, *Speaking in a Judicial Voice*, 67 N.Y.U. L. REV. 1185, 1206 (1992). *See generally* GORDON SILVERSTEIN, LAW'S ALLURE: HOW LAW SHAPES, CONSTRAINS, SAVES, AND KILLS POLITICS (2009) (discussing the interaction between legal and political institutions).

[80] *A Conversation with Justice Ruth Bader Ginsburg* (Public Radio Exchange broadcast Sept. 2, 2004), http://www.prx.org/piece/2952.

[81] *See generally* TOMIKO BROWN-NAGIN, COURAGE TO DISSENT: COURTS AND COMMUNITIES IN

then dashed expectations. It was the disappointment with "all deliberate speed" — the legal system's failure to live up to the promise of the Court's initial ruling — that inspired students to take to the streets and initiate some of the bold protest demonstrations at lunch counters and in streets in the 1960s.[82] Brown-Nagin emphasizes the multiple ways in which courts, lawyers and social movement actors are engaged in a dialogic and recursive discourse.[83]

Rosenberg's second misunderstanding deserves both a concession and a clarification. Rosenberg's criticism that my argument is too Court-centric is fair as far as it goes.[84] I appreciate (and to a great extent share) Rosenberg's skepticism regarding courts as the primary actors in forging the path of social change. Gerald Torres and I argue that social change involves denaturalizing prior assumptions, a process that must be continuously monitored under the watchful eye of engaged political and social actors.[85] Moreover, social change is only sustainable if it succeeds in changing cultural norms, is institutionalized through policy decisions and the oversight of administrative actors, and develops an internal and external constituency of accountability. I concede that courts are not necessarily central to social movement activism.

Why then do I focus on the dialogic relationship between the Supreme Court and other essential social change actors in the foreword? The foreword is designed to be, and has always been, *about the Court's Term*.[86] In this venue, I developed the idea of demosprudence *in application* to this particular organ of government. The inherent structural limitation of this particular art form was challenging but ultimately, in my view, productive. It pushed me to explore the ways that judicial actors, in conjunction with mobilized constituencies, can redefine their roles consistently with ideas of democratic accountability. Indeed, because the format of the foreword encouraged me to approach demosprudence from this angle, I discovered something important about demosprudence: judges, not just lawyers or legislators, speak to constituencies of accountability in a de-

---

THE CIVIL RIGHTS MOVEMENT (forthcoming 2009).

[82] *See id.*

[83] *See id.* Also, Reva Siegel, alone and with Robert Post, has produced several excellent articles on just this point. *See generally* Robert Post & Reva Siegel, Roe *Rage: Democratic Constitutionalism and Backlash*, 42 HARV. C.R.-C.L. L. REV. 373 (2007); Siegel, *Constitutional Culture, supra* note 32.

[84] *See* Rosenberg, *supra* note 54, at 573-77.

[85] *See generally* Guinier & Torres, *supra* note 37.

[86] Mark Tushnet & Timothy Lynch, *The Project of the Harvard* Forewords: *A Social and Intellectual Inquiry*, 11 CONST. COMMENT. 463, 463-64 (1995).

mocratically accountable and democracy-inspired legal system.

I argued that oral dissents (like Justice Ginsburg's in *Ledbetter*) reveal the existence of an alternative, and relatively unnoticed, source of judicial authority.[87] The Court's legitimacy in a democracy need not depend on the Court speaking with an "institutional voice" (that is, unanimously). Here I am influenced by Jane Mansbridge's idea that democratic power can be held to account through two-way interactions, a source of authority rooted in "deliberative accountability."[88] The demosprudential dissenter ideally provides greater transparency to the Court's internal deliberative process.[89] At the same time, the dissenter may disperse power "by appealing to the audience's own experience and by drafting or inspiring them to *participate* in a form of collective problem solving."[90] Thus, the Court gains constitutional authority when dissenters speak in a "democratic voice," potentially expanding their audience beyond legal elites. In Mark Tushnet's words, "the Constitution belongs to all of us collectively, *as we act together*."[91]

Third, Rosenberg's argument that oral dissents are ineffectual, are unlikely to ever be effectual, and should not be considered relevant, reflects his disciplinary allegiances.[92] His perspective depends on empirical evidence of causation. It has a substantive, a methodological and a technological dimension.

Rosenberg's substantive argument seems to rest on the assumption that law almost never influences politics or vice versa. His skeptical certitude reduces to insignificance the recursive interactions between the courts and the activists in the 1950s and '60s over civil rights, in the 1970s over the meaning of gender equality, in the 1990s over affirmative action, and in the 2000s over the meaning of marriage. In addition, Professor Rosenberg's certitude goes well beyond the evidence he cites. He believes demosprudential dissents "are not necessary because if there is an active social movement in place then no judicial help is needed."[93] At the same

---

[87] *See* Guinier, *supra* note 13, at 4.

[88] *Id.* at 111 n.509 (citing Jane Mansbridge, *The Fallacy of Tightening the Reins*, 34 ÖSTERREICHISCHE ZEITSCHRIFT FÜR POLITIKWISSENSCHAFT 233 (2005)).

[89] *See, e.g.*, James L. Gibson, Gregory A. Caldeira & Lester Kenyatta Spence, *Measuring Attitudes Towards the United States Supreme Court*, 47 AM. J. POL. SCI. 354, 364 (2003) (finding that increased awareness of the Court's activities may increase the public's confidence and the Court's institutional legitimacy).

[90] *See* Guinier, *supra* note 13, at 111.

[91] *See id.* at 115 n.528 (quoting MARK TUSHNET, TAKING THE CONSTITUTION AWAY FROM THE COURTS 181 (1999)).

[92] *See* Rosenberg, *supra* note 54, at 570-73.

[93] *Id.* at 572.

time, he quotes McCann approvingly despite the fact that McCann concludes law can in fact make a difference under the right circumstances.[94]

There is more than a friendly misunderstanding at work. Within Professor Rosenberg's critique of demosprudence lurks a deep disciplinary tension about the nature of causation and the primacy of uniform metrics of measurement, as well as the meaning of political participation and influence.[95] What I value about political engagement cannot simply be reduced to what can be measured. When judges participate openly in public discussion, whether through book tours or oral dissents, their words or ideas may have traction without causing measureable changes in public opinion.

As Robert Post notes, I am of the school that values "the texture and substance of dialogue."[96] I do not define politics, more generally, primarily by election outcomes or polling data. As I write elsewhere, opportunities for participation enhance democratic legitimacy in part because "democracy involves justice-based commitments to voice, not just votes: participation cannot be reduced to a single moment of choice."[97] Opportunities for formal and informal deliberation are important because of "the texture and meaning of the relationships among political actors, as well as the texture and substance of the values that emerge from public discussion."[98]

The methodological aspect of Rosenberg's critique involves his taste for numbers and other metrics of certainty.[99] Rosenberg would prefer that I treat the format of a dissent as something to be studied by literary critics

---

[94] *Id.* at 571-72 nn.80-82 (quoting MICHAEL W. MCCANN, RIGHTS AT WORK: PAY EQUITY REFORM AND THE POLITICS OF LEGAL MOBILIZATION 136-37, 305 (1994)). In challenging Rosenberg's "zero-sum account of law and social change," for example, Professor Tomiko Brown-Nagin cites multiple studies, including one by Michael McCann, that show how "law provides normative and strategic resources for social movements." Tomiko Brown-Nagin, *"One of These Things Does Not Belong": Intellectual Property and Collective Action Across Boundaries*, 117 YALE L.J. POCKET PART 280, 281 (2008) (citing MCCANN, *supra*; Marc Galanter, *The Radiating Effects of Courts*, in EMPIRICAL THEORIES ABOUT COURTS 117 (Keith O. Boyum & Lynn Mather eds., 1983)), http://thepocketpart. org/ 2008/06/01/brownnagin.htm. In addition, Rosenberg's certitude may also be based on evidence-gathering techniques that are less accurate than he assumes. *See* James L. Gibson & Gregory A. Caldeira, *Knowing the Supreme Court? A Reconsideration of Public Ignorance of the High Court*, J. POL. (forthcoming) (manuscript at 8-13, on file with author).

[95] *See* SILVERSTEIN, *supra* note 79, at 283-84.

[96] Post, *supra* note 51, at 585.

[97] Lani Guinier, *Beyond Electocracy: Rethinking the Political Representative as Powerful Stranger*, 71 MOD. L. REV. 1, 22 (2008). Demosprudence, in other words, is not a philosophy of unmediated preference gathering (like the populist initiative process or the market). Rather, it represents a philosophical commitment to the lawmaking force of meaningful participatory democracy.

[98] *See* Post, *supra* note 51, at 585.

[99] *See id.*

but as irrelevant to political or public relationships.[100] The notion that storytelling is not the stuff of politics ignores the important work of social psychologists and linguists who write at length about the processes by which the brain hears and evaluates information. For example, what people say they believe is not necessarily predictive of what they do.[101] Indeed, attitudes are not recalled like USB memory sticks, but are reconstructed in relationship to the environment.[102]

My argument assumes that the river of social change has many tributaries, from the strategic mobilization of diverse resources that Marshall Ganz identifies to the narratives of resistance that Fred Harris explores.[103] No single institution of government, acting alone, successfully controls or enables these mighty currents. For example, the Supreme Court, when it wields law to establish relationships of power and control, primarily legitimates rather than destabilizes existing relationships of power and control.[104] Thus I agree with Rosenberg that the Court rarely functions as the central power source for fundamental structural change.

Nevertheless, I argue that members of the Court can catalyze change when they help craft or expand the narrative space in which mobilized constituencies navigate the currents of democracy. That role may be hard to measure, especially when demosprudential politics do not use the same language or framing devices as ordinary politics.[105] That role may also be inaccurately interpreted if the evaluation tool is survey data that asks open-ended questions or miscodes respondents' answers.[106] For example, after

---

[100] See Rosenberg, supra note 54, at 569.

[101] And people can and do change their minds, especially as a result of deliberating with others. See generally BRUCE ACKERMAN & JAMES FISHKIN, DELIBERATION DAY (2004) (maintaining that robust debate and deliberation is good for democracy).

[102] See Gregory M. Walton & Mahzarin R. Banaji, Being What You Say: The Effect of Essentialist Linguistic Labels on Preferences, 22 SOC. COGNITION 193, 205 (2004). See generally Norbert Schwarz, Self Reports: How the Questions Shape the Answers, AM. PSYCHOLOGIST, Feb. 1999 (discussing the cognitive mechanisms that underlie the question-and-answer dynamic).

[103] See generally MARSHALL GANZ, WHY DAVID SOMETIMES WINS: LEADERSHIP, ORGANIZATION AND STRATEGY IN THE CALIFORNIA FARM WORKER MOVEMENT (forthcoming 2009); Fredrick C. Harris, Specifying the Mechanism Linking Dissent to Action, 89 B.U. L. Rev. 605, 605-07 (2009). Both Ganz and Harris find that disappointment can be channeled into collective action through narratives of injustice, agency and identity.

[104] See, e.g., Robin West, The Supreme Court, 1989 Term—Foreword: Taking Freedom Seriously, 104 HARV. L. REV. 43, 50 (1990).

[105] Fred Harris cites work on the role played by framing abstract concepts through narratives. See Harris, supra note 103, at 605 n.3 (citing David A. Snow & Robert D. Benford, Master Frames and Cycles of Protest, in FRONTIERS IN SOCIAL MOVEMENT THEORY 133, 136 (Aldon D. Morris & Carol McClurg Mueller eds., 1992)).

[106] See Gibson & Caldeira, supra note 94 (manuscript at 11-13) (arguing that open-ended questions underestimate the public's knowledge of the Supreme Court).

recalibrating the measurement tools on which conventional wisdom relies, Professors Gibson and Caldeira conclude that the American people may not be as woefully ignorant about the Court as has been consistently reported.[107] In addition, when members of the Court direct their dissents to social movement actors and other role-literate participants, the recursive nature of that discourse would be difficult to capture in national survey instruments.[108]

Rosenberg's technical claim dismisses the form of oral dissents because they are not readily available.[109] Yet the technology that presently limits the reach of dissenting opinions does not tell us what the future holds regarding wider dissemination of the ideas and values of Justices who dissent.[110] Justice Ginsburg already makes copies of her oral dissents available to the press, and Justice Scalia is a recognizable face on television and in the media. Fueled by video or simultaneous audio transmission, more people might actually read or hear the opinions, especially the oral dissents,[111] which are usually quite short. The technology of dissemination, like the technological framing of the story, is certainly relevant to who hears the story and who understands it. The inherent limitations on the current forms of outreach of demosprudential dissents, as well as the lack of public awareness of the majority's holdings, is incontrovertible. That oral dissents are not widely disseminated, however, does not establish their uselessness were more people to hear them.[112]

---

[107] *Id.* (manuscript at 27-29).

[108] Professor Rosenberg states that "[e]lites are seldom if ever motivated or inspired to act by the language of judicial opinions. Rather, they are motivated by the substantive holdings of cases." Rosenberg, *supra* note 54, at 564. Professor Post, in response, thoroughly dispatches this motivational claim that a demosprudential act is useless if it does not directly yield movement in the Gallup polls or produce some other immediately (and causally) quantifiable result. Post, *supra* note 51, at 585.

[109] *See* Rosenberg, *supra* note 54, at 567-68.

[110] *See* Guinier, *supra* note 13, at 120 (suggesting that videos of oral dissents may eventually reach a wider audience through YouTube); *supra* note 64 and accompanying text.

[111] Guinier, *supra* note 13, at 37 n.161; *cf. id.* at 24-25 (discussing the "humanizing approach" of having the Justices appear on screen, delivering opinions, in the film RECOUNT: THE STORY OF THE 2000 PRESIDENTIAL ELECTION (HBO Films 2008)).

[112] And it arguably suggests the opposite — a need for greater attention to the narrative style and accessibility of the opinions. *See id.* at 90-107 (evaluating various stylistic elements and the effectiveness of some recent Supreme Court dissents). I well understand how hard it is for these oral dissents to make a big impact; for example, I had difficulty obtaining the written transcripts of the oral dissents from the 2007-08 Term. Professor Rosenberg, however, misstates the lag time. I was able to listen to the oral dissents of the 2006-07 Term, including Justice Breyer's oral dissent in *Parents Involved* as well as Justice Ginsburg's oral dissent in *Ledbetter*. It was the audio of the oral dissents delivered in June 2008 that were not yet available at the time of my writing the foreword in the summer of 2008.

Consider two approaches to Justice Ginsburg's role in the passage of the Lilly Ledbetter Fair Pay Act. One way of viewing the Lilly Ledbetter Fair Pay Act is to discount almost entirely the role played by judicial elites (Ginsburg and her fellow dissenters). After all, it was legislative elites (the United States Congress) who passed a bill that was signed into law by an executive elite elected on a change agenda. Viewed this way, the Supreme Court dissenters were peripheral actors in a policy development orchestrated by executive and legislative change agents. The dissent and subsequent Act affected ordinary women, but the process of enacting the law did not include them. Few Americans in 2008 could name Ruth Bader Ginsburg as a Supreme Court Justice,[113] and it is difficult to imagine that figure would be any higher for those who could name Lilly Ledbetter. Without linear data identifying the precise trajectory of the bill's passage, we can assume that the Court played a unidirectional role that distracted attention from, undermined the importance of, and had little direct influence on the behavior of the other role-literate actors in this series of dramatic events.[114] This story suggests that Justice Ginsburg's dissent was mostly irrelevant because the political changes in the executive and the legislative branches, alone, could account for the Lilly Ledbetter Fair Pay Act. The framing effects of Justice Ginsburg's dissent were so small as to be insignificant.

Now consider an alternative. In this scenario, members of a judicial elite (Ginsburg and her fellow dissenters) sounded the alarm to get the immediate attention of "role-literate participants" who knew how to make themselves known among a watchful public. That alarm was heard by a middle elite of women's and civil rights advocates who helped organize a campaign to change the law. That campaign capitalized on, but also contributed to, the momentum of a historic presidential election campaign and emboldened a seventy-year-old grandmother from Alabama to jump onto the public stage. Not to be left out of the arc of change was the culture-changing effect of Hillary Clinton's "eighteen million cracks" in the glass ceiling during the Democratic primaries of 2008.[115] In this alternative, Lilly Ledbetter's willingness — after consulting with her husband — to step into the national stage reflected a complex process of which at least

---

[113] Findlaw.com, FindLaw's US Supreme Court Awareness Survey, http://public.findlaw. com/ussc/122005survey.html (last visited Feb. 20, 2009) (finding that just twelve percent of Americans could name Ruth Bader Ginsburg as a Supreme Court Justice).

[114] *See* Michael W. McCann, *Reform Litigation on Trial*, 17 LAW & SOC. INQUIRY 715, 731-32 (1992) (identifying and critiquing this analysis).

[115] *See* Dana Milbank, *A Thank-You for 18 Million Cracks in the Glass Ceiling*, WASH. POST, June 8, 2008, at A1.

one element was Justice Ginsburg's forceful oral dissent. Justice Ginsburg's dissent did not *cause* Congress to pass the Lilly Ledbetter Fair Pay Act, but did play a role. It articulated, in widely accessible terms, a storyline that was picked up in the mobilization that ultimately led to a new President signing a law enshrining Lilly Ledbetter's name in history.[116]

I subscribe to this more complex view in which a forceful dissent sounded the alarms as first responder. Indeed, the language of that dissent was audible to those outside the legal elite. The process that followed not only affected ordinary people. It included them.

Those who believe it is possible to calculate with precision the inputs and outputs of social change might find the first hypothesis more plausible. The first approach has the virtue of certainty and clarity. It views members of the Supreme Court as members of a weak and dependent branch of our government who are dependent upon support from other branches. By themselves, they are not credible agents of progressive change.[117] Thus, we can dismiss demosprudential dissenters as "neither necessary nor sufficient for democratic deliberation."[118]

However, those whose reality is closer to the second alternative imagine social change along a multifaceted trajectory that consists of competing yet interdependent stories, resources and means of exercising power. Although this narrative of change is concededly imprecise, it is not per se irrelevant. As Michael McCann writes: "[J]udicial decisions express a whole range of norms, logics, and signals that cannot be reduced to clear commands and rules . . . ."[119] Instead, their power comes from generating information and knowledge that reshape the tactical judgments of social change actors and "refin[e] the language of politics."[120] Through their opinions, judges send messages to social change activists as to what is possible. They "reshap[e] perceptions of when and how particular values are realis-

---

[116] That storyline "authorized" Ledbetter's delay in filing suit, a delay that the Court majority had used to justify its decision to overturn the favorable damage award below. *See* Ledbetter v. Goodyear Tire & Rubber Co., 127 S. Ct. 2162, 2168-70 (2007), *superseded by statute*, Lilly Ledbetter Fair Pay Act of 2009, Pub. L. No. 111-2, 123 Stat. 5. Although Lilly Ledbetter received no money as a result of the Ledbetter Bill she did get "personal satisfaction." *See* Times Topics: People, Lilly M. Ledbetter, N.Y. TIMES, http://topics.nytimes.com/top/reference/timestopics/people/l/lilly_m_ledbetter/index.html (last visited Mar. 11, 2009).

[117] *But see* McCann, *supra* note 114, at 727-28 (critiquing Rosenberg's zero-sum perspective and noting that discrete institutions are almost never "solitary organs of change").

[118] Rosenberg, *supra* note 54, at 564.

[119] McCann, *supra* note 114, at 732.

[120] *Id.* (quoting JOHN BRIGHAM, THE CULT OF THE COURT 196 (1991)).

tically actionable as claims of legal right."[121]

I defend the second hypothesis on the grounds that an important dialogic relationship exists between law and politics. Law does not substitute for politics. But politics is informed by and can inform law. Here, McCann is again on point when he says that court actions can play an important, though partial, role in "fashioning the different 'opportunity structures' and discursive frameworks within which citizens act."[122] Thus, in courting the people, Justice Ginsburg's Ledbetter dissent opened up an analytic space for productive dialogue and what Daniel HoSang terms "politically potent action" by the people themselves.[123]

Politically potent action, however, is not limited to casting a ballot or engineering policy outcomes that can be quickly aggregated and counted. Nor is it always precisely what the judicial dissenter imagines. As Martha Minow writes, "[l]egal language, like a song, can be hummed by someone who did not write it and changed by those for whom it was not intended."[124] Or, as I note in the foreword, the demosprudential dissenter's real power "comes when the dissenter is aligned with a social movement or community of accountability that mobilizes to change the meaning of the Constitution over time."[125]

We have often seen this dynamic on the right, where Justice Scalia is perhaps the most demosprudential of the Justices.[126] Were more dissenters on the left, not just the right, to participate self-consciously in a larger demosprudential project, a more dynamic set of "politically" potent relationships might emerge between legal elites and aggrieved community actors. In other words, judges (and other legal professionals) could play a more active and self-conscious role in creating "analytic" space for citizens to advance alternative interpretations of their own lived experience and

---

[121] Id. at 732.

[122] Id. at 733.

[123] See HoSang, supra note 57.

[124] MARTHA MINOW, MAKING ALL THE DIFFERENCE: INCLUSION, EXCLUSION, AND AMERICAN LAW 310 (1990).

[125] Guinier, supra note 13, at 114.

[126] Looking at the decisions over the past year, I concluded, along with a talented group of research assistants, that Justice Scalia was probably the Court's most demosprudential dissenter. In the same way Justice Ginsburg has a recursive relationship with women's rights advocates, Justice Scalia's dissents engage and mobilize advocates with a conservative viewpoint. He has an obvious constituency of accountability — and they listen. Within a few days of having published his dissent in Lawrence, right-wing activists were making, mimeographing and circulating copies of it. See Guinier, supra note 13, at 118 n.544. It is a phenomenon one rarely observes on the left. In fact, Justice Ginsburg notwithstanding, one might argue that Scalia has no liberal counterpart.

ultimately help change the law. Law and politics are not the same, but they constitute and shape each other over time through mass conversation as well as mass mobilization.

At the same time, I readily concede that the challenges of *courting* the people are neither captured by, nor limited to, what Justices say aloud and in dissent. Justices operate under multiple constraints that Professor Rosenberg painstakingly documents.[127] To the extent Supreme Court Justices appear to politicize their own internal decision-making process, they may lose legitimacy in the eyes of the public.[128]

How, then, might President Obama proceed were a vacancy to arise on the Court during his term? Consider these facts. Republicans, although now out of power in Congress and the White House, still enjoy a super-majority on the Supreme Court.[129] The age and the health of the Justices make it likely that President Obama, should a vacancy arise, will only get to replace one moderately liberal dissenter with another.[130] Even if President Obama gets to name two or three new Justices, his nominees will likely reflect their judicial philosophies primarily in dissent.

As President Obama considers candidates for a future Court vacancy, he may therefore find himself thinking demosprudentially, especially if his nominees reflect his commitment to engaging "We the People" in deliberation about the meaning of our democracy. Thinking demosprudentially has both a mobilizing and mirroring dimension. It is a call to understand the ongoing dialogue between constitutional law and constitutional culture. It invites public debate about the meaning of constitutional princi-

---

[127] *See* Rosenberg, *supra* note 54, at 574-75.

[128] Gibson, Caldeira & Spence, *supra* note 89, at 365.

[129] An electoral minority, in other words, is exercising dead-hand control. This dead-hand control of an electoral minority is more acute in the twenty-first century because Justices now live longer and thus serve for longer periods of time. In the eighteenth and nineteenth centuries, the average tenure for a Supreme Court Justice was fourteen years. Steven Calabresi & James Lindgren, *Term Limits for the Supreme Court: Life Tenure Reconsidered*, 29 HARV. J.L. & PUB. POL'Y 769, 770-71 (2006). Since 1970, the average tenure of a Supreme Court justice is over twenty-five years. *Id.*

[130] Justice Stevens, often the most liberal justice and a frequent dissenter, views himself as a moderate Republican. *See, e.g.*, Jeffrey Rosen, *The Dissenter*, N.Y. TIMES MAG., Sept. 7, 2007, at 50. Like six of his eight colleagues, he was appointed by a Republican President. Of his more conservative colleagues, five are Catholic. Only one member of the current Court is female. All of the Justices came to the Court from the federal courts of appeals. The current judicial career ladder, in some ways, acculturates them to think in narrow terms about what constitutional interpretation means. Life experience, as President Obama's advisors acknowledge, can matter. *See infra* notes 131-134 and accompanying text. Although most cases are decided based on precedents, "a handful of decisions can reflect judges' own life experiences." Patrick Healy, *Seeking to Shift Attention to Judicial Nominees*, N.Y. TIMES, Oct. 6, 2008, at A15.

ples. At the same time it is reflective. It raises to public consciousness the aspirational merits of deliberative accountability. It summons social movement actors to meditate on what it means for the Constitution to belong to the people and not just to the Supreme Court. Thinking demos-prudentially is a reminder that the people themselves have a role to play in the conversation about the conflicts at the core of our democracy.

Thinking demosprudentially is not a project of the left or the right. It is a project of democratic accountability. To the extent Justices root their disagreement about the meaning and interpretation of constitutional law in a more democratically accountable soil, they may spark a deliberative process that enhances public confidence in the legitimacy of the judicial process itself.

Considerations of demosprudence, however, are not invitations for judicial activism. There is a difference between a self-effacing judicial philosophy powered by democratic empathy, on the one hand, and a self-aggrandizing philosophy of judicial lawmaking that pre-empts the legislative or popular will. The former links the Court's authority to its democratic accountability; the latter is a form of juridification.

President Obama, as well as his advisors, recognize this distinction.[131] Indeed, when the bugaboo of judicial activism was leveled during the campaign,[132] Obama's advisors acted quickly to disaggregate a philosophy based on competence, empathy and democratic accountability from one based on judicial presumption.[133] They summoned *Ledbetter* as an example of the role that judicial biography and temperament already play in judicial

---

[131] David G. Savage, *Two Visions of the Supreme Court*, L.A. TIMES, May 19, 2008, at A8 (contrasting Senator McCain's criticism of "judicial activism" with then-Senator Obama's concern that the judiciary does not look out for "ordinary Americans").

[132] Conservative court watchers have already denounced President Obama for comments made during the presidential campaign as someone who would simply appoint "liberal activist judges." *See, e.g.*, Steven G. Calabresi, *Obama's 'Redistribution' Constitution*, WALL ST. J., Oct. 28, 2008, at A17; S.A. Miller, *Voting Record Clouds Obama's Judge Picks*, WASH. TIMES, Nov. 17, 2008, at A1 (reporting that "conservatives balk at Mr. Obama's pledge to fill the federal courts with judges in the mold of Justice Ruth Bader Ginsburg . . . [one of] the most liberal judges in the court's history").

[133] When President Obama was campaigning for the Democratic Party nomination, he spoke harshly about some of the decisions made by the conservative majority on the Supreme Court. At a Planned Parenthood Conference in Washington, D.C. on July 17, 2007, he suggested that judicial philosophy was a relevant consideration in evaluating nominees to the Court: "We need somebody who's got the heart . . . to recognize what it's like to be a young teenage mom. The empathy to understand what it's like to be poor, or African-American, or gay, or disabled, or old. And that's the criteria by which I'm going to be selecting my judges." Carrie Dann, *Obama on Judges, Supreme Court*, MSNBC.COM, July 17, 2007, http://firstread.msnbc.msn.com/archive/2007/07/17/274143.aspx.

preemption on the right, not the left.[134]

Demosprudential dissenters actually have an even stronger defense to charges of judicial activism. They will "avoid the problem of judicial activism . . . because they are not using 'the law' in Professor Robert Cover's 'jurispathic' sense, in order to kill alternative and inventive meanings, developed by citizens themselves, in favor of one restrictive mandate."[135] Having a constituency of accountability to whom a Justice speaks in dissent is quite different than over-reaching, backed by the coercive power of the state, to overrule established precedent as a member of the Court majority. As dissenters on a conservative Court, liberal Justices will not, by themselves, make law. Nor will they, by themselves, make politics.

Instead, demosprudential dissenters invite the people, not their judicial colleagues, to become activists in service of democracy. They attempt to provide an important check on the power of the Court majority, by inviting the people themselves to play a more active role in the interpretation of the law. A demosprudential dissenter can also bring greater transparency to the lawmaking process, providing openness that heightens public regard for the legal process and the Court as an institution. By themselves, demosprudential dissents are neither necessary nor sufficient to propel social change. But, as with Justice Ginsburg's oral dissent in *Ledbetter*, their voices in dissent can help frame a culturally resonant and democratically potent narrative of change.[136]

I would never argue that a single Justice in dissent could issue a poetic and inspired commentary that by itself could initiate action and be historically relevant in the same way as Martin Luther King's speech at Holt Street Baptist Church in Montgomery in 1955 or on the Washington Mall in 1963. I am not suggesting that Supreme Court Justices must or should recast themselves as orators, oracles or poets. I do suggest that at this historical moment Justices on the left, and not just the right, would do well to consider their demosprudential power as dissenters. Should they succeed, it is because "We the People" become the real democratic activists.

---

[134] *See* Healy, *supra* note 130.

[135] Guinier, *supra* note 13, at 58 (citing Cover, *supra* note 36, at 4, 9, 11, 40).

[136] *See, e.g.*, Posting of Dahlia Lithwick to The XX Factor (Feb. 10, 2009 16:39), http://www.slate.com/blogs/blogs/xxfactor/archive/2009/02/10/ledbetter-and-ginsburg-and-a-cheer-for-the-feisty-gals.aspx ("[W]ithout Ginsburg's lifelong commitment to women's equality and her passionate (and very personal) dissent in the *Ledbetter* case, the issue of pay parity would not have blossomed into the national Ledbetter tsunami that helped sweep Obama into office in November.").

HOME RUN HARLAN

19 Green Bag 558 (1907)

Justice Harlan of the U.S. Supreme Court, aged 74, made a home run and won the game in a baseball contest at the annual shad bake given by the Washington bar association at Marshall Hall, Md.

When Justice Harlan went to the bat the score was a tie, and the umpire had called two strikes and three balls. It was a critical and exciting moment. Justice Harlan smashed the sphere a wicked swat to deep center. He started around the bases, and his leg work was really marvelous. His sprinting qualities surprised and delighted the fans, who were wild with enthusiasm.

The ball went over the head of the center fielder and was lost in the tall grass. Before it was recovered Justice Harlan had reached the home plate, where he stood sipping a mint julep which had been prepared hurriedly for the agile Kentuckian as a reward for lining out a four-base hit.

TOP 10 LAW SCHOOL
HOME PAGES OF 2009

Roger V. Skalbeck[†]

Editor's note: It was a simultaneously pleasing and painful moment when Roger Skalbeck's study of law school home pages arrived at Green Bag World Headquarters. The study itself is pleasingly useful and interesting. But the position of the George Mason University School of Law at the top of Skalbeck's 2009 list might be especially interesting to readers who know that the editor of this Almanac works at that law school. All I can say is that I (a) had no hand in Skalbeck's work (other than soliciting it in the first place, after seeing his book, "Law School Website Design Study 2009"); (b) gave no thought to how he might treat my employer; and (c) have every reason to believe that he conducted his work in a thorough and thoroughly impartial way. Of course, it would be a lie to say that I am not proud of my colleagues whose good work Skalbeck recognizes below. Similarly, it would be a shame if the Green Bag were to adopt a practice of twisting its publication standards to squelch work that might be embarassing to someone associated with the Bag. And so we will not, which means you get to enjoy Skalbeck's work. Please do.

The website home page represents the virtual front door for any law school. It's the place many prospective students start in the application process. Enrolled students, law school faculty and other employees often start with the home page to find classes, curricula and compensation plans. Home page content changes constantly. Deciding which home pages are good is often very subjective. Creating a ranking system for "good taste" is perhaps impossible.

This brief ranking report attempts to identify the best law school home pages based entirely on objective criteria. The goal was to include elements that make websites easier to use for sighted as well as visually-impaired users. Most elements require no special design skills, sophisticated technology or significant expenses.

EVALUATION CRITERIA

Sites included in this report include 195 United States law schools accredited by the American Bar Association (ABA), as shown in the accompanying chart. Humans performed the more than 2700 data evaluation tasks, completed in late November and early December 2009. All screen shots for the top 10 sites were taken on December 11, 2009.

Thankfully technology tools can make an otherwise tedious analysis a bit easier. The primary tools used to assist in evaluating sites include four add-on programs for the Firefox browser:

[†] Associate Law Librarian for Electronic Resources & Services, Georgetown Law Library. Copyright © Roger V. Skalbeck, 2009.

Web Developer Toolbar
(https://addons.mozilla.org/en-US/firefox/addon/60)

Operator for finding Microformats
(https://addons.mozilla.org/en-US/firefox/addon/4106)

Dublin Core Viewer
(https://addons.mozilla.org/en-US/firefox/addon/528)

Wave Toolbar
(https://addons.mozilla.org/en-US/firefox/addon/6720)

All remaining analysis was done manually by humans with pretty good eyesight.

In scoring each of the websites, fourteen elements were selected for the evaluation. The goal was to select meaningful criteria that could be objectively evaluated. As some elements are more important than others, elements were prioritized by importance. Once prioritized, point values were assigned to add up to 100 for a perfect score. With two exceptions, analysis is essentially a binary task. For instance, a site either lists a physical address or it doesn't. Those sites containing selected elements receive full credit. Those lacking it get nothing. For two elements, half credit is possible.

Here is an overview of the elements and their respective weighted values.

Element	Weighted Value
Address [a]	10
Search Box [b]	10
Cascading Stylesheet (CSS)[*] [c]	10
News Headlines [d]	6
News Headlines with Images [e]	7
Embedded Media [f]	5
Favicon [g]	7
Smiles [h]	5
Social Network Link [i]	6
Content Carousel [j]	6
RSS Meta Information [k]	8
Microformats [l]	6
Dublin Core [m]	4
Hierarchal Organization[*] [n]	10
Perfect Score	**100**

---

[*] For [c] and [n] several sites partially implemented these elements. For instance, with Cascading Stylesheets, one site may have used a single HTML table to format content, or another may have used HTML headers out of order.

Address [a] – 10 points

A physical address for the law school is included in text. Post office boxes count, but there's no credit if an address is in a graphical image. Whether you're a prospective student using Google Earth or attending a guest lecture on campus, finding a physical address quickly is important.

Search Box [b] – 10 points

The site has a search box that users can type terms into without leaving the page. A link to a separate search page gets no points.

Cascading Stylesheet (CSS) [c] – 10 points

A good practice in web design is to use a Cascading Stylesheet (CSS) to control the site design, including layout, colors and typography. HTML is for content and CSS is for presentation. Sites that include very limited use of HTML tables receive half the point total.

News Headlines [d] – 5 points

The site has headlines about news or events relating to the law school.

News Headlines With Images [e] – 7 points

An effective way to improve text-based news headlines is to add graphics or images next to the news links. For this element, a site needs to have a news headline accompanied by a small image relating to that story or event.

Embedded Media [f] – 5 points

One effective way to make online media engaging is to make it playable directly from the home page. Points are awarded if a site has audio or video that can be played directly without leaving the site.

Favicon [g] – 7 points

A favorites icon (or "favicon") is a small graphic associated with a website, which appears in places such as the browser location bar or in your bookmarks or favorites file. The favicon is probably the most important tiny graphic any site can have, and it is a simple way to help identify a law school brand or image.

Smiles [h] – 5 points

Somebody is smiling in at least one picture on the site.

Social Network Link [i] – 6 points

If you are on Facebook, Twitter, YouTube or iTunes, having this information on the home page helps. If you're on Friendster, MySpace, Orkut, Hi5 or Kadoo, it's probably not worth the screen real estate to tell people. Points awarded for any social network link or icon.

Carousel Content [j] – 6 points

Multiple types of the same content can be viewed in a single space on the home page. This can be a slideshow, a series of stories about the school or a profile gallery of people important to the law school. To qualify for points here, the carousel needs to have content users can control, so it doesn't count to have galleries that automatically refresh or content that is randomly displayed when the page loads.

RSS Meta Information [k] – 8 points

If you distribute news through an RSS (Rich Site Summary) feed such as blog content or news stories, you should let people as well as computers know about it, to maximize the exposure. A single line of code in a document's header achieves this result. If a site has an RSS feed structured for automatic discovery, all points are awarded. If Firefox can't recognize the feed, the site gets no points.

Microformats [l] – 6 points

If you include the school address, contact details or event information on your site, using microformats (www.microformats.org) ensures that computers can recognize this. This is one aspect of the Semantic Web.

Dublin Core [n] – 4 points

Content in a website header is invisible in the browser, but it can be used to convey descriptive information such as key words and version information. Sites that want to display structured and deliberate descriptive information (typically called metadata) may want to use a format called Dublin Core (www.dublincore.org). There is debate as to whether Dublin Core is the best metadata standard, so this is the lowest-ranked element in the evaluation.

Hierarchal Structure [n] – 10 points

Header tags such as <h1> and <h2> should have meaning and relationships between site content. Having proper headings helps computers understand a website's logical organization, and many tools for visually impaired users can use header tags for navigation and to recognize site content.

● ● ● ●

TOP 10 HOME PAGES

#1: George Mason University School of Law

www.law.gmu.edu
Score: 85
Elements: [a] [b] [c] [d] [e] [g] [h] [i] [j] [k]

#2: University of Virginia School of Law

www.law.virginia.edu
Score: 80
Elements: [a] [b] [c] [d] [e] [f] [g] [h] [i] [j] [k]

#3: Wayne State University Law School

www.law.wayne.edu
Score: 78
Elements: [a] [b] [c] [d] [g] [h] [i] [k] [l] [n]

#4: University of Washington School of Law

www.law.washington.edu
Score: 77
Elements: [a] [b] [c] [d] [e] [g] [h] [i] [j] [n]

#5: Harvard Law School

www.law.harvard.edu
Score: 75
Elements: [b] [c] [d] [e] [g] [h] [i] [j] [k] [n]

#5: *Regent University School of Law*

www.regent.edu/acad/schlaw
Score: 75
Elements: [b] [c] [d] [e] [g] [h] [i] [j] [k] [n]

#7: Loyola University of Chicago School of Law

www.luc.edu/law
Score: 74
Elements: [a] [b] [c] [d] [e] [g] [h] [j] [k] [n*]
* Partially implemented

#7 *University of Notre Dame Law School*

http://law.nd.edu
Score: 74
Elements: [a] [b] [c] [d] [e] [g] [h] [j] [k] [n*]
* Partially implemented

#9: University of Illinois College of Law

www.law.illinois.edu
Score: 73
Elements: [a] [b] [c] [d] [g] [h] [i] [j] [k] [n*]
* Partially implemented

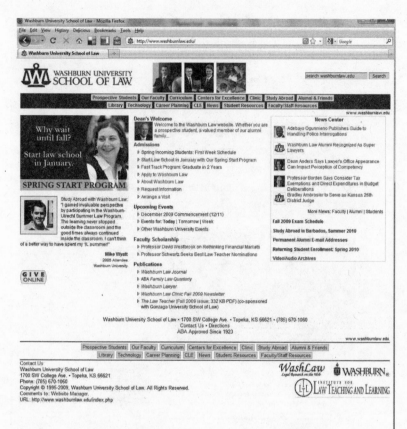

#9: *Washburn University School of Law*

www.washburnlaw.edu
Score: 73
Elements: [a] [b] [c] [d] [e] [g] [h] [k] [n]

ALL 195 HOME PAGES

Key:

R = Rank
S = Score
a = Address
b = Search box
c = Cascading stylesheet (CSS)
d = News headlines
e = News headlines with images
f = Embedded media

g = Favicon
h = Smiles
i = Social network link
j = Content carousel
k = RSS meta information
l = Microformats
m = Dublin core
n = Hierarchal organization

R	S	Law School Name	Law School URL	a	b	c	d	e	f	g	h	i	j	k	l	m	n
1	85	George Mason University	www.law.gmu.edu/	x	x	x	x	x		x	x	x	x	x			x
2	80	University of Virginia	www.law.virginia.edu	x	x	x	x	x	x	x	x	x	x	x			
3	78	Wayne State University	www.law.wayne.edu/	x	x	x	x			x	x	x		x	x		x
4	77	University of Washington	www.law.washington.edu/	x	x	x	x	x		x	x	x	x				x
5	75	Harvard Law School	www.law.harvard.edu/		x	x	x	x		x	x	x	x				x
5	75	Regent University	www.regent.edu/acad/schlaw/		x	x	x	x		x	x	x	x	x			x
7	74	Loyola University-Chicago	www.luc.edu/law.	x	x	x	x	x		x	x		x	x			½
7	74	University of Notre Dame	law.nd.edu/	x	x	x	x	x		x	x		x	x			½
9	73	University of Illinois	www.law.illinois.edu	x	x	x	x			x	x	x	x	x			½
9	73	Washburn University	www.washburnlaw.edu/	x	x	x	x			x	x		x				x
11	72	University of Chicago	www.law.uchicago.edu/	x	x	x	x			x	x		x				x
11	72	University of Utah	www.law.utah.edu/	x	x	x	x			x	x		x				x
11	72	Florida Coastal School of Law	www.fcsl.edu/	x	x	x	x			x	x		x				x
11	72	Pepperdine University	law.pepperdine.edu/	x	x	½	x	x		x	x	x	x				x
15	71	University of New Mexico	lawschool.unm.edu/	x	x	x	x			x	x		x				x
16	70	University of Akron	www.uakron.edu/law/	x	x	x	x			x	x	x	x				x
16	70	University of South Dakota	www.usd.edu/law/	x	x	x	x			x	x		x		x		x
16	70	University of Tennessee	www.law.utk.edu/	x	x	x	x			x	x	x	x				x
16	70	Univ. of California at Davis	www.law.ucdavis.edu/	x	x	½	x	x		x	x	x	x	x			x
16	70	Yale University	www.law.yale.edu/	x	x	x	x	x	x	x	x		x				x
21	69	University of North Carolina	www.law.unc.edu/	x	x	x	x	x		x	x	x		x			
21	69	Catholic Univ. of America	www.law.edu/	x	x	½	x	x			x	x			x	x	x
23	68	Wake Forest University	law.wfu.edu/	x	x	x	x		x		x	x	x				x
24	67	University of Kansas	www.law.ku.edu/	x	x	x	x			x	x	x		x			½
24	67	University of Texas at Austin	utexas.edu/law/	x	x	x	x			x				x	x		x
24	67	Univ. of Southern California	law.usc.edu/		x	x	x			x	x	x	x				x
27	66	American University	www.wcl.american.edu/	x	x	x	x			x	x		x				x
27	66	Columbia University	www.law.columbia.edu/		x	x	x	x	x	x	x		x				x
29	65	University of Hawaii	www.hawaii.edu/law/	x	x	x	x			x		x	x				x
29	65	St. Mary's University	www.stmarytx.edu/law/	x	x	x	x			x	x	x	x				½
29	65	Univ. of Cal. at Berkeley	www.law.berkeley.edu/	x	x	x	x	x		x	x						x
29	65	University of San Diego	www.sandiego.edu/usdlaw/	x	x	x	x	x		x	x						x
29	65	Lewis And Clark College	www.lclark.edu/LAW/	x	x	x	x	x		x	x						x
29	65	West Virginia University	law.wvu.edu/	x	x	x	x	x		x	x						x
29	65	Georgia State University	law.gsu.edu/	x	x	x	x	x		x	x						x
29	65	Western State School of Law	www.wsulaw.edu/	x	x	½	x	x	x	x	x						x
37	64	Univ. of California-Hastings	www.uchastings.edu/	x	x	x	x			x	x		x				x
37	64	Brooklyn Law School	www.brooklaw.edu/	x	x	x	x			x	x		x				x
37	64	New York University	www.law.nyu.edu	x	x	x	x			x	x		x				x
37	64	Cleveland State University	www.law.csuohio.edu/	x	x	x	x			x	x		x				x
41	63	Willamette University	www.willamette.edu/wucl/	x	x	x	x		x	x	x						x
42	61	William Mitchell Coll. of Law	www.wmitchell.edu/	x	x	x	x			x					x		x
42	61	Duke University	www.law.duke.edu/		x	x	x		x	x	x				x		x
42	61	Ohio State University	moritzlaw.osu.edu	x	x	½	x	x		x	x				x		x
42	61	Vermont Law School	www.vermontlaw.edu/	x	x	½	x			x	x				x		x
46	60	Rutgers University-Newark	www.law.newark.rutgers.edu/	x	x	½	x			x					x	x	x
46	60	University of Pennsylvania	www.law.upenn.edu/	x	x					x	x	x	x				x
46	60	University of South Carolina	usclaw.sc.edu/		x	x	x			x	x	x	x				x

R	S	Law School Name	Law School URL	a	b	c	d	e	f	g	h	i	j	k	l	m	n
46	60	University of Richmond	law.richmond.edu/	x	x					x	x			x			x
46	60	Michigan State University	www.law.msu.edu/	x	x	x	x	x		x	x						½
46	60	Faulkner University	www.faulkner.edu/admissions/jonesLaw.asp	x	x	½	x	x		x	x						x
52	59	University of Houston	www.law.uh.edu/	x	x	½	x			x	x	x					x
52	59	Villanova University	www.law.villanova.edu/	x	x	½	x	x			x		x				x
54	58	University of Florida	www.law.ufl.edu/	x	x	x	x			x	x						x
54	58	University of Detroit Mercy	www.law.udmercy.edu/	x	x	x	x			x	x						x
54	58	University of Tulsa	www.law.utulsa.edu/	x	x	x	x			x	x						x
54	58	Howard University	www.law.howard.edu/	x	x	x	x	x		x							x
58	56	Franklin Pierce Law Center	www.pierceLaw.edu/	x	x	½	x				x	x	x	x			
59	55	Southwestern University	www.swlaw.edu/	x	x		x	x		x	x						x
60	55	Indiana Univ. - Indianapolis	indylaw.indiana.edu/	x	x	x	x	x		x	x						
60	55	Vanderbilt University	law.vanderbilt.edu		x		x	x		x	x	x	x	x			
60	55	Seattle University	www.law.seattleu.edu/		x	x	x	x		x	x						x
60	55	Univ. of St. Thomas Sch. Law	www.stthomas.edu/law/	x	x		x	x		x	x						x
64	54	Depaul University	www.law.depaul.edu/	x	x	x	x			x	x	x					
64	54	University of Iowa	www.law.uiowa.edu/		x	x	x			x	x	x					
64	54	Northeastern University	www.northeastern.edu/law/	x	x	x	x			x	x	x					
64	54	St. Louis University	law.slu.edu/	x	x	x	x			x	x	x					
64	54	St. John's University	www.stjohns.edu/academics/graduate/law		x	x	x			x	x		x				x
64	54	University of North Dakota	www.law.und.nodak.edu/	x	x		x			x	x	x					x
64	54	Oklahoma City University	www.okcu.edu/law/	x	x	½	x		x	x	x	x					
64	54	University of Oregon	www.law.uoregon.edu/	x	x		x			x	x	x					x
64	54	Liberty University	law.liberty.edu/	x	x	x	x			x	x		x				
73	53	Univ. of Ark. at Little Rock	www.law.ualr.edu/	x	x	x	x			x							x
73	53	University of Maine	mainelaw.maine.edu/	x	x	½	x			x	x						x
73	53	University of Maryland	www.law.umaryland.edu	x	x	½	x			x	x						x
73	53	Albany Law Sch. of Union U.	www.albanylaw.edu/	x	x	x	x		x	x	x						
73	53	University of Cincinnati	www.law.uc.edu/	x	x	x	x			x	x						½
73	53	University of Oklahoma	www.law.ou.edu/	x	x	x	x			x							
79	52	City University of New York	www.law.cuny.edu/index.html		x		x			x	x		x	x			x
80	51	University of Colorado	www.colorado.edu/Law/		x	½	x			x	x			x			x
80	51	University of Georgia	www.lawsch.uga.edu/		x	½	x			x	x			x			x
80	51	Thomas Jefferson Sch. of Law	www.tjsl.edu/	x	x		x			x				x			x
80	51	University of Baltimore	law.ubalt.edu	x	x	x	x			x							x
80	51	Washington University	www.wulaw.wustl.edu/	x	x	x	x			x							x
80	51	Seton Hall University	law.shu.edu/	x	x	x	x			x							x
80	51	Southern Methodist Univ.	www2.law.smu.edu/		x		x	x		x	x		x				x
80	51	University of Wisconsin	www.law.wisc.edu/	x	x	x	x			x							x
88	50	Emory University	www.law.emory.edu/	x	x	½	x							x	x		½
88	50	William & Mary Sch. of Law	law.wm.edu		x	x	x	x		x	x						½
88	50	Chapman Univ. Sch. of Law	www.chapman.edu/law/	x	x	½	x	x		x	x						
91	49	New York Law School	www.nyls.edu/	x	x	½	x			x	x		x				
91	49	Florida Int'l School of Law	law.fiu.edu/		x	½	x			x	x		x				x
91	49	McGeorge School of Law	www.mcgeorge.edu/		x	x	x	x		x	x		x				½
94	48	University of Denver	www.law.du.edu/		x	x	x			x	x						x
94	48	University of Connecticut	www.law.uconn.edu/	x	x		x			x	x						x
94	48	Valparaiso University	www.valpo.edu/law/	x	x	½	x			x	x						½
94	48	Northern Kentucky Univ.	chaselaw.nku.edu/	x	x	x	x			x	x						
94	48	University of Kentucky	www.uky.edu/Law/	x	x		x			x	x						x
94	48	University of Louisville	www.law.louisville.edu/		x	x	x			x	x						x
94	48	Boston College	www.bc.edu/schools/law/home.html		x	x	x			x	x						x
94	48	Rutgers University-Camden	www-camlaw.rutgers.edu/	x	x	½	x			x	x						½
94	48	Northern Illinois University	law.niu.edu/law/		x	x	x			x	x						x
94	48	Capital University	www.law.capital.edu/	x	x		x	x		x							x
94	48	Widener Univ.-Harrisburg	law.widener.edu/	x	x	x	x	x		x							
105	47	Marquette University	law.marquette.edu	x	x		x			x	x						x
105	47	Quinnipiac College	law.quinnipiac.edu/	x	x	x	x			x		x					
107	46	Illinois Institute of Tech.	www.kentlaw.edu/	x	x		x			x	x			x			
107	46	New England School of Law	www.nesl.edu/	x	x		x			x	x			x			
107	46	University of Minnesota	www.law.umn.edu/	x	x		x			x	x			x			
107	46	Univ. of Missouri-Columbia	www.law.missouri.edu/	x	x	x	x			x							½
107	46	Brigham Young University	www.law2.byu.edu/		x	½	x	x		x	x			x			

R	S	Law School Name	Law School URL	a	b	c	d	e	f	g	h	i	j	k	l	m	n
112	45	Indiana Univ.-Bloomington	www.law.indiana.edu/		x		x	x•		x	x						x
112	45	Loyola Univ.-New Orleans	law.loyno.edu/	x	x	x					x						x
112	45	Western New England Coll.	www1.law.wnec.edu/		x	x	x	x		x	x						
112	45	University of Nebraska	law.unl.edu/home		x		x	x		x	x						x
112	45	Fordham University	law.fordham.edu/	x	x		x	x		x	x						
112	45	Mississippi College	www.mc.edu/law/	x	x		x	x		x	x						
112	45	Roger Williams University	law.rwu.edu/	x	x		x	x		x	x						
119	44	Georgetown University	www.law.georgetown.edu/	x	x		x			x	x	x					
119	44	Boston University	web.bu.edu/law/	x	x		x			x	x	x					
119	44	University of Michigan	www.law.umich.edu	x	x		x			x	x	x					
119	44	State Univ. of N.Y. at Buffalo	www.law.buffalo.edu/	x	x		x			x	x	x					
119	44	Ohio Northern University	www.law.onu.edu/	x			x			x	x	x					x
119	44	Texas Tech University	www.ttu.edu/	x	x		x			x	x	x					
119	44	North Carolina Central Univ.	web.nccu.edu/law/	x	x		x	x		x	x						
126	43	University of Miami	www.law.miami.edu/	x	x	½	x			x	x						
126	43	Creighton University	culaw2.creighton.edu/	x	x	x	x			x							
126	43	Cornell University	www.lawschool.cornell.edu/		x	½	x			x	x						x
126	43	University of Memphis	www.memphis.edu/law/index.php	x	x		x			x	x				x		
126	43	University of La Verne	law.ulv.edu/	x	x	½	x			x	x						
126	43	Washington & Lee University	law.wlu.edu/			x	x			x	x			x			x
126	43	Charleston School of Law	www.charlestonlaw.org/		x	½	x	x		x							x
133	42	Yeshiva University	www.cardozo.yu.edu/	x	x	x	x		x	x		x					
134	41	Widener University	law.widener.edu/	x	x	x	x			x							
134	41	Gonzaga University	www.law.gonzaga.edu/	x	x		x			x							x
136	39	Dickinson School of Law	www.dsl.psu.edu/		x		x			x	x		x				½
136	39	Univ. of Mo.-Kansas City	www.law.umkc.edu/		x		x	x		x	x						½
136	38	UCLA	www.law.ucla.edu/home/Default.aspx	x	x		x			x	x						
136	38	Loyola Marymount Univ.-LA	www.lls.edu/	x	x		x			x	x						
136	38	University of Idaho	www.law.uidaho.edu		x	x	x			x	x						
136	38	Northwestern University	www.law.northwestern.edu/	x	x	x	x			x	x						
136	38	Syracuse University	www.law.syr.edu/		x	x	x			x	x						
136	38	St. Thomas University	www.stu.edu/law	x	x		x			x	x						
136	38	Arizona State University	www.law.asu.edu/	x	x		x	x		x							
136	38	Florida State University	www.law.fsu.edu/	x	x		x	x		x							
136	38	Dwayne O. Andreas School	www.barry.edu/law/default.aspx	x	x		x	x									½
147	37	Samford University	cumberland.samford.edu/	x	x	x				x							
147	37	Stanford University	www.law.stanford.edu/		x	½				x	x						x
147	37	Hamline University	law.hamline.edu/	x	x		x			x	x					x	½
147	37	University of Toledo	www.law.utoledo.edu/	x		x	x			x	x						
151	36	S. Ill. Univ.-Carbondale	www.law.siu.edu/	x		½	x			x							x
151	36	Tulane University	www.law.tulane.edu/	x	x	½	x			x							
153	35	University of Arizona	www.law.arizona.edu/	x		x				x		x					
153	35	Mercer University	www.law.mercer.edu/	x			x	x		x	x						
153	35	University of Montana	www.umt.edu/law/	x			x	x		x	x						
156	34	Ave Maria Univ. Sch. of Law	www.avemarialaw.edu/	x			x			x	x		x				
157	33	Golden Gate University	www.ggu.edu/school_of_law/		x	x	x			x							
157	33	Suffolk University	www.law.suffolk.edu/	x	x		x			x							
157	33	Hofstra University	law.hofstra.edu		x	½	x			x	x						
157	33	University of Dayton	www.law.udayton.edu/	x	x		x			x							
157	33	Pontifical Catholic Univ. P.R.	www.pucpr.edu/	x	x		x			x							
157	33	Campbell University	law.campbell.edu/	x			x		x	x	x						
163	32	Thomas M. Cooley Law Sch.	www.cooley.edu/	x	x					x	x						
163	32	South Texas College of Law	www.stcl.edu/	x	x					x	x						
163	32	John Marshall Law School	www.jmls.edu/	x						x	x						½
163	32	University of Wyoming	uwadmnweb.uwyo.edu/law/			½	x			x	x						x
167	31	University of San Francisco	www.law.usfca.edu/		x		x			x							x
167	31	Santa Clara University	law.scu.edu/		x	x	x			x							
167	31	George Washington Univ.	www.law.gwu.edu/Pages/Default.aspx	x		x	x			x							
167	31	Stetson University	www.law.stetson.edu/	x	x	x	x										
167	31	Nova Southeastern Univ.	www.nsulaw.nova.edu/	x	x		x										½
167	31	Louisiana State University	www.law.lsu.edu/	x	x		x			x							
167	31	Temple University	www.law.temple.edu	x	x		x			x							
167	31	Inter American Univ. of P.R.	www.derecho.inter.edu/	x	x		x			x							

R	S	Law School Name	Law School URL	a	b	c	d	e	f	g	h	i	j	k	l	m	n
167	31	Pace University	www.law.pace.edu/	x	x		x				x						
167	31	District of Columbia	www.law.udc.edu/	x		x	x				x						
167	31	Florida A&M School of Law	law.famu.edu/			x	x				x						x
167	31	John Marshall Law Sch.-Atl.	www.johnmarshall.edu/				x	x		x	x	x					
179	30	Baylor University	law.baylor.edu/	x						x	x			x			
180	28	Drake University	www.law.drake.edu/	x			x			x	x						
180	28	Texas Wesleyan University	www.law.txwes.edu/	x			x			x	x						
180	28	Southern University	www.sulc.edu	x			x	x			x						
183	27	Univ. of Ark., Fayetteville	law.uark.edu/	x	x					x							
184	26	Texas Southern University	www.tsulaw.edu/	x	x		x										
185	22	University of Pittsburgh	www.law.pitt.edu/			x				x	x						
186	21	Cal. Western Sch. of Law	www.cwsl.edu/main/home.asp		x		x				x						
186	21	University of Mississippi	www.olemiss.edu/depts/law_school/	x			x				x						
186	21	Case Western Reserve Univ.	law.cwru.edu/		x		x				x						
186	21	Duquesne University	www.law.duq.edu/				x				x						x
186	21	William S. Boyd Sch. of Law	www.law.unlv.edu/	x			x				x						
191	17	University of Alabama	www.law.ua.edu/		x					x							
191	17	Appalachian School of Law	www.asl.edu/	x						x							
193	13	Whittier College	www.law.whittier.edu/				x			x							
193	13	Touro College	www.tourolaw.edu/				x			x							
195	6	University of Puerto Rico	www.law.upr.edu				x										

I went to State Teachers' College at Ada
for three years, although I didn't really
intend to be a teacher. Maybe for a little
while, but not forever. What I wanted to
be was a lawyer, and I figured sooner or
later I'd go to law school. Eventually I
was going to go to Harvard Law School,
I reckon. That was my ambition anyway.

But all at once baseball came up, and
that changed everything all around.

Paul Waner (ca. 1961)

SEPTEMBER

FRANK LELAND

Member, Cook County Board of Commissioners (1908).
See Leland, Frank C., in THOM LOVERRO,
THE ENCYCLOPEDIA OF NEGRO LEAGUE BASEBALL (2003).

Leland (8) and his 1905 Leland Giants team: Sherman Barton
(1), Dell Mathews (2), William Horn (3), George Taylor (4), Na-
than Harris (5), Charles Green (6), John Davis (7), William
Brown (trav. Mgr.) (9), William Binga (10), James Smith (11),
Arthur Ross (12), Mascot (13), Billy Holland (14), and Bob
Robinson (15).

❧ SEPTEMBER ❧

SUN	MON	TUES	WED	THUR	FRI	SAT
			1	2	3	4
5	6	7	8	9	10	11
12	13	14	15	16	17	18
19	20	21	22	23	24	25
26	27	28	29	30		

UNITED STATES V. HAYES

129 S. Ct. 1079 (2009)

Ruth Bader Ginsburg[†]

The federal Gun Control Act of 1968, 18 U.S.C. § 921 *et seq.*, has long prohibited possession of a firearm by any person convicted of a felony. In 1996, Congress extended the prohibition to include persons convicted of "a misdemeanor crime of domestic violence." § 922(g)(9). The definition of "misdemeanor crime of domestic violence," contained in § 921(a)(33)(A), is at issue in this case. Does that term cover a misdemeanor battery whenever the battered victim was in fact the offender's spouse (or other relation specified in § 921(a)(33)(A))? Or, to trigger the possession ban, must the predicate misdemeanor identify as an element of the crime a domestic relationship between aggressor and victim? We hold that the domestic relationship, although it must be established beyond a reasonable doubt in a § 922(g)(9) firearms possession prosecution, need not be a defining element of the predicate offense.

I

In 2004, law enforcement officers in Marion County, West Virginia, came to the home of Randy Edward Hayes in response to a 911 call reporting domestic violence. Hayes consented to a search of his home, and the officers discovered a rifle. Further investigation revealed that Hayes had recently possessed several other firearms as well. Based on this evidence, a federal grand jury returned an indictment in 2005, charging Hayes, under §§ 922(g)(9) and 924(a)(2), with three counts of possessing firearms after having been convicted of a misdemeanor crime of domestic violence.

The indictment identified Hayes's predicate misdemeanor crime of domestic violence as a 1994 conviction for battery in violation of West

---

[†] Justice, Supreme Court of the United States, joined by Justices John Paul Stevens, Anthony Kennedy, David Souter, Stephen Breyer, and Samuel Alito, and Clarence Thomas as to all but Part III. Chief Justice John Roberts dissented, joined by Justice Antonin Scalia.

Virginia law.[1] The victim of that battery, the indictment alleged, was Hayes's then-wife — a person who "shared a child in common" with Hayes and "who was cohabitating with . . . him as a spouse." App. 3.[2]

Asserting that his 1994 West Virginia battery conviction did not qualify as a predicate offense under § 922(g)(9), Hayes moved to dismiss the indictment. Section 922(g)(9), Hayes maintained, applies only to persons previously convicted of an offense that has as an element a domestic relationship between aggressor and victim. The West Virginia statute under which he was convicted in 1994, Hayes observed, was a generic battery proscription, not a law designating a domestic relationship between offender and victim as an element of the offense. The United States District Court for the Northern District of West Virginia rejected Hayes's argument and denied his motion to dismiss the indictment. 377 F.Supp.2d 540, 541-542 (2005). Hayes then entered a conditional guilty plea and appealed.

In a 2-to-1 decision, the United States Court of Appeals for the Fourth Circuit reversed. A § 922(g)(9) predicate offense, the Court of Appeals held, must "have as an element a domestic relationship between the offender and the victim." 482 F.3d 749, 751 (2007). In so ruling, the Fourth Circuit created a split between itself and the nine other Courts of Appeals that had previously published opinions deciding the same question.[3] Ac-

---

[1] West Virginia's battery statute provides: "[A]ny person [who] unlawfully and intentionally makes physical contact of an insulting or provoking nature with the person of another or unlawfully and intentionally causes physical harm to another person, . . . shall be guilty of a misdemeanor." W. Va. Code Ann. § 61-2-9(c) (Lexis 2005).

[2] The indictment stated, in relevant part:

"Defendant RANDY EDWARD HAYES' February 24, 1994 Battery conviction . . . constituted a misdemeanor crime of domestic violence because:

"a. Battery is a misdemeanor under State law in West Virginia;

"b. Battery has, as an element, the use and attempted use of physical force;

"c. Defendant RANDY EDWARD HAYES committed the offense of Battery against the victim:

"i. who was his current spouse; and

"ii. who was a person with whom he shared a child in common; and

"iii. who was cohabitating with and had cohabitated with him as a spouse." App. 2-3 (bold typeface deleted).

[3] See *United States v. Heckenliable*, 446 F.3d 1048, 1049 (CA10 2006); *United States v. Belless*, 338 F.3d 1063, 1067 (CA9 2003); *White v. Department of Justice*, 328 F.3d 1361, 1364-1367 (CA Fed.2003); *United States v. Shelton*, 325 F.3d 553, 562 (CA5 2003); *United States v. Kavoukian*, 315 F.3d 139, 142-144 (CA2 2002); *United States v. Barnes*, 295 F.3d 1354, 1358-1361 (CADC 2002); *United States v. Chavez*, 204 F.3d 1305, 1313-1314 (CA11 2000); *United States v. Meade*, 175 F.3d 215, 218-221 (CA1 1999); *United States v. Smith*, 171 F.3d 617, 619-621 (CA8 1999).

cording to those courts, § 922(g)(9) does not require that the offense predicate to the defendant's firearm possession conviction have as an element a domestic relationship between offender and victim. We granted certiorari, 552 U.S. ___ (2008), to resolve this conflict.

II

Section 922(g)(9) makes it "unlawful for any person . . . who has been convicted in any court of a misdemeanor crime of domestic violence . . . [to] possess in or affecting commerce, any firearm or ammunition." Section 921(a)(33)(A) defines "misdemeanor crime of domestic violence" as follows:

> "[T]he term 'misdemeanor crime of domestic violence' means an offense that —
>
> "(i) is a misdemeanor under Federal, State, or Tribal law; and
>
> "(ii) has, as an element, the use or attempted use of physical force, or the threatened use of a deadly weapon, committed by a current or former spouse, parent, or guardian of the victim, by a person with whom the victim shares a child in common, by a person who is cohabiting with or has cohabitated with the victim as a spouse, parent, or guardian, or by a person similarly situated to a spouse, parent, or guardian of the victim" (footnotes omitted).

This definition, all agree, imposes two requirements: First, a "misdemeanor crime of domestic violence" must have, "as an element, the use or attempted use of physical force, or the threatened use of a deadly weapon." Second, it must be "committed by" a person who has a specified domestic relationship with the victim. The question here is whether the language of § 921(a)(33)(A) calls for a further limitation: Must the statute describing the predicate offense include, as a discrete element, the existence of a domestic relationship between offender and victim? In line with the large majority of the Courts of Appeals, we conclude that § 921 (a)(33)(A) does not require a predicate-offense statute of that specificity. Instead, in a § 922(g)(9) prosecution, it suffices for the Government to charge and prove a prior conviction that was, in fact, for "an offense . . . committed by" the defendant against a spouse or other domestic victim.

We note as an initial matter that § 921(a)(33)(A) uses the word "element" in the singular, which suggests that Congress intended to describe only one required element. Immediately following the word "element," § 921(a)(33)(A)(ii) refers to the use of force (undoubtedly a required element) and thereafter to the relationship between aggressor and victim, *e.g.*, a current or former spouse. The manner in which the offender acts, and the offender's relationship with the victim, are "conceptually distinct attributes." *United States v. Meade*, 175 F.3d 215, 218 (CA1 1999).[4] Had Congress meant to make the latter as well as the former an element of the predicate offense, it likely would have used the plural "elements," as it has done in other offense-defining provisions. See, *e.g.*, 18 U.S.C. § 3559(c) (2)(A) ("[T]he term 'assault with intent to commit rape' means an offense that has as its elements engaging in physical contact with another person or using or brandishing a weapon against another person with intent to commit aggravated sexual abuse or sexual abuse."). Cf. Black's Law Dictionary 559 (8th ed. 2004) (defining "element" as "[a] constituent part of a claim that must be proved for the claim to succeed <Burke failed to prove the element of proximate cause in prosecuting his negligence claim>").[5]

Treating the relationship between aggressor and victim as an element of the predicate offense is also awkward as a matter of syntax. It requires the reader to regard "the use or attempted use of physical force, or the threatened use of a deadly weapon" as an expression modified by the relative clause "committed by." In ordinary usage, however, we would not say that a person "commit[s]" a "use." It is more natural to say that a person "commit[s]" an "offense." See, *e.g.*, *United States v. Belless*, 338 F.3d 1063, 1066 (CA9 2003) ("One can 'commit' a crime or an offense, but one does not 'commit' 'force' or 'use.'").

In reaching the conclusion that § 921(a)(33)(A) renders both the use of force and a domestic relationship between aggressor and victim necessary elements of a qualifying predicate offense, the Fourth Circuit majority

---

[4] Hayes observes, see Brief for Respondent 24-25, that Congress has used the singular "element" in defining a "crime of violence" to require both an action (the use of force) and its object (the person of another). See, *e.g.*, 18 U.S.C. § 16(a) (defining "crime of violence" as "an offense that has as an element the use, attempted use, or threatened use of physical force against the person or property of another"). Although one might conceive of an action and its object as separate elements, it is unsurprising that Congress would have chosen to denominate "the use of force against another" as a single, undifferentiated element. In contrast, the two requirements set out in § 921(a)(33)(A)(ii) — the use of force and the existence of a specified relationship between aggressor and victim — are not readily conceptualized as a single element.

[5] Invoking the Dictionary Act, Hayes contends that the singular "element" encompasses the plural "elements." See Brief for Respondent 25. The Dictionary Act provides that, "unless the context indicates otherwise," "words importing the singular include and apply to several persons, parties, or things." 1 U.S.C. § 1. On the rare occasions when we have relied on this rule, doing so was "necessary to carry out the evident intent of the statute." *First Nat. Bank in St. Louis v. Missouri*, 263 U.S. 640, 657 (1924). As we explain *infra*, at 10-12, Hayes's reading of 18 U.S.C. § 921(a)(33)(A) does not accord with Congress' aim in extending the gun possession ban.

relied on two textual arguments. First, the court noted that clause (ii) is separated from clause (i) by a line break and a semicolon; in contrast, the components of clause (ii) — force and domestic relationship — are joined in an unbroken word flow. See 482 F.3d, at 753.

Had Congress placed the "committed by" phrase in its own clause, set off from clause (ii) by a semicolon or a line break, the lawmakers might have better conveyed that "committed by" modifies only "offense" and not "use" or "element." Congress' less-than-meticulous drafting, however, hardly shows that the legislators meant to exclude from § 922(g)(9)'s firearm possession prohibition domestic abusers convicted under generic assault or battery provisions.

As structured, § 921(a)(33)(A) defines "misdemeanor crime of domestic violence" by addressing in clause (i) the meaning of "misdemeanor" and, in turn, in clause (ii), "crime of domestic violence." Because a "crime of domestic violence" involves both a use of force and a domestic relationship, joining these features together in clause (ii) would make sense even if Congress had no design to confine laws qualifying under § 921(a)(33)(A) to those designating as elements both use of force and domestic relationship between aggressor and victim. See *id.*, at 761 (Williams, J., dissenting). See also *United States v. Barnes*, 295 F.3d 1354, 1358-1360, 1361 (CADC 2002) ("The fact that the Congress somewhat awkwardly included the 'committed by' phrase in subpart (ii) (instead of adding a subpart (iii)) is not significant in view of the *un*natural reading that would result if 'committed by' were construed to modify 'use of force.'").

A related statutory provision, 25 U.S.C. § 2803(3)(C), indicates that Congress did not ascribe substantive significance to the placement of line breaks and semicolons in 18 U.S.C. § 921(a)(33)(A). In 2006, Congress amended § 921(a)(33)(A)(i) to include misdemeanors under "[t]ribal law" as predicate offenses. As a companion measure, Congress simultaneously enacted § 2803(3)(C), which employs use-of-force and domestic-relationship language virtually identical to the language earlier placed in § 921(a)(33)(A)(i), except that § 2803(3)(C) uses no semicolon or line break.

Section 2803(3)(C) authorizes federal agents to "make an arrest without a warrant for an offense committed in Indian country if —"

> "the offense is a misdemeanor crime of domestic violence . . . and has, as an element, the use or attempted use of physical force, or the threatened use of a deadly weapon, committed by a current or former spouse, parent, or guardian of the victim, by a person with whom the victim shares a child in common, by a person who

is cohabitating with or has cohabitated with the victim as a spouse, parent, or guardian, or by a person similarly situated to a spouse, parent or guardian of the victim . . . ."

At the time Congress enacted § 2803(3)(C), the Courts of Appeals uniformly agreed that § 921(a)(33)(A) did not limit predicate offenses to statutory texts specifying both a use of force and a domestic relationship as offense elements. Congress presumably knew how § 921(a)(33)(A) had been construed, and presumably intended § 2803(3)(C) to bear the same meaning. See *Merrill Lynch, Pierce, Fenner & Smith Inc. v. Dabit*, 547 U.S. 71, 85-86 (2006) ("[W]hen 'judicial interpretations have settled the meaning of an existing statutory provision, repetition of the same language in a new statute indicates, as a general matter, the intent to incorporate its . . . judicial interpretations as well.'" (quoting *Bragdon v. Abbott*, 524 U.S. 624, 645 (1998))). Relying on spacing and punctuation to hem in § 921(a)(33)(A), while reading § 2803(3)(C) to contain no similar limitation, would create a disjunction between these two provisions that Congress could not have intended.

As a second justification for its construction of § 921(a)(33)(A), the Court of Appeals invoked the "rule of the last antecedent," under which "a limiting clause or phrase . . . should ordinarily be read as modifying only the noun or phrase that it immediately follows." *Barnhart v. Thomas*, 540 U.S. 20, 26 (2003). The words "committed by" immediately follow the use-of-force language, the court observed, and therefore should be read to modify that phrase, not the earlier word "offense." See 482 F.3d, at 753-755. The rule of the last antecedent, however, "is not an absolute and can assuredly be overcome by other indicia of meaning." *Barnhart*, 540 U.S., at 26.[6]

Applying the rule of the last antecedent here would require us to accept two unlikely premises: that Congress employed the singular "element" to encompass two distinct concepts, and that it adopted the awkward construction "commi[t]" a "use." See *supra*, at 1084-1085. Moreover, as the dissent acknowledges, *post*, at 1090-1091, the last-antecedent rule would render the word "committed" superfluous: Congress could have conveyed the same meaning by referring simply to "the use . . . of physical

---

[6] As the United States points out, the Court of Appeals "itself recognized the flexibility of the rule [of the last antecedent]." Brief for United States 20, n. 7. Under a strict application of the rule, the "committed by" phrase would modify only its immediate antecedent, *i.e.*, "the threatened use of a deadly weapon," and not the entire phrase "use or attempted use of physical force, or the threatened use of a deadly weapon." The court rightly regarded such a reading as implausible. See 482 F.3d 749, 755 (CA4 2007).

force . . . by a current or former spouse . . . ." See Tr. of Oral Arg. 29. "Committed" retains its operative meaning only if it is read to modify "offense."

Most sensibly read, then, § 921(a)(33)(A) defines "misdemeanor crime of domestic violence" as a misdemeanor offense that (1) "has, as an element, the use [of force]," and (2) is committed by a person who has a specified domestic relationship with the victim. To obtain a conviction in a § 922(g)(9) prosecution, the Government must prove beyond a reasonable doubt that the victim of the predicate offense was the defendant's current or former spouse or was related to the defendant in another specified way. But that relationship, while it must be established, need not be denominated an element of the predicate offense.[7]

III

Practical considerations strongly support our reading of § 921(a)(33)(A)'s language. Existing felon-in-possession laws, Congress recognized, were not keeping firearms out of the hands of domestic abusers, because "many people who engage in serious spousal or child abuse ultimately are not charged with or convicted of felonies." 142 Cong. Rec. 22985 (1996) (statement of Sen. Lautenberg). By extending the federal firearm prohibition to persons convicted of "misdemeanor crime[s] of domestic violence," proponents of § 922(g)(9) sought to "close this dangerous loophole." *Id.*, at 22986.

Construing § 922(g)(9) to exclude the domestic abuser convicted under a generic use-of-force statute (one that does not designate a domestic relationship as an element of the offense) would frustrate Congress' manifest purpose. Firearms and domestic strife are a potentially deadly combination nationwide. See, *e.g.*, Brief for Brady Center to Prevent Gun Violence et al. as *Amici Curiae* 8-15; Brief for National Network to End Domestic Violence et al. as *Amici Curiae* 2-8. Yet, as interpreted by the Fourth Circuit, § 922(g)(9) would have been "a dead letter" in some two-thirds of the States from the very moment of its enactment. 482 F.3d, at 762 (Williams, J., dissenting).

As of 1996, only about one-third of the States had criminal statutes that specifically proscribed domestic violence. See Brief for United States

---

[7] We find it not at all "surprising" — indeed, it seems to us "most natural" — to read § 921(a)(33)(A) to convey that a person convicted of battering a spouse or other domestic victim has committed a "crime of domestic violence," whether or not the statute of conviction happens to contain a domestic-relationship element. Cf. *post*, at 1089.

23, n. 8.[8] Even in those States, domestic abusers were (and are) routinely prosecuted under generally applicable assault or battery laws. See Tr. of Oral Arg. 19. And no statute defining a distinct federal misdemeanor designated as an element of the offense a domestic relationship between aggressor and victim. Yet Congress defined "misdemeanor crime of domestic violence" to include "misdemeanor[s] under Federal . . . law." § 921(a)(33)(A)(i). Given the paucity of state and federal statutes targeting *domestic* violence, we find it highly improbable that Congress meant to extend § 922(g)(9)'s firearm possession ban only to the relatively few domestic abusers prosecuted under laws rendering a domestic relationship an element of the offense. See *Barnes*, 295 F.3d, at 1364 (rejecting the view that "Congress remedied one disparity — between felony and misdemeanor domestic violence convictions — while at the same time creating a new disparity among (and sometimes, within) states").[9]

The measure that became § 922(g)(9) and § 921(a)(33)(A), Hayes acknowledges, initially may have had a broadly remedial purpose, see Brief for Respondent 28-29, but the text of the proposal, he maintains, was revised and narrowed while the measure remained in the congressional hopper. The compromise reflected in the text that gained passage, Hayes argues, restricted the legislation to offenses specifically denominating a domestic relationship as a defining element. The changes Hayes identifies, however, do not corroborate his argument.

Congress did revise the language of § 921(a)(33)(A) to spell out the use-of-force requirement. The proposed legislation initially described the predicate domestic-violence offense as a "crime of violence . . . committed by" a person who had a domestic relationship with the victim. 142 Cong. Rec. 5840. The final version replaced the unelaborated phrase "crime of violence" with the phrase "has, as an element, the use or attempted use of physical force, or the threatened use of a deadly weapon." This apparently last-minute insertion may help to explain some of the syntactical awkwardness of the enacted language, but it does not evince an intention to convert the "committed by" phrase into a required element of the predicate offense.

---

[8] Additional States have enacted such statutes since 1996, but about one-half of the States still prosecute domestic violence exclusively under generally applicable criminal laws. See Brief for United States 23-24, and n. 9.

[9] Generally, as in this case, it would entail no "'elaborate factfinding process,'" cf. *post*, at 1092, to determine whether the victim of a violent assault was the perpetrator's "current or former spouse" or bore one of the other domestic relationships specified in § 921(a)(33)(A)(ii) to the perpetrator.

Indeed, in a floor statement discussing the revised version of § 922(g)(9), Senator Frank Lautenberg, the sponsor of the provision, observed that a domestic relationship between aggressor and victim often would not be a designated element of the predicate offense:

> "[C]onvictions for domestic violence-related crimes often are for crimes, such as assault, that are not explicitly identified as related to domestic violence. Therefore, it will not always be possible for law enforcement authorities to determine from the face of someone's criminal record whether a particular misdemeanor conviction involves domestic violence, as defined in the new law." *Id.*, at 26675.

The remarks of a single Senator are "not controlling," *Consumer Product Safety Comm'n v. GTE Sylvania, Inc.*, 447 U.S. 102, 118 (1980), but, as Hayes recognizes, the legislative record is otherwise "absolutely silent." See Tr. of Oral Arg. 32, 35. It contains no suggestion that Congress intended to confine § 922(g)(9) to abusers who had violated statutes rendering the domestic relationship between aggressor and victim an element of the offense.

IV

The rule of lenity, Hayes contends, provides an additional reason to construe § 922(g)(9) and § 921(a)(33)(A) to apply only to predicate offenses that specify a domestic relationship as an element of the crime. "[T]he touchstone of the rule of lenity is statutory ambiguity." *Bifulco v. United States*, 447 U.S. 381, 387 (1980) (internal quotation marks omitted). We apply the rule "only when, after consulting traditional canons of statutory construction, we are left with an ambiguous statute." *United States v. Shabani*, 513 U.S. 10, 17 (1994). Section 921(a)(33)(A)'s definition of "misdemeanor crime of domestic violence," we acknowledge, is not a model of the careful drafter's art. See *Barnes*, 295 F.3d, at 1356. But neither is it "grievous[ly] ambigu[ous]." *Huddleston v. United States*, 415 U.S. 814, 831 (1974). The text, context, purpose, and what little there is of drafting history all point in the same direction: Congress defined "misdemeanor crime of domestic violence" to include an offense "committed by" a person who had a specified domestic relationship with the victim, whether or not the misdemeanor statute itself designates the domestic relationship as an element of the crime.

• • • •

For the reasons stated, the judgment of the United States Court of Appeals for the Fourth Circuit is reversed, and the case is remanded for further proceedings consistent with this opinion.

THE MACMILLIAN BASEBALL ENCYCLOPEDIA, THE WEST SYSTEM, AND SWEAT EQUITY

Robert C. Berring[†]

There is beauty in finding that beneath a complex system, one so large and entrenched that it seems to operate under its own power, there is a history that is quite human. The work of a person, perhaps a small band of people, fueled by energy and sweat equity, and perhaps a dollop of obsessiveness, can create a mighty enterprise. Simon Winchester wrote a bestseller about how one man, John Murray, stood at the center of the *Oxford English Dictionary*. On an abstract level, one might claim that William Blackstone created the conceptual framework of the common law that still guides us. But those two are famous figures. The real fun lies in identifying those who, by sheer perseverance and drive, create mighty dreadnaughts that sail on under their own power, growing and changing, and yet remain anonymous. Two delightful examples, related on many levels, are the individuals behind the West System[1] and the *MacMillan Baseball Encyclopedia* (MBE).

Baseball and lawyers are intricately intertwined. This is no news to the reader of this article. The magic that pulls them together may not admit to easy characterization, but there is no denying that Stevens's *The Common Law Origins of the Infield Fly Rule* created an enthusiastic body of commentary all on its own, or that the intricacy of the Baseball Rule Book maps easily onto the technical pyrotechnics of the Internal Revenue Code for specificity and opaqueness. Lawyers love the intricacies of the game of baseball and the collection of statistics. More congruence is found in the fact that the guiding light of modern baseball statistics and the conceptual blueprint for legal analysis share similar origins. There are human stories behind these grand enterprises.

BUILDING THE WEST SYSTEM

The West Publishing Company was founded by two brothers: John and Horatio. John was a salesman who noticed that some of his customers, who were lawyers, were having trouble getting their hands on recent judicial decisions. West lived in Minnesota in the late 19th Century. Courts there were required to make written copies of judicial opinions available, and the state had an official printer of decisions, but getting access to these opinions was not easy.[2] The official printer was slow and not always reliable. This gave John West an idea.

[†] Walter Perry Johnson Professor of Law at the UC Berkeley School of Law.
[1] The West System will stand for both the National Reporter System and the American Digest System. Though it is the former that is primarily of interest here, like Ruth and Gehrig they are forever conjoined.
[2] For a short and charming description of the history of the distribution of legal information in the United States, see the text of the 2009 Opperman Lecture at Drake Law School, *Remarks of the Honorable John G. Roberts, Jr. Chief Justice of the United States*, in the Fall 2008 issue of the *Drake Law Review* at page 1. I am an admirer of any Chief Justice who can use the term "pneumatic tube" in a lecture.

The classic Supreme Court opinion in *Wheaton v. Peters* had established in 1834 that judicial opinions were in the public domain. These opinions could be published by anyone who wanted to do so. Many jurisdictions had official printers for their courts' decisions, but the office of official printer was often a sinecure. The resulting publications were incomplete and slow. John realized that one might make money by doing the sheer donkey work of going from court to court, making copies of the opinions, printing them, and distributing them.[3] Remember, the West brothers had no photocopy machines, let alone digital information. What they did have was an idea and the market incentive to perform the simple, hard work. It had to be done carefully and quickly. John was not a lawyer; he was an entrepreneur.

Armed with his idea and the raw materials to carry it out, he and his brother Horatio went into business. They produced the *Syllabus*, a collection of Minnesota decisions. It was a huge success. It was such a winner that the brothers began the *Northwestern Reporter*, which included decisions from courts in surrounding states. That quickly led to the full National Reporter System. This tale has been told in detail elsewhere, but what matters here is that the root from which it all grew was simple effort and obsessive attention to detail. The West Company produced and produces a more thorough and timely product than anything seen before.

The maraschino cherry on the chocolate sundae of the West story is the Key Number System. The West brothers realized that they should offer some organizational system for finding the judicial opinions in their *Reporters*. They bought a system developed by John Mallory and morphed it into the Key Number System. The Key Number System categorized opinions by classifying legal ideas. It was new and it allowed lawyers to find judicial opinions via an entirely new rubric. Several of us have contended that the Key Number System categories came to have an impact on the way lawyers think and judges write.

As the paper-based universe of information sinks slowly in the west, and the new dawn belongs to the texting, social networking, and Boolean searching generation of multi-taskers who sit in the classes that I teach, it is fitting to note that the mighty West system was the product of the obsessive work and simple plan of human beings.

THE MACMILLAN BASEBALL ENCYCLOPEDIA: THE BEGINNING OF A MAGNIFICENT OBSESSION

Growing up as a baseball fanatic,[4] I treasured the *MacMillan Baseball Encyclopedia*. As a boy contemplating it, I was filled with wonder. The MBE listed every player who ever had a cup of coffee in the majors. It was de-

---

[3] Marvin, *History of the West Publishing Company*, provides a full account of this story. This book is very hard to find. For a more easily located version of the story try *Collapse of the Structure of the Legal Research Universe: The Imperative of Digital Information*, 69 WASH. L. REV. 9 (1994). It is my youthful attempt at telling the story, complete with edifying footnotes.

[4] Growing up in northeastern Ohio, I was a Cleveland Indians fan. Since my team never won, focusing on statistics was a fine outlet for my enthusiasm. Did you know that Rocky Colavito once hit four home runs in one game? I thought not.

tailed and it was authoritative. For me it was an unquestioned source of information. Like the West System (of which I was ignorant in my elementary school years), it seemed an enterprise bigger than any human, but in fact it was the product of the work of a small band of zealots — humans who were willing to invest the sweat equity in its creation.

David Neft was a statistician who loved baseball. Growing up in the 1950s, he saw the *Official Encyclopedia of Baseball* as his lodestone of authority. But it was incomplete in coverage, and printed only batting averages for hitters and won-loss records for pitchers. He nurtured the dream of something better. When he went to work for Information Concepts Incorporated in 1965, he proposed the idea of a computerized baseball encyclopedia that would be complete and reliable. How Neft sold his concept to ICI and then to MacMillan is a great tale.[5] The statistics were out there, but before 1920 they were not in one place, and after 1920 they were unverified. Doing the job right would mean starting over. First, the new effort would need to be certain who the players were. For that there was another compulsive information maven, Lee Allen.

Lee Allen was the long-time historian of the Baseball Hall of Fame in Cooperstown, New York. Known as a walking encyclopedia of baseball knowledge, Allen had spent three decades collecting information on players. Allen did not care about statistics; he wanted biographical data. Though official records had been kept since 1903, there had been little quality control. Mr. Allen had supplemented these records through his own research, his own drive to be accurate and complete. He visited graveyards and pursued leads on players like a Sam Spade in search of information on the black bird. He compiled a massive library of books and materials that he took with him to Cooperstown when he assumed his position as librarian there.[6] Basing their encyclopedic work on the biographies compiled by Mr. Allen, Neft and his team went to work gathering up data. Neft hired a team of 21 researchers and set them to work, checking old newspapers and gathering up data. As Schwarz put it:

> The staff of 21 then began its Kerouakian odyssey all over the United States, from library microfilm rooms to long lost graveyards, mortar and spades always in tow, to build the greatest book of statistics sports had ever seen.[7]

The hard work of slogging was supplemented by the effort of programming a computer to sort and check each item. It was the middle of the 1960s. Computers were primitive creatures and the task was not simple. It fell to Neil Armann. Armann was not a baseball fan, much like John West was not a legal scholar, but he took on the challenge of creating a computer program that would pull together and cross-check all statistics. Given that these were early days for computing, there is another great story here, but we shall tip our cap to Mr. Armann and move on.

---

[5] The story is well told in Schwarz, *The Numbers Game*. Chapter 5 covers this territory but if one loves baseball and statistics, the whole book is worth a read. It is in print in paperback.

[6] Credit should also be given to John Tattersall, a shipping executive who spent his life collecting information on players from the 19th century. His work formed the basis of the reports on the earliest players of the game.

[7] Schwarz, p. 95. Kerouakian is my word of the month.

The first edition of the *MacMillan Baseball Encyclopedia*, which was published in 1969, sold an amazing 100,000 copies at $25 ($200 in the dollars of 2009). The *New York Times* reviewed it three times. It carried the day. Just as the West Key Number System set the accepted categories for legal thought, the *Baseball Encyclopedia* established the standard for statistical categories. If you look through the volume you will find 17 categories for hitters, and 19 for pitchers. They became the standard way of evaluating performance. In my family's basement back in Ohio, these were the numbers that meant something to me. The *Baseball Encyclopedia* was authoritative and it created an authoritative classification system. I knew that if Kelly Heath had one at bat in the major leagues, it would be in the MBE. As with the world of the West brothers, the information was there for the taking. It never occurred to me that actual people struggled to pull these sources together, they just existed.

Once the MBE was in place, a new world was opened. Having a source of reliable information available, others began to build. In its wake, those who were devoted to baseball statistics founded the Society for American Baseball Research (SABR),[8] which applies the tools of modern statistics and the power of computers to generate, refine, and parse new categories of information. Indeed, new statistical categories are now in vogue, but the rock upon which it was all built was the *MacMillan Baseball Encyclopedia*.

COMMON FATE

These two great enterprises share another characteristic. They are intellectual booster rockets carrying their missions forward. And now, having served their purposes, they are falling back to earth. Each has taken us to a new level where others have built upon them. Boolean searching has largely replaced the Key Number System at the center of the search function of legal research. New digital tools, web-pages, blogs and a deluge of specialty software applications have replaced the *Baseball Encyclopedia*. The 10th Edition, published in 1996, was its last hurrah. Just as law libraries are shipping the old *West Digest* and *National Reporter* volumes to storage, or perhaps to a nearby dumpster, no one wants to buy a ten-pound reference book on baseball statistics when a website can tell you everything you need to know and more.

Since you have read to this point, you must be a person of the old school. One who values the feel of pages and admires the heft of a ten-pound reference book. Let us take a moment, and raise a glass of fine single malt scotch to these two very human efforts to bring order out of chaos, and to the resulting books that represent the giants upon whose shoulders we now stand. Each was a masterpiece built on sweat, and each was a financial success in its day. As with so many other great authoritative tools of the 20th Century, their days are gone, but they should not be forgotten.

---

[8] See www.sabr.org/sabr.cfm?a=cms,c,110,39 for more information on this group.

A NOTE TO THE READER

AND

TWO KINDS OF PEOPLE

from

IN SEARCH OF JEFFERSON'S MOOSE:
NOTES ON THE STATE OF CYBERSPACE

David G. Post[†]

Editor's note: Post's book is in a distinctive format, and the text features some unusual conventions. These attributes of the book call for two editorial compromises.

First, intead of following our regular practice of re-typesetting the exemplary writing we present to you, we present below scanned images of the pages making up the excerpts of Post's book we are sharing with you. We lose the crispness of fresh type this way, as well as some of the consistency in the look of our Almanac. But we gain the pleasure of seeing slices of Post's book in its original and appealing design, as well as the comprehensibility that comes from seeing his words in the arrangements he intended.

Second, to make it easier for you, the reader, to appreciate the textual conventions used in Post's book, we begin with his introductory "A Note to the Reader" and follow it with the chapter titled "Two Kinds of People".

[†] I. Herman Stern Professor of Law, Temple University Beasley School of Law. Copyright © 2009 by Oxford University Press, Inc. This excerpt of *In Search of Jefferson's Moose: Notes on the State of Cyberspace* (Oxford University Press 2009) is reprinted with permission from the author and the publisher. For more information about this publication please visit www.oup.com.

A NOTE TO THE READER

A large work is difficult because it is large, even though all its parts might singly
be performed with facility; where there are many things to be done, each must be
allowed its share of time and labour, in the proportion only which it bears to the
whole; nor can it be expected, that the stones which form the dome of a temple,
should be squared and polished like the diamond of a ring.

SAMUEL JOHNSON, PREFACE TO HIS *DICTIONARY OF THE ENGLISH LANGUAGE*

Although this book is a work of "scholarship" (and a good one, I hope), it's not a
"scholarly" work, by which I mean two things. First, I have tried to stay focused on
the issues and ideas, rather than, in a more scholarly fashion, on the debate **about**
the issues, more on whether X is right or wrong than on what various scholars have
said previously about whether X is right or wrong, more on trying to make sense of
things and less on trying to explain how others have done so. I don't mean to slight
the scholarly debates—quite the opposite: I couldn't have written anything remotely
resembling this book without drawing upon, as best I could, the vigorous (to put it
mildly) scholarly debates that swirl around both of the twinned subject matters of
this book—Jefferson's system of thought, and the law of the Net. A book describing
and explaining the scholarly debates in those two fields would be a very interesting
book, but it's not this book. I find the ideas difficult enough to make sense of and to
convey to a reader, without also trying simultaneously to situate each one, to try to
explain where it came from, and who held it first, and what the opposing position
might be, and who has articulated that opposing position, and why I've chosen one
over another, and so on.

I'm assuming, in short, that you, my reader, care less (or not at all) about what
Professors X and Y have said about things than you do about the things themselves.
I **have** tried to give credit and attribution wherever they're due for the facts, and
ideas, and arguments presented in what follows; in the "References and Suggested
Readings" section for each chapter, I have tried to bring together enough information to permit the interested reader to uncover the provenance of all of the
facts, ideas, and arguments I present. But I have not attempted to provide what
every good scholarly work should provide, namely the full panoply of scholarly

citation and cross-citation and authoritative support for all of it. A colleague once remarked (only half-jokingly) that the perfect work of legal scholarship would have a footnote at the end of every sentence except the final one, the whole point of the scholarly enterprise being, as it were, to place every idea and every argument in its full context, to show the provenance of every fact asserted, and to give credit for the prior appearance of every idea and argument save the last, the one constituting the author's own original contribution. This is not that kind of work.

A word about Jefferson's words. I use them a lot (and I print them all *in italic type*), and in a somewhat unusual way: I'm trying to bring them inside the narrative, to get you to engage with them not as historical artifacts (though they are indeed historical artifacts) but as expressions of living ideas that are always interesting and sometimes, even, profound. (If I were **really** good at this, I would have written the whole book using **only** Jefferson's words, rearranged to tell the story I want to tell). Jefferson was one of history's greatest prose stylists, and one tinkers with his prose at one's peril. It is, though, eighteenth-century prose, and eighteenth-century prose has any number of peculiarities that can sometimes obscure its meaning to twenty-first-century readers. I have taken some (small) liberties with his words from time to time, in an effort to give it greater fluency for twenty-first-century eyes—altering punctuation (often), paragraph structure (occasionally), and even sentence order (rarely). I have done my best to keep its meaning intact—but even taking out the odd comma (and Jefferson's prose has some **very** odd commas in it) can have subtle and sometimes profound effects on meaning, and I cannot state with absolute certainty that I have always succeeded in doing so.[1] The original sources for all quotations are presented in the supplementary references; if you are unwilling to take my word for it, by all means have at it—nothing would delight me more than to have you checking back with the Jeffersonian originals to point out some nuance I have perhaps missed, or misstated. And if you come up with something interesting, I'd love to hear what it is—www.jeffersonsmoose.org.[2]

---

1 My favorite example: When Robert Frost's now-classic poem "Stopping by Woods on a Snowy Evening" appeared in the first edition of his *Collected Poems*, it read:

   The woods are lovely, dark, and deep
   But I have promises to keep

   In fact, what Frost had written was:

   The woods are lovely, dark and deep
   But I have promises to keep

2 I also apologize, in advance, for my use of the term "American" throughout to refer to the United States. It's unpleasantly chauvinistic, and I know that it drives Mexicans and Canadians and Brazilians and Peruvians and other "Americans" to distraction—but there is really no other adjective that works as well to describe United Statesian law, or United Statesesque history, or United Statesish patent procedures, or the like.

And finally, a word to those of you who are tempted to dismiss Jefferson and all things Jeffersonian out of hand—either on general "dead white guy" grounds, or because of his inability to solve, in his own life let alone for the nation as a whole, the terrible problem of slavery, or because of his (many) failures and compromises and defects of character. Jefferson has been the subject of much criticism of late—"viciously maligned," historian Sean Wilentz has written, "in ways normally reserved only for modern American presidents and liberals." Much of it, in my opinion (and Wilentz's), is wrongheaded—but my point here is not to persuade you of that. It's not his character, or even his reputation, that I'm trying to get my hands around, but his ideas, and I ask only that you keep your mind open to the possibility that he still has much to teach us about the world.

TWO KINDS OF PEOPLE

Men by their constitution are naturally divided into two parties. . . . The division is founded in the nature of man; it has existed from the first establishment of governments to the present day [and] will continue through all future time. . . . In every country these two parties exist; and in every one where they are free to think, speak, and write, they will declare themselves. Call them Whigs and Tories; Republicans and Federalists; Jacobins and Ultras; Liberals and Serviles; Aristocrats and Democrats, or by whatever name you please, they are the same parties still, and pursue the same objects.

TJ TO HENRY LEE, AUGUST 10, 1824/TJ TO JOEL BARLOW, MAY 3, 1802

There is an old joke: There are two kinds of people in the world—those who think there are two kinds of people in the world, and those who don't.[1]

But I'm with Jefferson on this one; I think there really **are** two kinds of people in the world (though I am not as certain as he was that the division is *founded in the nature of man*—part of *natural, as well as civil, history*, as he put it elsewhere). He usually called them, using language that is now decidedly out of style, "whigs" and "tories." I prefer "Jeffersonians" and "Hamiltonians."

They are the two great pole stars in American politics, Thomas Jefferson and Alexander Hamilton—each thoughtful, brilliant, often profound, always unafraid of new ideas and new intellectual challenges. You couldn't have made up a more extraordinary pair of combatants for the soul of the new nation—as Jonathan Spence put it, one of history's uses being to remind us how unlikely things can be. Their feud is the longest-running in American political history, for they stood on opposite shores of a great intellectual divide, a divide that encapsulates something fundamental in the way we think about society and government. In the "balance between liberty and authority," Merrill Peterson wrote, "Jefferson tipped the former scale, Hamilton the latter:

> One despised, the other idolized, rulership. One located the strength of the republic in the diffuse energies of a free society, the other in the consolidation of authority. . . . Hamilton feared most the ignorance and tumult of the people, Jefferson

---

1   Or, a variant I heard recently: There are 10 kinds of people in the world—those who understand binary notation and those who don't.

326

feared the irresponsibility of rulers independent of them. Hamilton labeled his rival a visionary and a demagogue, while Jefferson named his a corrupter, a monarchist, and an Angloman.

Jefferson and Jeffersonians think centrifugally, outwards from the center. End to end, as it were: Liberty, Chaos, The Many, Diffusion. Hamilton and Hamiltonians think centripetally, towards the center: Authority, Order, The Few, Concentration. Jeffersonians love turbulence—*I like a little rebellion now and then; it is like a storm in the atmosphere*—while Hamiltonians prize stability: when the "zeal for liberty becomes predominant and excessive," Hamilton wrote, "only the principle of strength and stability in the organization of our government," and the "vigor in its operations," could put things right. Jeffersonians mistrust concentrated power: *It is not by the consolidation or concentration of powers, but by their **distribution**, that good government is effected... Were we directed from Washington when to sow, and when to reap, we should soon want bread.* Hamiltonians counter that "too little power is as dangerous as too much; as too much power leads to despotism, too little leads to anarchy, and both eventually to the ruin of the people." Jeffersonians look forward, drawing inspiration from unpredictability and possibility; *I like the dreams of the future better than the history of the past.* Hamiltonians look back, drawing inspiration from the certainty of the past and from the ideas that have proven themselves over time.

Jeffersonians think that governments can be saved by their people: *The will of the people... is the only legitimate foundation of any government, [and] the people of every country are the only safe guardian of their own rights... No other depositories of power have ever yet been found, which did not end in converting to their own profit the earnings of those committed to their charge....* To Hamiltonians, it is the other way around: "The people are turbulent and changing; they seldom judge or determine right... Mankind in general [are] vicious... Our prevailing passions are ambition and interest; and it will ever be the duty of government to avail itself of those passions, in order to make them subservient to the public good."

It was an extraordinary conversation about (among other things) the shape of the network they were helping to build, with Hamiltonians in the center and Jeffersonians at the edge. Much of the history of the early days of the American republic can be (and has been) described in terms of the opposition between these two great competing visions. On virtually every issue, large and small, facing the new nation—states' rights versus a strong national government, the need for a central bank, free trade versus mercantilism, the location of the national capital, the value of naval versus land-based armed forces, agriculture versus manufacturing, legislative versus executive power, a foreign policy tilting toward France versus a foreign policy tilting toward England—the two men staked out opposing positions, and two parties, Republican and Federalist, coalesced around their views.

Jeffersonian energy and Hamiltonian power. Jeffersonian chaos and Hamiltonian order. Jeffersonian liberty and Hamiltonian authority. The challenge for the

BOX I.1

JEFFERSON	HAMILTON
Government wherein the will of every one has a just influence... has its evils, the principal one of which is the turbulence to which it is subject. But weigh this against the oppressions of monarchy, and it becomes nothing. **Malo periculosam libertatem quam quietam servitutem.** [*I prefer the tumult of liberty to the quiet of servitude.*]	The voice of the people has been said to be the voice of God; however generally this maxim has been quoted and believed, it is not true in fact. The people are turbulent and changing; they seldom judge or determine right.
TJ TO JAMES MADISON, JANUARY 30, 1787	The rights of government are as essential to be defended as the rights of individuals. The security of the one is inseparable from that of the other.... History is full of examples where...a jealousy of power has...subverted liberty by clogging government with too great precautions for its security, or by leaving too wide a door for sedition and popular licentiousness. In a government framed for durable liberty, no less regard must be paid to giving the magistrate a proper degree of authority, to make and execute the laws with vigour, than to guarding against encroachments upon the rights of the community. As too much power leads to despotism, too little leads to anarchy, and both eventually to the ruin of the people.
The people of every country are the only safe guardian of their own rights, [and] the will of the people... is the only legitimate foundation of any government. Whenever the people are well-informed, they can be trusted with their own government; whenever things get so far wrong as to attract their notice, they may be relied on to set them to rights.... The cherishment of the people was our [party's] principle, the fear and distrust of them that of the other party.	
TJ TO JOHN WYCHE, MAY 19, 1809	HAMILTON, LETTER TO JOHN DICKINSON (1783)
TJ TO DR. PRICE, JANUARY 8, 1789, AND	
TJ TO JUSTICE WILLIAM JOHNSON, JUNE 12, 1823	HAMILTON, *THE CONTINENTALIST* NO. 1 (1781)

new republic was to link them together, to find the sweet spot, the point of optimum tension, between the two. Determining who was right and who was wrong, who "won" and who "lost," is akin to determining whether the glass is actually half-full or half-empty.

Each had his triumphs (usually at the other's expense): Jefferson got Louisiana, Hamilton got a national bank; Jefferson got the Bill of Rights, Hamilton got his preferred interpretation of the powers "implied" by the Constitution; Jefferson got a national capital located far away from the dens of financial speculation in New York, Hamilton got debt financing.

It's as though the new country were oscillating between two great magnetic attractors, kept aloft by the powerful tug of two contrary forces.

> *Everyone takes his side, according to his constitution and the circumstances in which he is placed. Opinions, which are equally honest on both sides, should not affect personal esteem or social intercourse.... Difference of opinion leads to inquiry, and inquiry to truth....A truth that has never been opposed cannot acquire that firm and unwavering assent, which is given to that which has stood the test of a rigorous examination.*

LOOKING WEST

Kentucky, the great wilderness beyond the western edge of the world,... seemed to the colonists along the eastern North-American seaboard as far away, nearly, and as difficult of approach, as had the problematical world beyond the western ocean to the times prior to Columbus. "A country there was, of this none could doubt who thought at all; but whether land or water, mountain or plain, fertility or barrenness, preponderated; whether it was inhabited by men or beasts, or both, or neither, they knew not."... Clinging narrowly to their new foothold, dependent still on sailing vessels for a contact none too swift or certain with "home," the colonists looked with fear to the west... Opposed to this lay the forbidden wealth of the Unknown.

WILLIAM CARLOS WILLIAMS, "THE DISCOVERY OF KENTUCKY"

That the United States came to span the entire expanse of territory from the Atlantic to the Pacific Ocean is, when you stop to think about it, really quite remarkable. The sheer immensity of it is so audacious; against the background of eighteenth-century Europe, it looks like the fourth grader whose hormones have kicked in too early, and who towers over his or her peers in the class photograph.

Some philosophers of history say that it was all quite inevitable, that, in the grand sweep of things, unstoppable forces—economic, demographic, and political—were at work, driving people west and, simultaneously, driving the settlements they occupied into the arms of the United States. Others say that history has no "inevitability" to it, that small, quasi-random events can have large consequences, that it all could have played out quite differently had certain things not transpired as they did—had, say, Aaron Burr gotten that one extra vote in the House of Representatives that would have made **him** president in 1800 (instead of Jefferson), or had the railroad locomotive been invented a few years later than it was, or had Lewis and Clark drowned on the banks of the Missouri, or...

I don't have a good enough theory of history to take a position one way or another. But I do know one thing: it sure didn't **seem** inevitable to many people—many very smart people—in 1787. In fact, not only did it not seem inevitable, it seemed, to many, hardly possible at all.

The central problem was one of scale: the Problem of the Extended Republic. How could a government remain true to "republican" principles—that the governed rule their governors, and that ultimate power is lodged in the people themselves[2]—when spread over large territories and large numbers of people?

The best and most advanced thinking of the time had it that it couldn't be done—certainly not on a continental scale. To begin with, it had never **been** done. Republics had always been small-scale affairs—the Roman Republic, Carthage, Athens, Iceland, the Florentine and Venetian Republics, the Swiss cantons—far smaller than even the state of Virginia in 1787, let alone the thirteen United States taken together, and positively microscopic when measured against the vast expanse of the entire American continent from ocean to ocean.[3] Larger states had always been despotic affairs, empires, not republics, ruled by the whim of one man—Caesar, Alexander the Great, the Tsar, the Emperor of China, Genghis Khan, Montezuma—and his

---

2 *The term "republic,"* as Jefferson put it, *is of very vague application in every language.* Including our own. As Akhil R. Amar has noted, there has been a fundamental shift in our use and understanding of the term over the past two hundred years or so. These days, as we learn in junior high school social studies class, "republics" are distinguished from "democracies": the former has representative institutions, while the latter involves direct action by all citizens acting en masse (in the manner of a New England town meeting or the Athenian assembly). Viewed from this perspective, the Founders' frequent references to "republican government" and "republicanism"—for instance, in the guarantee of Article IV of the Constitution that every state shall have "a Republican Form of Government"—is seen by some as reflecting an antidemocratic impulse, a desire to take control of the government out of the hands of the people and into a more select band of rulers.

Nothing could be more misguided. In eighteenth-century usage, the two terms were largely indistinguishable and interchangeable; the critical distinction was not between "republican" and "democratic" governance, but between "republican" and "democratic" governance on the one hand and monarchical or aristocratic governance on the other, between sovereignty lodged in the people and sovereignty lodged in a select ruling class. The *mother principle of republicanism,* Jefferson called it: *that all power is inherent in the people* [*and*] *that they may exercise it by themselves in all cases to which they think themselves competent.*

Government by its own citizens in mass, acting directly and personally, according to rules established by the majority.... Governments are republican only in proportion as every member composing it has his equal voice in the direction of its concerns, and only in proportion as they embody the will of their people, and execute it. The true foundation of republican government is the equal right of every citizen in his person and property, and in their management.

3 "World history... furnished no model of a genuinely democratic regime stretching across a continental expanse.... No democracy in world history had ever spanned so vast a range encompassing such diverse weather zones, dominant sects, labor systems, and local temperaments. The widely admired French writer Montesquieu was commonly read as suggesting it could not be done" (Akhil R. Amar, *America's Constitution: A Biography* (2005), 41).

chosen confederates, held together only by the projection of powerful military force under their command.

"Montesquieu's Law," it was called, in honor of the great French political philosopher who explained most cogently and comprehensively why republican government could survive **only** in small communities. In Gordon Wood's words:

> The best political science of the century, as expressed most pointedly but hardly exclusively by Montesquieu, had told them "that so extensive a territory as that of the United States, including such a variety of climates, productions, interests; and so great differences of manners, habits, and customs" could never be a single republican state. "No government formed on the principles of freedom can pervade all North America." An extended republic ... could never be "so competent to attend to the various local concerns and wants, of every particular district, as well as the peculiar [local] governments who are nearer the scene and possessed of superior means of information" ... The idea of a single republic ... one thousand miles in length, and eight hundred in breadth, and containing six millions of white inhabitants ... [is] "in itself an absurdity, and contrary to the whole experience of mankind." "Nothing would support government, in such a case as that, but military coercion."

From this perspective—the "European perspective," we might call it—the size of the new American republic that had declared itself into existence in 1776 was **already** its most serious liability.[4] Surely, were it to get bigger and attempt to project its authority across the continent, republican institutions would, as Peter Onuf puts it, "have to be jettisoned in favor of the despotic forms that enabled the great European kingdoms to rule far-flung subject populations."

Writing to a friend in 1790 about the prospects for the newly formed United States, Hamilton referred to Florida "on our right" and Canada "on our left." It was a revealing turn of phrase, for Hamilton was always more comfortable facing east, toward Europe and the Old World; when he turned around, he didn't always like what he saw.

Hamilton had personal experience with Montesquieu's Law and the difficulties of governing the extended republic. In 1794, while he was serving as George Washington's secretary of treasury, the new nation faced its first great domestic crisis: the so-called Whiskey Rebellion, armed attacks by settlers in the hills of western Pennsylvania against federal agents attempting to collect the new federal tax on distilled spirits.

---

4 Even Jefferson's close colleague James Madison was apprehensive about expanding the Union westward. It is "fraught with danger," he wrote to Jefferson in 1784:

> As settlements become extended the members of the Confederacy must be multiplied, and along with them the wills which are to direct the machine. And as the wills multiply, so will the chances against a dangerous union of them. We experience every day the difficulty of drawing thirteen States into the same plans. Let the number be doubled and so will the difficulty." (James Madison to TJ, Aug. 20, 1784.)

The tax was very much Hamilton's tax—enacted at his urging by the first Congress in 1791, enforced by agents of his Treasury Department, and a critical piece of his great plan to have the federal government pay off the states' accumulated debts—and the Whiskey Rebellion became Hamilton's war. He wrote a confidential memorandum to President Washington warning of the "persevering and violent opposition to the law" and calling for "vigorous and decisive measures": "It is indispensable," he wrote, "to exert the full force of the law against the offenders, [and] to employ those means which in the last resort are put in the power of the executive." He drafted the stern words of the Presidential Proclamation issued by Washington, warning against interference with the tax collectors and declaring that "the laws will be strictly enforced against the offenders." At the emergency cabinet meeting called by the president in August 1794 as the crisis deepened, he argued forcefully (and ultimately persuasively) for swift military action against the rebels: "Moderation enough has been shown; 'tis time to assume a different tone."

He took, as he often did, to the newspapers in an attempt to marshal public opinion to his side, calling on all to reject the "apostles of anarchy" who were spreading "sedition and popular licentiousness" through the Pennsylvania hills.[5]

> Government is frequently and aptly classed under two descriptions, a government of FORCE and a government of LAWS; the first is the definition of despotism—the last, of liberty. But how can a government of laws exist where the laws are disrespected and disobeyed? **Government supposes control.** It is the POWER by which individuals in society are kept from doing injury to each other and are brought to co-operate to a common end. The instruments by which it must act are either the AUTHORITY of the Laws or FORCE. If the first be destroyed, the last must be substituted; and where this becomes the ordinary instrument of government there is an end to liberty.[6]

5 "Fresh symptoms every moment appear of a dark conspiracy, hostile to your government, to your peace abroad, to your tranquility at home.... Were it not that it might require too lengthy a discussion, it would not be difficult to demonstrate, that a large and well organized Republic can scarcely lose its liberty from any other cause than that of anarchy, to which a contempt of the laws is the high road.... [If] force is not to be used against the seditious combinations of parts of the community to resist the laws... this would be to give a carte blanche to ambition—to licentiousness... The goodly fabric you have established would be rent assunder [sic!], and precipitated into the dust. You knew how to encounter civil war, rather than surrender your liberty to foreign domination—you will not hesitate now to brave it rather than surrender your sovereignty to the tyranny of a faction—you will be as deaf to the apostles of anarchy now as you were to the emissaries of despotism then. Your love of liberty will guide you now as it did then—you know that the POWER of the majority and LIBERTY are inseparable—destroy that, and this perishes.... (Hamilton, *Letters to the American Daily Advertiser* [the "Tully Letters" nos. 3 and 4], Aug. 28, 1794, and Sept. 2, 1794.)

6 Ibid.

And last, but hardly least, when President Washington called for 15,000 federal troops to march on Pittsburgh—the first time in the country's history that the military was called into action against U.S. citizens—who rode into battle as commander of the troops but Hamilton himself!

There wasn't, as it turned, to be much of a battle—the rebellious settlers fled into the hills before the advancing troops, no shots were fired, and the rebellion quickly quieted down (enough so, at least, to allow Hamilton's tax collectors to operate more-or-less freely in the area).

To Hamilton, the Whiskey Rebellion episode was proof (if proof were needed) of the truth of Montesquieu's Law; the new United States was going to have its hands full keeping the peace and maintaining control over its already-enormous territory.[7] After the dust had settled, Hamilton wrote to Washington and called for **permanent** military occupation of the western Pennsylvania hills, a force of 500 infantry and 100 cavalrymen "to be stationed in the disaffected country."

---

7 Jefferson, predictably, saw things differently. To his eye, it was all much ado about nothing, an attempt *to slander the friends of popular rights,* an "excessive and unnecessary military response," as Joseph Ellis put it, "to a healthy and essentially harmless expression of popular discontent by American farmers, [and] his first instinct was to blame Hamilton for the whole sorry mess." *The excise tax,* he wrote to James Madison, *is an infernal one:*

> *You are all swept away in the torrent of governmental opinions. The first error was to admit it by the Constitution; the 2d., to act on that admission; the 3d & last will be to make it the instrument of dismembering the Union, & setting us all afloat to choose which part of it we will adhere to.*

The so-called "rebellion" had been *nothing more than riotous:*

> *There was indeed a meeting to consult about a separation [from the Union]. But to consult on a question does not amount to a determination of that question in the affirmative, still less to the acting on such a determination. But we shall see, I suppose, what the court lawyers, & courtly judges, & would-be ambassadors will make of it.*

> [Hamilton's army is] *the object of laughter, not of fear; 1000 men could have cut off their whole force in a thousand places of the Alleganey.*

> *But the settlers' detestation of the excise law is universal, and has now associated to it a detestation of the government; & that separation which perhaps was a very distant & problematical event, is now near, & certain, & determined in the mind of every man.*

Hamilton, it is probably fair to say in retrospect, won that round; although historians still debate the question, the military operation was largely a success: no shots were actually fired, there was a lot of noise but no real action, two "rebels" were convicted of treason (and later pardoned), federal tax collectors were able subsequently to go about their lawful business without too much interference, and Jefferson's fear—that the use of military force made separation from the Union *near, & certain, & determined in the mind of every man*—appears to have been unfounded.

Without this, the expense incurred will have been essentially fruitless ... The political putrefaction of Pennsylvania is greater than I had any idea of. [!] Without rigor everywhere, our tranquility is likely to be of very short duration, and the next storm will be infinitely worse than the present one.

You can imagine, then, his reaction when, less than a decade later, his old nemesis Jefferson, now president, acquired on behalf of the United States the entire Louisiana Territory—a chunk of territory so big nobody really had the faintest idea how big it was. (Around 827,000 square miles, as it turned out.)

"At best, extremely problematical," Hamilton wrote.

The western region [is] not valuable to the United States for settlement.... Should our own citizens, more enterprising than wise, become desirous of settling this country and emigrat[ing] thither, it must not only be attended with all the injuries of a too widely dispersed population, but, by adding to the great weight of the western part of our territory, must hasten [either] the **dismemberment** of a large portion of our country or a **dissolution** of the Government. (Emphasis Hamilton's]

The new nation, Hamilton wrote, had no need of more territory: "When we consider the **present** extent of the United States, and that not even one-sixteenth part of [our] territory is yet under occupation,"—a curious turn of phrase, that "under occupation"!—"the advantage of the acquisition [of the Louisiana Territory], as it relates to actual settlement, appears too distant and remote to strike the mind of a sober politician with force." The most that could be said for it was that it might allow the United States "at some distant period" to trade the whole territory to Spain in exchange for Florida, a territory "obviously of far greater value to us than all the immense, undefined region west of the [Mississippi] river."

Expansion of the Union, Hamilton believed, could only proceed hand-in-hand with federal power, the new government's ability to project force and to maintain order from its base of operations on the eastern seaboard. Overextend the union beyond that limit, and the result would be, as Hamilton put it, "despotism or anarchy ... dismemberment or dissolution."

Jefferson, of course, had other ideas. Unlike Hamilton, he liked looking west; although he would never actually set foot on the other side of the Alleghenies, he lived, in John Logan Allen's wonderful phrase, "farther west in his mind" than any other major political figure of the time. And when he looked west—with Canada on his right and the Floridas on his left—he saw a very different landscape there than Hamilton did. To Jefferson, the West wasn't a problem to be solved, it was an opportunity to be seized; not a bug, but a feature. He had a vision for the new American nation—remember those "New States" on his map?—and he had a plan to bring it into being.

He was convinced that Montesquieu had been wrong, Montesquieu's "Law" no law at all. Republican government **could** scale; in fact, it could get **stronger** as it got bigger.

> *I have much confidence that we shall proceed successfully for ages to come, and that, contrary to the principle of Montesquieu, it will be seen that **the larger the extent of country, the more firm its republican structure,** if founded, not on conquest, but in principles of compact and equality.*

Its size could be its strength, and its strength could be its size; Montesquieu, turned upside down. The New World, he was convinced, would *furnish proof of the falsehood of Montesquieu's doctrine that a republic can be preserved only in a small territory. The reverse is the truth.*

How would **that** work? How do you build a democratic system that would scale, that would get stronger as it got bigger, and bigger as it got stronger?

It was without historical precedent, and it was going to take some hard thinking, hard work, and new ideas to make it happen. Luckily, Jefferson was never afraid of hard thinking, hard work, or new ideas:

> *Our Revolution . . . presented us an album on which we were free to write what we pleased. We had no occasion to search into musty records, to hunt up royal parchments, or to investigate the laws and institutions of a semi-barbarous ancestry. We appealed to those of nature, and found them engraved on our hearts. . . .*
>
> *[This] chapter of our history furnishes a lesson to man perfectly new. We can no longer say there is nothing new under the sun, for this whole chapter in the history of man is new . . . The great extent of our Republic is new. Its sparse habitation is new. The mighty wave of public opinion which has rolled over it is new. . . . Before the establishment of the American States, nothing was known to history but the man of the Old World, crowded within limits either small or overcharged . . . A government adapted to such men would be one thing; but a very different one, that for the man of these States. . . .*
>
> *My hope of its duration is built much on the enlargement of the resources of life going hand in hand with the enlargement of territory, and the belief that men are disposed to live honestly, if the means of doing so are open to them. . . . I have [the consolation] of other prophets who foretell distant events, that I shall not live to see it falsified. My theory has always been that if we are to dream, the flatteries of hope are as cheap, and pleasanter, than the gloom of despair.*

LOOKING FORWARD

Cyberspace is not the American West of 1787, of course. But like the American West of 1787, cyberspace is (or at least it has been) a Jeffersonian kind of place. Jeffersonians always predominate in new places, because new places attract people who find new places attractive and repel people who do not. Jefferson biographer Joseph Ellis called cyberspace the "perfect Jeffersonian environment," all decentralization and disorder, growth and expansion, a frontier that is constantly expanding and seemingly illimitable. Hamiltonians, though, inevitably make their way to Jeffersonian places (certainly once gold is discovered there!), claims of order and authority and power assert themselves, and struggles over the shape of the place begin in earnest.

> **BOX I.2 JEFFERSON ON CYBERSPACE**
>
> *Were it left to me to decide whether we should have a government without newspapers or newspapers without government, I should not hesitate a moment to prefer the latter.*
> **TJ TO EDWARD CARRINGON, JANUARY 16, 1787**

And like the West of 1787, cyberspace poses some hard questions, and could use some new ideas, about governance, and law, and order, and scale. The engineers have bequeathed to us a remarkable instrument, one that has managed to solve prodigious technical problems associated with communication on a **global** scale. The problem is the one that Jefferson and his contemporaries faced: How do you build "republican" institutions—institutions that respect the equal worth of all individuals and their right to participate in the formation of the rules under which they live—that scale?

⁂

Like baseball players and law book writers, judges have their off days, and the day when Justice Holmes wrote his Carver [260 U.S. 482] opinion was one of his worst.

Grant Gilmore &
Charles L. Black, Jr. (1957)

OCTOBER

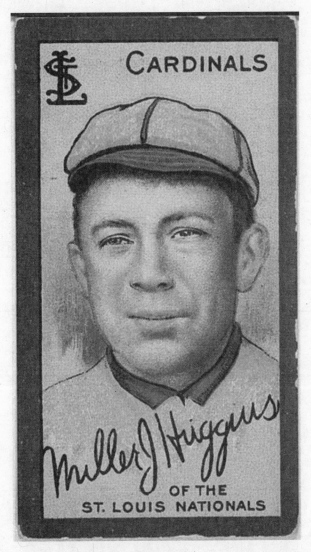

MILLER JAMES HUGGINS

Alumnus, University of Cincinnati College of Law (1902).
See Stuart Schimler, *Miller Huggins, in*
TOM SIMON, DEADBALL STARS OF THE NATIONAL LEAGUE (2004).

❦ OCTOBER ❧

SUN	MON	TUES	WED	THUR	FRI	SAT
31					1	2
3	4	5	6	7	8	9
10	11	12	13	14	15	16
17	18	19	20	21	22	23
24	25	26	27	28	29	30

The Republican mascot surrounded by players from both the Republican (elephant uniforms) and Democratic ("D" uniforms) teams before the game, May 1, 1926. Excitement ran especially high because, as the *Washington Post* had reported on April 14, "Political issues won't count when Democratic and Republican members of Congress go to bat May 1 to fight it out on a baseball diamond in their first game since 1918." The proceeds went to the Women's Congressional Club. *The Congress Ball Game*, WASH. POST., Apr. 28, 1926, at 6.

DEMOCRATS DEFEAT REPUBLICANS' TEAM IN BALL GAME, 12-9

Washington Post, May 2, 1926, at M2

The House of Representatives Republican-Democratic baseball game, at American League park yesterday afternoon, ended in an argument at the end of the seventh inning, when the Republicans, who were trailing on the short end of a 12-to-9 score, mistak[en]ly resorted to strategy and switched their batting order, which placed their heaviest hitters up.

More than 4,000 persons were present. Social and official Washington was well represented, while the House took a day off to attend the game, played for charity.

A baseball, autographed by President Coolidge, was sold for $650 to Representative Sol Bloom, of New York, after some lively bidding between Representative Sosnowski, of Michigan, and Representative Bloom.

Immediately before the game a big parade of the Republicans and Democrats took place, with an elephant and a mule leading the members of their respective parties. "Nick" Altrock, Washington coach and comedian, who was borrowed for the occasion, acted as marshal of the parade around the ball park, amusing the throng with his funny antics. Music was furnished by the army and navy bands.

SPEAKER IN BOX.

Speaker of the House Longworth and his wife, the former Alice Roosevelt, together with Representative and Mrs. Parker Corning, of New York; Senator Gillett and Representative Edith Nourse Rogers, of Massachusetts, occupied the President's box.

Speaker Longworth, who was much amused by the proceedings, displayed the enthusiasm of a sandlotter when he "warmed up" for his task of throwing out the first ball. His colleagues called for him to "sink 'em Nick" and Nick sank them too, although his well oiled soupbone became a trifle lame after more than a dozen heaves for the camera men.

American League park was draped with its best bunting and flags for the occasion. More than two score young girls of the Congressional set donned the white hats and coats of peanut and hot dog venders to help swell the fund for charity.

Representative Clyde Kelly, of Pennsylvania, was the recipient of a huge basket of flowers, presented to him by Speaker Longworth, on his first trip to the plate. Kelly then obliged by crashing out a two-base hit that scored the first run of the game.

Most of the crowd was at the park long before game time. There seemed to be as many women present as men and the women lost no opportunities to razz the "enemy."

The two teams displayed a lot of good, as well as bad baseball. Representative Busby, who pitched for the Democrats got off to a bad start when the Republicans started off with seven runs on six hits, two bases on balls and a hit batsman, but settled down and held his opponents safe thereafter.

Representatives Wilson, Mead and Busby were the hitting heroes of the winners, while Representatives Bachman, Kelly and Updyke collected a majority of the Republicans' hits.

The game proceeded without a hitch until the last half of the seventh inning. The trouble started when Representative Golder, hard-hitting catcher of the Republicans, batted out of turn, in place of Representative Sosnowski, who in his only turn at bat had struck out.

Representative Tolley also batted out of turn and took first when Representative Busby planted one in his ribs. When Representative Bachman, of West Virginia, who had made four consecutive hits, including a double, strode to the plate, the Democrats got a quorum together and besieged the umpires, claiming that the Republicans were trying to steam-roller them and that the side was automatically out.

Not to be outdone, the Republicans gathered their clan and started a filibuster that completely tied up the game. The umpires, unused to congressional "politics," appealed to the scribes in the press box for aid after they had listened to the arguments of the wrangling players for more than 15 minutes.

When the smoke of battle cleared away, the Republicans again were on the short end and the game was called.

DEMOCRATS DEFEAT REPUBLICANS

Republicans	AB	H	O	A	Democrats	AB	H	O	A
Talley, rf	4	1	0	0	Jones, 2b	5	1	2	2
Bachman, 1b	4	4	9	0	Vinson, ss	5	1	0	1
Kelly, 2b	4	3	1	2	Wilson, 1b.	4	3	6	0
Appleby, 3b	3	1	1	1	McMillan, c	4	1	8	0
Ketcham, cf	4	1	0	0	Mead, cf	4	3	1	0
Rowbot'm, lf	1	0	0	0	Lanham, 3b	5	0	0	0
Sosnowski, lf	1	0	0	0	Browning, rf	5	0	0	0
Reese, ss	2	0	1	0	Connery, lf	3	0	0	0
Brum, ss	1	1	0	0	O'Connell, lf	1	0	0	0
Updyke, c, cf	3	2	8	0	Busby, p	4	3	1	2
Golder, c	1	0	0	0	Totals	40	12	18	6
Montgom'y, p	3	0	1	2					
Crowther	1	0	0	0					
Totals	32	13*	21	5					

*Side retired in seventh. Republicans batted out of turn.

Republicans	7	0	0	0	0	2	0	—	9
Democrats	0	3	0	6	2	0	1	—	12

Runs — Jones, Vinson, Wilson (2), McMillan (3), Mead, Lanham, Browning, Connery, Busby, Tolley, Bachman (2), Kelly (2), Appleby, Ketcham, Rowbottom, Golder. Errors — Reese (4), Golder (2), Ketcham, Sosnowski, Vinson (2), Browning, Busby. Two-base hits — Wilson, Mead (2), Bachman, Kelley (2), Updyke. Three-base hit — Busby. Double play — Reese to Kelly to Bachman. Struck out — By Busby, 8; by Montgomery, 8. Passed balls — Updyke, Golder.

UNITED STATES V. CRUZ

Alex Kozinski[†]

Editor's note: As Judge Stephen Reinhardt explained in the opening paragraphs of his opinion for the court (footnote omitted),

> At first glance, there appears to be something odd about a court of law in a diverse nation such as ours deciding whether a specific individual is or is not "an Indian." Yet, given the long and complex relationship between the government of the United States and the sovereign tribal nations within its borders, the criminal jurisdiction of the federal government often turns on precisely this question — whether a particular individual "counts" as an Indian — and it is this question that we address once again today. . . .

> [O]ur circuit has distilled a specific test for determining whether an individual can be prosecuted by the federal government under 18 U.S.C. § 1153, a statute governing the conduct of Indians in Indian Country. We announced that test in United States v. Bruce, 394 F.3d 1215 (9th Cir. 2005), a case that both parties agree controls our analysis today. Because the evidence adduced during Christopher Cruz's trial does not satisfy any of the four factors outlined in the second prong of the Bruce test, we hold that, even when viewed in the light most favorable to the government, his conviction cannot stand. The district court's failure to grant Cruz's motion for judgment of acquittal was plain error, and accordingly we reverse.

Because defendant has the requisite amount of Indian blood, the only question is whether he has "tribal or government recognition as an Indian." *United States v. Bruce*, 394 F.3d 1215, 1223 (9th Cir. 2005) (quoting *United States v. Broncheau*, 597 F.2d 1260, 1263 (9th Cir. 1979) for the "generally accepted test," derived from *United States v. Rogers*, 45 U.S. (4 How.) 567, 573 (1846)). He plainly does. The record discloses that the Blackfeet tribal authorities have accorded Cruz "descendant" status, which entitles

---

[†] Alex Kozinski is chief judge of the United States Court of Appeals for the Ninth Circuit.

him to many of the benefits of tribal membership, including medical treatment at any Indian Health Service facility in the United States, certain educational grants, housing assistance and hunting and fishing privileges on the reservation.

That Cruz may not have taken advantage of these benefits doesn't matter because the test is whether the tribal authorities recognize him as an Indian, not whether he considers himself one. That they do is confirmed by the fact that, when he was charged with an earlier crime on the reservation, the tribal police took him before the tribal court rather than turning him over to state or federal authorities. How that case was finally resolved is irrelevant; what matters is that the tribal authorities protected him from a state or federal prosecution by treating him as one of their own. Finally, Cruz was living on the reservation when he was arrested, another piece of evidence supporting the jury's verdict.

The majority manages to work its way around all of this evidence by taking a stray comment in *Bruce* to the effect that certain factors have been considered in "declining order of importance" and turning it into a four-part balancing test. But *Bruce* was not announcing a rule of law; it was merely reporting what it thought other courts had done: "[C]ourts have considered, in declining order of importance, evidence of [four factors]." 394 F.3d at 1224. *Bruce* did not adopt this as any sort of standard, nor did it have any cause to do so, as nothing in *Bruce* turned on the relative weight of the factors. The majority strains hard to make this part of *Bruce*'s holding, but a fair reading of the opinion discloses that it's not even dicta because it's descriptive rather than prescriptive. We recognized this the last time we applied the test by omitting any reference to the declining order of importance. See *United States v. Ramirez*, 537 F.3d 1075, 1082 (9th Cir. 2008).

Bruce borrowed the "declining order of importance" language from *United States v. Lawrence*, 51 F.3d 150, 152 (8th Cir. 1995), and *Lawrence* itself was quoting the observation of a district judge in an earlier case, *St. Cloud v. United States*, 702 F. Supp. 1456, 1461-62 (D.S.D.1988). The district judge in *St. Cloud* did not cite most of the cases he relied on, so it's hard to tell whether his observation is correct, but he did offer a note of caution that my colleagues overlook: "These factors do not establish a precise formula for determining who is an Indian. Rather, they merely guide the analysis of whether a person is recognized as an Indian." *Id.* at 1461.

This is the opposite of what my colleagues do today: They turn the four factors into a rigid multi-part balancing test, with the various prongs reinforcing or offsetting each other, depending on how they are analyzed.

This is not what the judge in *St. Cloud* had in mind, and certainly nothing like what *Bruce* adopted as the law of our circuit. It is an invention of the majority in our case, designed to take power away from juries and district judges and give it to appellate judges. Nothing in the law, dating back to the Supreme Court's opinion in *Rogers*, justifies this fine mincing of the evidence. The question we must answer is whether there is enough evidence from which a rational jury could have concluded beyond a reasonable doubt that Cruz was recognized as an Indian. Clearly there was, and that's the end of our task.

The majority misreads *Bruce* and misrepresents my position: "Given *Bruce*'s clear admonition that 'tribal enrollment,' and therefore *a fortiori* descendant status, 'is not dispositive of Indian status,' we reject the dissent's argument that mere descendant status with the concomitant eligibility to receive benefits is effectively sufficient to demonstrate 'tribal recognition.'" Maj. op. at 847 (quoting *Bruce*, 394 F.3d at 1224-25). *Bruce* certainly doesn't hold that tribal enrollment is insufficient to support a finding of Indian status. *Bruce* holds the converse: that the absence of tribal enrollment does not preclude finding that defendant is an Indian — which was the question presented here. To suggest, as does the majority, that an individual who is enrolled as a member of a tribe might not be an Indian after all is not only preposterous, it's unnecessary, as no one claims that Cruz was enrolled.

Nor do I maintain, as the majority makes believe, that Cruz's descendant status is enough to make him an Indian. Whether or not it is, there are additional facts here: Cruz's residence on the reservation and the fact that he was previously arrested and brought before the tribal court. The latter is a fact that the *Bruce* majority held to be highly significant. *Bruce* did not consider the disposition of prior tribal court cases relevant and we are not free to disregard the arrest and prosecution by tribal authorities on this spurious basis.

Worse still, after huffing and puffing for 11 hefty paragraphs and 12 chubby footnotes trying to explain why the district court erred at all, the majority concludes in a single opaque sentence that the error is "plain." Just how plain can this error be when the majority has to struggle so long and hard to find any error at all? After complaining bitterly about pointy-headed judges who "slic[e] ever finer and finer distinctions whose practical consequences are seemingly minuscule, if not microscopic," maj. op. at 845, my colleagues pull out a scalpel of their own and proceed to engage in the same exercise, so that "our standards of review continue to multiply, the relationships between them growing more obscure with each iteration." *Id.* at 845. Before reading today's opinion, no one could have guessed its outcome and methodology. Saying that the error is plain eviscerates the "plain" part of the plain error standard. If this is plain error, no error isn't.

Not satisfied with merely reversing the verdict, the majority goes a bridge too far by converting its novel four-part test into a jury instruction. This is wholly unnecessary, as Cruz cannot be tried again for violating 18 U.S.C. § 1153 because of double jeopardy. It is also wrong. We don't instruct juries as to how to weigh the evidence; that is their function, not ours. Yet the majority now requires jurors to assign relative weight to various pieces of evidence presented to them. I am aware of no such instruction anywhere else in our jurisprudence and the majority points to none. It is a bold step into uncharted territory and, in my judgment, an unwise one.

• • • •

The majority engages in vigorous verbal callisthenics to reach a wholly counter-intuitive — and wrong — result. Along the way, it mucks up several already complex areas of the law and does grave injury to our plain error standard of review. I hasten to run in the other direction.

❋ ❋ ❋

As someone said, "Babe never heard the fine print in the promises." Nor did he consult a lawyer. "Hell," an oldtimer said, "you didn't talk to lawyers about things like contracts." [National League President Ford] Frick affirmed this, recalling that in his first year in office, the National League's fee for legal services was less than $500.

Robert W. Creamer (1974)

FIELDS OF LIENS

REAL PROPERTY DEVELOPMENT IN BASEBALL

Robert A. James[†]

Baseball is at one and the same time an idyllic game for children and a gravely serious business for adults. A sport that can be played on a pastoral commons requires, in the world of commerce, space to which some can be admitted and from which others can be excluded — in short, what lawyers call real property. Land must be acquired, grandstands and other improvements must be constructed, and parking and transportation access must be arranged. In these respects, ballparks are like other forms of American urban development.

Yet stadiums are a breed apart from shopping malls, office buildings or municipal centers. They represent the significance of a city, literally as a "major league town," above and beyond their bare economic data. They are founts of media content that create value well past their earnings from in-person attendance. And their reason for being is *baseball*, darn it; even crusty, hard-edged men and women in public life can get misty-eyed and perhaps not entirely rational just thinking about the subject.[1] It remains to be seen whether that peculiar bond between civic leaders and the sport, established by parents and kids entwined over the years in a single pastime, will survive as baseball competes for affection with football, basketball, soccer, skateboarding and video games.

A number of elements of real estate law and development can be illustrated by the country's ballparks. To that end, this article examines the two celebrated homes of the Dodgers, Ebbets Field in Brooklyn and Dodger Stadium in Los Angeles. The journey between these venues is one of the most surveyed subjects in all of the baseball literature. The story features metaphors of one city's decline and another's ascent, a Homeric struggle between two stubborn men, and a seemingly undying memory of monumental betrayal.[2] Transcending all this baggage, I believe that even

---

[†] Rob James is a partner in the San Francisco and Houston offices of Pillsbury Winthrop Shaw Pittman LLP and a lecturer at the University of California, Berkeley, School of Law. A lifelong San Francisco Giants fan, he was counsel for the ballclub on the design and construction contracts for the stadium completed in 2000 and now named AT&T Park. His title pays tribute to "Field of Liens," a story by Matt Smith in the Oct. 30, 2002 S.F. Weekly about an ill-fated minor league stadium.
[1] Several economists have questioned the value of sports clubs to cities and the wisdom of government policies designed to attract or retain them. See SPORTS, JOBS AND TAXES: THE ECONOMICS OF SPORTS TEAMS AND STADIUMS (Roger G. Noll & Andrew S. Zimbalist eds. 1997). Such policies have nonetheless proven resilient for decades.
[2] See, among many published sources with many more details than are covered here, MICHAEL D'ANTONIO, FOREVER BLUE: THE TRUE STORY OF WALTER O'MALLEY, BASEBALL'S MOST CONTROVERSIAL OWNER, AND THE DODGERS OF BROOKLYN AND LOS ANGELES (2009); MICHAEL SHAPIRO, THE LAST GOOD SEASON: BROOKLYN, THE DODGERS, AND THEIR FINAL PENNANT RACE TOGETHER (2003); DORIS KEARNS GOODWIN, WAIT TILL NEXT YEAR (1997); CARL E. PRINCE, BROOKLYN'S DODGERS: THE

the stadiums themselves offer lessons for lawyers and developers alike.

ACT I

A BALLPARK GROWS IN BROOKLYN

Assemblage. For urban infill projects, it is critical to employ a strategy of discreet land acquisition. Charles Ebbets, an architect by profession, became president of the team then known as the Brooklyns[3] in 1898, the year that the proudly independent city of Brooklyn merged into New York City.[4] Desiring to escape the all-wood Washington Park, he had nominees set up a shell corporation that anonymously purchased a number of lots along Bedford Avenue in the "Pigtown" district. Though he attempted to maintain secrecy, word leaked out and some of the forty lotholders were able to hike their sales prices.[5] The land assemblage took roughly four years to complete. Ebbets built a $750,000, 35,000-seat stadium bearing his name, which opened amid much local fanfare in 1913.[6]

Design. Commercial and civic projects often emphasize impressive, even awe-inspiring entryways and architecturally striking public areas, and ballparks are true to form. The design of Ebbets Field by the architect Charles Von Buskirk may not be suited to everyone's aesthetic taste, but a description of the opening defies the reports of later decay:

> Fans who arrived at the main entrance discovered an ornate rotunda with a soaring domed ceiling, gilded ticket booths, and a white Italian marble floor inlaid with red tiles in the pattern of the stitches on a baseball. Overhead, light came from a chandelier designed to look as if it were made of bats and balls. Valet parking service was offered to the swells who came by car, while businessmen were welcomed to use public phones equipped with desks and chairs.[7]

Maintenance. Even a cathedral requires upkeep; absent ongoing investment, a property can lose its reputation and value. The heirs of Ebbets and his partner Edward McKeever quarreled over the team's direction, while their loans from the Brooklyn Trust Company grew ever more precarious — the ballpark encumbered by its mortgages constituted an early example of a "field of liens." To reduce the likelihood of having to foreclose on those liens, the bank recommended that a lawyer named Walter

---

BUMS, THE BOROUGH, AND THE BEST OF BASEBALL, 1947-1957 (1996); NEIL J. SULLIVAN, THE DODGERS MOVE WEST (1987); Peter Ellsworth, The Brooklyn Dodgers' Move to Los Angeles: Was Walter O'Malley Solely Responsible?, 14 NINE 19 (2005). For its part, the O'Malley family has sponsored its own web site, www .walteromalley.com, with photographs, audio clips and documents; D'Antonio was granted access to additional family archives for his work cited above.

[3] Later the Bridegrooms and the Superbas, before they paid homage to their trolley-car environment and became the Dodgers. The name is as inapposite in their adopted city as are those of basketball's Los Angeles Lakers and Utah Jazz.

[4] See generally BROOKLYN USA: THE FOURTH LARGEST CITY IN AMERICA (Rita Seiden Miller ed. 1979); DAVID MCCULLOUGH, THE GREAT BRIDGE (1972).

[5] RED BARBER, RHUBARB PATCH: THE STORY OF THE BROOKLYN DODGERS 31 (1954).

[6] See D'ANTONIO, supra note 2, at 34.

[7] D'ANTONIO, supra note 2, at 36; see Ellsworth, supra note 2, at 20.

Parking at Ebbets Field, circa 1916.

Francis O'Malley join club management; along with Branch Rickey and others, he ultimately acquired equity interests in the team.[8] As a new executive, O'Malley learned that years of neglect had left the stadium both in poor repair and expensive to maintain. Reportedly, only "influence" with an assistant's sister's father-in-law in the New York Fire Department was saving the venue from hazard citations.[9]

Expansion. A developer often has expansions in mind even as the original improvements are being built. Ebbets Field had nowhere to grow, either out or up. While the Yankees could host 67,000 fans and the Giants 54,000, the Dodgers had no means of achieving similar gates for their most popular home games.[10]

Parking and Transportation. Some of the most contentious issues for urban projects revolve around parking and traffic impacts.[11] Unfortunately, the vacant lots around Ebbets accommodated only 700 automobiles. Such contraptions were novelties when the park was built. But as World War II ended and city-dwellers flocked to outer Long Island and New Jersey, the lack of vehicle access threatened to cut ties with the long-time Dodger fan

---

[8] See Andy McCue, "Walter O'Malley," Society for American Baseball Research, SABR Biography Project, available at bioproj.sabr.org (vis. Dec. 12, 2009).

[9] D'ANTONIO, supra note 2, at 90; see Ellsworth, supra note 2, at 20.

[10] The crosstown rivals depended to a great degree on their intra-city contests. The Giants' 11 annual home games against the Dodgers generated fully one-third of the team's revenues from all of its 77 home games. GOODWIN, supra note 2, at 223.

[11] Decades later, the environmental impact report and analysis for the new Giants ballpark in San Francisco required detailed studies of patterns of traffic on surface streets and highway onramps and offramps, and justifications for the omission from the project of a new parking garage. The stadium features access by railroad, rapid transit and municipal transit, bicycle racks, and even ferry service. See Metropolitan Transportation Commission, "Bay Area: A Showcase for Public Transit" (Sept./Oct. 2000), available at www.mtc.ca.gov/news/transactions (vis. Dec. 12, 2009).

base.[12] Attendance languished; for the potential title-clinching Game 6 of the 1952 World Series, there were five thousand empty Ebbets seats.[13] As O'Malley wrote, "Ebbets Field was built in the Trolley car era. There are no trolleys to speak of today but there are automobiles and intelligently planned parkways."[14]

ACT II

CLASH OF THE GOTHAM TITANS

From this point onward, the story of the Dodgers' homes becomes more idiosyncratic. The experience of the club may be in a league of its own, but it nonetheless has applications for other types of real property development.

By the 1950s, the specter of "community antenna" television haunted the entertainment industry. Still in its infancy, cable TV promised new revenues for baseball game broadcasts and uncertain positive and negative impacts on attendance. Installation of lighting for night games added to most teams' capital and operational expenses. The Dodgers fared better than other clubs with these changes in the short term. But a good investor like O'Malley was more concerned about the future, and he set his sights on a new location.[15]

Contrary to urban legend, O'Malley appears to have made good faith efforts to relocate within Brooklyn — albeit always with a businessman's eye for profit.[16] Given the vital importance of transportation access, the Dodgers focused on sites adjacent to the Long Island Rail Road and connecting transit lines. Futuristic designs were produced, including a retractable roof facility planned by Norman Bel Geddes and a translucent geodesic dome conceived by R. Buckminster Fuller.[17]

---

[12] See ROGER KAHN, THE BOYS OF SUMMER xv (1972). "Ebbets Field was located miles away from any expressway and, with insufficient rail facilities and limited parking, did not have the amenities necessary for a thriving ballpark." Ellsworth, supra note 2, at 22. See also EDWARD G. WHITE, CREATING THE NATIONAL PASTIME: BASEBALL TRANSFORMS ITSELF 1903-1953 at 46 (1996).

[13] See D'ANTONIO, supra note 2, at 250. Home attendance during the Dodgers' pennant-winning 1955 and 1956 seasons averaged only 16,000 per game.

[14] Quoted in SHAPIRO, supra note 2, at 73. See also David W. Chen, Nothing Sub About Us, Suburban Fans Say, N.Y. TIMES (Oct. 23, 2000) (most fans attending the 2000 Mets-Yankees "Subway Series" arrived by car).

[15] "Similar profits at that time certainly convinced the large American car companies that they had nothing to worry about. The difference in management foresight was apparent a decade later . . . . O'Malley was basking in higher profits in the Los Angeles sunshine because he had recognized that his 1950s profits cloaked problems that needed to be solved." McCue, supra note 8.

[16] "O'Malley was unquestionably a shrewd businessman unaffected by sentiment in his operation of the Dodgers, but he did not scheme to move the Dodgers to Los Angeles. . . . [He] did not move the [team] until it became evident that a stadium was not going to be built in New York." Ellsworth, supra note 2, at 35. He expected the city to condemn the land and build the stadium, but was prepared to pay significant rentals and gross receipt royalties. See D'ANTONIO, supra note 2.

[17] See SHAPIRO, supra note 2; GOODWIN, supra note 2, at 223. The designs were published in magazines such as Collier's and Mechanix Illustrated. See Ellsworth, supra note 2, at 24-25. Photographs of a retractable dome sketch, and of Fuller and O'Malley with geodesic dome models, are available on walteromalley.com.

Astride the path of O'Malley's proposals loomed Robert Moses, the "power broker" of all New York development in the era.[18] Again contrary to urban legend, Moses was no enemy of baseball itself, but he did firmly believe that a stadium should sit on the outskirts of the city, served by highways rather than by surface streets or public transit. Indeed, his early vision for a ballpark near the 1939 World's Fair site, in the Flushing Meadows district of Queens, was finally realized with Shea Stadium.[19] The two men maneuvered themselves into an intractable duel, thrusting and parrying for several years over many sites and mutual accusations.

A bilateral conflict during project development sometimes requires the intervention of a third party. The lawyer in O'Malley seized on the possibility of an external solution to the impasse. Title I of the Federal Housing Act of 1949 (the "FHA") offered federal funds for acquiring land for "development or redevelopment for predominantly residential uses."[20] The law would soon be used for private developments contributing in some manner to what became known as "urban renewal," and O'Malley suggested to Moses that the Dodgers were worthy recipients of such a program's benefits, courtesy of Uncle Sam. The cities of Baltimore and Milwaukee took advantage of the FHA for similar purposes. And in 1954 the U.S. Supreme Court held, in *Berman v. Parker*, that a District of Columbia law constitutionally allowed non-blighted private property in a blighted area to be taken for private development with a public purpose; the case is best known today as a prologue to the controversial *Kelo v. City of New London* decision.[21]

Moses expressed horror at the prospect of helping O'Malley in such a fashion. In correspondence, he stated flatly that a ballpark could not be included in a "slum-clearance project." In fact, Moses had his sights set on other forms of equally private improvements that would be funded by his FHA grants. (Among them was a project awarded to Fred Trump, a prominent developer who kept a lower profile than does his son Donald.) Mayor Robert Wagner's legal staff came forward with arguments for using public authority to build a stadium, but it was too little and too late. By 1957, Moses had made clear that he would not grant approval to support relocation in any part of Brooklyn that the Dodgers considered acceptable.[22]

---

[18] See generally ROBERT A. CARO, THE POWER BROKER: ROBERT MOSES AND THE FALL OF NEW YORK (1974). For 50 years, Moses oversaw almost every major improvement in the city, including the United Nations Headquarters and Lincoln Center, displacing some half-million residents in the process. His official titles included New York Parks commissioner and head of the Triborough Bridge and Tunnel Authority, Construction Commission and Slum Clearance Committee.

[19] According to Caro, Moses had envisioned a baseball park in Flushing Meadows "since the 1930s, if not the 1920s." Zack O'Malley Greenburg, Who Framed Walter O'Malley?, FORBES (Apr. 14, 2009). Shea Stadium opened in 1962 as the first home of the New York Mets, bearing the color blue for the departed Dodgers and the color orange for the departed Giants. Shea has been replaced with Citi Field, whose exterior is designed in turn to resemble that of Ebbets.

[20] Housing Act of 1949, Pub. L. No. 81-171, tit. I, § 110(c), 63 Stat. 413 (1949).

[21] Berman v. Parker, 348 U.S. 26 (1954); Kelo v. City of New London, 545 U.S. 469 (2005).

[22] Sites may have been available in the Bedford-Stuyvesant and Brownsville districts, which O'Malley rejected, possibly on grounds of the neighborhoods' eco-

The ultimate weapon of any real estate investor is the threatened alternative — the credible statement of a proponent, lessee or purchaser that it will go elsewhere if terms cannot be reached with the municipality, lessor or vendor. The Dodgers played seven games in Jersey City in 1956 and again in 1957, and sold Ebbets Field, reserving a three-year leaseback. With the fading of efforts of the St. Louis Browns, Washington Senators and Kansas City Athletics to move to Los Angeles, O'Malley opened up communications with representatives of the California city. He ostentatiously hosted Angelenos, with New York reporters present, at spring training in Vero Beach, Florida in 1957. He also encouraged Horace Stoneham, the owner of the New York Giants, to explore prospects in San Francisco rather than in Minneapolis. O'Malley rightly reasoned that the other team owners, concerned with travel expenses, would not approve a single West Coast move — but might approve two in tandem.

The Giants proclaimed their relocation to San Francisco in August 1957 while the Dodgers quietly announced their move to Los Angeles in October, whereupon O'Malley entered eternal ignominy in Brooklyn.[23] The last game at Ebbets Field was witnessed by 6,702 souls. A wrecking ball swung into the old ballpark in February 1960. On the site now stands the Ebbets Field Apartments, a high-rise housing project whose grounds feature a sign reading "NO BALLPLAYING."[24]

Act III

A Ballad of Chávez Ravine

The quest for major league baseball in Los Angeles pulled the Dodgers into the tortuous story of the Chávez Ravine district — the last vacant

---

nomic and racial makeup. On one of his preferred locations, at Flatbush and Atlantic, now stands the new Barclays Center basketball stadium designed by Frank Gehry.

The recent backlash against Moses rather than O'Malley as the proximate cause of Brooklyn's loss of the Dodgers, see SHAPIRO, supra note 2, may be overstated. The Dodgers had lukewarm support throughout the city government. "[Moses] may have been right to argue that a privately owned baseball stadium for a privately owned baseball team did not conform to the 'public purpose' and should not have been even partly financed with federal funds." David Nasaw, Hitler, Stalin, O'Malley and Moses, N.Y. TIMES (May 25, 2003) (review of SHAPIRO, supra note 2).

[23] Reactions expressing betrayal are legion. Three samples will suffice:

"In the hearts of Brooklyn fans, O'Malley had secured his place in a line of infamy which now crossed the centuries from Judas Iscariot to Benedict Arnold to Walter F. O'Malley. Effigies of the Dodgers owner were burned on the streets of Brooklyn." GOODWIN, supra note 2, at 226.

"O'Malley's reputation only worsens with the passage of time. There is no loss of emotion even in the twenty-first century. Such perpetuation of emotional loss into the next generation suggests just how strong the symbolic relationship between Brooklyn and the Dodgers was." Ellsworth, supra note 2, at 35.

"The Dodgers were more than a business. They represented a cultural totem, a tangible symbol of the community and its values." SULLIVAN, supra note 2, at 18.

[24] See D'ANTONIO, supra note 2, at 250; Greenburg, supra note 18.

downtown sector, lying between the Hollywood and Pasadena freeways. For decades, the neighborhood had filled with shacks and houses principally of Mexican-American families.[25] The city housing authority used an FHA grant to acquire properties for the express purpose of constructing 3,360 replacement residences, part of the "Elysian Park Heights" development designed by Richard Neutra. Those who sold out were often promised first priority on the planned units. But a 1952 referendum rejected a housing project in the Ravine, and the city acquired the properties in 1953 for a fraction of the acquisition cost, on condition that the land be used for "public purposes only."[26] Eminent domain was used to claim the final properties. In 1959, the last resident was televised being physically carried out of her home, which was quickly bulldozed.[27]

Mayor Norris Poulson, county supervisor Kenneth Hahn and city councilwoman Rosalind Wyman persistently courted O'Malley. However, the savvy negotiator once disembarked from his airplane at LAX wearing a lapel pin reading "Keep the Dodgers in Brooklyn," and professed a desire for a ballpark not in the Ravine but on the west side of town, the home of the entertainment industry and the wealthier enclaves. Similar strategies have been wielded by many tenants — their current property is a gem when speaking with other owners, and an eyesore when speaking with their current landlord.

In 1957, O'Malley acquired the Los Angeles Angels, formerly the farm club of the Chicago Cubs, and their ballpark. The stage was thus set for a grand exchange between local government and the Dodgers. The real estate terms (setting aside complex monetary commitments on both sides) were that the team would convey the Angels' "little Wrigley Field" to the city in return for fee simple absolute title to up to three hundred acres in the Ravine, complete with public promises to construct freeway access improvements.

The economics, wisdom and legality of the swap were all exposed to intense public scrutiny. After all, the voters in 1955 had rejected a bond proposal to use public funds for a ballpark on the very site. Petitions were circulated calling for a public vote on the Dodgers transaction — though the biggest detractors were owners of the San Diego Padres minor league club and other competing businesses, not the representatives of the evicted residents. Separate lawsuits alleged that the deal exceeded the city council's authority and was unconstitutional, and two superior courts ruled in the plaintiffs' favor. But the voters narrowly endorsed the exchange in a June 1958 referendum, after a pro-Dodger telethon featuring Debbie Reynolds, Dean Martin, Jerry Lewis and Ronald Reagan. Likewise,

---

[25] For artists' impressions of the district's social culture, see DON NORMARK, CHAVEZ RAVINE, 1949 (2003); RY COODER, CHAVEZ RAVINE (Nonesuch Records 2005); Lynn Becker, ArchitectureChicago Plus (review of Cooder's "ballads of Chavez Ravine"), available at arcchicago.blogspot.com (vis. Dec. 12, 2009).

[26] See Public Housing and the Brooklyn Dodgers: Los Angeles, Double Play by City Hall in the Ravine, FRONTIER (June 1957), available at www.library.ucla.edu/libraries/special/scweb (vis. Dec. 12, 2009).

[27] A documentary film narrated by Cheech Marin, CHÁVEZ RAVINE: A LOS ANGELES STORY (Bullfrog Films 2003), includes footage of the evictions. On condemnation for sports facilities generally, see Tyson E. Hubbard, For the Public's Use? Eminent Domain in Stadium Construction, 15 SPORTS LAW. J. 173 (2008).

the California Supreme Court reversed the lower court decisions, and the U.S. Supreme Court denied a writ of certiorari in October 1959.[28]

Many developers find that the entitlements process — the securing of rights to pursue the project from public authorities and from businesses affected by the development — is the largest challenge for the viability and cost of an urban project. Remaining properties not owned by the city, appraised at $93,000, wound up requiring over a half million dollars to acquire; the West Coast minor league clubs demanded and received compensation for the Giants' and Dodgers' entry into their markets. Unexpectedly high rent needed to be paid for the Los Angeles Coliseum while the new stadium was built. O'Malley found the interest rate and closing fees quoted by Los Angeles banks for the construction loans to be unattractive. The delays and logistical challenges of construction also complicated the financing of the new venue.

Help arrived from an unlikely source, the advertising appetite of Union Oil Company of California. The company's chairman, Reese Taylor, had been instrumental in the success of the "Bring Baseball to Los Angeles" drive. Union Oil became prime lender, advancing $8 million (interest-free and payment-free for the first two years) in return for broadcasting and publicity rights and — a natural in Southern California — a franchise for a Union 76 gasoline service station in the parking lot.[29]

The new "field of liens" was certainly more favorable for the club than was the mortgaged old park in Flatbush. The Union Oil arrangement illustrates the capability of a sports asset to generate revenue far beyond that gleaned from onsite visitors. It bears many characteristic aspects of ballpark development: an enthusiastic booster of civic pride, and of the game itself, had offered above-market value to be affiliated with the ballclub, the venue, and their associated media and transportation rights.

O'Malley's field was touted as the "last privately built baseball park"[30] until the completion of the San Francisco Giants' new stadium in 2000. It was conceived in a favorable property exchange and nurtured with generous commercial terms, all bestowed on an eagerly coveted market entrant. In any event, the park's design is undeniably classic. Of the facilities built in its era, the colorful Dodger Stadium most retains its appeal for players and spectators.[31]

In the park's inaugural 1962 season, the Dodgers sold a major league record 2.7 million tickets and continued their position as one of the stronger sports franchises. Walter O'Malley's son Peter became president in 1970; Walter died in 1979 and was inducted into the Hall of Fame in 2008. The O'Malley family sold the team in 1997 to Rupert Murdoch's News Corporation, which justified the acquisition as a source of content

---

[28] See Cary S. Henderson, Los Angeles and the Dodger War, 1957-62, S. CAL. Q., Fall 1980, at 261-86 (detailed description of terms and negotiations); City of Los Angeles v. Superior Court, 51 Cal. 2d 423, 333 P.2d 745, cert. denied, 361 U.S. 30 (1959).

[29] See D'ANTONIO, supra note 2, at 289-90.

[30] Steven A. Riess, Historical Perspectives on Sports and Public Policy, in THE ECONOMICS AND POLITICS OF SPORTS FACILITIES 1, 30 (Wilbur C. Rich ed. 2000).

[31] "From dugout seats to in-stadium restaurants, to a message board to terraced parking lots removing the need for people to climb stairs or ramps to their seats, Dodger Stadium was full of new ideas. It was the first large baseball stadium built without pillars that blocked the view from some seats." McCue, supra note 8.

This conveyance is made by the Grantor and is accepted by the Grantee upon the condition that the Grantee shall cause to be constructed on said real property, at Grantee's cost and expense, a modern baseball stadium, seating not less than fifty thousand (50,000) people; provided that a breach of said condition above set forth, or any re-entry by reason of such breach, shall not defeat or render invalid the lien of any mortgage or deed of trust made in good faith and for value as to said property or any part thereof; but said condition shall be binding upon and effective against any owner of said property whose title is acquired by foreclosure or trustee's sale or convey-

ance in lieu thereof; and provided further that said stadium shall be deemed to have been constructed in compliance with said condition and said condition shall thereupon be and become null and void upon the issuance of a Certificate of Occupancy with respect to said stadium by the Department of Building and Safety of The City of Los Angeles.

This deed is made in accordance with the provisions of Ordinance No. 116,489 of The City of Los Angeles.

IN WITNESS WHEREOF, The City of Los Angeles, by its City Council has caused these presents to be executed on its behalf, by its Mayor, and its corporate seal to be hereto affixed by its City Clerk, this _16th_ day of _August_ , 19_60_.

THE CITY OF LOS ANGELES

By _____
                          Mayor

From pages 13 and 14 of the grant deed for the Chávez Ravine property.

for its widespread media outlets, particularly in Asia.[32] The club and its stadium are now owned by Frank McCourt, who is by profession a real property developer.

🏰   🏰   🏰

The Dodgers' move from Brooklyn to Los Angeles had effects in a number of economic, political and legal dimensions. Scholars have noted that it anticipated the "issues that dominate contemporary stadium politics . . . public versus private development, eminent domain, competing economic development strategies, neighborhood resistance and fragmented local political processes."[33] As illustrated above, many of these issues come up in other forms of high-stakes real estate development. The signal differences between ballparks and other properties are rather less tangible: the capacity for producing value from afar through media both old and new, and the deeply rooted emotions and memories that connect communities and generations through sport.

✳ ✳ ✳

Before 1957, New York lawyers chose juries inexpensively and expeditiously by asking just one question: What baseball team do you root for?

    If the juror answered, "Yankees," the defense exercised a peremptory challenge. If the juror said, "Dodgers," the prosecution exercised the challenge. But Giants fans were eminently acceptable to both sides, under a tacit understanding that they were the only reasonable people in town.

Burt Neuborne (1983)

---

[32] See Robert V. Bellamy, Jr. & James R. Walker, Whatever Happened to Synergy? MLB as Media Product, 13 NINE 19 (2005); Sallie Hofmeister, Deal Shows Use of Teams to Build a Global TV Empire, L.A. TIMES (Mar. 20, 1998); Sallie Hofmeister, Murdoch Deal Sets Stage for Fox Challenge to ESPN, L.A. TIMES (June 24, 1997).

[33] Riess, supra note 30, at 29, citing CHARLES C. EUCHNER, PLAYING THE FIELD: WHY SPORTS TEAMS MOVE AND CITIES FIGHT TO KEEP THEM 19 (1993).

CONSTITUTIONALITY OF THE RONALD REAGAN CENTENNIAL COMMISSION ACT OF 2009

MEMORANDUM OPINION FOR THE ACTING ASSISTANT ATTORNEY
GENERAL FOR THE OFFICE OF LEGISLATIVE AFFAIRS

Martin S. Lederman[†]

The Ronald Reagan Centennial Commission Act of 2009 (H.R. 131, or the "Act") would create a Ronald Reagan Centennial Commission with responsibility to "plan, develop, and carry out such activities as the Commission considers fitting and proper to honor Ronald Reagan on the occasion of the 100th anniversary of his birth." *Id.* § 3(1). Six of the eleven commissioners would be members of Congress, appointed by congressional leadership (*id.* § 4(a)), raising concerns under the Appointments Clause, the Ineligibility Clause, and the separation of powers. To ameliorate these concerns, we recommend amending subsection 3(1) of the bill to make clear that the Commission would be responsible for making advice and recommendations as to the planning, developing, and carrying out of the contemplated commemorative activities. We further recommend designating an Executive Branch official as the officer responsible for considering the advice and recommendations of the Commission and then "planning, developing and carrying out" the ceremonial events. The Act could require that these events include participatory roles for members of both branches, but operational control should remain with the designated Executive Branch official.

I

The Ronald Reagan Centennial Commission (the "Commission") created by the Act would be composed of the following eleven members:

[†] Deputy Assistant Attorney General. This opinion was issued on April 21, 2009.

(1) The Secretary of the Interior.

(2) Four members appointed by the President after considering the recommendations of the Board of Trustees of the Ronald Reagan Foundation.

(3) Two Members of the House of Representatives appointed by the Speaker of the House of Representatives.

(4) One Member of the House of Representatives appointed by the minority leader of the House of Representatives.

(5) Two Members of the Senate appointed by the majority leader of the Senate.

(6) One Member of the Senate appointed by the minority leader of the Senate.

H.R. 131, § 4(a). Six of the eleven members, therefore, would be members of Congress, appointed by other members of Congress. The Commission would have responsibility to

(1) plan, develop, and carry out such activities as the Commission considers fitting and proper to honor Ronald Reagan on the occasion of the 100th anniversary of his birth;

(2) provide advice and assistance to Federal, State, and local governmental agencies, as well as civic groups to carry out activities to honor Ronald Reagan on the occasion of the 100th anniversary of his birth;

(3) develop activities that may be carried out by the Federal Government to determine whether the activities are fitting and proper to honor Ronald Reagan on the occasion of the 100th anniversary of his birth; and

(4) submit to the President and Congress reports pursuant to section 7.

Id. § 3. To fulfill these responsibilities, the Commission would be empowered to appoint an executive director and hire staff (*id.* § 5(a)-(b)), to "procure temporary and intermittent services" of experts and consultants (*id.* § 5(e)), and to "enter into contracts with and compensate government and private agencies or persons" (*id.* § 6(f)). Positions on the Commission would be uncompensated (*id.* § 4(f)) and would last until the duties of the Commission are complete, "but not later than May 30, 2011" (*id.* § 8(a)).

II

Legislation of this nature, creating a commemorative commission composed of representatives of multiple branches, has ample historical precedent.[1] It is not unconstitutional for such commissions to perform advisory

---

[1] *See, e.g.*, Pub. L. No. 91-332, § 2(a), 84 Stat. 427 (1970) (creating a National Parks Centennial Commission, consisting of four members of the Senate appointed by the President of the Senate;

functions. Nor is there any constitutional problem with representatives of multiple branches participating in ceremonial events. Congress also possesses the authority to plan, develop and carry out ceremonial activities of its own that are clearly in aid of the functions of the Legislative Branch.[2] However, when the responsibilities of members of hybrid commissions extend beyond providing advice or recommendations to the Executive Branch, or participating in ceremonial activities, to exercising operational control over a statutorily prescribed national commemoration, then the Executive Branch has consistently raised constitutional objections.[3] Spe-

---

four members of the House appointed by the Speaker of the House; the Secretary of the Interior; and six presidential appointees); Pub. L. No. 98-101, § 4(a), 97 Stat. 719 (1983) (creating a Commission on the Bicentennial of the Constitution, consisting of 20 presidential appointees; the Chief Justice of the United States; the President pro tempore of the Senate; and the Speaker of the House); Pub. L. No. 99-624, § 4(a), 100 Stat. 3497 (1986) (creating a Dwight David Eisenhower Centennial Commission, consisting of the President pro tempore of the Senate; the Speaker of the House; six Senators appointed by the President pro tempore of the Senate; six members of the House appointed by the Speaker; six Presidential appointees; and the Archivist of the United States); Pub. L. No. 105-389, § 4(a), 112 Stat. 3486 (1998) (creating a Centennial of Flight Commission, consisting of the Director of the National Air and Space Museum of the Smithsonian Institution; the Administrator of the National Aeronautics and Space Administration; the chairman of the First Flight Centennial Foundation of North Carolina; the chairman of the 2003 Committee of Ohio; the head of a United States aeronautical society; and the Administrator of the Federal Aviation Administration); Pub. L. No. 106-408, § 303(b)(1), 114 Stat. 1782 (2000) (creating a National Wildlife Refuge System Centennial Commission, consisting of the Director of the United States Fish and Wildlife Service; up to ten persons appointed by the Secretary of the Interior; the chairman and ranking minority member of the Committee on Resources of the House of Representatives and of the Committee on Environment and Public Works of the Senate; and the congressional representatives of the Migratory Bird Conservation Commission).

[2] See, e.g., Capitol Visitor Center Act, Pub. L. No. 110-437, § 402(b)(1), 122 Stat. 4983, 4991-92 (Oct. 20, 2008), to be codified at 2 U.S.C. § 2242(b)(1) ("In providing for the direction, supervision, and control of the Capitol Guide Service, the Architect of the Capitol, upon recommendation of the Chief Executive Officer, is authorized to . . . subject to the availability of appropriations, establish and revise such number of positions of Guide in the Capitol Guide Service as the Architect of the Capitol considers necessary to carry out effectively the activities of the Capitol Guide Service.").

[3] Constitutionality of Resolution Establishing United States New York World's Fair Commission, 39 Op. Att'y Gen. 61, 62 (1937) (Attorney General Cummings) ("In my opinion those provisions of the joint resolution establishing a Commission composed largely of members of the Congress and authorizing them to appoint a United States Commissioner General and two Assistant Commissioners for the New York World's Fair, and also providing for the expenditure of the appropriation made by the resolution and for the administration of the resolution generally amount to an unconstitutional invasion of the province of the Executive"); H.R. Doc. No. 75-252, at 2 (1937) (message of President Roosevelt vetoing joint resolution that would have authorized federal participation in 1939 World's Fair and quoting opinion of Attorney General Cummings above as basis); Statement on Signing the Bill Establishing a Commission on the Bicentennial of the United States Constitution, Sept. 29, 1983, in II Public Papers of the President: Ronald Reagan 1390 (1983) ("I welcome the participation of the Chief Justice, the President pro tempore of the

cifically, legislative involvement in the proposed Commission would be constitutionally problematic for several reasons.

First, the Appointments Clause requires that "Officers of the United States" be appointed by the President with the Senate's advice and consent or, in cases of inferior officers, either by that same process or by the President alone, by Courts of Law, or by Heads of Departments. U.S. Const. art. II, § 2, ¶ 2. An Officer of the United States is an appointee to an "office" whose duties constitute the exercise of "significant authority pursuant to the laws of the United States."[4]

For purposes of the Appointments Clause, an "office" "embraces the ideas of tenure, duration, emolument, and duties." *United States v. Hartwell*, 73 U.S. (6 Wall.) 385, 393 (1867). The commissioners here would not receive compensation for their services (H.R. 131, § 4(f) ("Members shall serve without pay")), and the positions they are to fill would exist for no longer than two years (*id.* § 8(a) ("The Commission may terminate on such date as the Commission may determine after it submits its final report pursuant to section 7(c), but not later than May 30, 2011")). Nevertheless, the duties of the commissioners would not be "occasional and intermittent."[5] They would be continuing during the period of time necessary for the exercise of the important government duties assigned to the

---

Senate, and the Speaker of the House of Representatives in the activities of the Commission [on the Bicentennial of the Constitution]. However, because of the constitutional impediments contained in the doctrine of the separation of powers, I understand that they will be able to participate only in ceremonial or advisory functions of the Commission, and not in matters involving the administration of the Act. Also, in view of the incompatibility clause of the Constitution, any Member of Congress appointed by me pursuant to Section 4(a)(1) of this Act may serve only in a ceremonial or advisory capacity."); *Appointments to the Commission on the Bicentennial of the Constitution*, 8 Op. O.L.C. 200 (1984) ("*Bicentennial Commission*") (proposing practical solution to constitutional concerns raised by presence of members of Congress on Commission on the Bicentennial of the Constitution).

[4] *Buckley v. Valeo*, 424 U.S. 1, 126 (1976); *see also United States v. Hartwell*, 73 U.S. (6 Wall.) 385, 393 (1867) ("An office is a public station, or employment, conferred by the appointment of government. The term embraces the ideas of tenure, duration, emolument, and duties."); *The Constitutional Separation of Powers Between the President and Congress*, 20 Op. O.L.C. 124, 148 (1996) ("Dellinger Memo") ("An appointee (1) to a position of employment (2) within the federal government (3) that carries significant authority pursuant to the laws of the United States is required to be an 'Officer of the United States.'").

[5] *See United States v. Germaine*, 99 U.S. 508, 511-12 (1879) ("If we look to the nature of [the civil surgeon's] employment, we think it equally clear that he is *not* an officer. . . . [T]he duties are not continuing and permanent, and they *are* occasional and intermittent.") (emphasis in original); *see also Auffmordt v. Hedden*, 137 U.S. 310, 326-27 (1890) ("[The merchant appraiser] has no general functions, nor any employment which has any duration as to time, or which extends over any case further than as he is selected to act in that particular case. . . . His position is without tenure, duration, continuing emolument, or continuous duties . . . . Therefore, he is not an 'officer,' within the meaning of the clause.").

Commission. In *Morrison v. Olson*, 487 U.S. 654 (1987), the Supreme Court held that it was "clear" that an "independent counsel" under the Ethics in Government Act of 1978, 28 U.S.C. §§ 591-599 (1982 & Supp V) — a position that was temporary and case-specific, but expected to last for an extended period, with ongoing, continuous duties, and termination only upon a determination that all matters within the counsel's jurisdiction were substantially complete — "is an 'officer' of the United States, not an 'employee.'" *Id.* at 671 n.12. Consistent with this holding, our Office has concluded that members of an unpaid commission similar to the Reagan Commission would hold offices in the constitutional sense.[6] Moreover, the Commissioners would exercise significant governmental authority. Although some of the functions of the Commission here would be merely advisory (H.R. 131, § 3(2), (3), (4)), the Commission would also have the authority to "plan, develop, and carry out such activities as the Commission considers fitting and proper to honor Ronald Reagan" (*id.* § 3(1)). This Office has previously indicated that "carrying out a limited number of commemorative events and projects" is a "clearly executive" function and that the planning and development of commemorative events constitutes "significant authority" for Appointments Clause purposes if the plans are final (i.e., not just advisory).[7] In light of these precedents, we conclude the Commissioners would be Officers of the United States. Therefore the bill's prescription that members of Congress shall appoint certain of the Commissioners would violate the Appointments Clause.

An additional constitutional problem arises from the fact that six of the Commissioners would not only be appointed by members of Congress but would themselves be members of Congress. The Ineligibility Clause states

---

[6] *See, e.g.*, Memorandum for L. Anthony Sutin, Acting Assistant Attorney General, Office of Legislative Affairs, from William Michael Treanor, Deputy Assistant Attorney General, Office of Legal Counsel, *Re: Centennial of Flight Commission — Airport Improvement Program Reauthorization, H.R. 4057*, at 1 (Oct. 1, 1998) ("*Centennial of Flight Commission*") (objecting on Appointments Clause grounds to H.R. 4057); *see also* H.R. 4057, 105th Cong. § 804(c)(1) (engrossed amendment as agreed to by Senate, Sept. 25, 1998) (providing that "members of the Commission shall serve without pay or compensation"). *Cf. Offices of Trust*, 15 Op. Att'y Gen. 187, 188 (1877) (concluding, for purposes of the Emoluments Clause and with respect to commissioners of the United States Centennial Commission, that "though their duties are of a special and temporary character, they may properly be called officers of the United States during the continuance of their official functions"); *In re Corliss*, 11 R.I. 639 (1877) (holding that member of same Centennial Commission held "Office of Trust or Profit" under U.S. Const., art. II, § 1, and was therefore disqualified from serving as a presidential elector).

[7] *Bicentennial Commission*, 8 Op. O.L.C. at 200; *Centennial of Flight Commission* at 1 ("The Commission is also authorized . . . to plan and develop commemorative activities itself . . . . In accordance with prior precedent of this Office, these functions have been understood to encompass significant authority for purposes of the Appointments Clause.").

that "[n]o Senator or Representative shall, during the Time for which he was elected, be appointed to any civil Office under the Authority of the United States, which shall have been created, or the Emoluments whereof shall have been increased during such time." U.S. Const. art. I, § 6, cl. 2. As we have previously advised, "[t]he most common problem under the Ineligibility Clause arises from legislation that creates a commission or other entity and simultaneously requires that certain of its members be Representatives or Senators, either *ex officio* or by selection or nomination by the congressional leadership. Unless the congressional members participate only in advisory or ceremonial roles, or the commission itself is advisory or ceremonial, the appointment of members of Congress to the commission would violate the Ineligibility Clause." Dellinger Memo, 20 Op. O.L.C. at 160. Here, the legislation contemplates that Commissioners would not simply be participating in or advising on ceremonial events but that they would also be responsible for planning, developing, and carrying out such events as part of a national commemoration. In such circumstances, the Commission's composition would run afoul of the Ineligibility Clause.

Finally, independent of the concerns under the Appointments and Ineligibility Clauses, the Commission's composition would raise constitutional concerns under the anti-aggrandizement principle. "[O]nce Congress makes its choice in enacting legislation, its participation ends. Congress can thereafter control the execution of its enactment only indirectly — by passing new legislation." *Bowsher v. Synar*, 478 U.S. 714, 733-34 (1986); *see also INS v. Chadha*, 462 U.S. 919 (1983). A statute may not give members of Congress, or congressional agents, the authority to perform Executive Branch functions. Accordingly, "designating a member of Congress to serve on a commission with any executive functions, even in what was expressly labeled a ceremonial or advisory role, may render the delegation of significant governmental authority to the commission unconstitutional as a violation of the anti-aggrandizement principle." Dellinger Memo, 20 Op. O.L.C. at 160 n.95 (citing *FEC v. NRA Political Victory Fund*, 6 F.3d 821 (D.C. Cir. 1993) (invalidating statute that authorized agents of Congress to be members of the Federal Election Commission)). This problem would persist, moreover, even if only a minority of Commissioners were members or agents of Congress, and even if the congressional members were not permitted to exercise voting authority. *See NRA Political Victory Fund*, 6 F.3d at 826-27 (members of Congress could not serve on the FEC even in non-voting capacity).[8]

To address these constitutional concerns, the functions of the Commission in subsection 3(1) should be limited to giving advice and making recommendations with respect to planning, developing and carrying out commemorative activities. In such an advisory capacity, the Commission could remain composed as it is under section 4(a) of the Act. The Act should then assign an Executive Branch official the responsibility to consider the advice of the Commission and then to "plan, develop and carry out such activities as [the official] considers fitting and proper to honor Ronald Reagan on the occasion of the 100th anniversary of his birth." The Act could still require that any ceremonial events include a role for members of Congress. As long as operational control remains with the Executive Branch official, the Appointments Clause and Ineligibility Clause concerns would be assuaged, and there would be no impermissible congressional aggrandizement.

Lawyers know better than to attempt to predict the outcome of lawsuits, but not being a lawyer, I am not handicapped by any such restraint. If Pete Rose ever sues baseball seeking to nullify the agreement he made with Giamatti, under which he agreed to accept a lifetime ban, he absolutely will win, and baseball will be ordered to remove him from their disqualified list, and to compensate him for the time he has spent there.

Bill James (1994)

---

[8] *See also* Memorandum for Robert Raben, Assistant Attorney General, Office of Legislative Affairs, from Evan Caminker, Deputy Assistant Attorney General, Office of Legal Counsel, *Re: National Wildlife Refuge System Centennial Commemoration Act of 2000* (Aug. 11, 2000) (objecting on anti-aggrandizement grounds to statute appointing members of Congress to serve as non-voting members of commission with responsibility to develop and carry out plan to commemorate 100th anniversary of National Wildlife Refuge System).

NOVEMBER

CHAS. W. BENNETT.
ALLEN & GINTER'S
RICHMOND. Cigarett s. VIRGINIA.

CHARLES WESLEY (CHARLIE) BENNETT

Respondent, *Allegheny Base-Ball Club v. Bennett*, 14 F. 257 (C.C. Pa. 1882).
See 49–Charlie Bennett, in
THE NEW BILL JAMES HISTORICAL ABSTRACT (2001).

❧ NOVEMBER ❧

SUN	MON	TUES	WED	THUR	FRI	SAT
	1	2	3	4	5	6
7	8	9	10	11	12	13
14	15	16	17	18	19	20
21	22	23	24	25	26	27
28	29	30				

J. Crawford Biggs, Baseball Fan

from Warner W. Gardner, Pebbles from the Paths Behind (1989) (excerpt)

[President Franklin D.] Roosevelt's first Solicitor General was a North Carolina lawyer and politician named J. Crawford Biggs. He was considered by the [Supreme] Court and his staff alike to be a man of uncommon incompetence.[1] Attorney General [Homer] Cummings must have come to the same view, since the Solicitor General argued neither of the major cases (*Panama v. Ryan* and *Gold Clause*) that arose during his term of office. Stanley Reed, who was General Counsel of the Reconstruction Finance Corporation and had joined Cummings in the *Gold Clause* arguments, was nominated to take Biggs' place and took office on March 23, 1935.

Adolph Berle, whom I had not seen since I left Columbia [Law School], was good enough to urge Reed to recruit me into the Solicitor General's Office. When Reed called me, sometime in the spring of 1935, I had just concluded that I would rather be a lawyer than an economist, but had given no thought at all to how and where I would be a lawyer. The Solicitor General's Office seemed a nice solution to all problems and I readily agreed.[2] Fortunately, in those days "conflict of interest" was examined in light of common sense rather than rigid rule, and the current requirement of two sanitizing years between Court [Gardner had clerked for Justice Harlan Fiske Stone in 1934-35] and Solicitor General would have been thought absurd.

---

[1] Justice Stone, who was not notably charitable to counsel, said that Biggs was not fit to argue a cow case before a justice of the peace, unless that is the cow was fatally sick. James M. Beck, Coolidge's Solicitor General, came off marginally better. Beck, Stone said, would get hopelessly lost in oral argument and would, if a Justice asked a question showing him the way out, quote Shakespeare and march off in the opposite direction.

[2] When I went to the Office for an interview Reed was for a while occupied and I was deflected to Biggs, who was either in the final days of office or was being phased out under the ubiquitous title "Special Assistant to the Attorney General," a blanket description covering alike a multitude of talent and a multitude of spavined politicians. He was jacketless, a condition rather more informal then than now, and his vest was covered with shells of the peanuts which he was devouring while he listened to a baseball game on radio. By mutual assent the interview never progressed beyond "hello" and he returned his attention to the ball game.

March 19, 1912.

My dear Judge:-

My mail last evening brought to me the reference of the enclosed communication.

As the application is to you as "Ex-Governor", I must respectfully decline to grant the writ. My own opinion is that the writer is a victim of too close study of the somewhat complicated rules and procedure concerning infield flies.

If you think I have not properly acted on this application, there is precedent for referring it to the court for action by a full bench.

Faithfully yours,

William R. Day

Mr. Justice Hughes,
2401 Massachusetts Avenue,
Washington, D.C.

A CRY FOR HELP

The *Green Bag* found the letter reproduced above in the William R. Day Papers at the Library of Congress, but we have no idea what Justice Charles Evans Hughes might have sent to Justice Day to inspire this response. We would welcome an answer, or even a clue, sent to editors@greenbag.org.

ARE OBAMA'S JUDGES REALLY LIBERALS?

Jeffrey Toobin[†]

The Obama Administration wanted to send a message with the President's first nomination to a federal court. "There was a real conscious decision to use that first appointment to say, 'This is a new way of doing things. This is a post-partisan choice,'" one White House official involved in the process told me. "Our strategy was to show that our judges could get Republican support." So on March 17th President Obama nominated David Hamilton, the chief federal district-court judge in Indianapolis, to the Seventh Circuit court of appeals. Hamilton had been vetted with care. After fifteen years of service on the trial bench, he had won the highest rating from the American Bar Association; Richard Lugar, the senior senator from Indiana and a leading Republican, was supportive; and Hamilton's status as a nephew of Lee Hamilton, a well-respected former local congressman, gave him deep connections. The hope was that Hamilton's appointment would begin a profound and rapid change in the confirmation process and in the federal judiciary itself.

The power to nominate federal judges is one of the great prizes of any Presidency, and Obama assumed office at a propitious moment. After Democrats won control of the Senate in 2006, the new chairman of the Judiciary Committee, Patrick Leahy, of Vermont, significantly slowed down the confirmation process for George W. Bush's appointees to the federal appeals courts. In addition, many federal judges appointed by President Clinton were waiting for the election of a Democratic President in order to resign. Now vacancies abound. Just eight months into his first term, Obama already has the chance to nominate judges for twenty-one

---

[†] Staff writer, *The New Yorker*. Copyright © 2009 by Jeffrey Toobin. This article was originally published in *The New Yorker* on September 21, 2009. It is reprinted here with the permission of the author and the publisher.

seats on the federal appellate bench — more than ten per cent of the hundred and seventy-nine judges on those courts. At least half a dozen more seats should open in the next few months. There are five vacancies on the Fourth Circuit alone; just by filling those seats, Obama can convert the Fourth Circuit, which has long been known as one of the most conservative courts in the country, into one with a majority of Democratic appointees. On the federal district courts, there are seventy-two vacancies, also about ten per cent of the total; home-state senators of the President's party generally take the lead in selecting nominees for these seats, but Obama will have influence in these choices as well. Seven appeals and ten district judges have been named so far. George W. Bush, in the first eight months of his Presidency, nominated fifty-two. But Obama, unlike Bush in his first year, has had the opportunity to place his first Justice on the Supreme Court, Sonia Sotomayor — and her confirmation has opened up another seat on the Second Circuit court of appeals. Justice John Paul Stevens, who is eighty-nine, has hired only one law clerk for the next Supreme Court term, so a second Obama appointment to the Court may be imminent as well.

"The unifying quality that we are looking for is excellence, but also diversity, and diversity in the broadest sense of the word," another Administration official said. "We are looking for experiential diversity, not just race and gender. We want people who are not the usual suspects, not just judges and prosecutors but public defenders and lawyers in private practice." Yet Hamilton and Sotomayor are the usual suspects — both sitting judges, who had already been confirmed by the Senate. Of Obama's seven nominees to the circuit courts, six are federal district-court judges. The group includes Gerard Lynch, a former Columbia Law School professor and New York federal prosecutor, and Andre Davis, who was nominated to the Fourth Circuit by Bill Clinton. (At the time, Republicans blocked any vote on Davis.) Two of the seven are African-American; two are women; all but one are in their fifties. (None are openly gay.) The one non-judge is Jane Stranch, who has represented labor unions and other clients at a Nashville law firm and is nominated for the Sixth Circuit. They are conventional, qualified, and undramatic choices, who were named, at least in part, because they were seen as likely to be quickly confirmed.

But then, as the first White House official put it, "Hamilton blew up." Conservatives seized on a 2005 case, in which Hamilton ruled to strike down the daily invocation at the Indiana legislature because its repeated references to Jesus Christ violated the establishment clause of the First Amendment. Hamilton had also ruled to invalidate a part of Indiana's abortion law that required women to make two visits to a doctor before undergoing the procedure. In June, Hamilton was approved by the Judiciary Committee on a straight party-line vote, twelve to seven, but his nomination has not yet been brought to the Senate floor. Some Republicans have already vowed a filibuster. (Republican threats of extended debate on nominees can stop the Democratic majority from bringing any of them up for votes.)

"The reaction to Hamilton certainly has given people pause here," the second White House official said. "If they are going to stop David Hamilton, then who won't they stop?"

Republicans in the Senate have not allowed a vote on any of the other nominees, either. So far, the only Obama nominee who has been confirmed to a lifetime federal judgeship is Sotomayor. The stalemate provides a revealing glimpse of the environment in Washington. Obama advisers (and Democratic Senate sources) aver that all the nominees, even Hamilton, will be confirmed eventually, but contrary to the President's early hope the struggle for his judges is likely to be long and contentious.

"The President did not set a good example when he was in the Senate," Orrin Hatch, the senior Republican senator from Utah, told me, pointing to Obama's votes against the confirmation of John G. Roberts, Jr., and Samuel A. Alito, Jr., to the Supreme Court. "You have to be a partisan ideologue not to support Roberts," Hatch said. "There is a really big push on by partisan Republicans to use the same things that they did against us." Hatch himself, who had voted for Ruth Bader Ginsburg, Stephen G. Breyer, and every other Supreme Court nominee in his Senate career, voted against Sotomayor. (The vote for her confirmation was sixty-eight to thirty-one.)

There is a certain irony in this, because Obama has long sought to define himself as something other than a traditional legal liberal. Starting about fifty years ago, after Earl Warren became Chief Justice, the concept of legal liberalism developed a clear meaning: a belief in what came to be called judicial activism. Liberals believed that the Constitution should be read expansively, and that the Supreme Court should recognize newly defined rights — the right, say, to attend an integrated public school, or, later, the right to choose abortion. Conservatives in this era believed in what they called judicial restraint, which suggested that courts should refrain from overruling decisions made by the elected parts of the government. Obama appears to be trying to move away from these old categories, which have, in any case, become scrambled in their meaning. Both sides now claim to embrace restraint and eschew activism.

Obama and his judge-pickers define their choices with the same post-partisan vocabulary that the President uses with most issues: excellence, competence, common sense. And so far Republicans have regarded Obama's claims in this realm with the same skepticism that they have displayed for his arguments on the economy and health care. Still, this is not just a replay of the usual ideological debate. Obama's choice of judges reflects ferment in the world of legal liberalism, which is tied ever more closely to the fate of Democrats in the executive and legislative branches of government. Liberals who once saw judges as the lone protectors of constitutional rights are now placing their hopes on elected politicians like Obama. At its core, Obama's jurisprudence may rest less on any legal theory or nomenclature than on a more primal political skill — the ability to keep winning elections.

Last August, after Obama had clinched the Democratic nomination for President, a lawyer in New York received a confidential assignment from the transition team. Preeta Bansal, who was then a partner at the law firm Skadden, Arps and formerly a solicitor general of New York State, was asked to prepare a series of memorandums about how a President Obama might transform the federal judiciary. She projected the number of likely vacancies, examined the ethnic and professional backgrounds of current judges, and compiled the first list of possible nominees for the new President to consider.

Through the final weeks of the campaign, Bansal refined and expanded her memos, and after Obama's victory she moved to Washington to work on the transition. There, joined by former campaign staffers, among them Danielle Gray and Michael Strautmanis, Bansal waded into the details of the project. Should Obama announce his first nominations as a group, as Bush did, or one at a time? (Obama chose one at a time.) Should the new Administration coöperate with the American Bar Association, which had traditionally rated nominees but which had been pushed out of the process by recent Republican Administrations? (Obama's team decided to reëstablish the connection, but only after securing a pledge from the A.B.A. that the group would act quickly.) A statistical analysis showed that Republican judicial appointees tended, on balance, to be younger than their Democratic counterparts — a finding that interested the future judge-pickers. (Soon after the Inauguration, the authors scattered: Bansal became general counsel and senior policy adviser at the Office of Management and Budget; Gray joined the staff of Gregory Craig, the White House counsel; and Strautmanis serves as chief of staff to Valerie Jarrett, a senior aide to Obama.)

John Podesta, the White House chief of staff under President Clinton, who was running Obama's transition process, arranged a few meetings for the President-elect to familiarize himself with judicial-selection issues. At one of these sessions, in the transition headquarters, on Sixth Street, the subject was possible Supreme Court vacancies, and Obama made a specific request. He wanted more information on a federal appeals-court judge in New York named Sonia Sotomayor.

It was no surprise that Sotomayor had caught Obama's eye. First appointed to the district court by George H. W. Bush, on the recommendation of Senator Daniel Patrick Moynihan, she had been promoted to the Court of Appeals by Bill Clinton, in 1998. At the time, her confirmation was stalled by Republicans who were concerned, even then, that she might make an appealing Democratic appointee to the Supreme Court. Raised poor in the Bronx, Sotomayor had an inspiring life story, experience as both a prosecutor and a judge, and the potential to be the first Hispanic on the High Court. To those inside the White House who followed the search process after David H. Souter announced his resignation, this spring, Sotomayor was the front-runner all along.

In recent years, the introduction of a Supreme Court nominee has become a major political undertaking. By the time the President announced his choice of Sotomayor, on May 26th, "there were two story tracks — 'eminently qualified' and 'an American story,'" an official who was involved with the rollout said. "The first part related to her judicial experience, which was more time as a federal judge than any nominee in a hundred years, but we also raised as a subtext her experience as a big-city prosecutor" — early in her career, Sotomayor was an assistant district attorney in Manhattan. "You always have to worry that a Democrat is going to be called soft on crime, but it's harder to do that if people know she was a big-city prosecutor." The American story related to her childhood, in public housing, followed by her academic success at Princeton and Yale Law School. At the time, several White House officials noted the similarities between Sotomayor's life story and that of Michelle Obama, who also had a working-class upbringing in an inner city and graduated from Princeton, nine years after Sotomayor.

On the question of Sotomayor's ideology — what she stood for — Administration officials used what may become the Obama template. A Supreme Court nomination, almost by definition, raises divisive social issues, like abortion and gay rights, but the White House tried to make Sotomayor sound like a post-partisan figure, much as Obama has tried to position himself. Part of Sotomayor's appeal to Obama was that she was not a law professor or a legal theorist, and on the bench she had written opinions that avoided broad pronouncements and stuck closely to the facts of each case. "Her judicial philosophy was to follow the rule of law, apply it in each case," the official said. "She was not going to be painted as an ivory-tower judge, but a real-world judge. I don't think that she has an ideology — that's what was so great about her."

Obama himself speaks as if pragmatism were a substitute for ideology, or at least an improvement on it. As he said in an interview with the Detroit Free Press in 2008, during the campaign, "When I think about the kinds of judges who are needed today, it goes back to the point I was making about common sense and pragmatism as opposed to ideology. I think that Justice Souter, who was a Republican appointee, Justice Breyer, a Democratic appointee, are very sensible judges. They take a look at the facts and they try to figure out: How does the Constitution apply to these facts? They believe in fidelity to the text of the Constitution, but they also think you have to look at what is going on around you and not just ignore real life."

Still, at times the post-partisan language of the White House sounded a lot like that of traditional judicial conservatism. In a set of talking points released before her confirmation hearing began, in July, the Obama team called Sotomayor "a nonideological and restrained judge." The statement noted that Sotomayor "wrote expressly about the importance of judicial restraint" in her Senate questionnaire when she became a circuit-court judge, and that her opinions "reflect a keen understanding of the appropriate limits of the judicial role."

Sotomayor elaborated on the theme when she testified before the Judiciary Committee. "It's important to remember that, as a judge, I don't make law," she said in her answers to Leahy's first round of questions. "And so the task for me as a judge is not to accept or not accept new theories; it's to decide whether the law, as it exists, has principles that apply to new situations."

Sotomayor's words amounted to an acknowledgment that conservative rhetoric, if not conservative views, had become the default mode for Supreme Court nominees. In the hearings of the two Clinton nominees, Ginsburg and Breyer, in the early nineteen-nineties, both candidates said, essentially, that the meaning of the Constitution had evolved with the times. Ginsburg herself, in her career as a litigator, had been among the first to persuade the Justices to recognize that the Constitution required equal treatment for women. Sotomayor and the Democratic senators who supported her portrayed a much less dynamic process of constitutional change — a fact that was noted by conservative legal scholars. "If you took the hearings we just had, as well as the statements that are being made on the Senate floor, you see a very different dialogue taking place than we saw in connection with Ginsburg or Thomas or Bork or Rehnquist," Leonard A. Leo, the executive vice-president of the Federalist Society, the conservative legal group, said. "It's an acknowledgment of the fact that that's the prevailing and conventional view of what the proper judicial role is in our democratic society. The Democrats said she was a non-ideological, restrained judge. They talked about her judicial modesty. That was language that the Bush White House coined to discuss John Roberts."

Nor did Sotomayor (or her Democratic supporters) offer much more than a tepid defense of the use of racial preferences in affirmative action, another traditional liberal cause. "The Constitution promotes and requires the equal protection of law of all citizens in its Fourteenth Amendment," Sotomayor told the senators. She went on:

> To ensure that protection, there are situations in which race in some form must be considered; the courts have recognized that. It is firmly my hope, as it was expressed by Justice O'Connor in her decision involving the University of Michigan Law School admissions criteria, that in twenty-five years race in our society won't be needed to be considered in any situation.

In the case that drew the most attention during the hearing, Sotomayor had ruled in favor of the city of New Haven, when it voided a promotion exam for firefighters; the results of the test left no African-Americans eligible for promotion, and the city feared a lawsuit charging that New Haven's policies had a "disparate impact." Scarcely any Democrats rose to Sotomayor's defense on the New Haven case, except to say that she had followed existing precedent. "We spent in previous confirmation hearings a very considerable amount of time probing Republican nominees about the extent to which they would entertain disparate-impact claims in the civil-rights arena," Leo said. "One has to assume that the calculation they made was that that is not an issue with which the American people are in agreement with them."

To some degree, the use of conservative language by Sotomayor and her allies was merely an attempt to forestall Republican opposition. (In any case, more than three-quarters of the Republicans in the Senate voted against her.) And it is true that the new Justice appears likely to embrace some traditional liberal positions on legal issues; for example, there is nothing in her background that would suggest any hostility to Roe v. Wade or to abortion rights. In her first case as a Justice, in August, she voted with the Court's three other liberals in an unsuccessful attempt to stop an execution. But the language and substance of Sotomayor's testimony, and the White House's advocacy for her, suggest that the progressive agenda in the Court is not the same as it once was. Not surprisingly, the change is best illustrated by the views and priorities of Barack Obama.

As the outgoing president of the Harvard Law Review, in 1991, Obama could have had his pick of judicial clerkships. "I asked him to apply to clerk for me," Abner Mikva, a former federal appeals-court judge in Washington, told me. "I was a feeder. At the time, I was sending clerks to work for Brennan, Marshall, Stevens, and Blackmun. I don't have any doubt that Obama would have got a Supreme Court clerkship if he wanted one."

But Obama decided against taking any clerkship and instead moved back to Chicago, where he joined a small law firm, started teaching law at the University of Chicago, and laid the groundwork for a political career. "He had decided at that point to go back to work in the community that he had worked in as a community organizer," Cassandra Butts, a law-school classmate of Obama's and now his deputy White House counsel, said. "He was very, very clear on that path. He obviously had an incredible number of opportunities to diverge from that path, but he decided that that's what he wanted to do." As Mikva remembered, "He wanted to go back to Chicago, and he wanted politics to be part of the mix."

David Strauss, who was a professor at the law school at the time, told me that Obama "didn't see himself as much as a legal intellectual as a community organizer and a politician. Even when he was teaching at our law school and practicing law, he was a politician — but not in a cheap sense. That's where he saw his future." In 1996, five years after his graduation, Obama won election to the Illinois State Senate, though he kept up his adjunct teaching at Chicago.

In short, Obama chose politics over law. This was a matter of personal preference and temperament, but it also reflected the times. "He came of age at a time when confidence in the judiciary as a vehicle of social change was very low," Geoffrey Stone, who was on the faculty at the University of Chicago when Obama taught there, said. "His generation of lawyers is much less confident of looking to the Court than an earlier one was. In the Rehnquist years, liberals didn't have a lot of confidence in the Court."

By the late eighties, the great activist years of the Warren Court had passed, and there appeared to be little prospect of a revival. When Obama moved back to Chicago, there was only one Democratic appointee on the Supreme Court — Byron White, hardly a liberal, who had been nominated by John F. Kennedy, in 1962. Obama believed that the Supreme Court wouldn't be remaking American society — and probably shouldn't be, either.

Over the years, Obama has expressed admiration for the great liberal Justices of the twentieth century, including William J. Brennan, Jr., and Thurgood Marshall, but he has nearly always distanced himself from their judicial philosophy. In the interview in Detroit last year, Obama described his view of the limits of judicial liberalism. "The Warren Court was one of those moments when, because of the particular challenge of segregation, they needed to break out of conventional wisdom because the political process didn't give an avenue for minorities and African Americans to exercise their political power to solve their problems. So the court had to step in and break that logjam," Obama said, adding, "I would be troubled if you had that same kind of activism in circumstances today."

A traditional liberal might see Obama's view of "that kind of activism" as heretical. Over the years, legal liberals in many respects have defined themselves by coming up with new rights for the Supreme Court to recognize. The most famous of these rights was the right to attend an integrated public school, which the Justices established in 1954 and then attempted, with mixed success, to enforce over subsequent decades. Later, thanks to Ginsburg and others, the Justices found that the Constitution generally forbade discrimination on the basis of gender. With *Roe v. Wade*, they recognized the right to obtain an abortion. Other claims were less successful. In an article in the Harvard Law Review, in 1969, Frank I. Michelman, a professor at Harvard, suggested that the Fourteenth Amendment might require a right to economic equality, not just freedom from discrimination. Some scholars posited a constitutional right to housing, or a right to health care. Many liberals tried for years to persuade the Supreme Court to step beyond desegregation orders and direct that public schools be funded equally. In an interview with Chicago public radio in 2001, Obama explained why he believed that approach had failed, citing the case of *San Antonio Independent School District v. Rodriguez*, in 1973. In *Rodriguez*, the Court found, by a 5-4 vote, that unequal funding of school districts in the same state did not amount to a violation of the equal-protection clause of the Fourteenth Amendment. As Obama described the decision, the Court "basically slaps those kinds of claims down and says, 'You know what — we as a court have no power to examine issues of redistribution and wealth inequalities with respect to schools. That's not a race issue, that's a wealth issue, and we can't get into this.'" The Court said that it was up to legislatures to make judgments about redistribution of wealth, not courts — which was fine with Obama. "Maybe I am show-ing my bias here as a legislator as well as a law professor," he went on, "but the institution just isn't structured that way."

Nor has Obama shown much enthusiasm for the traditional civil-rights agenda, particularly when it comes to voting rights and affirmative action. Obama taught a course on election law at Chicago, and he used the manu-script of a textbook co-written by Richard Pildes, a law professor then at the University of Michigan and now at New York University. In the early nineties, and even today, most liberals in the field supported the creation of so-called "majority-minority districts" — legislative districts that were gerrymandered to help minority politicians win elections. According to Pildes, Obama was skeptical about African-Americans relying on these districts as the sole route to political success. "He was very different from most younger academics, who had very conventional ways of looking at issues like this one," Pildes told me. "He was very interested in the facts on the ground, how this stuff was really playing out, rather than ideology."

Like Sotomayor in her hearing, Obama has expressed little enthusiasm for group-based affirmative action, the kind practiced by the city of New Haven in the firefighter case. As he notes in his second book, "The Audac-ity of Hope," "An emphasis on universal, as opposed to race-specific, pro-grams isn't just good policy; it's also good politics." Still, the President is a strong believer in redress for individual, as opposed to group, victims of discrimination; the first bill he signed in office, known as the Lilly Ledbet-ter Act, overturned a Supreme Court ruling that had restricted the statute of limitations for filing such cases.

There is another reason for Obama's skepticism about court-ordered change: that it distracts liberals and progressives from the hard work of winning elections. In the 2001 interview, he said that one of "the tragedies of the civil rights movement was because the civil rights movement be-came so court-focused — I think there was a tendency to lose track of the political and community-organizing activities on the ground that are able to put together the actual coalitions of power through which you bring about redistributive change. And in some ways we still suffer from that." Five years later, as a senator and all but declared Presidential candidate, Obama wrote in "The Audacity of Hope" that he had been reluctant to enter the political brawl over President Bush's judicial nominees. "I won-dered if, in our reliance on the courts to vindicate not only our rights but also our values, progressives had lost too much faith in democracy," he wrote. "Elections ultimately meant something. . . . Instead of relying on Senate procedures, there was one way to ensure that judges on the bench reflected our values, and that was to win at the polls."

Notwithstanding Obama's protestations, his brand of pragmatism is an ideology, and his reconsideration of what it means to be a judicial liberal has come at the same time as some in the legal academy are examining the same questions. One prominent effort in this vein, which began before Obama even became a candidate for President, has led to a complementary approach to that of the new President.

"The liberal-activist model of the nineteen-sixties and nineteen-seventies said that the Supreme Court would declare that there are rights, and then order the political branches to enforce them," Jack Balkin, a professor at Yale Law School, told me. That approach seemed both unattainable and undesirable to Balkin and Reva Siegel, a colleague at Yale, so they decided to try to rethink the liberal legal agenda. They were inspired in part by a series of memos and speeches that Edwin Meese III, as Ronald Reagan's attorney general in the eighties, had commissioned to articulate a conservative vision for the courts; over the years, the ideas in several of these memos have found their way into Supreme Court precedent. It was Meese, for instance, who first called Washington's attention to the view that the Constitution should be interpreted according to the "original intent" of the Framers, an approach that Antonin Scalia and Clarence Thomas have brought to the Supreme Court.

The main result of Balkin and Siegel's collaboration is a book, "The Constitution in 2020," published earlier this year, which includes contributions from more than a score of leading progressive law professors — some of whom now work in the Obama Administration. At the core of Balkin and Siegel's concept is the notion that "judges don't own the Constitution." By that, they mean that the Constitution, at any given point in history, is shaped by a broad array of forces, including elected officials, activists, and voters. "The Court decided Brown in 1954, but that didn't settle what 'equal protection of the laws' meant," Balkin said. "Politicians and the civil-rights movement shifted the meaning. Martin Luther King changed it. The Civil Rights Act changed it. The organized right changed the meaning when it reacted to busing. The history of race relations in this country is organized around each side claiming the mantle of Brown. But no one ever has the last word."

As proof of this hypothesis, the authors point to the history of the Second Amendment and gun control. The first clause of the amendment refers to the need for "a well regulated Militia" and the second states that "the right of the people to keep and bear Arms, shall not be infringed." For many decades, into the nineteen-eighties, it was widely agreed among judges and scholars that the right to bear arms belonged only to militias, and thus the Second Amendment imposed no limits on the ability of states and localities to enact gun-control laws. Warren E. Burger, the former Chief Justice (and no liberal), said that any other view of the law was a "fraud," and Robert Bork, the conservative hero, said much the same thing. But Meese and his allies in the National Rifle Association were indefatigable in pushing an opposing interpretation, and their position became widely adopted, first in the Republican Party and then among many Democrats. Finally, in 2008, the Supreme Court, in an opinion written by Antonin Scalia (who was appointed while Meese was attorney general), struck down a District of Columbia gun-control law as a violation of the Second Amendment. A fringe position — a "fraud" — two decades earlier had become the law of the land. To Balkin, this is an entirely appropriate example of what he, Siegel, and Robert Post, the dean of Yale Law School, call Democratic Constitutionalism. "Conservatives convinced other people that their vision of the Constitution was a better one, they won elections, they appointed their people to the Court," Balkin said. "This is not lawlessness. This is how the system works."

In a way, Democratic Constitutionalism goes back to the origin of the activism-vs.-restraint debate. In the late nineteenth century, a conservative majority on the Supreme Court embraced a kind of activism when it struck down several state and local measures intended to regulate the economy or to protect workers. In the nineteen-thirties, a conservative majority on the Supreme Court struck down several early New Deal measures; in these cases, the Justices ruled that Congress lacked the constitutional authority to launch such federal initiatives as the National Recovery Administration. Franklin D. Roosevelt initially responded to these defeats with his infamous court-packing plan, but in time he was able to appoint Justices who deferred to legislative judgments about how best to address the Depression. In other words, in that era liberals believed in restraint, and conservatives were the activists. (That flipped in the Warren era.) Notably, when Sotomayor was asked her favorite Supreme Court Justice, she named Benjamin Cardozo, who was a leader in fighting the conservative activism of the thirties on the Court.

"What you'll get with Obama is basically *Carolene Products* — 'Leave me alone on economic issues and protect me on civil rights,'" Richard Epstein, the conservative legal scholar who was interim dean of the Chicago Law School when Obama taught there, said. *Carolene Products* was a 1938 decision, involving skim milk spiked with non-milk fat, in which the Court set up a structure that would shape constitutional law for the next several generations. The Justices gave the elected branches a more or less free hand on economic issues but exercised greater scrutiny of measures that affected minorities. "Obama has nothing much he wants from the courts," Epstein told me. "He wants them to stay away from the statutes he passes, and he wants solidity on affirmative action and abortion. That's it."

As David Strauss observed, "Fighting over the courts is not going to be a high-priority issue for Obama or the Democratic coalition. The Republican coalition cares a lot more about it at this point, because they want the Court to change on issues like abortion, affirmative action, school prayer, gun rights. If the courts stay right where they are, that's fine with the Democrats. The Democratic agenda is more democratically focussed on legislation."

In recent years, thirties-style conservative judicial activism, targeting federal legislation, has been returning to the Court. As Cass Sunstein, a former professor at Harvard Law School, writes in the "2020" collection, "Increasingly, conservatives have been drawn to 'movement judges' — judges with no interest in judicial restraint, with a willingness to rule broadly and a demonstrated willingness to strike down the acts of Congress and state governments. Movement judges have an agenda, which, as it happens, overlaps a great deal with the extreme wing of the Republican Party." Sunstein notes that the Rehnquist Court struck down more than three dozen federal enactments between 1995 and 2004 — "a record of aggressiveness against the national legislature that is unequaled in the nation's history."

Last week, after a long delay, Sunstein was confirmed as director of the Office of Information and Regulatory Affairs in the Office of Management and Budget. Dawn E. Johnsen, another contributor, has been waiting for months for a Senate vote on her nomination as an assistant attorney general. Harold Hongju Koh, who was the dean of Yale Law School and another writer in the collection, was recently confirmed, also after a long delay, as legal adviser to the State Department. The trouble that these outspoken academics have had in winning confirmation for Administration posts offers another augury of major battles ahead if Obama nominates any of them, or anyone like them, for judgeships.

The Roberts Court, in addition to striking down the D.C. gun-control law, invalidated school-integration plans undertaken by local governments in Seattle and Louisville, and rejected part of the McCain-Feingold campaign-finance law. In an oral argument last week, in a case involving a film critical of Hillary Clinton, the Court appeared poised to strike down another part of the same law. An Obama Court would almost certainly defer more to congressional and other legislative judgments. "You start with the premise that the political branches are the first line of defense of constitutional rights," Balkin said. "If you think that health care is a very important right that people should enjoy, you think that the best way to enforce it is for Congress to pass a law and the President to sign it. This is a very different model from the late sixties." Obama's ambitious legislative agenda, combined with his stated devotion to judicial restraint, signals an approach in synch with this ideology.

During the campaign, Obama criticized George W. Bush for his aggressive use of the powers of the Presidency, particularly regarding the treatment of military detainees. Obama and other liberals saluted the Supreme Court's decisions, in the *Hamdan* and *Boumediene* cases, which rejected Bush Administration proposals regarding Guantánamo Bay. But, like most Presidents, Obama has now embraced a more robust conception of executive power than some traditional liberals would prefer. He has issued signing statements, noting his objections to certain legislation on constitutional grounds; he has expressed a willingness to create a system for trying detainees that offers fewer protections than criminal trials do; and his Administration has invoked the state-secrets privilege to keep information away from torture victims who have filed lawsuits. In these areas, Obama has taken less aggressive positions than the Bush Administration did, but the difference is of degree, not of kind.

In some respects, Democratic Constitutionalism, or the Obama version of it, still looks much like traditional liberalism. The deference to the will of the people will go only so far. If, for example, a state legislature were to ban all abortions, there would be little hesitation on the part of most liberals to strike that action down. Same-sex marriage, which many liberals favor, presents a similar dilemma, although Balkin can fit the current struggles into his template. "Same-sex marriage right now is a collaboration, where sometimes courts are leading, like in Massachusetts, and sometimes in other states the courts are teeing up the question and forcing the attention of the polity on it," he said. "But courts can only push so far out against what the people believe. They can lead, but they have to get some degree of take-up from the legislature, or nothing is going to change."

As Obama has said, the role of the Court is sometimes specifically to confront — not ratify — the will of the majority. "One of the roles of the courts is to protect people who don't have a voice. That's the special role of that institution," Obama said in Detroit. "The vulnerable, the minority, the outcast, the person with the unpopular idea, the journalist who is shaking things up. That's inherently the role of the court. And if somebody doesn't appreciate that role, then I don't think they are going to make a very good justice."

This is the paradox of the judiciary — that unelected judges must protect democratic values. Obama's belief that judges reflect the prevailing political environment raises a paradox of its own. He is launching his nominees into an atmosphere that is so poisoned that scarcely anyone can get confirmed. As one of his advisers said, "Post-partisanship has not yet arrived in judicial selection, or in anything else."

✳ ✳ ✳

AHEAD OF HIS TIME

from John Montgomery Ward, Base-Ball: How to Become a Player, With the Origin, History and Explanation of the Game (1888)

In the fall of 1885 the members of the New York team met and appointed a committee to draft a Constitution and By-laws for an organization of players, and during the season of 1886 the different "Chapters" of the "National Brotherhood of Ball-Players" were instituted by the mother New York Chapter. The objects of this Brotherhood as set forth by the Constitution are:

"To protect and benefit its members collectively and individually;

"To promote a high standard of professional conduct;

"To foster and encourage the interests of 'The National Game.'"

There was no spirit of antagonism to the capitalists of the game, except in so far as the latter might at any time attempt to disregard the rights of any member.

In November, 1887, a committee of the Brotherhood met a committee of the League, and a new form of players' contract was agreed upon. Concessions were made on both sides, and the result is a more equitable form of agreement between the club and players.

The time has not yet come to write of the effect of this new factor in base-ball affairs. It is organized on a conservative plan, and the spirit it has already shown has given nothing to fear to those who have the broad interests of the game at heart. That it has within it the capacity for great good, the writer has no manner of doubt.

TENER'S BASEBALL CREED

(excerpts)

Cleveland Plain Dealer, Jan. 11, 1914

Epigrams bunched from a running interview with John K. Tener, governor of Pennsylvania, and the new president of the National Baseball League.

Phrases taken from the language of baseball enrich the vocabulary of success. "Making a hit" and "putting one over" are generally accepted and widely popular forms of expressing accomplishment.

Baseball, like the constitution, follows the flag. The impact of the willow against the horsehide sphere is heard 'round the world. There are score boards in London, Paris, Berlin, Guam, Hong Kong and Tokio, and rooters in every known tongue.

Gallant Commodore Perry opened the ports of Japan to American commerce and globe-trotting nines opened the parks of Japan to the great American game. Thus are the peaceful messages of new world civilization carried to ancient peoples.

Modern civics finds one of its ablest allies in baseball. Executive, judicial and legislative branches of government year after year are recruited from the diamond. President Wilson was a ballplayer; so was President Taft. The distinguished chief justice of the supreme court of the United States never varies in his loyal support of the game, and so it is all along the line.

If all the ballplayers in the country were organized into an army, they would form a force that would be invincible. They would be a defense against the armies of the world.

DECISION IN THE APPEAL OF

KEVIN GROSS

A. Bartlett Giamatti[†]

The appeal of Mr. Kevin Gross of the Philadelphia Phillies of his ten day suspension for violating rule 8.02(b) is denied. He must begin serving his ten day suspension immediately.

The opinion that follows is more lengthy than is customary because the hearing giving rise to it was some five hours long and involved exhibits of considerable breadth, two entailing nearly 1,000 notations. Properly to deliberate upon the materials and arguments requires extended examination, as it required considerable time.

I.

SUMMARY OF APPEAL

The Players Association (hereinafter P.A.) conceded that Mr. Gross had violated Official Playing Rule 8.02(b) by having sandpaper affixed to his glove and a sticky substance on his glove in the game of August 10, 1987. P.A. did not dispute that the president of the National League had the overall authority to interpret playing rules and impose discipline for infractions as provided in the Official Playing Rules (2.00 and 9.05(c)) and the National League Constitution (V.3.a. and V.3.c). The burden of P.A.'s appeal was that the ten day suspension was unduly harsh; it was, P.A. contended, without precedent, inconsistent with past practice and not comparable with discipline for other offenses.

In order to provide the basis for these arguments, P.A. introduced exhibits, derived from P.A. records, listing infractions and discipline imposed from 1978 to 1987 in the American League and the National League, and, derived from National League records, a listing of ejections from games from 1977 to 1987 for reasons other than fighting, arguing, bench clearing, etc. and the discipline imposed.

II.

THE RECORD

Before weighing the arguments derived from this historical record, it is necessary — as with any historical record — to assess the reliability of the record itself. The record presented by P.A. shows omissions, inconsistencies and trivial errors. To wit:

P.A.'s exhibits omit any notation of the ten day suspension and fine imposed on 8/24/82 on Mr. G. Perry, appealed to the American League president on 9/9/82; appeal denied; suspension served and fine paid,

---

[†] President, The National League of Professional Baseball Clubs. The copyright in this decision is owned by the Office of the Commissioner of Major League Baseball, with whose permission it is reprinted here.

beginning 9/17/82. Mr. Perry was charged with violating rules 3.02 and 8.02.

P.A. exhibits omit any notation of the ten day suspension imposed on 10/01/80 on Mr. R. Honeycutt for violating rule 3.02; P.A. notes only the fine for that offense imposed on Mr. Honeycutt on 9/30/80. The letter of L.S. McPhail, Jr. to R. Honeycutt of 10/1/80 clarifies the record.

P.A. exhibits occasionally include discipline imposed on coaches and managers but more often omit suspensions and fines since 1978 on such non-playing personnel. Fuller data were available in the material requested by P.A. from the National League. One would have assumed such data to be relevant when one is searching for patterns or standards of league imposed discipline.

P.A. exhibits are also inconsistent as between themselves. The American League exhibit lists discipline only through 6/25/87, omitting at least two months of this season, while the National League exhibit lists discipline up through the case under appeal, that of Mr. Gross.

These comments would not be germane had not the exhibits formed the basis for the P.A.'s appeal on the ground of undue severity and had not the exhibits themselves occupied such a significant portion of the hearing. No adverse inference is intended or drawn from these omissions or inconsistencies.

III.

THE ARGUMENTS

A) That a ten day suspension is without precedent for violating rule 8.02(b) is true. Any discipline for violating rule 8.02(b) would be without precedent because all the exhibits show that in the last ten years of major league baseball, there have been no recorded violations of 8.02(b). Severity of discipline, or mildness of discipline, cannot be fruitfully argued from a vacuum.

B) We must consider the argument of P.A. counsel that the ten day suspension of Mr. Gross is harsh or unduly severe because it is not comparable to discipline historically imposed for other offenses. The record (excluding Mr. Gross) shows there to have been 39 disciplinary acts in major league baseball since 1978 involving suspensions and fines — 21 in the A.L., 18 in the N.L. Of the 21 cases in the American League, 17 saw discipline imposed for in some way physically abusing umpires (9 instances) or for fighting with players or fans (8 instances). All 18 instances of discipline in the National League were imposed for some form of physical abuse to umpires (11) or for fighting with players or fans (7). For these physical and abusive acts, discipline in each case in both leagues included monetary fines and suspensions. Suspensions in the American League ran from two to four days; in the National League, from two to fifteen days.

The four cases in the American League not falling into the category of physical and abusive acts included the aforementioned ten day suspensions and fines imposed for violating rule 3.02 on R. Honeycutt and imposed for violating rule 3.02 and 8.02 on G. Perry.

The vast majority (35 of 39) of instances of discipline involving suspension and fines in the last ten years were for some sort of violent or impulsive act. This is not surprising in a physical game played intensely by highly skilled and competitive professional athletes. While such acts, whatever their nature, can never be condoned or tolerated, it must be recognized that they grow often out of impulse, and the aggressive, volatile nature of the game and of those who play it. It would be most surprising if the preponderance of serious infractions, and attendant discipline, were of a different kind.

C) There is, however, in the record another category of offenses and discipline, which involve cheating. Such acts are the result not of impulse, borne of frustration or anger or zeal as violence is, but are rather acts of a cool, deliberate, premeditated kind. Unlike acts of impulse or violence, intended at the moment to vent frustration or abuse another, acts of cheating are intended to alter the very conditions of play to favor one person. They are secretive, covert acts that strike at and seek to undermine the basic foundation of any contest declaring the winner — that all participants play under identical rules and conditions. Acts of cheating destroy that necessary foundation and thus strike at the essence of a contest. They destroy faith in the games' integrity and fairness; if participants and spectators alike cannot assume integrity and fairness, and proceed from there, the contest cannot in its essence exist.

Acts of physical excess, reprehensible as they are, often represent extensions of the very forms of physical exertion that are the basis for playing the game; regulation and discipline seek to contain, not expunge, violent effort in sport. Cheating, on the other hand, has no organic basis in the game and no origins in the act of playing. Cheating is contrary to the whole purpose of playing to determine a winner fairly and cannot simply be contained; if the game is to flourish and engage public confidence, cheating must be clearly condemned with an eye to expunging it.

D) The ten year history of discipline in the American League shows acts of cheating dealt with more severely than various physical acts of impulse or abuse. The ten year history of discipline in the National League offers no guidance whatever for cheating, save for a warning to D. Sutton in 1978; it shows that on two occasions longer suspensions were imposed than that given to Mr. Gross. The ten year history of major league baseball shows that regardless of the kind of offense, all 39 suspensions were accompanied by monetary fines.

To summarize broad categories of comparison: across ten years of major league baseball, where discipline included a suspension, we find cases of cheating treated very seriously, usually more seriously than other offenses; and we find suspensions of greater duration than the suspension imposed on Mr. Gross.

E) Is Mr. Gross to be compared to all previous offenders receiving suspensions and fines? If so, the data do not support the charge of excessive severity, for some have been suspended longer and all have been fined.

What of comparable cases of cheating? Messrs. Honeycutt and Sutton were suspended for damaging a baseball or delivering damaged balls in violation of rule 3.02, wherein it is mandated that a pitcher "shall be suspended automatically for ten days," whereas Mr. Gross was suspended under rule 8.02(b) where no suspension is mandated. P.A. counsel argued that the rule makers must have considered a violation of rule 3.02 a more serious offense than a violation of rule 8.02(b) because the former mandates a suspension beyond ejection, while the latter mandates only ejection. Therefore, either by imposing a sentence not mandated, or by imposing a sentence under rule 8.02(b) by inappropriate analogy to rule 3.02, the National League has imposed an improper, and unduly severe, punishment on Mr. Gross.

The arguments are not persuasive. If only those penalties prescribed in the Official Playing Rules should be imposed, then all past discipline which has exceeded prescribed penalties was in error. But that is manifestly not the case.

In the particular instance of arguing by analogy from rule 3.02, in order to say that rule 8.02(b) must be read as limiting the league president only to the penalty prescribed, one most ignore the fact that 3.02 does not prescribe a monetary fine such as was imposed on Messrs. Honeycutt and Perry. The argument from analogy fails because the analogy contradicts precisely the point P.A. counsel seemed to wish to establish by analogy. If the prescriptions of rule 3.02 did not constrain the American League president, it is therefore specious to argue that the model of prescriptions in rule 3.02 constrains a league president under 8.02(b), particularly where there is not contrary past practice.

It is impossible to argue seriousness of offense, or severity of discipline, by analogy or by whether the Official Playing Rules prescribe a penalty or not. Infractions must be judged in the light of the applicable rule on a case by case basis. Past practice must be taken into account, if and when it exists. So also must current circumstances be carefully considered. A league president must neither be captivated by the past nor indifferent to it, any more than he may be capricious in imposing discipline, either on the side of severity or of laxity.

IV.

CONCLUSION

What did Kevin Gross do? He deliberately and flagrantly violated rule 8.02(b) by affixing a round piece of apparently heavy duty sandpaper to the lower thumb or heel area of his glove. He also had a sticky substance on the top of the glove's thumb. Sandpaper is not some foreign substance (like shampoo or chewing gum) that conceivably could have been inadvertently acquired by storing a glove in a clubhouse locker. Clearly the sandpaper was not acquired and affixed to the lower thumb by accident nor does sandpaper come in that shape, or adhere to the heel area of a baseball glove in nature. A premeditated effort is required to affix sandpaper to a glove. Because those bringing the appeal on behalf of Mr. Gross chose not to call him as a witness, though he was present, we cannot know if Mr. Gross had any explanation to counter the presumption that he deliberately brought onto the field an illegal glove for any reason than the one the rule is intended to forbid.

Among other substances, sandpaper is used to deface baseballs. That is why foreign substances are forbidden under rule 8.02(b). The intent of the rule is to prevent a pitcher from having on his person or in his possession any foreign substance that could mar or deface or be used to mar or deface a baseball in that game or in any game.

It is cheating *per se* to have such a glove with sandpaper and sticky substance on the field. On August 10, 1987, Mr. Gross cheated by bringing on the field an illegal glove. It is not necessary actively or even inadvertently (such as could have occurred, given the placement of the sandpaper in the glove) to have defaced a baseball. That contingency is covered elsewhere in the rules. Mr. Gross is neither charged with defacing a baseball nor with throwing a defaced baseball. To be guilty of cheating it is enough to have flagrantly and willfully violated 8.02(b).

Cheating is a very serious offense and merits serious discipline. I have expressed myself above as to the reasons why cheating has always been considered destructive of the essence of a contest designed to declare a winner. Cheating corrodes the integrity of any game. It undermines the assumption necessary to any game declaring a winner, that the contestants are playing fairly, i.e. under identical rules and conditions. It destroys public and participant confidence, morale and goodwill. Mr. Gross acted with indifference to these principles.

Amidst a season marred, in my view, by allegations of "scuffed" balls and "corked" bats, amidst all the warnings against cheating of various kinds, Mr. Gross exhibited a reckless disregard for the reputation and good name of his teammates, club and league and for the integrity of the game. He acted wrongly, in a serious fashion and his suspension is merited. The appeal is denied.

September 1, 1987

A. Bartlett Giamatti
President
The National League of
Professional Baseball Clubs

❋ ❋ ❋

THERE WERE CZARS IN THE EARTH THEN, TOO

During the April 7, 1926 meeting of the U.S. House of Representatives, Congressman Loring Milton Black, Jr. a Columbia JD from New York, spoke on the question of regulation of the coal industry:

> A coal "czar" similar to those governing baseball and motion picture industries, was advocated by Mr. Black, of New York.[*]

---

[*] Washington Post, Apr. 8, 1926, at 5.

General view of Sarasota, Florida trailer park alongside baseball park, circa 1941.

A CRITICAL GUIDE TO

VEHICLES IN THE PARK

Frederick Schauer[†]

INTRODUCTION

It is the most famous hypothetical in the common law world. And it is part of one of the more memorable debates in the history of jurisprudence. Stunning in its simplicity, H.L.A. Hart's example of a rule prohibiting vehicles from a public park was intended primarily as a response to the claims of the legal realists about the indeterminacy of legal rules.[1] Hart believed that many of the realists were obsessed with difficult appellate cases at the fragile edges of the law and, as a result, overestimated law's epiphenomenal indeterminacy and vastly underestimated its everyday determinacy. Through the example of the rule excluding vehicles from the park, Hart hoped to differentiate the straightforward applications of a rule at what Hart called the rule's "core" from the hard cases at a rule's edge, the area that he labeled the "penumbra."[2] For Hart, the fundamental flaw of the realist perspective was in taking the often-litigated problems of the penumbra as representative of the operation of law itself.[3] And insofar as

---

[†] Copyright © 2008 by Frederick Schauer, David and Mary Harrison Distinguished Professor of Law, University of Virginia; Visiting Professor of Law, Harvard Law School; George Eastman Visiting Professor and Fellow of Balliol College, University of Oxford. This Article was prepared for the Symposium on the Hart-Fuller Debate at Fifty, held at the New York University School of Law on February 1-2, 2008. The audience comments on that occasion were especially helpful, as was research support from the Harvard Law School. This article originally appeared at 83 N.Y.U. L. Rev. 1109 (2009). It is reprinted here with permission from the author and the publisher.

[1] H.L.A. Hart, *Positivism and the Separation of Law and Morals*, 71 HARV. L. REV. 593, 606-15 (1958) [hereinafter Hart, *Positivism and the Separation of Law and Morals*]. The example is reprised in modified form in H.L.A. HART, THE CONCEPT OF LAW 125-27 (Penelope A. Bulloch & Joseph Raz eds., 2d ed. 1994) [hereinafter HART, THE CONCEPT OF LAW].

[2] Hart, *Positivism and the Separation of Law and Morals, supra* note 1, at 607.

[3] Although Hart's charge rings true with respect to some of the realists, others, especially Karl Llewellyn, explicitly acknowledged that their observations about legal indeterminacy were restricted to the skewed sample consisting of only those cases that were worth litigating. *See*

judicial decisions in the penumbra necessarily involve determinations of what the law ought to be, it was important for Hart the positivist to stress that the interconnection between what the law is and what the law ought to be in the penumbra was not an accurate characterization of how law operated at the core, where the separation between the "is" and the "ought," between law and morality, could still obtain.

Although Hart's target was legal realism, the response came from a different direction. Lon Fuller was no legal realist himself,[4] but Hart's almost offhand observations about the clear cases at the rule's core — ordinary automobiles, for example — spurred Fuller to respond.[5] Believing Hart to be claiming that the core of a rule's application was determined by the ordinary meaning of individual words in a rule's formulation[6] — if something like an automobile was straightforwardly a vehicle in ordinary language, then an automobile would plainly fall within the scope of the rule — Fuller offered a gripping counterexample. What if a group of patriots, Fuller asked, sought to "mount on a pedestal" in the park, as a war memorial, a military truck "in perfect working order"?[7] Although the truck would plainly count as a vehicle in ordinary talk, it was hardly plain to Fuller that the truck ought to be excluded. Indeed, for Fuller it was not even clear whether the truck qualified as a vehicle at all in the particular context of this rule. We could not know whether the truck was within the scope of the rule, Fuller argued, without consulting the rule's deeper purpose. His challenge was thus not to Hart's conception of the penumbra,

---

K.N. LLEWELLYN, THE BRAMBLE BUSH: ON OUR LAW AND ITS STUDY 58 (1930) (observing that litigated cases bear same relationship to underlying pool of disputes "as does homicidal mania or sleeping sickness, to our normal life"); *see also* KARL N. LLEWELLYN, THE COMMON LAW TRADITION: DECIDING APPEALS 6, 64-68 (1960) (noting that "demonstrations will be undertaken not on cases carefully selected to convenience" but "on stuff from the daily grist"); WILLIAM TWINING, KARL LLEWELLYN AND THE REALIST MOVEMENT 245-69 (1973). In this respect, Llewellyn anticipated by many years the phenomenon now known as the selection effect. *See, e.g.*, RICHARD A. POSNER, THE ECONOMIC ANALYSIS OF LAW § 21.4, at 567-71, § 21.15, at 600 (6th ed. 2003); George L. Priest & Benjamin Klein, *The Selection of Disputes for Litigation*, 13 J. LEGAL STUD. 1 (1984); Frederick Schauer, *Judging in a Corner of the Law*, 61 S. CAL. L. REV. 1717 (1988). An excellent analytical overview of the literature is in Leandra Lederman, *Which Cases Go to Trial?: An Empirical Study of Predictions of Failure to Settle*, 49 CASE W. RES. L. REV. 315 (1999).

[4] *See* L.L. Fuller, *American Legal Realism*, 82 U. PA. L. REV. 429, 430-31 (1934); *see also* Myres S. McDougal, *Fuller v. the American Legal Realists: An Intervention*, 50 YALE L.J. 827, 828 (1941).

[5] Lon L. Fuller, *Positivism and Fidelity to Law — A Reply to Professor Hart*, 71 HARV. L. REV. 630, 661-69 (1958) [hereinafter Fuller, *Positivism and Fidelity to Law*]. Fuller addresses similar themes in a broader way in LON L. FULLER, THE MORALITY OF LAW 81-91 (rev. ed. 1969) [hereinafter FULLER, THE MORALITY OF LAW].

[6] Fuller, *Positivism and Fidelity to Law*, *supra* note 5, at 662.

[7] *Id.* at 663.

with which Fuller presumably would have had little quarrel.[8] Rather, the hypothetical truck/memorial was a challenge to the idea of a language-determined core. In offering this example, Fuller meant to insist that it was *never* possible to determine whether a rule applied without understanding the purpose that the rule was supposed to serve.[9]

The debate over this simple example has spawned numerous interpretations, applications, variations, and not a few misunderstandings.[10] The

---

[8] But not no quarrel: When making decisions in the penumbra, Hart argued, judges would exercise "discretion" to make decisions in more or less legislative (or administrative agency) style. HART, THE CONCEPT OF LAW, *supra* note 1, at 135-36. By contrast, Fuller's belief that judges should look to "purpose," FULLER, THE MORALITY OF LAW, *supra* note 5, at 145-51, 189-90, was, in theory if not in practice, more focused and more constraining than Hart's open-ended approach.

[9] In using the phrase "supposed to," I attempt, with only limited success, to avoid terms having a meaning similar to that of "intended to." Throughout his life, Fuller remained committed to law's overall purpose, *see supra* note 8, and also to the particular purpose behind particular laws. The purpose that a reasonable person might see a presumably reasonable law as serving (which is how Fuller might well have put it), however, is very different from the intentions or mental states of the people who actually drafted or enacted the law. *See* Richards v. United States, 369 U.S. 1, 9 (1962) ("[W]e are faced with . . . a problem which Congress apparently did not explicitly consider . . . ."); AHARON BARAK, PURPOSIVE INTERPRETATION IN LAW 265-68 (2005); Felix Frankfurter, *Some Reflections on the Reading of Statutes*, 47 COLUM. L. REV. 527 (1947); Max Radin, *Statutory Interpretation*, 43 HARV. L. REV. 863 (1930).

[10] Among the more extended discussions, some of which qualify as misunderstandings, are FREDERICK SCHAUER, PLAYING BY THE RULES: A PHILOSOPHICAL EXAMINATION OF RULE-BASED DECISION-MAKING IN LAW AND IN LIFE 212-15 (1991) [hereinafter SCHAUER, PLAYING BY THE RULES]; STEVEN L. WINTER, A CLEARING IN THE FOREST: LAW, LIFE, AND MIND 200-06 (2001); Larry Alexander, *All or Nothing at All: The Intentions of Authorities and the Authority of Intention*, in LAW AND INTERPRETATION 357 (Andrei Marmor ed., 1995); Bernard W. Bell, *R-E-S-P-E-C-T: Respecting Legislative Judgments in Interpretive Theory*, 78 N.C. L. REV. 1253, 1333-41 (2000); Paul Brest, *The Misconceived Quest for the Original Understanding*, 60 B.U. L. REV. 204, 209-13 (1980); Anthony D'Amato, *Can Legislatures Constrain Judicial Interpretation of Statutes?*, 75 VA. L. REV. 561, 595-602 (1989); Kent Greenawalt, *The Nature of Rules and the Meaning of Meaning*, 72 NOTRE DAME L. REV. 1449, 1460, 1463, 1474 (1997); Heidi M. Hurd, *Sovereignty in Silence*, 99 YALE L.J. 945, 984, 989-99 (1990); Robert E. Keeton, *Statutory Analogy, Purpose, and Policy in Legal Reasoning: Live Lobsters and a Tiger Cub in the Park*, 52 MD. L. REV. 1192 (1993); Andrei Marmor, *No Easy Cases?*, CANADIAN J.L. & JURISPRUDENCE, July 1990, at 61, 65-68; Michael S. Moore, *A Natural Law Theory of Interpretation*, 58 S. CAL. L. REV. 277, 338-46 (1985); Samuel C. Rickless, *A Synthetic Approach to Legal Adjudication*, 42 SAN DIEGO L. REV. 519, 520-23 (2005); Frederick Schauer, *Formalism*, 97 YALE L.J. 509, 514, 524-26, 533-34 (1988) [hereinafter Schauer, *Formalism*]; Pierre Schlag, *No Vehicles in the Park*, 23 SEATTLE U. L. REV. 381 (1999); Anthony J. Sebok, *Finding Wittgenstein at the Core of the Rule of Recognition*, 52 SMU L. REV. 75, 76-77, 89, 96-101 (1999); Peter M. Tiersma, *A Message in a Bottle: Text, Autonomy, and Statutory Interpretation*, 76 TUL. L. REV. 431, 441, 456-57, 462-64, 473-77 (2001); William N. Eskridge, Jr., *The Circumstances of Politics and the Application of Statutes*, 100 COLUM. L. REV. 558, 563-71 (2000) (reviewing JEREMY WALDRON, LAW AND DISAGREEMENT (1999)); William N. Eskridge, Jr., *No Frills Textualism*, 119 HARV. L. REV. 2041, 2041-43 (2006) (reviewing ADRIAN VERMEULE, JUDGING UNDER UNCERTAINTY (2006)).

fiftieth anniversary of the debate, therefore, seems the appropriate occasion on which to offer a guide to understanding a seemingly simple example that has mushroomed into something far larger. The hypothetical rule prohibiting vehicles in the park, and Fuller's response to what Hart likely initially believed to be its least controversial dimension, has become a lens through which many commentators have viewed more recent debates, including those about statutory interpretation, law's determinacy, the role of rules in law, and the nature of legal language, among others. If we can get clear about the issues involved in Hart and Fuller's disagreement over this one example, and if we can understand the strongest arguments on either side (only some of which were actually offered by either Fuller or Hart), we will have learned something important about numerous questions of legal theory and legal practice, questions that transcend what initially may appear to be a rather limited debate.

I. A Debate Within a Debate

The Hart-Fuller debate was focused principally neither on Hart's example nor on Fuller's counterexample. Nor was this larger debate significantly one about legal rules, or about rules in general, or even about the interpretation of rules. Rather, the bulk of the debate consisted of a comprehensive and eventually defining controversy about legal positivism and its opponents, with Hart championing the former against Fuller's procedural variation on traditional natural law theory.[11] Conducted when Nazi atrocities committed in the name of the law were a recent memory,[12] the debate over the question whether a broadly positivist or instead a broadly natural law vision of law would be more conducive to morally right action figured prominently in the articles of both men,[13] as did an even deeper disagreement about the fundamental nature of law itself.

In discussing legal interpretation, and in using the rule prohibiting ve-

---

[11] In addition to the works cited in notes 1 and 5, *supra*, the debate also includes H.L.A. Hart, Book Review, 78 HARV. L. REV. 1281 (1965) (reviewing FULLER, THE MORALITY OF LAW, *supra* note 5).

[12] *See* David Dyzenhaus, *The Grudge Informer Revisited*, 83 N.Y.U. L. REV. 1000, 1003-08 (2008).

[13] Although Hart retreated slightly from such an overtly instrumentalist position in THE CONCEPT OF LAW, *supra* note 1, in 1958, he and Fuller shared the view that the worth of a theory of law lay partly in its tendency to foster the correct attitude towards morally iniquitous official action. *See* Frederick Schauer, *The Social Construction of the Concept of Law: A Reply to Julie Dickson*, 25 OXFORD J. LEGAL STUD. 493 (2005). See also Liam Murphy, *The Political Question of the Concept of Law, in* HART'S POSTSCRIPT: ESSAYS ON THE POSTSCRIPT TO THE CONCEPT OF LAW 371 (Jules Coleman ed., 2001), a position subsequently modified in Liam Murphy, *Better To See Law This Way*, 83 N.Y.U. L. REV. 1088 (2008).

hicles from the park to further that discussion, Hart does not appear to have taken very seriously the connection between the issue of interpretation and these larger moral and conceptual themes. Hart had something he wanted to say to the legal realists, and, like the chapter of *The Concept of Law*[14] that the discussion of the no-vehicles-in-the-park example spawned, the debate about interpretation, with the example as its focal point, seems oddly removed from much of the surrounding debate about legal positivism and natural law.

This is not to say there was no connection at all. The question of how to understand and interpret a rule such as one prohibiting vehicles from the park does link to Hart's larger jurisprudential position, and he strains — albeit with less than complete success — to demonstrate this. If law is to be understood as not necessarily incorporating moral criteria for legal validity,[15] then there must exist some possible rules in some possible legal systems that can be identified as legal without resort to moral criteria. And what better example could there be than a rule whose principal operative terms appear morally neutral, and whose application, at least at the core, would seem to avoid any recourse to morality? If the clear applications of the no-vehicles-in-the-park rule were plainly law, Hart appears to be arguing, then the inevitable use of morality (or justice, equity, policy, efficiency, or something else he would have considered nonlegal) in the interpretation of unclear rules (or largely clear rules in the region of their murkiness) would not undercut the basic positivist claim. No sensible positivist, even in Hart's time (or in Austin's for that matter, as Hart himself makes clear[16]), would claim that morality is never relevant or necessary for legal interpretation.[17] But in order to support his case that moral-

---

[14] HART, THE CONCEPT OF LAW, *supra* note 1, at 124-27.

[15] The characterization of positivism in the text owes less to what Hart wrote in either 1958 or 1961 than to subsequent debates and interpretations about the character and forms of legal positivism. The flavor of these debates — ones that tend to treat *The Concept of Law* as the canonical legal positivist text — can be seen in the various contributions in, for example, ANALYZING LAW: NEW ESSAYS ON LEGAL THEORY (Brian Bix ed., 1998), THE AUTONOMY OF LAW: ESSAYS ON LEGAL POSITIVISM (Robert P. George ed., 1996), and HART'S POSTSCRIPT, *supra* note 13. Useful overviews of existing conceptions of legal positivism can be found in John Gardner, *Legal Positivism: 5½ Myths*, 46 AM. J. JURIS. 199 (2001), Stephen R. Perry, *The Varieties of Legal Positivism*, 9 CANADIAN J.L. & JURISPRUDENCE 361 (1996), and Leslie Green, *Legal Positivism*, STANFORD ENCYCLOPEDIA OF PHILOSOPHY (2003), http://plato.stanford.edu/entries/legal-positivism/.

[16] Hart, *Positivism and the Separation of Law and Morals*, *supra* note 1, at 609 n.34.

[17] Some so-called "exclusive" positivists might say that even if recourse to morality is often part of what judges and other legal actors in legal systems do, they are not actually "doing law" or engaging in legal reasoning when they do it. *See* Joseph Raz, *Postema on Law's Autonomy and Public Practical Reason: A Critical Comment*, 4 LEGAL THEORY 1, 4-7 (1998). For a discussion of this

ity is not always or necessarily relevant, Hart needs an example in which recourse to morality is unnecessary (or impermissible) to the performance of an act that is plainly — at least to Hart — deserving of the name "law." The rule excluding vehicles from the park was just that example, and the application of that rule to clear cases in the core was for Hart just that morality-free legal act.

Making the link between the no-vehicles-in-the-park example and Hart's side of the debate about legal positivism is something of a reach, not least because of Hart's dual agenda of challenging the realists and challenging Blackstone.[18] Much the same can be said about Fuller's side of the debate. Fuller's lifelong focus on the purpose of *a* law and the purpose *of* law provides an obvious connection between the interpretive debate and the debate about the nature of law,[19] especially from Fuller's more or less natural law perspective. If law itself is by (Fuller's) definition just, then the demands of law would require that it understand particular legal acts in just or sensible or otherwise morally desirable ways. A legal outcome excluding the truck/memorial from the park would thus for Fuller not only be a silly one, but also one inconsistent with the deeper nature of law itself. This aspect of the connection between the interpretive debate and the debate about the nature of law is closer for Fuller than its counterpart is for Hart. Still, the connection is neither obvious nor necessary, and it seems fair to conclude that the no-vehicles-in-the-park example and its surrounding debate were largely, even if not completely, detached on

---

aspect of exclusive positivism, see JULES L. COLEMAN, THE PRACTICE OF PRINCIPLE: IN DEFENSE OF A PRAGMATIST APPROACH TO LEGAL THEORY 105-07 (2001), and Brian Bix, *Patrolling the Boundaries: Inclusive Legal Positivism and the Nature of Jurisprudential Debate*, 12 CANADIAN J.L. & JURISPRUDENCE 17, 27-28 (1999).

[18] I take Blackstone, along with Cicero and Fuller, but not Aquinas, as exemplary proponents of the "unjust law is not law" position often taken to be a central tenet of a prominent version of natural law theory. 1 WILLIAM BLACKSTONE, COMMENTARIES *41, *70; CICERO, THE LAWS, at bk. 2, para. 13, *translated in* THE REPUBLIC AND THE LAWS 95, 126 (Jonathan Powell & Niall Rudd eds., Niall Rudd trans., 1998) (arguing that "unjust" law should not "be given the status or even the name of law"); *see* JOHN FINNIS, NATURAL LAW AND NATURAL RIGHTS 25-29, 364 (1980) (maintaining that Aquinas recognizes status and value of positive law as well as natural law); *see also* Frederick Schauer, *Positivism as Pariah*, *in* THE AUTONOMY OF LAW, *supra* note 15, at 31 (describing common caricatures of positivism and natural law). For a recent defense of the position taken by Blackstone and Cicero, see generally Philip Soper, *In Defense of Classical Natural Law in Legal Theory: Why Unjust Law Is No Law at All*, 20 CANADIAN J.L. & JURISPRUDENCE 201 (2007).

[19] Fuller's preoccupation with purpose is evident in, for example, FULLER, THE MORALITY OF LAW, *supra* note 5, at 145-51, 189-90, LON L. FULLER, ANATOMY OF THE LAW 26-40 (1968), LON L. FULLER, THE LAW IN QUEST OF ITSELF 55-59 (1940), and Lon L. Fuller, *Human Purpose and Natural Law*, 53 J. PHIL. 697 (1956).

both sides from many of the loftier moral and conceptual issues that were an important part of the larger debate.

The lack of a close connection between the interpretive debate and the conceptual one, however, is better seen as a strength than as a weakness. The value of Hart's example transcends his own use of it, and so too for Fuller's counterexample. For not only would one be hard-pressed to find a question about legal reasoning that is unconnected with one or the other position in the interpretive debate, but the questions of interpretation over which Hart and Fuller tussled are also serious and enduring ones, even when the issue of the nature of the concept of law is far in the distance.

II. AN UNFORTUNATE EXAMPLE

Fuller was of course compelled to take Hart's example as Hart presented it. But in terms of how we can best understand Fuller's larger point, an example using the word "vehicle" may have presented an unfortunate distraction.[20] In order to see why this is so, we must take the debate to a higher level of generality. That is, we have to understand that the question was not only the familiar one about the potential conflict between the text of a rule and its purpose[21] — between the letter of the law and its spirit — but about legal formality in all of its (defensible) guises.[22] The question

---

[20] Hart almost certainly drew the example from *McBoyle v. United States*, 283 U.S. 25 (1931), a case in which the question was whether an airplane was a vehicle for purposes of a federal statute prohibiting transporting a stolen vehicle across state lines. *See id.* at 26. I suspect that Hart learned of the case while at the Harvard Law School in 1956-1957, and in particular that he learned of it from Henry Hart, Albert Sacks, or possibly even from Fuller himself. On Hart's sojourn at Harvard and the circumstances in which the article was written, see NICOLA LACEY, A LIFE OF H.L.A. HART: THE NIGHTMARE AND THE NOBLE DREAM 179-208 (2004) [hereinafter LACEY, A LIFE OF H.L.A. HART], and Nicola Lacey, *Philosophy, Political Morality, and History: Explaining the Enduring Resonance of the Hart-Fuller Debate*, 83 N.Y.U. L. REV. 1059, 1060-63 (2008).

[21] *See* AHARON BARAK, PURPOSIVE INTERPRETATION IN LAW 77-80, 143-44 (Sari Bashi trans., 2005).

[22] *See* Schauer, *Formalism, supra* note 10, at 520-38 (defending possibility of constraint by literal meaning of rules); Cass R. Sunstein, *Must Formalism Be Defended Empirically?*, 66 U. CHI. L. REV. 636, 643-44, 669 (1999) (defending formalism when it produces fewer errors). Legal formalism is defensible not when it is the instrument for denying the extent to which a judge is exercising a genuine choice — when it treats choice as compulsion, as in Justice Peckham's opinion in *Lochner v. New York*, 198 U.S. 45, 53 (1905) — but when it recognizes that guidance and constraint by precise language is often possible and sometimes desirable. In this latter sense, what some call "formalism" others would label "objectivity." *See* KENT GREENAWALT, LAW AND OBJECTIVITY 14-15, 48-49, 71-73, 207-31 (1992) (connecting objectivity in interpretation with shared understandings of meaning); Kent Greenawalt, *How Law Can Be Determinate*, 38 UCLA L. REV. 1 *passim* (1990) (same).

that the debate about vehicles in the park raises is the question of the ever-present potential for conflict between the letter of the law (about which much more will be said in the following Part) and what would otherwise be the best (fairest, wisest, most just, most optimal, etc.) resolution of a legal question. If the straightforward reading of the law produces a ridiculous or even merely suboptimal outcome, are legal actors required or even permitted to reach the right outcome instead of the outcome seemingly mandated by the plain meaning of the words on the page?

In order to frame this recurring conflict in the crispest possible way, it is important that following the letter of the law really does produce a poor outcome. And for this purpose the word "vehicle" might not do the trick. It is a colorable understanding of the word "vehicle" that something is not a vehicle unless, at the time we are applying the label, the thing we are describing has the capacity for self-propulsion, or at least for movement. If it cannot move, it might be said, it is not a vehicle.[23] It might be a former vehicle, or a quasi-vehicle, or even a vehicle-in-progress, but to be a real vehicle it must be able to move.

If this understanding of at least one meaning of the word "vehicle" is plausible, then it is no longer clear that the truck which has been "mount[ed] on a pedestal" as a military memorial is even a vehicle at all. We have all seen bronzed cannons, immobilized tanks, and flightless airplanes used as war memorials, and a tank — or a truck, for that matter — with all of its moving parts removed or welded fixed might not strike everyone as being a vehicle at all. That conclusion might not be much different if the truck used as a war memorial consisted of an otherwise fully functioning vehicle — Fuller did use the description "in perfect working order" — that was placed in a locked enclosure, or bolted to a base, or even simply had its battery or keys removed. At some point on a continuum these former vehicles move from nonvehicles (the bronzed and welded tank) to vehicles (the fully operational truck with the keys removed), but the point is that the issue might be seen as debatable.[24] Some degree of functionality may, and only may, be one of the necessary conditions for something being a vehicle at all and, insofar as this is so, then the

---

[23] Not only might it be said, it has been said. *The Shorter Oxford English Dictionary* includes within its definition of "vehicle" that the thing must be a "means of conveyance" and must be used "for transporting people, goods, etc." 2 THE SHORTER OXFORD ENGLISH DICTIONARY 3512 (5th ed. 2002).

[24] But only barely. The familiar phrase "disabled vehicle" makes sense only because vehicles that do not work are still vehicles. In an imaginary debate between Fuller and the person who objects that the truck is no longer a vehicle, Fuller has the better of it, but not by so much as to render the example perfect for his purposes.

example becomes a bit murky on the conflict between what the rule clearly requires and what the best result would be. If the truck/memorial is possibly not a vehicle at all, then the conflict dissolves, and the point of the example is lost.

Not so, however, with various other examples. Indeed, Fuller himself, perhaps recognizing the potential complications of the word "vehicle," provides a different example. A page after talking about trucks being used as war memorials, he asks us to imagine a tired passenger who nods off in the station late at night while waiting for a delayed train.[25] In doing so, the passenger runs afoul of a "no sleeping in the station" rule, a rule plainly designed, says Fuller, as a restriction on the homeless (this being 1958, Fuller calls them "tramps"), who might seek to use the station as their residence.[26]

This turns out to be a better example. Sleep is a physiological state, and as a matter of physiology Fuller's businessman was sleeping. Period. It is true that there are uses of the word "sleep" that do not require physiological sleep, as when sleep is a euphemism for "have sex" or when it is used to describe a computer that has gone into low-power mode, but there are few instances of the reverse. If you are physiologically sleeping you are almost always sleeping in ordinary language, even if sometimes when you are sleeping in ordinary language you are not always physiologically sleeping. The no-sleeping-in-the-station example thus turns out to be a better one than the prohibition on vehicles in the park, because now the conflict between what the rule on its face requires and what a good outcome would be becomes much crisper and substantially less open to challenge on definitional grounds.

The same crispness of conflict is equally apparent in the now-prominent example of *Riggs v. Palmer*.[27] The force of using *Riggs* as an example of one dilemma of legal reasoning is that the case also presents a well-defined opposition between what a rule says and what the morally right or sensibly right or all-things-considered right answer should be. Insofar as New York's Statute of Wills, as it existed in 1889, said plainly that anyone named in a will would inherit except in cases of fraud, duress, or incapacity at the time the will was made,[28] Elmer Palmer should clearly

---

[25] Fuller, *Positivism and Fidelity to Law, supra* note 5, at 664.

[26] *Id.*

[27] 22 N.E. 188 (N.Y. 1889).

[28] It is noteworthy that both the majority and the dissent in *Riggs* share this understanding of what the plain meaning of the statute required. Judge Earl for the majority said that "[i]t is quite true that statutes regulating the making, proof, and effect of wills and the devolution of prop-

inherit according to the language of the statute,[29] even though his killing of the testator, his grandfather, makes this a morally abhorrent result. We now associate the case with Ronald Dworkin,[30] and with the Hart and Sacks materials on the Legal Process,[31] but both *Riggs* and the sleeping businessman would have been clearer examples for Fuller than one using the word "vehicle," a word that is linguistically problematic for Fuller in just the wrong way.

So although some might therefore quibble over whether the military truck ceased being a vehicle at the moment it was mounted on a pedestal to become a war memorial, this is a peculiarity only of the example. The literature on statutory interpretation is replete with instances in which the conflict between the plain meaning of the most immediately applicable legal item and simple good sense is far less escapable, whether they be real cases like *United States v. Kirby*[32] and *Church of the Holy Trinity v. United States*,[33] or hypothetical ones like Pufendorf's surgeon, who, in performing an emergency operation, runs afoul of the prohibition on drawing blood in the streets.[34] Consequently, we should not get hung up on the word "vehicle," for the point of Fuller's counterexample of the vehicle that has become a war memorial is a point that far transcends the peculiarities of the particular word.

The example of the no-vehicles-in-the-park rule turns out to be doubly unfortunate because it also allows Fuller mistakenly to suppose that Hart's argument turns on the meaning of individual words taken in isolation. Fuller stresses that Hart's mistake is in thinking that a single word by itself

---

erty, if literally construed, and if their force and effect can in no way and under no circumstances be controlled or modified, give this property to the murderer." *Id.* at 189. And in dissent Judge Gray insisted that "the very provision defining the modes of alteration and revocation implies a prohibition of alteration or revocation in any other way." *Id.* at 192. For both the majority and the dissent, therefore, the facts of *Riggs* presented an inescapable conflict between the plain meaning of the statute and the best, fairest, or most just result.

[29] This is decidedly not the same as saying "should clearly inherit according to the law," for that is precisely the matter at issue.

[30] *See* RONALD DWORKIN, LAW'S EMPIRE 15-20 (1986); RONALD DWORKIN, TAKING RIGHTS SERIOUSLY 23-31 (1978).

[31] *See* HENRY M. HART & ALBERT M. SACKS, THE LEGAL PROCESS: BASIC PROBLEMS IN THE MAKING AND APPLICATION OF LAW 68-102 (William N. Eskridge, Jr. & Philip P. Frickey eds., 1994).

[32] 74 U.S. (7 Wall.) 482, 487 (1868) (finding that statute prohibiting obstruction of mail did not extend to law enforcement officer arresting mail carrier).

[33] 143 U.S. 457, 472 (1892) (finding that statute prohibiting paying passage of foreign labor was not violated when church hired new pastor from abroad).

[34] SAMUEL VON PUFENDORF, DE JURE NATURAE ET GENTIUM LIBRO OCTO (1672), *as described in* 1 WILLIAM BLACKSTONE, COMMENTARIES *60.

can tell us what a rule means, but Hart makes no such claim. Indeed, had Hart anticipated that Fuller would challenge him on this point, he might have used a better example, such as the language in *Riggs*, or, better yet, *Kirby*. For although it is pretty clear what the language in the statute at issue in *Kirby* — "willfully obstruct or retard the passage of the mail, or of any driver or carrier"[35] — means, very few questions of meaning, and certainly not the question at issue in *Kirby* itself, would focus on any one of those words in isolation. So while Hart used an example that turned out to be susceptible to Fuller's misaimed charge, nothing in Hart's larger point is inconsistent with the (correct) view that it is sentences, not individual words, that are the principal carriers of meaning.[36] Hart's claim, at least in 1958, was that the statutory language, as language, would generate some number of clear or core applications, and this is a claim that does not at all depend on whether it is this or that particular word in a rule or statute that is expected to carry most of the load.

III. THE MEANING OF MEANING[37]

Fuller's challenge to Hart's theory of meaning is broader than just the question whether it is the word or the sentence that is the principal transmitter of meaning. For Fuller, Hart's mistake in believing that words can have meanings in isolation is the mistake of ignoring the importance of context, of ignoring the maxim that meaning is use, and, in essence, of not having read his Wittgenstein.[38] Once we recognize that meaning is use, Fuller appears to argue, we cannot avoid the fact that it is the use in the particular context that is the appropriate unit of understanding. If we appreciate this understanding of contextual definition, he seems to be saying, then we must realize that, in the *particular* context of applying a rule prohibiting vehicles from the park to a *particular* military truck used as a war memorial, the alleged vehicle may simply not be a vehicle at all.

But even if Fuller were right (which he was not) about Hart being committed to a so-called pointer theory of meaning and about Hart believing that the chief unit of meaning was the word, it does not follow that

---

[35] 4 Stat. 104 (1825), *quoted in Kirby*, 74 U.S. at 483.

[36] *See* W.V. Quine, *Epistemology Naturalized, in* ONTOLOGICAL RELATIVITY AND OTHER ESSAYS 69, 72 (1969) (understanding "contextual definition" as "recognition of the sentence as the primary vehicle of meaning").

[37] With apologies to Ogden and Richards. *Cf.* C.K. OGDEN & I.A. RICHARDS, THE MEANING OF MEANING (1923).

[38] *See* LUDWIG WITTGENSTEIN, PHILOSOPHICAL INVESTIGATIONS (G.E.M. Anscombe trans., 2d ed. 1958).

meaning resides solely or even principally in the full immediate context in which words and sentences are used. This is a common view,[39] but its ubiquity, like the ubiquity of belief in the explanatory validity of astrology, is no indicator of its soundness. For if meaning only existed in the particular context in which words and sentences are used, it is hard to see how we could talk to each other. It is true that the compositional nature of language — the ability to understand sentences we have never heard before — is one of the hardest and most complex of questions concerning the nature of language. But anything even residing in the neighborhood of the "meaning is use on a particular occasion" view of language fails even to address the compositional problem: Without knowing something about words and sentences and grammar and syntax as general or acontextual rules (or, even better, conventions), we could never hope to understand each other. The full particular context may indeed add something or even a great deal to our understanding, but we will understand virtually nothing at all about "the cat is on the mat" unless we understand that this sentence carries meaning by drawing on shared acontextual understandings of the facts that the word "cat" refers to cats, that the word "mat" refers to mats, and that the words "is on" refer to a certain kind of relationship that differs from the relationship described by phrases such as "is under," "is near," or "is a."[40]

When Wittgenstein, J.L. Austin,[41] and all of their fellow travelers in Cambridge and Oxford, respectively, talked about meaning being use, they were talking not about particulars but about rules or conventions. And they were talking about the rules or conventions that constitute any language. The way the word "cat" is used in a particular linguistic community is what determines the meaning of the word "cat," but it is the *community* that is the key. That linguistic community could decide (in a nonconscious sense of that word) over time that the word "cat" would refer instead to dogs or sheep or sealing wax, and in just that sense the meaning of

---

[39] *See, e.g.*, James Boyle, *The Politics of Reason: Critical Legal Theory and Local Social Thought*, 133 U. PA. L. REV. 685, 709-13, 759-60 (1985) (insisting that linguistic meaning depends on subjective intention); Stanley Fish, *Almost Pragmatism: Richard Posner's Jurisprudence*, 57 U. CHI. L. REV. 1447, 1456 (1990) ("No act of reading can stop at the plain meaning of a document . . . ."); Stanley Fish, *Fish v. Fiss*, 36 STAN. L. REV. 1325, 1332 (1984) (claiming that all interpretation is inside context and that external constraint by rules is impossible).

[40] *See* JOHN R. SEARLE, EXPRESSION AND MEANING: STUDIES IN THE THEORY OF SPEECH ACTS 117-26 (1979); P.F. Strawson, *On Referring*, in ESSAYS IN CONCEPTUAL ANALYSIS 21, 30-31 (Antony Flew ed., 1956); *see also* MICHAEL DUMMETT, THE INTERPRETATION OF FREGE'S PHILOSOPHY 364 (1981); Paul Ziff, *On H.P. Grice's Account of Meaning*, 28 ANALYSIS 1, 7 (1967).

[41] *See* J.L. AUSTIN, HOW TO DO THINGS WITH WORDS (J.O. Urmson & Marina Sbisa'eds., 2d ed. 1975).

a word or, better, a sentence is a function of how that sentence is now used by the relevant linguistic community.

Still, nothing in the view that linguistic communities determine meaning by how they in fact use language entails the view that meaning is entirely or even largely a function of how particular individuals use language on particular occasions. In baseball there used to be, prior to the modern era of interleague play, a difference between a strike in the American League and a strike in the National League, even though the umpires in the respective leagues both purported to be interpreting the same words in the same written book of rules.[42] Yet no one suggested that an American League umpire was free to call balls and strikes according to National League criteria. If he did, he would have been criticized or sanctioned for violating a rule that reflected a continuously changing practice, but which possessed sufficient short-term fixity in the face of longer-term flexibility that we could usually understand at any point of time who was following the rules and who was breaking them. The fact that the Constitution adopted in 1787 referred to a "*Republican* Form of Government"[43] does not mean that we cannot now distinguish the party affiliation of Barack Obama from that of John McCain. And it is hardly nonsense to speak of standing still while on a moving train. Although the conventions of language change over time or in different contexts, they still have the capacity to carry meaning at any given time, and this conclusion applies no less to the language of the law than it does to language in general.

In misunderstanding the lessons of "use" and "context" that dominated the philosophy of language of his times,[44] Fuller failed to understand the basic problem of language — our ability to understand sentences we have never heard, people we have never met, and propositions we have never previously encountered. And thus Fuller failed to understand why as an American English-speaking lawyer I can understand far more on a first reading of a New Zealand statute about corporate insolvency, a topic about which I am completely ignorant, than I can on a first reading of a French code provision about freedom of expression, a subject about which I have considerably more knowledge.

Fuller's misguided foray into the philosophy of language is ironic, because it damaged his own case. Insofar as he wished to employ the military

---

[42] *See* Murray Chass, *In the Early Returns, American League Hitters Have the Upper Hand*, N.Y. TIMES, Apr. 13, 1997, § 8, at 8; Tim Sullivan, *High Time for "New" Strike Zone*, CINCINNATI ENQUIRER, Feb. 25, 2001, at 1C.

[43] U.S. CONST. art. IV, § 4 (emphasis added).

[44] *See* Fuller, *Positivism and Fidelity to Law*, *supra* note 5, at 669.

truck/war memorial example to demonstrate how legal language may not always produce the correct all-things-considered result or to show that language may not always accurately reflect a rule's purpose, Fuller needed to rely on the fact that legal language transmitted meaning apart from its particular application. The vividness of Fuller's counterexample stems precisely from the fact that the truck *is* a vehicle.[45] If Fuller had instead offered the counterexample of a veterans group that wished to plant a bed of poppies as a war memorial, we would have thought him daft, because it is implausible that a bed of poppies would be prohibited by a "no vehicles in the park" rule. Only because a truck is a vehicle in the way that a bed of poppies is not does the example have its sting. Like pitchers trying to explain the physics of the curveball or artists venturing into philosophical aesthetics, Fuller's examples demonstrated an intuitive and correct understanding of the problem which his explanations served only to undercut.

●   ●   ●   ●

A related problem arises with respect to the distinction between plain and ordinary meaning. Putting aside any question about words as opposed to sentences, Hart's point was basically one about plain meaning, although he did not explicitly take up the question of the linguistic community or sub-community within which the meaning would be plain. An automobile is plainly a vehicle, Hart argues, but the fact that what counts as a vehicle in ordinary language is (usually) the same as what counts as a vehicle in legal language does not mean that law is committed to the ordinary meaning of ordinary terms.

There are times when law uses language of its own making, often in Latin — replevin, assumpsit, quantum meruit, habeas corpus, res judicata — and sometimes even in English — bailment, demurrer, due process, joinder, interpleader, easement. Such terms have little if any meaning for the layperson, but they can still have plain meanings in law and for lawyers and judges. So as long as one believes in anything close to plain or literal meaning at all,[46] such terms, when used inside the legal world, do not present special problems. Like the words of ordinary language, the meaning here is determined by the rules of use of the relevant linguistic community, but here that community is the community of legal actors rather than the men on the Clapham omnibus.

---

[45] Subject to the qualifications in Part II, *supra*.

[46] For my own longer discussion of plain or literal meaning in the context of rules, see SCHAUER, PLAYING BY THE RULES, *supra* note 10, at 53-64.

Things become somewhat more problematic, however, when terms have both ordinary and technical legal meanings. We know that "due process" in the Fifth and Fourteenth Amendments has a legal/constitutional meaning with no ordinary counterpart. The women on the D train are no more likely ever to use the term than are the men on the Clapham omnibus. But the same does not hold true for "speech" and "religion" in the First Amendment[47] or "arms" in the Second[48] or "searches" in the Fourth.[49] Here there are both ordinary and legal meanings, and the question is about the relation between them. So too outside of constitutional law, where words such as "trespass," "complaint," and even "contract" have legal meanings that diverge from their nonlegal ones.

This is not the place to engage in an in-depth analysis of the relationship between ordinary language and legal language.[50] My point here is only that there is nothing about the existence of law itself as a relevant linguistic community that entails that every person is his or her own linguistic community. Just as there can be plain (legal) meanings of terms like replevin and bailment, so too can there be plain (legal) meanings of terms like speech and contract. That Hart and Fuller were debating, in part, about the extent to which plain meaning is dispositive in the interpretation or application of a formulated rule says nothing about whether that meaning need be ordinary or technical — whether the terms be everyday ones or terms of art. And although Fuller does not exactly say this, one senses in his challenge a flavor of the belief that if law can be a relevant linguistic community and a relevant linguistic context, then there is no limit to the smallness of the context that should concern us. This is a mistake about the relationships between language and community and between language and rules, but it is not a mistake that detracts from the basic problem: Sometimes language will simply give the wrong answer, and the problem for law is the problem of what, if anything, to do about it.

IV. Cores, Penumbras, and Open Texture

Hart employs the "no vehicles in the park" rule as a way of explaining the problem of the penumbra, but it is important to distinguish two very different types of penumbral problems, problems signaled in Hart's 1958 contribution but not developed fully until *The Concept of Law* three years

---

[47] U.S. CONST. amend. I.

[48] U.S. CONST. amend. II.

[49] U.S. CONST. amend. IV.

[50] A good exploration of the issues is Mary Jane Morrison, *Excursions into the Nature of Legal Language*, 37 CLEV. ST. L. REV. 271 (1989).

later.

One type of penumbral problem, if we can even call it that, is the problem of pervasive vagueness.[51] Although Hart focused on statutes with a clear core and a vague penumbra, some legal rules resemble penumbra all the way through. It is true that there exist intentionalist theories of interpretation that would find in the drafters' mental states a clear set of intended applications even when the language of a legal text is unclear,[52] and in that way "cure" the vagueness of a vague text. But if we put aside such an approach and focus just on the language, we find that on occasion legal language is so vague by itself that there is nothing clear at all. Without recourse to the original intentions of the drafters (or possibly, as Justice Scalia would have it, to potentially narrower contemporaneous meanings[53]), there may be *no* clear instances of which searches and seizures are "unreasonable" under the Fourth Amendment; which forms of inequality are the focus of the Fourteenth Amendment's prohibition on the denial of the "equal protection of the laws"; when a "contract, combination, . . . or conspiracy" is "in restraint of trade or commerce" for purposes of the Sherman Antitrust Act;[54] which custody decisions are in the "best interests" of the child;[55] and just how fast one may drive when the only relevant rule says simply that one's driving must be "reasonable" and "prudent."[56]

---

[51] Vagueness in law is a far larger issue than I can hope to deal with in this Article. For comprehensive analytic discussions of the topic, see TIMOTHY A.O. ENDICOTT, VAGUENESS IN LAW (2000), Timothy A.O. Endicott, *Vagueness and Legal Theory*, 3 LEGAL THEORY 37 (1997), and Jeremy Waldron, *Vagueness in Law and Language: Some Philosophical Issues*, 82 CAL. L. REV. 509 (1994). And for a collection of valuable attempts to link legal with philosophical thinking about vagueness, see Symposium, *Vagueness and Law*, 7 LEGAL THEORY 369 (2001).

[52] *See, e.g.*, RAOUL BERGER, GOVERNMENT BY JUDICIARY: THE TRANSFORMATION OF THE FOURTEENTH AMENDMENT 4, 9, 404-05, 410-27 (2d ed. 1997) (insisting that original intentions are "binding" and can clear up meaning of otherwise indeterminate language); Richard S. Kay, *Adherence to the Original Intentions in Constitutional Adjudication: Three Objections and Responses*, 82 NW. U. L. REV. 226, 228-35 (1988) (distinguishing use of original intentions from interpretive approach that looks only to words of legal text); Earl M. Maltz, *Federalism and the Fourteenth Amendment: A Comment on* Democracy and Distrust, 42 OHIO ST. L.J. 209, 210 (1981) (explaining that recourse to original intentions can limit judicial authority when constitutional text is indeterminate).

[53] *See* ANTONIN SCALIA, A MATTER OF INTERPRETATION: FEDERAL COURTS AND THE LAW 38 (1997). For a careful and balanced exploration of the "original meaning" position and the differences between it and an "original intentions" approach, see Caleb Nelson, *Originalism and Interpretive Conventions*, 70 U. CHI. L. REV. 519, 553-78 (2003).

[54] 15 U.S.C. § 1 (2000).

[55] *E.g.*, ARIZ. REV. STAT. ANN. § 25-403 (2007); MASS. GEN. LAWS ch. 119, § 23 (2003); MICH. COMP. LAWS ANN. § 722.23 (West 2002); *accord* CAL. FAM. CODE § 3011 (West 2004) (using phrase "the best interest of the child").

[56] MONT. CODE ANN. § 61-8-303(1) (1995), *invalidated by* State v. Stanko, 974 P.2d 1132 (Mont. 1998). The history of Montana's experience with and without numerical speed limits is

With respect to examples like these, there is no reason to believe that Hart would not have taken the position that *all* applications (questions of precedent and *stare decisis* aside) of such rules require an exercise of judicial discretion, and that judicial discretion necessarily requires recourse to extralegal factors. And there is no reason to believe that Fuller would have disagreed, except of course with the designation of such factors as "extralegal." So although this kind of pervasive vagueness is widespread, and although it requires the type of judicial behavior that Hart saw in the penumbras around clearer cores, this is not an issue about which Hart and Fuller, except perhaps for terminology, would have had much disagreement.

So what, then, *is* a penumbra, whether in the context of language generally or of legal language specifically? In explaining the idea of penumbral language, Hart borrows in part from Bertrand Russell, who in his enduring article on "vagueness" drew a distinction between the core and the fringe.[57] He borrows even more, however, from Friedrich Waismann, whose elaboration of Wittgensteinian themes brought us the idea of "open texture."[58] Russell was concerned principally with line-drawing and boundaries, and he relied on the example of baldness as a way of showing that the inability to draw a sharp demarcation between two words or concepts does not mean that there was no distinction to be had. So in this companion to the classic paradox of *sorites*,[59] Russell asked us to recognize that although there might be some cases in which we would be unsure about whether a man was bald or not,[60] this does not mean that there are not men who are clearly bald and men who are clearly not. And so too with vehicles: The line between a vehicle and a nonvehicle is fuzzy — and this is presumably what Hart had in mind in offering bicycles, roller skates, and toy automobiles as examples — but this does not mean, Hart argued, that standard ordinary automobiles are not clearly vehicles, nor, he might have said, that lovers quietly strolling hand-in-hand in the park

---

recounted in great detail in Robert E. King & Cass R. Sunstein, *Doing Without Speed Limits*, 79 B.U. L. REV. 155 (1999).

[57] Bertrand Russell, *Vagueness*, 1 AUSTRALASIAN J. PHIL. 84 (1923).

[58] Friedrich Waismann, *Verifiability*, in LOGIC AND LANGUAGE: FIRST AND SECOND SERIES 122, 125 (Antony Flew ed., Anchor Books 1965) (1951).

[59] General discussions of linguistic vagueness and the *sorites* paradox can be found in, for example, LINDA CLAIRE BURNS, VAGUENESS: AN INVESTIGATION INTO NATURAL LANGUAGES AND THE SORITES PARADOX (1991), TIMOTHY WILLIAMSON, VAGUENESS (1994), and Dominic Hyde, *Sorites Paradox*, STANFORD ENCYCLOPEDIA OF PHILOSOPHY (2005), http://plato.stanford.edu/entries/sorites-paradox/. The paradox of baldness, *falakros*, in fact has the same origin — Eubulides of Miletus — as the paradox of *sorites*, the heaper. *Id.*

[60] Ten or so years ago, I used to see an example of this when I looked in the mirror.

are not nonvehicles. In this respect, the penumbra consists of those anticipated applications of a term that we know now will present uncertainties or indeterminacies, just as we know now that a rule requiring drivers to have their lights on after dark will be vague with respect to dusk and that the mostly clear distinction between frogs and tadpoles will become vague at some point on a tadpole's journey towards becoming a frog. In offering the example of the no-vehicles-in-the-park rule, and in speaking of the core and the penumbra, Hart was presumably asking us to see that for many or even most rules we can, even at the time of drafting, imagine that there will be hard cases as well as easy ones,[61] but that the existence of the hard ones — the indeterminacy claims of the legal realists notwithstanding — does not mean that there are not easy ones as well, just as there are clear examples of frogs, tadpoles, night, day, and, of course, vehicles.

Waismann's valuable addition to what was in his time well known about vagueness was the conclusion that it is impossible to eliminate the *potential* for vagueness in even nonvague terms, and this is the phenomenon he called "open texture."[62] Even the most precise term has the potential for becoming vague upon confronting the unexpected, Waismann argued, and so no amount of precision can wall off every possibility of future but now unforeseen and even unforeseeable vagueness. When Hart's friend and Waismann's contemporary J.L. Austin talked of the exploding goldfinch,[63] he vividly captured the same idea, for his point was that even if we could now describe with total precision the necessary and sufficient conditions for "goldfinchness," "we [would not] know what to say" — "words [would] literally fail us" — when confronting a creature that was a goldfinch according to all of the existing criteria, but which proceeded to explode before our eyes.[64] In other words, the unexpectedly exploding goldfinch would render vague what we had previously thought clear, just

---

[61] Which is not to say that there will be clear lines between the hard cases and the easy ones. The boundary between the core and the penumbra is itself a fuzzy one, and it is towards precisely this issue that the longstanding debates about the *sorites* paradox are directed.

[62] A generation of law professors (who shall remain unnamed here), perhaps attempting to look sophisticated, has used "open texture" as a synonym for "vagueness." As Waismann made very clear, the two are not the same, and he used the term "open texture" to refer to the ineliminable potential for vagueness surrounding even the clearest of terms. Waismann, *supra* note 58, at 126-27. Hart unfortunately fostered some of the problem, for in *The Concept of Law* we see the phrase "vagueness or 'open texture,'" which in context was ambiguous as to whether Hart was describing two different phenomena or whether he was merely providing two terms for the same idea. HART, THE CONCEPT OF LAW, *supra* note 1, at 123.

[63] J.L. AUSTIN, *Other Minds*, in PHILOSOPHICAL PAPERS 76, 88 (J.O. Urmson & G.J. Warnock eds., 3d ed. 1979).

[64] *Id.*

as the unexpectedly vehicle-like war memorial would render vague what might have been thought to be the clear part of the no-vehicles-in-the-park rule.

Fuller's example of the truck/memorial thus presents an interesting question with respect to the idea of open texture. Fuller presented the example as a case involving legal uncertainty arising from linguistic certainty — or at least should have — and it raises an important question with respect to the relationship between linguistic open texture and what we might think of as legal open texture.[65] It is certainly possible to imagine legal uncertainty arising out of unexpected linguistic uncertainty: If we had a statute that protected goldfinches as, say, endangered species or national symbols,[66] a sudden awareness of the existence of an exploding goldfinch would have made the law uncertain — it would have produced an indeterminate application — just because that event would have made the language in which the law was written uncertain as well.

More commonly, however, and this is the point of Fuller's example, as well as Pufendorf's, as well as of real cases like *Riggs*,[67] *Kirby*,[68] and *Church of the Holy Trinity*,[69] our language does not fail us but our law does. The language is clear, and the application is linguistically clear, but following the clear language will lead to what appears to be a wrong or unjust or unwise or inequitable or silly result. In such cases we do not have linguistic open texture, but we might have legal open texture, and it is in such cases that legal decisionmakers must decide what to do. For Fuller, the law should always in such cases seek to come up with the reasonable result, and from this premise Fuller derives the conclusion that there are no purpose-independent, clear, easy, or core cases.

Interestingly, Hart may not have completely disagreed with Fuller

---

[65] *See* Frederick Schauer, *On the Supposed Defeasibility of Legal Rules*, in CURRENT LEGAL PROBLEMS 1998 (M.D.A. Freeman ed., 1998); *see also* Neil MacCormick, *Defeasibility in Law and Logic*, in INFORMATICS AND THE FOUNDATIONS OF LEGAL REASONING 99 (Zenon Bankowski, Ian White & Ulrike Hahn eds., 1995); Richard H.S. Tur, *Defeasibilism*, 21 OXFORD J. LEGAL STUD. 355 (2001).

[66] Imagine, if you will, the case of the exploding bald eagle.

[67] Riggs v. Palmer, 22 N.E. 188 (N.Y. 1889); *see supra* notes 27-29 and accompanying text.

[68] United States v. Kirby, 74 U.S. (7 Wall.) 482 (1868); *see supra* note 32.

[69] Church of the Holy Trinity v. United States, 143 U.S. 457 (1892); *see supra* note 33. An important and interesting disagreement about the actual facts and legislative history can be found in Adrian Vermeule, *Legislative History and the Limits of Judicial Competence: The Untold Story of* Holy Trinity Church, 50 STAN. L. REV. 1833, 1885-96 (1998) (challenging Supreme Court's understanding of pertinent legislative history), and Carol Chomsky, *Unlocking the Mysteries of* Holy Trinity: *Spirit, Letter, and History in Statutory Interpretation*, 100 COLUM. L. REV. 901 (2000) (supporting Court's historical understanding and *Church of the Holy Trinity* outcome).

about the proper outcome of the truck/memorial case, although he might have disagreed with the route that Fuller took to get there. When Hart says in *The Concept of Law* that legal rules are necessarily always subject to exceptions, and that the grounds for creating such exceptions cannot be specified in advance,[70] we see in Hart the through-and-through mentality of the common law lawyer. Common law rules are always subject to modification at the moment of application, and it is characteristic of the common law that it treats a ridiculous or even somewhat suboptimal outcome generated by an existing common law rule as the occasion for changing the rule. If "no vehicles in the park" were a common law rule, there is little doubt that Hart would have expected the common law judge to change the rule into "no vehicles in the park except for war memorials," or something of that sort. Indeed, Hart verges on suggesting in his discussion of the always open "unless" clause that this is not only a characteristic of the common law, but a necessary feature of law and a necessary feature of rules.

In this Hart was mistaken. As most civil lawyers would understand, and as Jeremy Bentham would have applauded,[71] sometimes the language of a rule generates a bad result, and sometimes we have to live with that bad result as the price to be paid for refusing to empower judges or bureaucrats or police officers with the authority to modify the language of a rule in the service of what they think, perhaps mistakenly, is the best outcome.[72] This is the argument for a plausible formalism, and in this respect

---

[70] Hart had made a seemingly similar claim earlier when he said that legal concepts could not be defined except "with the aid of a list of exceptions or negative examples." H.L.A. Hart, *The Ascription of Responsibility and Rights*, 49 PROC. ARISTOTELIAN SOC'Y (NEW SERIES) 171, 174 (1948-49). But by itself this is a mild and almost certainly sound claim. It was not until Hart added in *The Concept of Law* that the list of exceptions could never be specified in advance — that law was necessarily continuously open to new exceptions — that the claim became more debatable. A claim similar to Hart's can be found in Neil MacCormick, *Law as Institutional Fact*, 90 LAW Q. REV. 102, 125 (1974).

[71] Bentham would have preferred a code so precise and prescient that such a thing would almost never occur. *See, e.g.*, Letter from Jeremy Bentham to Pres. James Madison (Oct. 1811), *in* THE COLLECTED WORKS OF JEREMY BENTHAM 5, 7-15 (Philip Schofield & Jonathan Harris eds., 1998) (stressing importance in legal code of correctness, completeness, and ability to impart clear knowledge of what law requires). Moreover, Bentham's skepticism about judges, judicial power, and the common law was so pervasive that he would hardly have approved of allowing to judges the updating function that is well-recognized in common law countries. *Compare* JEREMY BENTHAM, TRUTH VERSUS ASHHURST (1823), *reprinted in* 5 THE WORKS OF JEREMY BENTHAM 231, 235-37 (photo. reprint, Russell & Russell, Inc. 1962) (John Bowring ed., 1843) (castigating almost all aspects of common law and common law judges), *with* GUIDO CALABRESI, A COMMON LAW FOR THE AGE OF STATUTES 170-74 (1982) (sympathetically describing updating function).

[72] *See* John F. Manning, *The Absurdity Doctrine*, 116 HARV. L. REV. 2387 (2003); Adrian Ver-

Hart's commitment to the continuous flexibility of the common law may have made him no more of a formalist than Fuller.

V. THE NATURE OF THE DEBATE

So what, precisely, were Hart and Fuller fighting about? What really were their differences regarding the no-vehicles-in-the-park rule? These questions are even more relevant in light of what might appear to some to be Hart's "concession" in the Preface to *Essays in Jurisprudence and Philosophy*.[73] Here, Hart acknowledged that the distinction between the core and the penumbra was not necessarily, at least in law, located in the language in which a rule is written. The law could, Hart concedes, distinguish the core from the penumbra on the basis of purpose or of intent, and were the law to do so, it might very well exclude the truck/vehicle from the reach of the rule, thus allowing it to be erected in the park.

At this point, it appears that the debate has become, in part, an empirical one. Fuller can be best understood as claiming that the reasonable and purpose-based interpretation of the no-vehicles-in-the-park rule is a *necessary* feature of law properly so called.[74] And, if we forgive Hart for what he said about "unless" in *The Concept of Law*, Hart might now be understood, postconcession, as saying that the recourse to purpose or common sense is a possible and even arguably desirable feature of a legal system, but that it is not a necessary component of the concept of law.

This is a real disagreement about the concept of law, but there is also an empirical disagreement between Hart and Fuller. Fuller is arguing not only that his purpose-focused approach is a necessary feature of law properly so called, but also that it is an accurate description of what most judges and other legal actors would actually do in most common law jurisdictions. On this point Hart might well be read as being agnostic, but there is still a tone in Hart of believing that Fuller not only overestimates the role of purpose in understanding the concept of law, but may well also be overestimating the role of purpose and underestimating the role of plain language in explaining the behavior of lawyers and judges. And if this is not what Hart would have said, and it may not have been, then it may

---

meule, *Interpretive Choice*, 75 N.Y.U. L. REV. 74 (2000); *cf.* Robert E. Scott, *The Case for Formalism in Relational Contract*, 94 NW. U. L. REV. 847 (2000) (applying same theme to judicial interpretation of contracts).

[73] H.L.A. HART, ESSAYS IN JURISPRUDENCE AND PHILOSOPHY 8 (1983).

[74] For a similar argument that an equitable override of inequitable statutory or common law outcomes is a necessary feature of law itself, see Tur, *supra* note 65.

well be what he should have said.[75]

Thus, although much of the debate appears to be a nonempirical one, it also has an empirical side, a side in which Fuller and Hart hint at opposing descriptions of the role of language-determined cores in producing actual legal outcomes in actual legal systems. Moreover, even as Hart conceded that the core of a rule might be determined by something other than the plain meaning of the rule's language, he did not go so far as conceding that anything other than first-level purpose — the purpose of a particular rule — might take the place of language in distinguishing the core from the penumbra. In this respect, Hart would almost certainly have bridled at the prospect of a judge setting aside both the purpose and the language of a rule when the two together produced a poor outcome from the perspective of broader conceptions of justice, fairness, efficiency, or wise policy. And here we suspect that Fuller may well have been more sympathetic to such an outcome because of his commitment to purpose, not only to the particular purpose behind particular rules, but also to the idea that law as a whole had a purpose — the reasonable regulation and organization of human conduct — the frustration of which was always to be avoided.[76]

Seen in this way, the example of the no-vehicles-in-the-park rule also suggests a real debate about the role of the judge. One way of understanding Fuller, and possibly theorists such as Ronald Dworkin[77] and Michael Moore[78] as well, is as believing that the good judge is one who sets aside the plain language of the most directly applicable legal rule in the service of purpose, or of reasonableness, or of making law the best it can be, or of integrity, or simply of doing the right thing. Dworkin's sympathy with the outcome in *Riggs* makes this clear for him,[79] and Fuller's only slightly less overt sympathy for his mythical Justice Foster in *The Case of the Speluncean*

---

[75] On the extent to which Hart can be understood as making empirical claims, admittedly sub silentio, about the operation of the legal systems he knew best, see Frederick Schauer, *The Limited Domain of the Law*, 90 VA. L. REV. 1909, 1912 (2004) [hereinafter Schauer, *The Limited Domain of the Law*], and Frederick Schauer, *(Re)Taking Hart*, 119 HARV. L. REV. 852, 860-61 (2006) (reviewing LACEY, A LIFE OF H.L.A. HART, *supra* note 20).

[76] *See* sources cited *supra* note 19.

[77] DWORKIN, LAW'S EMPIRE, *supra* note 30, at 37-43; DWORKIN, TAKING RIGHTS SERIOUSLY, *supra* note 30, at 23-39.

[78] Michael S. Moore, *A Natural Law Theory of Interpretation*, 58 S. CAL. L. REV. 277, 381-96 (1985) (arguing that judge has responsibility to pursue morally correct outcome even if ordinary meaning of legal language indicates otherwise); Michael S. Moore, *The Semantics of Judging*, 54 S. CAL. L. REV. 151, 178-202 (1981) (discussing necessary role of moral considerations in legal interpretation).

[79] *E.g.*, DWORKIN, TAKING RIGHTS SERIOUSLY, *supra* note 30, at 23.

Explorers[80] is in the same vein.

So then the question is a slightly different one. If the plain meaning of a rule, or of "the law" positivistically understood,[81] generates a wrong, silly, absurd, unjust, inequitable, unwise, or suboptimal outcome (and these are not all the same thing), then is it the job of the judge to do something about it? This is a question of role morality, and just as some would argue that justice is best done if lawyers fight for their clients and not justice,[82] that truth may emerge from the clash of often false ideas,[83] and that economic progress for all comes from the invisible hand of the market while individual economic actors pursue only their own well-being,[84] it might be the case that the best legal system is one in which individual judges do not seek — or at least do not always seek — to obtain the all-things-considered best outcome.[85] Neither Hart nor Fuller addresses this issue directly, but one cannot help believing that on this question it is Fuller who far more likely prefers the justice-seeking judge and Hart who might understand that in law, seeking justice is not always or necessarily part of the job description of either the lawyer or the judge.[86]

VI. WHO WON?

There are, to be sure, people who cannot see a debate without insisting that we pick a winner and a loser. Many of those same people cannot see a list or collection of two or more items without ranking the items on the list. But we are not choosing between Hart and Fuller for a single position on a law faculty. They are, after all, both dead, and that appears to make

---

[80] Lon L. Fuller, *The Case of the Speluncean Explorers*, 62 HARV. L. REV. 616, 620-26 (1949).

[81] For the conception of positivism that informs this statement, a conception that finds its roots in Bentham, Austin, and, more controversially, Hart, but a conception that is decidedly non-standard in some of the current debates, see Schauer, *The Limited Domain of the Law, supra* note 75.

[82] *See, e.g.*, MONROE H. FREEDMAN, LAWYERS' ETHICS IN AN ADVERSARY SYSTEM (1975); Lon L. Fuller & John D. Randall, *Professional Responsibility: Report of the Joint Conference*, 44 A.B.A. J. 1159 (1958); Simon H. Rifkind, *The Lawyer's Role and Responsibility in Modern Society*, 30 REC. ASS'N B. CITY N.Y. 534, 535-45 (1975).

[83] *See, e.g.*, JOHN STUART MILL, ON LIBERTY ch. II (Prometheus Books 1986) (1859).

[84] *E.g.*, ADAM SMITH, THE WEALTH OF NATIONS: BOOKS IV-V 32-33 (Andrew Skinner ed., Penguin Books 1999) (1776).

[85] And something like this claim is implicit in any serious defense of legal formalism. *See supra* note 22.

[86] This difference of opinion between Fuller and Hart may have been partly a function of the fact that Fuller seems more focused on an audience of lawyers and law students, while Hart is interested more in an external description of the operation of the law, albeit one that includes an external description of a judge's internal point of view. Frederick Schauer, *Fuller's Internal Point of View*, 13 LAW & PHIL. 285, 298-308 (1994).

them unlikely candidates for faculty appointments.[87] Thus, it may not really matter whether anyone won or lost the debate. Much more important is what the debate as a whole illuminated' and what the particular example of the no-vehicles-in-the-park rule revealed about one of the central dilemmas of law. Most of what we have learned comes not from Hart's original example itself, nor solely from Fuller's counterexample, but from the conjunction of the two. Looking at the conjunction, we might say that Hart's basic point about the core and the penumbra was properly influential, and demonstrated not only his firsthand knowledge of how law worked,[88] but also the sophistication, for the times, of his philosophical knowledge.

Although Fuller's philosophical forays were far clumsier, it may be important to remember that Fuller offered a highly resonant picture of modern common law legal systems, especially (though not exclusively) in the United States. In an environment in which law professors who urge judges to rewrite statutes to make them less obsolete can go on to become judges themselves;[89] in which the instrumentalist, anti-literal, and anti-formal approach exemplified by cases like *Riggs*, *Kirby*, and *Church of the Holy Trinity* is a major component of the legal and judicial arsenal; and in which judges may without fear of impeachment set aside the plain language of even the Constitution in the service of something larger or deeper,[90] Fuller may have correctly captured something important about the legal system he knew best. Even with respect to Great Britain, a legal environment more formal than that of the United States but in which judges still sometimes use broad conceptions of equity to defeat an other-

---

[87] Which is not to say that we might not prefer to have them, even dead, over some of our colleagues.

[88] Hart spent almost nine years as a barrister, specializing in equity. *See* LACEY, A LIFE OF H.L.A. HART, *supra* note 20, at 45-46, 84. And although as a barrister he presumably spent some time in court, he was likely, given the nature of his practice, to have spent a considerable amount of time writing opinions about the core meanings of complex trusts and related documents. *Id.* at 46.

[89] *See* CALABRESI, *supra* note 71, at 163-66. For similar arguments supporting a statute-revising function for the courts, see Donald C. Langevoort, *Statutory Obsolescence and the Judicial Process: The Revisionist Role of the Courts in Federal Banking Regulation*, 85 MICH. L. REV. 672 (1987), and Note, *Intent, Clear Statements, and the Common Law: Statutory Interpretation in the Supreme Court*, 95 HARV. L. REV. 892, 912-15 (1982).

[90] *See* U.S. Trust Co. v. New Jersey, 431 U.S. 1, 21 (1977) (quoting Home Bldg. & Loan Ass'n v. Blaisdell, 290 U.S. 398, 428 (1934)) (holding that literal meaning of Contract Clause is not conclusive); *see also* Principality of Monaco v. Mississippi, 292 U.S. 313, 322 (1934) (holding that state cannot be sued by own citizens despite Eleventh Amendment's literal meaning); Hans v. Louisiana, 134 U.S. 1, 10-11, 15 (1890) (same).

wise unfortunate application of a legal rule,[91] Fuller's description may capture an element of actual adjudication and legal practice that Hart had neglected or slighted.

Riggs, *Kirby*, and *Church of the Holy Trinity* are of course not all or even most of American law, to say nothing of law in jurisdictions more formal and less instrumentalist than the United States.[92] Even in America, cases like *United States v. Locke*[93] and *Tennessee Valley Authority v. Hill*[94] represent part of the fabric of the law, and although *Riggs* has become famous, there are in fact numerous decisions in which unworthy beneficiaries who were in some way responsible for the testator's death have been permitted to inherit.[95] Moreover, the United States is also a legal environment in which the formal constitutional separation of powers as specified in the document often is outcome-determinative,[96] in which a court can believe that a statute that produces an obsolete and morally problematic result can nevertheless be changed only by the legislature,[97] and in which prominent

---

[91] *See, e.g.*, Lloyds Bank Ltd. v. Bundy, [1975] Q.B. 326, 339 (1974) (U.K.) (holding that standard contract law will not be enforced where there is "inequality of bargaining power" and terms are "very unfair"); *In re* Vandervell's Trust (No.2), [1974] Ch. 269, 322 (U.K.) ("If the law should be in danger of doing injustice, then equity should be called in to remedy it."); Central London Prop. Trust Ltd. v. High Trees House Ltd., [1947] K.B. 130, 134-35 (1946) (U.K.) (concluding that "fusion of law and equity" allows enforcement of promise even where there is no consideration); *see also* PATRICK DEVLIN, THE JUDGE 90-93 (1979) (discussing more examples of such cases in English law). For an analysis of the even more common American equivalent, see Doug Rendleman, *The Trial Judge's Equitable Discretion Following* eBay v. MercExchange, 27 REV. LITIG. 63, 68, 72-80 (2007).

[92] *See generally* P.S. ATIYAH & ROBERT S. SUMMERS, FORM AND SUBSTANCE IN ANGLO-AMERICAN LAW: A COMPARATIVE STUDY IN LEGAL REASONING, LEGAL THEORY, AND LEGAL INSTITUTIONS (1987) (concluding that formal approaches to law are more common in English than in American law); INTERPRETING STATUTES: A COMPARATIVBE STUDY (D. Neil MacCormick & Robert S. Summers eds., 1991) (surveying approaches to statutory interpretation throughout world).

[93] 471 U.S. 84, 93-96 (1985) (enforcing literal meaning of "prior to December 31" statutory filing deadline despite argument that Congress obviously intended to say "on or prior to December 31").

[94] 437 U.S. 153 (1978) (enforcing plain meaning of Endangered Species Act to protect habitat of three-inch-long brown fish called snail darter, even at what majority conceded was sacrifice of great public benefit and millions of dollars), *superseded by statute*, Endangered Species Act Amendments of 1978, Pub. L. No. 95-632, 92 Stat. 3753.

[95] The cases are described in Schauer, *The Limited Domain of the Law*, *supra* note 75, at 1937-38.

[96] *See, e.g.*, Bowsher v. Synar, 478 U.S. 714 (1986); INS v. Chadha, 462 U.S. 919 (1983).

[97] *See In re* Blanchflower, 834 A.2d 1010 (N.H. 2003) (construing statutory definition of adultery as limited to opposite-sex partners because term had been limited to opposite-sex partners in other statutory contexts); *see also* Ga. Forestry Comm'n v. Taylor, 526 S.E.2d 373, 374-75 (Ga. Ct. App. 1999) (correcting even a "weakness" in statute is for legislature and not court); Hauser v. Reilly, 536 N.W.2d 865, 869 (Mich. Ct. App. 1995) (admittedly "unfortunate" consequences for divorced parent must be remedied by legislature and not court); Todd v. Bigham,

political figures who might otherwise have had presidential aspirations[98] never consider the possibility solely because they would run afoul of the Constitution's "natural born" requirement to be President.[99] So although the example of the truck/memorial that falls within the literal language of a statute tells us something important about modern common law legal systems, so too does the automobile that is plainly a vehicle. Indeed, if we seek to understand law and not just judging — and that was what Hart wanted us to understand by using the example in the first place — it is important that we not forget about the driver of a pickup truck, with family and picnic preparations in tow, who sees the "No Vehicles in the Park" sign at the entrance to the park and simply turns around.

Once we see how often law is formal, and once we see how often (especially in the United States) it is not, we can appreciate that the best understanding of rule interpretation in particular, and an important part of law in general, may come neither exclusively from Hart's example of the automobile, nor from Fuller's counterexample of the military truck. Rather, we learn a great deal from the conjunction of both examples and both sides, and from an appreciation that each of the two examples captures an important feature of the legal systems we know best. To the extent that this is so, the real winner of the debate is not Hart, nor is it Fuller, for both neglected something important. Instead, insofar as the two perspectives complemented each other and remedied the too-narrow descriptive account of the other, the real winner turns out to be all of us.

* * *

One of the baseball-team owners approached me and said: "If you become baseball commissioner, you're going to have to deal with 28 big egos," and I said, "For me, that's a 72 percent reduction."

U.S. Senator George Mitchell (1994)

---

395 P.2d 163, 165 (Or. 1964) (court may not depart from statute even to accomplish "desirable result"); N. Marianas Hous. Corp. v. Flores, 2006 MP 23, ¶ 5 (N. Mar. I. 2006) ("[E]mpathy does not trump legislation.").

[98] Including, for example, Jennifer Granholm, Christian Herter, Henry Kissinger, Madeleine Albright, and Arnold Schwarzenegger. And maybe Bob Hope.

[99] U.S. CONST. art. II, § 1, cl. 4.

DECEMBER

Supreme Court Sluggers ◆ October Term 2009

John Glover Roberts, Jr.　　Pitcher

JOHN G. ROBERTS, JR.

Chief Justice of the United States (2005–).
See THE JUSTICES OF THE SUPREME COURT,
supremecourtus.gov/about/biographiescurrent.pdf.

❦ December ❦

SUN	MON	TUES	WED	THUR	FRI	SAT
			1	2	3	4
5	6	7	8	9	10	11
12	13	14	15	16	17	18
19	20	21	22	23	24	25
26	27	28	29	30	31	

U.S. v. Navajo Nation

David H. Souter[†]

I am not through regretting that my position in *United States v. Navajo Nation*, 537 U.S. 488, 514-521 (2003) (dissenting opinion), did not carry the day. But it did not, and I agree that the precedent of that case calls for the result reached here.

[†] Justice, Supreme Court of the United States, joined by Justice John Paul Stevens.

RUTH'S RULE OF LAW

from the New York Telegram, May 30, 1920

From now on I intend to organize my own law out there in right field.

From now on any fan who thinks he has a license to use bad language in the right field bleacher is going to get a fine surprise.

Anybody who thinks he gets the privilege of calling me all sorts of nasty names when he pays 50 cents to go into the bleachers is in for another thought.

If any fan in the future uses indecent language, either to me or any other Yankee, I will stop the game, call a policeman, and have the fan thrown out of the park. I am going to be my own law from now on.

LAW REVIEW CIRCULATION 2009
THE COMBOVER

For our second annual study of the law review business,[1] we added circulation data for four flagship law reviews (UCLA, Texas, USC, and Washington University) and two specialty journals (NYU's *Tax Law Review* and Duke's *Law and Contemporary Problems*). We also corrected a few errors in the tables in our first study and filled in a few blanks. And, finally, we noticed something that might be worth thinking about: the possibility that the law school combover culture has infected law reviews.

In our first study, we wondered why some law reviews sometimes exaggerate their paid circulation numbers, and noted that

> [t]he *Harvard Law Review*, for example, boasts on its website that, "A circulation of about 8,000 enables the *Review* to pay all of its own expenses." We doubt this is one of those forgot-to-update-the-website oversights. The last time the *HLR* had 8,000 subscribers was in 1985. But who knows?[2]

That study appeared in print in February 2009. By March, the *Harvard Law Review* (*HLR*) website was reporting that "A circulation of about 4,000 enables the *Review* to pay all of its own expenses." The same words are still there as this article goes to press.[3] Why, in March 2009, change 8,000 to 4,000? The last time the *HLR* had 4,000 subscribers was in 2001. What was the *HLR* thinking? Perhaps it depends on what the meaning of the word "circulation" is.

While exploring this problem, keep in mind the following numbers from the *HLR*'s 2006, 2007, and 2008 circulation reports to the U.S. Postal Service (the original reports are reproduced on pages 421-423 below):

	2006	2007	2008
Total paid and/or requested circulation:	2,837	2,853	2,610
Total free distribution:	382	286	295
Copies not distributed:	843	923	957
Total:	4,062	4,062	3,862

First, a dictionary might help: it suggests that the *HLR*'s circulation is either much lower or much higher than 4,000. According to the *Oxford English Dictionary*, "circulation" in this context means either (a) "[t]he extent to which copies of a newspaper, periodical, etc., are distributed," or (b) "the number of readers which it reaches."[4] If the *HLR* is using definition (a), then it is inflating its circulation. It cannot plausibly include the copies it reports as "Copies not distributed" — they are not "copies [that] ... are distributed" — and thus its circulation is nowhere near 4,000. Using numbers in the *HLR*'s 2006, 2007, and 2008 reports to the USPS, its "Total" circulation minus "Copies not distributed" equals 3,219 for 2006, 3,139 for 2007, or 2,905 for 2008. If by "circulation" the *HLR* means "the extent to which copies of [the *HLR*] ... are distributed," why not say something more accurate on its website, like: "A circulation of about 2,900

---

[1] For the first study, see *Law Review Circulation*, 2009 GREEN BAG ALM. 164.

[2] *Id.* at 167 (quoting www.harvardlawreview.org/about.shtml (vis. Dec. 7, 2008)).

[3] *See* www.harvardlawreview.org/about.shtml (vis. Mar. 10); *id.* (vis. Dec. 27, 2009).

[4] *See* circulation, 7.b., OED Online (vis. Dec. 27, 2009).

enables the *Review* to pay all of its own expenses." On the other hand, if the *HLR* is using definition (b), then it is understating its circulation. After all, the journal does sell more than 2,000 copies, is available on Westlaw and Lexis (and in the many libraries that subscribe), and is cited every year in hundreds of articles and briefs.[5] Surely the "number of readers which it reaches" is greater than 4,000. Of course, if the USPS wanted to know how many readers the *HLR* has, it would ask, and if the *HLR* wanted to tell us how many readers it has, it would say so.

Second, the text might help: it suggests that the *HLR*'s circulation is much lower than 4,000. Recall that the website says, "A circulation of about 4,000 enables the *Review* to pay all of its own expenses." This sentence appears to be an effort to explain to us where the money comes from to pay the *HLR*'s expenses. It is not plausible that "Total free distribution" would bring in any money (we leave it to you to look up "free" in the dictionary if you have any doubts). And unless the *HLR* has found people willing to pay it to refrain from distributing itself, then "Copies not distributed" surely do not generate revenue either. That leaves "Total paid and/or requested circulation." Assuming (generously) that the numbers under this heading are exclusively for "paid" circulation, the *HLR*'s circulation was 2,837 in 2006, 2,853 in 2007, and 2,610 in 2008. Far away from "about 4,000" and getting farther. So why not say something even more accurate on its website, like: "A circulation of about 2,600 enables the *Review* to pay all of its own expenses." (If the *HLR* were aiming for full and accurate disclosure, it might also mention income from *Bluebook* sales, from West, Lexis, and other on-line distributors, and so on.)

Third, context might help: it suggests that the *HLR*'s circulation is whatever the *HLR* can convince you it is. The *HLR*, like all law reviews, operates within a larger world driven in substantial part by *USNews* rankings and related creatures. It is a world in which some law school leaders — that is, the people in charge of teaching law review editors and other students about the law, its practice, and its values — are committed to being in the elite, to being highly ranked, even if that means also being not fully forthright about the numbers on which rankings are based.[6] Perhaps law review editors internalize that kind of commitment, if not from their own schools, then perhaps from the law school world at large. Perhaps the propriety of fudging your way toward first place in the law is being simultaneously booted out the front door via lectures in Professional Responsibility classes and welcomed in at the back gate via role-modeling in law school administration and media coverage of it.

Perhaps in March 2009 the *HLR* was thinking that "about 8,000" had become laughably implausible, but "about 4,000," while not accurate, (1) could pass the laugh test and would be believed by most readers, and (2) was more impressive than an accurate "about 2,600" (2,600 being not much more than the *Yale Law Journal*'s 1,915).[7] But who knows?

---

[5] For example, in 2008, the *HLR* was cited in at least 354 briefs and 201 law review articles (search for "'harv. l. rev.' & da(aft 2007 & bef 2009)" in brief-all and jlr Westlaw databases) (Dec. 27, 2009).

[6] *See, e.g.*, Alex Wellen, *The 8.78 Million Maneuver*, N.Y. TIMES, July 31, 2005.

[7] The differences are more striking now, with journals' release of 2008-09 numbers. The *HLR*'s "paid and/or requested circulation" is now 2,029; the *YLJ*'s is 1,725.

LAW REVIEW CIRCULATION

STATEMENT OF OWNERSHIP, MANAGEMENT, AND CIRCULATION

1. Publication title: Harvard Law Review
2. Publication number: 0017-811X
3. Filing date: September 7, 2006
4. Issue frequency: Monthly, November–June
5. Number of issues published annually: Eight
6. Annual subscription price: Individual: $55.00; Institution: $200.00; Non-Profit: $95.00
7. Complete mailing address of known office of publication: Gannett House, 1511 Massachusetts Ave., Cambridge, MA 02138
   Contact person: Colleen Verner, (617) 495-4650
8. Complete mailing address of headquarters or general business office of publisher: Harvard Law Review, Gannett House, 1511 Massachusetts Ave., Cambridge, MA 02138
9. Full names and complete mailing addresses of Publisher, Editor, and Managing Editor:
   Publisher: Harvard Law Review, Gannett House, 1511 Massachusetts Ave., Cambridge, MA 02138
   Editor:
       86 student editors
       President — Aileen M. McGrath, Gannett House, 1511 Massachusetts Ave., Cambridge, MA 02138
   Managing Editor:
       Managing Editor — Alex N. Wong, Gannett House, 1511 Massachusetts Ave., Cambridge, MA 02138
       Treasurer — David C. Newman, Gannett House, 1511 Massachusetts Ave., Cambridge, MA 02138
10. Owner: The Harvard Law Review Association, Gannett House, 1511 Massachusetts Ave., Cambridge, MA 02138, a non-profit educational membership organization
11. Known bondholders, mortgagees, and other security holders owning or holding one percent or more of total amount of bonds, mortgages, or other securities: None
12. The purpose, function, and nonprofit status of this organization and the exempt status for federal income tax purposes have not changed during preceding twelve months.
13. Publication title: Harvard Law Review
14. Issue date for circulation data below: Volume 119, November 2005–June 2006
15. Extent and nature of circulation

		Average no. copies each issue during preceding 12 months	No. copies of single issue published nearest to filing date
A.	Total number of copies (net press run)	4062	4000
B.	Paid and/or requested circulation		
	1. Paid/requested outside-county mail subscriptions	2777	3071
	2. Paid in-county subscriptions	0	0
	3. Sales through dealers and carriers, street vendors, counter sales, and other non-USPS paid distribution	0	0
	4. Other classes mailed through the USPS	60	68
C.	Total paid and/or requested circulation	2837	3139
D.	Free distribution by mail (samples, complimentary, and other free copies)		
	1. Outside-county	45	45
	2. In-county	0	0
	3. Other classes mailed through the USPS	0	0
E.	Free distribution outside the mail (carriers or other means)	337	200
F.	Total free distribution (sum of D and E)	382	245
G.	Total distribution (sum of C and F)	3219	3384
H.	Copies not distributed	843	616
I.	Total (sum of G and H)	4062	4000
J.	Percent paid and/or requested circulation	88%	93%

16. Publication of statement of ownership is required.
17. I certify that all information furnished on this form is true and complete.

Aileen M. McGrath
President
September 7, 2006

STATEMENT OF OWNERSHIP, MANAGEMENT, AND CIRCULATION

1. Publication title: Harvard Law Review
2. Publication number: 0017-811X
3. Filing date: September 12, 2007
4. Issue frequency: Monthly, November–June
5. Number of issues published annually: Eight
6. Annual subscription price: Individual: $55.00; Institution: $200.00; Nonprofit: $95.00
7. Complete mailing address of known office of publication: Gannett House, 1511 Massachusetts Ave., Cambridge, MA 02138
   Contact person: Colleen Verner, (617) 495-4650
8. Complete mailing address of headquarters or general business office of publisher: Harvard Law Review, Gannett House, 1511 Massachusetts Ave., Cambridge, MA 02138
9. Full names and complete mailing addresses of Publisher, Editor, and Managing Editor:
   Publisher: Harvard Law Review, Gannett House, 1511 Massachusetts Ave., Cambridge, MA 02138
   Editor:
   > 86 student editors
   > President — Andrew Manuel Crespo, Gannett House, 1511 Massachusetts Ave., Cambridge, MA 02138
   Managing Editor:
   > Managing Editor — Andrea J. Paul, Gannett House, 1511 Massachusetts Ave., Cambridge, MA 02138
   > Treasurer/Vice President — Adam C. Jed, Gannett House, 1511 Massachusetts Ave., Cambridge, MA 02138
10. Owner: The Harvard Law Review Association, Gannett House, 1511 Massachusetts Ave., Cambridge, MA 02138, a nonprofit educational membership organization
11. Known bondholders, mortgagees, and other security holders owning or holding one percent or more of total amount of bonds, mortgages, or other securities: None
12. The purpose, function, and nonprofit status of this organization and the exempt status for federal income tax purposes have not changed during preceding twelve months.
13. Publication title: Harvard Law Review
14. Issue date for circulation data below: Volume 120, November 2006–June 2007
15. Extent and nature of circulation

		Average no. copies each issue during preceding 12 months	No. copies of single issue published nearest to filing date
A.	Total number of copies (net press run)	4062	4000
B.	Paid circulation		
	1. Mailed outside-county paid subscriptions	2488	2688
	2. Mailed in-county paid subscriptions	0	0
	3. Paid distribution outside the mails including sales through dealers and carriers, street vendors, counter sales, and other paid distribution outside USPS	307	307
	4. Paid distribution by other classes of mail through the USPS	58	67
C.	Total paid distribution	2853	3119
D.	Free or nominal rate distribution		
	1. Outside-county	50	50
	2. In-county	0	0
	3. Copies mailed at other classes through the USPS	0	0
	4. Outside the mail (carriers or other means)	236	236
E.	Total free or nominal rate distribution (sum of D)	286	286
F.	Total distribution (sum of C and E)	3139	3405
G.	Copies not distributed	923	595
H.	Total (sum of F and G)	4062	4000
I.	Percent paid	91%	92%

16. Publication of statement of ownership is required.
17. I certify that all information furnished on this form is true and complete.

> Andrew Manuel Crespo
> *President*
> September 12, 2007

STATEMENT OF OWNERSHIP, MANAGEMENT, AND CIRCULATION

1. Publication title: Harvard Law Review
2. Publication number: 0017-811X
3. Filing date: September 30, 2008
4. Issue frequency: Monthly, November–June
5. Number of issues published annually: Eight
6. Annual subscription price: Individual: $55.00; Institution: $200.00; Non-Profit: $95.00
7. Complete mailing address of known office of publication: Gannett House, 1511 Massachusetts Ave., Cambridge, MA 02138
   Contact person: Colleen Verner, (617) 495-4650
8. Complete mailing address of headquarters or general business office of publisher: The Harvard Law Review, Gannett House, 1511 Massachusetts Ave., Cambridge, MA 02138
9. Full names and complete mailing addresses of Publisher, Editor, and Managing Editor:
   Publisher: Harvard Law Review, Gannett House, 1511 Massachusetts Ave., Cambridge, MA 02138
   Editor:
   > 87 student editors
   > President — Robert W. Allen, Gannett House, 1511 Massachusetts Ave., Cambridge, MA 02138
   Managing Editor:
   > Managing Editor — Jonathan G. Cooper, Gannett House, 1511 Massachusetts Ave., Cambridge, MA 02138
   > Treasurer/Vice President — Portia D. Pedro, Gannett House, 1511 Massachusetts Ave., Cambridge, MA 02138
10. Owner: The Harvard Law Review Association, Gannett House, 1511 Massachusetts Ave., Cambridge, MA 02138, a nonprofit educational membership organization
11. Known bondholders, mortgagees, and other security holders owning or holding one percent or more of total amount of bonds, mortgages, or other securities: None
12. The purpose, function, and nonprofit status of this organization and the exempt status for federal income tax purposes have not changed during preceding twelve months.
13. Publication title: The Harvard Law Review
14. Issue date for circulation data below: Volume 121, November 2007–June 2008
15. Extent and nature of circulation

	Average no. copies each issue during preceding 12 months	No. copies of single issue published nearest to filing date
A. Total number of copies (net press run)	3862	3800
B. Paid and/or requested circulation		
1. Mailed outside-county paid subscriptions	2136	2706
2. Mailed in-county paid subscriptions	0	0
3. Paid distribution outside the mails including sales through dealers and carriers, street vendors, counter sales, and other paid distribution outside USPS	0	0
4. Paid distribution by other classes of mail through the USPS	474	593
C. Total paid distribution	2610	3299
D. Free or nominal rate distribution		
1. Outside-county	50	50
2. In-county	0	0
3. Copies mailed at other classes through the USPS	0	0
4. Outside the mail (carriers or other means)	245	245
E. Total free or nominal rate distribution (sum of D)	295	295
F. Total distribution (sum of C and E)	2905	3594
G. Copies not distributed	957	206
H. Total (sum of G and H)	3862	3800
I. Percent paid and/or requested circulation	89%	91%

16. Publication of statement of ownership is required.
17. I certify that all information furnished on this form is true and complete.

Robert W. Allen
President
September 30, 2008

"TOTAL PAID CIRCULATION"
1979-2009 FOR THE FLAGSHIPS OF THE U.S. NEWS TOP 19, PLUS OTHERS

	Yale	Harvard	Stanford	Columbia	NYU	Boalt	Chicago	Penn
1979-80	*	8760	*	3795	2100	2549	2068	2176
1980-81	4051	8836	*	3790	2173	2342	1827	2150
1981-82	4126	9767	2056	3790	2092	2342	1993	2150
1982-83	4199	8389	2350	3561	2074	2342	2150	1900
1983-84	4092	8762	*	4046	2069	2200	2300	2080
1984-85	3950	7390	*	3227	*	2168	2617	1996
1985-86	3755	7705	*	3164	*	2014	*	*
1986-87	3755	7694	*	2938	*	1990	*	1708
1987-88	3700	7325	*	2947	*	1990	*	1762
1988-89	3700	6995	*	2337	*	1816	*	1628
1989-90	3700	7016	*	2913	*	*	2229	1864
1990-91	3700	7768	*	2676	*	1740	2205	1719
1991-92	3700	6517	*	2798	*	1694	2454	1781
1992-93	3600	6070	*	2525	*	1690	*	1673
1993-94	3500	6018	*	2463	*	1701	1979	1673
1994-95	3300	5204	*	2381	*	1696	2048	1551
1995-96	3300	5029	*	2497	*	1595	1959	1446
1996-97	3300	5454	*	2365	*	1507	1922	1408
1997-98	3300	4367	*	2273	1362	1422	1875	1334
1998-99	3300	4574	*	2227	1222	1639	1872	1347
1999-00	2705	4223	8850	2174	1200	*	1870	1191
2000-01	2705	4013	*	2082	1183	1305	2062	1043
2001-02	2677	3735	1434	2069	1159	1253	1769	1293
2002-03	2577	3491	1280	2029	1211	1196	1845	1233
2003-04	2579	3451	1112	1875	1209	1045	*	1180
2004-05	2712	2945	1112	1743	867	1040	*	1056
2005-06	2296	2837	1112	1638	999	992	*	1101
2006-07	1782	2853	1089	1578	990	1178	*	1093
2007-08	1915	2610	1008	*	*	884	1525	923
2008-09	1725	2029	*	1364	763	820	*	844

* Form 3526 report not found for this year.

"TOTAL PAID CIRCULATION"
1979-2009 FOR THE FLAGSHIPS OF THE U.S. NEWS TOP 19, PLUS OTHERS

	Michigan	Duke	N'western	Virginia	Cornell	G'town	UCLA
1979-80	2950	1326	1771	*	3350	3197	1536
1980-81	2979	1296	1610	2396	*	3058	1563
1981-82	2985	1411	1520	2387	*	2950	1277
1982-83	2844	1440	1416	2443	3603	3100	1251
1983-84	2771	1378	1440	2400	*	3200	1361
1984-85	2727	1412	1354	2161	*	3000	1400
1985-86	2657	1445	1251	*	3682	1116	1400
1986-87	2604	1469	1268	2200	*	1116	*
1987-88	2535	1335	1264	2029	*	*	1192
1988-89	2481	1295	1223	1958	*	*	1192
1989-90	2426	1268	1178	*	*	3043	1192
1990-91	2382	1255	951	1882	*	2782	1134
1991-92	2332	1253	*	*	*	2260	1192
1992-93	2263	1187	887	1840	*	3955	1083
1993-94	2256	*	*	1680	3250	1514	940
1994-95	2227	*	723	1670	3252	1462	940
1995-96	2125	*	*	1550	2958	*	990
1996-97	*	*	*	1552	2890	1536	1000
1997-98	1925	*	*	1536	2803	1487	1000
1998-99	2010	*	*	*	2805	1471	1000
1999-00	1841	*	*	*	2859	*	921
2000-01	1697	*	*	*	2845	1398	922
2001-02	1654	*	*	1849	2816	*	695
2002-03	1571	*	1017	1068	2288	*	650
2003-04	1419	*	997	644	1766	*	563
2004-05	1207	*	660	616	1827	*	648
2005-06	925	*	466	483	1712	1027	520
2006-07	862	*	575	526	1497	924	521
2007-08	783	957	584	530	1458	1068	*
2008-09	711	790	*	542	1319	*	*

* Form 3526 report not found for this year.

"Total Paid Circulation"
1979-2009 for the Flagships of the U.S. News Top 19, Plus Others

	Texas	Vanderbilt	USC	Wash U	Tax L Rev	L&C Probs
1979-80	*	1995	1614	1091	5310	*
1980-81	2349	2046	1519	1190	5685	2000
1981-82	2347	2046	1532	1096	5664	2441
1982-83	2396	1995	1435	1120	5235	2628
1983-84	2396	1995	1333	1107	5189	2543
1984-85	*	2001	1204	1106	4505	2443
1985-86	1960	2020	1082	508.5	4064	2459
1986-87	1684	1996	1054	701	3863	2720
1987-88	*	1550	1199	706	3545	2523
1988-89	*	1359	1133	714	3442	2887
1989-90	*	1253	1133	725	3315	2068
1990-91	1548	1281	1215	502	3000	2106
1991-92	1489	1330	830	490	1544	*
1992-93	1407	1220	980	490	*	*
1993-94	1261	1252	772	490	2016	*
1994-95	881	1252	795	490	1772	*
1995-96	1137	1267	4770	560	*	*
1996-97	1123	1287	*	560	1517	*
1997-98	1645	1265	*	672	1176	*
1998-99	1628	1165	795	660	1149	*
1999-00	1526	952	760	644	*	*
2000-01	1488	960	4100	*	*	*
2001-02	1449	855	680	*	*	*
2002-03	1372	*	698	*	*	*
2003-04	1125	800	680	*	741	*
2004-05	1056	850	670	*	*	*
2005-06	963	850	700	*	746	*
2006-07	963	850	720	*	620	*
2007-08	941	850	740	*	684	1810
2008-09	860	850	*	*	*	1393

* Form 3526 report not found for this year.

JUSTICE CINCINNATUS

DAVID SOUTER — A DYING BREED, THE YANKEE REPUBLICAN

Kermit Roosevelt[†]

Few justices have been as consistently misunderstood as David Souter. Even at the end of his service on the Supreme Court, the conventional view is that he is a shy and bookish recluse, hiding from the modern world. This characterization misunderstands the man.

It has, of course, a grain of truth. Souter is bookish, and he is no great fan of modern gizmos or even basic tools. He does not use a computer or even a typewriter; I clerked for him during the court's 1999-2000 term, and I vividly remember trying to decipher his ornate longhand script. Once I went into his office for a discussion and found myself wandering about in the dark. Only after my eyes had adjusted could I make out the justice standing by the window with an open book, reading in the weak light that filtered through the glass.

It is not that Souter can't cope with modernity. When the Supreme Court considered a copyright case involving the latest file-sharing methods in 2005, Souter's opinion for a unanimous court showed a deep understanding of peer-to-peer Internet applications. It has won praise from both the legal and the high-tech communities.

Why would a man who can understand Grokster read by the window rather than turn on a light? Souter has a characteristic New England thriftiness and a distrust of luxury that verges on the spartan. He can keep a suit for decades, and he gently mocked me and my fellow clerks for wearing overcoats in the winter, claiming that his view was shared by that other great Yankee justice, Oliver Wendell Holmes. Souter is also deeply unpretentious. It would never occur to him that because he is a Supreme

---

[†] Kermit Roosevelt is a professor of law at the University of Pennsylvania Law School and clerked for Justice Souter during the 1999-2000 term. Copyright © 2008 Washingtonpost.Newsweek Interactive Co. LLC. This article originally appeared in *Slate* on May 1, 2009, and is reprinted here with permission of the author and the publisher.

Court justice he's entitled to waste a bit of the taxpayers' electricity. (He once wrote me a note on a napkin I'd left on my desk rather than using a new sheet of paper.)

I suspect that Souter's down-to-earth humility is the source of much of his famed distaste for Washington, which seems to have finally gotten the better of him. Talking to clerks, he always spoke without a sense of status or hierarchy, as one person or one mind to another. The fetish that Washington makes of position must have grated on him. In New Hampshire, his neighbors knew him as simply David Souter. I think he did not enjoy the fact that so many people in the capital found it far more important that he was a Supreme Court justice.

Certainly, it was not a lack of sociability that kept Souter on the outskirts of Washington society. When I arrived at the court, given what I had read about the man, I expected my interactions with him to be intellectually stimulating but interpersonally awkward. It was a surprise and a delight to learn how warm and witty he was. Nearly every afternoon he would emerge from his office to take a cup of coffee and chat with the clerks, and invariably he'd have us in stitches with some anecdote about New Hampshire or Oxford. His reunions are always well-attended, and I think there are few justices who command such filial affection from their clerks.

Souter has also been misunderstood as a judge. From the very beginning, partisans on both sides of the political spectrum projected onto him their hopes and fears. For the right, when President George H.W. Bush chose him, he was the stealth candidate whose lack of a paper trail would frustrate opposition but whose hidden political views would make him a "home run" for the conservative cause. For the left, he was the same thing. Demonstrators outside his confirmation hearings, fearing that he would prove a crucial vote to overturn *Roe v. Wade*, waved posters reading "Stop Souter, or Women Will Die." (Years later, we clerks found some of these on eBay and snapped them up as souvenirs.)

When Souter did not follow the narrative both sides had crafted for him, the left felt relieved and the right betrayed. He had lurched to the left, as a conservative judge once put it to me. Again, there is, of course, some truth to this story. On the court, Souter has voted mostly with the center-left justices in controversial cases, and his track record certainly does not follow the Republican Party platform.

But Souter's current position on the left wing of the court owes much more to movement by the court and the country than to any lurch on his part. The current court, after all, has seven Republican appointees and has been on a steady rightward drift since the Reagan years. The Republican Party has, too. I think Souter is indeed in many ways a Republican; it's just that his sort of Republican no longer really exists.

More important, Souter's performance on the court tracked his testimony during his confirmation hearings, for anyone who was paying close attention. Souter described himself as a cautious moderate, conservative in his distaste for drastic change and the importance he attached to precedent. On the controversial issue of the right to privacy, he described himself as a follower of Justice John Marshall Harlan, who wrote that constitutional due process of law includes protection against "all substantial arbitrary impositions and purposeless restraints." Souter believed that judges should not substitute their views of wise policy for those of the legislature but also that judges must play a meaningful role if legislative action becomes oppressive. It was not astonishing, then, when in the 1992 case *Planned Parenthood v. Casey*, he joined Justices Sandra Day O'Connor and Anthony Kennedy to reaffirm the central abortion-rights holding of Roe, basing his decision in significant part on respect for precedent.

Of course, other justices have sounded similar notes at their confirmation hearings and gone on to perform quite differently than promised. Souter's hearings, perhaps, offered a rather too handy template for what a justice seeking confirmation should say, regardless of his or her actual beliefs. Other nominees have promised humility and pledged their fealty to Justice Harlan, only to become wrecking balls once appointed. It is hard to escape the conclusion that one of Souter's distinguishing characteristics is his honesty.

That is something that the Supreme Court and the nation will miss. It will not be very hard to replace Souter's vote. Any Obama appointee will most likely vote roughly the same way, at least on the most contested issues that capture public attention. But it will be much harder to find someone with the same judicial temperament as Souter, the same open-mindedness, desire to learn, and willingness to take each case as it comes and reconsider past positions when necessary.

Souter was never an agenda-driven justice. If he had been, I think he would have stayed longer. With the replacement of just one conservative member of the court, Souter's frequent four-justice dissents, from the court's liberal-moderate wing, could have become majorities. I'd hoped he would stay long enough to see that happen. But I think he feels he has done his duty.

The comparable figure that comes to my mind is Cincinnatus, the Roman hero called to leadership who cast off his authority and returned home to his farm as soon as the crisis was past. Souter did not seek out his position, nor, it now seems clear, did he value it for its own sake. He did not go to the court to effect change; instead he did us a great service by resisting it. Reading the long and heated opinions in *Casey*, now, has something of the drama of a visit to Gettysburg. That was the closest the enemies of *Roe* came to overturning legal abortion. They came close indeed. But the charge fell short in the end, turned back by just a few people, Souter crucially among them, who found themselves in the right place at the right time. Some of the recent rulings limiting presidential power in the face of the Bush administration's protestations were 5-4 decisions as well; there, too, the vote of a single justice made the difference.

I am sorry to see Justice Souter go. The court will miss his intelligence, his integrity, and his humor. But he has earned his release, if that is what he wants. He leaves with his honor, and he should have our thanks as well.

✳ ✳ ✳

A baseball fan has every right to voice his or her prejudices in or out of the ball park, but there is no room for intolerance in the chambers of the wise appellate judge.

John Paul Stevens (1989)

ILLUSTRATIONS & CREDITS

ILLUSTRATIONS

Cover: The American national game of base ball: Grand match for the championship at the Elysian Fields, Hoboken, N.J., by Currier & Ives. Courtesy of Library of Congress, Prints & Photographs Div., repr. no. LC-DIG-pga-00600 (ca. 1866).

Page i: Detail from A baseball match at the Elysian Fields, Hoboken, Harper's Weekly, Oct. 15, 1859, at 664-65. Courtesy of Library of Congress, Prints & Photographs Div., repr. no. LC-DIG-ppmsca-17524.

Pages iv, 39, 52, 99, 153, 256, 263, 337 & 363: Baseball cards from the Benjamin K. Edwards Collection. Courtesy of Library of Congress, Prints & Photographs Div., repr. nos. LC-DIG-bbc-0006f, LC-DIG-bbc-0924f, LC-DIG-bbc-2038f, LC-DIG-bbc-0158f, LC-DIG-bbc-0570f, LC-DIG-bbc-1486f, LC-DIG-bbc-0946f, LC-DIG-bbc-1449f & LC-DIG-bbc-0003f (ca. 1887-1912).

Pages x & 432: The Judge. From H. Stacy Marks et al., Mr. Punch in Wig and Gown: The Lighter Side of Bench and Bar (ca. 1910).

Page 11: Bryan A. Garner. Reprinted by permission of Bryan A. Garner.

Page 23: Tony Mauro. Reprinted by permission of Tony Mauro.

Page 29: Kevin Underhill. Reprinted by permission of Kevin Underhill.

Page 42: Smoky Joe Wood. Courtesy of Library of Congress, Prints & Photographs Div., repr. no. LC-DIG-ggbain-33123 (ca. 1920).

Page 50: Preston Woodlock's "Souvenir of First Yale-Waseda International Series 1935." Courtesy of Douglas P. Woodlock.

Page 69: Octavius V. Catto. Harper's Weekly, Oct. 28, 1871, at 1005. Courtesy of Library of Congress, Prints & Photographs Div., repr. no. LC-DIG-ppmsca-18480.

Page 81: The Athenaeum, Pittsfield, Mass. Courtesy of Library of Congress, Prints & Photographs Div., repr. no. LC-DIG-det-4a13123 (ca. 1900-06).

Page 101: "Bean Him," by Donald McKee, Life magazine, July 9, 1914, at 71. Courtesy of Library of Congress, Prints & Photographs Div., repr. no. LC-USZ62-108047.

Pages 112 & 114: George Wharton Pepper et al. Courtesy of Library of Congress, Prints & Photographs Div., repr. nos. LC-DIG-npcc-30246 & LC-USZ62-34138 (ca. 1921-1924).

Page 119: Moe Berg. Public domain.

Page 121: Congressional baseball teams. Courtesy of Library of Congress, Prints & Photographs Div., repr. no. LC-DIG-hec-09155 (1917).

Page 124: OPA hearing. Courtesy of Library of Congress, Prints & Photographs Div., repr. no. LC-USW3-030777-D (1943).

Page 152: "The little boy and the big boys prepare for the baseball season." Courtesy of Library of Congress, Prints & Photographs Div., repr. no. LC-USZ62-63121 (ca. 1901).

Page 162: Ty Cobb and Joe Jackson. Courtesy of Library of Congress, Prints & Photographs Div., repr. no. LC-DIG-ppmsca-18474 (ca. 1913).

Page 167: Muddy Ruel et al. Courtesy of Library of Congress, Prints & Photographs Div., repr. no. LC-DIG-ggbain-37515 (1924).

Page 195: Myrtle Rowe. Courtesy of Library of Congress, Prints & Photographs Div., repr. no. LC-DIG-ggbain-04721 (1910).

Pages 212-218: Fred M. Vinson et al. Courtesy of University of Kentucky Libraries, Special Collections and Archives, and, for those on page 214, courtesy of Centre College as well (ca. 1909-1953).

Page 241: Branch Rickey. Courtesy of Library of Congress, Prints & Photographs Div., repr. no. LC-DIG-npcc-19279 (ca. 1909-1919).

Page 246: A. Lawrence Lowell. Courtesy of Library of Congress, Prints & Photographs Div., repr. no. LC-DIG-ggbain-06180.

Page 288: John Marshall Harlan. Courtesy of Library of Congress, Prints & Photographs Div., repr. no. LC-DIG-hec-14623 (ca. 1905-1911).

Page 307: Frank Leland et al. From Spalding's Chicago Amateur Baseball Annual and Inter-City Baseball Association Year Book 36 (1905).

Page 339 & 341: Congressional baseball teams. Courtesy of Library of Congress, Prints & Photographs Div., repr. nos. LC-USZ62-94505 & LC-DIG-npcc-15774 (1926).

Page 348: Parking at Ebbets Field. Courtesy of Library of Congress, Prints & Photographs Div., repr. no. LC-DIG-ggbain-22423 (1916).

Page 365: J. Crawford Biggs. Courtesy of Library of Congress, Prints & Photographs Div., repr. no. LC-DIG-npcc-10445 (1924).

Page 382: John K. Tener et al. Courtesy of Library of Congress, Prints & Photographs Div., repr. no. LC-DIG-ggbain-15765 (1914).

Page 388: Sarasota trailer park alongside baseball park. Courtesy of Library of Congress, Prints & Photographs Div., repr. no. LC-USF34-057041-D (1941).
Page 415: John G. Roberts, Jr.
Page 418: Babe Ruth et al. Courtesy of Library of Congress, Prints & Photographs Div., repr. no. LC-DIG-ggbain-32385 (1921).
Page 433: A ball player (2009).

CREDITS

Amy Bach. Excerpt of *Chapter One* from ORDINARY JUSTICE: HOW AMERICA HOLDS COURT by Amy Bach (pp. 11-40). Copyright © 2009 by Amy Bach. Reprinted by permission of Henry Holt and Company, LLC. (And of the author.)

Eugene R. Fidell, *Appellate Review of Military Commissions*, BALKINIZATION, http://balkin.blogspot.com/2009/10/in-coming-weeks-there-will-be-no.html (Oct. 8, 2009). Copyright © 2009. Reprinted with permission from the author and the publisher.

Annette Gordon-Reed. Excerpt from THE HEMINGSES OF MONTICELLO BY ANNETTE GORDON-REED. Copyright © 2008 by Annette Gordon-Reed. Used with permission of the publisher, W.W. Norton & Company, Inc. (And of the author.)

Lani Guinier, *Courting the People: Demosprudence and the Law/Politics Divide*, 89 BOSTON UNIVERSITY LAW REVIEW 539 (2009). Copyright © 2009. Reprinted with permission from the author and the publisher.

Pamela S. Karlan, *Voting Rights and the Third Reconstruction*, in THE CONSTITUTION IN 2020 (Oxford University Press 2009) (Jack M. Balkin & Reva B. Siegel, eds.). Copyright © 2009. Reprinted with permission from the author and the publisher.

David F. Levi, *Autocrat of the Armchair*, 58 DUKE LAW JOURNAL 1791 (2009). Copyright © 2009 by David F. Levi. Reprinted with permission from the author and the publisher.

Dahlia Lithwick, *Shit Doesn't Happen: The Supreme Court's 100 percent dirt-free exploration of potty words*, SLATE, Nov. 4, 2008. Copyright © 2008. Reprinted with permission from the author and the publisher.

Michael J. Morrissey, *Dead Men Sometimes Do Tell Tales*, in YOUR WITNESS: LESSONS ON CROSS-EXAMINATION AND LIFE FROM GREAT CHICAGO TRIAL LAWYERS (Law Bulletin 2008) (Steven F. Molo & James R. Figliulo, eds.). Copyright © 2008. Law Bulletin Publishing Company. All rights reserved. This work is one of 50 chapters in the book Your Witness: Lessons on Cross-Examination and Life from Great Chicago Trial Lawyers, available at yourwitnessbook.com. Reprinted with permission from the author and the publisher.

David G. Post. Excerpt of IN SEARCH OF JEFFERSON'S MOOSE: NOTES ON THE STATE OF CYBERSPACE (Oxford University Press 2009) reprinted with permission from the author and the publisher. Copyright © 2009 by Oxford University Press, Inc. For more information about this publication please visit www.oup.com.

Kermit Roosevelt, *Justice Cincinnatus: David Souter—a dying breed, the Yankee Republican*, SLATE, May 1, 2009. Copyright © 2008 Washingtonpost.Newsweek Interactive Co. LLC. Reprinted with permission from the author and the publisher.

Frederick Schauer, *A Critical Guide to Vehicles in the Park*, 83 NYU LAW REVIEW 1109 (2008). Copyright © 2008 by Frederick Schauer. Reprinted with permission from the author and the publisher.

Jeffrey Toobin, *Are Obama's judges really liberals?*, THE NEW YORKER, Sept. 21, 2009. Copyright © 2009 by Jeffrey Toobin. Reprinted with permission from the author and the publisher.

G. Edward White, *Introduction* to OLIVER WENDELL HOLMES, JR., THE COMMON LAW (1881; Harvard University Press 2009 prtg.). Reprinted by permission of the publisher from The Common Law by Oliver Wendell Holmes, Jr., pp. vii-xxxiii, Cambridge, Mass.: The Belknap Press of Harvard University Press, Copyright © 2009 by the President and Fellows of Harvard College.

Little League baseball is a very good thing
because it keeps the parents off the streets.

Yogi Berra

Available now . . .

Subscription Information

Domestic subscriptions to the *Green Bag, An Entertaining Journal of Law* cost $40 for one year (four issues), $80 for two years (eight issues), $120 for three years (twelve issues), and $200 for four years (sixteen issues). Foreign subscriptions are $60 per year. All subscriptions start with the next issue to be published after we receive payment. For gift subscriptions, please specify to whom renewal notices should be sent. A nice notice of a gift subscription is available on our website. For back-issues, please call W.S. Hein at (800) 828-7571. For other subscription matters, please email us at subscriptions@greenbag.org.

When you buy a subscription to the *Green Bag*, that is all you are buying — one copy of each issue of the journal for the duration of your order. Everything else we make is a gift we may or may not bestow on some or all of our subscribers (*e.g.*, an almanac, bobblehead, or trading card) or a product you may purchase separately (*e.g., Judge Dave & the Rainbow People*). In addition, to the extent that the *Green Bag* does occasionally and arbitrarily give away goodies, we do not give multiple goodies to anyone carrying more than one *Green Bag* subscription.

To subscribe online, please visit our web site, www.greenbag.org. (Paypal is the only form of electronic payment we accept.) Otherwise, please send the following information, or a completed copy of this form, together with your check payable to the *Green Bag*, to the address below.

Name: _____

Address: _____

City: _____

State/Zip: _____

Email: _____

The Green Bag, 6600 Barnaby Street NW, Washington, DC 20015

Thank you.